Lecture Notes in Computer Science   10001

Commenced Publication in 1973
Founding and Former Series Editors:
Gerhard Goos, Juris Hartmanis, and Jan van Leeuwen

More information about this series at http://www.springer.com/series/7408

Wolfgang Ahrendt · Bernhard Beckert
Richard Bubel · Reiner Hähnle
Peter H. Schmitt · Mattias Ulbrich (Eds.)

Deductive Software Verification – The KeY Book

From Theory to Practice

 Springer

Editors

Wolfgang Ahrendt
Chalmers University of Technology
Gothenburg
Sweden

Bernhard Beckert
Karlsruher Institut für Technologie (KIT)
Karlsruhe
Germany

Richard Bubel
Technische Universität Darmstadt
Darmstadt
Germany

Reiner Hähnle
Technische Universität Darmstadt
Darmstadt
Germany

Peter H. Schmitt
Karlsruher Institut für Technologie (KIT)
Karlsruhe
Germany

Mattias Ulbrich
Karlsruher Institut für Technologie (KIT)
Karlsruhe
Germany

ISSN 0302-9743   ISSN 1611-3349   (electronic)
Lecture Notes in Computer Science
ISBN 978-3-319-49811-9   ISBN 978-3-319-49812-6   (eBook)
DOI 10.1007/978-3-319-49812-6

Library of Congress Control Number: 2016957483

LNCS Sublibrary: SL2 – Programming and Software Engineering

Printed on acid-free paper

This Springer imprint is published by Springer Nature
The registered company is Springer International Publishing AG
The registered company address is: Gewerbestrasse 11, 6330 Cham, Switzerland

Authors' Affiliations

Wolfgang Ahrendt (Chalmers University of Technology, Gothenburg, Sweden, email: ahrendt@chalmers.se)

Bernhard Beckert (Karlsruher Institut für Technologie (KIT), Germany, email: beckert@kit.edu)

Richard Bubel (Technische Universität Darmstadt, Germany, email: bubel@cs.tu-darmstadt.de)

Frank S. de Boer (Centrum voor Wiskunde en Informatica, Amsterdam, The Netherlands, email: f.s.de.boer@cwi.nl)

Stijn de Gouw (Open University, Heerlen, The Netherlands, email: stijn.degouw@ou.nl)

Christoph Gladisch (Karlsruher Institut für Technologie (KIT), Germany, email: gladisch@ira.uka.de)

Daniel Grahl (Karlsruher Institut für Technologie (KIT), Germany, email: daniel.grahl@alumni.kit.edu)

Sarah Grebing (Karlsruher Institut für Technologie (KIT), Germany, email: grebing@ira.uka.de)

Simon Greiner (Karlsruher Institut für Technologie (KIT), Germany, email: simon.greiner@kit.edu)

Reiner Hähnle (Technische Universität Darmstadt, Germany, email: haehnle@cs.tu-darmstadt.de)

Martin Hentschel (Technische Universität Darmstadt, Germany, email: hentschel@cs.tu-darmstadt.de)

Mihai Herda (Karlsruher Institut für Technologie (KIT), Germany, email: herda@kit.edu)

Marieke Huisman (University of Twente, The Netherlands, email: m.huisman@utwente.nl)

Ran Ji (Technische Universität Darmstadt, Germany, email: rj82cnus@cs.cmu.edu)

Vladimir Klebanov (Karlsruher Institut für Technologie (KIT), Germany,
email: klebanov@kit.edu)

Wojciech Mostowski (Halmstad University, Sweden,
email: wojciech.mostowski@hh.se)

Jurriaan Rot (Radboud University, Nijmegen, The Netherlands,
email: jrot@cs.ru.nl)

Philipp Rümmer (Uppsala University, Sweden,
email: philipp.ruemmer@it.uu.se)

Christoph Scheben (Karlsruher Institut für Technologie (KIT), Germany,
email: scheben@ira.uka.de)

Peter H. Schmitt (Karlsruher Institut für Technologie (KIT), Germany,
email: pschmitt@ira.uka.de)

Mattias Ulbrich (Karlsruher Institut für Technologie (KIT), Germany,
email: ulbrich@kit.edu)

Nathan Wasser (Technische Universität Darmstadt, Germany,
email: nate@sharpmind.de)

Benjamin Weiß (Karlsruher Institut für Technologie (KIT), Germany,
email: benjamin.weiss@alumni.uni-karlsruhe.de)

Foreword

Program verification has a long and distinguished history in computer science. As early as 1949, Alan Turing, in a technical report titled *On Checking a Large Routine*, raised the question of how to verify computer programs. Ever since that time, this problem has been investigated by several researchers. Some of them earned the ACM Turing Award for their work on the subject.

With this concerted effort of several scientists in mind, one would think that the "problem" of software correctness has been "solved" by now, whatever the qualification "solved" is supposed to mean. Nothing is further from the truth.

In books on algorithms, for example, those covering the standard material on algorithms on data structures, the correctness of the presented algorithms is ignored or glossed over. At best a justification of the selected algorithms is given by presenting a mathematical argument without a rigorous explanation of why this argument can be applied to the program in question. The point is that a program is just a piece of text, while the presented mathematical argument refers to the program execution. The reasoning then tacitly presupposes an implementation that conforms to the informal description of the program meaning given in English. This subtle gap in reasoning is especially acute if one deals with recursive programs or programs involving dynamic data structures.

An alternative is to rely on a large body of literature on program verification and use one of the formal systems developed to provide rigorous correctness proofs using axioms and proof rules. Unfortunately, formal correctness proofs are very tedious and hence error prone. This raises a natural question: If we do not trust the correctness of a program, why should we trust its correctness proof?

A possible answer lies in relying on *mechanized verification* that provides a programming environment allowing us to check the correctness proof of a program in the sense that each step of the proof is mechanically verified. Such a programming environment, when properly built, allows us to treat the underlying proof system as a parameter, just as the program that is to be verified.

Mechanized verification has a distinguished history as well, and this is not the place to trace it. It suffices to say that the KeY project, the subject of this book, is possibly the most ambitious endeavor in this area. It started in 1998 and gradually evolved into, what the authors call, the *KeY framework*.

This framework goes beyond mechanized verification by also providing a means of program specification, a test case generation, a teaching tool for a number of courses on software engineering, and a debugging tool. The current book is a substantial revision and extension of the previous edition that takes into account this evolution of the KeY system. It systematically explains several facets of the KeY framework, starting with the theoretical underpinning and ending with a presentation of nontrivial case studies.

I would like to congratulate the authors not only for the outcome but also for their persistence and their vision. The current scientific climate aiming at maximizing your number of publications and your H-index does not bode well with long-term projects. It is refreshing to see that not everybody has yielded to it.

October 2016   Krzysztof R. Apt

Preface

Wer hat an der Uhr gedreht? Ist es wirklich schon so spät?—Every child growing up in the 1970s in Germany (like the author of this text) is familiar with these lines. They are from a theme song played during the closing credits of the German version of the *Pink Panther Show*. The ditty conveys the utter bafflement ("Who advanced the clock?") of the listener about 30 minutes of entertainment having passed in what seemed to be mere seconds. And it is exactly this feeling that we editors have now: What? Ten years since the first book about KeY [Beckert et al., 2007] was published? Impossible! But of course it is possible, and there are good reasons for a new book about KeY, this time simply called *The KeY Book*.

What Is New in The KeY Book?

In short: almost everything! This is not merely an overhaul of the previous book, but a completely different volume: only eight of 15 chapters from the previous edition are still around with a roughly similar function, while there are 11 completely new chapters. But even most of the chapters retained were rewritten from scratch. Only three chapters more or less kept their old structure. What happened?

First of all, there were some major technical developments in the KeY system that required coverage as well as changes in the theoretical foundations:

- With KeY 2.x we moved from a memory model with an implicit heap to one with explicit heaps, i.e., heaps have a type in our logic, can be quantified over, etc. As a consequence, it was possible to:
- Implement better support for reasoning about programs with heaps [Weiß, 2011, Schmitt et al., 2010], essentially with a variant of dynamic frames [Kassios, 2011].
- We dropped support for specification with the Object Constraint Language (OCL) and drastically improved support for the Java Modeling Language (JML) [Leavens et al., 2013].
- Rules and automation heuristics for a number of logical theories were added, including finite sequences, strings [Bubel et al., 2011], and bitvectors.
- Abstract interpretation was tightly integrated with logic-based symbolic execution [Bubel et al., 2009].

In addition, the functionality of the KeY was considerably extended. This concerns not merely the kind of analyses that are possible, but also usability.

- Functional verification is now only one of many analyses that can be performed with the KeY system. In addition, there is support for debugging and visualization [Hentschel et al., 2014a,b], test case generation [Engel and Hähnle, 2007, Gladisch, 2008], information flow analysis [Darvas et al., 2005, Grahl, 2015, Do et al., 2016], program transformation [Ji et al., 2013], and compilation [Ji, 2014].

- There are IDEs for KeY, including an Eclipse extension, that make it easy to keep track of proof obligations in larger projects [Hentschel et al., 2014c].
- A stripped down version of KeY, specifically developed for classroom exercises with Hoare logic, was provided [Hähnle and Bubel, 2008].

Finally, the increased maturity and coverage of the KeY system permitted us to include much more substantial case studies than in the first edition.

Inevitably, some of the research strands documented in the first edition did not reach the maturity or importance we hoped for and, therefore, were dropped. This is the case for specification patterns, specification in natural language, induction, and proof reuse. There is also no longer a dedicated chapter about Java integers: The relevant material is now, in much condensed form, part of the 'chapters on "First-Order Logic" and "Theories."'

A number of topics that are actively researched have not yet reached sufficient maturity to be included: merging nodes in symbolic execution proof trees, KeY for Java bytecode, certification, runtime verification, regression verification, to name just a few. Also left out is a variant of the KeY system for the concurrent modeling language ABS called KeY-ABS, which allows one to prove complex properties about unbounded programs and data structures. We are excited about all these developments, but we feel that they have not yet reached the maturity to be documented in the KeY book. We refer the interested reader to the research articles available from the KeY website at www. key-project.org.

Also not covered in this book is KeYmaera, a formal verification tool for hybrid, cyber-physical systems developed in André Platzer's research group at CMU and that has KeY as an ancestor. It deserves a book in its own right, which in fact has been written [Platzer, 2010].

The Concept Behind This Book

Most books on foundations of formal specification and verification orient their presentation along traditional lines in logic. This results in a gap between the foundations of verification and its application that is too wide for most readers. The main presentation principles of the KeY book is something that has *not* been changed between the first book about KeY and this volume:

- The material is presented on an advanced level suitable for graduate (MSc level) courses, and, of course, active researchers with an interest in verification.
- The dependency graph on the chapters in the book is not deep, such that the reader does not have to read many chapters before the one (s)he is most interested in. Moreover, the dependencies are not all too strong. More advanced readers may not have to strictly follow the graph, and less advanced readers may decide to follow up prerequisites on demand. The graph shows that the chapters on First-Order Logic, the Java Modeling Language, and Using the KeY Prover are entirely self-contained. The same holds for each chapter not appearing in the following graph.

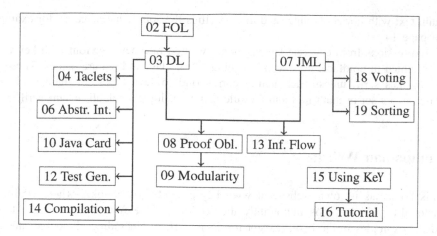

- The underlying verification paradigm is deductive verification in an expressive program logic.
- As a rule, the proofs of theoretical results are not contained here, but we give pointers on where to find them.
- The logic used for reasoning about programs is not a minimalist version suitable for theoretical investigations, but an industrial-strength version. The first-order part is equipped with a type system for modeling of object hierarchies, with underspecification, and with various built-in theories. The program logic covers full Java Card and substantial parts of Java. The main omissions are: generics (a transformation tool is available), floating-point types, threads, lambda expressions.
- Much emphasis is on specification, including the widely used JML. The generation of proof obligations from annotated source code is discussed at length.
- Two substantial case studies are included and presented in detail.

Nevertheless, we cannot and do not claim to have fully covered formal reasoning about (object-oriented) software in this book. One reason is that the choice of topics is dependent on our research agenda. As a consequence, important topics in formal verification, such as specification refinement or model checking, are out of our scope.

Typographic Conventions

We use a number of typesetting conventions to give the text a clearer structure. Occasionally, we felt that a historical remark, a digression, or a reference to material outside the scope of this book is required. In order to not interrupt the text flow we use gray boxes, such as the one on page 40, whenever this is the case.

In this book a considerable number of specification and programming languages are referred to and used for illustration. To avoid confusion we usually typeset multiline expressions from concrete languages in a special environment that is set apart from the main text with horizontal lines and that specifies the source language as, for example, on page 14.

Expressions from concrete languages are written in typewriter font with keywords highlighted in boldface, the exception being UML class and feature names. These are set in sans serif, unless class names correspond to Java types. Mathematical meta symbols are set in math font and the rule names of logical calculi in sans serif.

Companion Website

This book has its own website at www.key-project.org/thebook2, where additional material is provided: most importantly, the version of the KeY tool that was used to run all the examples in the book (except for Chaps. 10,19) including all source files, for example, programs and specifications (unless excluded for copyright reasons), various teaching materials such as slides and exercises, and the electronic versions of papers on KeY.

Acknowledgments We are very grateful to all researchers and students who contributed with their time and expertise to the KeY project. We would like to acknowledge in particular the editorial help of Dr. Daniel Grahl and Dr. Vladimir Klebanov during the production of this book.

Many current and former KeY project members made valuable contributions to the KeY project, even though they are not directly involved as chapter authors: Prof. Thomas Baar (HTW Berlin), Dr. Thorsten Bormer, Dr. Ádám Darvas, Dr. Crystal Din, Huy Qouc Do, Dr. Christian Engel, Dr. Tobias Gedell, Dr. Elmar Habermalz, Dr. Kristofer Johannisson, Michael Kirsten, Daniel Larsson, Prof. Wolfram Menzel (KIT; emeritus, co-founder of the KeY project), Gabriele Paganelli, Prof. Aarne Ranta (Gothenburg University), Dr. Andreas Roth, Prof. Ina Schaefer (TU Braunschweig), Dominic Scheurer, Prof. Steffen Schlager (HS Offenburg), Prof. Shmuel Tyszberowicz (The Academic College Tel Aviv-Yaffo), Dr. Bart van Delft, Dr. Isabel Tonin, Angela Wallenburg, and Dr. Dennis Walter.

Besides the current and former project members and the chapter authors of this book, many students helped with implementing the KeY system, to whom we extend our sincere thanks: Gustav Andersson, Dr. Marcus Baum, Hans-Joachim Daniels, Marco Drebing, Marius Hillenbrand, Eduard Kamburjan, Stefan Käsdorf, Dr. Bastian Katz, Uwe Keller, Stephan Könn, Achim Kuwertz, Denis Lohner, Moritz von Looz, Martin Möller, Dr. Ola Olsson, Jing Pan, Sonja Pieper, Prof. André Platzer (CMU Pittsburgh), Friedemann Rößler, Bettina Sasse, Dr. Ralf Sasse, Prof. Gabi Schmithüsen (Universität des Saarlandes), Max Schröder, Muhammad Ali Shah, Alex Sinner, Hubert Schmid, Holger Stenger, Kai Wallisch, Claus Wonnemann, and Zhan Zengrong.

The authors acknowledge support by the Deutsche Forschungsgemeinschaft (DFG) under projects "Program-level Specification and Deductive Verification of Security Properties" (DeduSec) and " Fully Automatic Logic-Based Information Flow" within Priority Programme 1496 "Reliably Secure Software Systems – RS^3" and under project "Deductive Regression Verification for Evolving Object-Oriented Software" within Priority Programme 1593 "Design for Future: Managed Software Evolution," as well as support by the German Federal Ministry of Education and Research (Bundesministerium für Bildung und Forschung, BMBF) for project "Formale Informationsflussspezifikation und -analyse in komponentenbasierten Systemen" as part of Software Campus. We also acknowledge support by the European Commission (EC) under FP7 Integrated Project "Highly Adaptable & Trustworthy Software using Formal Methods" and STREP "Engineering Virtualized Services."

The authors have done their job. The success of the result of their toil will now be judged by the readers. We hope they will find the text easily accessible, illuminating, stimulating and, yes, fun to read. What can be more fun than gaining insight into what was nebulous before or solving a problem at hand that defied a solution so far? We will not fail to admit that besides all the labor, writing this book was fun. Putting in words often helped us reach a better understanding of what we were writing about. Thus, it is not easy to say who profits more, the authors in writing the book or the readers from reading it. In the end this may be irrelevant, authors and readers together constitute the scientific community and together they advance the state of the art. It would be the greatest reward for us to see this happening and perhaps after another ten years, or even earlier, a return of the pink panther.

August 2016

Wolfgang Ahrendt
Bernhard Beckert
Richard Bubel
Reiner Hähnle
Peter H. Schmitt
Mattias Ulbrich

Contents

Part I Foundations

Part II Specification and Verification

Part III From Verification to Analysis

List of Figures

List of Tables

List of Listings

Chapter 1
Quo Vadis Formal Verification?

Reiner Hähnle

The KeY system has been developed for over a decade. During this time, the field of Formal Methods as well as Computer Science in general has changed considerably. Based on an analysis of this trajectory of changes we argue why, after all these years, the project is still relevant and what the challenges in the coming years might be. At the same time we give a brief overview of the various tools based on KeY technology and explain their architecture.

1.1 What KeY Is

There is the KeY project, the KeY system, and a collection of software productivity tools based on the KeY system that we call the KeY framework (see Figure 1.1 below).

The KeY *project* is a long-term research project started in 1998 by Reiner Hähnle, Wolfram Menzel, and Peter Schmitt at University of Karlsruhe (now Karlsruhe Institute of Technology). After Menzel's retirement Bernhard Beckert joined the project leader team which has been unchanged ever since. This proves that long-term research on fundamental problems is possible—despite dramatic changes in the academic funding landscape—provided that the people involved think it is worthwhile. The question is: why should they think it is?

From the very first publication [Hähnle et al., 1998] the aim of the KeY project was to integrate formal software analysis methods, such as formal specification and formal verification, into the realm of mainstream software development. This has always been—and still is—a very ambitious goal that takes a long-time perspective to realize. In the following we argue why we are still optimistic that it can be reached.

The KeY *system* was originally a formal verification tool for the Java programming language, to be coupled with a UML-based design tool. Semantic constraints expressed in the Object Constraint Language (OCL) [Warmer and Kleppe, 1999] were intended as a common property specification language. This approach had to be abandoned, because UML and OCL never reached a level of semantic foundation

© Springer International Publishing AG 2016
W. Ahrendt et al. (Eds.): Deductive Software Verification, LNCS 10001, pp. 1–19, 2016
DOI: 10.1007/978-3-319-49812-6_1

that was sufficiently rigorous for formal verification [Baar, 2003]. In addition, OCL is not an object-oriented language and the attempt to formally specify the behavior of Java programs yields clumsy results.

To formally specify Java programs KeY currently uses the result of another long-term project: the *Java Modeling Language* (JML) [Leavens et al., 2013] which enjoys wide acceptance in the formal methods and programming languages communities.

From the mid 2000s onward, a number of application scenarios for deductive verification technology beyond functional verification have been realized on the basis of the KeY system. These include test case generation, an innovative debugging tool, a teaching tool for Hoare logic, and an Eclipse extension that integrates functional verification with mainstream software development tools. Even though they share the same code base, these tools are packaged separately to cater for the different needs of their prospective users.

1.2 Challenges To Formal Verification

First, let us clarify that in this book we are concerned with *formal* software verification. With this we mean a formal, even mechanical argument, typically expressed in a formal logical system, that a given program satisfies a given property which also had been formalized. In contrast to this, most software engineers associate heuristic, informal techniques such as testing or code reviews with the term "verification" [Sommerville, 2015, Chapter 8].

Formal verification of nontrivial programs is tedious and error-prone. Therefore, it is normally supported by tools which might be dedicated verification tools, such as KeY, or general purpose interactive theorem provers such as Isabelle [Nipkow et al., 2002] or Coq [Dowek et al., 1993]. One can further distinguish between interactive tools where a verification proof is built in dialogue with a human user and tools that work in "batch mode," not unlike a compiler, where a program is incrementally annotated with specifications and hints until its correctness can be automatically proven. Examples of the latter are the systems Dafny [Leino, 2010] and VeriFast [Jacobs and Piessens, 2008]. A full discussion of possible architectures of verification systems, as well as their pros and cons, is found in the survey [Beckert and Hähnle, 2014].

For a long time the term *formal verification* was almost synonymous with *functional verification*. In the last years it became more and more clear that full functional verification is an elusive goal for almost all application scenarios. Ironically, this happened *because of* advances in verification technology: with the advent of verifiers, such as KeY, that mostly cover and precisely model industrial languages and that can handle realistic systems, it finally became obvious just how difficult and time consuming the specification of functionality of real systems is. Not verification but specification is the real bottleneck in functional verification [Baumann et al., 2012]. This becomes also very clear from the case studies in Chapters 18 and 19.

Even though formal verification of industrial target languages made considerable progress, *complete* coverage of languages such as Java, Scala, or C++ in any formal verification tool is still a significant challenge. The KeY tool, while fully covering Java Card (see Chapter 10), makes similar restrictions to most other verification tools: floating-point types are not supported, programs are assumed to be sequential, and generic types are expected to have been compiled away. On the other hand, Java integer types, exceptions and static initialization all are faithfully modeled in KeY.

Some of the restrictions will be, at least partially, addressed in the future. First approaches to formal verification of concurrent Java have been presented [Amighi et al., 2012] and are on their way into KeY [Mostowski, 2015]. On the other hand, to the best of my knowledge, all existing formalizations of Java concurrency assume sequential consistency. A full formalization of the Java memory model seems far away at this moment.

Floating-point types seem a more achievable goal, because formal models of the IEEE floating-point standard are available today [Yu, 2013] and it is only a matter of time until they are supported in verification tools. A more difficult question, however, appears to be how to formally specify floating-point programs.

A major challenge for all formal verification approaches, most of which are part of academic research projects, is the evolution of industrial languages such as Java. This evolution takes place at a too fast pace for academic projects with their limited resources to catch up quickly. Moreover, the design of new language features takes into account such qualities as usability, marketability, or performance, but never verifiability. Many recent additions to Java, for example, lambda expressions, pose considerable challenges to formal verification. Many others, while they would be straightforward to realize, do not yield any academic gain, i.e., publishable papers. This results in a considerable gap between the language supported by a verification tool and its latest version. KeY, for example, reflects mostly Java 1.5, while the latest Java version at the time of writing this article is 1.8.

A problem of a somewhat different kind constitute the vast APIs of contemporary programming languages. The API of a language is among its greatest assets, because it is the basis of programmer productivity, but it presents a major problem for program analysis: in general neither the source code of an API method is available nor a formal contract describing its behavior. For special cases like Java Card [Mostowski, 2007] or for specific aspects such as concurrency [Amighi et al., 2014b] it is possible to provide formal specifications of API classes, however, in general the usage of APIs poses a serious problem for program analysis. To be fair, though, this is the case not only in formal verification, but already for test case generation or much simpler static analyses. That formal verification of APIs is, in principle, feasible shows the recent complete verification of Eiffel's container library [Polikarpova et al., 2015].

The preceding discussion gives a somewhat mixed prospect for formal verification of functional properties of Java. So, why do we carry on with KeY? As a matter of fact, we believe that there are many good reasons and one can even argue that deductive verification is just beginning to become an interesting technology (see also [Beckert and Hähnle, 2014]). Let us see why.

1.3 Roles of Deductive Verification

A central insight from the last decade or so is that deductive verification technology is not only useful for functional verification, but is applicable to a large number of further scenarios, many of which avoid the problems discussed in the previous section.

1.3.1 Avoid the Need for Formal Specification

If full-fledged functional verification is no longer the main focus, but deductive verification technology is used for analyses that do not require to compare a program against its functionality, then the problem of providing formal specifications is at least alleviated or even vanishes completely.

For example, it is very useful to know that a program does not throw any runtime exceptions, that it terminates, or that it only accesses a certain part of the heap. Such *generic properties* can be specified in a uniform manner for a given program. In the last years a number of specialized verification tools appeared for this class of problems that scale up to real-world problems [Beyer, 2015]. Note, however, that it might still be necessary to provide detailed specifications in order to avoid too many false positives.

Closely related is the problem of *resource analysis*, where the best-case or worst-case consumption for a target program of a given resource is computed. Analyzed resources include runtime and memory, but also bandwidth or the number of parallel threads. Cost analysis tools involve complex constraint solving and typically do not include a formal semantics of the target language. Therefore, the question of soundness arises. In this context, verification tools such as KeY were successfully employed as "proof checkers" [Albert et al., 2012]. This is possible, because the resource analyzer can infer enough annotations (such as the invariants) required for automating the verification process and because resource properties can be expressed in a uniform manner.

About ten years ago, several research groups independently proposed to generate glass-box test cases with code coverage guarantees by symbolic execution of the program under test [Tillmann and Schulte, 2005, Engel and Hähnle, 2007, Albert et al., 2009].[1] In Chapter 12 we describe how test cases can be obtained from a verification attempt in KeY. The embedding into a deductive framework has a number of advantages over using symbolic execution alone:

- full first-order simplification can eliminate unreachable code and hence irrelevant test cases, in particular, when combined with preconditions;
- with suitable loop invariants and contracts even programs with loops and recursive programs can be fully symbolically executed, thus increasing coverage;

---

[1] None of them had realized at the time that this idea had in essence been already suggested by King [1976].

- test oracles can be specified declaratively and can be implemented by deductive inference.

Yet another application of deductive verification that can dispense with detailed specifications are *relational properties*. Relational properties became increasingly important as an application scenario for verification in recent years. They compare the behavior of two or more programs when run with identical inputs. The crucial point is that it is not necessary to fully specify the behavior of the target programs, but only compare their respective behaviors and ensure they maintain a certain relation (e.g., bisimilarity). That relation is typically fixed and can be expressed in a uniform manner for all given target programs. Therefore, the specification can either be written once and for all or at least it can be computed automatically. This observation was used, for example, by Benton [2004] to formalize program properties and the soundness of program transformations in relational Hoare logic.

Examples of relational properties include information flow [Darvas et al., 2003, 2005], where the property to be proven takes the form of a security policy; another is the correctness of compiler optimizations [Barthe et al., 2013a] and program transformations [Ji et al., 2013] where it must be shown that the original and the compiled/transformed program behave identically on all observable outputs. These scenarios are supported by KeY and are discussed in Chapters 13 and 14, respectively, in this book.

What makes relational properties attractive as an application of verification technology, besides the fact that extensive specifications are not needed, is the high degree of automation that is achievable. The main obstacle against automation is the need to provide suitable specification annotations in the form of loop invariants (or contracts in the case of recursive calls). To prove relational properties, the required invariants are often simple enough to be inferred automatically. In KeY a combination of symbolic execution and abstract interpretation proved to be effective [Do et al., 2016]. How this works is explained in Chapter 6.

Uniform specifications and simple invariants contribute towards automation in another crucial way: the resulting proof obligations tend not to require complex quantifier instantiations. Given sufficient support for reasoning over theories that occur in the target program, full automation is achievable for many relational problems. Chapter 5 explains by selected examples how theory reasoning has been integrated into the deduction machinery of KeY.

1.3.2 Restricted Target Language

In Section 1.2 we pointed out that real-world languages, such as Java, C++, or Scala with their vast scope, their idiosyncrasies and the dynamics of their development pose significant challenges to formal verification. One obvious reaction to this is to focus on programming languages that are smaller and less prone to change. Examples include Java Card [JavaCardRTE], a Java dialect for small, mobile devices, Real-Time Java [Bollella and Gosling, 2000], and SPARK [Jennings, 2009], an Ada dialect for safety-critical software. For these languages complete formalizations, including their APIs exist. In KeY we support Java Card (see [Mostowski, 2007] and Chapter 10) and Real-Time Java [Ahrendt et al., 2012].

A different approach is to design a *modeling language* that retains the essential properties of the underlying implementation language, but abstracts away from some of its complexities. Verification of abstract models of the actual system is standard in model checking [Clarke et al., 1999]; PROMELA [Holzmann, 2003], for example, is a widely used modeling language for distributed systems. In the realm of object-oriented programming with concurrency the language ABS (for *Abstract Behavioral Specification*) [Johnsen et al., 2011] was recently suggested as an abstraction for languages such as Java, Scala, C++, or Erlang, several of which it supports with code generator backends. ABS has a concurrency model based on cooperative scheduling that permits compositional verification of concurrent programs [Din, 2014]. It also enforces strong encapsulation, programming to interfaces, and features abstract data types and a functional sublanguage. This allows a number of scalable analyses tools, including resource analysis, deadlock analysis, test generation, as well as formal verification [Wong et al., 2012]. A version of KeY that supports ABS is available [Chang Din et al., 2015].

The formal verification system KeYmaera[2] [Platzer and Quesel, 2008, Fulton et al., 2015] targets a modeling language that combines an abstract, imperative language with continuous state transitions that are specified by partial differential equations. It can be used to formally specify and verify complex functional properties of realistic hybrid systems [Loos et al., 2013] that cannot be expressed in model checking tools.

1.3.3 Formal Verification in Teaching

One important application area of formal verification is education in formal approaches to software development. Here the coverage of the target language and of the APIs are not a critical issue, because the teacher can avoid features that are not supported and is able to supply specifications of the required APIs.

On the other hand, different issues are of central importance when deductive verification systems are used in teaching. The main challenge in teaching formal methods is to convey to students that the learning outcomes are useful and worthwhile. Students should not be force-fed with a formal methods course they find to be frustrating or irrelevant. This puts high demands on the usability and the degree of automation in the used tools. It is also crucial to present the course material in a manner that connects formal verification with relevant every-day problems that one has to solve as a developer. Finally, one has to take care that not too many mathematical prerequisites are needed.

Since 2004 we use the KeY system in a variety of mandatory and specialized courses, where we try to address the issues raised in the previous paragraph. In

---

[2] KeYmaera branched off from KeY, see also Section 1.5.1.

2007 we created a B.Sc. level course called *Testing, Debugging, and Verification* [Ahrendt et al., 2009a] where we present formal specification and verification as part of a continuous spectrum of software quality measures. This being a B.Sc. course, we wanted to illustrate formal verification in Hoare style [Hoare, 1969], and with a simple while-language, not Java. To our amazement, we could not find any tool support with automatic discharge of first-order verification conditions (after all, we did not want to include automated theorem proving in our course as well!). Therefore, we decided to create a version of the KeY system that combines forward symbolic execution with axiomatic reasoning on a while-language with automatic first-order simplification [Hähnle and Bubel, 2008]. Incidentally, when we were looking for examples for our course to be done with KeY Hoare, we found that a large number of Hoare logic derivations published in lectures notes and text books are slightly wrong: forgotten preconditions, too weak invariants, etc. This is practically inevitable when formal verification is attempted by hand and demonstrates that tool support is absolutely essential in a formal methods course. The KeY Hoare tool is discussed in this book in Chapter 17. The aforementioned course is currently still taught at Chalmers University[3] (with KeY having been replaced by Dafny [Leino, 2010]).

Another course worth mentioning is called *Software Engineering using Formal Methods*. It was created in 2004 by the author of this chapter, initially conceived as a first year computer science M.Sc. course and it is still being taught[4] in this fashion at Chalmers University and elsewhere. The course introduces model checking with PROMELA and SPIN [Holzmann, 2003] in its first part and functional verification of Java with KeY in the second. It is a mix between theoretical foundations and hands-on experimentation. By 2012 KeY was considered to be stable and usable enough (SPIN had reached that state over a decade earlier) to design a somewhat stripped down version of the course for 2nd year B.Sc. students. Since Fall 2012 that course is compulsory for Computer Science majors at TU Darmstadt and taught annually to 250–300 students.[5] The response of the students is on the whole encouraging and evaluation results are in the upper segment of compulsory courses. Other versions of the course, based on material supplied by the KeY team, are or were taught at CMU, Polytechnic University of Madrid, University of Rennes, University of Iowa, RISC Linz, to name a few.

What this shows is that formal verification can be successfully taught even in large classes and to students without a strong background or interest in mathematics. The user interface of the KeY system, in particular its GUI, plays a major role here. Another important issue is ease of installation: KeY installs via Java webstart technology on most computers with only one click.[6] In this context it cannot be overestimated how important usability and stability are for user acceptance. Students later become professionals and are the prospective users of our technology. Their feedback has been taken very seriously in the development of KeY. In fact, the results

---

[3] www.cse.chalmers.se/edu/course/TDA567

[4] www.cse.chalmers.se/edu/course/TDA293

[5] www.se.informatik.tu-darmstadt.de/teaching/courses/formale-methoden-im-softwareentwurf

[6] If you want to try it out right now, jump to Section 15.2 to see how.

of systematic usability studies done with KeY [Beckert and Grebing, 2012, Hentschel et al., 2016] are reflected in the design of its user interface. KeY's user interface and its various features are explained in Chapter 15. A systematic tutorial to get you started with the verification of actual Java programs is found in Chapter 16.

1.3.4 Avoid the Need for Fully Specified Formal Semantics

There is one application scenario for deductive verification technology that not only dispenses with the need for formal specification, but does not even require any prior knowledge in formal methods and does not necessarily rest on a full axiomatization of all target language constructs. First experiments with a prototype of an interactive debugger based on KeY's symbolic execution engine [Hähnle et al., 2010] resulted in a dedicated, mature tool called *Symbolic Execution Debugger* (SED) [Hentschel et al., 2014a]. It offers all the functionality of a typical Java debugger, but in addition, it can explore all symbolic execution paths through a given program, which it visualizes as a tree. Full exploration of all paths is possible, because the SED can handle loop invariants and method contracts. Also the symbolic environment and heap at each execution step can be visualized. The SED is realized as an Eclipse extension and is as easy to use as the standard Java debugger of Eclipse. The SED is explained in Chapter 11.

In the future we plan to support concurrent Java programs in the SED and programs with floating-point types, both of which are not axiomatized in KeY's program logic. But for the purpose of debugging and visualization this is also not really necessary. To debug concurrent programs it is already useful to concentrate on one thread—this is what debuggers normally do. The underlying verification machinery of KeY can give additional hints that go beyond the capabilities of standard debuggers, for example, which values might have been changed by other threads.

Floating-point data can be represented simply by symbolic terms that contain the operations performed to obtain a current value. As floating-point operations raise no `ArithmeticExcpetion` besides "divide by zero," they do not create control flow that is not represented already in a symbolic execution tree over integer types. Of course, a symbolic execution tree over "uninterpreted" floating-point terms may contain infeasible paths. But this could be detected by test case generation.

1.3.5 Where Are We Now?

Where does deductive verification with KeY stand at this moment? What about our original goal to bring formal verification into the realm of mainstream software development? I believe we are on the right track: with the Symbolic Execution Debugger, with the Eclipse integration of KeY, and with mostly automatic tools such as test case generation. Other research groups are also working towards the general goal, even though by different means: several test case generation tools based on symbolic execution are commercially used; a static analysis tool using deduction is part of Microsoft's developer tools, a termination analyzer will soon follow; the Spec# programming system includes a verifier and bug finding tool for the C# programming language.

As explained in Section 1.3.1 above, deductive verification technology is also a base technology for security analysis, sound compilation and program transformation, resource analysis and, in the future, to regression test generation, fault propagation as well as possibly other scenarios. We predict that in ten years from now, deductive verification will be the underlying technology, largely invisible to the end-user, in a wide range of software productivity products used in different phases of the development chain.

But what about functional verification—the supposed gold standard? Routine functional specification and formal verification is possible—for restricted languages such as Java Card or SPARK that can be fully formalized, or for languages such as ABS that have been developed with verifiability in mind. Partial functional verification of medium-sized, real C programs is possible [Alkassar et al., 2010, Klein et al., 2010]—with huge effort and with limited reusability. Most importantly, functional verification of complex Java library methods is possible, provided that they fall into Java fragments covered by verification tools: with the help of KeY we found a subtle bug in the default sorting method of Java (as well as Python, Haskell, and several other programming languages and frameworks) and we showed that our fix actually eliminates the bug [De Gouw et al., 2015]. The proof required over two million steps and an effort of several person weeks.

A central limitation of all approaches to functional verification so far is their brittleness in the presence of evolution of the verification target: any change to the program under verification may necessitate to redo a large amount of the verification effort already spent. Even though first approaches to alleviate this problem have been presented [Bubel et al., 2014b], it is far from being solved.

For the reasons spelled out above, we expect that functional verification of executable source code remains a niche application of deductive verification in the foreseeable future, suitable for safety-critical software, where restricted programming languages are acceptable and changes to the verification target are carefully controlled. Another area where formal verification will become widely used are model-centric approaches, where verification of a software model is combined with code generation. The latter is particularly interesting for industry, where model-driven development approaches have been well received.

But then, who knows? Probably, the world (of verification) will have changed again, when we prepare the third edition of the KeY book in 2025 or so. Already now we see that the view on deductive verification of software became much more differentiated than it was at the start of the KeY project. The question is no longer *whether* deductive verification is useful, but *how* to make best use of it. These are exciting times to work with Formal Methods in Software Engineering!

1.4 The Architecture of KeY

We emphasize that KeY is an integrated, standalone system that doesn't need any external components to function. This is in contrast to, for example, verification condition generators such as Dafny [Leino, 2010] that are part of a tool chain (in Dafny's case Boogie [Barnett et al., 2006] and various SMT solvers). Nevertheless, KeY can be advantageously integrated with other deduction and software productivity tools, as we shall see.

1.4.1 Prover Core

How does the architecture of KeY support the extended application scenarios of deductive verification sketched above? Let us start at the core. Here we find a pretty standard *sequent* or *Gentzen* calculus: a set of schematic rules that manipulate structured implications, called *sequents*, of the form

$$\varphi_1, \ldots, \varphi_m \implies \psi_1, \ldots, \psi_n$$

where $0 \leq m$, $0 \leq n$ and the φ_i, ψ_j are formulas. The semantics of sequents is that the *meaning formula* of the sequent, i.e., the universal closure of the formula $\bigwedge_{i=1}^{m} \varphi_i \to \bigvee_{j=1}^{n} \varphi_j$, is valid in all models. This setup is a standard choice for many interactive theorem provers [Balser et al., 2000, Nipkow et al., 2002].

A specific choice of KeY, however, is that formulas φ_i are from a *program logic* that includes correctness modalities over actual Java source code fragments. Before we come to that, let us note some important design decisions in KeY's logic. First of all, the program logic of KeY is an extension of typed first-order classical logic. All KeY formulas that fall into its first-order fragment are evaluated relative to classical model semantics and all sequent rules over first-order formulas are classically sound and complete. In particular, we assume that all structural sequent rules are valid so that associativity, order, and multiplicity of formulas occurring in sequents are irrelevant. The first-order fragment of KeY's logic and its calculus is explained in detail in Chapter 2. Figure 2.1, for example, lists the rules for classical connectives and quantifiers.

A central design issue for any interactive verifier is how the rules of its calculus are composed into proofs. Here we come to a second peculiarity of KeY that sets it apart from most other systems: the rule set is parametric to the system and can be arbitrarily chosen during initialization. Many verifiers let the system user build new rules from existing ones with the help of meta-rules, so-called tactics [Gordon et al., 1979] with the restriction that only rules whose validity can be proven inside the system are available [Nipkow et al., 2002, Paulin-Mohring, 2012]. This requires some form of higher-order logic. The main advantage is that soundness of the rule base can be reduced to a small set of trusted axioms, for example, those of set theory in the case of Isabelle/HOL [Nipkow et al., 2002].

In KeY we decided to follow a different path and trade off a small trusted foundation for more flexibility and a less steep learning curve for users of the system. Schematic sequent rules in KeY are specified as so-called *taclets* [Beckert et al., 2004]. They contain the declarative, logical content of the rule schemata, but also *pragmatic* information: in which context and when a rule should be applied by an automated reasoning strategy and how it is to be presented to the user. Taclets constitute in essence a tiny domain-specific language for typed, first-order schematic rules. This is explained in detail in Chapter 4. At the core of the KeY system is an efficient interpreter that applies taclets to goal sequents and thereby constructs proof trees. It is called *KeY Prover* in Figure 1.1.

The language of taclets and the KeY Prover are intentionally restricted for efficiency reasons: for example, taclets always have exactly one main formula of a sequent in focus that can be manipulated and automated proof search does not implement backtracking (though proofs can be pruned interactively). As a consequence, one cannot describe most calculi for modal and substructural logics [D'Agostino et al., 1999] with taclets; one could represent a calculus for intuitionistic logic, but not automated proof search in it, etc. In other words, taclets are optimized for their main use case: automated proof search in typed first-order logic and logic-based symbolic execution in JavaDL.

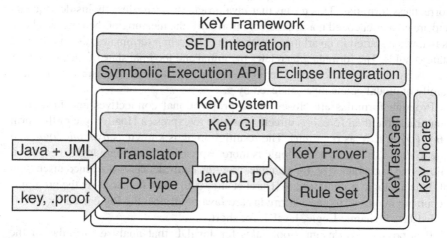

Figure 1.1 Architecture of the KeY tool set

Taclets provide the kind of flexibility we need for the various application scenarios in KeY: there are different rule sets tailored to functional verification, to information flow analysis, etc. Moreover, taclets dispense with the need to support higher-order quantification in the logic. This makes interaction with the prover easier, both for humans and with other programs: for example, as first-order logic is taught in introductory courses on discrete math, it is possible to expose second-year B.Sc. students to KeY in a compulsory course at Technische Universität Darmstadt (see Section 1.3.3). But also the proximity of modeling languages such as JML and of the language of SMT solvers [Barrett et al., 2010] to typed first-order logic make it simple to import and export formulas from KeY's program logic. On the one hand, this makes it possible to have JML-annotated Java as an input language of KeY, on the other hand, using SMT solvers as a backend increases the degree of automation.

An important question is how to ensure soundness of the more than 1,500 taclets loaded in a standard configuration of KeY. Many of them are first-order rewrite rules and have been proven to be sound in KeY itself relative to the few rules given in Chapter 2. Rules that manipulate programs, however, can in general not be validated in KeY's first-order logic. Instead, soundness of a large part of the rules dealing with programs has been proven against a formal semantics of Java external to KeY [Ahrendt et al., 2005]. That paper, as well as Section 3.5.3, discusses the pros and cons of KeY's taclet approach versus the foundational approach implemented in higher-order logic proof assistants.

1.4.2 Reasoning About Programs

The program logic of KeY contains "correctness formulas" of the form $[p]\varphi$, where p is an executable fragment of a Java program and φ a formula that may in turn contain correctness formulas. This means that Java programs occur directly inside sequents and are neither encoded nor abstracted. Informally, the meaning of the formula above is that when started in an arbitrary state, if the program p terminates, then in its final state φ holds. The formula $[p]\varphi$ relates the initial and the final state of the program p, i.e., its big step semantics $[\![p]\!]$. Therefore, the $[\cdot]\cdot$ operator can be seen as an (infinite) family of modal connectives, indexed by p.

Program formulas are closed under propositional connectives and first-order quantification, therefore, it is directly possible to express a Hoare triple of the form $\{\theta\}p\{\varphi\}$ in KeY as $\theta \to [p]\varphi$. The resulting logic is known as *dynamic logic* and due to Pratt [1977]. Dynamic logic is more expressive than Hoare logic, because it allows one to characterize, for example, program equivalence. A deepened discussion of dynamic logic is contained in [Harel et al., 2000] and Chapter 3. As the programs occurring in our correctness formulas are Java programs, the logic used by KeY is called Java Dynamic Logic, JavaDL for short.

It is possible to design proof rules for JavaDL that analyze formulas of the form $[p; \omega]\varphi$, where p is a single Java statement and ω the remaining (possibly empty) program. For example, p might be a simple assignment of the form $x=e$, where x is an int variable and e a simple int expression. Chapter 3 discusses rules that reduce such a program to a statement about the remaining program $[\omega]\varphi$ plus first-order verification conditions. Other rules decompose complex Java statements into simple ones. The rules for program formulas in KeY are designed in such a way that they constitute a symbolic execution engine for Java. Together with an induction principle (in KeY: loop invariants), symbolic execution becomes a complete verification method [Burstall, 1974, Heisel et al., 1987]: Any valid program formula, for example, $n \geq i \to [\texttt{while (i<n) \{i++\};}]i \doteq n$ can be syntactically reduced

to a finite set of valid first-order formulas with arithmetic. In contrast to model checking, it is neither necessary to abstract the target program, nor can spurious counter examples occur. The price is, of course, that Java programs must be annotated with suitable specifications, including loop invariants. In addition, some quantifier instantiations might not be found automatically, but must be supplied by the user. This requires a certain amount of expertise, at least if KeY is used for functional verification.

While (logic-based) symbolic execution plus invariant reasoning is, in principle, sufficient to formally verify programs, it is not feasible to verify anything but toy programs without a modularization principle, because the number of branches in a symbolic execution tree grows exponentially with the number of decision conditions in a program. For an imperative, object-oriented language such as Java the most common approach to decompose its verification problem into chunks of manageable size is to provide for each method implementation a declarative specification of its behavior in the form of a *contract*. The idea is that a method call is replaced by the contract which the implementer of the method promises to honor. Thus the caller of a method is the contract's client and the callee is its supplier. This idea goes back to Meyer [1992] who propagated it as *design-by-contract* and implemented a runtime assertion checker in the Eiffel language, but did not use contracts for the purpose of verification. Contracts became also part of the OCL [Warmer and Kleppe, 1999] and in this form were implemented in KeY [Ahrendt et al., 2000].

JML introduced contracts systematically to the Java language; a method contract consists of three parts: a *precondition* specifies when the callee considers the contract to be applicable; a *postcondition* specifies what the callee promises to guarantee in the final state after it returns; finally, an *assignable* clause records the program locations that might have been changed during the execution. Many of the examples in the JML specification and tutorials [Leavens et al., 2013] are geared towards the use of JML in runtime verification. For this reason we found it useful to include Chapter 7 in this book that explains in detail how JML can be used to formally specify functional correctness of Java programs. It can be read with benefit even if one is not interested in KeY and simply wants to learn about formal specification of object-oriented programs.

While contracts provide a natural and effective way to reason about a program by looking at one method at a time, there are two serious challenges in practice: the first is technical and is related to the question of how to specify succinctly the state change effected by a method execution. For example, assignable clauses in practice are not static, but depend on the symbolic heap at call time. There are several technical solutions to this problem, including ownership types [Clarke et al., 1998] and dynamic frames [Kassios, 2006]. The approach of KeY is a variation of the latter and discussed in Chapter 9. The second challenge is to come up with suitable contracts in the first place. As pointed out above this is, at least partially, still an open research issue.

1.4.3 Proof Obligations

A minimal input file of a verification task for KeY might look as simple as this:

—— KeY ——————————————————————————————————

```
\problem{
  \[{ ... a Java program ... }\] φ
}
```

————————————————————————————————————— KeY ——

The system will offer the user to prove validity of the formula given as the problem specification, i.e., partial correctness of the given Java program with respect to the postcondition φ (the square brackets are rendered in ASCII as \[, \]). How this is done is explained in detail in Chapter 15. It is possible to load such a file with the extension .key directly into the prover (see Figure 1.1). In most cases, however, the JavaDL formula to be proven is the result of a translation and a selection of a specific proof obligation. Consider the following snippet from a .java file with JML annotations:

—— Java + JML ————————————————————————————————

```
class C {
  /*@ invariant ι; @*/
  ...
  /*@
    @ requires θ;
    @ ensures φ;
    @*/
  void m(Object o) { ... method body ... }
  ...
}
```

————————————————————————————————— Java + JML ——

At first glance, this looks similar to the .key file above. But there might be many methods declared in it as well as class invariants. One of them has to be selected. And then what to prove? That a selected method satisfies its contract? That the contract is well-defined? But it is also possible to prove *nonfunctional* properties about a given program (see Section 1.3.1), such as secure information flow (see Chapter 13) and correctness of program transformations (see Chapter 14).

So for each given .java file there are a plethora of different proof obligations (PO) one might want to look at. It is necessary to first select one of them and then to translate it into JavaDL. This translation is far from trivial: the Java name space must be flattened into a first-order signature, default assumptions of JML (for example, o!=null above) must be ensured, well-formedness of the heap and default values must be assumed. Implicit declarations in Java, such as default constructors or "extends Object" must be made explicit, etc. The translation of JML (or, rather, the KeY-specific extension of JML) to JavaDL and the generation of various proof obligations is a fully automatic process and explained in Chapter 8.

1.4.4 The Frontends

When you download, install, and start up the KeY system you will see its graphical user interface (GUI), see Figure 1.2. This is the standard frontend of the KeY system. The KeY GUI is a stand-alone Java application. Its usage scenario is to perform functional verification of JML-annotated Java programs. Upon loading a `.java` file the proof obligation selector is launched and selected POs are automatically translated into JavaDL.

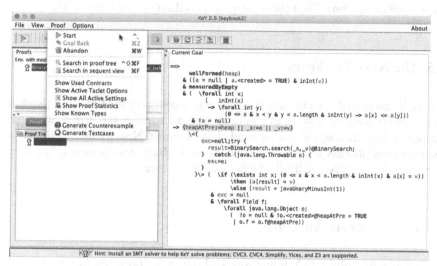

Figure 1.2 GUI of the KeY system with a loaded proof obligation

The test case generation tool, discussed in Chapter 12, is integrated into the KeY GUI (and into the Eclipse GUI, see below), but test case generation typically requires much less user interaction than functional verification. On the other hand, the generated test cases need to be connected to JUNIT (see junit.org) or other unit test frameworks to be executed and managed.

For some of the application scenarios of deductive verification discussed in Section 1.2 the KeY GUI is not suitable. The various tools based on the KeY system also address a variety of different user communities. Therefore, they are packaged separately from the KeY system and provide alternative frontends.

The teaching tool KeY Hoare is a stripped down version of the KeY system that lets students perform formal verification exercises on a simple while-language and provides a Hoare logic-like view of JavaDL proofs [Hähnle and Bubel, 2008]. KeY Hoare has an interface that is similar to the KeY GUI, but is much simplified.

There are two KeY frontends in the shape of extensions of the popular software development environment Eclipse: the Symbolic Execution Debugger, mentioned above in Section 1.3.4 and discussed more fully in Chapter 11, is fully immersed into Eclipse. Generation of POs and proving them happens in the background, the

KeY system is completely invisible to the user. This is made possible by a dedicated symbolic execution API which exports the capabilities of the KeY system (described in the previous subsections) to external programs without having to go via the KeY GUI. Finally, the Eclipse integration of the KeY system attempts to integrate formal verification with KeY into the standard development workflow. Currently, there are two Eclipse extensions: the KeY 4 Eclipse Starter that connects existing Java projects with the KeY system so it can be invoked from within Eclipse to verify methods. The second extension is called KeY Resources and extends a standard Eclipse Java project into a KeY project that permits to run proofs in the background and to manage open proof obligations. The Eclipse integration is discussed in Chapter 15.

1.5 The Next Ten Years

A decade has passed since the first lines of the first edition of the KeY book [Beckert et al., 2007] were written. In this introduction we tried to summarize what has happened since then and where we stand at the moment. Now we take a glimpse at the future and discuss what appear to be the most likely developments. The third edition of the KeY book will tell whether we are on target.

1.5.1 Modular Architecture

The architecture of the KeY framework laid out in the previous section suggests that the KeY system can be reused and instantiated for its various incarnations and usage scenarios. To tell the truth, this is not quite the case. In reality, there are a number of *profiles* of the KeY system: for functional verification, for Hoare logic, for information flow, etc. They all started from the same basis, but live in different development branches. The problem with this is obvious: it is difficult to propagate bug fixes and other improvements. The system KeYmaera [Platzer and Quesel, 2008], now developed by André Platzer at CMU Pittsburgh, branched off from KeY at around 2007 and soon the differences between the systems became too large to attempt a merge. This is regrettable, because a lot of improvements were made for each system over the years that would have benefited both of them, but are now too expensive to transfer.

To avoid this situation in the future, a major refactoring of the KeY system has been initiated. There will be an extensible common core, into which all major development branches eventually will be remerged.

A closely related architectural issue concerns the target language. KeY has been developed to verify Java programs, but currently supports at least also the modeling language ABS [Bubel et al., 2014a] and the while-language used in KeY Hoare. A version of KeY for a subset of C was once available [Mürk et al., 2007], but was abandoned: the lack of multi-language support in KeY made it impossible to attempt a merge and maintaining a separate branch was too expensive. Finally, the sound compilation approach detailed in Chapter 14 requires at least to support Java bytecode. All this suggests that KeY should strive to enable support for multiple target languages. This seems possible, because the language-specific frontends (parsers, pretty-printers) are largely separate and the internal data structures dealing with ASTs are fairly general. Importantly, the taclet concept and the prover core can be made generic.

We expect that the next major release of KeY will have a unified architecture for different extensions and will offer multi-target language support.

1.5.2 Relational Properties Are Everywhere

Two of the various kinds of proof obligations currently supported by KeY are relational in their nature (see Section 1.3.1): information flow and sound program transformation. We argued above that relational properties are a highly interesting scenario for deductive verification, because specifications are uniform and coupling invariants are much easier to derive than functional invariants. We predict that relational verification problems will become a hotspot for research in formal verification in the coming years. Not only are they feasible and practically relevant, but after a closer look they are very widespread, even ubiquitous in software development. To name just three examples:

1. Fault injection is an import testing strategy against external faults for safety-critical systems. Using deductive verification, it can be generalized to a symbolic fault analysis [Larsson and Hähnle, 2007]. In analogy to verification of information flow properties one can then prove properties about the *fault propagation* for a given program.
2. A growing problem for software that must work in many different environments and configurations is to detect and to exclude unwanted feature interactions [Apel et al., 2010]. To compare the behavior of two versions of a program with different features again is a relational problem.
3. Regression verification is a problem of huge practical interest, particularly in modern software development processes, such as continuous deployment. As pointed out above in Section 1.3.1, it is much easier to verify the preservation of behavior among two closely related programs than to establish functional correctness. Therefore, automatic regression verification is an interesting and feasible goal of deductive verification [Felsing et al., 2014].

And there is another important reason why relational verification problems are interesting: they provide a natural bridge to test-based approaches. For example, from a failed attempt at verifying secure information flow, it is possible to extract a candidate for an attack on privacy, an *exploit* [Do et al., 2015]; from a failed attempt to show behavioral equivalence of two versions of a program one can generate a regression test, and so on.

1.5.3 Learning from Others

Recently there has been substantial progress in the field of automata learning related
to the problem of learning behavioral structures from sets of computation traces
[Isberner et al., 2014]. It is possible to learn automata with at least a limited notion
of data types as part of their state. Formal verification tools at the moment almost
completely ignore the potential of machine learning, even though, as some first work
demonstrates [Howar et al., 2013], it should be possible to alleviate the specification
authoring problem (Section 1.2). Vice versa, learning algorithms for state machines
typically suffer from slow convergence and from scaling issues. Why not try to
import successful techniques from formal verification, such as contracts or symbolic
values, to machine learning? Clearly, here lie vast research opportunities.

1.5.4 Code Reviews

Code inspections and code reviews [Fagan, 1976] are popular and important software
quality assurance measures [Sommerville, 2015]. One of their downsides is that they
are very time-intensive. Tools such as the SED (see Chapter 11) can and should
be further developed into Code Review Assistants that efficiently guide through all
possible behaviors, animate execution paths and data structures and can find potential
problems or code smells not merely based on metrics and syntactic analyses, but
based on deductive verification technology. A recent experimental user case study
[Hentschel et al., 2016] showed that this is a promising path.

1.5.5 Integration

When writing an overview article on deductive verification [Beckert and Hähnle,
2014], we realized to which large extent the verification community suffers from a
fragmentation of tools. There are well over one hundred verification tools currently
available with widely varying scopes, theoretical bases, and usage scenarios. Only
a few subcommunities organize competitions or systematic tool comparisons [Kle-
banov et al., 2011, Beyer, 2015]. In most cases, larger case studies are not publicly
available. With the exception of SMT solvers that are integrated via the SMT-LIB
standard (smt-lib.org) [Barrett et al., 2010], virtually no generally accepted interface languages or APIs exist. Even programs annotated in JML cannot be readily
exchanged, because of slightly different interpretation of the semantics of some JML
constructs in different tools and because of different coverage of Java.

  Even though it is natural to combine, for instance, symbolic execution with
invariant generation and termination analysis, this is exceedingly time consuming in
practice. It is important to work on exchange standards that would allow, for example,

to transfer symbolic program states or invariants at a certain point of execution in a semantically sound manner.

Acknowledgments and Disclaimer

I would like to thank Richard Bubel and Martin Hentschel for helping to clarify the KeY architecture discussed in Section 1.4 and for drafting the first version of Figure 1.1. Daniel Grahl, Martin Hentschel, Peter Schmitt, and Shmuel Tyszberowicz all proofread this chapter and gave valuable feedback. More generally, this chapter could not have been written without the continuing efforts of the whole KeY team. Nevertheless, the opinions and judgments expressed here are the author's and do not necessarily reflect those of everyone else involved in KeY.

Part I
Foundations

Chapter 2
First-Order Logic

Peter H. Schmitt

2.1 Introduction

The ultimate goal of first-order logic in the context of this book, and this applies
to a great extent also to Computer Science in general, is the formalization of and
reasoning with natural language specifications of systems and programs. This chapter
provides the logical foundations for doing so in three steps. In Section 2.2 basic
first-order logic (FOL) is introduced much in the tradition of Mathematical Logic
as it evolved during the 20th century as a universal theory not tailored towards a
particular application area. Already this section goes beyond what is usually found
in textbooks on logic for computer science in that type hierarchies are included
from the start. In the short Section 2.3 two features will be added to the basic logic,
that did not interest the mathematical logicians very much but are indispensable for
practical reasoning. In Section 2.4 the extended basic logic will be instantiated to
Java first-order logic (JFOL), tailored for the particular task of reasoning about Java
programs. The focus in the present chapter is on statements; programs themselves
and formulas talking about more than one program state at once will enter the scene
in Chapter 3.

2.2 Basic First-Order Logic

2.2.1 Syntax

Definition 2.1. A *type hierarchy* is a pair $\mathcal{T} = (\text{TSym}, \sqsubseteq)$, where

1. TSym is a set of type symbols;
2. $\sqsubseteq$ is a reflexive, transitive relation on TSym, called the subtype relation;
3. there are two designated type symbols, the *empty* type $\bot \in \text{TSym}$ and the
   universal type $\top \in \text{TSym}$ with $\bot \sqsubseteq A \sqsubseteq \top$ for all $A \in \text{TSym}$.

© Springer International Publishing AG 2016
W. Ahrendt et al. (Eds.): Deductive Software Verification, LNCS 10001, pp. 23–47, 2016
DOI: 10.1007/978-3-319-49812-6_2

We point out that no restrictions are placed on type hierarchies in contrast to other approaches requiring the existence of unique lower bounds.

Two types A, B in $\mathscr{T}$ are called *incomparable* if neither $A \sqsubseteq B$ nor $B \sqsubseteq A$.

Definition 2.2. A *signature*, which is sometimes also called *vocabulary*, $\Sigma =$ (FSym, PSym, VSym) for a given type hierarchy $\mathscr{T}$ is made up of

1. a set FSym of typed function symbols,
   by $f : A_1 \times \ldots \times A_n \rightarrow A$ we declare the argument types of $f \in$ FSym to be $A_1, \ldots, A_n$ in the given order and its result type to be A,
2. a set PSym of typed predicate symbols,
   by $p(A_1, \ldots, A_n)$ we declare the argument types of $p \in$ PSym to be $A_1, \ldots, A_n$ in the given order,
   PSym obligatory contains the binary dedicated symbol $\doteq(\top, \top)$ for equality. and the two 0-place predicate symbols *true* and *false*.
3. a set VSym of typed variable symbols,
   by $v : A$ for $v \in$ VSym we declare v to be a variable of type A.

All types A, A_i in this definition must be different from $\bot$. A 0-ary function symbol $c : \rightarrow A$ is called a constant symbol of type A. A 0-ary predicate symbol $p()$ is called a propositional variable or propositional atom. We do not allow overloading: The same symbol may not occur in FSym $\cup$ PSym $\cup$ VSym with different typing.

The next two definitions define by mutual induction the syntactic categories of terms and formulas of typed first-order logic.

Definition 2.3. Let $\mathscr{T}$ be a type hierarchy, and Σ a signature for $\mathscr{T}$. The set Trm_A of *terms of type A*, for $A \neq \bot$, is inductively defined by

1. $v \in \mathrm{Trm}_A$ for each variable symbol $v : A \in$ VSym of type A.
2. $f(t_1, \ldots, t_n) \in \mathrm{Trm}_A$ for each $f : A_1 \times \ldots \times A_n \rightarrow A \in$ FSym and all terms $t_i \in \mathrm{Trm}_{B_i}$ with $B_i \sqsubseteq A_i$ for $1 \leq i \leq n$.
3. (if ϕ then t_1 else t_2) $\in \mathrm{Trm}_A$ for $\phi \in$ Fml and $t_i \in \mathrm{Trm}_{A_i}$ such that $A_2 \sqsubseteq A_1 = A$ or $A_1 \sqsubseteq A_2 = A$.

If $t \in \mathrm{Trm}_A$ we say that t is of (static) type A and write $\alpha(t) = A$.

Note, that item (2) in Definition 3 entails $c \in \mathrm{Trm}_A$ for each constant symbol $c : \rightarrow A \in$ FSym. Since we do not allow overloading there is for every term only one type A with $t \in \mathrm{Trm}_A$. This justifies the use of the function symbol α.

Terms of the form defined in item (3) are called *conditional terms*. They are a mere convenience. For every formula with conditional terms there is an equivalent formula without them. More liberal typing rules are possible. The theoretically most satisfying solution would be to declare the type of (if ϕ then t_1 else t_2) to be the least common supertype $A_1 \sqcup A_2$ of A_1 and A_2. But, the assumption that $A_1 \sqcup A_2$ always exists would lead to strange consequences in the program verification setting.

Definition 2.4. The set Fml of *formulas* of first-order logic for a given type hierarchy $\mathscr{T}$ and signature Σ is inductively defined as:

1. $p(t_1,\ldots,t_n) \in \text{Fml}$ for $p(A_1,\ldots,A_n) \in \text{PSym}$, and $t_i \in \text{Trm}_{B_i}$ with $B_i \sqsubseteq A_i$ for all $1 \le i \le n$.

   As a consequence of item 2 in Definition 2.2 we know

   $t_1 \doteq t_2 \in \text{Fml}$ for arbitrary terms t_i and *true* and *false* are in Fml.
2. $(\neg\phi), (\phi \wedge \psi), (\phi \vee \psi), (\phi \to \psi), (\phi \leftrightarrow \psi)$ are in Fml for arbitrary $\phi, \psi \in \text{Fml}$.
3. $\forall v; \phi, \exists v; \phi$ are in Fml for $\phi \in \text{Fml}$ and $v : A \in \text{VSym}$.

As an inline footnote we remark that the notation for conditional terms can also be used for formulas. The *conditional formula* (if ϕ_1 then ϕ_2 else ϕ_3) is equivalent to $(\phi_1 \wedge \phi_2) \vee (\neg\phi_1 \wedge \phi_3)$.

If need arises we will make dependence of these definitions on Σ and $\mathcal{T}$ explicit by writing $\text{Trm}_{A,\Sigma}$, Fml_Σ or $\text{Trm}_{A,\mathcal{T},\Sigma}$, $\text{Fml}_{\mathcal{T},\Sigma}$. When convenient we will also use the redundant notation $\forall A\, v; \phi$, $\exists A\, v; \phi$ for a variable $v : A \in \text{VSym}$.

Formulas built by clause (1) only are called *atomic formulas*.

Definition 2.5. For terms t and formulas ϕ we define the sets $var(t)$, $var(\phi)$ of all variables occurring in t or ϕ and the sets $fv(t), fv(\phi)$ of all variables with at least one free occurrence in t or ϕ:

$$
\begin{array}{llll}
var(v) = & \{v\} & fv(v) = & \{v\} & \text{for } v \in \text{VSym} \\[4pt]
var(t) = & \bigcup_{i=1}^n var(t_i) & fv(t) = & \bigcup_{1=i}^n fv(t_i) & \text{for } t = f(t_1,\ldots,t_n) \\[4pt]
var(t) = & var(\phi) \cup & fv(t) = & fv(\phi) \cup & \text{for } t = \\
 & var(t_1) \cup var(t_2) & & fv(t_1) \cup fv(t_2) & \text{(if } \phi \text{ then } t_1 \text{ else } t_2) \\[4pt]
var(\phi) = & \bigcup_{i=1}^n var(t_i) & fv(\phi) = & \bigcup_{i=1}^n fv(t_i) & \text{for } \phi = p(t_1,\ldots,t_n) \\[4pt]
var(\neg\phi) = & var(\phi) & fv(\neg\phi) = & fv(\phi) & \\[4pt]
var(\phi) = & var(\phi_1) \cup var(\phi_2) & fv(\phi) = & fv(\phi_1) \cup fv(\phi_2) & \text{for } \phi = \phi_1 \circ \phi_2 \\
 & & & & \text{where } \circ \text{ is any binary Boolean operation} \\[4pt]
var(Q\, v.\phi) = var(\phi) & & fv(Q\, v.\phi) = var(\phi) \setminus \{v\} & & \text{where } Q \in \{\forall,\exists\}
\end{array}
$$

A term without free variables is called a *ground term*, a formula without free variables a *ground formula* or *closed formula*.

It is an obvious consequence of this definition that every occurrence of a variable v in a term or formula with empty set of free variables is within the scope of a quantifier $Q\, v$.

One of the most important syntactical manipulations of terms and formulas are substitutions, that replace variables by terms. They will play a crucial role in proofs of quantified formulas as well as equations.

Definition 2.6. A *substitution* τ is a function that associates with every variable v a type compatible term $\tau(v)$, i.e., if v is of type A then $\tau(v)$ is a term of type A' such that $A' \sqsubseteq A$.

We write $\tau = [u_1/t_1,\ldots,u_n/t_n]$ to denote the substitution defined by $\text{dom}(\tau) = \{u_1,\ldots,u_n\}$ and $\tau(u_i) = t_i$.

A substitution τ is called a *ground substitution* if $\tau(v)$ is a ground term for all $v \in \text{dom}(\tau)$.

We will only encounter substitutions τ such that $\tau(v) = v$ for all but finitely many variables v. The set $\{v \in \text{VSym} \mid \tau(v) \neq v\}$ is called the *domain* of τ. It remains to make precise how a substitution τ is applied to terms and formulas.

Definition 2.7. Let τ be a substitution and t a term, then $\tau(t)$ is recursively defined by:

1. $\tau(x) = x$ if $x \notin \text{dom}(\tau)$
2. $\tau(x)$ as in the definition of τ if $x \in \text{dom}(\tau)$
3. $\tau(f(t_1,\ldots,t_k)) = f(\tau(t_1),\ldots,\tau(t_k))$ if $t = f(t_1,\ldots,t_k)$

Let τ be a ground substitution and ϕ a formula, then $\tau(\phi)$ is recursive defined

4. $\tau(true) = true$, $\tau(false) = false$
5. $\tau(p(t_1,\ldots,t_k)) = p(\tau(t_1),\ldots,\tau(t_k))$ if ϕ is the atomic formula $p(t_1,\ldots,t_k)$
6. $\tau(t_1 \doteq t_k) = \tau(t_1) \doteq \tau(t_k)$
7. $\tau(\neg\phi) = \neg\tau(\phi)$
8. $\tau(\phi_1 \circ \phi_2) = \tau(\phi_1) \circ \tau(\phi_2)$ for propositional operators $\circ \in \{\land, \lor, \to, \leftrightarrow\}$
9. $\tau(Qv.\phi) = Qv.\tau_v(\phi)$ for $Q \in \{\exists, \forall\}$ and $\text{dom}(\tau_v) = \text{dom}(\tau) \setminus \{v\}$ with $\tau_v(x) = \tau(x)$ for $x \in \text{dom}(\tau_v)$.

There are some easy conclusions from these definitions:

- If $t \in \text{Trm}_A$ then $\tau(t)$ is a term of type A' with $A' \sqsubseteq A$. Indeed, if t is not a variable then $\tau(t)$ is again of type A.
- $\tau(\phi)$ meets the typing restrictions set forth in Definition 2.4.

Item 9 deserves special attention. Substitutions only act on free variables. So, when computing $\tau(Qv.\phi)$, the variable v in the body ϕ of the quantified formula is left untouched. This is effected by removing v from the domain of τ.

It is possible, and quite common, to define also the application of nonground substitutions to formulas. Care has to be taken in that case to avoid *clashes*, see Example 2.8 below. We will only need ground substitutions later on, so we sidestep this difficulty.

Example 2.8. For the sake of this example we assume that there is a type symbol $int \in \text{TSym}$, function symbols $+ : int \times int \to int$, $* : int \times int \to int$, $- : int \to int$, $exp : int \times int \to int$ and constants $0 : int$, $1 : int$, $2 : int$, in FSym. Definition 2.3 establishes an abstract syntax for terms. In examples we are free to use a concrete, or pretty-printing syntax. Here we use the familiar notation $a + b$ instead of $+(a,b)$, $a * b$ or ab instead of $*(a,b)$, and a^b instead of $exp(a,b)$. Let furthermore $x : int$, $y : int$ be variables of sort int. The following table shows the results of applying the substitution $\tau_1 = [x/0, y/1]$ to the given formulas

$$\phi_1 = \forall x; ((x+y)^2 \doteq x^2 + 2xy + y^2) \quad \tau_1(\phi_1) = \forall x; ((x+1)^2 \doteq x^2 + 2*x*1 + 1^2)$$
$$\phi_2 = (x+y)^2 \doteq x^2 + 2xy + y^2 \quad\quad \tau_1(\phi_2) = (0+1)^2 \doteq 0^2 + 2*0*1 + 1^2$$
$$\phi_3 = \exists x; (x > y) \quad\quad\quad\quad\quad\quad\quad \tau_1(\phi_3) = \exists x; (x > 1)$$

Application of the nonground substitution $\tau_2 = [y/x]$ on ϕ_3 leads to $\exists x; (x > x)$. While $\exists x; (x > y)$ is true for all assignments to y the substituted formula $\tau(\phi_3)$ is not.

Validity is preserved if we restrict to clash-free substitutions. A substitution τ is said to create a *clash* with formula ϕ if a variable w in a term $\tau(v)$ for $v \in \text{dom}(\tau)$ ends up in the scope of a quantifier Qw in ϕ. For τ_2 the variable x in $\tau_2(y)$ will end up in the scope of $\forall x$;

The concept of a substitution also comes in handy to solve the following notational problem. Let ϕ be a formula that contains somewhere an occurrence of the term t_1. How should we refer to the formula arising from ϕ by replacing t_1 by t_2? E.g. replace $2xy$ in ϕ_2 by $xy2$. The solution is to use a new variable z and a formula ϕ_0 such that $\phi = [z/t_1]\phi_0$. Then the replaced formula can be referred to as $[z/t_2]\phi_0$. In the example we would have $\phi_0 = (x+y)^2 \doteq x^2 + z + y^2$. This trick will be extensively used in Figure 2.1 and 2.2.

2.2.2 Calculus

The main reason nowadays for introducing a formal, machine readable syntax for formulas, as we did in the previous subsection, is to get machine support for logical reasoning. For this, one needs first a suitable calculus and then an efficient implementation. In this subsection we present the rules for basic first-order logic. A machine readable representation of these rules will be covered in Chapter 4. Chapter 15 provides an unhurried introduction on using the KeY theorem prover based on these rules that can be read without prerequisites. So the reader may want to step through it before continuing here.

The calculus of our choice is the *sequent calculus*. The basic data that is manipulated by the rules of the sequent calculus are *sequents*. These are of the form $\phi_1, \ldots, \phi_n \Longrightarrow \psi_1, \ldots, \psi_m$. The formulas $\phi_1, \ldots, \phi_n$ at the left-hand side of the sequent separator $\Longrightarrow$ are the antecedents of the sequent; the formulas $\psi_1, \ldots, \psi_m$ on the right are the succedents. In our version of the calculus antecedent and succedent are sets of formulas, i.e., the order and multiple occurrences are not relevant. Furthermore, we will assume that all ϕ_i and ψ_j are ground formulas. A sequent $\phi_1, \ldots, \phi_n \Longrightarrow \psi_1, \ldots, \psi_m$ is valid iff the formula $\bigwedge_{1=i}^{n} \phi_i \rightarrow \bigvee_{1=j}^{m} \psi_j$ is valid.

The concept of sequent calculi was introduce by the German logician Gerhard Gentzen in the 1930s, though for a very different purpose.

Figures 2.1 and 2.2 show the usual set of rules of the sequent calculus with equality as it can be found in many text books, e.g. [Gallier, 1987, Section 5.4]. Rules are written in the form

$$\text{ruleName} \quad \frac{P_1, \ldots P_n}{C}$$

The P_i is called the *premisses* and C the *conclusion* of the rule. There is no theoretical limit on n, but most of the time $n = 1$, sometimes $n = 2$, and in rare cases $n = 3$. Note, that premiss and conclusion contain the schematic variables Γ, Δ for set of formulas, ψ, ϕ for formulas and t, c for terms and constants. We use Γ, ϕ and ψ, Δ to stand for $\Gamma \cup \{\phi\}$ and $\{\psi\} \cup \Delta$. An instance of a rule is obtained by consistently replacing the

$$\text{andLeft } \frac{\Gamma,\phi,\psi \Longrightarrow \Delta}{\Gamma,\phi \wedge \psi \Longrightarrow \Delta} \qquad \text{andRight } \frac{\Gamma \Longrightarrow \phi,\Delta \quad \Gamma \Longrightarrow \psi,\Delta}{\Gamma \Longrightarrow \phi \wedge \psi,\Delta}$$

$$\text{orRight } \frac{\Gamma \Longrightarrow \phi,\psi,\Delta}{\Gamma \Longrightarrow \phi \vee \psi,\Delta} \qquad \text{orLeft } \frac{\Gamma,\phi \Longrightarrow \Delta \quad \Gamma,\psi \Longrightarrow \Delta}{\Gamma,\phi \vee \psi \Longrightarrow \Delta}$$

$$\text{impRight } \frac{\Gamma,\phi \Longrightarrow \psi,\Delta}{\Gamma \Longrightarrow \phi \to \psi,\Delta} \qquad \text{impLeft } \frac{\Gamma \Longrightarrow \phi,\Delta \quad \Gamma,\psi \Longrightarrow \Delta}{\Gamma,\phi \to \psi \Longrightarrow \Delta}$$

$$\text{notLeft } \frac{\Gamma \Longrightarrow \phi,\Delta}{\Gamma,\neg\phi \Longrightarrow \Delta} \qquad \text{notRight } \frac{\Gamma,\phi \Longrightarrow \Delta}{\Gamma \Longrightarrow \neg\phi,\Delta}$$

$$\text{allRight } \frac{\Gamma \Longrightarrow [x/c](\phi),\Delta}{\Gamma \Longrightarrow \forall x;\phi,\Delta} \qquad \text{allLeft } \frac{\Gamma,\forall x;\phi,[x/t](\phi) \Longrightarrow \Delta}{\Gamma,\forall x;\phi \Longrightarrow \Delta}$$

with $c : \to A$ a new constant, if $x{:}A$ with $t \in \mathrm{Trm}_{A'}$ ground, $A' \sqsubseteq A$, if $x{:}A$

$$\text{exLeft } \frac{\Gamma,[x/c](\phi) \Longrightarrow \Delta}{\Gamma,\exists x;\phi \Longrightarrow \Delta} \qquad \text{exRight } \frac{\Gamma \Longrightarrow \exists x;\phi,[x/t](\phi),\Delta}{\Gamma \Longrightarrow \exists x;\phi,\Delta}$$

with $c : \to A$ a new constant, if $x{:}A$ with $t \in \mathrm{Trm}_{A'}$ ground, $A' \sqsubseteq A$, if $x{:}A$

$$\text{close } \frac{*}{\Gamma,\phi \Longrightarrow \phi,\Delta}$$

$$\text{closeFalse } \frac{*}{\Gamma,\text{false} \Longrightarrow \Delta} \qquad \text{closeTrue } \frac{*}{\Gamma \Longrightarrow \text{true},\Delta}$$

Figure 2.1 First-order rules for the logic FOL

schematic variables in premiss and conclusion by the corresponding entities: sets of formulas, formulas, etc. Rule application in KeY proceeds from bottom to top. Suppose we want to prove a sequent s_2. We look for a rule R such that there is an instantiation *Inst* of the schematic variables in R such that the instantiation of its conclusion $Inst(S_2)$ equals s_2. After rule application we are left with the task to prove the sequent $Inst(S_1)$. If S_1 is empty, we succeeded.

Definition 2.9. The rules close, closeFalse, and closeTrue from Figure 2.1 are called *closing rules* since their premisses are empty.

Since there are rules with more than one premiss the proof process sketched above will result in a proof tree.

Definition 2.10. A *proof tree* is a tree, shown with the root at the bottom, such that

1. each node is labeled with a sequent or the symbol $*$,
2. if an inner node n is annotated with $\Gamma \Longrightarrow \Delta$ then there is an instance of a rule whose conclusion is $\Gamma \Longrightarrow \Delta$ and the child node, or children nodes of n are labeled with the premiss or premisses of the rule instance.

A branch in a proof tree is called *closed* if its leaf is labeled by $*$. A proof tree is called *closed* if all its branches are closed, or equivalently if all its leaves are labeled with $*$.

We say that a sequent $\Gamma \Longrightarrow \Delta$ can be derived if there is a closed proof tree whose root is labeled by $\Gamma \Longrightarrow \Delta$.

As a first simple example, we will derive the sequent $\Longrightarrow p \wedge q \rightarrow q \wedge p$. The same formula is also used in the explanation of the KeY prover in Chapter 15. As its antecedent is empty, this sequent says that the propositional formula $p \wedge q \rightarrow q \wedge p$ is a tautology. Application of the rule impRight reduces our proof goal to $p \wedge q \Longrightarrow q \wedge p$ and application of andLeft further to $p, q \Longrightarrow q \wedge p$. Application of andRight splits the proof into the two goals $p, q \Longrightarrow q$ and $p, q \Longrightarrow p$. Both goals can be discharged by an application of the close rule. The whole proof can concisely be summarized as a tree

$$
\cfrac{
\cfrac{
\cfrac{*}{p, q \Longrightarrow q} \qquad \cfrac{*}{p, q \Longrightarrow p}
}{
\cfrac{p, q \Longrightarrow q \wedge p}{
\cfrac{p \wedge q \Longrightarrow q \wedge p}{
\Longrightarrow p \wedge q \rightarrow q \wedge p
}}}
}{}
$$

Let us look at an example derivation involving quantifiers. If you are puzzled by the use of substitutions $[x/t]$ in the formulations of the rules you should refer back to Example 2.8. We assume that $p(A, A)$ is a binary predicate symbol with both arguments of type A. Here is the, nonbranching, proof tree for the formula $\exists v; \forall w; p(v, w) \rightarrow \forall w; \exists v; p(v, w)$:

$$
\cfrac{
\cfrac{
\cfrac{*}{\forall w; p(c, w), p(c, d) \Longrightarrow p(c, d), \exists v; p(v, d)}
}{
\cfrac{\forall w; p(c, w) \Longrightarrow \exists v; p(v, d)}{
\cfrac{\exists v; \forall w; p(v, w) \Longrightarrow \forall w; \exists v; p(v, w)}{
\Longrightarrow \exists v; \forall w; p(v, w) \rightarrow \forall w; \exists v; p(v, w)
}}}
}{}
$$

The derivation starts, from bottom to top, with the rule impRight. The next line above is obtained by applying exLeft and allRight. This introduces new constant symbols $c : \rightarrow A$ and $d : \rightarrow A$. The top line is obtained by the rules exRight and allLeft with the ground substitutions $[w/d]$ and $[v/c]$. The proof terminates by an application of close resulting in an empty proof obligation. An application of the rules exLeft, allRight is often called *Skolemization* and the new constant symbols called *Skolem constants*. The rules involving equality are shown in Figure 2.2. The rules eqLeft and eqRight formalize the intuitive application of equations: if $t_1 \doteq t_2$ is known, we may replace wherever we want t_1 by t_2. In typed logic the formula after substitution might not be well-typed. Here is an example for the rule eqLeft without restriction. Consider two types $A \neq B$ with $B \sqsubseteq A$, two constant symbols $a : \rightarrow A$ and $b : \rightarrow B$, and a unary predicate $p(B)$. Applying unrestricted eqLeft on the sequent $b \doteq a, p(b) \Longrightarrow$ would result in $b \doteq a, p(b), p(a) \Longrightarrow$. There is in a sense logically nothing wrong with this, but $p(a)$ is not well-typed. This motivates the provisions in the rules eqLeft and eqRight.

$$\text{eqLeft}\ \frac{\Gamma, t_1 \doteq t_2, [z/t_1](\phi), [z/t_2](\phi) \Longrightarrow \Delta}{\Gamma, t_1 \doteq t_2, [z/t_1](\phi) \Longrightarrow \Delta}$$
provided $[z/t_2](\phi)$ is well-typed

$$\text{eqRight}\ \frac{\Gamma, t_1 \doteq t_2 \Longrightarrow [z/t_2](\phi), [z/t_1](\phi), \Delta}{\Gamma, t_1 \doteq t_2 \Longrightarrow [z/t_1](\phi), \Delta}$$
provided $[z/t_2](\phi)$ is well-typed

$$\text{eqSymmLeft}\ \frac{\Gamma, t_2 \doteq t_1 \Longrightarrow \Delta}{\Gamma, t_1 \doteq t_2 \Longrightarrow \Delta} \qquad \text{eqReflLeft}\ \frac{\Gamma, t \doteq t \Longrightarrow \Delta}{\Gamma \Longrightarrow \Delta}$$

Figure 2.2 Equality rules for the logic FOL

Let us consider a short example of equational reasoning involving the function symbol $+ : int \times int \rightarrow int$.

7 *

6 $(a+(b+c))+d) \doteq a+((b+c)+d), \forall x,y,z; ((x+y)+z \doteq x+(y+z))$
$(b+c)+d \doteq b+(c+d), a+(b+c))+d) \doteq a+(b+(c+d)) \Longrightarrow$
$(a+(b+c))+d) \doteq a+(b+(c+d))$

5 $(a+(b+c))+d) \doteq a+((b+c)+d), \forall x,y,z; ((x+y)+z \doteq x+(y+z))$
$(b+c)+d \doteq b+(c+d) \Longrightarrow$
$(a+(b+c))+d) \doteq a+(b+(c+d))$

4 $(a+(b+c))+d) \doteq a+((b+c)+d), \forall x,y,z; ((x+y)+z \doteq x+(y+z)) \Longrightarrow$
$(a+(b+c))+d) \doteq a+(b+(c+d))$

3 $\forall x,y,z; ((x+y)+z \doteq x+(y+z)) \Longrightarrow (a+(b+c))+d \doteq a+(b+(c+d))$

2 $\forall x,y,z; ((x+y)+z \doteq x+(y+z)) \Longrightarrow$
$\forall x,y,z,u; (((x+(y+z))+u) \doteq x+(y+(z+u)))$

1 $\Longrightarrow \forall x,y,z; ((x+y)+z \doteq x+(y+z)) \rightarrow$
$\forall x,y,z,u; (((x+(y+z))+u) \doteq x+(y+(z+u)))$

Line 1 states the proof goal, a consequence from the associativity of $+$. Line 2 is obtained by an application of impRight while line 3 results from a four-fold application of allRight introducing the new constant symbol a, b, c, d for the universally quantified variables x, y, z, u, respectively. Line 4 in turn is arrived at by an application of allLeft with the substitution $[x/a, y/(b+c), z/d]$. Note, that the universally quantified formula does not disappear. In Line 5 another application of allLeft, but this time with the substitution $[x/b, y/c, z/d]$, adds the equation $(b+c)+d \doteq b+(c+d)$ to the antecedent. Now, eqLeft is applicable, replacing on the left-hand side of the sequent the term $(b+c)+d$ in $(a+b)+(c+d) \doteq a+(b+(c+d))$ by the right-hand side of the equation $(b+c)+d \doteq b+(c+d)$. This results in the same equation as in the succedent. Rule close can thus be applied.

Already this small example reveals the technical complexity of equational reasoning. Whenever the terms involved in equational reasoning are of a special type one would prefer to use decision procedures for the relevant specialized theories, e.g., for integer arithmetic or the theory of arrays.

We will see in the next section, culminating in Theorem 2.20, that the rules from Figures 2.1 and 2.2 are sufficient with respect to the semantics to be introduced in that section. But, it would be very inefficient to base proofs only on these first principles. The KeY system contains many derived rules to speed up the proof process. Let us just look at one randomly chosen example:

$$\text{doubleImpLeft} \quad \frac{\Gamma \Longrightarrow b, \Delta \qquad \Gamma \Longrightarrow c, \Delta \qquad \Gamma, d \Longrightarrow \Delta}{\Gamma, b \to (c \to d) \Longrightarrow \Delta}$$

It is easy to see that doubleImpLeft can be derived.

There is one more additional rule that we should not fail to mention:

$$\text{cut} \quad \frac{\Gamma \Longrightarrow \phi, \Delta \qquad \Gamma, \phi \Longrightarrow \Delta}{\Gamma \Longrightarrow \Delta}$$

provided ϕ is a ground formula

On the basis of the notLeft rule this is equivalent to

$$\text{cut}' \quad \frac{\Gamma, \neg \phi \Longrightarrow \Delta \qquad \Gamma, \phi \Longrightarrow \Delta}{\Gamma \Longrightarrow \Delta}$$

provided ϕ is a ground formula

It becomes apparent that the cut rule allows at any node in the proof tree proceeding by a case distinction. This is the favorite rule for user interaction. The system might not find a proof for $\Gamma \Longrightarrow \Delta$ automatically, but for a cleverly chosen ϕ automatic proofs for both $\Gamma, \phi \Longrightarrow \Delta$ and $\Gamma \Longrightarrow \phi, \Delta$ might be possible.

2.2.3 Semantics

So far we trusted that the logical rules contained in Figures 2.1 and 2.2 are self-evident. In this section we provide further support that the rules and the deduction system as a whole are sound, in particular no contradiction can be derived. So far we also had only empirical evidence that the rules are sufficient. The semantical approach presented in this section will open up the possibility to rigorously prove completeness.

Definition 2.11. A *universe* or *domain* for a given type hierarchy $\mathscr{T}$ and signature Σ consists of

1. a set D,

2. a typing function $\delta : D \to \mathrm{TSym} \setminus \{\bot\}$ such that for every $A \in \mathrm{TSym}$ the set
   $D^A = \{d \in D \mid \delta(d) \sqsubseteq A\}$ is not empty.

The set $D^A = \{d \in D \mid \delta(d) \sqsubseteq A\}$ is called the type universe or type domain for A.
Definition 2.11 implies that for different types $A, B \in \mathrm{TSym} \setminus \{\bot\}$ there is an element
$o \in D^A \cap D^B$ only if there exists $C \in \mathrm{TSym}$, $C \neq \bot$ with $C \sqsubseteq A$ and $C \sqsubseteq B$.

Lemma 2.12. *The type domains for a universe* (D, δ) *share the following properties*

1. $D^\bot = \emptyset$, $D^\top = D$,
2. $D^A \subseteq D^B$ *if* $A \sqsubseteq B$,
3. $D^C = D^A \cap D^B$ *in case the greatest lower bound* C *of* A *and* B *exists.*

Definition 2.13. A first-order *structure* $\mathcal{M}$ for a given type hierarchy $\mathcal{T}$ and signature Σ consists of

   - a domain (D, δ),
   - an interpretation I

such that

1. $I(f)$ is a function from $D^{A_1} \times \cdots \times D^{A_n}$ into D^A for $f : A_1 \times \ldots \times A_n \to A$ in
   FSym,
2. $I(p)$ is a subset of $D^{A_1} \times \cdots \times D^{A_n}$ for $p(A_1, \ldots, A_n)$ in PSym,
3. $I(\doteq) = \{(d, d) \mid d \in D\}$.

For constant symbols $c : \to A \in \mathrm{FSym}$ requirement (1) reduces to $I(c) \in D^A$. It has
become customary to interpret an empty product as the set $\{\emptyset\}$, where $\emptyset$ is deemed
to stand for the empty tuple. Thus requirement (2) reduces for $n = 0$ to $I(p) \subseteq \{\emptyset\}$.
Only if need arises, we will say more precisely that $\mathcal{M}$ is a $\mathcal{T}$-Σ-structure.

Definition 2.14. Let $\mathcal{M}$ be a first-order structure with universe D.
   A *variable assignment* is a function $\beta : \mathrm{VSym} \to D$ such that $\beta(v) \in D^A$ for
$v : A \in \mathrm{VSym}$.
   For a variable assignment β, a variable $v : A \in \mathrm{VSym}$ and a domain element
$d \in D^A$, the following definition of a modified assignment will be needed later on:

$$\beta_v^d(v') = \begin{cases} d & \text{if } v' = v \\ \beta(v') & \text{if } v' \neq v \end{cases}$$

   The next two definitions define the evaluation of terms and formulas with respect
to a structure $\mathcal{M} = (D, \delta, I)$ for given type hierarchy $\mathcal{T}$, signature Σ, and variable
assignment β by mutual recursion.

Definition 2.15. For every term $t \in \mathrm{Trm}_A$, we define its evaluation $\mathrm{val}_{\mathcal{M}, \beta}(t)$ inductively by:

   - $\mathrm{val}_{\mathcal{M}, \beta}(v) = \beta(v)$ for any variable v.

- $\text{val}_{\mathcal{M},\beta}(f(t_1,\ldots,t_n)) = I(f)(\text{val}_{\mathcal{M},\beta}(t_1),\ldots,\text{val}_{\mathcal{M},\beta}(t_n))$.
- $\text{val}_{\mathcal{M},\beta}(\text{if } \phi \text{ then } t_1 \text{ else } t_2) = \begin{cases} \text{val}_{\mathcal{M},\beta}(t_1) & \text{if } (\mathcal{M},\beta) \models \phi \\ \text{val}_{\mathcal{M},\beta}(t_2) & \text{if } (\mathcal{M},\beta) \not\models \phi \end{cases}$

Definition 2.16. For every formula $\phi \in \text{Fml}$, we define when ϕ is considered to be true with respect to $\mathcal{M}$ and β, which is denoted with $(\mathcal{M},\beta) \models \phi$, by:

1. $(\mathcal{M},\beta) \models true$, $\quad (\mathcal{M},\beta) \not\models false$
2. $(\mathcal{M},\beta) \models p(t_1,\ldots,t_n)$ iff $(\text{val}_{\mathcal{M},\beta}(t_1),\ldots,\text{val}_{\mathcal{M},\beta}(t_n)) \in I(p)$
3. $(\mathcal{M},\beta) \models \neg\phi$ iff $(\mathcal{M},\beta) \not\models \phi$
4. $(\mathcal{M},\beta) \models \phi_1 \wedge \phi_2$ iff $(\mathcal{M},\beta) \models \phi_1$ and $(\mathcal{M},\beta) \models \phi_2$
5. $(\mathcal{M},\beta) \models \phi_1 \vee \phi_2$ iff $(\mathcal{M},\beta) \models \phi_1$ or $(\mathcal{M},\beta) \models \phi_2$
6. $(\mathcal{M},\beta) \models \phi_1 \rightarrow \phi_2$ iff $(\mathcal{M},\beta) \not\models \phi_1$ or $(\mathcal{M},\beta) \models \phi_2$
7. $(\mathcal{M},\beta) \models \phi_1 \leftrightarrow \phi_2$ iff $((\mathcal{M},\beta) \models \phi_1$ and $(\mathcal{M},\beta) \models \phi_2)$ or
                               iff $((\mathcal{M},\beta) \not\models \phi_1$ and $(\mathcal{M},\beta) \not\models \phi_2)$
8. $(\mathcal{M},\beta) \models \forall A\, v; \phi$ iff $(\mathcal{M},\beta_v^d) \models \phi$ for all $d \in D^A$
9. $(\mathcal{M},\beta) \models \exists A\, v; \phi$ iff $(\mathcal{M},\beta_v^d) \models \phi$ for at least one $d \in D^A$

For a 0-place predicate symbol p, clause (2) says $\mathcal{M} \models p$ iff $\emptyset \in I(p)$. Thus the interpretation I acts in this case as an assignment of truth values to p. This explains why we have called 0-place predicate symbols propositional atoms.

Given the restriction on $I(\dot{=})$ in Definition 2.13, clause (2) also says $(\mathcal{M},\beta) \models t_1 \dot{=} t_2$ iff $\text{val}_{\mathcal{M},\beta}(t_1) = \text{val}_{\mathcal{M},\beta}(t_2)$.

For a set Φ of formulas, we use $(\mathcal{M},\beta) \models \Phi$ to mean $(\mathcal{M},\beta) \models \phi$ for all $\phi \in \Phi$.

If ϕ is a formula without free variables, we may write $\mathcal{M} \models \phi$ since the variable assignment β is not relevant here.

To prepare the ground for the next definition we explain the concept of extensions between type hierarchies.

Definition 2.17. A type hierarchy $\mathcal{T}_2 = (\text{TSym}_2, \sqsubseteq_2)$ is an *extension* of a type hierarchy $\mathcal{T}_1 = (\text{TSym}_1, \sqsubseteq_1)$, in symbols $\mathcal{T}_1 \sqsubseteq \mathcal{T}_2$, if

1. $\text{TSym}_1 \subseteq \text{TSym}_2$
2. $\sqsubseteq_2$ is the smallest subtype relation containing $\sqsubseteq_1 \cup \Delta$ where Δ is a set of pairs (S,T) with $T \in \text{TSym}_1$ and $S \in \text{TSym}_2 \setminus \text{TSym}_1$.

So, new types can only be declared to be subtypes of old types, never supertypes. Also, $\bot \sqsubseteq_2 A \sqsubseteq_2 \top$ for all new types A.

Definition 2.17 forbids the introduction of subtype chains like $A \sqsubseteq B \sqsubseteq T$ into the type hierarchy. However, it can be shown that relaxing the definition in that respect results in an equivalent notion of logical consequence. We keep the restriction here since it simplifies reasoning about type hierarchy extensions.

For later reference, we note the following lemma.

Lemma 2.18. Let $\mathcal{T}_2 = (\text{TSym}_2, \sqsubseteq_2)$ be an extension of $\mathcal{T}_1 = (\text{TSym}_1, \sqsubseteq_1)$ with $\sqsubseteq_2$ the smallest subtype relation containing $\sqsubseteq_1 \cup \Delta$, for some $\Delta \subseteq (\text{TSym}_2 \setminus \text{TSym}_1) \times \text{TSym}_1$.

Then, for $A, B \in \text{TSym}_1$, $C \in \text{TSym}_2 \setminus \text{TSym}_1$, $D \in \text{TSym}_2$

1. $A \sqsubseteq_2 B$ iff $A \sqsubseteq_1 B$
2. $C \sqsubseteq_2 A$ iff $T \sqsubseteq_1 A$ for some $(C,T) \in \Delta$.
3. $D \sqsubseteq_2 C$ iff $D = C$ or $D = \bot$

Proof. This follows easily from the fact that no supertype relations of the form $A \sqsubseteq_2 C$ for new type symbols C are stipulated. $\square$

Definition 2.19. Let $\mathcal{T}$ be a type hierarchy and Σ a signature, $\phi \in \text{Fml}_{\mathcal{T},\Sigma}$ a formula without free variables, and $\Phi \subseteq \text{Fml}_{\mathcal{T},\Sigma}$ a set of formulas without free variables.

1. ϕ is a *logical consequence* of Φ, in symbols $\Phi \models \phi$, if for all type hierarchies $\mathcal{T}'$ with $\mathcal{T} \sqsubseteq \mathcal{T}'$ and all $\mathcal{T}'$-Σ-structures $\mathcal{M}$ such that $\mathcal{M} \models \Phi$, also $\mathcal{M} \models \phi$ holds.
2. ϕ is *universally valid* if it is a logical consequence of the empty set, i.e., if $\emptyset \models \phi$.
3. ϕ is satisfiable if there is a type hierarchy $\mathcal{T}'$, with $\mathcal{T} \sqsubseteq \mathcal{T}'$ and a $\mathcal{T}'$-Σ-structure $\mathcal{M}$ with $\mathcal{M} \models \phi$.

The extension of Definition 2.19 to formulas with free variables is conceptually not difficult but technically a bit involved. The present definition covers however all we need in this book.

The central concept is universal validity since, for finite Φ, it can easily be seen that:

- $\Phi \models \phi$ iff the formula $\bigwedge \Phi \to \phi$ is universally valid.
- ϕ is satisfiable iff $\neg \phi$ is not universally valid.

The notion of *logical consequence* from Definition 2.19 is sometimes called *super logical consequence* to distinguish it from the concept $\Phi \models_{\mathcal{T},\Sigma} \phi$ denoting that for any $\mathcal{T}$-Σ-structure $\mathcal{M}$ with $\mathcal{M} \models \Phi$ also $\mathcal{M} \models \phi$ is true.

To see the difference, let the type hierarchy $\mathcal{T}_1$ contain types A and B such that the greatest lower bound of A and B is $\bot$. For the formula $\phi_1 = \forall A\, x; (\forall B\, y; (x \neq y))$ we have $\models_{\mathcal{T}_1} \phi_1$. Let $\mathcal{T}_2$ be the type hierarchy extending $\mathcal{T}_1$ by a new type D and the ordering $D \sqsubseteq A, D \sqsubseteq B$. Now, $\models_{\mathcal{T}_2} \phi_1$ does no longer hold true.

The phenomenon that the tautology property of a formula ϕ depends on symbols that do not occur in ϕ is highly undesirable. This is avoided by using the logical consequence defined as above. In this case we have $\not\models \phi_1$.

Theorem 2.20 (Soundness and Completeness Theorem). *Let $\mathcal{T}$ be a type hierarchy and Σ a signature, $\phi \in \text{Fml}_{\mathcal{T},\Sigma}$ without free variables. The calculus for FOL is given by the rules in Figures 2.1 and 2.2. Assume that for every type $A \in \mathcal{T}$ there is a constant symbol of type A' with $A' \sqsubseteq A$.*

Then:

- *if there is a closed proof tree in FOL for the sequent $\implies \phi$ then ϕ is universally valid*
  i.e., FOL is sound.
- *if ϕ is universally valid then there is a closed proof tree for the sequent $\implies \phi$ in FOL.*
  i.e., FOL is complete.

For the untyped calculus a proof of the sound- and completeness theorem may be found in any decent text book, e.g. [Gallier, 1987, Section 5.6]. Giese [2005] covers the typed version in a setting with additional cast functions and type predicates. His proof does not consider super logical consequence and requires that type hierarchies are lower-semi-lattices.

Concerning the constraint placed on the signature in Theorem 2.20, the calculus implemented in the KeY system takes a slightly different but equivalent approach: instead of requiring the existence of sufficient constants, it allows one to derive via the rule ex_unused, for every $A \in \mathcal{T}$ the formula $\exists x(x \doteq x)$, with x a variable of type A.

Definition 2.21. A rule

$$\frac{\Gamma_1 \Longrightarrow \Delta_1 \qquad \Gamma_2 \Longrightarrow \Delta_2}{\Gamma \Longrightarrow \Delta}$$

of a sequent calculus is called

- *sound* if whenever $\Gamma_1 \Longrightarrow \Delta_1$ and $\Gamma_2 \Longrightarrow \Delta_2$ are universally valid so is $\Gamma \Longrightarrow \Delta$.
- *complete* if whenever $\Gamma \Longrightarrow \Delta$ is universally valid then also $\Gamma_1 \Longrightarrow \Delta_1$ and $\Gamma_2 \Longrightarrow \Delta_2$ are universally valid.

For nonbranching rules and rules with side conditions the obvious modifications have to be made.

An inspection of the proof of Theorem 2.20 shows that if all rules of a calculus are sound then the calculus itself is sound. This is again stated as Lemma 4.7 in Section 4.4 devoted to the soundness management of the KeY system. In the case of soundness also the reverse implication is true: if a calculus is sound then all its rules will be sound.

The inspection of the proof of Theorem 2.20 also shows that the calculus is complete if all its rules are complete. This criterion is however not necessary, a complete calculus may contain rules that are not complete.

2.3 Extended First-Order Logic

In this section we extend the Basic First-Order Logic from Section 2.2. First we turn our attention in Subsection 2.3.1 to an additional term building construct: *variable binders*. They do not increase the expressive power of the logic, but are extremely handy.

An issue that comes up in almost any practical use of logic, are partial functions. In the KeY system, partial functions are treated via underspecification as explained in Subsection 2.3.2. In essence this amounts to replacing a partial function by all its extensions to total functions.

2.3.1 Variable Binders

This subsection assumes that the type *int* of mathematical integers, the type *LocSet* of sets of locations, and the type *Seq* of finite sequences are present in TSym. For the logic JFOL to be presented in Subsection 2.4 this will be obligatory.

A typical example of a variable binder symbol is the sum operator, as in $\Sigma_{k=1}^{n} k^2$. Variable binders are related to quantifiers in that they *bind* a variable. The KeY system does not provide a generic mechanism to include new binder symbols. Instead we list the binder symbols included at the moment.

A more general account of binder symbols is contained in the doctoral thesis [Ulbrich, 2013, Subsection 2.3.1]. Binder symbols do not increase the expressive power of first-order logic: for any formula ϕ_b containing binder symbols there is a formula ϕ without such that ϕ_b is universally valid if and only if ϕ is, see [Ulbrich, 2013, Theorem 2.4]. This is the reason why one does not find binder symbols other than quantifiers in traditional first-order logic text books.

Definition 2.22 (extends Definition 2.3).

4. If vi is a variable of type *int*, b_0, b_1 are terms of type *int* not containing vi and s is an arbitrary term in Trm$_{int}$, then $bsum\{vi\}(b_0, b_1, s)$ is in Trm$_{int}$.
5. If vi is a variable of type *int*, b_0, b_1 are terms of type *int* not containing vi and s is an arbitrary term in Trm$_{int}$, then $bprod\{vi\}(b_0, b_1, s)$ is in Trm$_{int}$.
6. If vi is a variable of arbitrary type and s a term of type *LocSet*, then $infiniteUnion\{vi\}(s)$ is in Trm$_{LocSet}$.
7. If vi is a variable of type *int*, b_0, b_1 are terms of type *int* not containing vi and s is an arbitrary term in Trm$_{any}$, then $seqDef\{vi\}(b_0, b_1, s)$ is in Trm$_{Seq}$.

It is instructive to observe the role of the quantified variable vi in the following syntax definition:

Definition 2.23 (extends Definition 2.5). If t is one of the terms $bsum\{vi\}(b_0, b_1, s)$, $bprod\{vi\}(b_0, b_1, s)$, $infiniteUnion\{vi\}(s)$, and $seqDef\{vi\}(b_0, b_1, s)$ we have

$$var(t) = var(b_0) \cup var(b_1) \cup var(s) \text{ and } fv(t) = var(t) \setminus \{vi\} \ .$$

We trust that the following remarks will suffice to clarify the semantic meaning of the first two symbols introduced in Definition 2.22. In mathematical notation one would write $\Sigma_{b_0 \leq vi < b_1} s_{vi}$ for $bsum\{vi\}(b_0, b_1, s)$ and $\Pi_{b_0 \leq vi < b_1} s_{vi}$ for $bprod\{vi\}(b_0, b_1, s)$. For the corner case $b_1 \leq b_0$ we stipulate $\Sigma_{b_0 \leq vi < b_1} s_{vi} = 0$ and $\Pi_{b_0 \leq vi < b_1} s_{vi} = 1$. The name *bsum* stands for *bounded sum* to emphasize that infinite sums are not covered. The proof rules for *bsum* and *bprod* are the obvious recursive definitions plus the stipulation for the corner cases which we forgo to reproduce here.

For an integer variable vi the term $infiniteUnion\{vi\}(s)$ would read in mathematical notation $\bigcup_{-\infty < vi < \infty} s$, and analogously for variables vi of type other than integer. The precise semantics is part of Figure 2.11 in Section 2.4.4 below.

The semantics of $seqDef\{vi\}(b_0, b_1, s)$ will be given in Definition 5.2 on page 151. But, it makes an interesting additional example of a binder symbol. The term

$seqDef\{vi\}(b_0,b_1,s)$ is to stand for the finite sequence $\langle s(b_0), s(b_0+1), \ldots, s(b_1-1)\rangle$. For $b_1 \le b_0$ the result is the empty sequence, i.e., $seqDef\{vi\}(b_0,b_1,s) = \langle\rangle$. The proof rules related to *seqDef* are discussed in Chapter 5.

2.3.2 Undefinedness

In KeY all functions are total. There are two ways to interpret a function symbol f in a structure $\mathcal{M}$ at an argument position $\bar{a}$ outside its intended range of definition:

1. The value of the function $val_{\mathcal{M}}(f)$ at position $\bar{a}$ is set to a default within the intended range of f. E.g., $bsum\{vi\}(1,0,s)$ evaluates to 0 (regardless of s).
2. The value of the function $val_{\mathcal{M}}(f)$ at position $\bar{a}$ is set to an arbitrary value b within the intended range of f. For different structures different b are chosen. When we talk about universal validity, i.e., truth in all structures, we assume that for every possible choice of b there is a structure $\mathcal{M}_b$ such that $val_{\mathcal{M}_b}(f)(\bar{a}) = b$. The prime example for this method, called *underspecification*, is division by 0 such that, e.g., $\frac{1}{0}$ is an arbitrary integer.

Another frequently used way to deal with undefinedness is to choose an error element that is different from all defined values of the function. We do not do this. The advantage of underspecification is that no changes to the logic are required. But, one has to know what is happening. In the setting of underspecification we can prove $\exists\, i; (\frac{1}{0} \doteq i)$ for an integer variable i. However, we cannot prove $\frac{1}{0} \doteq \frac{2}{0}$. Also the formula $cast_{int}(c) \doteq 5 \rightarrow c \doteq 5$ is not universally valid. In case c is not of type *int* the underspecified value for $cast_{int}(c)$ could be 5 for $c \neq 5$.

The underspecification method gives no warning when undefined values are used in the verification process. The KeY system offers a well-definedness check for JML contracts, details are described in Section 8.3.3.

2.4 First-Order Logic for Java

As already indicated in the introduction of this chapter, Java first-order logic (JFOL) will be an instantiation of the extended classical first-order logic from Subsection 2.3 tailored towards the verification of Java programs. The precise type hierarchy $\mathcal{T}$ and signature Σ will of course depend on the program and the statements to be proved about it. But we can identify a basic vocabulary that will be useful to have in almost every case. Figure 2.3 shows the type hierarchy $\mathcal{T}_J$ that we require to be at least contained in the type hierarchy $\mathcal{T}$ of any instance of JFOL. The mandatory function and predicate symbols Σ_J are shown in Figure 2.4. Data types are essential for formalizing nontrival program properties. The data types of the integers and the theory of arrays are considered so elementary that they are already included here. More precisely what is covered here are the mathematical integers. There are of course also Java integers types. Those and their relation to the mathematical integers are covered in Section 5.4 on page 161. Also the special data type *LocSet* of sets of memory locations will already be covered here. Why it is essential for the verification of Java programs will become apparent in Chapters 8 and 9. The data type of *Seq* of finite sequences however will extensively be treated later in Section 5.2.

2.4.1 Type Hierarchy and Signature

The mandatory type hierarchy $\mathcal{T}_J$ for JFOL is shown in Figure 2.3. Between *Object* and *Null* the class and interface types from the Java code to be investigated will appear. In the future there might be additional data types at the level immediately below *Any* besides *boolean*, *int*, *LocSet* and *Seq*, e.g., *maps*.

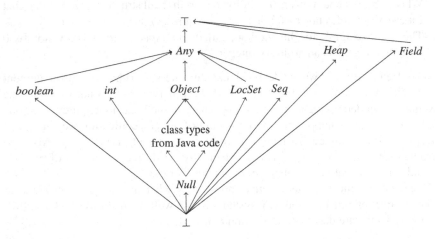

Figure 2.3 The mandatory type hierarchy $\mathcal{T}_J$ of JFOL

The mandatory vocabulary Σ_J of JFOL is shown in Figure 2.4 using the same notation as in Definition 2.2. In the subsections to follow we will first present the axioms that govern these data types one by one and conclude with their model-theoretic semantics in Subsection 2.4.5.

As mentioned above, in the verification of a specific Java program the signature Σ may be a strict superset of Σ_J. To mention just one example: for every model field m of type T contained in the specification of a Java class C an new symbol $f_m : Heap \times C \to T$ is introduced. We will in Definition 9.7 establish the terminology that function symbols with at least one, usually the first, argument of type *Heap* are called *observer function symbols*.

int and *boolean*	all function and predicate symbols for *int*, e.g., $+,*,<,\ldots$
	boolean constants *TRUE, FALSE*
Java types	*null* : *Null*
	length : *Object* → *int*
	$cast_A$: *Object* → *A* for any *A* in $\mathscr{T}$ with $\bot \sqsubset A \sqsubseteq Object$.
	$instance_A$: *Any* → *boolean* for any type $A \sqsubseteq Any$
	$exactInstance_A$: *Any* → *boolean* for any type $A \sqsubseteq Any$
Field	*created* : *Field*
	arr : *int* → *Field*
	f : *Field* for every Java field *f*
Heap	$select_A$: *Heap* × *Object* × *Field* → *A* for any type $A \sqsubseteq Any$
	store : *Heap* × *Object* × *Field* × *Any* → *Heap*
	create : *Heap* × *Object* → *Heap*
	anon : *Heap* × *LocSet* × *Heap* → *Heap*
	wellFormed(*Heap*)
LocSet	ε(*Object,Field,LocSet*)
	empty, allLocs : *LocSet*
	singleton : *Object* × *Field* → *LocSet*
	subset(*LocSet,LocSet*)
	disjoint(*LocSet,LocSet*)
	union, intersect, setMinus : *LocSet* × *LocSet* → *LocSet*
	allFields : *Object* → *LocSet*, *allObjects* : *Field* → *LocSet*
	arrayRange : *Object* × *int* × *int* → *LocSet*
	unusedLocs : *Heap* → *LocSet*

Figure 2.4 The mandatory vocabulary Σ_J of JFOL

2.4.2 Axioms for Integers

polySimp_addComm0	$k+i \doteq i+k$	add_zero_right	$i+0 \doteq i$
polySimp_addAssoc	$(i+j)+k \doteq i+(j+k)$	add_sub_elim_right	$i+(-i) \doteq 0$
polySimp_elimOne	$i*1 \doteq i$	mul_distribute_4	$i*(j+k) \doteq (i*j)+(i*k)$
mul_assoc	$(i*j)*k \doteq i*(j*k)$	mul_comm	$j*i \doteq i*j$
less_trans	$i<j \wedge j<k \rightarrow i<k$	less_is_total_heu	$i<j \vee i \doteq j \vee j<i$
less_is_alternative_1	$\neg(i<j \wedge j<i)$	less_literals	$0<1$
add_less	$i<j \rightarrow i+k<j+k$	multiply_inEq	$i<j \wedge 0<k \rightarrow i*k<j*k$

$$\text{int\_induction} \quad \frac{\Gamma \Longrightarrow \phi(0),\Delta \quad \Gamma \Longrightarrow \forall n;(0 \leq n \wedge \phi(n) \rightarrow \phi(n+1)),\Delta}{\Gamma \Longrightarrow \forall n;(0 \leq n \rightarrow \phi(n)),\Delta}$$

Figure 2.5 Integer axioms and rules

Figure 2.5 shows the axioms for the integers with $+$, $*$ and $<$. Occasionally we use the additional symbol $\leq$ which is, as usual, defined by $x \leq y \leftrightarrow (x<y \vee x \doteq y)$. The implication multiply_inEq does in truth not occur among the KeY taclets. Instead multiply_inEq0 $i \leq j \wedge 0 \leq k \rightarrow i*k \leq j*k$ is included. But, multiply_inEq can be derived from , multiply_inEq0 although by a rather lengthy proof (65 steps) based on a normal form transformation. The reverse implication is trivially true.

Figure 2.5 also lists in front of each axiom the name of the taclet that implements it. The KeY system not only implements the shown axioms but many useful consequences and defining axioms for further operations such as those related to integer division and the modulo function. How the various integer data types of the Java language are handled in the KeY system is explained in Section 5.4.

Incompleteness

Mathematically the integers $(\mathbb{Z}, +, *, 0, 1, <)$ are a commutative ordered ring satisfying the well-foundedness property: every nonempty subset of the positive integers has a least element. Well-foundedness is a second-order property. It is approximated by the first-order induction schema, which can be interpreted to say that every nonempty definable subset of the positive integers has a least element. The examples known so far of properties of the integers that can be proved in second-order logic but not in its first-order approximation, see e.g. [Kirby and Paris, 1982] are still so arcane that we need not worry about this imperfection.

2.4.3 Axioms for Heap

The state of a Java program is determined by the values of the local variables and the heap. A heap assigns to every pair consisting of an object and a field declared for this object an appropriate value. As a first step to model heaps, we require that a type *Field* be present in JFOL. This type is required to contain the field constant *created* and the fields $arr(i)$ for array access for natural numbers $0 \le i$. In a specific verification context there will be constants f for every field f occurring in the Java program under verification. There is no assumption, however, that these are the only elements in *Field*; on the contrary, it is completely open which other field elements may occur. This feature is helpful for modular verification: when the contracts for methods in a Java class are verified, they remain true when new fields are added. The data type *Heap* allows us to represent more functions than can possibly occur as heaps in states reachable by a Java program:

1. Values may be stored for arbitrary pairs (o, f) of objects o and fields f regardless of the question if f is declared in the class of o.
2. The value stored for a pair (o, f) need not match the type of f.
3. A heap may assign values for infinitely many objects and fields.

On one hand our heap model allows for heaps that we will never need, on the other hand this generality makes the model simpler. Relaxation 2 in the above list is necessary since JFOL does not use dependent types. To compensate for this shortcoming there has to be a family of observer functions $select_A$, where A ranges over all subtypes of *Any*.

The axiomatization of the data type *Heap*, shown in Figure 2.6, follows the pattern well known from the theory of arrays. The standard reference is [McCarthy, 1962]. There are some changes however. One would expect the following rule $select_A(store(h,o,f,x),o2,f2) \rightsquigarrow$ if $o \doteq o2 \wedge f \doteq f2$ then x else $select_A(h,o2,f2)$. Since the type of x need not be A this easily leads to an ill-typed formula. Thus we need $cast_A(x)$ in place of x. In addition the implicit field *created* gets special treatment. The value of this field should not be manipulated by the *store* function. This explains the additional conjunct $f \neq created$ in the axiom. The rule selectOfStore as it is shown below implies $select_A(store(h,o,created,x),o2,f2) \doteq select_A(h,o2,f2)$. Assuming extensionality of heaps this entails $store(h,o,created,x) \doteq h$. The *created* field of a heap can only be changed by the *create* function as detailed by the rule selectOfCreate. This ensures that the value of the *created* field can never be changed from *TRUE* to *FALSE*. Note also, that the object *null* is considered to be created from the start, so it can be excepted from rule selectOfCreate.

selectOfStore $select_A(store(h,o,f,x),o2,f2) \rightsquigarrow$
$\qquad$ if $o \doteq o2 \wedge f \doteq f2 \wedge f \neq created$ then $cast_A(x)$ else $select_A(h,o2,f2)$

selectOfCreate $select_A(create(h,o),o2,f) \rightsquigarrow$
$\qquad$ if $o \doteq o2 \wedge o \neq null \wedge f \doteq created$ then $cast_A(TRUE)$ else $select_A(h,o2,f)$

selectOfAnon $select_A(anon(h,s,h'),o,f) \rightsquigarrow$
$\qquad$ if$(\varepsilon(o,f,s) \wedge f \neq created) \vee \varepsilon(o,f,unusedLocs(h))$
$\qquad$ then $select_A(h',o,f)$ else $select_A(h,o,f)$

with the typing $o,o1,o2 : Object, f, f2 : Field, h, h' : Heap, s : LocSet$

Figure 2.6 Rules for the theory of arrays.

There is another operator, named $anon(h,s,h')$, that returns a *Heap* object. Its meaning is described by the rule selectOfAnon in Figure 2.6: at locations (o,f) in the location set s the resulting heap coincides with h' under the proviso $f \neq created$, otherwise it coincides with h. To get an idea when this operator is useful imaging that h is the heap reached at the beginning of a while loop that at most changes locations in a location set s and that h' is a totally unknown heap. Then $anon(h,s,h')$ represents a heap reached after an unknown number of loop iterations. This heap may have more created objects than the initial heap h. Since location sets are not allowed to contain locations with not created objects, see onlyCreatedObjectsAreInLocSets in Figure 2.7, this has to be added as an addition case in rule selectOfAnon. This application scenario also accounts for the name which is short for *anonymize*.

A patiently explained example for the use of *store* and *select* functions can be found in Subsection 15.2.3 on page 526. While SMT solvers can handle expressions containing many occurrences of *store* and *select* quite efficiently, they are a pain in the neck for the human reader. The KeY interface therefore presents those expressions in a pretty printed version, see explanations in Section 16.2 on page 544.

The taclets in Figure 2.6 are called *rewriting taclets*. We use the $\leadsto$ notation to distinguish them from the other sequent rules as, e.g., in Figures 2.1 and 2.2. A rewriting rule $s \leadsto t$ is shorthand for a sequent rule $\frac{\Gamma' \Longrightarrow \Delta'}{\Gamma \Longrightarrow \Delta}$ where $\Gamma' \Longrightarrow \Delta'$ arises from $\Gamma \Longrightarrow \Delta$ by replacing one or more occurrences of the term s by t. Rewriting rules will again be discussed in Subsection 4.2.3, page 116.

onlyCreatedObjectsAreReferenced
$wellFormed(h) \rightarrow select_A(h,o,f) \doteq null \vee select_{boolean}(h, select_A(h,o,f), created) \doteq TRUE$

onlyCreatedObjectsAreInLocSets
$wellFormed(h) \wedge \varepsilon(o2, f2, select_{LocSet}(h,o,f)) \rightarrow o2 \doteq null \vee$
$\qquad\qquad\qquad\qquad\qquad\qquad select_{boolen}(h, o2, created) \doteq TRUE$

narrowSelectType
$wellFormed(h) \wedge select_B(h,o,f) \rightarrow select_A(h,o,f)$ $\qquad$ where type of f is A and $A \sqsubseteq B$

narrowSelectArrayType
$wellFormed(h) \wedge o \neq null \wedge select_B(h,o,arr(i)) \rightarrow select_A(h,o,arr(i))$
$\qquad\qquad\qquad\qquad$ where type of o is $A[]$ and $A \sqsubseteq B$

wellFormedStoreObject
$wellFormed(h) \wedge (x \doteq null \vee (select_{boolean}(h,x,created) \doteq TRUE \wedge instance_A(x) \doteq TRUE))$
$\qquad \rightarrow wellFormed(store(h,o,f,x))$ $\qquad$ where type of f is A

wellFormedStoreArray
$wellFormed(h) \wedge (x \doteq null \vee (select_{boolean}(h,x,created) \doteq TRUE \wedge arrayStoreValid(o,x)))$
$\qquad \rightarrow wellFormed(store(h,o,arr(idx),x)))$

wellFormedStoreLocSet
$wellFormed(h) \wedge \forall ov; \forall fv; (\varepsilon(ov, fv, y) \rightarrow ov \doteq null \vee select_{boolean}(h, ov, created) \doteq TRUE)$
$\qquad \rightarrow wellFormed(store(h,o,f,y))$ $\qquad$ where type of f is A and $LocSet \sqsubseteq A$

wellFormedStorePrimitive
$wellFormed(h) \rightarrow wellFormed(store(h,o,f,x))$
provided f is a field of type A, x is of type B, and $B \sqsubseteq A, B \not\sqsubseteq Object, B \not\sqsubseteq LocSet$

wellFormedStorePrimitiveArray
$wellFormed(h) \rightarrow wellFormed(store(h,o,arr(idx),x))$
provided o is of sort A, x is of sort $B, B \not\sqsubseteq Object, B \not\sqsubseteq LocSet, B \sqsubseteq A$

wellFormedCreate
$wellFormed(h) \rightarrow wellFormed(create(h,o))$

wellFormedAnon
$wellFormed(h) \wedge wellFormed(h2) \rightarrow wellFormed(anon(h,y,h2))$

In the above formulas the following implicitly universally quantified variables are used: $h, h2 : Heap$, $o, x : Object$, $f : Field$, $i : int$, $y : LocSet$

Figure 2.7 Rules for the predicate *wellFormed*

Our concept of heap is an overgeneralization. Most of the time this does no harm. But, there are situations where it is useful to establish and depend on certain well-formedness conditions. The predicate *wellFormed*(*heap*) has been included in the vocabulary for this purpose. No effort is made to make the *wellFormed*(*h*) predicate so strong that it only is true of heaps *h* that can actually occur in Java programs. The axioms in Figure 2.7 were chosen on a pragmatic basis. There is e.g., no axiom that guarantees for a created object *o* of type *A* with *select*(*h*,*o*,*f*) defined that the field *f* is declared in class *A*.

The first four axioms in Figure 2.7 formalize properties of well-formed heaps while the rest cover situations starting out with a well-formed heap, manipulate it and end up again with a well-formed heap. The formulas are quite self-explanatory. Reading though them you will encounter the auxiliary predicate `arrayStoreValid`: `arrayStoreValid(o,x)` is true if *o* is an array object of exact type *A*[] and *x* is of type *A*.

The meaning of the functions symbols *instance$_A$*(*x*), *exactInstance$_A$*(*x*), *cast$_A$*(*x*), and *length*(*x*) is given by the axioms in Figure 2.8. This time we present the axioms in mathematical notation for conciseness. The axiom scheme, (Ax-I) and (Ax-C) show that adding *instance$_A$* and *cast$_A$* does not increase the expressive power. These functions can be defined already in the basic logic plus underspecification. The formulas (Ax-E_1) and (Ax-E_2) completely axiomatize the *exactInstance$_A$* functions, see Lemma 2.24 on page 47. The function *length* is only required to be not negative. Axioms (Ax-E_1), (Ax-E_2), and (Ax-L) are directly formalized in the KeY system as

$\forall Object\ x; (instance_A(x) \doteq TRUE \leftrightarrow \exists y; (y \doteq x))$ with $y : A$	(Ax-I)
$\forall Object\ x; (exactInstance_A(x) \doteq TRUE \rightarrow instance_A(x) \doteq TRUE)$	(Ax-E_1)
$\forall Object\ x; (exactInstance_A(x) \doteq TRUE \rightarrow instance_B(x) \doteq FALSE)$ with $A \not\sqsubseteq B$	(Ax-E_2)
$\forall Object\ x; (instance_A(x) \doteq TRUE \rightarrow cast_A(x) \doteq x)$	(Ax-C)
$\forall Object\ x; (length(x) \geq 0)$	(Ax-L)

Figure 2.8 Axioms for functions related to Java types

taclets instance_known_dynamic_type, exact_instance_known_dynamic_type and arrayLengthNotNegative. The other two axioms families have no direct taclet counterpart. But, they can easily be derived.

2.4.4 Axioms for Location Sets

The data type *LocSet* is a very special case of the set type in that only sets of heap locations are considered, i.e., sets of pairs (o, f) with *o* an object and *f* a field. This immediately guarantees that the is-element-of relation ε is well-founded for *LocSet*. Problematic formulas such as $a\varepsilon a$ are already syntactically impossible.

The rules for the data type *LocSet* are displayed in Figure 2.9. The only constraint on the membership relation ε is formulated in rule equalityToElementOf. One could view this rule as a definition of equality for location sets. But, since equality is a built in relation in the basic logic it is in fact a constraint on ε. All other rules in this figure are definitions of the additional symbols of the data type, such as, e.g., *allLocs*, *union*, *intersect*, and *infiniteUnion*$\{av\}(s1)$.

elementOfEmpty	$\varepsilon(o1,f1,empty)$	$\rightsquigarrow$ FALSE
elementOfAllLocs	$\varepsilon(o1,f1,allLocs)$	$\rightsquigarrow$ TRUE
equalityToElementOf	$s1 \doteq s2$	$\rightsquigarrow \forall o; \forall f; (\varepsilon(o,f,s1) \leftrightarrow \varepsilon(o,f,s2))$
elementOfSingleton	$\varepsilon(o1,f1,singleton(o2,f2))$	$\rightsquigarrow o1 \doteq o2 \wedge f1 \doteq f2$
elementOfUnion	$\varepsilon(o1,f1,union(t1,t2))$	$\rightsquigarrow \varepsilon(o1,f1,t1) \vee \varepsilon(o1,f1,t2)$
subsetToElementOf	$subset(t1,t2)$	$\rightsquigarrow \forall o; \forall f; (\varepsilon(o,f,t1) \rightarrow \varepsilon(o,f,t2))$
elementOfIntersect	$\varepsilon(o1,f1,intersect(t1,t2))$	$\rightsquigarrow \varepsilon(o1,f1,t1) \wedge \varepsilon(o1,f1,t2)$
elementOfAllFields	$\varepsilon(o1,f1,allFields(o2))$	$\rightsquigarrow o1 \doteq o2$
elementOfSetMinus	$\varepsilon(o1,f1,setMinus(t1,t2))$	$\rightsquigarrow \varepsilon(o1,f1,t1) \wedge \neg\varepsilon(o1,f1,t2)$
elementOfAllObjects	$\varepsilon(o1,f1,allObjects(f2))$	$\rightsquigarrow f1 \doteq f2$
elementOfInfiniteUnion	$\varepsilon(o1,f1,infiniteUnion\{av\}(s1))$	$\rightsquigarrow \exists av; \varepsilon(o1,f1,s1)$

with the typing $o, o1, o2 : Object, f, f1 : Field, s1, s2, t1, t2 : LocSet, av$ of arbitrary type.

Figure 2.9 Rules for data type *LocSet*

2.4.5 Semantics

As already remarked at the start of Subsection 2.2.3, a formal semantics opens up the possibility for rigorous soundness and relative completeness proofs. Here we extend and adapt the semantics provided there to cover the additional syntax introduced for JFOL (see Section 2.4.1).

We take the liberty to use an alternative notion for the interpretation of terms. While we used val$_{\mathcal{M},\beta}(t)$ in Section 2.2.3 to emphasize also visually that we are concerned with evaluation, we will write $t^{\mathcal{M},\beta}$ for brevity here.

The definition of a FOL structure $\mathcal{M}$ for a given signature in Subsection 2.2.3 was deliberately formulated as general as possible, to underline the universal nature of logic. The focus in this subsection is on semantic structures tailored towards the verification of Java programs. To emphasize this perspective we call these structures JFOL structures.

A decisive difference to the semantics from Section 2.2.3 is that now the interpretation of some symbols, types, functions, predicates, is constrained. Some functions are completely fixed, e.g., addition and multiplication of integers. Others are almost fixed, e.g., integer division n/m that is fixed except for $n/0$ which may have different interpretations in different structures. Other symbols are only loosely constrained, e.g., *length* is only required to be nonnegative.

The semantic constraints on the JFOL type symbols are shown in Figure 2.10. The restriction on the semantics of the subtypes of *Object* is that their domains contain for every $n \in \mathbb{N}$ infinitely many elements o with $length^{\mathcal{M}}(o) = n$. The reason for this is the way object creation is modeled. When an array object is created an element o in the corresponding type domain is provided whose *created* field has value *FALSE*. The created field is then set to *TRUE*. Since the function *length* is independent of the heap it cannot be changed in the creation process. So, the element picked must already have the desired length. This topic will be covered in detail in Subsection 3.6.6. The semantics of *Seq* will be given in Chapter 5.

- $D^{int} = \mathbb{Z}$,
- $D^{boolean} = \{tt, ff\}$,
- $D^{ObjectType}$ is an infinite set of elements for every *ObjectType* with $Null \sqsubseteq ObjectType \sqsubseteq Object$, subject to the restriction that for every positive integer n there are infinitely many elements o in $D^{ObjectType}$ with $length^{\mathcal{M}}(o) = n$.
- $D^{Null} = \{null\}$,
- D^{Heap} = the set of all functions $h : D^{Object} \times D^{Field} \to D^{Any}$,
- D^{LocSet} = the set of all subsets of $\{(o, f) \mid o \in D^{Object}$ and $f \subset D^{Field}\}$,
- D^{Field} is an infinite set.

Figure 2.10 Semantics on type domains

Constant Domain

Let T be a theory, that does not have finite models. By definition $T \vdash \phi$ iff $\mathcal{M} \models \phi$ for all models $\mathcal{M}$ of T. The Löwenheim-Skolem Theorem, which by the way follows easily from the usual completeness proofs, guarantees that $T \vdash \phi$ iff $\mathcal{M} \models \phi$ for all countably infinite models $\mathcal{M}$ of T. Let S be an arbitrary countably infinite set, then we have further $T \vdash \phi$ iff $\mathcal{M} \models \phi$ for all models $\mathcal{M}$ of T such that the universe of $\mathcal{M}$ is S. To see this assume there is a countably infinite model $\mathcal{N}$ of T with universe N such that $\mathcal{N} \models \neg\phi$. For cardinality reasons there is a bijection b from N onto S. So far, S is just a set. It is straightforward to define a structure $\mathcal{M}$ with universe S such that b is an isomorphism from $\mathcal{N}$ onto $\mathcal{M}$. This entails the contradiction $\mathcal{M} \models \neg\phi$.

The interpretation of all the JFOL function and predicate symbols listed in Figure 2.4 is at least partly fixed. All JFOL structures $\mathcal{M} = (M, \delta, I)$ are required to satisfy the constraints put forth in Figure 2.11.

Some of these constraints are worth an explanation. The semantics of the *store* function, as stated above, is such that it cannot change the implicit field *created*. Also there is no requirement that the type of the value x should match with the type of the

1. $TRUE^{\mathcal{M}} = tt$ and $FALSE^{\mathcal{M}} = ff$
2. $select_A^{\mathcal{M}}(h,o,f) = cast_A^{\mathcal{M}}(h(o,f))$
3. $store^{\mathcal{M}}(h,o,f,x) = h^*$, where the function h^* is defined by

$$h^*(o',f') = \begin{cases} x & \text{if } o' = o, f = f' \text{ and } f \neq created^{\mathcal{M}} \\ h(o',f') & \text{otherwise} \end{cases}$$

4. $create^{\mathcal{M}}(h,o) = h^*$, where the function h^* is defined by

$$h^*(o',f) = \begin{cases} tt & \text{if } o' = o, o \neq null \text{ and } f = created^{\mathcal{M}} \\ h(o',f) & \text{otherwise} \end{cases}$$

5. $arr^{\mathcal{M}}$ is an injective function from $\mathbb{Z}$ into $Field^{\mathcal{M}}$
6. $created^{\mathcal{M}}$ and $f^{\mathcal{M}}$ for each Java field f are elements of $Field^{\mathcal{M}}$, which are pairwise different and also not in the range of $arr^{\mathcal{M}}$.
7. $null^{\mathcal{M}} = null$
8. $cast_A^{\mathcal{M}}(o) = \begin{cases} o & \text{if } o \in A^{\mathcal{M}} \\ \text{arbitrary element in } A^{\mathcal{M}} & \text{otherwise} \end{cases}$
9. $instance_A(o)^{\mathcal{M}} = tt \Leftrightarrow o \in A^{\mathcal{M}} \Leftrightarrow \delta(o) \sqsubseteq A$
10. $exactInstance_A^{\mathcal{M}} = tt \Leftrightarrow \delta(o) = A$
11. $length^{\mathcal{M}}(o) \in \mathbb{N}$
12. $\langle o,f,s \rangle \in \varepsilon^{\mathcal{M}}$ iff $(o,f) \in s$
13. $empty^{\mathcal{M}} = \emptyset$
14. $allLocs^{\mathcal{M}} = Object^{\mathcal{M}} \times Field^{\mathcal{M}}$
15. $singleton^{\mathcal{M}}(o,f) = \{(o,f)\}$
16. $\langle s_1,s_2 \rangle \in subset^{\mathcal{M}}$ iff $s_1 \subseteq s_2$
17. $\langle s_1,s_2 \rangle \in disjoint^{\mathcal{M}}$ iff $s_1 \cap s_2 = \emptyset$
18. $union^{\mathcal{M}}(s_1,s_2) = s_1 \cup s_2$
19. $infiniteUnion\{av\}(s)^{\mathcal{M}} = \{(a \in D^T \mid s^{\mathcal{M}}[a/av]\}$ with T type of av
20. $intersect^{\mathcal{M}}(s_1,s_2) = s_1 \cap s_2$
21. $setMinus^{\mathcal{M}}(s_1,s_2) = s_1 \setminus s_2$
22. $allFields^{\mathcal{M}}(o) = \{(o,f) \mid f \in Field^{\mathcal{M}}\}$
23. $allObjects^{\mathcal{M}}(f) = \{(o,f) \mid o \in Object^{\mathcal{M}}\}$
24. $arrayRange^{\mathcal{M}}(o,i,j) = \{(o,arr^{\mathcal{M}}(x) \mid x \in \mathbb{Z}, i \leq x \leq j\}$
25. $unusedLocs^{\mathcal{M}}(h) = \{(o,f) \mid o \in Object^{\mathcal{M}}, f \in Field^{\mathcal{M}}, o \neq null, h(o,created^{\mathcal{M}}) = false\}$
26. $anon^{\mathcal{M}}(h_1,s,h_2) = h^*$, where the function h^* is defined by:

$$h^*(o,f) = \begin{cases} h_2(o,f) \text{ if } (o,f) \in s \text{ and } f \neq created^{\mathcal{M}}, \text{ or} \\ \qquad (o,f) \in unusedLocs^{\mathcal{M}}(h_1) \\ h_1(o,f) \text{ otherwise} \end{cases}$$

Figure 2.11 Semantics for the mandatory JFOL vocabulary (see Figure 2.4)

field f. This liberality necessitates the use of the $cast_A$ functions in the semantics of $select_A$.

It is worth pointing out that the *length* function is defined for all elements in D^{Object}, not only for elements in D^{OT} where OT is an array type.

Since the semantics of the wellFormed predicate is a bit more involved we put it separately in Figure 2.12

The integer operations are defined as usual with the following versions of integer division and the modulo function:

$h \in wellFormed^{\mathcal{M}}$ iff (a) if $h(o,f) \in D^{Object}$ then $h(o,f) = null$ or $h(h(o,f), created^{\mathcal{M}}) = tt$
(b) if $h(o,f) \in D^{LocSet}$ then $nh(o,f) \cap unusedLocs^{\mathcal{M}}(h) = \emptyset$
(c) if $\delta(o) = T[]$ then $\delta(h(o, arr^{\mathcal{M}}(i))) \sqsubseteq T$ for all $0 \le i < length^{\mathcal{M}}(o)$
(d) there are only finitely many $o \in D^{Object}$ for which $h(o, created^{\mathcal{M}}) = tt$

Figure 2.12 Semantics for the predicate *wellFormed*

$$n /^{\mathcal{M}} m = \begin{cases} \begin{array}{l} \text{the uniquely defined } k \text{ such that} \\ |m| * |k| \le |n| \text{ and } |m| * (|k| + 1) > |n| \text{ and} \\ k \ge 0 \text{ if } m,n \text{ are both positive or both negative and} \\ k \le 0 \text{ otherwise} \end{array} & \text{if } m \ne 0 \\ \\ \text{unspecified} & \text{otherwise} \end{cases}$$

Thus integer division is a total function with arbitrary values for $x /^{\mathcal{M}} 0$. Division is an example of a partially fixed function. The interpretation of $/$ in a JFOL structure $\mathcal{M}$ is fixed except for the values $x /^{\mathcal{M}} 0$. These may be different in different JFOL structures. The modulo function is defined by

$$mod(n,d) = n - (n/d) * d$$

Note, that this implies $mod(n,0) = n$ as $/$ is – due to using underspecification – a total function.

Lemma 2.24. *The axioms in Figure 2.8 are sound and complete with respect to the given semantics.*

For a proof see [Schmitt and Ulbrich, 2015].

Chapter 3
Dynamic Logic for Java

Bernhard Beckert, Vladimir Klebanov, and Benjamin Weiß

3.1 Introduction

In the previous chapter, we have introduced JFOL a variant of classical first-order logic tailored for reasoning about (single) states of Java programs (Section 2.4). Now, we extend this logic such that we can reason about the behavior of programs, which requires to consider not just one but several program states. As a trivial example, consider the Java statement x++. We want to be able to express that this statement, when started in a state where x is zero, terminates in a state where x is one.

We use an instance of dynamic logic (DL) [Harel, 1984, Harel et al., 2000, Kozen and Tiuryn, 1990, Pratt, 1977] for this purpose, which we will call JavaDL. The principle of dynamic logic is the formulation of assertions about program behavior by integrating programs and formulas within a single language. To this end, the *modalities* $\langle p \rangle$ and $[p]$ can be used in formulas, where p can be any sequence of legal program statements (i.e., DL is a multi-modal logic). These operators refer to the final state of p and can be placed in front of any formula. The formula $\langle p \rangle \phi$ expresses that the program p terminates in a state in which ϕ holds, while $[p]\phi$ does not demand termination and expresses that, *if* p terminates, then ϕ holds in the final state. For example, "when started in a state where x is zero, x++ terminates in a state where x is one" can in DL be expressed as $x \doteq 0 \rightarrow \langle x\texttt{++} \rangle (x \doteq 1)$.

Nondeterministic programs can have more than one final state; but here, since we consider Java programs to be deterministic, there is exactly one final state (if p terminates normally, i.e., does not terminate abruptly due to an uncaught exception) or there is no final state (if p does not terminate or terminates abruptly). "Deterministic" here means that a program, for the same initial state and the same inputs, always has the same behavior—in particular, the same final state (if it terminates) and the same outputs. Assuming Java to be deterministic is justified as we do not consider concurrency, which is the main source of nondeterminism in Java.

In exact terms, the programming language supported by JavaDL, as defined in this chapter, is not full Java. It lacks features like concurrency, floating-point arithmetic, and dynamic class loading, but retains the essentials of object-orientation. In fact,

© Springer International Publishing AG 2016
W. Ahrendt et al. (Eds.): Deductive Software Verification, LNCS 10001, pp. 49–106, 2016
DOI: 10.1007/978-3-319-49812-6_3

JavaDL supports all features that occur in both Java Card (version 2.2.2 or 3.0.x, classic edition)—a Java dialect for smart cards—and Java (version 1.4). Beyond Java Card features, JavaDL supports Java's dynamic object creation and initialization, assertions, the primitive types `char` and `long`, strings, multi-dimensional arrays, the enhanced `for`-loop, and more. Extending JavaDL to cover Java Card-specific extensions like transactions is the topic of Chapter 10.

Deduction in DL, and in particular in JavaDL is based on symbolic program execution and simple program transformations and is, thus, close to a programmer's understanding of Java (see Section 3.5.6).

Dynamic Logic and Hoare Logic

Dynamic logic can be seen as an extension of Hoare logic. The DL formula $\phi \rightarrow [p]\psi$ is similar to the Hoare triple $\{\phi\}p\{\psi\}$. But in contrast to Hoare logic, the set of formulas of DL is closed under the usual logical operators: In Hoare logic, the formulas ϕ and ψ are pure first-order formulas, whereas in DL they can contain programs. Using a program in ϕ, for example, it is easy to specify that an input data structure is not cyclic, which is impossible in pure first-order logic.

A version of KeY that, for teaching purposes, supports a variant of Hoare logic, is described in Chapter 17.

Structure of this Chapter

We first define syntax and semantics of JavaDL in Sections 3.2 and 3.3, respectively. In Section 3.4, we add another type of modal operators to JavaDL, called *updates*, that (like programs) can be used to describe state changes. Then, in Sections 3.5–3.7, we present the JavaDL calculus, which is used in the KeY system for verifying Java programs. Section 3.5 gives an overview, Section 3.6 describes the basic rules of the calculus, and Section 3.7 gives an introduction to the rules for unbounded loops and replacing method invocations by specifications. These latter rules use program abstraction, which is described in more detail in Chapter 9.

3.2 Syntax of JavaDL

In this section, we define the syntax—and later in the chapter, semantics—of JavaDL for a given Java program *Prg*. By *Java program* we mean, as usual, a set of source files containing a set of class definitions. We assume that *Prg* can be compiled without errors.

It is worth noting that while the syntax and semantics of the logic are tied to a fixed and completely known program, the calculus is "modular" and does not have this restriction. Individual methods are soundly verified without the rest of the program being taken into particular consideration—unless the user deliberately chooses to forego modularity.

3.2.1 Type Hierarchies

The minimal type hierarchy $\mathscr{T}_J$ for JFOL was already introduced in Section 2.4.1. A JavaDL type hierarchy for a given Java program *Prg* is any hierarchy $\mathscr{T} = (\mathrm{TSym}, \sqsubseteq)$ that contains $\mathscr{T}_J$ as a subhierarchy (see Figure 2.3 on page 38). That is, it contains (at least) the class and interface types from *Prg* in addition to the types *Any, boolean, int, Null, LocSet, Field, Heap,* $\bot$, $\top$.

We map the finite-width Java integer types byte, short, int, etc. to the unbounded JavaDL type *int* $\in$ TSym. This mapping does *not* necessarily mean that integer overflows are ignored. Instead, the handling of overflow depends on the semantics and rules for reasoning about the arithmetical operators of Java, which are configurable in KeY. The KeY system allows the user to choose between several different ways of reasoning about the Java integers: (i) ignoring integer overflows, (ii) checking that no integer overflows can occur, and (iii) using the actual modulo semantics of Java. The details can be found in Section 5.4 and, ultimately, in [Beckert and Schlager, 2004, 2005].

Note that Java Card and KeY do not support the Java floating-point types float and double, so there are also no corresponding types in $\mathscr{T}_J$.

3.2.2 Signatures

In JavaDL, symbols can be either *rigid* or *nonrigid*. The intuition is that the interpretation of nonrigid symbols can be changed by the program, while rigid symbols maintain their interpretation throughout program execution. The class of nullary nonrigid function symbols has a particular importance—we will refer to such symbols as *program variables*.

Definition 3.1. Let $\mathscr{T}$ be a JavaDL type hierarchy for a Java program *Prg*. A JavaDL *signature* w.r.t. $\mathscr{T}$ is a tuple

$$\Sigma = (\mathrm{FSym}, \mathrm{PSym}, \mathrm{VSym}, \mathrm{ProgVSym})$$

where

- (FSym, PSym, VSym) is a JFOL signature, i.e., Σ includes the vocabulary from Σ_J (see Figure 2.4);

- the set ProgVSym of nullary nonrigid function symbols, which we call *program variables*, contains all local variables a declared in *Prg*, where the type of $a\!:\!A \in$ ProgVSym is given by the declared Java type T as follows:

  - $A = T$ if T is a reference type,
  - $A = boolean$ if $T = $ boolean,
  - $A = int$ if $T \in \{$byte, short, int, long, char$\}$.

- ProgVSym contains an infinite number of symbols of every typing.
- ProgVSym contains the "special" program variable

$$\text{heap}\!:\!Heap \in \text{ProgVSym} .$$

There is an important difference between *logical variables* in VSym and *program variables* in ProgVSym: logical variables can be universally or existentially quantified but never occur in programs, while program variables can occur in programs but cannot be quantified.

3.2.3 Syntax of JavaDL Program Fragments

The programs p occurring in modal operators $\langle p \rangle$ and $[p]$ in JavaDL formulas are written in Java, or, more precisely, in the intersection between Java and Java Card. Thus, for full formal rigor, the definitions of JavaDL would have to include definitions of the syntax and semantics of this subset of Java. However, this is beyond the scope of this text. Instead, Definition 3.2 below defines the admissible programs p rather informally, by referring to the *Java language specification* (JLS) [Gosling et al., 2013].

Definition 3.2 (Legal program fragments). Let *Prg* be a Java program. A *legal program fragment p in the context of Prg* is a sequence of Java statements, where there are local variables $a_1, \ldots, a_n \in$ ProgVSym of Java types $T_1, \ldots, T_n$ such that extending *Prg* with an additional class

```
class C {
    static void m(T₁ a₁, ..., Tₙ aₙ) throws Throwable { p }
}
```

yields a legal program according to the rules of the Java language specification (with certain deviations outlined below).

The purpose of the parameter declarations T_1 a_1, ..., T_n a_n of m is to bind *free* occurrences of the program variables $a_1, \ldots, a_n$ in p, i.e., occurrences not bound by a declaration within p itself. For example, in the legal program fragment "int a = b;" there is a free occurrence of the program variable $b \in$ ProgVSym. The throws Throwable clause is included to accommodate any uncaught checked exceptions originating from p.

The deviations from the program legality in the sense of the JLS, include the following syntactical extensions:

- p may contain *method frames* in addition to normal Java statements. A method frame is a statement of the form

```
method-frame(result=r,source=m(T_1,...,T_n)@T,this=t):{ body }
```

where (a) r is a local variable (in case of a void method `result=r` is omitted), (b) $m(T_1,\ldots,T_n)@T$ is a class and method context (method m with given signature of class T), (c) t is an expression free of side-effects and without method calls, and (d) *body* is a legal program fragment in the context of *Prg*. The semantics of a method frame is that, inside *body* (but outside of any nested method frames that might be contained in *body*), the visibility rules for the given class and method context $m(T_1,\ldots,T_n)@T$ are applicable, keyword `this` evaluates to the value of t, and the meaning of a `return` statement is to assign the returned value to r and to then exit the method frame.

- p may contain *method body statements*

$$retvar=target.m(t_1,\ldots,t_n)@T;$$

where

- $target.m(t_1,\ldots,t_n)$ is a method invocation expression,
- the type T points to a class declared in *Prg*,
- the result of the method is assigned to *retvar* after return (if the method is not void).

Intuitively, a method body statement is a shorthand notation for the precisely identified implementation of method $m(\ldots)$ in class T (in other words, for the unambiguously resolved corresponding method invocation). In contrast to a normal method call where the implementation to be taken is determined by dynamic binding, a method body statement is a call to a method declared in a type that is precisely identified by the method body statement.

Typically, method body statements are already contained in initial proof obligations for functional contracts (Definition 8.4), while method frames are only created during symbolic execution.

We also deviate from the JLS by relaxing its requirements in certain aspects, among them:

- Outside method frames, p may refer to fields, methods, and classes that are not visible in C. Inside a method frame, KeY follows the visibility rules of the JLS, except that when resolving a method invocation by inlining, the inlined code may refer to classes not visible in the calling method.
- We do not require *definite assignment*. In Java, the value of a local variable or a `final` field must have a definitely assigned value when any access of its value occurs [Gosling et al., 2013, Section 16]. In JavaDL we allow sequences of

statements that violate this condition (the variable then has a well-defined but unknown value).

- We do not ban *unreachable statements* [Gosling et al., 2013, Section 14.21]. For example, we consider

```
throw new RuntimeException(); int i = 0;
```

a legal program fragment.

3.2.4 Syntax of JavaDL Terms and Formulas

JavaDL *terms* are defined in the same way as FOL terms (Definition 2.3). However, the resulting set of terms is a strict superset of the terms of FOL, as the definitions of terms and formulas are mutually recursive, and JavaDL admits formulas that contain the modal operators $\langle p \rangle$ and $[p]$ and are, thus, not part of FOL.

Definition 3.3 (Terms and Formulas of JavaDL). Let *Prg* be a Java program, $\mathscr{T}$ a type hierarchy for *Prg*, and Σ a signature w.r.t. $\mathscr{T}$.

The set DLTrm_A of JavaDL terms of type A, for $A \neq \bot$, and the set DLFml of JavaDL formulas are defined as in first-order logic (Definitions 2.3 and 2.4, page 24) except for the following differences:

- The signature Σ now refers to the JavaDL signature.
- The mutual recursive references to Trm_X and Fml are now to DLTrm_X and DLFml, respectively.
- The following fourth clause is added to the definition of formulas:

  4. $\langle p \rangle \phi$, $[p]\phi \in$ DLFml for all legal program fragments p.

A term or formula is called rigid if it does not contain any occurrences of program variables.

We use the shorthand notation $o.a$ for $select_A(\mathtt{heap}, o, a)$, where the declared type of attribute a is A. Similarly, $a[i]$ is shorthand for $select_A(\mathtt{heap}, a, arr(i))$. These notations are also used by the KeY pretty printer; see Section 16.2.

Definition 3.4. The definition of the sets *var* of variables and *fv* of free variables in a term or formula is extended to JavaDL by adding the following clauses to the FOL version of their definition (Definition 2.5):

- $var(\mathtt{a}) = \emptyset, fv(\mathtt{a}) = \emptyset$ for $\mathtt{a} \in$ ProgVSym
- $var(\langle p \rangle \phi) = var(\phi), fv(\langle p \rangle \phi) = fv(\phi)$ for $\phi \in$ DLFml
- $var([p]\phi) = var(\phi), fv([p]\phi) = fv(\phi)$ for $\phi \in$ DLFml

3.3 Semantics

To define the syntax of JavaDL, we have extended first-order logic with program variables and program modalities. On the semantic level, the difference is that JavaDL formulas are not evaluated in a single first-order structure but in a so-called Kripke structure, which is a collection of first-order structures.

3.3.1 Kripke Structures

Different first-order structures within a Kripke structure assign different values to program variables. Accordingly, they are called *program states* or simply *states*. We demand that states in the *same* Kripke structure differ only in the interpretation of the *nonrigid* symbols (i.e., the program variables). Two different Kripke structures, on the other hand, may differ in the choice of domain or interpretation of the predicate and (rigid) function symbols.

Definition 3.5 (JavaDL Kripke structure). Let *Prg* be a Java program, $\mathcal{T}$ a type hierarchy for *Prg* and Σ a signature w.r.t. $\mathcal{T}$. A *JavaDL Kripke structure* for Σ is a tuple

$$\mathcal{K} = (\mathcal{S}, \rho)$$

consisting of

- an infinite set $\mathcal{S}$ of first-order structures over Σ (Definition 2.13), which we will call *states*, such that:
  - Any two states $s_1, s_2 \in \mathcal{S}$ coincide in their domain and in the interpretation of predicate and function symbols.
  - $\mathcal{S}$ is closed under the above property, i.e., any FOL structure coinciding with the states in $\mathcal{S}$ in the domain and the interpretation of the predicate and function symbols is also in $\mathcal{S}$.

- a function ρ that associates with every legal program fragment p a *transition relation* $\rho(p) \subseteq \mathcal{S} \times \mathcal{S}$ such that $(s_1, s_2) \in \rho(p)$ iff p, when started in s_1, terminates normally in s_2 (i.e., not by throwing an exception). (We consider Java programs to be deterministic, so for all legal program fragments p and all $s_1 \in \mathcal{S}$, there is at most one s_2 such that $(s_1, s_2) \in \rho(p)$.)

Here, we do not give a formal definition of the transition relation ρ and, thus, no formalization of the semantics of Java. Instead, we treat the function ρ as a black box that captures the behavior of the legal program fragments p and is informally described by the Java Language Specification [Gosling et al., 2013]. We do, however, explicitly formalize the behavior of Java programs on the level of the calculus, in the form of symbolic execution rules (Section 3.6).

The fact that all states of a JavaDL Kripke structure $\mathcal{K}$ share a common domain is sometimes referred to as the *constant domain assumption*. This simplifies, for example, reasoning about quantifiers in the presence of modal operators and updates. On the other hand, the Java programs appearing in formulas may allocate new objects (i.e., elements of D^{Object}) that did not exist previously. This apparent contradiction is resolved with the help of the special field *created*: given a heap $h \in D^{Heap}$ and an object $o \in D^{Object}$, the object o is considered "created" in h in the sense of Java if and only if *created* is set to true for this object in h, i.e., if $h(o, I(created)) = tt$. An allocation statement in a program is understood as choosing a previously noncreated object in D^{Object}, and setting its *created* field to true in the heap. The alternative of abandoning the constant domain assumption has been investigated by Ahrendt et al. [2009b].

3.3.2 Semantics of JavaDL Terms and Formulas

Similar to the first-order case, we inductively define the semantics of JavaDL terms and formulas. Since program variables can have different meanings in different states, the valuation function is parameterized with a Kripke structure $\mathcal{K}$ and a state s in $\mathcal{K}$.

The semantics of terms and formulas without modalities matches that of first-order logic.

Definition 3.6 (Semantics of JavaDL terms and formulas). Let *Prg* be a Java program, $\mathcal{T}$ a type hierarchy for *Prg*, Σ a signature w.r.t. $\mathcal{T}$, $\mathcal{K} = (\mathcal{S}, \rho)$ a Kripke structure for Σ, $s \in \mathcal{S}$ a state, and $\beta : \text{VSym} \to D$ a variable assignment.
For every JavaDL term $t \in \text{DLTrm}_A$, we define its evaluation by

$$val_{\mathcal{K},s,\beta}(t) = val_{s,\beta}(t) \ ,$$

where $val_{s,\beta}$ is defined as in the first-order case (Definition 2.15).
For every JavaDL formula $\phi \in \text{Fml}$, we define when ϕ is considered to be true with respect to $\mathcal{K}, s, \beta$, which is denoted with $(\mathcal{K}, s, \beta) \models \phi$, by Clauses 1–9 as shown in the definition of the semantics of FOL formulas (Definition 2.16)—with $\mathcal{M} = s$ and $(\mathcal{K}, s, \beta)$ replaced for $(\mathcal{M}, \beta)$——in combination with the two new clauses:

$$10 \ (\mathcal{K}, s, \beta) \models [p]\phi \quad \text{iff} \quad \text{there is no } s' \text{ with } (s, s') \in \rho(p) \text{ or}$$
$$(\mathcal{K}, s', \beta) \models \phi \text{ for } s' \text{ with } (s, s') \in \rho(p)$$
$$11 \ (\mathcal{K}, s, \beta) \models \langle p \rangle \phi \quad \text{iff} \quad \text{there is an } s' \text{ with } (s, s') \in \rho(p) \text{ and}$$
$$(\mathcal{K}, s', \beta) \models \phi \text{ for } s' \text{ with } (s, s') \in \rho(p)$$

As said above, we consider Java programs to be deterministic, such that there is at most one s' with $(s, s') \in \rho(p)$ for each $s \in \mathcal{S}$.

Finally, we define what it means for a JavaDL formula to be satisfiable, respectively valid. A first-order formula is satisfiable (respectively valid) if it holds in some (all) model(s) for some (all) variable assignment(s). Similarly, a JavaDL formula is satisfiable (respectively valid) if it holds in some (all) state(s) of some (all) Kripke structure(s) $\mathcal{K}$ for some (all) variable assignment(s).

Definition 3.7. Let *Prg* be a Java program, $\mathcal{T}$ a type hierarchy for *Prg*, Σ a signature w.r.t. $\mathcal{T}$, and $\phi \in$ Fml a formula.

ϕ is *satisfiable* if there is a Kripke structure $\mathcal{K} = (\mathcal{S}, \rho)$, a state $s \in \mathcal{S}$ and a variable assignment β such that $(\mathcal{K}, s, \beta) \models \phi$.

ϕ is *logically valid*, denoted by $\models \phi$, if $(\mathcal{K}, s, \beta) \models \phi$ for all Kripke structures $\mathcal{K} = (\mathcal{S}, \rho)$, all states $s \in \mathcal{S}$, and all variable assignments β.

3.4 Describing Transitions between States: Updates

3.4.1 Syntax and Semantics of JavaDL Updates

JavaDL extends classical logic with another syntactical category besides modal operators with program fragments, namely *updates*. Like program fragments, updates denote state changes. The difference between updates and program fragments is that updates are a simpler and more restricted concept. For example, updates always terminate, and the expressions occurring in updates never have side effects.

Definition 3.8 (Updates). Let *Prg* be a Java program, $\mathcal{T}$ a type hierarchy for *Prg*, and Σ a signature for $\mathcal{T}$. The set Upd of updates is inductively defined by:

- $(\mathtt{a} := t) \in$ Upd for each program variable symbol $\mathtt{a} : A \in$ ProgVSym and each term $t \in$ DLTrm$_{A'}$ such that $A' \sqsubseteq A$.
- $\mathtt{skip} \in$ Upd.
- $(u_1 \,\|\, u_2) \in$ Upd for all updates $u_1, u_2 \in$ Upd.
- $(\{u_1\} \, u_2) \in$ Upd for all updates $u_1, u_2 \in$ Upd.

An expression of the form $\{u\}$, where $u \in$ Upd, is called an *update application*.

Intuitively, an *elementary update* $\mathtt{a} := t$ assigns the value of the term t to the program variable $\mathtt{a}$. The *empty update* that does not change anything is denoted by $\mathtt{skip}$. A *parallel update* $u_1 \,\|\, u_2$ executes the subupdates u_1 and u_2 in parallel (as parallel composition is associative, e.g., $(u_1 \,\|\, (u_2 \,\|\, u_3))$ can be written as $u_1 \,\|\, u_2 \,\|\, u_3$). The semantics of $\{u\} \, x$, i.e., prefixing an expression x with an update application, is that x is to be evaluated in the state produced by the update u (the expression x can be a term, a formula, or another update). The precise definition of the semantics of updates is given in Definition 3.11 below.

We extend the definition of occurring and free variables to include updates, which is straightforward.

Definition 3.9. In extension of Definitions 2.5 and 3.4:

$$var(\mathtt{a}:=t) \; = var(t)$$
$$var(\mathtt{skip}) \; = \emptyset$$
$$var(u_1 \,\|\, u_2) = var(u_1) \cup var(u_2)$$
$$var(\{u\}\, x) \; = var(u) \cup var(x)$$

$$fv(\mathtt{a}:=t) \; = fv(t)$$
$$fv(\mathtt{skip}) \; = \emptyset$$
$$fv(u_1 \,\|\, u_2) = fv(u_1) \cup fv(u_2)$$
$$fv(\{u\}\, x) \; = fv(u) \cup fv(x)$$

for $\mathtt{a} \in \mathrm{ProgVSym}$, $t \in \mathrm{DLTrm}_\top$ $u, u_1, u_2 \in \mathrm{Upd}$, $x \in \mathrm{DLTrm}_\top \cup \mathrm{DLFml} \cup \mathrm{Upd}$.

To include updates, we extend the definitions of terms and formulas of JavaDL (Definition 3.3) with additional clauses:

Definition 3.10 (Terms and formulas of JavaDL with updates). The definition of terms (Definition 3.3 and Definition 2.3) is extended with a fourth clause:

4. $\{u\}\, t \in \mathrm{DLTrm}_A$ for all updates $u \in \mathrm{Upd}$ and all terms $t \in \mathrm{DLTrm}_A$.

The definition of formulas (Definition 3.3) is extended with a fifth clause:

5. $\{u\}\, \phi \in \mathrm{DLFml}$ for all formulas $\phi \in \mathrm{DLFml}$ and updates $u \in \mathrm{Upd}$.

Updates transform one state into another. The meaning of $\{u\}t$, where u is an update and t is a term, a formula, or an update, is that t is evaluated in the state produced by u. Note the *last-win semantics* of parallel updates $u_1 \,\|\, u_2$: if there is a "clash," where u_1 and u_2 attempt to assign conflicting values to a program variable, then the value written by u_2 prevails.

Definition 3.11 (Semantics of JavaDL updates). Let *Prg* be a Java program, $\mathscr{T}$ a type hierarchy for *Prg*, Σ a signature for $\mathscr{T}$, $\mathscr{K}$ a Kripke structure for Σ, $s \in \mathscr{S}$ a state, and $\beta : \mathrm{VSym} \to D$ a variable assignment.

The valuation function $val_{\mathscr{K},s,\beta} : \mathrm{Upd} \to (\mathscr{S} \to \mathscr{S})$ is defined as follows:

$$val_{\mathscr{K},s,\beta}(a := t)(s')(\mathtt{b}) = \begin{cases} val_{\mathscr{K},s,\beta}(t) & \text{if } \mathtt{b} = \mathtt{a} \\ s'(\mathtt{b}) & \text{otherwise} \end{cases}$$

$$\text{for all } s' \in \mathscr{S}, \mathtt{b} \in \mathrm{ProgVSym}$$

$$val_{\mathscr{K},s,\beta}(\mathtt{skip})(s') = s' \quad \text{for all } s' \in \mathscr{S}$$

$$val_{\mathscr{K},s,\beta}(u_1 \,\|\, u_2)(s') = val_{\mathscr{K},s,\beta}(u_2)(val_{\mathscr{K},s,\beta}(u_1)(s')) \quad \text{for all } s' \in \mathscr{S}$$

$$val_{\mathscr{K},s,\beta}(\{u_1\}\, u_2) = val_{\mathscr{K},s',\beta}(u_2) \quad \text{where } s' = val_{\mathscr{K},s,\beta}(u_1)(s)$$

Moreover, the definition of the semantics of JavaDL terms and formulas (Definition 3.6) is extended for terms with the clause

$$val_{\mathscr{K},s,\beta}(\{u\}\, t) = val_{\mathscr{K},s',\beta}(t) \quad \text{where } s' = val_{\mathscr{K},s,\beta}(u)(s)$$

and it is extended for formulas with the clause

$$(\mathscr{K},s,\beta) \models val_{\mathscr{K},s,\beta}(\{u\}\, \phi) \quad \text{iff} \quad (\mathscr{K},s',\beta) \models \phi \quad \text{where } s' = val_{\mathscr{K},s,\beta}(u)(s)$$

Table 3.1 Simplification rules for updates

$$\{\ldots \| \, \mathtt{a} := t_1 \, \| \ldots \| \, \mathtt{a} := t_2 \, \| \ldots \} \, t$$
$$\leadsto \{\ldots \| \, \mathtt{skip} \, \| \ldots \| \, \mathtt{a} := t_2 \, \| \ldots \} \, t \qquad\qquad \text{dropUpdate}_1$$
$$\text{where } t \in \text{DLTrm}_A \cup \text{DLFml} \cup \text{Upd}$$

$$\{\ldots \| \, \mathtt{a} := t' \, \| \ldots \} \, t \leadsto \{\ldots \| \, \mathtt{skip} \, \| \ldots \} \, t \qquad\qquad \text{dropUpdate}_2$$
$$\text{where } t \in \text{DLTrm}_A \cup \text{DLFml} \cup \text{Upd}, \ \mathtt{a} \notin \mathit{fpv}(t)$$

$$\{u\} \, \{u'\} \, t \leadsto \{u \, \| \, \{u\} \, u'\} \, t \qquad\qquad \text{seqToPar}$$
$$\text{where } t \in \text{DLTrm}_A \cup \text{DLFml} \cup \text{Upd}$$

$$\{u \, \| \, \mathtt{skip}\} \, t \leadsto \{u\} \, t \quad \text{where } t \in \text{DLTrm}_A \cup \text{DLFml} \cup \text{Upd} \qquad \text{parallelWithSkip}_1$$
$$\{\mathtt{skip} \, \| \, u\} \, t \leadsto \{u\} \, t \quad \text{where } t \in \text{DLTrm}_A \cup \text{DLFml} \cup \text{Upd} \qquad \text{parallelWithSkip}_2$$

$$\{\mathtt{skip}\} \, t \leadsto t \quad \text{where } t \in \text{DLTrm}_A \cup \text{DLFml} \cup \text{Upd} \qquad \text{applySkip}$$

$$\{u\} \, x \leadsto x \quad \text{where } x \in \text{VSym} \cup \{\mathit{true}, \mathit{false}\} \qquad \text{applyOnRigid}_1$$

$$\{u\} \, f(t_1, \ldots, t_n) \leadsto f(\{u\} t_1, \ldots, \{u\} t_n) \quad \text{where } f \in \text{FSym} \cup \text{PSym} \qquad \text{applyOnRigid}_2$$

$$\{u\} \, (\text{if } \phi \text{ then } t_1 \text{ else } t_2) \leadsto \text{if } \{u\} \, \phi \text{ then } \{u\} \, t_1 \text{ else } \{u\} \, t_2 \qquad \text{applyOnRigid}_3$$

$$\{u\} \, \neg \phi \leadsto \neg \{u\} \, \phi \qquad \text{applyOnRigid}_4$$

$$\{u\} \, (\phi_1 \bullet \phi_2) \leadsto \{u\} \, \phi_1 \bullet \{u\} \, \phi_2 \quad \text{where } \bullet \in \{\wedge, \vee, \rightarrow, \leftrightarrow\} \qquad \text{applyOnRigid}_5$$

$$\{u\} \, \mathcal{Q}Ax; \phi \leadsto \mathcal{Q}Ax; \{u\} \, \phi \text{ where } \mathcal{Q} \in \{\forall, \exists\}, \ x \notin \mathit{fv}(u) \qquad \text{applyOnRigid}_6$$

$$\{u\} \, (\mathtt{a} := t) \leadsto \mathtt{a} := \{u\} \, t \qquad \text{applyOnRigid}_7$$

$$\{u\} \, (u_1 \, \| \, u_2) \leadsto (\{u\} \, u_1) \, \| \, (\{u\} \, u_2) \qquad \text{applyOnRigid}_8$$

$$\{\mathtt{a} := t\} \, \mathtt{a} \leadsto t \qquad \text{applyOnTarget}$$

3.4.2 Update Simplification Rules

The part of the JavaDL calculus that deals with simplification of updates is shown in Table 3.1.

The dropUpdate$_1$ rule simplifies away an ineffective elementary subupdate of a larger parallel update: if there is an update to the same program variable a further to the right of the parallel composition, then this second elementary update overrides the first due to the last-win semantics of parallel updates (Definition 3.11).

The dropUpdate$_2$ rule allows dropping an elementary update a := t' where the term, formula, or update in scope of the update cannot depend on the value of the program variable a, because it does not contain any free occurrences of a. A *free* occurrence of a program variable is any occurrence, except for an occurrence inside a program fragment p that is bound by a declaration within p. In addition to explicit occurrences, we consider program fragments p to always contain an implicit free occurrence of the program variable heap. The function $\mathit{fpv} : \text{DLTrm}_A \cup \text{DLFml} \cup \text{Upd} \to 2^{\text{ProgVSym}}$ is defined accordingly. For example, we have $\mathit{fpv}([\mathtt{int} \ \mathtt{a} \ = \ \mathtt{b};](\mathtt{b} \doteq \mathtt{c})) = \{\mathtt{b}, \mathtt{c}, \mathtt{heap}\}$. Java's rules for *definite assignment*

[Gosling et al., 2013, Chapter 16] ensure that within a program fragment p, a declared program variable (such as a in the example) is always written before being read, and that the behavior of p thus cannot depend on its initial value.

The seqToPar rule converts a cascade of two update applications—which corresponds to sequential execution of the two updates—into the application of a single parallel update. Due to the last-win semantics for parallel updates, this is possible by applying the first update to the second, and replacing the sequential composition by parallel composition.

The rules parallelWithSkip$_i$ and applySkip remove the effect-less skip update from parallel updates or apply it as identity to any term, formula, or update.

The remaining rules are responsible for applying updates to terms, formulas and (other) updates as substitutions. The various applyOnRigid rules propagate an update to the subterms below a (rigid) operator. Ultimately, the update can either be simplified away with dropUpdate$_2$, or it remains as an elementary update a $:= t$ applied to the target program variable a itself. In the latter case, the term t is substituted for a by the applyOnTarget rule.

The only case not covered by the rules in Table 3.1 is that of applying an update to a modal operator, as in $\{u\} [p]\phi$ or $\{u\} \langle p\rangle\phi$. For these formulas, the program p must first be eliminated using the symbolic execution rules. Only afterwards can the resulting update be applied to ϕ.

3.5 The Calculus for JavaDL

The calculus for JavaDL follows the same basic logical principles as the calculus for first-order logic (FOL) introduced in Chapter 2. We do thus not repeat them here but only explain extensions and restrictions in comparison to the FOL case. The remaining bulk of this chapter is concerned with explaining in detail how the JavaDL calculus formalizes symbolic execution of Java programs.

3.5.1 JavaDL Rule Schemata and First-Order Rules

Since first-order logic (FOL) is part of JavaDL, all the axioms and rule schemata of the first-order calculus introduced in Chapter 2 are also part of the JavaDL and its calculus. This inclusion pertains, inter alia, Figure 2.1 (classical first-order rules), Figure 2.2 (equality rules), Figure 2.5 (integer axioms and rules), and Figure 2.8 (axioms about types). As a consequence, these rules can be applied to JavaDL sequents—even if the formulas to which they are applied are not purely first-order.

Compared to Section 2.2.2 on FOL calculus, we do simplify and generalize the rule schema notation in two ways, though. First, we leave out the explicit context (in form of formula sets Γ and Δ), which is added on-the-fly during rule application.

Second, we extend the notion of context in that, when writing a rule schema, an update that is common to all premisses can be left out as well.

Definition 3.12. If

$$\phi_1^1, \ldots, \phi_{m_1}^1 \implies \psi_1^1, \ldots, \psi_{n_1}^1$$

$$\vdots$$

$$\frac{\phi_1^k, \ldots, \phi_{m_k}^k \implies \psi_1^k, \ldots, \psi_{n_k}^k}{\phi_1, \ldots, \phi_m \implies \psi_1, \ldots, \psi_n}$$

is an instance of a rule schema, then

$$\Gamma, \mathcal{U}\phi_1^1, \ldots, \mathcal{U}\phi_{m_1}^1 \implies \mathcal{U}\psi_1^1, \ldots, \mathcal{U}\psi_{n_1}^1, \Delta$$

$$\vdots$$

$$\frac{\Gamma, \mathcal{U}\phi_1^k, \ldots, \mathcal{U}\phi_{m_k}^k \implies \mathcal{U}\psi_1^k, \ldots, \mathcal{U}\psi_{n_k}^k, \Delta}{\Gamma, \mathcal{U}\phi_1, \ldots, \mathcal{U}\phi_m \implies \mathcal{U}\psi_1, \ldots, \mathcal{U}\psi_n, \Delta}$$

is an inference rule of our DL calculus, where $\mathcal{U}$ is the application of an arbitrary syntactic update (it may be empty), and Γ, Δ are finite sets of context formulas.

If, however, the symbol $(*)$ is added to the rule schema, the context $\Gamma, \Delta, \mathcal{U}$ must be empty, i.e., only instances of the schema itself are inference rules. Later in the book we will present a few rules, e.g., the loop invariant rule (Section 3.7.2), where the context cannot be omitted.

Example 3.13. Consider, for example, the rule impRight, which made a first appearance in Figure 2.1 on page 28. In the just introduced notation, the rule schema for this rule takes the following form:

$$\text{impRight} \quad \frac{\phi \implies \psi}{\implies \phi \to \psi}$$

When this schema is instantiated for JavaDL, a context consisting of Γ, Δ and an update $\mathcal{U}$ can be added, and the schema variables ϕ, ψ can be instantiated with formulas that are not purely first-order. For example, the following is an instance of impRight:

$$\frac{x \doteq 1, \{x := 0\}(x \doteq y) \implies \{x := 0\}\langle \mathtt{m}(); \rangle(y \doteq 0)}{x \doteq 1 \implies \{x := 0\}(x \doteq y \to \langle \mathtt{m}(); \rangle(y \doteq 0))}$$

where $\Gamma = (x \doteq 1)$, Δ is empty, and the context update is $\mathcal{U} = \{x := 0\}$.

Due to the presence of modalities and program variables, which do not exist in purely first-order formulas, different parts of a formula may have to be evaluated in different states. Therefore, the application of some first-order rules that rely on the identity of terms in different parts of a formula need to be restricted. That affects rules for universal quantification and equality rules.

3.5.1.1 Restriction of Rules for Universal Quantification

The rules for universal quantification have the following form:

$$\text{allLeft} \ \frac{\forall x.\phi, \ [x/t](\phi) \Longrightarrow}{\forall x.\phi \Longrightarrow} \qquad \text{exRight} \ \frac{\Longrightarrow \exists x.\phi, \ [x/t](\phi)}{\Longrightarrow \exists x.\phi}$$

where $t \in DLTrm_{A'}$ is a rigid ground term
whose type A' is a subtype of the type A of x

In the first-order case, the term t that is instantiated for the quantified variable x can be an arbitrary ground term. In JavaDL, however, we have to add the restriction that t is a *rigid* ground term (Definition 3.3). The reason is that, though an arbitrary value can be instantiated for x as it is universally quantified, all occurrences of x must have the same value in each individual instantiation.

Example 3.14. The formula $\forall x.(x \doteq 0 \rightarrow \langle \text{i++;} \rangle (x \doteq 0))$ is logically valid, but instantiating the variable x with the nonrigid program variable i is wrong as it leads to the unsatisfiable formula $\text{i} \doteq 0 \rightarrow \langle \text{i++;} \rangle (\text{i} \doteq 0))$.

In practice, it is often very useful to instantiate a universally quantified variable x with the value of a nonrigid term t. That, however, is not easily possible as a quantified variable, which is a rigid term, must not be instantiated with a nonrigid term. To solve that problem, one can add the logically valid formula $\exists y.(y \doteq t)$ to the left of the sequent, Skolemize that formula, which yields $c_{sk} \doteq t$, and then instantiate x with the rigid constant c_{sk}.

Rules for existential quantification do not have to be restricted because they introduce *rigid* Skolem constants anyway.

3.5.1.2 Restriction of Rules for Equalities

The equality rules (Figure 2.2) are part of the JavaDL calculus but an equality $t_1 \doteq t_2$ may only be used for rewriting if

- both t_1 and t_2 are rigid terms (Definition 3.3), or
- the equality $t_1 \doteq t_2$ and the occurrence of t_i that is being replaced are (a) not in the scope of two different program modalities and (b-1) not in the scope of two different updates or (b-2) in the scope of syntactically identical updates (in fact, it is also sufficient if the two updates are only semantically identical, i.e., have the same effect). This same-update-level property is explained in more detail in Section 4.3.1.

Example 3.15. The sequent

$$\text{x} \doteq \text{v} + 1 \Longrightarrow \{\text{v} := 2\}(\text{x} \doteq 3)$$

is satisfiable, but not valid. According to the above restriction on the equality rule, the equality $\text{x} \doteq \text{v} + 1$ must not be applied to the occurrence of x on the right side of the sequent: (a) The terms are nonrigid; and (b) while the equation is not in the scope of any update, the occurrence of x is below an update.

The example demonstrates that this restriction is crucial for soundness of the calculus as, if we allow the equality to be applied, this would lead to the *valid* sequent

$$x \doteq v + 1 \Longrightarrow \{v := 2\}(v + 1 \doteq 3) \ .$$

Thus, we would have turned an invalid into a valid sequent.

In the sequent

$$\{v := 2\}(x \doteq v + 1) \Longrightarrow \{v := 2\}(x \doteq 3) \ ,$$

however, both the equality and the term being replaced occur in the scope of identical updates and, thus, the equality rule can be applied.

3.5.2 Nonprogram Rules for Modalities

The JavaDL calculus contains some rules that apply to modal operators and, thus, are not first-order rules but that are neither related to a particular Java construct.

The most important representatives of this rule class are the following two rules for handling empty modalities:

$$\text{emptyDiamond} \ \frac{\Longrightarrow \phi}{\Longrightarrow \langle\rangle\phi} \qquad \text{emptyBox} \ \frac{\Longrightarrow \phi}{\Longrightarrow [\,]\phi}$$

The rule

$$\text{diamondToBox} \ \frac{\Longrightarrow [p]\phi \qquad \Longrightarrow \langle p\rangle\text{true}}{\Longrightarrow \langle p\rangle\phi}$$

relates the diamond modality to the box modality. It allows one to split a total correctness proof into a partial correctness proof and a separate proof for termination. Note, that this rule is only sound for deterministic programming languages like Java.

3.5.3 Soundness and Completeness of the Calculus

3.5.3.1 Soundness

The most important property of the JavaDL calculus is soundness, i.e., only valid formulas are derivable.

Proposition 3.16 (Soundness). *If a sequent $\Gamma \Longrightarrow \Delta$ is derivable in the JavaDL calculus (Definition 2.10), then it is valid, i.e., the formula $\bigwedge \Gamma \to \bigvee \Delta$ is logically valid (Definition 3.7).*

It is easy to show that the whole calculus is sound if and only if all its rules are sound. That is, if the premisses of any rule application are valid sequents, then the conclusion is valid as well.

Given the soundness of the existing core rules of the JavaDL calculus, the user can add new rules, whose soundness must then be proven w.r.t. the existing rules (see Section 4.4).

Validating the Soundness of the JavaDL Calculus

So far, we have no intention of formally proving the soundness of the JavaDL calculus, i.e., the core rules that are not user-defined (the soundness of user-defined rules can be verified within the KeY system, see Section 4.4). Doing so would first require a formal specification of the Java language. No *official* formal semantics of Java is available though. Furthermore, proving soundness of the calculus requires the use of a higher-order theorem proving tool, and it is a tedious task due to the high number of rules. Resources saved on a formal soundness proof were instead spent on further improvement of the KeY system. We refer to [Beckert and Klebanov, 2006] for a discussion of this policy and further arguments in its favor. On the other hand, the KeY project performs cross-verification against other Java formalizations to ensure the faithfulness of the calculus.

One such effort compares the KeY calculus with the Bali semantics [von Oheimb, 2001], which is a Java Hoare logic formalized in Isabelle/HOL. KeY rules are translated manually into Bali rules. These are then shown sound with respect to the rules of the standard Bali calculus. The published result [Trentelman, 2005] describes in detail the examination of the rules for local variable assignment, field assignment, and array assignment.

Another validation was carried out by Ahrendt et al. [2005]. A reference Java semantics from [Farzan et al., 2004] was used, which is formalized in Rewriting Logic [Meseguer and Rosu, 2004] and mechanized in the input language of the MAUDE system. This semantics is an executable specification, which together with MAUDE provides a Java interpreter. Considering the nature of this semantics, we concentrated on using it to verify our program transformation rules. These are rules that decompose complex expressions, take care of the evaluation order, etc. (about 45% of the KeY calculus). For the cross-verification, the MAUDE semantics was "lifted" in order to cope with schematic programs like the ones appearing in calculus rules. The rewriting theory was further extended with means to generate valid initial states for the involved program fragments, and to check the final states for equivalence. The result is used in automated validation runs, which is beneficial, since the calculus is constantly extended with new features.

Furthermore, the KeY calculus has been tested against the compiler test suite Jacks (part of the Java compiler Jikes). The suite is a collection of intricate programs covering many difficult features of the Java language. These programs are symbolically executed with the KeY calculus and the output is compared to the reference provided by the suite. To what extent testing of verification systems is able to provide evidence for the correctness of the rule base has been examined in [Beckert et al., 2013].

3.5.3.2 Relative Completeness

Ideally, one would like a program verification calculus to be able to prove all statements about programs that are true, which means that all valid sequents should be derivable. That, however, is *impossible* because JavaDL includes first-order arithmetic, which is already inherently incomplete as established by Gödel's Incompleteness Theorem [Gödel, 1931] (see the box on page 40). Another, equivalent, argument is that a complete calculus for JavaDL would yield a decision procedure for the Halting Problem, which is well-known to be undecidable. Thus, a logic like JavaDL cannot ever have a calculus that is both sound and complete.

Still, it is possible to define a notion of *relative completeness* [Cook, 1978], which intuitively states that the calculus is complete "up to" the inherent incompleteness in its first-order part. A relatively complete calculus contains all the rules that are necessary to prove valid program properties. It only may fail to prove such valid formulas whose proof would require the derivation of a nonprovable first-order property (being purely first-order, its provability would be independent of the program part of the calculus).

Proposition 3.17 (Relative Completeness). *If a sequent $\Gamma \implies \Delta$ is valid, i.e., the formula $\bigwedge \Gamma \to \bigvee \Delta$ is logically valid (Definition 3.7), then there is a finite set Γ_{FOL} of logically valid first-order formulas such that the sequent*

$$\Gamma_{FOL}, \Gamma \implies \Delta$$

is derivable in the JavaDL calculus.

The standard technique for proving that a program verification calculus is relatively complete [Harel, 1979] hinges on a central lemma expressing that for all JavaDL formulas there is an equivalent purely first-order formula.

A completeness proof for the object-oriented dynamic logic ODL [Beckert and Platzer, 2006], which captures the essence of JavaDL, is given by Platzer [2004]. ODL captures the essence of JavaDL, consolidating its foundational principles into a concise logic. The ODL programming language is a While language extended with an object type system, object creation, and nonrigid symbols that can be used to represent program variables and object attributes. However, it does not include the many other language features, built-in operators, etc. of Java.

3.5.4 Schema Variables for Program Constructs

The schema variables used in rule schemata are all assigned a kind that determines which class of concrete syntactic elements they represent. In the following sections, we often do not explicitly mention the kinds of schema variables but use the name of the variables to indicate their kind. Table 3.2 gives the correspondence between names of schema variables that represent pieces of Java code and their kinds. In addition, we use the schema variables ϕ, ψ to represent formulas and Γ, Δ to represent sets of formulas. Schema variables of corresponding kinds occur also in the *taclets* used to implement rules in the KeY system (see Section 4.2).

Table 3.2 Correspondence between names of schema variables and their kinds

π	nonactive prefix of Java code (Section 3.5.5)
ω	"rest" of Java code after the active statement (Section 3.5.5)
p, q	Java code (arbitrary sequence of statements)
e	arbitrary Java expression
se	simple expression, i.e., any expression whose evaluation, a priori, does not have any side-effects. It is defined as one of the following: (a) a local variable (b) `this.a`, i.e., an access to an instance attribute via the target expression `this` (or, equivalently, no target expression) (c) an access to a static attribute of the form $t.a$, where the target expression t is a type name or a simple expression (d) a literal (e) a compile-time constant (f) an `instanceof` expression with a simple expression as the first argument (g) a `this` reference (h) expressions of types *LocSet* (location sets), *Seq* (finite sequences) etc., provided that their subexpressions are simple expressions (e.g., $union(r, s)$ is a simple expression if r, s are simple). An access to an instance attribute $o.a$ is not simple because a `NullPointerException` may be thrown
nse	nonsimple expression, i.e., any expression that is not simple (see above)
lhs	simple expression that can appear on the left-hand-side of an assignment. This amounts to the items (a)–(c) from above
$v, v_0, \ldots$	local program variables
a	attribute
l	label
$args$	argument tuple, i.e., a tuple of expressions
cs	sequence of catch clauses
$mname$	name of a method
T	type expression
C	name of a class or interface

If a schema variable T representing a type expression is indexed with the name of another schema variable, say e, then it only matches the Java type of the expression with which e is instantiated. For example, "$T_w \; v = w$" matches the Java code "`int i = j`" if and only if the type of j is int (and not, e.g., `byte`).

3.5.5 *The Active Statement in a Modality*

The rules of our calculus operate on the first *active* statement p in a modality $\langle \pi p \omega \rangle$ or $[\pi p \omega]$. The nonactive prefix π consists of an arbitrary sequence of opening braces "{", labels, beginnings "try{" of try-catch-finally blocks, and beginnings "method-frame(...){" of method invocation blocks. The prefix is needed to (i) keep track of the blocks that the (first) active command is part of, such that the abruptly terminating statements throw, return, break, and continue can be handled appropriately; and (ii) to correctly resolve field and method bindings.

The postfix ω denotes the "rest" of the program, i.e., everything except the nonactive prefix and the part of the program the rule operates on (in particular, ω contains closing braces corresponding to the opening braces in π). For example, if a rule is applied to the following Java block operating on its first active command i=0;, then the nonactive prefix π and the "rest" ω are the indicated parts of the block:

$$\underbrace{\texttt{l:\{try\{}}_{\pi} \texttt{ i=0; } \underbrace{\texttt{j=0; \} finally\{ k=0; \}\}}}_{\omega}$$

No Rule for Sequential Composition

In versions of dynamic logic for simple programming languages, where no prefixes are needed, any formula of the form $\langle pq \rangle \phi$ can be replaced by $\langle p \rangle \langle q \rangle \phi$. In our calculus, decomposing of $\langle \pi pq\omega \rangle \phi$ into $\langle \pi p \rangle \langle q\omega \rangle \phi$ is not possible (unless the prefix π is empty) because πp is not a valid program; and the formula $\langle \pi p\omega \rangle \langle \pi q\omega \rangle \phi$ cannot be used either because its semantics is in general different from that of $\langle \pi pq\omega \rangle \phi$.

3.5.6 *The Essence of Symbolic Execution*

Our calculus works by reducing the question of a formula's validity to the question of the validity of several simpler formulas. Since JavaDL formulas contain programs, the JavaDL calculus has rules that reduce the meaning of programs to the meaning of simpler programs. For this reduction we employ the technique of *symbolic execution* [King, 1976]. Symbolic execution in JavaDL resembles playing an accordion: you make the program longer (though simpler) before you can make it shorter.

For example, to find out whether the sequent[1]

$$\Longrightarrow \langle \texttt{o.next.prev=o;} \rangle \texttt{o.next.prev} \doteq \texttt{o}$$

---

[1] The expression o.next.prev is shorthand for $select_A(\texttt{heap}, select_A(\texttt{heap}, \texttt{o}, \texttt{next}), \texttt{prev})$; see Section 3.2.4 and 16.2.

is valid, we symbolically execute the Java code in the diamond modality. At first, the calculus rules transform it into an equivalent but longer—albeit in a sense simpler—sequence of statements:

$$\Longrightarrow \langle \texttt{ListEl v; v=o.next; v.prev=o;} \rangle \texttt{o.next.prev} \doteq \texttt{o} \ .$$

This way, we have reduced the reasoning about the expression `o.next.prev=o` to reasoning about several simpler expressions. We call this process *unfolding*, and it works by introducing fresh local variables to store intermediate computation results.

Now, when analyzing the first of the simpler assignments (after removing the variable declaration), one has to consider the possibility that evaluating the expression `o.next` may produce a side effect if o is `null` (in that case an exception is thrown). However, it is not possible to unfold `o.next` any further. Something else has to be done, namely a case distinction. This results in the following two new goals:

$$\texttt{o} \not\doteq \texttt{null} \Longrightarrow \{\texttt{v} := \texttt{o.next}\} \langle \texttt{v.prev=o;} \rangle \texttt{o.next.prev} \doteq \texttt{o}$$

$$\texttt{o} \doteq \texttt{null} \Longrightarrow \langle \texttt{throw new NullPointerException();} \rangle \texttt{o.next.prev} \doteq \texttt{o}$$

Thus, we can state the essence of symbolic execution: the Java code in the formulas is step-wise unfolded and replaced by case distinctions and syntactic updates.

Of course, it is not a coincidence that these two ingredients (case distinctions and updates) correspond to two of the three basic programming constructs. The third basic construct are loops. These cannot in general be treated by symbolic execution, since using symbolic values (as opposed to concrete values), the number of loop iterations is unbounded. Symbolically executing a loop, which is called "unwinding," is useful and even necessary, but unwinding cannot eliminate a loop in the general case. To treat arbitrary loops, one needs to use induction or loop invariants (see Section 3.7.2). (A different method for treating certain loops of a simple, uniform structure is described in [Gedell and Hähnle, 2006].)

Method invocations can be symbolically executed, replacing a method call by the method's implementation. However, it is often useful to instead use a method's contract so that it is only symbolically executed once—during the proof that the method satisfies its contract—instead of executing it for each invocation.

3.5.7 Components of the Calculus

Our JavaDL calculus has several major components, which are described throughout this book. However, since the calculus, as implemented in the KeY system, consists of hundreds of rules, we cannot list them all in this book. Instead, we give typical examples for the different rule types and classes.

The major components of the JavaDL calculus are:

1. Nonprogram rules, i.e., rules that are not related to particular program constructs. This component contains first-order rules (see Chapter 2), which include rules

for reasoning about heaps; rules for data-types, such as integers, sequences and strings (see Chapter 5); rules for modalities (e.g., rules for empty modalities); and the induction rule.

2. Update simplification rules (see Section 3.4.2).

3. Rules for symbolic execution of programs. These rules work towards reducing/simplifying the program and replacing it by a combination of case distinctions (proof branches) and sequences of updates. These rules always (and only) apply to the first active statement. Note that a "simpler" program *may* be syntactically longer; it is simpler in the sense that expressions are not as deeply nested or have less side-effects.

   When presenting these rules, we usually only give the rule versions for the diamond modality $\langle \cdot \rangle$. The rules for box modality $[\cdot]$ are mostly the same—notable exceptions are the rules for handling abrupt termination (Section 3.6.7) and the loop invariant rule that, in fact, belongs to the next component.

4. Rules for program abstraction and modularization. This component contains the loop invariant rule for reasoning about loops for which no fixed upper bound on the number of iterations exists and the rules that replace a method invocation by the method's contract (Section 3.7, see also Chapter 9).

Component 3 is the core for handling Java programs occurring in formulas. These rules can be applied automatically, and they can do everything needed for handling programs except evaluating loops and using method specifications.

The overall strategy for proving a formula containing a program is to use the rules in Component 3, interspersed with applications of rules in Component 4 for handling loops and methods, to step-wise eliminate the program and replace it by updates and case distinctions. After each step, Component 2 is used to simplify/eliminate updates. The final result of this process are sequents containing pure first-order formulas. These are then handled by Component 1.

The symbolic execution process is, for the most part, done automatically by the KeY system. Usually, only handling loops and methods may require user interaction. Also, for solving the first-order problems that are left at the end of the symbolic execution process, the KeY system often needs support from the user (or from the decision procedures integrated into KeY, see Chapter 15).

3.6 Rules for Symbolic Execution of Java Programs

3.6.1 The Basic Assignment Rule

In Java—like in other object-oriented programming languages—different object variables can refer to the same object. This phenomenon, called aliasing, causes serious difficulties for handling assignments in a calculus (a similar problem occurs with syntactically different array indices that may refer to the same array element).

For example, whether or not the formula o1.a $\doteq$ 1 still holds after the execution of
the assignment "o2.a = 2;" depends on whether or not o1 and o2 refer to the same
object. Therefore, Java assignments cannot be symbolically executed by syntactic
substitution, as done, for instance, in classical Hoare Logic. Solving this problem
naively—by doing a case split—is inefficient and leads to heavy branching of the
proof tree.

In the JavaDL calculus we use a different solution. It is based on the concept of
updates, which can be seen as "semantic substitutions." Evaluating $\{loc := value\}\phi$
in a state is equivalent to evaluating ϕ in a modified state where loc evaluates
to *value*, i.e., loc has been "semantically substituted" with *value* (see Section 3.4 for
a discussion and a comparison of updates to assignments and substitutions).

The KeY system uses special simplification rules to compute the result of applying
an update to terms and formulas that do not contain programs (see Section 3.4.2).
Computing the effect of an update to a formula $\langle p\rangle\phi$ is delayed until p has been
symbolically executed using other rules of the calculus. Thus, case distinctions
are not only delayed but can often be avoided altogether, since (a) updates can be
simplified *before* their effect has to be computed, and (b) their effect is computed
when a maximal amount of information is available (namely *after* the symbolic
execution of the whole program).

The basic assignment rule thus takes the following simple form:

$$\text{assignment} \quad \frac{\Longrightarrow \{loc := value\}\langle\pi \ \ \omega\rangle\phi}{\Longrightarrow \langle\pi \ \ loc \ = \ value; \ \ \omega\rangle\phi}$$

That is, it just turns the assignment into an update. Of course, this does not solve the
problem of computing the effect of the assignment. This problem is postponed and
solved later by the rules for simplifying updates.

Furthermore—and this is important—this "trivial" assignment rule is correct only
if the expressions *loc* and *value* satisfy certain restrictions. The rule is only applicable
if neither the evaluation of *loc* nor that of *value* can cause any side effects. Otherwise,
other rules have to be applied first to analyze *loc* and *value*. For example, those other
rules would replace the formula $\langle\text{x} \ = \ \text{++i;}\rangle\phi$ with $\langle\text{i} \ = \ \text{i+1;} \ \ \text{x} \ = \ \text{i;}\rangle\phi$, before
the assignment rule can be applied to derive first $\{\text{i} := \text{i+1}\}\langle\text{x} \ = \ \text{i;}\rangle\phi$ and then
$\{\text{i} := \text{i+1}\}\{\text{x} := \text{i}\}\langle\rangle\phi$.

3.6.2 Rules for Handling General Assignments

In the following we use the notion *(program) location* to refer to local program
variables, instance or static fields and array elements.

There are four classes of rules in the JavaDL calculus for treating general assignment expressions (that may have side-effects). These classes—corresponding to steps
in the evaluation of an assignment—are induced by the evaluation order rules of
Java:

1. Unfolding the left-hand side of the assignment.
2. Saving the location.
3. Unfolding the right-hand side of the assignment.
4. Generating an update.

Of particular importance is the fact that though the right-hand side of an assignment can change the variables appearing on the left-hand side, it cannot change the location scheduled for assignment, which is saved before the right-hand side is evaluated.

3.6.2.1 Step 1: Unfolding the Left-Hand Side

In this first step, the left-hand side of an assignment is unfolded if it is a nonsimple expression, i.e., if its evaluation may have side-effects. One of the following rules is applied depending on the form of the left-hand side expression. In general, these rules work by introducing a new local variable v_0, to which the value of a subexpression is assigned.

If the left-hand side of the assignment is a nonatomic field access—which is to say it has the form $nse.a$, where nse is a nonsimple expression—then the following rule is used:

$$\text{assignmentUnfoldLeft} \quad \frac{\Longrightarrow \langle \pi \ T_{nse} \ v_0 = nse; \ v_0.a = e; \ \omega \rangle \phi}{\Longrightarrow \langle \pi \ nse.a = e; \ \omega \rangle \phi}$$

Applying this rule yields an equivalent but simpler program, in the sense that the two new assignments have simpler left-hand sides, namely a local variable or an atomic field access.

Unsurprisingly, in the case of arrays, two rules are needed, since both the array reference and the index have to be treated. First, the array reference is analyzed:

$$\text{assignmentUnfoldLeftArrayReference}$$
$$\frac{\Longrightarrow \langle \pi \ T_{nse} \ v_0 = nse; \ v_0[e] = e_0; \ \omega \rangle \phi}{\Longrightarrow \langle \pi \ nse[e] = e_0; \ \omega \rangle \phi}$$

Then, the rule for analyzing the array index can be applied:

$$\text{assignmentUnfoldLeftArrayIndex}$$
$$\frac{\Longrightarrow \langle \pi \ T_v \ v_a = v; \ T_{nse} \ v_0 = nse; \ v_a[v_0] = e; \ \omega \rangle \phi}{\Longrightarrow \langle \pi \ v[nse] = e; \ \omega \rangle \phi}$$

3.6.2.2 Step 2: Saving the Location

After the left-hand side has been unfolded completely (i.e., has the form v, $v.a$ or $v[se]$), the right-hand side has to be analyzed. But before doing this, we have to memorize the location designated by the left-hand side. The reason is that the location affected by the assignment remains fixed even if evaluating the right-hand side of the assignment has a side effect changing the location to which the left-hand side points. For example, if $i \doteq 0$, then $a[i] = ++i;$ has to update the location $a[0]$ even though evaluating the right-hand side of the assignment changes the value of i to 1.

Since there is no universal "location" or "address-of" operator in Java, this memorizing looks different for different kinds of expressions appearing on the left. The choice here is between field and array accesses. For local variables, the memorizing step is not necessary, since the "location value" of a variable is syntactically defined and cannot be changed by evaluating the right-hand side.

We will start with the rule variant where a field access is on the left. It takes the following form; the components of the premiss are explained in Table 3.3:

$$
\text{assignmentSaveLocation}
$$
$$
\frac{\Longrightarrow \langle \pi \ \textit{memorize}; \ \textit{unfoldr}; \ \textit{update}; \ \omega \rangle \phi}{\Longrightarrow \langle \pi \ v.a\texttt{=}nse; \ \omega \rangle \phi}
$$

Table 3.3 Components of rule assignmentSaveLocation for field accesses $v.a\texttt{=}nse$

memorize	$T_v \ v_0 = v;$	
unfoldr	$T_{nse} \ v_1 = nse;$	set up Step 3
update	$v_0.a = v_1;$	set up Step 4

There is a very similar rule for the case where the left-hand side is an array access, i.e., the assignment has the form $v[se]\texttt{=}nse$. The components of the premiss for that case are shown in Table 3.4.

Table 3.4 Components of rule assignmentSaveLocation for array accesses $v[se]\texttt{=}nse$

memorize	$T_v \ v_0 = v; \ T_{se} \ v_1 = se;$	
unfoldr	$T_{nse} \ v_2 = nse;$	set up Step 3
update	$v_0[v_1] = v_2;$	set up Step 4

[a] This includes an implicit test that v is not `null` when $v.$`length` is analyzed.

3.6.2.3 Step 3: Unfolding the Right-Hand Side

In the next step, after the location that is changed by the assignment has been memorized, we can analyze and unfold the right-hand side of the expression. There are several rules for this, depending on the form of the right-hand side. As an example, we give the rule for the case where the right-hand side is a field access $nse.a$ with a nonsimple object reference nse:

assignmentUnfoldRight

$$\frac{\Longrightarrow \langle \pi \ T_{nse} \ v_0 \ = \ nse; \ v \ = \ v_0.a; \ \omega \rangle \phi}{\Longrightarrow \langle \pi \ v \ = \ nse.a; \ \omega \rangle \phi}$$

The case when the right-hand side is a method call is discussed in the section on method calls (Section 3.6.5).

3.6.2.4 Step 4: Generate an Update

The fourth and final step of treating assignments is to turn them into an update. If both the left- and the right-hand side of the assignment are simple expressions, the basic assignment rule applies:

$$\text{assignment} \ \frac{\Longrightarrow \{lhs := se^*\}\langle \pi \ \omega \rangle \phi}{\Longrightarrow \langle \pi \ lhs \ = \ se; \ \omega \rangle \phi}$$

The value se^* appearing in the update is not identical to the se in the program because creating the update requires replacing any Java operators in the program expression se by their JavaDL counterparts in order to obtain a proper logical term. For example, the Java division operator / is replaced by the function symbol $javaDivInt$ (or $javaDivLong$ depending on the promoted type of its arguments). These function symbols are then further replaced according to the chosen integer semantics (see Section 5.4). The KeY system performs this conversion automatically to construct se^* from se. The complete list of predefined JavaDL operators is given in Appendix B.

If there is an atomic field access $v.a$ either on the left or on the right of the assignment, no further unfolding can be done and the possibility has to be considered here that the object reference may be null—which would result in a NullPointerException. Depending on whether the field access is on the left or on the right of the assignment one of the following rules applies:

assignment

$$\frac{v \not\doteq \texttt{null} \Longrightarrow \{v_0 := select_A(\text{heap}, v, Class::\$a)\}\langle \pi \ \omega \rangle \phi}{v \doteq \texttt{null} \Longrightarrow \langle \pi \ \texttt{throw new NullPointerException(); } \omega \rangle \phi}$$
$$\Longrightarrow \langle \pi \ v_0 \ = \ v.a; \ \omega \rangle \phi$$

assignment

$$\frac{v \not\doteq \texttt{null} \Longrightarrow \{\text{heap} := store(\text{heap}, v, Class::\$a, se^*)\}\langle \pi \ \omega \rangle \phi}{v \doteq \texttt{null} \Longrightarrow \langle \pi \ \texttt{throw new NullPointerException(); } \omega \rangle \phi}$$
$$\Longrightarrow \langle \pi \ v.a \ = \ se; \ \omega \rangle \phi$$

In the rules you may have noticed that the field a is referred to by its unique field constant $Class::\$a$. This field constant unambiguously refers to the field named a of type A declared in the class $Class$ (where $Class$ is the fully qualified name). Determining $Class$ can be nontrivial, in particular in the presence of field hiding. Hiding occurs when derived classes declare fields with the same name as in the superclass. Inside a program the exact field reference can be determined from the short name a using the static type of the target expression and the program context, in which the reference appears. Since logical terms do not have a program context, hidden fields have to be immediately disambiguated by the assignment rule.

The KeY system's pretty-printer tries to improve readability of these terms by displaying the shorthand $v.a$ for $select_A(\text{heap}, o, a)$, whenever the select expression is in a defined normalform and no hiding occurs (for a thorough description of pretty printing see Section 16.2). In the following, we use this shorthand notation unless there is a danger of confusion.

For array access, we have to consider the possibility of an `ArrayIndexOutOf-BoundsException` in addition to that of a `NullPointerException`. Thus, the rule for array access on the right of the assignment takes the following form (there is a slightly more complicated rule for array access on the left as it needs to account for `ArrayStoreExceptions`):

assignment
$$
\frac{
\begin{array}{l}
v \not\doteq \text{null}, se^* \geq 0, se^* < v.\text{length} \Longrightarrow \\
\quad \{v_0 := select_A(\text{heap}, v, arr(se^*))\}\langle \pi\ \omega\rangle\phi \\
v \doteq \text{null} \Longrightarrow \\
\quad \langle \pi\ \text{throw new NullPointerException();}\ \omega\rangle\phi \\
v \not\doteq \text{null}, (se^* < 0 \vee se^* \geq v.\text{length}) \Longrightarrow \\
\quad \langle \pi\ \text{throw new ArrayIndexOutOfBoundsException();}\ \omega\rangle\phi
\end{array}
}{
\Longrightarrow \langle \pi\ v_0\ \texttt{=}\ v\,\texttt{[}se\texttt{]};\ \omega\rangle\phi
}
$$

Please note that, if possible, KeY's pretty-printer uses the shorthand notation $v[se^*]$ for $select_A(\text{heap}, v, arr(se^*))$; see Section 16.2.

The JVM throws exceptions such as the `ArrayIndexOutOfBoundsException` and the `NullPointerException` to signal an error condition during program execution. The assignment rules shown above faithfully model this behavior by introducing explicit `throw` statements during symbolic execution for those cases where the JVM would throw an exception.

However, the KeY system actually contains three user-selectable calculus variations for reasoning about such exceptions. The three variations are: *ban*, *allow*, and *ignore* (see Section 15.2.3 for an explanation of how to select different rule sets). The variation of assignment shown above is *allow*—it is both sound and complete. The variation *ban* requires to prove that no JVM-thrown exceptions can occur—it is sound but incomplete, as programs relying on catching such exceptions cannot be proved correct. The upside of *ban* is smaller proof size, as less symbolic execution is necessary. The third calculus variation is *ignore*; it makes the assumption that all operations succeed and neither checks for nor generates JVM-thrown exceptions. This variation is yet more efficient but neither sound nor complete.

A variability similar in spirit can be observed in the part of the calculus for reasoning about integer arithmetic (see Section 5.4.3).

Example 3.18. Consider the JavaDL formula

$$pre \rightarrow \langle \text{i = 0; try \{ o.a = null; i = 1; \}}$$
$$\text{catch(Exception e) \{\}}$$
$$\rangle post$$

The following table shows the differences in provability of this formula for different combinations of *pre* and *post* and different choices for exception handling in the calculus:

		provable		
pre	*post*	*allow*	*ban*	*ignore*
$o \doteq \text{null}$	$i \doteq 0$	Yes	No	No
$o \doteq \text{null}$	$i \doteq 1$	No	No	Yes
$o \not\doteq \text{null}$	$i \doteq 0$	No	No	No
$o \not\doteq \text{null}$	$i \doteq 1$	Yes	Yes	Yes

3.6.3 Rules for Conditionals

Most if-else statements have a nonsimple expression (i.e., one with potential side-effects) as their condition. In this case, we unfold it in the usual manner first. This is achieved by the rule

ifElseUnfold
$$\frac{\Longrightarrow \langle \pi \text{ boolean } v = nse; \text{ if } (v) \, p \text{ else } q \, \omega \rangle \phi}{\Longrightarrow \langle \pi \text{ if } (nse) \, p \text{ else } q \, \omega \rangle \phi}$$

where v is a fresh Boolean variable.

After dealing with the nonsimple condition, we will eventually get back to the if-else statement, this time with the condition being a variable and, thus, a simple expression. Now it is time to take on the case distinction inherent in the statement. That can be done using the following rule:

ifElseSplit
$$\frac{se^* \doteq TRUE \Longrightarrow \langle \pi \, p \, \omega \rangle \phi}{se^* \doteq FALSE \Longrightarrow \langle \pi \, q \, \omega \rangle \phi}{\Longrightarrow \langle \pi \text{ if } (se) \, p \text{ else } q \, \omega \rangle \phi}$$

While perfectly functional, this rule has several drawbacks. First, it unconditionally splits the proof, even in the presence of additional information. However, the program or the sequent may contain the explicit knowledge that the condition is true (or false). In that case, we want to avoid the proof split altogether. Second, after the split, the condition *se* appears on both branches, and we then have to reason about the same expression twice.

A different solution is the following rule that translates a program with an if-else statement into a conditional formula:

$$\text{ifElse} \; \frac{\implies \text{if}(se^* \doteq TRUE) \text{then} \; \langle \pi \; p \; \omega \rangle \phi \; \text{else} \; \langle \pi \; q \; \omega \rangle \phi}{\implies \langle \pi \; \text{if} \; (se) \; p \; \text{else} \; q \; \omega \rangle \phi}$$

Note that the if-then-else in the premiss of this rule is a logical and not a program language construct (Definition 3.3).

The ifElse rule solves the problems of the ifElseSplit rule described above. The condition *se* only has to be considered once. And if additional information about its truth value is available, splitting the proof can be avoided. If no such information is available, however, it is still possible to replace the propositional if-then-else operator with its definition, resulting in

$$((se^* \doteq TRUE) \to \langle \pi \; p \; \omega \rangle \phi) \quad \wedge \quad ((se^* \not\doteq TRUE) \to \langle \pi \; q \; \omega \rangle \phi)$$

and carry out a case distinction in the usual manner.

A problem that the above rule does not eliminate is the duplication of the code part ω. Its double appearance in the premiss means that we may have to reason about the same piece of code twice. Leino [2005] proposes a solution for this problem within a verification condition generator system. However, to preserve the advantages of a symbolic execution, the KeY system here sacrifices some efficiency for the sake of usability. And, fortunately, this issue is hardly ever limiting in practice.

The rule for the `switch` statement, which also is conditional and leads to case distinctions in proofs, is not shown here. It transforms a `switch` statement into a sequence of `if` statements.

3.6.4 Unwinding Loops

The following rule "unwinds" `while` loops.[2] Its application is the prerequisite for symbolically executing the loop body. Unfortunately, just unwinding a loop repeatedly is only sufficient for its verification if the number of loop iterations has a known upper bound. And it is only practical if that number is small (as otherwise the proof gets too big).

If the number of loop iterations is not bounded, the loop has to be verified using (a) induction or (b) an invariant rule (see Sections 3.7.2 and 9.4.2). If induction is used, the unwind rule is also needed as the loop has to be unwound once in the step case of the induction.

In case the loop body does not contain `break` or `continue` statements (which is the standard case), the following simple version of the unwind rule can be applied:

$$\text{loopUnwind} \; \frac{\implies \langle \pi \; \text{if} \; (e) \; \{ \; p \; \text{while} \; (e) \; p \; \} \; \omega \rangle \phi}{\implies \langle \pi \; \text{while} \; (e) \; p \; \omega \rangle \phi}$$

---

[2] Occurrences of `for` loops, enhanced `for` loops, and `do-while` loops are transformed into `while` loops by means of dedicated rules.

Otherwise, in the general case where `break` and/or `continue` occur, the following more complex rule version has to be used:

loopUnwind
$$\frac{\Longrightarrow \langle \pi \; \text{if} \; (e) \; l':\{ \; l'':\{ \; p' \; \} \; l_1:...l_n:\text{while} \; (e) \; \{ \; p \; \} \; \} \; \omega\rangle \phi}{\Longrightarrow \langle \pi \; l_1:...l_n:\text{while} \; (e) \; \{ \; p \; \} \; \omega\rangle \phi}$$

where

- l' and l'' are new labels,
- p' is the result of (simultaneously) replacing in p

  - every "`break` l_i" (for $1 \leq i \leq n$) and every "`break`" (with no label) that has the `while` loop as its target by "`break` l'," and
  - every "`continue` l_i" (for $1 \leq i \leq n$) and every "`continue`" (with no label) that has the `while` loop as its target by "`break` l''."

(The target of a `break` or `continue` statement with no label is the loop that immediately encloses it.)

The label list $l_1:...l_n$: usually has only one element or is empty, but in general a loop can have more than one label.

In the "unwound" instance p' of the loop body p, the label l' is the new target for `break` statements and l'' is the new target for `continue` statements, which both had the `while` loop as target before. This results in the desired behavior: `break` abruptly terminates the whole loop, while `continue` abruptly terminates the current instance of the loop body.

A `continue` (with or without label) is never handled directly by a JavaDL rule, because it can only occur in loops, where it is always transformed into a `break` statement by the loop rules.

3.6.5 Replacing Method Calls by their Implementation

Symbolic execution deals with method invocations by syntactically replacing the call by the called implementation (verification via contracts is described in Section 3.7.1). To obtain an efficient calculus we have conservatively extended the programming language (see Section 3.2.3) with two additional constructs: a method body statement, which allows us to precisely identify an implementation, and a `method-frame` block, which records the receiver of the invocation result and marks the boundaries of the inlined implementation.

3.6.5.1 Evaluation of Method Invocation Expressions

The process of evaluating a method invocation expression (method call) within our
JavaDL calculus consists of the following steps:

1. Identifying the appropriate method.
2. Computing the target reference.
3. Evaluating the arguments.
4. Locating the implementation (or throwing a `NullPointerException`).
5. Creating the method frame.
6. Handling the `return` statement.

Since method invocation expressions can take many different shapes, the calculus
contains a number of slightly differing rules for every step. Also, not every step is
necessary for every method invocation.

3.6.5.2 Step 1: Identify the Appropriate Method

The first step is to identify the appropriate method to invoke. This involves determining the right method signature and the class where the search for an implementation
should begin. Usually, this process is performed by the compiler according to the
(quite complicated) rules of the Java language specification and considering only
static information such as type conformance and accessibility modifiers. These rules
have to be considered as a background part of our logic, which we will not describe
here though, but refer to the Java language specification instead. In the KeY system
this process is performed internally (it does not require an application of a calculus
rule), and the implementation relies on the Recoder metaprogramming framework to
achieve the desired effect (Recoder is available at recoder.sourceforge.net).

For our purposes, we discern three different method invocation modes:

Instance or "virtual" mode.   This is the most common mode. The target expression
    references an object (it may be an implicit `this` reference), and the method is not
    declared static or private. This invocation mode requires dynamic binding.
Static mode.   In this case, no dynamic binding is required. The method to invoke is
    determined in accordance with the declared static type of the target expression and
    not the dynamic type of the object to which this expression may point. The static
    mode applies to all invocations of methods declared `static`. The target expression
    in this case can be either a class name or an object referencing expression (which
    is evaluated and then discarded). The static mode is also used for instance methods
    declared `private` (in which case the evaluated target reference is not discarded
    but used to identify the object on which to invoke the method).
Super mode.   This mode is used to access the methods of the immediate superclass.
    The target expression in this case is the keyword `super`. The super mode bypasses
    any overriding declaration in the class that contains the method invocation.

Below, we present the rules for every step in a method invocation. We concentrate on the virtual invocation mode and discuss other modes only where significant differences occur.

3.6.5.3 Step 2: Computing the Target Reference

The following rule applies if the target expression of the method invocation is not a simple expression and may have side-effects. In this case, the method invocation gets unfolded so that the target expression can be evaluated first.

methodCallUnfoldTarget
$$\frac{\Longrightarrow \langle \pi \; T_{nse} \; v_0 \; = \; nse; \; lhs \; = \; v_0.mname(args); \; \omega \rangle \phi}{\Longrightarrow \langle \pi \; lhs \; = \; nse.mname(args); \; \omega \rangle \phi}$$

This step is not performed if the target expression is the keyword super or a class name. For an invocation of a static method via a reference expression, this step *is* performed, but the result is discarded later on.

3.6.5.4 Step 3: Evaluating the Arguments

If a method invocation has arguments that need to be evaluated, i.e., if at least one of the arguments is not a simple expression, then the arguments have to be evaluated before control is transferred to the method body. This is achieved by the following rule:

methodCallUnfoldArguments
$$\frac{\Longrightarrow \langle \pi \; T_{e_1} \; a_1 = e_1; \; \ldots; \; T_{e_n} \; a_n = e_n; \atop lhs \; = \; se.mname(a_1, \ldots, a_n); \atop \omega \rangle \phi}{\longrightarrow \langle \pi \; lhs \; = \; se.mname(e_1, \ldots, e_n); \; \omega \rangle \phi}$$

The rule unfolds the arguments using fresh variables in the usual manner.

In the *instance* invocation mode, the target expression se must be simple (otherwise the rules from Step 2 apply). Furthermore, argument evaluation has to happen even if the target reference is null, which is not checked until the next step.

3.6.5.5 Step 4: Locating the Implementation

This step has two purposes in our calculus: to bind the argument values to the formal parameters and to simulate dynamic binding (for *instance* invocations). Both are achieved with the following rule:

methodCall
$$\frac{se \neq \texttt{null} \Longrightarrow \langle \pi \ T_{lhs} \ v_0; \ paramDecl; \ ifCascade; \ lhs = v_0; \ \omega \rangle \phi}{\Longrightarrow \langle \pi \ lhs = se.mname(se_1,\ldots,se_n); \ \omega \rangle \phi}$$
$$se \doteq \texttt{null} \Longrightarrow \langle \pi \ \texttt{throw new NullPointerException(); } \omega \rangle \phi$$

The code piece *paramDecl* introduces and initializes new local variables that later replace the formal parameters of the method. That is, *paramDecl* abbreviates

$$T_{se_1} \ p_1 = se_1; \ \ldots \ T_{se_n} \ p_n = se_n;$$

The code schema *ifCascade* simulates dynamic binding. Using the signature of *mname*, we extract the set of classes that implement this particular method from the given Java program. Due to the possibility of method overriding, there can be more than one class implementing a particular method. At runtime, an implementation is picked based on the dynamic type of the target object—a process known as dynamic binding. In our calculus, we have to do a case distinction as the dynamic type is in general not known. We employ a sequence of nested `if` statements that discriminate on the type of the target object, cast the callee variable to the static type in which the method implementation is found, and refer to the distinct method implementations via method body statements (see Section 3.2.3). Thus, *ifCascade* abbreviates:

```
if (se instanceof C₁) {
    C₁ target = (C₁)se;    v₀ = target.mname(p₁,...,pₙ)@C₁;
} else if (se instanceof C₂) {
    C₂ target = (C₂)se;    v₀ = target.mname(p₁,...,pₙ)@C₂;
    ⋮
} else if (se instanceof Cₖ₋₁) {
    Cₖ₋₁ target = (Cₖ₋₁)se;    v₀ = target.mname(p₁,...,pₙ)@Cₖ₋₁;
else {
    Cₖ target = (Cₖ)se;    v₀ = target.mname(p₁,...,pₙ)@Cₖ;
}
```

The order of the if statements is a bottom-up latitudinal search over all classes $C_1,\ldots,C_k$ of the class inheritance tree that implement *mname*$(\ldots)$. In other words, the more specialized classes appear closer to the top of the cascade. Formally, if $i < j$ then $C_j \not\sqsubseteq C_i$.

If the invocation mode is *static* or *super* no *ifCascade* is created. The single appropriate method body statement takes its place. Furthermore, the check whether *se* is `null` is omitted in these modes, though not for private methods.

Please note that this step in method invocation and its associated rule forfeit modular correctness: The rule is only sound if the constructed if-cascade is complete, which requires all relevant methods to be known at the time of rule application (see Section 9.1.3).

3.6.5.6 Step 5: Creating the Method Frame

In this step, the method body statement v_0=*se* . *mname* (...) @*Class* is replaced by the implementation of *mname* from the class *Class* and the implementation is enclosed in a method frame:

methodBodyExpand

$$\Longrightarrow \langle \pi \text{ method-frame(result->}lhs,$$
$$\text{source=}mname\,(T_1,\ldots,T_n)\,@Class,$$
$$\text{this=}se$$
$$) : \{ body \} \,\omega\rangle\phi$$

$$\overline{\langle \pi \ lhs=se.mname\,(v_1,\ldots,v_n)\,@Class; \ \omega\rangle\phi \Longrightarrow}$$

in the implementation *body* the formal parameters of types $T_1,\ldots,T_n$ of *mname* are syntactically replaced by $v_1,\ldots,v_n$.

3.6.5.7 Step 6: Handling the `return` Statement

The final stage of handling a method invocation, after the method body has been symbolically executed, involves committing the return value (if any) and transferring control back to the caller. We postpone the description of treating method termination resulting from an exception (as well as the intricate interaction between a `return` statement and a `finally` block) until the following section on abrupt termination.

The basic rule for the `return` statement is:

methodCallReturn

$$\Longrightarrow \langle \pi \text{ method-frame(}\ldots\text{)}:\{ v=se; \} \,\omega\rangle\phi$$

$$\overline{\Longrightarrow \langle \pi \text{ method-frame(result->}v, \ \ldots\text{)} : \{ \text{ return } se; \ p \} \,\omega\rangle\phi}$$

We assume that the return value has already undergone the usual unfolding analysis, and is now a simple expression *se*. Now, we need to assign it to the right variable v within the invoking code. This variable is specified in the head of the method frame. A corresponding assignment is created and v disappears from the method frame. Any trailing code p is also discarded.

After the assignment of the return value is symbolically executed, we are left with an empty method frame, which can now be removed altogether. This is achieved with the rule

methodCallEmpty $\dfrac{\Longrightarrow \langle \pi \ \ \omega\rangle\phi}{\Longrightarrow \langle \pi \text{ method-frame(}\ldots\text{)} : \{ \} \,\omega\rangle\phi}$

In case the method is void or if the invoking code simply does not assign the value of the method invocation to any variable, this fact is reflected by the variable v missing from the method frame. Then, slightly simpler versions of the return rule are used, which do not create an assignment.

3.6.5.8 Example for Handling a Method Invocation

Consider the example program from Figure 3.1. The method nextId() returns for a given integer value id some next available value. In the Base class this method is implemented to return id+1. The class SubA inherits and retains this implementation. The class SubB overrides the method to return id+2, which is done by increasing the result of the implementation in Base by one.

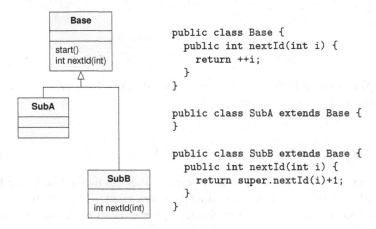

```
public class Base {
    public int nextId(int i) {
        return ++i;
    }
}

public class SubA extends Base {
}

public class SubB extends Base {
    public int nextId(int i) {
        return super.nextId(i)+1;
    }
}
```

Figure 3.1 An example program with method overriding

We now show step by step how the following code, which invokes the method nextId() on an object of type SubB, is symbolically executed:

—— Java ————————————————————————————————————
```
Base o = new SubB();
res = o.nextId(i);
```
———————————————————————————————————— Java ——

First, the instance creation is handled, after which we are left with the actual method call. The effect of the instance creation is reflected in the updates attached to the formula, which we do not show here. Since the target reference o is already *simple* at this point, we skip Step 2. The same applies to the arguments of the method call and Step 3. We proceed with Step 4, applying the rule methodCall. This gives us two branches. One corresponds to the case where o is null, which can be discharged using the knowledge that o points to a freshly created object. The other branch assumes that o is not null and contains a formula with the following Java code (in the following, program part A is transformed into A', B into B' etc.):

—— Java ———————————————————————————————

```
int j; {                                   Ⓐ
    int i_1 = i;
    if (o instanceof SubB) {
        SubB target = (SubB)o;
        j=target.nextId(i_1)@SubB;
    } else {
        Base target = (Base)o;
        j=target.nextId(i_1)@Base;
    }
}
res=j;
```

——————————————————————————————— Java ——

After dealing with the variable declarations, we reach the if-cascade simulating dynamic binding. In this case we happen to know the dynamic type of the object referenced by o. This eliminates the choice and leaves us with assigning o to a variable of the same static type where the implementation is been found, and finally, the method body statement pointing to the implementation from SubB:

—— Java ———————————————————————————————

```
SubB target = (SubB)o;      Ⓐ'
j=target.nextId(i_1)@SubB;
res=j;
```

——————————————————————————————— Java ——

After executing the variable declaration of target and assigning it the value of o (the cast succeeds because of the if-statement guard in the previous step), it is time for Step 5: unfolding the method body statement and creating a method frame. This is achieved by the rule methodBodyExpand:

—— Java ———————————————————————————————

```
method-frame(result->j,source=nextId(int)@SubB,this=target):{ Ⓐ'
    return super.nextId(i_1)+1;      Ⓑ
}
res=j;
```

——————————————————————————————— Java ——

The method implementation has been inlined above. We start to execute it symbolically, unfolding the expression in the return statement in the usual manner, which gives us after some steps:

—— Java ——————————————————————————————————
```
method-frame(result->j, source=nextId(int)@SubB, this=target):{
    int j_2 = super.nextId(i_1);   Ⓒ      Ⓑ'
    j_1=j_2+1;
    return  j_1;
}
res=j;
```
——————————————————————————————————— Java ——

The active statement is now again a method invocation, this time with the super keyword. The method invocation process starts again from scratch. Steps 2 and 3 can be omitted for the same reasons as above. Step 4 gives us the following code. Note that there is no if-cascade, since no dynamic binding needs to be performed.

—— Java ——————————————————————————————————
```
method-frame(result->j, source=nextId(int)@SubB, this=target):{
    int j_3; {                                  Ⓒ'
        int i_2 = i_1;
        j_3=target.nextId(i_2)@Base;
    }
    j_2=j_3;
    j_1=j_2+1;
    return  j_1;
}
res=j;
```
——————————————————————————————————— Java ——

Now it is necessary to remove the declarations and perform the assignments to reach the method body statement j_3=target.nextId(i_2)@Base;. Then, this statement can be unpacked (Step 5), and we obtain two nested method frames. The second method frame retains the value of this, while the implementation source is now taken from the superclass:

```
—— Java ————————————————————————————————
method-frame(result->j, source=nextId(int)@SubB, this=target):{
    method-frame(result->j_3,                                    C"
                  source=nextId(int)@Base, this=target)  : {
        return ++i_2;  D
    }
    j_2=j_3;
    j_1=j_2+1;
    return j_1;
}
res=j;
————————————————————————————————————— Java ——
```

The return expression is unfolded until we arrive at a simple expression. The actual return value is recorded in the updates attached to the formula. The code in the formula then is:

```
—— Java ————————————————————————————————
method-frame(result->j, source=nextId(int)@SubB, this=target):{
    method-frame(result->j_3,                                    E
                  source=nextId(int)@Base, this=target) : {
        return j_4;  D'
    }
    j_2=j_3;
    j_1=j_2+1;
    return j_1;
}
res=j;
————————————————————————————————————— Java ——
```

Now we can perform Step 6 (rule methodCallReturn), which replaces the return statement of the inner method frame with the assignment to the variable j_3. We know that j_3 is the receiver of the return value, since it was identified as such by the method frame (this information is removed with the rule application).

```
—— Java ——
method-frame(result->j, source=nextId(int)@SubB, this=target):{
    method-frame(source=nextId(int)@Base, this=target) : { Ⓔ
        j_3=j_4;
    }
    j_2=j_3;
    j_1=j_2+1;
    return j_1;
}
res=j;
———————————————————————————————————— Java ——
```

The assignment j_3=j_4; can be executed as usual, generating an update, and we obtain an empty method frame.

```
—— Java ——
method-frame(result->j, source=nextId(int)@SubB, this=target):{
    method-frame(source=nextId(int)@Base, this=target):{ Ⓔ'
    }
    j_2=j_3;
    j_1=j_2+1;
    return j_1;
}
res=j;
———————————————————————————————————— Java ——
```

The empty frame can be removed with the rule methodCallEmpty, completing Step 6. The invocation depth has now decreased again. We obtain the program:

```
—— Java ——
method-frame(result->j, source=nextId(int)@SubB, this=target):{
    j_2=j_3;
    j_1=j_2+1;
    return j_1;
}
res=j;
———————————————————————————————————— Java ——
```

From here, the execution continues in an analogous manner. The outer method frame is eventually removed as well.

3.6.6 *Instance Creation and Initialization*

In this section we cover the process of instance creation and initialization. We do not go into details of array creation and initialization, since it is sufficiently similar.

3.6.6.1 Instance Creation and the Constant Domain Assumption

JavaDL, like many modal logics, operates under the technically useful constant domain semantics (all program states have the same universe). This means, however, that all instances that are ever created in a program have to exist a priori. To resolve this seeming paradox, we introduce *implicit fields* that allow to change and query the program-visible instance state (created, initialized, etc.); see Table 3.5. These implicit fields behave as the usual class or instance attributes, except that they are not declared by the user but by the logic designer. To distinguish them from normal (user-declared) fields, their names are enclosed in angled brackets.

Table 3.5 Implicit object repository and status fields

Modifier	Implicit field	Declared in	Explanation
`protected boolean <created>`		Object	indicates whether the object has been created
`protected boolean <initialised>`		Object	indicates whether the object has been initialized

Example 3.19. To express that the field `head` declared in some class A is nonnull for all created and initialized objects of type A, one can use the following formula:

$$\forall a : A.(a \neq \texttt{null} \land a.\texttt{<created>} \doteq \mathit{TRUE} \;\rightarrow\; (a.\texttt{head} \neq \texttt{null}))$$

In future, we use the easier to read *created* to refer to the field `<created>`, except for syntax used as part of KeY input files or similar.

3.6.6.2 Overview of the Java Instance Creation and Initialization Process

We use an approach to handle instance creation and initialization that is based on program transformation. The transformation reduces a Java program p to a program p' such that the behavior of p (with initialization) is the same as that of p' when initialization is disregarded. This is done by inserting code into p that explicitly executes the initialization.

The transformation inserts code for explicitly executing all initialization processes. To a large extent, the inserted code works by invoking implicit class or instance methods (similar to implicit fields), which do the actual work. An overview of all implicit methods introduced is given in Table 3.6.

Table 3.6 Implicit methods for object creation and initialization declared in every nonabstract type T (syntactic conventions from Figure 3.2)

Static methods	
`public static T <createObject>()`	main method for instance creation and initialisation
`private static T <allocate>()`	allocation of an unused object from the object repository

Instance methods	
`protected void <prepare>()`	assignment of default values to all instance fields
mods T `<init>`(*params*)	execution of instance initializers and the invoked constructor

The transformation covers all details of initialization in Java, except that we only consider nonconcurrent programs and no reflection facilities (in particular no instances of `java.lang.Class`). Initialization of classes and interfaces (also known as static initialization) is fully supported for the single threaded case. KeY passes the static initialization challenge stated by Jacobs et al. [2003].

In the following, we use the schematic class form shown in Figure 3.2.

$$
\begin{aligned}
&mods_0 \text{ class } T \ \{ \\
&\quad mods_1 \ T_1 \ a_1 \ = \ initExpression_1; \\
&\quad \vdots \\
&\quad mods_m \ T_m \ a_m \ = \ initExpression_m; \\
&\quad \{ \\
&\qquad initStatement_{m+1}; \\
&\qquad \vdots \\
&\qquad initStatement_l; \\
&\quad \} \\
&\quad mods \ T(params) \ \{ \\
&\qquad st_1; \\
&\qquad \vdots \\
&\qquad st_n; \\
&\quad \} \\
&\quad \vdots \\
&\}
\end{aligned}
$$

Figure 3.2 Initialization part in a schematic class

Example 3.20. Figure 3.3 shows a class `Person` and its mapping to the schematic class declaration of Figure 3.2. There is only one initializer statement in class `Person`, namely "`id = 0`," which is induced by the corresponding field declaration of `id`.

```
class Person {
  private int id = 0;

  public Person(int persID) {
    id = persID;
  }
}
```

$$
\begin{aligned}
mods_0 &\mapsto - \\
T &\mapsto \texttt{Person} \\
mods_1 &\mapsto \texttt{private} \\
T_1 &\mapsto \texttt{int} \\
a_1 &\mapsto \texttt{id} \\
initExpression_1 &\mapsto \texttt{0} \\
mods &\mapsto \texttt{public} \\
params &\mapsto \texttt{int persID} \\
st_1 &\mapsto \texttt{id = persID}
\end{aligned}
$$

Figure 3.3 Example for the mapping of a class declaration to the schema of Figure 3.2

To achieve a uniform presentation we also stipulate that:

1. The default constructor `public T()` exists in T in case no explicit constructor has been declared.
2. Unless $T = \texttt{Object}$, the statement st_1 must be a constructor invocation. If this is not the case in the original program, "`super();`" is added explicitly as the first statement.

Both of these conditions reflect the actual semantics of Java.

3.6.6.3 The Rule for Instance Creation and Initialization

The instance creation rule

$$
instanceCreation \;\; \frac{\begin{aligned}
&\Longrightarrow \langle \pi \; T \; v_0 \; \texttt{= T.<createObject>();} \\
&\quad T_1 \; a_1 \; \texttt{=} \; e_1; \; \ldots; \; T_1 \; a_n \; \texttt{=} \; e_n; \\
&\quad v_0.\texttt{<init>}(a_1,\ldots,a_n)\texttt{@T;} \\
&\quad v_0.\texttt{<initialised> = true;} \\
&\quad v \; \texttt{=} \; v_0; \\
&\quad \omega \rangle \phi
\end{aligned}}{\Longrightarrow \langle \pi \; v \; \texttt{= new } T(e_1,\ldots,e_n); \; \omega \rangle \phi}
$$

replaces an instance creation expression "$v = \texttt{new } T(e_1,\ldots,e_n)$" by a sequence of statements. The implicit static method `<createObject>()` is declared in each nonabstract class T as follows:

```
public static T <createObject>() {
    T newObject = T.<allocate>();
            // Invoke the preparation method to assign default values to
            // instance fields
    newObject.<create>();
            // Return the newly created object in order to initialize it:
    return newObject;
}
```

`<createObject>()` delegates its work to a series of other helper methods. The generated code can be divided into three phases, which we examine in detail below:

1. `<allocate>()`: Allocate space on the heap, mark the object as created (as explained above, it is not really "created"), and assign the reference to a temporary variable v_0.
2. `<create>()`: Prepare the object by assigning all fields their default values.
3. `<init>()`: Initialize the object and subsequently mark it as initialized. Note that the rule uses the method body statement instead of a normal method invocation. This is possible as we exactly know which constructor has been invoked and it allows us to achieve an improved performance as we do not need to use dynamic dispatch.

The reason for assigning v_0 to v in the last step is to ensure correct behavior in case initialization terminates abruptly due to an exception.[3]

3.6.6.4 Phase 1: Instance Allocation: `<allocate>`

During the first phase, an implicit method called `<allocate>()`, performs the central interaction with the heap. The `<allocate>()` method has no Java implementation; its semantics is given by the following rule instead:

allocateInstance

$$
\begin{array}{c}
o' \neq \texttt{null}, \; exactInstance_T(o') \doteq TRUE, \\
\left(wellFormed(\texttt{heap}) \rightarrow select_{boolean}(\texttt{heap}, o', created) \doteq FALSE\right) \\
\implies \{\texttt{heap} := create(\texttt{heap}, o')\} \\
\{lhs := o'\} \\
\langle \pi \;\; \omega \rangle \phi \\
\hline
\implies \langle \pi \;\; lhs = T.\texttt{<allocate>}(); \;\; \omega \rangle \phi
\end{array}
$$

where $o' : T \in$ FSym is a fresh symbol

---

[3] Java does not prevent creating and accessing partly initialized objects. This can be done, for example, by assigning the object reference to a static field during initialization. This behavior is modeled faithfully in the calculus. In such cases the preparation phase guarantees that all fields have a definite value.

The rule introduces a *fresh* constant symbol o' to represent the new object, i.e., a constant symbol not occurring anywhere in the conclusion. The rule adds three assumptions about the otherwise unknown object represented by o': (i) it is different from *null*; (ii) its dynamic type is T; and (iii) if the heap is well-formed, then the object is not yet created. These assumptions are always satisfiable, because there is an infinite reservoir of objects of every type, and because in a well-formed heap only a finite number of them is created.

The new object is then marked as "created" by setting its *created* field to true, and the reference to the newly created object is assigned to the program variable *lhs*.

3.6.6.5 Phase 2: Preparation: `<create>`

During the second phase, an implicit method called `<create>` marks the object as not yet initialized (`this.<initialized>=false;`) and calls the implicit method `<prepare>()`, which makes sure that all fields, including the ones declared in the superclasses, are assigned their default values.[4] Up to this point no user code is involved, which ensures that all field accesses by the user observe a definite value. This value is given by the function *defaultValue* that maps each type to its default value (e.g., `int` to 0). The concrete default values are specified in the Java language specification [Gosling et al., 2013, § 4.5.5]. The method `<prepare>()` used for preparation is shown in Figure 3.4.[5]

```
protected void <prepare>() {
        // Prepare the fields declared in the superclass...
    super.<prepare>();              // unless T = Object
        // Then assign each field a_i of type T_i declared in T
        // to its default value:
    a_1 = defaultValue(T_1);

    a_m = defaultValue(T_m);
}
```

Figure 3.4 Implicit method `<prepare>()`

---

[4] Since class declarations are given beforehand this is possible with a simple enumeration. In case of arrays, a quantified update is used to achieve the same effect, even when the actual array size is not known.

[5] In the KeY system, `<create>()` does not call `<prepare>()` on the new object directly. Instead it invokes another implicitly declared method called `<prepareEnter>()`, which has private access and whose body is identical to the one of `<prepare>()`. The reason is that due to the super call in `<prepare>()`'s body, its visibility must be at least `protected` such that a direct call would trigger dynamic method dispatching, which is unnecessary and would lead to a larger proof.

3.6.6.6 Instance Initialization: `<init>`

After the preparation of the new object, the user-defined initialization code can be processed. Such code can occur

- as a field initializer expression "T *attr* = *val*;" (e.g., (*) in Figure 3.5); the corresponding initializer statement is *attr* = *val*;
- as an instance initializer block (similar to (**) in Figure 3.5); such a block is also an initializer statement;
- within a constructor body (like (***) in Figure 3.5).

```
class A {
  (*)    private int a = 3;           private <init>() {
  (**)   {a++;}                         super.<init>();
         public int b;                   a = 3;
                                         {a++;}
                                         a = a + 2;
  (***) private A() {                  }
          a = a + 2;
        }                            public <init>(int i) {
  (***) public A(int i) {              this.<init>();
          this();                      a = a + i;
          a = a + i;                 }
        }                          }
  ...
```

Figure 3.5 Example for constructor normal form

For each constructor *mods* T(*params*) of T we provide a constructor normal form *mods* T `<init>`(*params*), which includes (1) the initialization of the superclass, (2) the execution of all initializer statements in source code order, and finally (3) the actual constructor body. In the initialization phase the arguments of the instance creation expression are evaluated and passed on to this constructor normal form. An example of the normal form is given in Figure 3.5.

The exact blueprint for building a constructor normal form is shown in Figure 3.6, using the conventions of Figure 3.2. Due to the uniform class form assumed above, the first statement st_1 of every original constructor is either an alternate constructor invocation or a superclass constructor invocation (with the notable exception of $T = $ Object). Depending on this first statement, the normal form of the constructor is built to do one of two things:

1. $st_1 = $ super(*args*): Recursive restart of the initialization phase for the superclass of T. If $T = $ Object stop. Afterwards, initializer statements are executed in source code order. Finally, the original constructor body is executed.
2. $st_1 = $ this(*args*): Recursive restart of the initialization phase with the alternate constructor. Afterwards, the original constructor body is executed.

If one of the above steps fails, the initialization terminates abruptly throwing an exception.

```
mods T <init>(params) {                    mods T <init>(params) {
       // invoke constructor
       // normal form of superclass              // constructor normal form
       // (only if T ≠ Object)                    // instead of this(args)
    super.<init>(args);                        this.<init>(args);
                                                   // no initializer statements
       // add the initializer                      // if st₁ is an explicit
       // statements:                              // this() invocation
    initStatement₁;
    ...
    initStatementₗ;
       // append constructor body                  // append constructor body
    stₛ; ... stₙ;                              st₂; ... stₙ;
       // if T = Object then s = 1                  // starting with its second
       // otherwise s = 2                          // statement
}                                           }
```

$$(a)\ st_1 = \texttt{super}(args)$$
in the original constructor

$$(b)\ st_1 = \texttt{this}(args)$$
in the original constructor

Figure 3.6 Building the constructor normal form

3.6.7 Handling Abrupt Termination

3.6.7.1 Abrupt Termination in JavaDL

In Java, the execution of a statement can terminate *abruptly* (besides terminating normally and not terminating at all). Possible reasons for an abrupt termination are (a) that an exception has been thrown, (b) that a statement (usually a loop or a switch) is terminated with break, (c) that a single loop iteration is terminated with the continue statement, and (d) that the execution of a method is terminated with the return statement. Abrupt termination of a statement either leads to a redirection of the control flow after which the program execution resumes (for example, if an exception is caught), or the whole program terminates abruptly (if an exception is not caught).

Note, that the KeY system contains three user-selectable calculus variations for reasoning about run-time exceptions that may be thrown by the JVM (e.g., NullPointerException); see Section 3.6.2 and 15.2.3.

3.6.7.2 Evaluation of Arguments

If the argument of a throw or a return statement is a nonsimple expression, the statement has to be unfolded first such that the argument can be (symbolically) evaluated:

$$\text{throwEvaluate} \; \frac{\Longrightarrow \langle \pi \; T_{nse} \; v_0 = nse; \; \texttt{throw} \; v_0; \; \omega \rangle \phi}{\Longrightarrow \langle \pi \; \texttt{throw} \; nse; \; \omega \rangle \phi}$$

3.6.7.3 If the Whole Program Terminates Abruptly

In JavaDL, an *abruptly* terminating statement—where the abrupt termination does not just change the control flow but actually terminates the whole program p in a modal operator $\langle p \rangle$ or $[p]$—has the same semantics as a *nonterminating* statement (Definition 3.5). For that case rules such as the following are provided in the JavaDL calculus for all abruptly terminating statements:

throwDiamond

$$\frac{\implies false}{\implies \langle \texttt{throw } se; \ \omega \rangle \phi}$$

throwBox

$$\frac{\implies true}{\implies [\texttt{throw } se; \ \omega] \phi}$$

Note, that in these rules, there is no inactive prefix π in front of the throw statement. Such a π could contain a try with accompanying catch clause that would catch the thrown exception. However, the rules throwDiamond, throwBox etc. must only be applied to uncaught exceptions. If there is a prefix π, other rules described below must be applied first.

3.6.7.4 If the Control Flow is Redirected

The case where an abruptly terminating statement does not terminate the whole program in a modal operator but only changes the control flow is more difficult to handle and requires more rules. The basic idea for handling this case in our JavaDL calculus are rules that *symbolically* execute the change in control flow by syntactically rearranging the affected program parts.

The calculus rules have to consider the different combinations of prefix-context (beginning of a block, method-frame, or try) and abruptly terminating statement (break, continue, return, or throw). Below, rules for all combinations are discussed—with the following exceptions:

- The rule for the combination method frame/return is part of handling method invocations (Step 6 in Section 3.6.5.1).
- Due to restrictions of the Java language specification, the combination method frame/break does not occur.
- Since the continue statement can only occur within loops, all occurrences of continue are handled by the loop rules.

Moreover, switch statements, which may contain a break, are not considered here; they are transformed into a sequence of if statements.

3.6.7.5 Rule for Method Frame and throw

In this case, the method is terminated, but no return value is assigned. The throw statement remains unchanged (i.e., the exception is handed up to the invoking code):

$$\text{methodCallThrow} \; \frac{\Longrightarrow \langle \pi \; \texttt{throw} \; se; \; \omega \rangle \phi}{\Longrightarrow \langle \pi \; \texttt{method-frame}(\ldots) \; : \; \{\texttt{throw} \; se; \; p \; \} \; \omega \rangle \phi}$$

3.6.7.6 Rules for try and throw

The following rule allows us to handle `try-catch-finally` blocks and the `throw` statement:

tryCatchFinallyThrow
$$\begin{aligned} \Longrightarrow \langle \pi \; &\texttt{if} \; (se \; \texttt{==} \; \texttt{null}) \; \{ \\ &\quad \texttt{try} \; \{ \; \texttt{throw new NullPointerException()}; \; \} \\ &\quad \texttt{catch} \; (T \; v) \; \{ \; q \; \} \; cs \; \texttt{finally} \; \{ \; r \; \} \\ &\texttt{\} else if} \; (se \; \texttt{instanceof} \; T) \; \{ \\ &\quad \texttt{try} \; \{ \; T \; v; \; v \; \texttt{=} \; (T)se; \; q \; \} \; \texttt{finally} \; \{ \; r \; \} \\ &\texttt{\} else} \; \{ \\ &\quad \texttt{try} \; \{ \; \texttt{throw} \; se; \; \} \; cs \; \texttt{finally} \; \{ \; r \; \} \\ &\texttt{\}} \\ \omega \rangle \phi& \end{aligned}$$

$$\begin{aligned} \Longrightarrow \langle \pi \; &\texttt{try} \; \{ \; \texttt{throw} \; se; \; p \} \\ &\quad \texttt{catch} \; (\; T \; v \;) \; \{ \; q \; \} \; cs \; \texttt{finally} \; \{ \; r \; \} \\ \omega \rangle \phi& \end{aligned}$$

The schema variable cs represents a (possibly empty) sequence of catch clauses. The rule covers three cases corresponding to the three cases in the premiss:

1. The argument of the `throw` statement is the null pointer (which, of course, in practice should not happen). In that case everything remains unchanged except that a `NullPointerException` is thrown instead of *null*.
2. The first catch clause catches the exception. Then, after binding the exception to v, the code q from the catch clause is executed.
3. The first catch clause does *not* catch the exception. In that case the first clause gets eliminated. The same rule can then be applied again to check further clauses.

Note, that in all three cases the code p after the `throw` statement gets eliminated.
    When all catch clauses have been checked and the exception has still not been caught, the following rule applies:

tryFinallyThrow
$$\begin{aligned} \Longrightarrow \langle \pi \quad &\texttt{if} \; (se \; \texttt{==} \; \texttt{null}) \; \{ \; v_{se} \; \texttt{=} \; \texttt{new NullPointerException()}; \; \} \\ &\texttt{else} \qquad \qquad \{ \; v_{se} \; \texttt{=} \; se; \; \} \\ &r \\ &\texttt{throw} \; v_{se}; \\ \omega \rangle \phi& \end{aligned}$$

$$\Longrightarrow \langle \pi \; \texttt{try} \; \{ \; \texttt{throw} \; se; \; p \; \} \; \texttt{finally} \; \{ \; r \; \} \rangle \phi$$

This rule moves the code r from the finally block to the front. The `try`-block gets eliminated so that the thrown exception now may be caught by other `try` blocks in π (or remain uncaught). The value of se has to be saved in v_{se} before the code r is executed as r might change se.

There is also a rule for `try` blocks that have been symbolically executed without throwing an exception and that are now empty and terminate normally (similar rules exist for empty blocks and empty method frames). Again, cs represents a finite (possibly empty) sequence of catch clauses:

$$\text{tryEmpty} \quad \frac{\Longrightarrow \langle \pi \ r \ \omega \rangle \phi}{\Longrightarrow \langle \pi \ \texttt{try\{ \} } cs \texttt{ \{ } q \texttt{ \} finally \{ } r \texttt{ \} } \omega \rangle \phi}$$

3.6.7.7 Rules for `try`/`break` and `try`/`return`

A `return` or a `break` statement within a `try-catch-finally` statement causes the immediate execution of the `finally` block. Afterwards the `try` statement terminates abnormally with the `break` or the `return` statement (a different abruptly terminating statement that may occur in the `finally` block takes precedence). This behavior is simulated by the following two rules (here, also, cs is a finite, possibly empty sequence of catch clauses):

$$\text{tryBreak} \quad \frac{\Longrightarrow \langle \pi \ r \ \texttt{break } l; \ \omega \rangle \phi}{\Longrightarrow \langle \pi \ \texttt{try\{ break } l; \ p \texttt{ \} } cs \texttt{ \{ } q \texttt{ \} finally\{ } r \texttt{ \} } \omega \rangle \phi}$$

$$\text{tryReturn} \quad \frac{\Longrightarrow \langle \pi \ T_{v_r} \ v_0 = v_r; \ r \ \texttt{return } v_0; \ \omega \rangle \phi}{\Longrightarrow \langle \pi \ \texttt{try\{ return } v_r; \ p \texttt{ \} } cs \texttt{ \{ } q \texttt{ \} finally\{ } r \texttt{ \} } \omega \rangle \phi}$$

3.6.7.8 Rules for block/`break`, block/`return`, and block/`throw`

The following two rules apply to blocks being terminated by a `break` statement that does not have a label, or by a break statement with a label l identical to one of the labels $l_1, \ldots, l_k$ of the block ($k \geq 1$).

$$\text{blockBreakNoLabel} \quad \frac{\Longrightarrow \langle \pi \quad \omega \rangle \phi}{\Longrightarrow \langle \pi \ l_1 : \ldots l_k : \texttt{\{ break; } p \texttt{ \} } \omega \rangle \phi}$$

$$\text{blockBreakLabel} \quad \frac{\Longrightarrow \langle \pi \quad \omega \rangle \phi}{\Longrightarrow \langle \pi \ l_1 : \ldots l_i : \ldots l_k : \texttt{\{ break } l_i; \ p \texttt{ \} } \omega \rangle \phi}$$

To blocks (labeled or unlabeled) that are abruptly terminated by a `break` statement with a label l not matching any of the labels of the block, the following rule applies:

$$\text{blockBreakNomatch} \quad \frac{\implies \langle \pi \ \texttt{break} \ l; \ \omega \rangle \phi}{\implies \langle \pi \ l_1 : \ldots l_k : \{ \ \texttt{break} \ l; \ p \} \ \omega \rangle \phi}$$

Similar rules exist for blocks that are terminated by a `return` or `throw` statement:

$$\text{blockReturn} \quad \frac{\implies \langle \pi \ \texttt{return} \ v; \ \omega \rangle \phi}{\implies \langle \pi \ l_1 : \ldots l_k : \{ \ \texttt{return} \ v; \ p \} \ \omega \rangle \phi}$$

$$\text{blockThrow} \quad \frac{\implies \langle \pi \ \texttt{throw} \ v; \ \omega \rangle \phi}{\implies \langle \pi \ l_1 : \ldots l_k : \{ \ \texttt{throw} \ v; \ p \} \ \omega \rangle \phi}$$

3.7 Abstraction and Modularization Rules

The symbolic execution rules presented so far are sufficient to verify many safety properties of Java programs. With these rules, method declarations are inlined at the invocation site and loops are unwound. Verifying programs this way is very similar to using a bounded model checker, such as, for example, CBMC [Kroening and Tautschnig, 2014].

Yet, in order for program verification to scale up, *abstraction* is in general required. With abstraction, certain pieces of code being verified are replaced with an approximation. The term "abstraction" refers to both the process and the approximation used.

Before we give a definition, let's recall that every program fragment p induces a transition relation $\rho(p)$ on states (Definition 3.5).

Definition 3.21 (Abstraction). We call a relation $\alpha(p)$ on states an *abstraction* of p, iff

$$\rho(p) \subseteq \alpha(p) \ , \tag{3.1}$$

i.e., iff the abstraction $\alpha(p)$ contains all behaviors that the program p exhibits (or more).

The two major kinds of abstractions in KeY are method contracts and loop invariants. They are user-supplied but machine-checked for correctness. The user describes an abstraction syntactically using JavaDL or, more often, JML. KeY generates a proof obligation that the abstraction is correct, i.e., that it fulfills (3.1). In parallel, the abstraction can be used in place of the abstracted method or loop.

Abstraction offers several advantages:

1. Not all aspects of the code are crucial to establish a given correctness property. Abstraction allows eliding irrelevant aspects, thus reducing proof size and complexity.

2. Abstractions can be used to facilitate inductive reasoning, such as is the case with loop invariants.
3. Abstractions can be checked once and used multiple times, potentially saving proof effort.
4. When a part of the program is extended or modified, it is sufficient to check that the new version conforms to the same abstraction as the old one. It is not necessary to reverify the rest of the program.
5. For certain program parts (library code, native code) the source code may be unavailable. A user-provided abstraction is a convenient way to capture some or all of the missing code's functionality.

Advantages 3 and 4 are typically what is referred to as *modularization*.

At the same time, there are also costs to using abstraction. One of them is associated overhead. For simple methods, it might be more efficient to inline the method implementation instead of writing, proving, and using a contract. Another one is incompleteness. If a proof attempt cannot be completed, an insufficiently precise abstraction can be the reason. The user needs to diagnose the issue and refine the abstraction.

In the following, we briefly introduce the method contract and the loop invariant rules of JavaDL.

3.7.1 Replacing Method Calls by Specifications: Method Contracts

The specification of a method is called *method contract* and is defined as follows (this definition is identical to Definition 8.2 on page 268, where the translation of JML contracts into JavaDL is presented).

Definition 3.22 (Functional method contract). A functional JavaDL method contract for a method or constructor

$$R \ \texttt{m}(T_1 \ \texttt{p}_1, \ \ldots, \ T_n \ \texttt{p}_n)$$

declared in class C is a quadruple

$$(pre, post, mod, term)$$

that consists of

- a precondition $pre \in$ DLFml,
- a postcondition $post \in$ DLFml,
- a modifier set $mod \in \text{Trm}_{LocSet} \cup \{\text{STRICTLYNOTHING}\}$, and
- a termination witness $term \in \text{Trm}_{Any} \cup \{\text{PARTIAL}\}$.

Contract components may contain special program variables referring to the execution context:

- `self` : C for references to the receiver object (not available if m is a static method),

- $p_1 : T_1, \ldots, p_n : T_n$ representing the method's formal parameters,
- heap : *Heap* to access heap locations,
- heap^{pre} : *Heap* to access heap locations in the state in which the operation was invoked (in the postcondition only),
- exc : *Exception* to refer to the exception in case the method terminates abruptly with a thrown exception (in the postcondition only),
- res : *R* to refer to the result value of a method with a return type different from void (in the postcondition only).

While *pre*, *mod*, *term* (only) refer to the state before method invocation, the postcondition *post* refers (also) to the state after termination of the invoked method. Therefore, *post* has more expressive means to its avail: Besides two heap representations (heap and heap^{pre}), the result value, and a possibly thrown exception can be used in the postcondition. In some situations, certain context variables are not available. For instance, there is no result value for a constructor invocation.

Usually (especially when employing JML as specification language), the postcondition *post* ∈ DLFml is of the form

$$(\text{exc} \doteq \text{null} \rightarrow \phi) \wedge (\text{exc} \not\doteq \text{null} \rightarrow \psi) \ ,$$

where ϕ is the postcondition for the case that the method terminates normally and ψ is the postcondition in case the method terminates abruptly with an exception.

The formulas *pre* and *post* are JavaDL formulas. However, in most cases, they do not contain modal operators. This is in particular true if they are automatically generated translations of JML specifications.

The termination marker *term* can be the special value PARTIAL, indicating that the contract is partial and does not require the method to terminate. Alternatively, *term* is an expression whose value needs to be decreasing according to some well-founded ordering with every recursive call. If the method does not involve recursive calls, any expression can be used for *term* (e.g., zero). More on termination proofs for recursive methods can be found in Section 9.1.4.

Below, we give the rule methodContractPartial that replaces a method invocation during symbolic execution with the method's contract. The rule assumes that the given method contract is a correct abstraction of the method. There must be a separate argument (i.e., a separate proof) establishing this fact. Chapter 8 gives details on such correctness arguments for method contracts.

The rule methodContractPartial applies to a box-modality and, thus, the question of whether the method terminates is ignored.

The above rule is applicable to a method invocation in which the receiver se_{target} and the arguments se_i are simple expressions. This can be achieved by using the rules methodCallUnfoldTarget and methodCallUnfoldArguments introduced in Section 3.6.5.3.

In the first premiss, we have to show that the precondition *pre* holds in the state in which the method is invoked after updating the program variables self and p_i with the receiver object se_{target} and with the parameters se_i. This guarantees that the

methodContractPartial
$$\Longrightarrow \mathcal{U}^{pre}_{cont}\, pre$$
$$\frac{\mathcal{U}^{post}_{cont}\,\mathcal{A}_{mod}(\texttt{exc} \doteq \texttt{null}) \Longrightarrow \mathcal{U}^{post}_{cont}\,\mathcal{A}_{mod}(post \rightarrow \{lhs := \texttt{res}\}\,[\pi\ \omega]\phi)}{\mathcal{U}^{post}_{cont}\,\mathcal{A}_{mod}(\texttt{exc} \not\doteq \texttt{null}) \Longrightarrow \mathcal{U}^{post}_{cont}\,\mathcal{A}_{mod}(post \rightarrow [\pi\ \texttt{throw}\ exc;\ \omega]\phi)}$$
$$\Longrightarrow [\pi\ lhs\texttt{=}se_{target}.method(se_1,\dots,se_n)\,;\ \omega]\phi$$

where

- $(pre, post, mod, term)$ is a contract for $method$;
- $\mathcal{U}^{pre}_{cont} = \{\texttt{self} := se_{target}\,||\,p_1 := se_1\,||\,\cdots\,||\,p_n := se_n\}$ is an update application setting up the precondition-context variables;
- $\mathcal{U}^{post}_{cont} = \mathcal{U}^{pre}_{cont}\{\texttt{heap}^{pre} := \texttt{heap}\,||\,\texttt{res} := c_r\,||\,\texttt{exc} := c_e\}$ is an update application setting up the postcondition-context variables; c_r and c_e are fresh constants of the result type of $method$ or of type $\texttt{Throwable}$;
- $\mathcal{A}_{mod}$ is an anonymizing update w.r.t. the modifier set mod.

Figure 3.7 Method contract rule

method contract's precondition is fulfilled and, according to the contract, we can use the postcondition *post* to describe the effects of the method invocation—where two cases must be distinguished.

In the first case (second premiss), we assume that the invoked method terminates normally, i.e., the context variable $\texttt{exc}$ is $\texttt{null}$ after termination. If the method is nonvoid the return value $\texttt{res}$ is assigned to the variable lhs. The second case deals with the situation that the method terminates abruptly (third premiss). As in the normal-termination case, the context variables are updated with the corresponding terms. But now, there is no result value to be assigned, but the exception $\texttt{exc}$ is thrown explicitly.

Note that, in both cases, the locations that the method possibly modifies are updated with an anonymizing update $\mathcal{A}_{mod}$. Such an update, which replaces the values of the locations in *mod* with new anonymous values can be constructed using the function $anon : Heap \times LocSet \times Heap \rightarrow Heap$ (see Section 2.4.3). The heap update

$$\{\texttt{heap} := anon(\texttt{heap}, mod, h)\}\ ,$$

where h is a new constant of type *Heap*, ensures that, in its scope, the heap coincides with h on all locations in *mod* and all not yet created locations and coincides with $\texttt{heap}$ before the update elsewhere.

Anonymizing the locations in *mod* ensures that the only knowledge that can be used about these locations when reasoning about the poststate is the knowledge contained in *post*—and not any knowledge that may be contained in other formulas in the sequence, which in fact refers to the prestate. Otherwise, without anonymization, knowledge about the pre- and the poststate would be mixed in an unsound way. See Section 9.4.1 for further information on the concept of anonymizing updates.

The method contract rule for the box modality is similar. It can be applied independently of the value of the termination marker.

3.7.2 *Reasoning about Unbounded Loops: Loop Invariants*

Loops with a small bound on the number of iterations can be handled by loop unwinding (see Section 3.6.4). If, however, there is no bound that is known a priori or if that bound is too high, then unwinding does not work. In that case, a loop-invariant rule has to be used.

A loop invariant is a formula describing an overapproximation of all states reachable by repeated execution of a loop's body while the loop condition is true. Using a loop invariant essentially is an inductive argument, proving that the invariant holds for any number of loop iterations—and, thus, still holds when the loop terminates.

Loop invariant rules are probably the most involved and complex rules of the KeY system's JavaDL calculus. This complexity results from the inductive structure of the argument but also from the features of Java loops, which include the possibility of side effects and abrupt termination in loop conditions and loop bodies.

In this section, we present basic versions of the loop invariant rules; in particular, loop termination and using the loop's modifier set for framing is not considered in the following. Enhanced loop invariant rules are presented in Chapter 9. Moreover, Section 16.3 provides a more intuitive introduction to formal verification of while loops with invariants and contains a tutorial on systematic development of loop invariants.

Also, automatic invariant generation is a hot research topic—a particular approach to this challenge is described in Section 6.3.

The loop invariant rule has been cross-verified against another language framework for an earlier version of JavaDL [Widmann, 2006].

3.7.2.1 Loop Specifications

A loop specification is similar to a method contract in that it formalizes an abstraction of the relationship between the state before a method or loop is executed and the state when the method or loop body, respectively, terminates. In that sense, a loop invariant is both the pre- and the postcondition of the loop body. Yet, in most cases, a useful loop invariant is more difficult to find than a method contract because it relates the initial state with the states after *every* loop iteration.

Like method contracts, loop specifications contain two additional elements: (a) a modifier set describing which parts of the state the loop body can modify and (b) a termination witness providing an argument for the loop's termination. As said above, the basic rules presented in this chapter do not make use of this additional information. Extended rules considering modifier sets and termination are presented in Chapter 9.

Definition 3.23. A *loop specification* is a tuple

$$(inv, mod, term)$$

that consists of

- a loop invariant $inv \in$ DLFml,
- a modifier set $mod \in \text{Trm}_{LocSet} \cup \{\text{STRICTLYNOTHING}\}$.
- a termination witness $term \in \text{Trm}_{Any} \cup \{\text{PARTIAL}\}$.

Specification components may make use of special program variables which allow them to refer to the execution context:

- all local variables that are defined in the context of the loop,
- $\text{self} : C$ for references to the receiver object of the current method frame (not available if that frame belongs to a static method),
- $\text{heap} : Heap$ referring to the heap in the state after the current iteration,
- $\text{heap}^{pre} : Heap$ referring to the heap in the initial state of the immediately enclosing method frame.

3.7.2.2 Basic Version of the Loop Invariant Rule

The first basic loop invariant rule we consider makes two assumptions: It is only applicable if (1) the loop guard is a simple expression se, i.e., the loop condition cannot have side effects and cannot terminate abruptly. And (2) the loop body p_{norm} must be guaranteed to always terminate normally, i.e.,

1. execution of p_{norm} does not raise an exception, and
2. p_{norm} does not contain break, continue, return statements.

The rule takes the form shown in Figure 3.8.

$$\text{simpleInv} \; \frac{\begin{array}{l} \Longrightarrow inv \\ \Longrightarrow \mathscr{A}_{heap}\mathscr{A}_{local}\big((inv \wedge se \doteq TRUE) \;\rightarrow\; [p_{norm}]inv\big) \\ \Longrightarrow \mathscr{A}_{heap}\mathscr{A}_{local}\big((inv \wedge se \doteq FALSE) \;\rightarrow\; [\pi\,\omega]\varphi\big) \end{array}}{\Longrightarrow [\pi\,\texttt{while(se)} \; \{\; p_{norm}\; \}\,\omega]\varphi}$$

where
- se is a simple expression and p_{norm} cannot terminate abruptly;
- $(inv, mod, term)$ is a loop specification for the loop to which the rule is applied;
- $\mathscr{A}_{heap} = \{\texttt{heap} := c_h\}$ anonymizes the heap; c_h:$Heap$ is a fresh constant;
- $\mathscr{A}_{local} = \{l_1 := c_1 \,\|\, \cdots \,\|\, l_n := c_n\}$ anonymizes all local variables $l_1, \ldots, l_n$ that are the target of an assignment (left-hand side of an assignment statement) in p_{norm}; each c_i is a fresh constant of the same type as l_i.

Figure 3.8 Basic loop invariant rule

When a method contract is used for verification, the validity of the contract is not part of the premisses of the contract rule but a separate proof obligation. In contrast to that, the loop invariant rule combines both aspects in its three premisses.

- *Base case:* The first premiss is the base case of the inductive argument. One has to show that the invariant is satisfied whenever the loop is reached.

- *Step case:* The second premiss is the inductive step. One has to show that, if the invariant holds before execution of the loop body, then it still holds afterwards.[6]
- *Use case:* The third premiss uses the inductive argument and continues the symbolic execution for the code $\pi\ \omega$ following the loop but now with the knowledge that the invariant holds.

Note that, in the step case, one can assume the loop condition *se* to be *TRUE* (i.e., the loop is iterated once more). In the use case, on the other hand, one can assume that the loop condition *se* is *FALSE* (i.e., the loop has terminated).

The combination $\mathscr{A}_{heap}\mathscr{A}_{local}$ is called the *anonymizing update application* of the loop rule. It needs to be added to the second and the third premiss of the rule, which refer to the state after an unknown number of loop iterations. Its application ensures that only the knowledge encoded in *inv* can be used to reason about the heap locations and the local variables changed by the loop. Instead, of using the update application $\mathscr{A}_{heap}$ that anonymizes all heap locations, one can use a more precise update $\mathscr{A}_{mod}$ that only anonymizes the locations in *mod* (see the previous section on method contracts and Section 9.4.1 for more information). This requires, however, the additional proof that the loop body does indeed not modify any other locations than those in *mod*.

3.7.2.3 Loop Conditions with Side-effects

In Java, loop conditions may have side effects. For example, the loop condition in

```
while(a[i++] > 0) { ... }
```

has a side effect on the local variable i.

In Figure 3.9, we present a loop invariant rule that allows the loop condition to be a nonsimple expression *nse*, i.e., to have side effects. The idea is to capture the value of *nse* in a fresh Boolean program variable b. To account for the effects of the condition, its evaluation is repeated right before the loop body.

While the rule sideEffectInv takes into account any state changing side effects in *nse*, it does not yet capture the exceptions that it might throw. For example, the possibility that the loop condition a[i++] in the above example can throw an ArrayIndexOutOfBoundsException is not considered.

3.7.2.4 Loops with Abrupt Termination

In the loop invariant rules shown above (simpleInv and sideEffectInv), the loop body is executed outside its usual context $\pi\ \omega$. Thus, a continue or a break statement does not make sense. Likewise, a return statement is not sensible since it is not

---

[6] Note that the loop body in the step case is not enclosed in the execution context $\pi\ \omega$. Nevertheless, the innermost method frame that is part of π has to be added implicitly so that method invocations within p_{norm} can be resolved correctly.

$$\Longrightarrow inv$$
$$\Longrightarrow \mathscr{A}_{heap}\mathscr{A}_{local}\big((inv \wedge [\mathsf{b}=nse;]\mathsf{b} \doteq TRUE) \rightarrow [\mathsf{b}=nse; p_{norm}]inv\big)$$
$$\Longrightarrow \mathscr{A}_{heap}\mathscr{A}_{local}\big((inv \wedge [\mathsf{b}=nse;]\mathsf{b} \doteq FALSE) \rightarrow [\pi\,\mathsf{b}=nse;\, \omega]\varphi\big)$$

sideEffectInv $\dfrac{}{\Longrightarrow [\pi\,\mathtt{while}(nse)\ \{\ p_{norm}\ \}\,\omega]\varphi}$

where

- p_{norm} and nse cannot terminate abruptly;
- $(inv, mod, term)$ is a loop specification for the loop to which the rule is applied;
- $\mathscr{A}_{heap} = \{\mathtt{heap} := c_h\}$ anonymizes the heap; $c_h{:}Heap$ is a fresh constant;
- $\mathscr{A}_{local} = \{l_1 := c_1 \,\|\, \cdots \,\|\, l_n := c_n\}$ anonymizes all local variables $l_1, \ldots, l_n$ that are the target of an assignment (left-hand side of an assignment statement) in p_{norm} or in nse; each c_i is a fresh constant of the same type as l_i;
- b is a fresh Boolean variable.

Figure 3.9 Invariant rule for loops with side effects in the loop condition

embedded into the original method frames, and exceptions do not occur within the right `try-catch-finally` block.

In order to be able to deal with loop bodies in isolation, we transform them in such a way that abnormal termination is turned into normal termination in which certain flags are set signaling the abnormal termination. We will not go into details of this transformation here, but illustrate it using one synthetic example loop, which exhibits all possible reasons for abnormal termination:

```
while(x >= 0) {
    if(x == 0) break;
    if(x == 1) return 42;
    if(x == 2) continue;
    if(x == 3) throw e;
    if(x == 4) x = -1;
}
```

We use the Boolean variables BREAK and RETURN, and a variable EXCEPTION of type `Throwable` to store and signal the termination state of the loop body. In the example, the original loop body is translated into the block

```
loopBody: {
  try {
    BREAK=false; RETURN=false; EXCEPTION=null;
    if(x == 0) { BREAK=true; break loopBody; }
    if(x == 1) { res=42; RETURN=true; break loopBody; }
    if(x == 2) { break loopBody; }
    if(x == 3) { throw e; }
    if(x == 4) { x = -1; }
  } catch(Throwable e) {
    EXCEPTION = e;
  }
}
```

The result of the transformation is guaranteed to terminate normally, with the original termination reason caught in the Boolean flags.

In general, this transformation can be more involved if it has to deal with nested labeled blocks and loops. It then resembles the translation outlined in Section 3.6.4 for loop unwinding.

Using the above transformation, the loop invariant rules that can handle both abrupt termination and side effects in the loop condition takes the form shown in Figure 3.10.

In the second premiss of this rule (subformula *post*), if a loop is left via abnormal termination rather than by falsifying the loop condition, the loop invariant does not need be reestablished but the execution of the program in its original context $\pi\ \omega$ is resumed—retriggering an exception or return statement if they were observed in the loop body. The rationale behind this is that loop invariants are supposed to hold whenever the loop is potentially reentered, which is not the case if a return, throw, or break statement has been executed. If, however, a continue statement is executed in the loop body p, the transformation b=nse; p terminates normally and the invariant has to hold before the next loop iteration is started (as in the NORMAL case).

In this chapter, we have not presented a loop invariant rule that handles loops in $\langle\cdot\rangle$-modalities and, thus, needs to guarantee program termination; this issue is addressed in Section 9.4.2. One aspect shall be mentioned here nonetheless: When termination matters, the modality $\langle\cdot\rangle$ is used instead of $[\cdot]$. However, the box modality $[b=nse]$, which occurs on the left-hand side of the second and the third premiss in rules sideEffectInv (Figure 3.9) and abruptTermInv (Figure 3.10), must remain a box modality. If it were to be changed into a diamond modality, then a nonterminating loop condition would make these two premisses of the loop invariant rules trivially valid; the calculus would be unsound.

$$\begin{aligned}
&\Longrightarrow inv\\
&\Longrightarrow \mathscr{A}_{heap}\mathscr{A}_{local}\big((inv \wedge [\mathtt{b}{=}nse;]\mathtt{b} \doteq \mathit{TRUE}) \;\rightarrow\; [\widehat{\mathtt{b}{=}nse};\,p]post\big)\\
&\Longrightarrow \mathscr{A}_{heap}\mathscr{A}_{local}\big((inv \wedge [\mathtt{b}{=}nse;]\mathtt{b} \doteq \mathit{FALSE}) \;\rightarrow\; [\pi\ \mathtt{b}{=}nse;\ \omega]\varphi\big)
\end{aligned}$$

abruptTermInv $\dfrac{}{\Longrightarrow [\pi\ \mathtt{while}(nse)\ \{\ p\ \}\ \omega]\varphi}$

where
- $(inv, mod, term)$ is a loop specification for the loop to which the rule is applied;
- $\mathscr{A}_{heap} = \{\mathtt{heap} := c_h\}$ anonymizes the heap; $c_h{:}Heap$ is a fresh constant;
- $\mathscr{A}_{local} = \{l_1 := c_1 \parallel \cdots \parallel l_n := c_n\}$ anonymizes all local variables $l_1, \ldots, l_n$ that are the target of an assignment (left-hand side of an assignment statement) in p_{norm} or in nse; each c_i is a fresh constant of the same type as l_i;
- $\mathtt{b}$ is a fresh Boolean variable;
- $\widehat{\mathtt{b}{=}nse};\,p$ is the result of transforming $\mathtt{b}{=}nse;\,p$ as described above to handle abrupt termination;
- $post$ is the formula

$$\begin{aligned}
&(\mathrm{EXCEPTION} \neq null \rightarrow [\pi\ \mathtt{throw}\ \mathrm{EXCEPTION};\ \omega]\varphi)\\
\wedge\ &(\mathrm{BREAK} \doteq \mathit{TRUE} \rightarrow \quad [\pi\ \omega]\varphi)\\
\wedge\ &(\mathrm{RETURN} \doteq \mathit{TRUE} \rightarrow \quad [\pi\ \mathtt{return}\ \mathtt{res};\ \omega]\varphi)\\
\wedge\ &(\mathrm{NORMAL} \rightarrow \qquad\quad inv)
\end{aligned}$$

with

$$\begin{aligned}
\mathrm{NORMAL} \equiv\ &\mathrm{BREAK} \doteq \mathit{FALSE}\ \wedge\\
&\mathrm{RETURN} \doteq \mathit{FALSE}\ \wedge\\
&\mathrm{EXCEPTION} \doteq null
\end{aligned}$$

Figure 3.10 Invariant rule for loops with abrupt termination

Chapter 4
Proof Search with Taclets

Philipp Rümmer and Mattias Ulbrich

4.1 Introduction

The primary means of reasoning in a logic are *calculi*, collections of purely syntactic operations that allow us to determine whether a given formula is valid. Two such calculi are defined in Chapter 2 and 3 for first-order predicate logic and for dynamic logic (DL). Having such calculi at hand enables us, in principle, to create proofs of complex conjectures, using pen and paper, but it is obvious that we need computer support for realistic applications. Such a mechanized *proof assistant* primarily helps us in two respects: 1. The assistant ensures that rules are applied correctly, e.g., that rules can only be applied if their side-conditions are not violated, and 2. the assistant can provide guidance for selecting the right rules. Whereas the first point is a necessity for making calculi and proofs meaningful, the second item covers a whole spectrum from simple analyses to determine which rules are applicable in a certain situation to the complete automation that is possible for many first-order problems.

Creating a proof assistant requires formalizing the rules that the implemented calculus consists of. In our setting—in particular looking at calculi for dynamic logic—such a formalization is subject to a number of requirements:

- JavaDL has a complex syntax (subsuming the actual Java language) and a large number of rules: first-order rules, rules for the reduction of programs and rules that belong to theories like integer arithmetic. Besides that, in many situations it is necessary to introduce derived rules (*lemmas*) that are more convenient or that are tailored to a particular complex proof. This motivates the need for a language in which new rules can easily be written, rather than hard-coding rules as it is done in high-performance automated provers (for first-order logic). It is also necessary to ensure the soundness of lemmas, i.e., we need a mechanized way to reason about the soundness of rules.
- Because complete automation is impossible for most aspects of program verification, the formalization has to support interactive theorem proving. KeY provides a graphical user interface (GUI) that makes most rules applicable only using mouse clicks and drag and drop. This puts a limit on the complexity that a single

© Springer International Publishing AG 2016
W. Ahrendt et al. (Eds.): Deductive Software Verification, LNCS 10001, pp. 107–147, 2016
DOI: 10.1007/978-3-319-49812-6_4

rule should have for keeping the required user interaction clear and simple, and it requires that rules also contain "pragmatic" information that describes how the rules are supposed to be applied. Accounts on the user interface in KeY are Chapter 15 and [Giese, 2004].

- The formalization also has to enable the automation of as many proof tasks as possible. This covers the simplification of formulas and proof goals, the symbolic execution of programs (which usually does not require user interaction) as well as automated proof or decision procedures for simpler fragments of the logic and for theories. The approach followed in KeY is to have global *strategies* that give priorities to the different applicable rules and automatically apply the rule that is considered most suitable. This concept is powerful enough to implement proof procedures for first-order logic and to handle theories like linear integer arithmetic or polynomial rings mostly automatically.

This chapter is devoted to the formalism called *taclets* that is used in KeY to meet these requirements. The concept of taclets provides a notation for rules of sequent calculi, which has an expressiveness comparable to the "textbook-notation" that is used in Chapters 2 and 3, while being more formal. Compared to textbook-notation, taclets inherently limit the degrees of freedom (nondeterminism) that a rule can have, which is important to clarify user interaction. Furthermore, an *application mechanism*—the semantics of taclets—is provided that describes when taclets can be applied and what the effect of an application is.

Historically, taclets have first been devised by Habermalz [2000b,a] under the name "Schematic Theory Specific Rules," with the main purpose of capturing the axioms of theories and algebraic specifications as rules. The language is general enough, however, to also cover all rules of a first-order sequent calculus and most rules of calculi for dynamic logic. The development of taclets as a way to build interactive provers was influenced to a large degree by the theorem prover InterACT [Geisler et al., 1996], but also has strong roots in more traditional methods like tactics and derived rules that are commonly used for higher-order logics (examples for such systems are Isabelle/HOL, see [Nipkow et al., 2002], Coq, see [Dowek et al., 1993], or PVS, see [Owre et al., 1996]). Compared to tactics, the expressiveness of taclets is very limited, for the reasons mentioned above. A further difference is that taclets do not (explicitly) build on a small and fixed set of primitive rules, as tactics do in (foundational) higher-order frameworks like Isabelle. It nevertheless is a good idea to add comments in files containing taclets that signal which are meant to be axioms and which are derived rules that require a proof from the axioms. This has, e.g., been consistently done for the data type of finite sequences, see Section 5.2.

4.1.1 Purpose and Organization of this Chapter

The purpose of this chapter is twofold: on the one hand, it provides new KeY users an introduction to the way calculus rules are implemented in the KeY system; on the other hand, it is a reference manual of the taclet formalism, targeting more experienced users as well as developers. The main sections of the chapter are:

- A *taclet tutorial* (Section 4.2): a high-level overview of the most important features provided by the taclet language, and the methodology how taclets are used for introducing new theories.
- *The taclet reference manual* (Section 4.3): a detailed description of the taclet language, and its semantics.
- *Reasoning about the soundness of taclets* (Section 4.4): techniques to mechanically prove the soundness of taclets, by deriving a formula representation of the logical content of a taclet.

4.2 A Taclet Tutorial

The next pages give a tour through the taclet language and illustrate the most important taclet features by means of a case study. Taclets are used in the KeY system for multiple purposes: for the definition of first-order calculus rules, for the rules of the JavaDL calculus, to introduce data types and decision procedures, and to give users the possibility to define and reason about new logical theories. Users typically encounter taclets in the context of the last scenario, which is why our tutorial will describe the introduction of a new theory in KeY: we consider a simplified version of a theory of *lists,* and refer the reader to a more complete and practical version of *finite sequences* in Chapter 5 .

Theories are introduced by declaring a vocabulary of *types* and (interpreted) *functions,* a set of basic *axioms* defining the semantics of the theory, as well as a set of *derived rules* that are suitable for the construction of actual proofs. Both axioms and derived rules are formulated as taclets in KeY, with the difference that axioms are assumed and cannot be proven to be correct, while derived rules logically follow from the axioms.

4.2.1 A Basic Theory of Lists

We will work with a simple data structure of lists resembling the data type found in Lisp and functional programming languages. The core theory, in the following sections denoted by T_{List}, is defined through a type *List*; elements of the data type are generated by two *constructor* symbols, *nil* and *cons*, representing the empty list and extension of a list by adding a new head element respectively. For simplicity we consider only elements of type *int* here. The theory of lists is in no way affected by the type of its elements.

$$nil : List$$

$$cons : int \times List \to List$$

For instance, the sequence $\langle 3, 5, -2 \rangle$ of integers will be represented through the term $cons(3, cons(5, cons(-2, nil)))$.

The symbols *nil* and *cons* are the only constructors of lists, and lists furthermore represent a *free algebraic data type,* which implies that:

- every list can be represented as a term only consisting of *nil* and *cons*, and possibly functions needed to construct the list elements (the first argument of *cons*);
- the representation of a list using *nil* and *cons* is *unique* assuming a unique representation of the integers.

Those properties are typically expressed with the help of *axioms*, which eliminate all interpretations of the constructor symbols that are inconsistent with the two properties. Axioms are formulas that are *assumed* to hold in all considered interpretations of the theory symbols; there is no way to prove that axioms are correct, since they are independent assumptions and cannot be derived from any other rules or axioms of the logic. The *consistency* of the axioms can be shown by defining a model in which all axioms are true: one such model is obtained by considering the set of ground terms over the constructors *nil* and *cons* and a unique representation of all integers as universe, and interpreting *nil* and *cons* and all integer ground terms as themselves. More details are given in Chapter 5 on theories. For our core theory of lists, we need three axioms:

$$\left(\phi[l/nil] \;\wedge\; \forall List\; l;\; \forall int\; a;\; \left(\phi \to \phi[l/cons(a,l)] \right) \right) \;\to\; \forall List\; l;\; \phi \qquad (4.1)$$

$$\forall List\; l;\; \forall int\; a;\; \left(nil \neq cons(a,l) \right) \qquad (4.2)$$

$$\forall List\; l_1, l_2;\; \forall int\; a_1, a_2;\; \left(cons(a_1, l_1) \doteq cons(a_2, l_2) \;\to\; a_1 \doteq a_2 \wedge l_1 \doteq l_2 \right) \qquad (4.3)$$

The axiom (4.1) reflects the assumption that any element of the list data type can be constructed using the symbols *nil* and *cons*. It can be shown that this assumption cannot precisely be captured using an axiom in first-order logic, it can only be approximated using weaker formulas, for instance using the induction axiom (4.1) shown here. The formula represents an *axiom schema,* since it is formulated with the help of a schematic variable ϕ that stands for an *arbitrary* formula that has to be chosen when using the axiom in a proof; this formula ϕ will usually contain the free variable l of type *List*.

In other words, (4.1) should be read as an infinite set of first-order formulas, one for each possible choice of the symbol ϕ. The axiom schema introduces an induction principle for lists, resembling the one for natural numbers (nonnegative integers) defined in Section 2.4.2: if it is possible to show that some formula ϕ holds for the empty list $l = nil$ (denoted by the substitution $[l/nil]$ replacing every occurrence of l with *nil*), and that ϕ implies that also $\phi[l/cons(a,l)]$ holds for any a, then it can be concluded that ϕ holds *for all* lists l.

```
—— Taclet ————————————————————————————————————————————
\sorts {
   List;
}

\functions {
   \unique List nil;
   \unique List cons(any, List);
}

\axioms {
   list_induction {
      \schemaVar \formula phi;
      \schemaVar \variable List lv;
      \schemaVar \variable any  av;

      \find( ==> \forall lv; phi )
      \varcond(\notFreeIn(av, phi))

      \replacewith( ==> {\subst lv; nil} phi
                    & \forall lv; \forall av;
                          (phi -> {\subst lv; cons(av, lv)}phi) )
   };
}
                                                                  Taclet ——
```

Figure 4.1 Vocabulary and induction axiom for a simplified theory of lists

Induction axioms are relevant for all theories that are assumed to be generated by some set of function symbols, in the sense that all elements can be written as terms over this set of functions. In particular, every algebraic data type (an example of which are lists) comes with a predefined induction axiom similar to (4.1).

The axioms (4.2) and (4.3) represent uniqueness of the representation of a list using *nil* and *cons*. (4.2) expresses that the ranges of *nil* and *cons* do not overlap, whereas (4.3) states that *cons* is an injective function; in combination, the axioms imply that two lists are equal only if they contain the same number of elements, and the elements coincide.

4.2.2 The List Theory in Concrete Syntax

We now explain how the theory T_{List} of lists (as introduced so far) can be modeled in the concrete syntax of the KeY system. We first use declarations and taclets in order to model the vocabulary and axioms of the theory in a direct way, and then describe how further rules can be derived to make the theory more convenient to work with in practice. Derived rules are also essential for automating the construction of proofs.

The taclet syntax is explained in Section 4.3.1, and a complete description of the KeY syntax is given in Appendix B.

Figure 4.1 shows the *List* type, the function symbols *nil* and *cons*, as well as the induction axiom (4.1) in taclet syntax. The \sorts block is used to declare the types of the theory, whereas \functions contains the declaration of available function symbols and their signature (the result type and the type of arguments), in syntax inspired by Java. The declarations and definitions would normally be placed in the beginning of a KeY problem file, and can then be used for formulating and proving formulas involving T_{List}; the concrete steps to do this are described in Chapter 15, and later chapters of the book.

Figure 4.1 also captures the two axioms (4.2)–(4.3) of lists. KeY provides a built-in keyword for specifying the uniqueness of functions, so that the axioms (4.2) and (4.3) do not have to be written by hand; it suffices to add the flag \unique in the function declarations. A function declared to be \unique is injective, and the values of two distinct \unique functions are never equal. The \unique flag implies that KeY will internally generate (and automatically apply) rules that capture those assumptions.

The \rules block contains the taclet list_induction representing the induction axiom (4.1). Operationally, the rule list_induction is applied to an existing formula $\forall List\ l;\ \phi$, and replaces this formula with $\phi[l/nil]\ \wedge\ \forall List\ l;\ \forall int\ a;\ (\phi \rightarrow \phi[l/cons(a,l)])$:

$$\text{list\_induction}\ \ \frac{\Gamma \Longrightarrow \phi[l/nil] \wedge \forall List\ l;\ \forall int\ a;\ (\phi \rightarrow \phi[l/cons(a,l)]),\Delta}{\Gamma \Longrightarrow \forall List\ l;\ \phi,\Delta}$$

In order to specify this transformation, the taclet uses a number of features of the taclet language, which are explained in the following paragraphs.

- \find defines a pattern that must occur in the sequent to which the taclet is supposed to be applied. In this taclet, the pattern ==> \forall lv; phi matches on quantified list formulas in the succedent of a sequent; accordingly, list_induction can be applied whenever such a quantified formula turns up in a proof goal. The expression matched by \find is called the *focus* of a taclet application.

- \replacewith tells how the focus of the taclet application will be altered: a new proof goal is created from the previous one by replacing the expression matched in the \find part with the expression in the \replacewith part.

For list_induction, the quantified list formula in the succedent will be replaced by the somewhat complicated expression after the arrow ==>; upon closer inspection, it can be seen that the expression indeed represents the conjunction $\phi[l/nil]\ \wedge\ \forall List\ l;\ \forall int\ a;\ (\phi \rightarrow \phi[l/cons(a,l)])$. The operator {\subst x; t} expresses substitution of a variable x with a term t.

Note 4.1. The keywords of the taclet language reflect the direction in which sequent calculus proofs are constructed: we start with a formula that is supposed to be proven and create a tree upwards by *analyzing* the formula and taking it apart. Taclets describe expansion steps (or, as a border case, closure steps), and by the *application* of a taclet we mean the process of adding new nodes to a leaf of a proof tree following this description.

The taclet illustrates a further important feature of the taclet language, namely the use of *schema variables* in order to create flexible rules that can be instantiated in many concrete ways. The taclet list_induction contains three such schema variables, phi, lv, and av. Every schema variable is of a certain *kind,* defining which expressions the variable can stand for (a precise definition is given in Section 4.3.2). In our example, phi represents an arbitrary formula, while lv represents bound variables of type *List,* and av bound variables of type *int.* The possible valuations of schema variables are controlled with the help of *variable conditions,* and the \varcond clause in list_induction:

- \varcond specifies conditions that have to hold for admissible instantiations of the schema variables of a taclet. The condition \notFreeIn in list_induction, in particular, expresses that the bound variable av must not occur as a free variable in the formula phi.

Note that some, but not all occurrences of the schema variable phi in the rule list_induction are in the scope of a quantifier binding av. Without the variable condition \notFreeIn(av, phi) it would be ambiguous whether av is allowed to occur in phi or not.

Example 4.2. We illustrate how the rule list_induction can be used to prove a theorem in our theory T_{List}, the fact that every list is constructed using either *nil* or *cons*:

$$\forall List\ l;\ \left(l \doteq nil \vee \exists List\ m, int\ b;\ l \doteq cons(b,m)\right) \qquad (4.4)$$

For this, we apply the sequent calculus notation introduced in Section 2.2.2. This sentence already has the shape of the formula \forall lv; phi in the \find part of the taclet list_induction, so that the taclet can directly be applied; this has been done in step $(*)$ in the proof in Figure 4.2. It should be noted, however, that inductive proofs often require appropriate *strengthening* of the formula to be proven: in order to show that $\forall x; \phi$ is a theorem, first a formula that implies $\forall x; \psi$ is introduced using the cut rule, and proven by means of induction. Luckily, no such strengthening is necessary in the example at hand.

When applying list_induction at $(*)$, all schema variables occurring in the taclet have to be instantiated with concrete syntactic objects: the variable lv is mapped to the bound variable l, the variable av to the (fresh) variable a, and the formula variable phi to the body $l \doteq nil \vee \exists List\ m, int\ b;\ l \doteq cons(b,m)$. When constructing the proof in the KeY system, the tool is able to determine those instantiations automatically, it is only necessary to tell KeY to apply list_induction to the formula (4.4) in the antecedent of the proof goal.

The rest of the proof can be constructed in a comparatively straightforward way (and can in fact be found automatically by KeY). At $(**)$, it can be observed that $nil \doteq nil$ holds, so that the whole conjunct $nil \doteq nil \vee \exists List\ m, int\ a;\ nil \doteq cons(a,m)$ can be reduced to *true* and eliminated. Finally, at $(***)$, we can observe that the

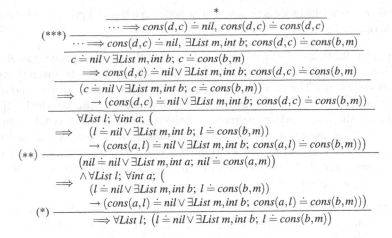

Figure 4.2 Inductive example proof

existentially quantified variables m, b can be instantiated with the terms c and d, respectively, concluding the proof.

4.2.3 Definitional Extension of the List Theory

At this point we have a fully defined, albeit very minimalist theory T_{List} of lists available, which could in principle be used to state and prove conjectures about lists in KeY, or to reason about programs operating on lists or sequences. Most practical applications require a richer set of operations on lists, however; a general strategy to introduce such operations, without putting the consistency of the theory at risk, is known as *definitional extension*, and proceeds by introducing further functions or predicates over lists, and defining their intended meaning through recursive axioms according to the list constructors. Again, for more details we refer to the dedicated Chapter 5 on theories.

In the scope of our taclet tutorial, we consider two defined functions for computing *length* and *concatenation* of lists; the resulting extension of T_{List} will be denoted by T_{List}^{LA}, and include the following additional function symbols:

$$length : List \rightarrow Int$$
$$append : List \times List \rightarrow List$$

The semantics of the functions can be formulated by simple recursion over one of the *List* arguments of each function, in mathematical notation leading to equations as follows:

—— Taclet ——————————————————————————

```
\functions {
    int length(List);
    List append(List, List);
}

\axioms {
    length_nil {
        length(nil) = 0
    };

    length_cons {
        \forall List l; \forall any a; length(cons(a, l)) = 1 + length(l)
    };

    append_nil {
        \schemaVar \term List l;
        \find( append(nil, l) )
        \replacewith( l )
    };

    append_cons {
        \schemaVar \term any a;
        \schemaVar \term List l1;
        \schemaVar \term List l2;
        \find( append(cons(a, l1), l2) )
        \replacewith( cons(a, append(l1, l2)) )
    };
}
```

—————————————————————————————————— Taclet ——

Figure 4.3 Vocabulary and axioms for defined list functions

$$length(l) = \begin{cases} 0 & \text{if } l = nil \\ length(l') + 1 & \text{if } l = cons(a, l') \end{cases} \tag{4.5}$$

$$append(l_1, l_2) = \begin{cases} l_2 & \text{if } l_1 = nil \\ cons(a, append(l'_1, l_2)) & \text{if } l_1 = cons(a, l'_1) \end{cases} \tag{4.6}$$

The corresponding declarations and axioms in KeY syntax are shown in Figure 4.3. The definitions can again be put in a KeY problem file, normally right after the definitions from Figure 4.1, and extend the basic list theory with the two additional functions *length* and *append* (as a technical detail, it is indeed necessary that the new axioms appear textually *after* the declarations of the constructors *nil* and *cons* in the KeY file, since KeY adopts a single-pass parsing approach).

Figure 4.3 illustrates that axioms can be written in two different styles. The first two axioms length_nil and length_cons are formulated as (quantified) formulas, and closely capture the recursive equation (4.5). When applying either rule in a proof, the

KeY prover will add the given formula to the antecedent of a proof goal; afterwards, quantifiers in the formula can be eliminated by instantiating with ground terms occurring in the goal, and the resulting equation can be used for equational rewriting. An example showing the rules is the following proof; after application of length_nil and length_cons, the proof can be closed using equational and arithmetic reasoning (not shown here):

$$
\text{length\_nil} \cfrac{
\text{length\_cons} \cfrac{
\cfrac{
\cfrac{*}{
length(cons(1,nil)) \doteq 1 + length(nil), length(nil) = 0 \implies length(cons(1,nil)) \doteq 1
}
}{
length(cons(1,nil)) \doteq 1 + length(nil) \implies length(cons(1,nil)) \doteq 1
}
}{
\forall List\ l.\ \forall int\ a.\ length(cons(a,l)) \doteq 1 + length(l) \implies length(cons(1,nil)) \doteq 1
}
}{
\implies length(cons(1,nil)) \doteq 1
}
$$

In contrast, the axioms append_nil and append_cons are formulated in a similar operational style as the induction axiom in Figure 4.1; the main difference to the induction axiom is the fact that \find expressions in Figure 4.3 are no longer *sequents* but *terms* (they do not contain an arrow ==>). Rules of this form are called *rewriting taclets* in the KeY terminology, and represent transformations that modify subexpressions (either a formula or a term) of arbitrary formulas in a proof, both in the antecedent and succedent, leaving the surrounding formula unchanged. For instance, the rule append_nil can be used to rewrite any term $append(nil, l)$ to the simpler expression l, and rule append_cons is applicable to any expression of the form $append(cons(a, l_1), l_2)$. An example proof is:

$$
\text{append\_nil} \cfrac{
\text{append\_cons} \cfrac{
\cfrac{
\cfrac{*}{
\implies cons(a,l) \doteq cons(a,l)
}
}{
\implies cons(a, append(nil, l)) \doteq cons(a,l)
}
}{
\implies append(cons(a, nil), l) \doteq cons(a,l)
}
}{}
$$

Compared to the declarative style of length_nil and length_cons, the taclets append_nil and append_cons have both advantages and disadvantages: in particular, rewriting taclets are usually a lot more convenient to apply when constructing proofs interactively, since expressions can be simplified (or "evaluated") with only a few mouse clicks, in contrast to the multiple rule applications needed when using axiom length_nil. In addition, the rewriting taclet append_nil also captures the direction in which the corresponding equation append(nil, 1) = 1 should be applied, namely rewriting the more complicated left-hand side to the simpler right-hand side, and can therefore also be applied automatically by the KeY system (see Section 4.3.1.10).

On the other hand, since the rules length_nil and length_cons are closer to the recursive mathematical formulation, the introduction of axioms in this style tends to be less error-prone. In the exceedingly rare case that a user wants to rewrite l to append(nil, l) when constructing a proof, append_nil is actually less practical than the axiom length_nil, since the simple equation introduced by the latter rule can be applied in both directions. Rewriting from right to left is still possible even with append_nil, however, by means of introducing a *cut* in the proof.

4.2.4 Derivation of Lemmas

An important feature of the taclet language, and of the KeY prover, is the ability to easily add further *derived* rules to a theory. Such rules represent lemmas that logically follow from the theory axioms, and can help structure proofs because the lemmas can be proven once and for all, and later be applied repeatedly for proving theorems. The number of derived rules often exceeds the number of axioms of a theory by far: to reduce the risk of inconsistencies, the set of axioms is usually kept minimalist, whereas any number of derived rules can be added for reasons of convenience. The soundness of derived rules can be verified using the same calculus as for proving theorems, by translating taclets to *meaning formulas* that capture the logical content of a rule (see Section 4.4).

A small selection of derived rules for the theory T_{List}^{LA} is shown in Figure 4.4; many more relevant lemmas exist. The first difference to earlier taclets is the fact that rules are now formulated within a \rules block, and no longer as \axioms, to indicate that the rules are lemmas.[1] The definitions from Figure 4.4 can again be put in a KeY problem file, either after the contents of Figures 4.1 and 4.3, or in a separate file that KeY users can load on demand. In the latter case, the KeY system will request that the soundness of the newly introduced rules is immediately justified by showing that their meaning formula is valid (Section 4.4).

The rewriting rules length_nil_rw and length_cons_rw in Figure 4.4 are operational versions of the axioms length_nil and length_cons, and correspond to the way the axioms append_nil and append_cons are written. Since rewriting rules are usually more convenient than axioms in the form of formulas, as illustrated by the examples in the previous section, length_nil_rw and length_cons_rw are useful derived rules; their correctness is directly implied by the theory axioms, of course.

The rule append_nil_right captures the fact that *nil* is also a right-neutral element for concatenation *append*, and complements the axiom append_nil. The soundness of append_nil_right has to be shown by induction over the first argument of *append*, with the help of the axiom list_induction. Similarly, length_append expresses that *length* distributes over concatenation, and can be proven correct by induction over the first argument of *append*. Both append_nil_right and length_append are rules that are frequently needed when proving theorems over lists, and present in every self-respecting list theory.

---

[1] In built-in rules of the KeY system, moreover the annotation \lemma can be added in front of a rule to indicate that a correctness proof has been conducted; the proof will then be checked automatically during regression testing.

```
────── Taclet ───────────────────────────────────────────────
\rules {
  length_nil_rw {
      \find( length(nil) )
      \replacewith( 0 )
  };

  length_cons_rw {
      \schemaVar \term any a;
      \schemaVar \term List l;
      \find( length(cons(a, l)) )
      \replacewith( 1 + length(l) )
  };

  append_nil_right {
      \schemaVar \term List l;
      \find( append(l, nil) )
      \replacewith( l )
  };

  length_append {
      \schemaVar \term List l1, l2;
      \find( length(append(l1, l2)) )
      \replacewith( length(l1) + length(l2) )
  };

  length_cons_assume {
      \schemaVar \term List l, l1;
      \schemaVar \term any  a;
      \assumes( l = cons(a, l1) ==> )
      \find( length(l) ) \sameUpdateLevel
      \replacewith( 1 + length(l1) )
  };

  list_ctor_split {
      \schemaVar \term        List l;
      \schemaVar \skolemTerm List skl;
      \schemaVar \skolemTerm any  ska;
      \find( l ) \sameUpdateLevel
      \varcond( \new(ska, \dependingOn(l)), \new(skl, \dependingOn(l)) )
      \replacewith( nil )                    \add( l = nil ==> );
      \replacewith( cons(ska, skl) ) \add( l = cons(ska, skl) ==> )
  };
}
─────────────────────────────────────────────────── Taclet ──
```

Figure 4.4 Derived taclets for the list theory T^{IA}_{List}

The rules length_cons_assume and list_ctor_split are more sophisticated, and show several further features of the taclet language. The rule length_cons_assume is similar to length_cons_rw, but is (also) applicable to list terms that are not of the form $cons(a,l)$: replacing $length(l)$ with $1 + length(l_1)$ is admissible provided that the equality $l \doteq cons(a,l_1)$ holds for some element a. This can be expressed using the keyword \assumes:

- \assumes imposes a condition on the applicability of a taclet, and has a sequent as parameter. In the case of length_cons_assume, the \assumes clause states that the taclet must only be applied if an equation $l \doteq cons(a,l_1)$ appears in the antecedent of a goal (the sequent may contain further formulas).
- \sameUpdateLevel is a *state condition* that can be added to rewriting taclets, and is relevant in the case of taclets in JavaDL proofs. The flag ensures that the focus of the taclet application (the term that is represented by $length(l)$ in rule length_cons_assume) does not occur in the scope of modal operators apart from updates. Updates are allowed above the focus, but in this case the equation $l \doteq cons(a,l_1)$—or, more generally, all formulas referred to using \assumes, \replacewith and \add—have to be in the scope of the same update.

This flag \sameUpdateLevel is necessary to ensure the soundness of the rule length_cons_assume in dynamic logic, and in fact required for most rewriting rules that contain any \assumes or \add clauses. In order to illustrate the effect of \sameUpdateLevel, we consider two potential applications of length_cons_assume:

Illegal:

$$\frac{v \doteq cons(a,w) \Longrightarrow \{w := nil\}p(1 + length(w))}{v \doteq cons(a,w) \Longrightarrow \{w := nil\}p(length(v))}$$

Legal:

$$\frac{\{w := nil\}(v \doteq cons(a,w)) \Longrightarrow \{w := nil\}p(1 + length(w))}{\{w := nil\}(v \doteq cons(a,w)) \Longrightarrow \{w := nil\}p(length(v))}$$

The first application of length_cons_assume has to be ruled out, and is prevented by KeY in the presence of the \sameUpdateLevel flag, since the application would incorrectly move the term w into the scope of the update $w := nil$ redefining the meaning of w: in the equation $v \doteq cons(a,w)$, the term w represents arbitrary lists, whereas the update defines w to denote the empty list. The application illustrates the case of a symbol changing its meaning due to the presence of modal operators.[2] The second application of length_cons_assume is correct and possible in KeY, because all formulas involved are in the scope of the same update.

The rule list_ctor_split enables users to introduce case splits for arbitrary list expressions l in a proof: either such an expression has to denote an empty list ($l = nil$), or the list must have length at least one and can be represented in the

---

[2] It should be noted, however, that KeY will usually apply updates immediately and thus simplify the formula $\{w := nil\}p(length(v))$ to $p(length(v))$; the illegal situation shown here therefore requires some mischievous energy to construct in an actual proof. Rule length_cons_assume without flag \sameUpdateLevel would be unsound nevertheless.

form $l = cons(a, l_1)$. In sequent notation, such case splits can be described using the following rule, in which c, d are required to be fresh constants, and $\phi[l]$ expresses that the list expression l occurs anywhere in the conclusion:

$$\frac{\Gamma, l \doteq nil \Longrightarrow \phi[nil], \Delta \qquad \Gamma, l \doteq cons(c,d) \Longrightarrow \phi[cons(c,d)], \Delta}{\Gamma \Longrightarrow \phi[l], \Delta}$$

In contrast to all taclets shown up to this point, list_ctor_split contains two *goal templates* separated by a semicolon ;, each with one \replacewith and one \add clause, corresponding to the two cases (or premises) to be generated when applying the rule. The \add clauses take care of adding the equations $l = nil$ and $l = cons(a, l_1)$ in the antecedent:

- \add specifies formulas that are added to a sequent when the taclet is applied. The argument of \add is a sequent with the formulas to be added to the antecedent and the succedent, respectively.

The taclet also states, by means of the variable condition \new, that ska and skl have to be instantiated with fresh *Skolem symbols* each time the taclet is applied. The correctness of list_ctor_split can again be proven by means of induction: the meaning formula of the taclet is essentially the formula discussed in Example 4.2.

Derived taclets can be used not only to augment user-defined theories, but also for all built-in data types and logics of the KeY system: for each proof to be constructed, a set of tailor-made taclets can be loaded into the system. The soundness of the derived taclets has to be shown as outlined before, by first producing a proof of the meaning formula of the taclets. For instance, a user might choose to introduce the following rule for *modus ponens* of antecedent formulas:

—— Taclet —————————————————————————————

```
\rules {
  mpLeft {
    \formula phi, psi;
    \assumes( phi ==> ) \find( phi -> psi ==> )
                        \replacewith( psi ==> )
  };
}
```

————————————————————————————————— Taclet ——

This rule is subsumed by propositional rules that already exist in KeY (since the KeY calculus is complete for propositional logic), but might sometimes be more natural to use in proofs than the built-in rules. The soundness of the rule can easily be shown automatically be KeY.

4.3 A Reference Manual of Taclets

This section introduces the concrete syntax of the taclet language and explains its semantics. It is written in the style of a reference manual for the different taclet constructs and provides most of the information that is necessary for writing one's own taclets to implement a new theory.

4.3.1 The Taclet Language

Taclets formalize sequent calculus rule schemata (see Section 3.5.1) within the KeY system. They define elementary proof goal expansion steps and describe

1. to which parts of a sequent and
2. under which conditions the taclet can be applied, and
3. in which way the sequent is modified yielding new proof goals.

This information is declared in the different parts of the body of a taclet. Figure 4.5 shows the syntax of the taclet language, which is explained in more detail on the following pages. The taclet language is part of the language for KeY input files whose grammar is described in Appendix B. The nonterminal symbols of the grammar that are not further expanded in Figure 4.5 (in particular $\langle schematicSequent \rangle$, $\langle schematicFormula \rangle$, and $\langle schematicTerm \rangle$) can be found in the appendix.

4.3.1.1 A Taclet Section

$\langle taclets \rangle$ ::= \rules { ($\langle taclet \rangle$)* }
          | \axioms { ($\langle taclet \rangle$ | $\langle axiom \rangle$)* }

KeY input files are divided into different section that define various parts of the syntactical language that can be used (functions, predicates, sorts, ...). Taclets are declared in their own sections headed by either rules or axioms. The header should be used to differentiate between rules which define the semantics of a newly introduced logical theory and theorems and lemma rules which follow from the axioms. Rules consisting only of a single formula (see Section 4.3.1.3) are only allowed in sections headed axioms .

―― KeY Syntax ――――――――――――――――――――――――――

⟨*taclets*⟩ ::= \rules { (⟨*taclet*⟩)∗ }
        | \axioms { (⟨*taclet*⟩ | ⟨*axiom*⟩)∗ }

⟨*taclet*⟩ ::=
  ⟨*identifier*⟩ {
    ⟨*localSchemaVarDecl*⟩∗
    ⟨*contextAssumptions*⟩? ⟨*findPattern*⟩?
    ⟨*applicationRestriction*⟩? ⟨*variableConditions*⟩?
    (⟨*goalTemplateList*⟩ | \closegoal)
    ⟨*ruleSetMemberships*⟩?
  }

⟨*axiom*⟩ ::= ⟨*identifier*⟩ { ⟨*formula*⟩ }

⟨*localSchemaVarDecl*⟩ ::= \schemaVar ⟨*schemaVarDecl*⟩
⟨*schemaVarDecl*⟩ ::= ⟨*schemaVarType*⟩ ⟨*identifier*⟩ (, ⟨*identifier*⟩)∗ ;

⟨*contextAssumptions*⟩ ::= \assumes (⟨*schematicSequent*⟩)

⟨*findPattern*⟩ ::= \find (⟨*schematicExpression*⟩)
⟨*schematicExpression*⟩ ::=
    ⟨*schematicSequent*⟩ | ⟨*schematicFormula*⟩ | ⟨*schematicTerm*⟩

⟨*applicationRestriction*⟩ ::= \inSequentState | \sameUpdateLevel
        | \antecedentPolarity | \succedentPolarity

⟨*variableConditions*⟩ ::= \varcond (⟨*variableConditionList*⟩)
⟨*variableConditionList*⟩ ::= ⟨*variableCondition*⟩ (, ⟨*variableCondition*⟩)∗
⟨*variableCondition*⟩ ::= \notFreeIn(⟨*identifier*⟩ , ⟨*identifier*⟩)
        | \new(⟨*identifier*⟩ , \dependingOn(⟨*identifier*⟩))

⟨*goalTemplateList*⟩ ::= ⟨*goalTemplate*⟩ (; ⟨*goalTemplate*⟩)∗
⟨*goalTemplate*⟩ ::=
    ⟨*branchName*⟩?
    (\replacewith (⟨*schematicExpression*⟩))?
    (\add (⟨*schematicSequent*⟩))?
    (\addrules (⟨*taclet*⟩ (, ⟨*taclet*⟩)∗))?
⟨*branchName*⟩ ::= ⟨*string*⟩ :

⟨*ruleSetMemberships*⟩ ::= \heuristics (⟨*identifierList*⟩)
⟨*identifierList*⟩ ::= ⟨*identifier*⟩ (, ⟨*identifier*⟩)∗

――――――――――――――――――――――――――――――――――――――― KeY Syntax ――

Figure 4.5 The taclet syntax

4.3.1.2 A Taclet Declaration

⟨*taclet*⟩ ::=
  ⟨*identifier*⟩ {
    ⟨*localSchemaVarDecl*⟩∗
    ⟨*contextAssumptions*⟩? ⟨*findPattern*⟩?
    ⟨*applicationRestriction*⟩? ⟨*variableConditions*⟩?
    (⟨*goalTemplateList*⟩ | \closegoal)
    ⟨*ruleSetMemberships*⟩?
  }

Every taclet has got a unique name and a body containing elements describing how the taclet is to be matched against a sequent followed by a description of what action will then take place. The order of elements matters in taclet definitions, the system will not accept taclet definitions that disobey this order of declaration.

4.3.1.3 Special Case: Axiom Declarations

⟨*axiom*⟩ ::=
  ⟨*identifier*⟩ {
    ⟨*formula*⟩
  }

When defining a logical theory, it is often clearer to state the axiomatic basis as a set of individual formulas rather than as inference rules that are matched against the current proof state. The semantics of axiom rules is very similar to rules that consist of a single \add clause. The first axiom length_nil from Figure 4.3, for instance, is semantically equivalent to the rule

—— Taclet ————————————————————————————————

```
length_nil {
  \add( length(nil) = 0 ==> )
}
```

———————————————————————————————————— Taclet ——

A special situation arises if quantified axioms are to be defined as taclets. The formula patterns in nonaxiomatic rule definitions are schematic formulas in which only schema variables can be quantified. The second example from the same figure, would hence have to be reformulated more lengthily when composed as a usual rule:

—— Taclet ————————————————————————————————

```
length_cons {
  \schemaVar \variable List l;
  \schemaVar \variable any a;
  \add( \forall l; \forall a;
          length(cons(a, l)) = 1 + length(l) ==> )
```

}

_____ Taclet ___

Not all axioms can be stated as individual first-order formulas. The induction rule
`list_induction` from Figure 4.1, for instance, *is* a schematic rule (standing for the
infinite set of all possible instantiations of the schema variable `phi`) that cannot be
formulated using this notation.

4.3.1.4 Schema Variables: Declaring Matching Placeholders

⟨*localSchemaVarDecl*⟩ ::= \schemaVar ⟨*schemaVarDecl*⟩
⟨*schemaVarDecl*⟩ ::= ⟨*schemaVarType*⟩ ⟨*identifier*⟩ (, ⟨*identifier*⟩)* ;

The patterns within the clauses of taclet definitions are templates which can
be applied to many concrete instantiations. They may, hence, contain placeholder
symbols called *schema variables* which are instantiated during rule application either
by matching the template description containing schematic entities to a part of the
current proof sequent or through user input.

Schema variables can be declared locally at the beginning of a taclet or globally
in a separate section before the taclet definitions. The available types of schema
variables are listed and explained in Section 4.3.2.

4.3.1.5 Context Assumptions: What Has to Be Present in a Sequent

⟨*contextAssumptions*⟩ ::= \assumes (⟨*schematicSequent*⟩)

Context assumptions are—together with the \find part of a taclet—the means
of expressing that a goal modification can only be performed if certain formulas
are present in the goal. If a taclet contains an \assumes clause, then the taclet may
only be applied if the specified formulas are part of the goal that is supposed to be
modified. Assumptions specify side conditions for the application of taclets. The
formulas specified as assumptions are not modified[3] by the taclet application.

4.3.1.6 Find Pattern: To Which Expressions a Taclet Can Be Applied

⟨*findPattern*⟩ ::= \find (⟨*schematicExpression*⟩)
⟨*schematicExpression*⟩ ::=
        ⟨*schematicSequent*⟩ | ⟨*schematicFormula*⟩ | ⟨*schematicTerm*⟩

More specifically than just to a goal of a proof, taclets are usually applied to an
occurrence of either a formula or a term within this goal. This occurrence is called

_____

[3] It is possible, however, that an assumption is also matched by the \find pattern of the taclet. In
this situation a taclet application can modify or remove an assumption.

the *focus* of the taclet application and is the only place in the goal where the taclet can modify an already existing formula.

There are three different kinds of patterns a taclet can match on:

- A schematic sequent that contains a formula: this either specifies that the taclet can be applied if the given formula is an element of the antecedent, or if it is an element of the succedent, with the formula being the focus of the application. It is allowed, however, that the occurrence of the formula is preceded by updates (see the section on "State Conditions" and Section 3.5.1).

  The question how many formulas may appear in a schematic sequent is not settled by the grammar. The KeY implementation insists that there is exactly one formula in schematic sequents in find patterns while in assumes patterns multiple occurrences are possible, e.g., \assumes (phi1, phi2 ==>).
- A formula: the focus of the application can be an arbitrary occurrence of the given formula (also as subformula) within a goal.
- A term: the focus of the application can be any occurrence of the given term within a goal.

Taclets with the last two kinds of \find patterns are commonly referred to as *rewriting taclets*.

The find pattern is an optional part of a taclet definition. However, most taclets possess a find pattern which acts as a hook for the strategy during automatic proof search by which it finds applicable rules. There are only few taclets without find clause with the cut rule that allows for case distinction being the most prominent example. Axioms (in Figure 4.3, e.g.) are also taclets without find clause since they add knowledge unconditionally onto the sequent.

4.3.1.7 State Conditions: Where a Taclet Can Be Applied

⟨*applicationRestriction*⟩ ::= \inSequentState | \sameUpdateLevel | \antecedentPolarity | \succedentPolarity

In JavaDL—like in any modal logic—, the same expression may evaluate differently depending on the modalities in whose context it occurs. A finer control over where the focus of a taclet application may be located is needed. For rewriting rules it is, for instance, often necessary to forbid taclet applications within the scope of modal operators in order to ensure soundness. Likewise, some rewrite rules are only sound if the matched focus lies within a context of a certain polarity.

There are three different "modes" that a taclet can have and that restrict its applicability:

- \inSequentState: the most restrictive mode, in which the focus of a taclet application must not be located within the scope of *any* modal operator.Likewise, the assumptions that match the \assumes pattern must not be under the influence of any modality.

  There are two submodes for this mode that restrict under which logical connectives a formula may appear. These modes anticipate on which side of the

Table 4.1 Matrix of the different taclet modes and the different \find patterns

	\find pattern is sequent	\find pattern is term or formula	No \find
Operators that are allowed above focus			
\inSequentState	None	All nonmodal operators	*Forbidden combination*
\sameUpdateLevel	*Forbidden combination*	All nonmodal operators, updates	*Forbidden combination*
Default	Updates	All operators	—
Which updates occur above \assumes *and* \add *formulas*			
\inSequentState	None	None	*Forbidden combination*
\sameUpdateLevel	*Forbidden combination*	Same updates as above focus	*Forbidden combination*
Default	Same updates as above focus	None	None
Which updates occur above \replacewith *formulas*			
\inSequentState	None	None	*Forbidden combination*
\sameUpdateLevel	*Forbidden combination*	Same updates as above focus	*Forbidden combination*
Default	Same updates as above focus	Same updates as above focus	None

For each combination, it is shown (1) where the focus of the taclet application can be located, and (2) which updates consequently have to occur above the formulas that are matched or added by \assumes, \add or \replacewith.

sequent a subformula would end up if the top-level formula were fully expanded using the basic propositional sequent calculus rules. For example, in the sequent $\neg a \Longrightarrow b \wedge \neg c$, the formula c has "antecedent polarity" while a and b have "succedent polarity" since the fully expanded equivalent sequent reads $c \Longrightarrow b, a$. The mode flags \antecedentPolarity or \succedentPolarity can be added to constrain the application of a taclet to the one polarity or the other.

- \sameUpdateLevel: this mode is only allowed for rewriting taclets and allows the application focus of a taclet to lie within the scope of updates, but not in the scope of other modal operators. The same updates that occur in front of the application focus must also occur before the formulas referred to using \assumes. The same update context is used when the \replacewith and \add patterns are expanded.
- Default: the most liberal mode. For rewriting taclets, this means that the focus can occur arbitrarily deeply nested and in the scope of any modal operator. If the \find pattern of the taclet is a sequent, then the application focus may occur below updates, but not in the scope of any other operator.

While there are no restrictions on the location of the focus, for rewriting taclets in default mode, formulas that are described by \assumes or \add must *not* be in the scope of updates.

An important representative for rules which require the mode \sameUpdateLevel is the rule applyEq:

—— Taclet ————————————————————————————

```
applyEq {
  \schemaVar \variable \term int t1, t2
  \assumes( t1 = t2 ==> )
  \find( t1 ) \sameUpdateLevel
  \replacewith( t2 )
}
```

———————————————————————————————— Taclet ——

The mode flag \sameUpdateLevel is mandatory for the soundness of the rule as it prevents the rule from illegally replacing terms which are influenced by an update. In the sequent $c \doteq 3 \Longrightarrow \{c := 0\}(c > 0)$, the term $c > 0$ cannot soundly be replaced with $3 > 0$ since the equality $c \doteq 3$ does not hold in the scope of the update. see also the examples on page 119.

As an example for a taclet that must be declared using the state condition \antecedentPolarity, consider the taclet

—— Taclet ————————————————————————————

```
weaken {
  \schemaVar \formula phi;
  \find( phi )
  \antecedentPolarity
  \replacewith( true )
}
```

———————————————————————————————— Taclet ——

that allows replacing of any subformula ϕ within the goal by true. In general, replacing a subformula by true is not a sound proof step. The taclet becomes, however, a sound rule if the polarity restriction is added: Replacing a formula in the antecedent by true strengthens the proof obligation and is thus a valid proof step. Using the modifier \antecedentPolarity, one can strengthen the obligation without having to fully expand its propositional structure. State conditions also affect the formulas that are required or added by \assumes, \add or \replacewith clauses. The relation between the positions of the different formulas is also shown in Table 4.1.

4.3.1.8 Variable Conditions: How Schema Variables May Be Instantiated

⟨*variableConditions*⟩ ::= \varcond (⟨*variableConditionList*⟩)
⟨*variableConditionList*⟩ ::= ⟨*variableCondition*⟩ (, ⟨*variableCondition*⟩)∗
⟨*variableCondition*⟩ ::= \notFreeIn(⟨*identifier*⟩ , ⟨*identifier*⟩)
                          | \new(⟨*identifier*⟩ , \dependingOn(⟨*identifier*⟩))

Schema variables are declared with a *kind* restricting how they can be instantiated.
Many kinds additionally support sorts limiting instantiation even further (see Section 4.3.2). In many cases, one has to impose further restrictions on the instantiations
of schema variables, for instance, state that certain logical variables must not occur
free in certain terms. The taclet formalism is hence equipped with a simple language
for expressing such conditions, *variable conditions*. To each taclet, a list of variable
conditions can be attached which will be checked when the taclet is about to be
applied.

Many variable conditions are available in KeY, but only two are of importance
when defining new theories. See Appendix B.2.3.3 for a list of all available variable
conditions.

notFreeIn The variable condition \notFreeIn(*lv*, *te*) is satisfied if the logical
variable which is the instantiation of the schema variable *lv* does *not* occur (freely)
in the instantiation of *te* (which is a term or a formula). The following rule, for
instance, removes a universal quantifier if the quantified variable *x* does not occur
in the matrix *b*.

—— Taclet ——————————————————————————————————————

```
deleteForall {
    \schemaVar \formula b;
    \schemaVar \variable int x;
    \find( \forall x; b )
    \varcond( \notFreeIn(x, b) )
    \replacewith( b )
}
```

——— Taclet ——

new The variable condition \new(sk, \dependingOn(t)) is used to indicate
that the schema variable sk is to be instantiated with a fresh symbol which has
not yet been used anywhere else within the proof. A fresh symbol not yet present
is surely not constrained by a formula on the sequent and can thus stand in for an
arbitrary value. After naming the schema variable sk which is to be instantiated,
one has to include a \dependingOn() clause listing all schema variables on
which the value of sk may depend. This variable condition used to be mandatory
in older versions of KeY, but is optional now. It is still valuable for documentation
purposes.

As an example consider the following taclet pullOut which allows the user
to replace a concrete integer expression *t* by a fresh constant *sk*. The equality

between the two is added as assumption to the antecedent of the sequent:

—— Taclet ——————————————————————————————————

```
pullOut {
  \schemaVar \term int t;
  \schemaVar \skolemTerm int sk;
  \find( t )
  \sameUpdateLevel
  \varcond( \new(sk, \dependingOn(t)) )
  \replacewith( sk )
  \add( t = sk ==> )
}
```

————————————————————————————————————— Taclet ——

4.3.1.9 Goal Templates: The Effect of the Taclet Application

$\langle goalTemplateList \rangle ::= \langle goalTemplate \rangle\ (\ ;\ \langle goalTemplate \rangle\ )*$
$\langle goalTemplate \rangle ::=$
    $\langle branchName \rangle$?
    (**\replacewith** ($\langle schematicExpression \rangle$))?
    (**\add** ($\langle schematicSequent \rangle$))?
    (**\addrules** ($\langle taclet \rangle$ (, $\langle taclet \rangle$)*))?
$\langle branchName \rangle ::= \langle string \rangle$:

If the application of a taclet on a certain goal and a certain focus is permitted and is carried out, the *goal templates* of the taclet describe in which way the goal is altered. Generally, the taclet application will first create a number of new proof goals (split the existing proof goal into a number of new goals) and then modify each of the goals according to one of the goal templates. A taclet without goal templates will close a proof goal. In this case the keyword \closegoal is written instead of a list of goal templates to clarify this behavior syntactically.

Goal templates are made up of three kinds of operations:

- \replacewith: if a taclet contains a \find clause, then the focus of the taclet application can be replaced with new formulas or terms. \replacewith has to be used in accordance with the kind of the \find pattern: if the pattern is a sequent, then also the argument of the keyword \replacewith has to be a sequent, etc. In contrast to \find patterns, there is no restriction concerning the number of formulas that may turn up in a sequent being argument of \replacewith. It is possible to remove a formula from a sequent by replacing it with an empty sequent, or to replace it with multiple new formulas.
- \add: independently of the kind of the \find pattern, the taclet application can add new formulas to a goal.
- \addrules: a taclet can also create new taclets when being applied. We will not go into this subject any deeper in this chapter.

Apart from that, each of the new goals (or branches) can be given a name using a `<branchName>` rule in order to improve readability of proof trees. Observe that this rule has to be terminated by `:`.

Note that a semicolon separates goal templates. The action of the taclet whose goal template is defined as `\find(A) \replacewith(B) \add(C==>)` has a single goal template: it replaces A with B and adds C to the antecedent of the sequent. In contrast to this, the taclet defined as `\find(A) \replacewith(B) ; \add(C==>)` has got two goal templates such that this rules spawns two child sequences, one replacing A with B and one with adding C to the sequent.

4.3.1.10 Rule Sets: Control How Taclets are Applied Automatically

⟨*ruleSetMemberships*⟩ ::= **\heuristics** (⟨*identifierList*⟩)
⟨*identifierList*⟩ ::= ⟨*identifier*⟩ (, ⟨*identifier*⟩)∗

Each taclet can be declared to be element of one or more rule sets, which are used by the *proof strategies* in KeY to choose the taclets which are applied automatically. Rule sets describe collections of taclets that should be treated in the same way by the strategies. The strategies work by assigning weights (called "costs") to all possible rule application and by choosing that applicable taclet for a sequent that has the lowest cost. The cost of an applicable rule application decreases over time (i.e., while other taclets take precedence), thus guaranteeing that every possible rule application will eventually be taken (fairness).

There exists a number of rule sets in KeY, of which only a few are relevant for creating new data types definitions. Most rule sets are special-purpose indicators used by the strategies. Table 4.2 lists those rule sets interesting for the design of data types and theories. Of particular interest are the rule sets 'userTaclets1', 'userTaclets2' and 'userTaclets3' whose priority can be chosen by the user and even modified at runtime during an interactive KeY proof.

There is one strategy optimization implemented to increase the performance of KeY's JavaDL calculus: the *One-Step-Simplifier*. This built-in aggregator rule accumulates taclet applications of the 'concrete' and 'simplify' rule sets and applies them as one modification to a formula within the sequent. The rules applied by the one-step-simplifier are the same as are applied by the strategies; however, proofs with and without activated One-Step-Simplifier may sometimes differ due to the order in which the individual rules are applied.

4.3.2 Schema Variables

Schema variables are placeholders for different kinds of syntactic entities that can be used in taclets. Despite their name *variable*, schema variables are a very broad concept in KeY. Schema variables can stand in for different kinds of variables (like

Table 4.2 Most important rule sets in KeY

concrete	Rules that simplify expressions containing concrete *constant* values are subsumed into this rule set. This includes, for instance, the rules that simplify $x \wedge true$ to x or $2+4$ to 6. Taclets for computations with concrete values have the highest priority and are applied eagerly.
simplify	Rules that simplify expressions locally, without making additional assumptions, are collected into this rule set. This includes a large number of taclets, for instance, the one that simplifies the expression $elementOf(o, f, union(A, B))$ into $elementOf(o, f, A) \vee elementOf(o, f, B)$ for location sets A and B. Taclets in set 'simplify' are applied eagerly, but with less priority than taclets in 'concrete'.
simplify_enlarging	Simplification taclets that expand a definition such that the resulting expression is considerably longer than the original one go into this rule set. It is applied with more reluctance than the above rule sets since it makes sequents grow. The rules which expand the predicate *wellFormed* (modeling the well-formedness of reachable Java heap models) belong to this set, for instance.
inReachableState-Implication	Taclets that add new formulas onto the sequent go into this set. The strategies make sure that the same formula is not added twice onto the same branch which could make the prover run round in circles. Rules in this rule set are applied more reluctantly and only if no rule of the above rule sets can be applied. The name of this rule set is historic, a more appropriate name would be 'adding'.
userTaclets1 userTaclets2 userTaclets3	These three rule sets are empty by default and are meant to be inhabited by user-defined taclets implemented for new theories and data types. Their priority can be controlled interactively by the user in the user interface of KeY.

logical variables or program variables), terms, formulas, programs or more abstract things like types or modal operators.

Schema variables are used in taclet definitions. When a taclet is applied, the contained schema variables will be replaced by *concrete* syntactic entities. This process is called *instantiation* and ensures that schema variables never occur in proof sequents. Some schema variables are instantiated by *matching* schematic expressions against concrete expressions on the goal sequent, other instantiations come up only during taclet application (through user interaction or by the automatic proof strategies).

In order to ensure that no ill-formed expressions occur while instantiating schema variables with concrete expressions, e.g., that no formula is inserted at a place where only terms are allowed, the *kind* of a schema variable defines which entities the schema variable can represent and may be replaced with. Schema variables can be declared locally at the beginning of a taclet definition or globally at the beginning of a file.

Example 4.3. In KeY syntax, we globally declare phi to be a schema variable representing formulas and n a variable for terms of type *int*. The taclet definition for

Table 4.3 Kinds of schema variables in the context of a type hierarchy $(\text{TSym}, \sqsubseteq)$

\variable A	Logical variables of type $A \in \text{TSym}$
\term A	Terms of type $B \sqsubseteq A$ (with $A \in \text{TSym}$)
\formula	Formulas
\skolemTerm A	Skolem constants/functions of type $A \in \text{TSym}$
\program t	Program entities of type t

impRight locally declares another schema variables psi for formulas and makes use of it and the global phi.

```
—— KeY ——————————————————————————————————————————————
\schemaVariables {
  \formula phi;
  \term int n;
}

\rules {
  impRight {
    \schemaVar \formula psi;
    \find( ==> phi -> psi )
    \replacewith( phi ==> psi )
  };
}
                                                            —— KeY ——
```

4.3.2.1 Schema Variable Kinds

The most important kinds of schema variables in the KeY system are given in Table 4.3. A more detailed explanation of each of the different categories is given on the following pages. Out of the kinds of schema variables in the table, the first four are relevant if you want to introduce user-defined logical theories and calculus rules. The last one is needed only when taclets are introduced that deal with JavaDL program modalities. Many subkinds of program schema variables exist and the kind is listed here only for completeness' sake and will not be explained in detail.

Variables: \variable A

Schema variables for variables can be instantiated with logical variables (*not* with program variables) that have static type A. In contrast to schema variables for terms, logical variables of subtypes of A are not allowed for instantiation.[4] Schema variables

---

[4] Such a semantics is hardly ever desired and would make development of sound taclets difficult.

of this kind can also be bound by quantifiers or variable-binding function symbols (see Section 2.3.1). Bound occurrences of such schema variables will also be replaced with concrete logical variables when instantiations are applied.

Terms: \term *A*

Schema variables for terms can be instantiated with arbitrary terms that have the static type *A* or a subtype of *A*. Subtypes are allowed because this behavior is most useful in practice: there are only very few rules for which the static type of involved terms has to match some given type *exactly*.[5] In general, there are no conditions on the logical variables that may occur (free) in terms substituted for such schema variables. When a term schema variable is in the scope of a quantifier, logical variables can be "captured" when applying the instantiation, which needs to be considered when writing taclets. The occurrence of variables within the instantiation of a term can be restricted using the variable condition notFreeIn (see Section 4.3.1.8).

Formulas: \formula

Schema variables for formulas can be instantiated with arbitrary JavaDL formulas. As for schema variables for terms, the substituted concrete formulas may contain free variables, and during instantiation variable capture can occur.

Skolem Terms: \skolemTerm *A*

A schema variable for Skolem terms is instantiated with a fresh constant c_{sk} of type *A* that has not occurred anywhere in the proof, yet.

The taclet application mechanism in KeY creates a fresh constant symbols every time a taclet with such a schema variable is applied. This ensures that the inserted symbols are always new, and, hence, can be used as Skolem constants. Compare the remarks on page 30 in Chapter 2 and at the end of Section 3.5.1.1 on page 62 in Chapter 3.

There are only few rules that require schema variables for Skolem terms. Sometimes it is helpful to be able to talk about a witnessing object which has some property. One can realize that using a Skolem schema variable. An alternative would be to state a corresponding quantified formula.

Schema variables of this kind always require a corresponding variable condition \new (see Section 4.3.1.8).

---

[5] In case the reader needs to implement a schema variable with exact type *A*, they may use the modifier strict after \term.

Other schema variable types

Three schema variable kinds are concerned with matching program constructs and modalities. They are usually not required to define new data types and theories. Schema variables of type \program match against syntactical entities[6] within Java programs, and they can be used to compose new rules for symbolic execution (see Section 3.5.6) of Java modalities in JavaDL formulas.

Moreover, there exist a few special purpose schema variable types to match other syntactical entities like updates or term labels, but we will not discuss them here since they are not relevant for data type definitions.

4.3.2.2 Schema Variable Instantiation

Schema variables are replaced with concrete entities when a taclet is applied. This replacement can be considered as a generalization of the notion of *ground substitutions* from Section 2.2.1 in Chapter 2, and like substitutions the replacement is carried out in a purely syntactic manner. A mapping from schema variables to concrete expressions is canonically extended to terms and formulas.

Definition 4.4 (Instantiation of Schema Variables). Let $(\text{FSym}, \text{PSym}, \text{VSym})$ be a signature for a type hierarchy $\mathscr{T} = (\text{TSym}, \sqsubseteq)$ and SV a set of schema variables over $\mathscr{T}$. An *instantiation* of SV is a partial mapping[7]

$$\iota : SV \nrightarrow \left(\text{DLFml} \cup \bigcup_{A \in \text{TSym}} \text{DLTrm}_A \right)$$

that maps schema variables to syntactic entities without schema variables in accordance with Table 4.3. An instantiation is called *complete* for SV if it is a total mapping on SV.

For sake of brevity, we also talk about instantiations of schematic terms or formulas, which really are instantiations of the set of schema variables that occur in the expression. Given a complete instantiation of a schematic expression, we can turn it into a concrete one by replacing all schema variables sv with the expression $\iota(\text{sv})$. To this end we can extend ι to expressions which may also contain schema variables. In such expressions, a schema variable of type \formula can be used in places where a formula is admissible, for instance.

Example 4.5. Table 4.4 illustrates the instantiation of the different kinds of schema variables for first-order logic. We assume that $f, g : A \rightarrow A$ are function symbols, $a, c : A$ are constants, $p : A$ and q, r are predicates and $x{:}A$ is a logical variable.

---

[6] like Java expressions, local variables, method or field references, types, switch labels, ...

[7] This is for the schema variables presented here. The domain of ι must be extended if schema variables for program elements, or modalities are considered.

Table 4.4 Examples of schematic expressions and their instantiations

Expression t	Instantiation ι	Instance $\iota(t)$
$f(\texttt{te})$	$\{\texttt{te} \mapsto g(a)\}$	$f(g(a))$
$f(\texttt{va})$	$\{\texttt{va} \mapsto x\}$	$f(x)$
$\forall \texttt{va}; p(\texttt{va})$	$\{\texttt{va} \mapsto x\}$	$\forall x; p(x)$
$\forall \texttt{va}; p(\texttt{te})$	$\{\texttt{va} \mapsto x, \texttt{te} \mapsto x\}$	$\forall x; p(x)$
$\forall \texttt{va}; \texttt{phi}$	$\{\texttt{va} \mapsto x, \texttt{phi} \mapsto p(x)\}$	$\forall x; p(x)$
$\texttt{phi} \wedge p(\texttt{te})$	$\{\texttt{phi} \mapsto q \vee r, \texttt{te} \mapsto f(a)\}$	$(q \vee r) \wedge p(f(a))$
$p(\texttt{sk}) \rightarrow \exists \texttt{va}; p(\texttt{va})$	$\{\texttt{sk} \mapsto c, \texttt{va} \mapsto x\}$	$p(c) \rightarrow \exists x; p(x)$

Schema variables:
`\variables A va; \term A te;`
`\formula phi; \skolemTerm A sk;`

4.3.2.3 Well-formedness Conditions

Not all taclets that can be written using the syntax of Section 4.3.1 are meaningful or desirable descriptions of rules. We want to avoid, in particular, rules whose application could destroy well-formedness of formulas or sequents.

Following Chapter 2, we do not allow sequents of our proofs to contain free logical variables. Unfortunately, this is a property that can easily be destroyed by incorrect taclets:

—— Taclet ——
```
illegalTac1 { \find(==> \forall va; p(va))
            \replacewith(==> p(va)) };
illegalTac2 { \find(==> \forall va; phi)
            \replacewith(==> phi) };
```
——— Taclet ——

In both examples, the taclets remove quantifiers and possibly inject free variables into a sequent: (1) schema variables of kind `\variable` could occur free in clauses `\add` or `\replacewith`, or (2) a logical variable $\iota(\texttt{va})$ could occur free in the concrete formula $\iota(\texttt{phi})$ that a schema variable `phi` represents, and after removing the quantifier, the variable would be free in the sequent (the same can happen with schema variables for terms). We will rule out both taclets by imposing suitable constraints.

To avoid that taclets like `illegalTac1` endanger the well-formedness of proof sequents, schema variables of kind `\variable` must not occur free in `\find`, `\assumes`, `\replacewith` and `\add` clauses. To forbid taclets like `illegalTac2`, schema variables must be used consistently: If a schema variable t is in the scope of a quantification over a schema variable `va`, then

1. every occurrence of t must also be in the scope of `va`, *or*
2. the taclet must be annotated with the variable condition `\notFreeIn(t, va)`.

Both properties can be checked statically, and the KeY implementation rejects ill-formed taclets immediately; they cannot even be loaded.

4.3.3 Application of Taclets

This section informally explains the process of how taclets are applied as sequent calculus rules on JavaDL sequents in KeY. A more formal introduction of the semantics of taclets can be found in Section 4.4 on reasoning about the soundness of taclets.

A taclet schematically describes a set of sequent calculus rules. By instantiating the schema variables in its clauses with concrete syntactical elements, it becomes a concrete applicable rule in the calculus (see Section 2.2.2). When applying a taclet, *all* schema variables must be instantiated according to their declaration. Many instantiations are determined by *matching* schematic expressions against concrete expressions on the goal sequent. Thus, it is determined if (and by which instantiation) the schematic and the concrete expression can be unified.

But if schema variables occur in the taclet but not in the \find or \assumes clauses, they cannot be instantiated by matching. In interactive proofs, the user is then asked to provide suitable instantiations; in automatic proofs, heuristics are invoked to come up with instantiations (e.g., for finding suitable ground instances of quantified statements).

An important role in the taclet application process is played by the \find clause since it determines *where* on the sequent the taclet performs rewriting actions. Both in automatic and interactive reasoning, this clause chooses the application focus (see Section 4.3.1.6) and thus triggers the rule application. We write *focus* to denote the located application focus of a rule application, that is, *focus* refers actually to a position within the sequent. We will use the notation *focus* also for the matched term or formula. The side conditions (variable conditions, \assumes clause, state conditions) are checked afterwards, and only if all of them are satisfied will the rule be applied.

Consider a well-formed taclet t and let SV denote the set of schema variables in t. An *applicable instantiation of* t is a tuple $(\iota, \mathcal{U}, \Gamma \Longrightarrow \Delta, \underline{focus})$ consisting of

- a complete instantiation ι of SV,
- an update $\mathcal{U}$ describing the context of the taclet application ($\mathcal{U}$ can be empty),
- a sequent $\Gamma \Longrightarrow \Delta$ to which the taclet is supposed to be applied, and
- an application focus $\underline{focus}$ within $\Gamma \Longrightarrow \Delta$ that is supposed to be modified (we write $\underline{focus} = \bot$ if t does not have a \find clause)

that satisfies the following conditions:

1. ι is an admissible instantiation of SV,
2. ι satisfies all variable conditions of taclet t,
3. all logical variables $\iota(\text{va})$ represented by schema variables va of kind \variable in t are distinct,
4. if t has a \find clause, then the position of $\underline{focus}$ is consistent with the state conditions of t (Table 4.1),
5. $\mathcal{U}$ is derived from $\underline{focus}$ according to the middle part "Which updates have to occur above \assumes and \add formulas" of Table 4.1 (for $\underline{focus} = \bot$ and the fields "forbidden combination" we choose the empty update skip),

6. for each formula ϕ of an \assumes clause of t, $\Gamma \implies \Delta$ contains a corresponding formula $\mathcal{U}\iota(\phi)$ (on the correct side),
7. if t has a clause \find(f), where f is a formula or a term, then $\iota(f) = \underline{focus}$ (the \find pattern has to match the focus of the application),
8. if t has a clause \find(f), where f is a sequent containing a single formula ϕ, then $\iota(\phi) = \underline{focus}$ and the formulas ϕ and $\underline{focus}$ occur on the same sequent side (both antecedent or both succedent),
9. if a state condition \antecedentPolarity or \succedentPolarity is part of the rewrite taclet t (see Section 4.3.1.7), then $\underline{focus}$ must have antecedent/-succedent polarity,
10. for every schema variable sv of t of kind \term or \formula and all free variables $x \in \mathit{fv}(\iota(\text{sv}))$,

   - sv is in the scope of a schema variable of type \variable with $\iota(\text{va}) = x$, or
   - t contains at most one \replacewith clause, sv turns up only in \find, \replacewith or \varcond clauses of t, and x is bound above $\underline{focus}$.

Once a complete taclet instantiation has been found applicable, it can be used to perform a step in the sequent calculus. Applying it onto a focus within an open proof goal spawns a set of new sequents, which are new proof goals after the application. The emerging sequents are obtained by modification of the original, carrying out the modification descriptions in the taclet's goal templates. The following informally describes the effects that the application of a taclet t together with an applicable instantiation $(\iota, \mathcal{U}, \Gamma \implies \Delta, \underline{focus})$ has on the goal.

First, the sequent is duplicated into new goals according to the number of goal templates (see Section 4.3.1.9) declared in the taclet. Every new goal corresponds to one goal template in t where its effects will be carried out. The new goals become children of the original goal in the sequent calculus proof tree. The following steps are then repeated for every new goal. If there are no goal templates in the taclet (indicated by \closegoal) the rule application successfully closes the proof branch.

1. If the goal template has a clause \replacewith(rw), where rw is a formula or a term, then $\underline{focus}$ is replaced with $\iota(rw)$. If rw is a term and the type A_{new} of $\iota(rw)$ is not a subtype of the type A_{old} of $\underline{focus}$, in symbols $A_{new} \not\sqsubseteq A_{old}$, then $\underline{focus}$ is replaced with $(A_{old})\iota(rw)$ instead of $\iota(rw)$ (a cast has to be introduced to prevent ill-formed terms).
2. If the goal template has a clause \replacewith(rw), where rw is a sequent, then the formula containing $\underline{focus}$ is removed from $\Gamma \implies \Delta$, and for each formula ϕ in rw the formula $\mathcal{U}\iota(\phi)$ is added (on the correct side).
3. If the goal template has a clause \add(add), then for each formula ϕ in add the formula $\mathcal{U}\iota(\phi)$ is added (on the correct side).

It is important to note that it is not possible to modify parts of the sequent other than through the focus. Formulas can be *added* to the sequent, but never can formulas that are not in the focus be *removed*. In terms of schematic sequent calculus rules, this means that the *context* of the sequent (Γ and Δ) is always retained through taclet application.

4.4 Reflection and Reasoning about Soundness of Taclets

This section summarizes results published by Bubel et al. [2008]. See the paper for further details.

Taclets are a general language for describing proof modification steps. In order to ensure that the rules that are implemented using taclets are correct, we can consider the definitions of the previous sections and try to derive that no incorrect proofs can be constructed using taclets. This promises to be tedious work, however, and is for a larger number of taclets virtually useless if the reasoning is performed informally: we are bound to make mistakes.

For treating the correctness of taclets in a more systematic way, we would rather like to have some *calculus* for reasoning about soundness of taclets. This is provided in this section for some of the features of taclets. To this end, a two-step translation will be presented that define *first-order soundness proof obligations* for taclets.

- We describe a translation of taclets into formulas (the *meaning formulas* of taclets), such that a taclet is sound if the formula is valid. This translation captures the semantics of the different clauses that a taclet can consist of. Meaning formulas do, however, still contain schema variables, which means that for proving their validity, (higher-order) proof methods like induction over terms or programs are necessary.
- A second transformation handles the elimination of schema variables in meaning formulas, which is achieved by replacing schema variables with Skolem terms or formulas. The result is a formula in first-order logic, such that the original formula is valid if the derived formula is valid.

The two steps can be employed to validate taclets in different theorem prover contexts:

- Only the first step can be carried out, and one can reason about the resulting formula using an appropriate proof assistant in which the semantics of schema entities can be modeled, e.g., based on higher-order logic.
- Both steps can be carried out, which opens up for a wider spectrum of provers or proof assistants with which the resulting formulas can be tackled. The formulas can in particular be treated by KeY itself.

Proving KeY taclets within KeY is an interesting feature for *lemma* rules, i.e., taclets can be proven sound referring to other—more basic—taclets. The complete translation from taclets to formulas of dynamic logic can automatically be performed by KeY and makes it possible to write and use lemmas whenever this is useful, see [Bubel et al., 2008].

Proof obligations cannot be generated for all taclets in KeY. At the time of writing this, the following artifacts within a taclet definition keep it from being verifiable within KeY:

- program modalities in any clause,
- variable conditions other than \new and \notFreeIn (see Section B.2.3.3),
- meta-functions (symbols which are evaluated at rule application time by executing Java code),
- generic sorts, or
- schema variables other \term, \formula, \variable.

In the following, we first give a recapitulation about when rules of a sequent calculus are sound, and then show how this notion can be applied to the taclet concept. It has to be noted, however, that although reading the following pages in detail is not necessary for defining new taclets, it might help to understand what happens when lemmas are loaded in KeY.

4.4.1 Soundness in Sequent Calculi

This section continues the discussion of Sequent Calculi begun in Section 2.2.2 by introducing a concept of soundness and criteria for it. In the whole section we write $(\Gamma \Longrightarrow \Delta)^* := \bigwedge \Gamma \to \bigvee \Delta$ for the formula that expresses the meaning of the sequent $\Gamma \Longrightarrow \Delta$. This formula is, in particular:

$$(\Longrightarrow \phi)^* = \phi \ , \qquad (\phi \Longrightarrow)^* = \neg \phi \ .$$

By the validity of a sequent we thus mean the validity of the formula $(\Gamma \Longrightarrow \Delta)^*$.

A further notation that we are going to use is the following "union" of two sequents:

$$(\Gamma_1 \Longrightarrow \Delta_1) \cup (\Gamma_2 \Longrightarrow \Delta_2) \quad := \quad \Gamma_1 \cup \Gamma_2 \Longrightarrow \Delta_1 \cup \Delta_2 \ .$$

Because antecedents and succedents are defined to be sets, duplicate formulas will not appear twice.

Definition 4.6 (Soundness). A sequent calculus C is *sound* if only valid sequents are derivable in C, i.e., if the root $\Gamma \Longrightarrow \Delta$ of a closed proof tree is valid.

This general definition does not refer to particular rules of a calculus C, but treats C as an abstract mechanism that determines a set of derivable sequents. For practical purposes, however, it is advantageous to formulate soundness in a more "local" fashion and to talk about the rules (or taclets implementing the rules) of C. Such a local criterion can already be given when considering rules in a very abstract sense: a rule R can be considered as an arbitrary (but at least semi-decidable) relation between tuples of sequents (the premisses) and single sequents (the conclusions). Consequently, $(\langle P_1, \ldots, P_k \rangle, Q) \in R$ means that the rule R can be applied in an expansion step

$$\frac{P_1 \quad \cdots \quad P_k}{Q}$$

The following lemma relates the notion of soundness of a calculus with rules:

Lemma 4.7. *A calculus C is sound, if for each rule $R \in C$ and also for all tuples $(\langle P_1, \ldots, P_k \rangle, Q) \in R$ the following implication holds:*

$$\text{if } P_1, \ldots, P_k \text{ are valid, then } Q \text{ is valid.} \tag{4.7}$$

If condition (4.7) holds for all tuples $(\langle P_1, \ldots, P_k \rangle, Q) \in R$ of a rule R, then this rule is also called *sound*.

4.4.2 Meaning Formulas of Sequent Taclets

In our case, the rules of a calculus C are defined through taclets t over a set SV of schema 15variables, and within the next paragraphs we discuss how Lemma 4.7 can be applied considering such a rule. For a start, we consider a taclet whose \find pattern is a sequent (without implicit update) and that has the following basic shape:

```
—— Taclet ————————————————————————————
t1 { \assumes(assum) \find(findSeq) \inSequentState
     \replacewith(rw1) \add(add1);
     ...
     \replacewith(rwk) \add(addk) };
————————————————————————————————— Taclet ——
```

Using text-book notation for rules in sequent calculi (as in Chapter 2), the taclet describes the rule

$$\frac{\texttt{rw1} \cup \texttt{add1} \cup \texttt{assum} \cup (\Gamma \Longrightarrow \Delta) \quad \cdots \quad \texttt{rwk} \cup \texttt{addk} \cup \texttt{assum} \cup (\Gamma \Longrightarrow \Delta)}{\texttt{findSeq} \cup \texttt{assum} \cup (\Gamma \Longrightarrow \Delta)}$$

In order to apply Lemma 4.7, it is then necessary to show implication (4.7) for all possible applications of the rule, i.e., essentially for all possible ways the schema variables that now turn up in the sequents can be instantiated. If ι is an applicable schema variable instantiation, and if $\Gamma \Longrightarrow \Delta$ is an arbitrary sequent, then

$$\begin{aligned} P_i &= \iota(\texttt{rw}i \cup \texttt{add}i \cup \texttt{assum}) \cup (\Gamma \Longrightarrow \Delta) \quad (i = 1, \ldots, k), \\ Q &= \iota(\texttt{findSeq} \cup \texttt{assum}) \cup (\Gamma \Longrightarrow \Delta) \end{aligned} \tag{4.8}$$

Implication (4.7) can be replaced with:

$$\left(P_1^* \wedge \ldots \wedge P_k^* \to Q^*\right) \text{ is valid.} \tag{4.9}$$

Implication (4.7) is a *global* soundness criterion since validity of the premises implies validity of the conclusion while the implication (4.9) is *local* in the sense that the premises implies the conclusion in any single structure.

This new condition is stronger than (4.7), however not significantly stronger because of the side formulas $\Gamma \Longrightarrow \Delta$ that can be chosen arbitrarily. Inserting the sequents (4.8) extracted from taclet $\mathtt{t1}$ into (4.9) leads to a formula whose validity is sufficient for implication (4.7):

$$P_1^* \wedge \ldots \wedge P_k^* \to Q^* = \bigwedge_{i=1}^{k} \left(\imath(\mathtt{rw}i \cup \mathtt{add}i \cup \mathtt{assum}) \cup (\Gamma \Longrightarrow \Delta)\right)^* \qquad (4.10)$$
$$\to \left(\imath(\mathtt{findSeq} \cup \mathtt{assum}) \cup (\Gamma \Longrightarrow \Delta)\right)^*$$

In order to simplify the right hand side of Equation (4.10), we can now make use of the fact that $\imath$ distributes through all propositional connectives ($\to$, $\wedge$, $\vee$, etc.) and also through the union of sequents. Thus, the formulas of Equation (4.10) are equivalent to

$$\imath\left(\bigwedge_{i=1}^{k} \left(\mathtt{rw}i^* \vee \mathtt{add}i^*\right) \to \left(\mathtt{findSeq}^* \vee \mathtt{assum}^*\right)\right) \vee (\Gamma \Longrightarrow \Delta)^*.$$

Showing that this formula holds for all sequents $\Gamma \Longrightarrow \Delta$, i.e., in particular for the empty sequent, is equivalent to proving

$$\imath\left(\bigwedge_{i=1}^{k} \left(\mathtt{rw}i^* \vee \mathtt{add}i^*\right) \to \left(\mathtt{findSeq}^* \vee \mathtt{assum}^*\right)\right)$$

for all possible instantiations $\imath$. We call the formula

$$M(\mathtt{t1}) = \bigwedge_{i=1}^{k} \left(\mathtt{rw}i^* \vee \mathtt{add}i^*\right) \to \left(\mathtt{findSeq}^* \vee \mathtt{assum}^*\right) \qquad (4.11)$$

the *meaning formula* of $\mathtt{t1}$. From the construction of $M(\mathtt{t1})$, it is clear that if $M(\mathtt{t1})$ is valid whatever expressions we replace its schema variables with, then the taclet $\mathtt{t1}$ will be sound. Note that the disjunctions $\vee$ in the formula stem from the union operator on sequents. Intuitively, given that the premisses of a rule application are true (the formulas on the left side of the implication), it has to be shown that at least one formula of the conclusion is true.

We can easily adapt Equation (4.11) if some of the clauses of $\mathtt{t1}$ are missing in a taclet:

- If the \find clause is missing: in this case, $\mathtt{findSeq}$ can simply be considered as the empty sequent, which means that we can set $\mathtt{findSeq}^* = \mathrm{false}$ in Equation (4.11).
- If \assumes or \add clauses are missing: again we can assume that the respective sequents are empty and set

$$\mathtt{assum}^* = \mathrm{false}, \qquad \mathtt{add}i^* = \mathrm{false}$$

- If a clause \replacewith($\mathtt{rw}i$) is not present: then we can normalize by setting $\mathtt{rw}i = \mathtt{findSeq}$, which means that the taclet will replace the focus of the application with itself. If both \replacewith and \find are missing, we can simply set $\text{rw}i^* = \text{false}$.

Example 4.8. We consider the taclet impRight from Ex. 4.3 that eliminates implications within the succedent. The taclet represents the rule schema

$$\frac{\text{phi} \Longrightarrow \text{psi}}{\Longrightarrow \text{phi} \rightarrow \text{psi}}$$

and the meaning formula is the logically valid formula

$M(\text{impRight})$
$$= (\underbrace{\neg\text{phi} \vee \text{psi}}_{=\text{rw1}^*}) \rightarrow (\underbrace{\text{phi} \rightarrow \text{psi}}_{=\text{findSeq}^*}) \equiv \neg(\text{phi} \rightarrow \text{psi}) \vee (\text{phi} \rightarrow \text{psi}) \;.$$

4.4.3 Meaning Formulas for Rewriting Taclets

The construction given in the previous section can be carried over to rewriting taclets.

—— Taclet ——————————————————————————————
```
t2 { \assumes(assum) \find(findTerm) \inSequentState
     \replacewith(rw1) \add(add1);
     ...
     \replacewith(rwk) \add(addk) };
```
————————————————————————————————— Taclet ——

In this case, findTerm and rw1, ..., rwk are schematic *terms*. We can, in fact, reduce the taclet t2 to a nonrewriting taclet (note, that the union operator $\cup$ is not part of the actual taclet language).

—— Taclet ——————————————————————————————
```
t2b { \assumes(assum) \inSequentState
      \add( (findTerm=rw1 ==>) ∪ add1 );
      ...
      \add( (findTerm=rwk ==>) ∪ addk ) };
```
————————————————————————————————— Taclet ——

We create a taclet that adds equations findTerm=rw1, ..., findTerm=rwk to the antecedent. Using taclet t2b and a general rule for applying equations in the antecedent, the effect of t2 can be simulated. On the other hand, also taclet t2b can be simulated using t2 and standard rules (cut, reflexivity of equality), which means that it suffices to consider the soundness of t2b. Equation (4.11) and some propositional simplifications then directly give us the meaning formula

$$M(\texttt{t2b}) \;\equiv\; M(\texttt{t2}) \;=\; \bigwedge_{i=1}^{k} \left(\texttt{findTerm} \doteq \texttt{rw}i \rightarrow \texttt{add}i^*\right) \rightarrow \texttt{assum}^* \;. \qquad (4.12)$$

We have looked at rewriting taclets for terms so far. In the same way, rewriting taclets for formulas can be treated, if equations in (4.12) are replaced with equivalences:

$$\bigwedge_{i=1}^{k} \left((\texttt{findFor} \leftrightarrow \texttt{rw}i) \rightarrow \texttt{add}i^*\right) \rightarrow \texttt{assum}^* \qquad (4.13)$$

For a taclet like t2 but with mode flag \succedentPolarity (instead of \inSequentSate), the taclet application is limited to occurrences with positive polarity; the meaning formula is hence weaker and has the equivalence of (4.13) replaced by an implication:

$$\bigwedge_{i=1}^{k} \left((\texttt{findFor} \rightarrow \texttt{rw}i) \rightarrow \texttt{add}i^*\right) \rightarrow \texttt{assum}^*$$

Likewise, for a taclet which is annotated with \succedentPolarity, the meaning formula has this implication reversed:

$$\bigwedge_{i=1}^{k} \left((\texttt{rw}i \rightarrow \texttt{findFor}) \rightarrow \texttt{add}i^*\right) \rightarrow \texttt{assum}^*$$

Example 4.9. Let us go back to the taclet applyEq introduced in Section 4.3.1.7 on page 127. According to (4.12) its meaning formula is

$$M(\texttt{applyEq}) \;=\; (\texttt{t1} \doteq \texttt{t2} \rightarrow \textit{false}) \rightarrow \texttt{t1} \doteq \texttt{t2} \qquad (4.14)$$

with t1 and t2 schema variables. The implication of *false* is introduced since the taclet does not specify an \assumes clause. The next section will elaborate how the schematic meaning formula is refined into a concrete proof obligation.

4.4.4 Elimination of Schema Variables

Meaning formulas of taclets in general contain schema variables, i.e., placeholders for syntactic constructs like terms, formulas or programs. In order to prove a taclet sound, it is necessary to show that its meaning formula is valid for all possible instantiations of the schema variables.

Let us once more look at taclet applyEq ($\Rightarrow$ Ex. 4.9). In order to prove the taclet sound, we would have to prove the meaning formula (4.14) valid for all possible terms $\iota(\texttt{t1})$, $\iota(\texttt{t2})$ that we can substitute for t1, t2. Note that this *syntactic* quantification ranges over terms and is completely different from a first-order formula

$\forall int\ x; p(x)$, which is *semantic* and expresses that x ranges over all elements in the set of integers.

Instead of explicitly enumerating instantiations using techniques like induction over terms, it is to some degree possible, however, to replace the syntactic quantification with an implicit semantic quantification through the introduction of Skolem symbols. For $M(\texttt{applyEq})$, it is sufficient to prove validity of the formula

$$\phi \quad = \quad (c \doteq d \rightarrow \text{false}) \rightarrow c \doteq d$$

in which c, d are fresh constant symbols. The validity of $M(\texttt{applyEq})$ for all other instantiations follows, because the symbols c, d can take the values of arbitrary terms $\iota(\texttt{t1}), \iota(\texttt{t2})$. Fortunately, ϕ is only a first-order formula that can be tackled with a calculus as defined in Chapter 2.

We will only sketch how Skolem symbols can be introduced for some of the schema variable kinds that are described in Section 4.3.2, more details can be found in [Bubel et al., 2008]. For the rest of the section, we assume that a taclet t and its meaning formula $M(t)$ are fixed. We then construct an instantiation ι_{sk} of the schema variables that turn up in t with Skolem expressions. In the example above, this instantiation would be

$$\iota_{\mathrm{sk}} = \{\texttt{t1} \mapsto c,\ \texttt{t2} \mapsto d\}$$

Variables: \variable A

KeY makes the names of bound variables unique by internally renaming them[8]. Thus we need only consider instantiations ι that map different schema variables va to distinct logical variables. Such variables only occur bound in taclets and the identity of bound variables does not matter. Therefore, this instantiation $\iota_{\mathrm{sk}}(\texttt{va})$ of a \variable schema variable va can simply be chosen to be a fresh logical variable $\iota_{\mathrm{sk}}(\texttt{va}) = x$ of type A.

Terms: \term A

As already shown in the example above, a schema variable te for terms can be eliminated by replacing it with a term. While it sufficed to choose Skolem constants in the above case, in general, also the logical variables $\Pi(\texttt{te})$ that are bound in the context of te have to be taken into account and have to appear as arguments of the Skolem functions symbol. The reason is that such variables can occur in the term that is represented by te. We choose the instantiation $\iota_{\mathrm{sk}}(\texttt{te}) = f_{\mathrm{sk}}(x_1, \ldots, x_l)$, where

- $x_1, \ldots, x_l$ are the instantiations of the schema variables $\texttt{va}_1, \ldots, \texttt{va}_l$, i.e., $x_i = \iota_{\mathrm{sk}}(\texttt{va}_i)$,

---

[8] applying so-called *α-conversions*

- $va_1,\ldots,va_l$ are the (distinct) context variables of the variable te in the taclet t: $\Pi(te) = \{va_1,\ldots,va_l\}$,
- $f_{sk} : A_1,\ldots,A_l \to A$ is a fresh function symbol,
- $A_1,\ldots,A_l$ are the types of $x_1,\ldots,x_l$ and te is of kind $\backslash term\, A$.

An example motivating the more complex Skolem expression will follow after the next paragraph which first describes a very similar situation.

Formulas: \formula

The elimination of schema variables phi for formulas is very similar to the elimination of term schema variables. The main difference is, obviously, that instead of a program variable, which is a nonrigid function symbol, a nonrigid predicate symbol has to be introduced: $\iota_{sk}(\texttt{phi}) = p_{sk}(x_1,\ldots,x_l)$, where

- $x_1,\ldots,x_l$ are the instantiations of the schema variables $va_1,\ldots,va_l$, i.e., $x_i = \iota_{sk}(va_i)$,
- $va_1,\ldots,va_l$ are the (distinct) context variables of the variable te in the taclet t: $\Pi_t(te) = \{va_1,\ldots,va_l\}$,
- $p_{sk} : A_1,\ldots,A_l$ is a fresh predicate symbol,
- $A_1,\ldots,A_l$ are the types of $x_1,\ldots,x_l$.

As an example to demonstrate the necessity of the arguments $x_1,\ldots,x_l$, consider the following unsound[9] taclet:

—— Taclet ——————————————————————————————————

```
swapMixedQuants {
  \schemaVar \variable int x;
  \schemaVar \variable int y;
  \schemaVar \formula phi;

  \find(\exists y; \forall x; phi)
  \replacewith(\forall x; \exists y; phi)
}
```

————————————————————————————————————— Taclet ——

Its meaning formula (according to (4.12)) is

$$M(\texttt{swapMixedQuants}) = (\exists x; \forall y; \texttt{phi}) \leftrightarrow (\forall y; \exists x; \texttt{phi})$$

with x, y and phi schema variables. Were phi replaced by a Skolem (propositional) constant $\iota(\texttt{phi}) = c$ and x, y by logical variables x, y, then the instantiated meaning formula $\iota(M(\texttt{swappedMixedQuants})) = (\exists x; \forall y; c) \leftrightarrow (\forall y; \exists x; c) \equiv c \leftrightarrow c$ would be valid although the taclet is clearly unsound.

---

[9] This taclet can, e.g., be used to prove $\exists int\, x; \forall int\, y; x \doteq y$ which is *not* a valid formula.

If, on the over hand, the instantiation for phi is chosen as $\iota'(\text{phi}) = b(x,y)$ with x and y as dependencies to a fresh Skolem predicate symbol $b : int, int$, the resulting formula $\iota'(M(\text{swapMixedQuants})) = (\exists x; \forall y; b(x,y)) \leftrightarrow (\forall y; \exists x; b(x,y))$ is not valid.

Skolem Terms: \skolemTerm A

Schema variables of kind \skolemTerm A are responsible for introducing fresh constant or function symbols in a proof. Such variables could in principle be treated like schema variables for terms, but this would strengthen meaning formulas excessively (often, the formulas would no longer be valid even for sound taclets).

We can handle schema variables sk for Skolem terms more faithfully: if in implication (4.7) the sequents $P_1, \ldots, P_k$ contain symbols that do not occur in Q, then these symbols can be regarded as universally quantified. Because a negation occurs in front of the quantifiers in (4.9) (the quantifiers are on the left side of an implication), the symbols have to be considered as existentially quantified when looking at the whole meaning formula. This entails that schema variables for Skolem terms can be eliminated and replaced with existentially quantified variables: $\iota_{sk}(\text{sk}) = x$, where x is a fresh variable of type A.[10] At the same time, an existential quantifier $\exists x;$ has to be added in front of the whole meaning formula.

Example 4.10. The taclet pullout allows replacing any ground term t with a fresh Skolem constant sk; equality between them is guaranteed by an added assumption.

—— Taclet ——————————————————————————————————

```
pullout {
  \schemaVar \term G t;
  \schemaVar \skolemTerm G sk;

  \find( t ) \sameUpdateLevel
  \varcond( \new(sk, \dependingOn(t)) )

  \replacewith( sk )
  \add( t = sk ==> )
};
```

——————————————————————————————————— Taclet ——

The meaning formula of the taclet pullout is

$$M(\text{pullout}) \quad = \quad (\text{t} \doteq sk \rightarrow \neg t \doteq sk) \rightarrow \text{false} \quad \equiv \quad t \doteq sk$$

---

[10] Strictly speaking, this violates Definition 4.4, because schema variables for Skolem terms must not be instantiated with variables according to this definition. The required generalization of the definition is, however, straightforward.

according to (4.12). In order to eliminate the schema variables of this taclet, we first assume that the schematic type[11] G of the taclet is instantiated with a concrete type A.

If both schema variables t and sk were replaced by Skolem constants c and d, the resulting formula $c \doteq d$ would be far from valid—though the taclet pullout *is* sound.

To overcome this imprecision, the schema variable sk can be replaced with a fresh logical variable $\iota_{sk}(sk) = x$ of type A. The schema variable t is eliminated through the instantiation by a Skolem constant $\iota_{sk}(t) = d$. Finally, we add an existential quantifier $\exists x$. The resulting formula without schema variables is

$$\exists x; \iota_{sk}(M(\texttt{pullout})) \quad \equiv \quad \exists x; (x \doteq d)$$

which is obviously universally valid.

The Order Matters

To establish the soundness of taclets for a theory, validity of the meaning formulas of all taclets in the theory must be shown. To this end, it would be convenient if already proved taclets could be used in the soundness proofs of the remaining taclets.

Such taclet applications must be restricted however: If taclets could be used unconditionally in each other's soundness proofs, two unsound taclets could be abused to mutually establish their validity. The consistency of the taclet rule base could thus be compromised.

A simple heuristics guarantees that such cyclic dependencies within the set of taclets of a theory are impossible: For the verification of the soundness of taclet, only taclets which are defined *before* it in the input file may be used.

This requires that the order of taclets is well thought of for the design of a theory to simplify the proof workload. Naturally, the axioms which fix the semantics, go first; followed by taclets capturing reusable lemmas, optimized special purpose taclets follow last.

---

[11] Schematic types, known as *generic sorts* in KeY, are like schema variables for type references that can be instantiated by concrete types.

Chapter 5
Theories

Peter H. Schmitt and Richard Bubel

5.1 Introduction

For a program verification tool to be really useful it needs to be able to reason about at least the most important data types, both abstract data types and those built into the programming language. In Section 5.2 below the theory of finite sequences of arbitrary objects, allowing in particular arbitrary nestings of sequences in sequences, is presented. This presentation covers axioms for a core theory plus definitional extensions plus consistency considerations.

Section 5.3 contains an axiomatization of Java's String data type. The theory of the mathematical integers has already been dealt with in Subsection 2.4.2. Section 5.4 below explains how the KeY system deals with the Java integer data types.

5.2 Finite Sequences

This section develops and explains the theory T_{seq} of finite sequences. By *Seq* we denote the type of finite sequences. The vocabulary Σ_{seq} of the theory is listed in Figure 5.1. We will start with a simple core theory CoT_{seq} and incrementally enrich it via definitional extensions. Typing of a function symbol f is given as $f : A_1 \times \ldots \times A_n \to R$ with argument types A_i and result type R, typing of a predicate symbol p as $p(A_1 \times \ldots \times A_n)$.

Our notion of a sequence is rather liberal, e.g., $\langle 5,6,7,8 \rangle$ is a sequence, in fact a sequence of integers. But the heterogeneous and nested list $\langle 0, \langle \emptyset, seqEmpty, null \rangle, true \rangle$ is also allowed.

The semantics of the symbols of the core theory will be given in Definition 5.3. We provide here a first informal account of the intended meaning. The function value $seqLen(s)$ is the length of list s. Since for heterogeneous lists there is no way the type of an entry can be recovered from the type of the list, we provide a family of access functions $seqGet_A$ that yields the cast to type A of the i-th entry in list s.

© Springer International Publishing AG 2016
W. Ahrendt et al. (Eds.): Deductive Software Verification, LNCS 10001, pp. 149–166, 2016
DOI: 10.1007/978-3-319-49812-6_5

Core Theory

$A::seqGet : Seq \times int \to A$ for any type $A \sqsubseteq Any$

$seqGetOutside : Any$

$seqLen : Seq \to int$

Variable Binder

$seqDef : int \times int \times Seq \to Seq$

Definitional Extension

$seqDepth : Seq \to int$

$seqEmpty : Seq$

$seqSingleton : Any \to Seq$

$seqConcat : Seq \times Seq \to Seq$

$seqSub : Seq \times int \times int \to Seq$

$seqReverse : Seq \to Seq$

$seqIndexOf : Seq \times Any \to int$

$seqNPerm(Seq)$

$seqPerm(Seq, Seq)$

$seqSwap : Seq \times int \times int \to Seq$

$seqRemove : Seq \times int \to Seq$

$seqNPermInv : Seq \to Seq$

Figure 5.1 The vocabulary Σ_{seq} of the theory T_{seq} of finite sequences

(The concrete, ASCII syntax is $A::seqGet$, but we stick here with the slightly shorter notation $seqGet_A$.) The constant $seqGetOutside$ is an arbitrary element of the top type Any. It is, e.g., used as the value of any attempt to access a sequence outside its range. $seqDef$ is a variable binder symbol, check Section 2.3.1 for explanation. Its precise semantics is given in Definition 5.2 below. The reader may get a first intuition from the simple example $seqDef\{u\}(1, 5, u^2)$ that represents the sequence $\langle 1, 4, 9, 16 \rangle$. We will comment on the symbols in the definitional extension, when we are finished with the core theory following page 152.

lenNonNegative

$\forall Seq\ s; (0 \leq seqLen(s))$

equalityToSeqGetAndSeqLen

$\forall Seq\ s_1, s_2; (s_1 \doteq s_2 \leftrightarrow seqLen(s_1) \doteq seqLen(s_2) \land$
$\qquad\qquad\qquad \forall int\ i; (0 \leq i < seqLen(s_1) \to seqGetAny(s_1, i) \doteq seqGet_{Any}(s_2, i)))$

getOfSeqDef

$\forall int\ i, ri, le; \forall Any\ \bar{x}; ($
$\qquad ((0 \leq i \land i < ri - le) \to seqGet_A(seqDef\{u\}(le, ri, t), i) \doteq cast_A(t\{(le + i)/u\})) \land$
$\qquad (\neg(0 \leq i \land i < ri - le) \to seqGet_A(seqDef\{u\}(le, ri, t), i) \doteq cast_A(seqGetOutside)))$

lenOfSeqDef

$\forall int\ ri, le; ((le < ri \to seqLen(seqDef\{u\}(le, ri, t)) \doteq ri - le) \land$
$\qquad (ri \leq le \to seqLen(seqDef\{u\}(le, ri, t)) \doteq 0))$

Figure 5.2 Axioms of the core theory CoT_{seq} (in mathematical notation)

The axioms of the core theory CoT_{seq} are shown in Figure 5.2 in mathematical notation together with the names of the corresponding taclets. In getOfSeqDef the quantifier $\forall Any\ \bar{x}$ binds the variables that may occur in term t.

Definition 5.1 below extends the semantics of type domains given in Figure 2.10 on page 45. More precisely, the definition gives the construction to obtain D^{Seq} when all other type domains are fixed.

Definition 5.1 (The type domain D^{Seq}). The type domain D^{Seq} is defined via the following induction:

$$D^{Seq} \quad := \quad \bigcup_{n \geq 0} D^n_{Seq}$$

where

$$
\begin{aligned}
U &= D^{Any} \setminus D^{Seq} \\
D^0_{Seq} &= \{\langle\rangle\} \\
D^{n+1}_{Seq} &= \{\langle a_0, \ldots, a_{k-1}\rangle \mid k \in \mathbb{N} \text{ and } a_i \in D^n_{Seq} \cup U, 0 \leq i < k\} \quad \text{for } n \geq 0
\end{aligned}
$$

The type domain for *Seq* being fixed we now may deliver on the forward reference after Definition 2.22 and define precisely the meaning of the variable binder symbol $seqDef\{iv\}(le, ri, e)$ in the JFOL structure $\mathcal{M}$. As already done in Section 2.4.5 we will use the notation $t^{\mathcal{M},\beta}$ for term evaluation instead of $val_{\mathcal{M},\beta}(t)$. We further will suppress β and write $t^{\mathcal{M}}$ if it is not needed or not relevant.

Definition 5.2.

$$
seqDef\{iv\}(le, ri, e)^{\mathcal{M},\beta} = \begin{cases} \langle a_0, \ldots a_{k-1}\rangle & \text{if } (ri - le)^{\mathcal{M},\beta} = k > 0 \text{ and } a_i = e^{\mathcal{M},\beta_i} \\ & \text{with } \beta_i = \beta[le+i/iv] \text{ and all } 0 \leq i < k \\ \langle\rangle & \text{otherwise} \end{cases}
$$

Remember, that $\beta[le+i/iv]$ is the variable assignment that coincides with β expect for the argument iv where it takes the value $le+i$.

The core vocabulary of CoT_{seq} is interpreted as follows:

Definition 5.3.

1. $seqGet^{\mathcal{M}}_A(\langle a_0, \ldots, a_{n-1}\rangle, i) = \begin{cases} cast^{\mathcal{M}}_A(a_i) & \text{if } 0 \leq i < n \\ cast^{\mathcal{M}}_A(seqGetOutside^{\mathcal{M}}) & \text{otherwise} \end{cases}$
2. $seqLen^{\mathcal{M}}(\langle a_0, \ldots, a_{n-1}\rangle) = n$
3. $seqGetOutside^{\mathcal{M}} \in D^{Any}$ arbitrary.

To have a name for it we might call a structure $\mathcal{M}$ in the vocabulary Σ_J (see Figure 2.4) plus the core vocabulary of finite sequences a *CoreSeq* structure, if its restriction to the JFOL vocabulary is a JFOL structure as defined in Section 2.4.5 and, in addition $\mathcal{M}$ satisfies Definition 5.3. We observe, that the expansion of a JFOL structure $\mathcal{M}_0$ to a *CoreSeq* structure is uniquely determined once an interpretation $seqGetOutside^{\mathcal{M}_0}$ is chosen.

Theorem 5.4. *The theory CoT$_{seq}$ is consistent.*

Proof. It is easily checked that the axioms in Figure 5.2 are true in all *CoreSeq* structures. The explicit construction guarantees that there is at least one *CoreSeq* structure.

$$\forall Seq\ s; (\forall int\ i; ((0 \le i < seqLen(s) \rightarrow \neg instance_{Seq}(seqGet_{Any}(s,i))) \rightarrow seqDepth(s) \doteq 0) \wedge$$
$$\forall Seq\ s; (\forall int\ i; ((0 \le i < seqLen(s) \wedge instance_{Seq}(seqGet_{Any}(s,i))) \rightarrow$$
$$seqDepth(s) > seqDepth(seqGet_{Seq}(s,i))) \wedge$$
$$\forall Seq\ s; (\exists int\ i; (0 \le i < seqLen(s) \wedge instance_{Seq}(seqGet_{Any}(s,i))) \rightarrow$$
$$\exists int\ i; (0 \le i < seqLen(s) \wedge instance_{Seq}(seqGet_{Any}(s,i)) \wedge$$
$$seqDepth(s) \doteq seqDepth(seqGet_{Seq}(s,i)) + 1)$$

Figure 5.3 Definition of *seqDepth*

We observe that *seqDepth*(s) as defined in Figure 5.3 equals the recursive definition

$$seqDepth(s) = \max\{seqDepth(seqGet_{Seq}(s,i)) \mid 0 \le i < seqLen(s) \wedge$$
$$instance_{Seq}(seqGet_{Seq}(s,i))\}$$

with the understanding that the maximum of the empty set is 0. Since we have not introduced the maximum operator we had to resort to the formula given above. The function *seqDepth* is foremost of theoretical interest and at the moment of this writing not realized in the KeY system. *seqDepth*(s) is an integer denoting the *nesting depth* of sequence s. If s has no entries that are themselves sequences then *seqDepth*(s) $\doteq 0$. For a sequence s_{int} of sequences of integers we would have *seqDepth*(s_{int}) $\doteq 0$.

In Figure 5.4 the mathematical formulas defining the remaining noncore vocabulary are accompanied by the names of the corresponding taclets. A few explaining comments will help the reader to grasp their meaning. The subsequence *seqSub*(s,i,j) from i to j of sequence s includes the i-th entry, but excludes the j-th entry. In the case $\neg(i < j)$ it will be the empty sequence, this is a consequence of the semantics of *seqDef*. The term *seqIndexOf*(s,t) denotes the least index n such that *seqGet*$_{Any}$(s,n) $\doteq t$ if there is one, and is undefined otherwise. See Section 2.3.2 on how undefinedness is handled in our logic. A sequence s satisfies the predicate *seqNPerm*(s) if it is a permutation of the integers $\{0,\dots,seqLen(s)-1\}$. The binary predicate *seqPerm*(s_1,s_s) is true if s_2 is a permutation of s_1. Thus *seqNPerm*($\langle 5,4,0,2,3,1\rangle$) and *seqPerm*($\langle a,b,c\rangle,\langle b,a,c\rangle$) are true.

Careful observation reveals that the interpretation of the vocabulary outside the core vocabulary is uniquely determined by the definitions in Figures 5.3 and 5.4.

We establish the following notation:

Definition 5.5. By T_{seq} we denote the theory given by the core axioms CoT_{seq} plus the definitions from Figures 5.3 and 5.4.

On the semantic side we call a structure $\mathcal{M}$ in the vocabulary Σ_J plus Σ_{Seq} a *Seq* structure if the restriction of $\mathcal{M}$ to Σ_J is a JFOL structure and $\mathcal{M}$ satisfies Definitions 5.3 and 5.4.

defOfEmpty
$seqEmpty \doteq seqDef\{iv\}(0,0,x)$
x is an arbitrary term of type *Any* not containing the variable iv.

defOfSeqSingleton
$\forall Any\ x; (seqSingleton(x) \doteq seqDef\{iv\}(0,1,x))$

defOfSeqConcat
$\forall Seq\ s_1, s_2; (seqConcat(s_1, s_2) \doteq$
$\qquad seqDef\{iv\}(0, seqLen(s_1) + seqLen(s_2),\ \text{if}\ iv < seqLen(s_1)$
$\qquad\qquad\qquad\qquad \text{then}\ seqGet_{Any}(s_1, iv)$
$\qquad\qquad\qquad\qquad \text{else}\ seqGet_{Any}(s_2, iv - seqLen(s_1)))))$

defOfSeqSub
$\forall Seq\ s; \forall int\ i, j; (seqSub(s, i, j) \doteq seqDef\{iv\}(i, j, seqGet_{Any}(s, iv)))$

defOfSeqReverse
$\forall Seq\ s; (seqReverse(s) \doteq seqDef\{iv\}(0, seqLen(s), seqGet_{Any}(s, seqLen(s) - iv - 1)))$

seqIndexOf
$\forall Seq\ s; \forall Any\ t; \forall int\ n; (0 \leq n < seqLen(s) \wedge seqGet_{Any}(s, n) \doteq t\ \wedge$
$\qquad\qquad \forall int\ m; (0 \leq m < n \rightarrow seqGet_{Any}(s, m) \neq t)$
$\qquad\qquad \rightarrow seqIndexOf(s, t) \doteq n)$

seqNPermDefReplace
$\forall Seq\ s; (seqNPerm(s) \leftrightarrow$
$\qquad\qquad \forall int\ i; (0 \leq i < seqLen(s) \rightarrow \exists int\ j; (0 \leq j < seqLen(s) \wedge seqGet_{int}(s, j) \doteq i)))$

seqPermDef
$\forall Seq\ s_1, s_2; (seqPerm(s_1, s_2) \leftrightarrow seqLen(s_1) \doteq seqLen(s_2)\ \wedge$
$\qquad\qquad \exists Seq\ s; (seqLen(s) \doteq seqLen(s_1) \wedge seqNPerm(s)\ \wedge$
$\qquad\qquad \forall int\ i; (0 \leq i < seqLen(s) \rightarrow$
$\qquad\qquad\qquad seqGet_{Any}(s_1, i) \doteq seqGet_{Any}(s_2, seqGet_{int}(s, i)))))$

defOfSeqSwap
$\forall Seq\ s; \forall int\ i, j; (seqSwap(s, i, j) \doteq$
$\qquad seqDef\{iv\}(0, seqLen(s),\ \text{if}\ \neg(0 \leq i < seqLen(s) \wedge 0 \leq j < seqLen(s))$
$\qquad\qquad\qquad\qquad \text{then}\ seqGet_{Any}(s, iv)$
$\qquad\qquad\qquad\qquad \text{else if}\ iv \doteq i$
$\qquad\qquad\qquad\qquad\qquad \text{then}\ seqGet_{Any}(s, j)$
$\qquad\qquad\qquad\qquad\qquad \text{else if}\ iv \doteq j$
$\qquad\qquad\qquad\qquad\qquad\qquad \text{then}\ seqGet_{Any}(s, i)$
$\qquad\qquad\qquad\qquad\qquad\qquad \text{else}\ seqGet_{Any}(s, iv)))$

defOfSeqRemove
$\forall Seq\ s; \forall int\ i; (seqRemove(s, i) \doteq\ \text{if}\ i < 0 \vee seqLen(s) \leq i$
$\qquad\qquad\qquad \text{then}\ s$
$\qquad\qquad\qquad \text{else}\ seqDef\{iv\}(0, seqLen(s) - 1,\ \text{if}\ iv < i$
$\qquad\qquad\qquad\qquad\qquad\qquad \text{then}\ seqGet_{Any}(s, iv)$
$\qquad\qquad\qquad\qquad\qquad\qquad \text{else}\ seqGet_{Any}(s, iv + 1)))$

defOfSeqNPermInv
$\forall Seq\ s; (seqNPermInv(s) \doteq seqDef\{iv\}(0, seqLen(s), seqIndexOf(s, iv)))$

Figure 5.4 Definition for noncore vocabulary in mathematical notation

Theorem 5.6. *The theory T_{Seq} is consistent.*

Proof. The consistency of T_{Seq} follows from the consistency of CoT_{Seq} since it is a definitional extension.

A proof of Theorem 5.6 together with a detailed review of the concept of definitional extensions, plus statement and proof of the relative completeness of T_{Seq} can be found in the technical report on first-order logic available from the companion website to this book www.key-project.org/thebook2.

1 seqSelfDefinition
$\forall Seq\ s; (s \doteq seqDef\{u\}(0, seqLen(s), seqGet_{Any}(s, u)))$

2 seqOutsideValue
$\forall Seq\ s; (\forall int\ i; ((i < 0 \vee seqLen(s) \leq i) \rightarrow seqGet_{\alpha}(s, i) \doteq (\alpha)seqGetOutside))$

3 castedGetAny
$\forall Seq\ s; \forall int\ i; ((\beta)seqGet_{Any}(s, i) \doteq seqGet_{\beta}(s, i))$

4 getOfSeqSingleton
$\forall Any\ x; \forall int\ i; (seqGet_{\alpha}(seqSingleton(x), i) \doteq$ if $i \doteq 0$ then $(\alpha)x$ else $(\alpha)seqGetOutside)$

5 getOfSeqConcat
$\forall Seq\ s, s2; \forall int\ i; (seqGet_{\alpha}(seqConcat(s, s2), i) \doteq$ if $i < seqLen(s)$
$\qquad\qquad$ then $seqGet_{\alpha}(s, i)$
$\qquad\qquad$ else $seqGet_{\alpha}(s2, i - seqLen(s)))$

6 getOfSeqSub
$\forall Seq\ s; \forall int\ from, to, i; (seqGet_{\alpha}(seqSub(s, from, to), i) \doteq$ if $0 \leq i \wedge i < (to - from)$
$\qquad\qquad$ then $seqGet_{\alpha}(s, i + from)$
$\qquad\qquad$ else $(\alpha)seqGetOutside$

7 getOfSeqReverse
$\forall Seq\ s; \forall int\ from, to, i; (seqGet_{\alpha}(seqReverse(s), i) \doteq seqGet_{\alpha}(s, seqLen(s) - 1 - i))$

8 lenOfSeqEmpty
$seqLen(seqEmpty) \doteq 0$

9 lenOfSeqSingleton
$\forall Any\ x; (seqLen(seqSingleton(x)) \doteq 1)$

10 lenOfSeqConcat
$\forall Seq\ s, s2; (seqLen(seqConcat(s, s2)) \doteq seqLen(s) + seqLen(s2))$

11 lenOfSeqSub
$\forall Seq\ s; \forall in\ from, to; (seqLen(seqSub(s, from, to)) \doteq$ if $from < to$ then $(to - from)$ else $0)$

12 lenOfSeqReverse
$\forall Seq\ s; (seqLen(seqReverse(s)) \doteq seqLen(s))$

13 seqConcatWithSeqEmpty
$\forall Seq\ s; (seqConcat(s, seqEmpty) \doteq s)$

14 seqReverseOfSeqEmpty
$seqReverse(seqEmpty) \doteq seqEmpty$

Figure 5.5 Some derived rules for finite sequences

Figure 5.5 lists some consequences that can be derived from the definitions in Figure 5.4 and the Core Theory. The entry 1 is a technical lemma that is useful in the derivation of the following lemmas in the list. The entry 2 clarifies the role of the default value *seqGetOutside*; it is the default or error value for any out-of-range access. Rules 2 to 7 are schematic rule. These rules are applicable for any instantiations of the schema variable α by a type. Entry 3 addresses an important issue: on one hand there is the family of function symbols $seqGet_\alpha$, on the other hand there are the cast expressions $(\alpha)seqGet_{Any}$. The lemma says that both coincide. The entries 4 to 12 allow to determine the access function and the length of the empty sequence, singleton, concatenation, subsequence and reverse constructors. The last two entries 13 and 14 are examples for a whole set of rules that cover corner cases of the constructors involved.

1 seqNPermRange
$\forall Seq\ s; (seqNPerm(s) \rightarrow$
$\forall int\ i; (0 \leq i \wedge i < seqLen(s) \rightarrow (0 \leq seqGet_{int}(s,i) \wedge seqGet_{int}(s,i) < seqLen(s))))$

2 seqNPermInjective
$\forall Seq\ s; (seqNPerm(s) \wedge$
$\quad \forall int\ i,j; (0 \leq i \wedge i < seqLen(s) \wedge 0 \leq j \wedge j < seqLen(s) \wedge seqGet_{int}(s,i) \doteq seqGet_{int}(s,j))$
$\quad \rightarrow i \doteq j)$

3 seqNPermEmpty
$seqNPerm(seqEmpty)$

4 seqNPermSingleton
$\forall int\ i; (seqNPerm(seqSingleton(i)) \leftrightarrow i \doteq 0)$

5 seqNPermComp
$\forall Seq\ s1,s2; (seqNPerm(s1) \wedge seqNPerm(s2) \wedge seqLen(s1) \doteq seqLen(s2) \rightarrow$
$seqNPerm(seqDef\{u\}(0,seqLen(s1),seqGet_{int}(s1,seqGet_{int}(s2,u)))))$

6 seqPermTrans
$\forall Seq\ s1,s2,s3; (seqPerm(s1,s2) \wedge seqPerm(s2,s3) \rightarrow seqPerm(s1,s3))$

7 seqPermRefl
$\forall Seq\ s; (seqPerm(s,s))$

Figure 5.6 Some derived rules for permutations

Figure 5.6 lists some derived rules for the one-place predicate *seqNPerm* and the two-place predicate *seqPerm* that follow from the definitions in Figure 5.4. Surprisingly, none of the proofs apart from the one for seqNPermRange needs induction. This is mainly due to the presence of the $seqDef\{\}(,,)$ construct. The lemma seqNPermRange itself is a kind of pigeon-hole principle and could only be proved via induction.

Applications of the theory of finite sequences can be found in Section 16.5 and foremost in Chapter 19.

5.3 Strings

Java strings are implemented as objects of their own and they are not identified
with arrays of characters. This eases treatment of strings in our program logic as we
can reuse all the mechanisms already in place for objects. So, do we need special
treatment for them at all? Why not simply use contracts as for other API classes?

To answer the first question: Although strings are normal objects, the Java Language Specification [Gosling et al., 2013] provides some additional infrastructure
not available for other kinds of objects. In particular, the existence of string literals like "Hello␣World" requires additional thought. A string literal is a reference
to a string object whose content coincides with the string literal name within the
quotation marks. The problem to be solved is to make string literals 'behave' like integer or Boolean literals. For instance, the expression "Hello" == "Hello" should
always be true. To solve this issue, Java ensures that all occurrences of the same
literal reference the same object. To ensure this behavior Java manages a *pool* of
strings in which all strings referenced by string literals (actually, all compile time
constants of type String) are put. Nevertheless, the taken solution does not hide
completely that string literals are different from other literals, e.g., the expression
new String("Hello") == "Hello" evaluates to false. To represent the pool, we
could model it in Java itself. This solution would allow us to be mostly ignorant to
strings on the logic level, but introduce a lot of clutter in the reasoning process when
string literals are involved. Instead we use an alternative route and model the pool
purely on the logic level, which allows us a more streamlined representation and
deemphasizes the use of a pool.

We go a step further and introduce a kind of "ghost" field for Java string objects that
assigns each string a finite sequence of characters based on the Sequence data type
introduce in the previous section. As specifications about strings express properties
about their content, e.g., that the content equals or matches a given expression (e.g.,
a regular expression), providing an abstract data type for strings allows us to separate
concerns and to ease writing of specifications.

In this section we describe three parts that constitute our handling of Java strings:
The theory T_{cl} of sequences of characters representing the content of a Java string as
an extension of the theory of finite sequences, a theory T_{rex} of regular expressions to
express and reason conveniently about the content of strings, and finally we conclude
with the actual theory $T_{\texttt{java.lang.String}}$ of Java strings, which uses the previous two
theories to model Java strings.

5.3.1 Sequences of Characters

Characters are not represented as a distinct type, but as integers which are interpreted
as the characters unicode (UTF-16) representation. A finite sequence of characters
is used to model the underlying theory to support Java Strings. The length of the
sequence is the number of 16-bit unicode values. This value might not coincide with

the number of actual characters as some unicode characters need to be represented by two 16-bit numbers. The presentation below and the actual implementation assumes that only unicode characters in the range 0x0000 − 0xFFFF are used.

We extend the theory of finite sequences by the additional functions and predicates shown in Table 5.1. They allow us later to specify the behavior of the String's method concisely. The first four functions return the first (or last) index of a sequence

Table 5.1 The additional functions and predicates of T_{cl} (int^* is used to indicate that a character's UTF-16 unicode representation is expected as argument; the actual type is int)

Extensions

$$clIndexOfChar : Seq \times int^* \times int \to int$$
$$clIndexOfCl : Seq \times int \times Seq \to int$$
$$clLastIndexOfChar : Seq \times int^* \times int \to int$$
$$clLastIndexOfCl : Seq \times int \times Seq \to int$$
$$clReplace : Seq \times int^* \times int^* \to Seq$$
$$clTranslateInt : int \to Seq$$
$$clRemoveZeros : Seq \to Seq$$
$$clHashCode : Seq \to int$$

$$clStartsWith : Seq \times Seq$$
$$clEndsWith : Seq \times Seq$$
$$clContains : Seq \times Seq$$

starting from the position given as third argument at which to find the specified character (start of the given character sequence) or −1 if no such character (character sequence) exists (this differs from $seqIndexOf$, which is undefined for elements not occurring in a sequent). Function $clReplace(s, c_1, c_2)$ evaluates to a sequence equal to s except that all occurrences of character c_1 have been replaced by character c_2. Function $clTranslateInt$ takes a character sequence specifying a number and translates it into the corresponding integer. It comes paired with the auxiliary function $clRemoveZero$ which removes any leading zeros, as in "000123", first, before the result can be handed over to $clTranslateInt$ in order to rewrite it into the integer 123.

The predicates $clContains$, $clStartsWith$, and $clEndsWith$ evaluate to true if the character sequence given as first argument contains, starts or ends with the character sequence given as second argument, respectively.

The actual axiomatizations are rather technical, but not complicated. Those for $clIndexOfChar$ and $clContains$ are shown in Figure 5.7. The axiomatization of $clIndexOfChar$ makes use of JavaDL's ifEx operator to determine the minimal (first) index of the searched character, if one exists.

For convenience reasons, we write short "abc" instead of the actual term $seqConcat(seqSingleton('a'), seqConcat(seqSingleton('b'), seqSingleton('c')))$. The pretty printer of KeY outputs a character sequence in this way (outside of modalities), and the parser accepts string literals as an alternative syntax for character sequences.

indexOf
$\forall Seq\ l,c;\forall int\ i;\ \big(clIndexOfChar(l,c,i) \doteq$
  ifEx $int\ iv;(i \geq 0 \wedge iv \geq i \wedge iv < seqLen(l) \wedge\ seqGet_{int}(l,iv) \doteq c)$
  then(iv) else$(-1)\big)$

containsAxiom
$\forall Seq\ textString,\ searchString;\ \big($
  $clContains(textString, searchString) \leftrightarrow$
    $\exists int\ iv;\ \big(iv \geq 0\ \wedge\ iv + seqLen(searchString) \geq seqLen(textString)$
      $\wedge\ seqSub(textString,iv,iv + seqLen(searchString)) \doteq searchString\big)\big)$

Figure 5.7 Axioms for *clIndexOfChar* and *clContains*

5.3.2 Regular Expressions for Sequences

To be able to conveniently specify methods manipulating strings, the theory T_{rex} allows one to match elements of type *Seq* using regular expression.[1] Pattern expressions (PExp) are represented as terms of type `rex`. Table 5.2 lists the PExp constructors. For instance, the pattern represented by the term $repeatStar(rex("ab"))$ matches a

Table 5.2 Pattern expressions (PExp) with $cl : Seq$ and $pe, pe1, pe2 : rex$.

constructor (of type `rex`)		constructor	
$rex(cl)$	matches exactly cl	$repeatStar(pe)$	pe^*
$opt(pe)$	$pe?$	$repeatPlus(pe)$	pe^+
$alt(pe1,pe2)$	$pe1 + pe2$	$repeat(pe,n)$	pe^n
$regConcat(pe1,pe2)$	$pe1 \cdot pe2$		

finite but arbitrary repetition of the word "*ab*". Match expressions are constructed using the predicate $match(rex, Seq)$. The predicate *match* takes two arguments: a PExp as first argument and the concrete character sequence to be matched against the pattern as second argument. The match expression is true if and only if the provided pattern matches the complete Seq.

Our calculus features a complete axiomatization of the pattern and matching language. Further, there are a number of derived rules to reduce and simplify pattern and match expression terms as far as possible. We give here only a few typical representatives of these axioms and rules.

The first axiom maps the alternative pattern constructor back to a logical disjunction:

  altAxiom
    $\forall rex\ pe1,pe2; \forall Seq\ cl;$
      $match(alt(pe1,pe2),cl) \leftrightarrow (match(pe1,cl) \vee match(pe2,cl))$

---

[1] Remark: T_{rex} goes actually beyond regular expressions.

The second axiom removes the pattern concatenation by guessing the index where to split the text to be matched into two parts. Each part is then independently matched against the corresponding subpattern:

regConcatAxiom
$$\forall rex\ pe1, pe2; \forall Seq\ cl; \big($$
$$match(regConcat(pe1, pe2), cl) \leftrightarrow \big(\exists int\ i; (i \geq 0 \wedge i \leq seqLen(cl)$$
$$\wedge\ match(pe1, seqSub(cl, 0, i)) \wedge match(pe2, seqSub(cl, i, seqLen(cl)))))\big)$$

A typical reduction rule aiming to reduce the complexity of is for instance:

regConcatConcreteStringLeft
$$\exists rex\ pre; \exists Seq\ s, cl; \big($$
$$match(regConcat(rex(s), pe), cl)$$
$$\leftrightarrow \big(seqLen(s) \leq seqLen(cl)$$
$$\wedge\ match(rex(s), seqSub(cl, 0, seqLen(s)))$$
$$\wedge\ match(pe, seqSub(cl, seqLen(s), seqLen(cl)))))\big)$$

5.3.3 Relating Java String Objects to Sequences of Characters

The previous sections introduced the logic representation of character sequences and regular expressions. To achieve our goal to specify and verify programs in presence of Strings, the abstract representation of a string's content and the implementation of Java's `String` class need to be related.

This could be simply achieved by introducing a ghost field and keeping the content on the heap. We choose a similar but slightly different modeling, which simplifies verification down the road by exploiting that once a String instance is created, its content does not change. This is the same situation as for the length field of an array, and we use the same idea. The function $strContent$: `java.lang.String` $\rightarrow Seq$ maps each String instance to a sequence of characters. It is left unspecified initially and upon creation of a new String instance s representing, e.g., the character list sc, the formula $strContent(s) \doteq sc$ is added to the antecedent of the formula. This is well-defined as the content of a `String` instance cannot be changed. The following sequent calculus rule illustrates this mechanism:

stringConcat
$$\cfrac{\Gamma, strContent(sk) \doteq seqConcat(strContent(s1), strContent(s2)), sk \neq \texttt{null} \Longrightarrow \{v := sk\}\,\{\texttt{heap} := create(\texttt{heap}, sk)\}\,\langle\pi\omega\rangle\phi, \Delta}{\Gamma \Longrightarrow \langle\pi\ v = s1 + s2;\ \omega\rangle\phi, \Delta}$$

Schema variables $v, s1, s2$ match local program variables of type `java.lang.String` and sk is a fresh Skolem-constant.

5.3.4 String Literals and the String Pool

The Java string pool caches `String` instances using their content as key. On start-up of the virtual machine and after class loading all compile-time constant of type `String` (in particular all string literals) are resolved to an actual String object. New elements can be added to the cache at run-time with method `intern()`, but Java programs cannot remove elements from the cache.

We model the string pool as an injective function

$$\text{strPool}: Seq \rightarrow \text{java.lang.String}$$

The assignment rule for string literals in the presence of the string pool can now be defined as follows:

> stringAssignment
> $$\frac{\begin{array}{l} \Gamma, strContent(\text{strPool}(sLit_{CL})) \doteq sLit_{CL}, \\ \text{strPool}(sLit_{CL}) \not\doteq null, \\ select_{\text{boolean}}(\text{heap}, \text{strPool}(strContent(sLit_{CL})), created) \doteq TRUE \\ \Longrightarrow \\ \{v := \text{strPool}(sLit_{CL})\} \langle \pi\ \omega \rangle \phi, \Delta \end{array}}{\Gamma \Longrightarrow \langle \pi\ v = sLit;\ \omega \rangle \phi, \Delta}$$

Here *sLit* is a schema variable matching string literals and $sLit_{CL}$ denotes the finite sequence *Seq* representation of the matched string literal *sLit*.

One side remark at this point concerning the concatenation of string literals, i.e., how a program fragment of the kind `v = "a" + "b";` is treated. In this case the expression `"a" + "b"` is a compile time constant, which are as their name suggests evaluated at compile time. Hence, any such expression has already been replaced by the result `"ab"` when reading in the program (in other words, in JavaDL all compile time constants are already replaced by their fully evaluated literal expression).

Finally, we give one of the rules for updating the Java string pool with a new element. Note, this rule is actually specified as a contract of method `intern()` of class `String`:

> updatePool
> $$\frac{\begin{array}{l} \Gamma, \neg(v \doteq null), \text{strPool}(strContent(v)) \not\doteq null, \\ select_{\text{boolean}}(\text{heap}, \text{strPool}(strContent(v)), created) \doteq TRUE \\ \Longrightarrow \{r := \text{strPool}(strContent(v))\} \langle \pi\ \omega \rangle \phi, \Delta \end{array}}{\Gamma, \neg(v \doteq null) \Longrightarrow \langle \pi\ r = .\text{intern}();\ \omega \rangle \phi, \Delta}$$

5.3.5 Specification of the Java String API

To obtain a complete calculus for Java strings, additional rules have to be created which translate an integer or the `null` reference to its String representation. The formalization of the necessary translate functions is rather tedious, but otherwise straightforward. The technical details are described in [Geilmann, 2009].

Based on the formalization described in this section, we specified the majority of the methods declared and implemented in the `java.lang.String` class. The Seq ADT functions have been chosen to represent closely the core functionality provided by the String class. The specification of the methods required then merely to consider the border cases of most of the methods. Border cases are typically those cases where the ADT has been left underspecified and that cause an exception in Java.

5.4 Integers

Arithmetic reasoning is required for a number of verification tasks like proving that a certain index is within the array's bounds, that no arithmetic exception occurs and, of course, that a method computes the correct value. Mathematical integers have already been covered in Section 2.4.5, in this section we highlight the axiomatization of integers with respect to their finite integral counterparts used in Java.

In lieu of the whole numbers $\mathbb{Z}$, programming languages usually use finite integral types based on a two-complement representation. For instance, Java's integral types (`byte`, `char`, `short`, `int` and `long`) are represented in 8-bit, 16-bit, 32-bit and 64-bit two-complement representation (with the exception of `char` which is represented as an unsigned 16-bit number).

The finiteness of integral types and the often used modulo arithmetics entail the possibility of underflows and overflows. While sometimes intended, they are also a source of bugs leading to unexpected behavior. As pointed out by Joshua Bloch[2] most binary search algorithms are broken because of an overflow that might happen when computing the middle of the interval `lower...upper` by `(upper+lower)/2` (e.g., for `lower` equal to 100 and `upper` equal to the maximal value of its integral type).

The question arises: How do we model finite integral types within the program logic. One possibility is to define new sorts to model the required fixed-precision numbers together with functions for addition and subtraction, e.g., as a general fixed-width bit-vector theory. Another approach, and that is the one we pursued in JFOL, is to map all Java arithmetic operations to standard arithmetic operations without the need to introduce new additional sorts.

---

[2] googleresearch.blogspot.se/2006/06/extra-extra-read-all-about-it-nearly.html

5.4.1 Core Integer Theory

The predefined sort `int` is evaluated to the set of whole numbers $\mathbb{Z}$. Table 5.3 shows a selection of the most important interpreted core functions. All of them are interpreted canonically. In case of division, *div* rounding towards the nearer lower number takes place, and *mod* is interpreted as the modulo function.

On top of these core functions, derived functions (shown in Table 5.3 as extensions) are defined. Their domain is still the whole numbers, i.e., no modulo arithmetics are involved, but otherwise they reflect the division and modulo semantics in Java more closely. Namely, function *jdiv* is interpreted as the division on $\mathbb{Z}$ rounding towards zero, while *jmod* is interpreted as the remainder function in opposite to the modulo function.

Finally, functions like *addJint*, *addJlong* etc. are defined in such a way that they reflect the modulo semantics of the Java operations. They are axiomatized solely using the functions shown in Table 5.3

Table 5.3 Core and extension functions for the `int` data type

Core		
add	'+'	addition on $\mathbb{Z}$
sub	'-'	subtraction on $\mathbb{Z}$
div	'/'	division on $\mathbb{Z}$ (Euclidean semantics)
mod	'%'	modulo on $\mathbb{Z}$
mul	'*'	multiplication on $\mathbb{Z}$
Extensions		
jdiv	n/a	division on $\mathbb{Z}$ (rounding towards zero)
jmod	n/a	remainder on $\mathbb{Z}$

Table 5.4 Functions for Java arithmetics

addJint/addJLong	addition with overflow for `int/long`
divJint/divJLong	modulo with overflow for `int/long`
moduloByte/moduloChar/moduloShort/...	modulo operation mapping numbers into their respective range
...	

On the calculus side the axiom for e.g. *addJlong* is given as rewrite rule

$$addJlong(fst, snd) \rightsquigarrow moduloLong(add(fst, snd))$$

and expresses the meaning of addition with overflow w.r.t. the value range of `long` in terms of the standard arithmetic addition and a modulo operation. The calculus rewrite rule defining function *moduloLong* is

$$moduloLong(i) \rightsquigarrow$$
$$add(long\_MIN, mod(add(long\_HALFRANGE, i), long\_RANGE))$$

Its definition refers only to the standard arithmetic functions for addition and modulo. The only other elements *long_MIN*, *long_HALFRANGE* and *long_RANGE* are constants like the smallest number of type `long` or the cardinality of the set of all numbers in `long`.

In our logic all function symbols are interpreted as total functions. There are several possibilities to deal with terms like $div(x,0)$ like (a) returning a default value, (b) returning a special named error element or (c) using underspecification. Solution (a) might easily hide an existing problem in the specification as it might render it provable but not matching the specifiers intuition, solution (b) would require to extend the definition of all functions defined on the integers to deal with the special error element. For these reasons, we choose underspecification, i.e., the semantics of logic does not fix a specific value for *div* in case of a division by zero. Instead each JFOL structure $\mathcal{M}$ assigns $div^{\mathcal{M}}(d,0)$ a fixed but unknown integer value for each dividend $d \in \mathbb{Z}$. These values may differ between different Kripke structures but are not state-dependent in the sense that $div(1,0)$ is assigned a different value in different states.

Besides the avoidance of a proliferation of special error cases or dealing with partial functions, the use of underspecification in the sketched manner provides additional advantages, e.g., a formula like

- $div(x,0) \doteq div(x+1,0)$ is neither a tautology nor unsatisfiable, but
- $div(x,0) \doteq div(x,0)$ remains a tautology.

5.4.2 Variable Binding Integer Operations

Variable binding operators are used to express sums and products. Our theory of integers supports the general versions $sum\{T\ x\}(\varphi(x),t), prod\{T\ x\}(\varphi(x),t)$ as well as their bounded variants $bsum\{int\ x\}(start,end,t)$ and $bprod\{int\ x\}(start,end,t)$. These functions are defined as follows:

$$sum\{T\ x\}(\varphi(x),t)^{\mathcal{M}} = \sum_{\phi(x)^{\mathcal{M}}} t^{\mathcal{M}} \qquad prod\{T\ x\}(\varphi(x),t)^{\mathcal{M}} = \prod_{\phi(x)^{\mathcal{M}}} t^{\mathcal{M}}$$

$$bsum\{int\ x\}(start,end,t)^{\mathcal{M}} = \sum_{x=start^{\mathcal{M}}}^{end^{\mathcal{M}}-1} t^{\mathcal{M}} \qquad (\text{if } start > end \text{, otherwise } 0)$$

$$bprod\{int\ x\}(start,end,t)^{\mathcal{M}} = \prod_{x=start^{\mathcal{M}}}^{end^{\mathcal{M}}-1} t^{\mathcal{M}} \qquad (\text{if } start > end \text{, otherwise } 1)$$

The logic axiomatization for the bounded sum is given as: For any int-typed term t

$\forall int\ start, end; (bsum\{int\ x\}(start,end,t) \doteq$
    $if(start < end)\ then\ bsum\{int\ x\}(start,end-1,t) + (\{\backslash subst\ x;\ start\}t)\ else(0))$

The bounded sum and bounded product are inclusive for the first argument *start* and exclusive for the second argument *end*. Besides the axioms there are as usual a large number of lemmas that ease reasoning and increase automation. We show here the Taclet definition for the splitting a bounded sum as it highlights a feature of Taclet language that allows one to specify triggers:

```
—— KeY ————————————————————————————————————
bsum_split {
  \schemaVar \term int low, middle, high;
  \schemaVar \variables int x;

  \find(bsum{x;} (low, high, t))
  \varcond ( \notFreeIn(x, low), \notFreeIn(x, middle),
             \notFreeIn(x, high) )
  \replacewith (
     \if(low <= middle & middle <= high)
     \then(bsum{x;}(low, middle, t) + bsum{x;}(middle,high,t))
     \else(bsum{x;}(low, high, t)) )

  \heuristics(comprehension_split, triggered)
  \trigger{middle} bsum{x;}(low, middle, t)
                   \avoid middle <= low, middle >= high;
};
                                                      —— KeY ——
```

The above rule splits the bounded sum expression somewhere between the lower and upper bound. The trigger specification is used by the strategies to determine good candidates for the splitting point. A trigger consists of three parts: (i) the schema variables to be instantiated by the trigger (trigger variables) (here: middle); (ii) the pattern to be matched against an existing term (or formula) in the sequent (here: bsum{x;}(low, middle, t)) (the match determines the value of the trigger variables) and (iii) an optional part \avoid that specifies the condition under which a candidate should be rejected. In the above case the trigger searches for positions at which to split the bounded sum into two parts such that the first summand already occurs in the sequent. The optional avoid part prevents superfluous splits outside the bounds (or directly at the start).

5.4.3 Symbolic Execution of Integer Expressions in Programs

In the following section, we explain how integer expressions are translated into logic terms. One obstacle to overcome is that there are several integral types in Java but only the logic type *int*. Given the following sequent

$$\Longrightarrow \langle \texttt{i = i + 1;} \rangle \texttt{i} > 0$$

and assume i is a program variable that had been declared to be of program type long (the logic type of i is *int*). As one of summands is of program type long the addition is widened to type long, i.e., it results only in an overflow (or underflow) if the normal mathematical addition results in a value outside of the range of type long.

The assignment is obviously side-effect free and can be directly moved into an update. Modeling the Java semantics faithfully, the application of the according assignment rule should result in

$$\Longrightarrow \{i := addJLong(i,1)\}\langle\rangle i > 0$$

using the addition with overflow function for long. However, performing this step within KeY results instead in the sequent

$$\Longrightarrow \{i := javaAddLong(i,1)\}\langle\rangle i > 0$$

where the Java operator + has been translated using the function *javaAddLong* : *int* × *int* → *int* (if i would have been declared of program type int the function *javaAddInt* : *int* × *int* → *int* would have been used).

These functions are intermediate representations which are used to represent the translation result of an integer program operation. The reason that we support three different integer semantics to cater for different usage scenarios. The three semantics are

Integer ignoring overflow semantics: All Java integral types and their operations are interpreted as the normal arithmetic operations without overflow. In this semantics the function *javaAddLong* would be interpreted as the arithmetic addition on $\mathbb{Z}$ (the same holds for *javaAddLong*). On the calculus level the corresponding rule would simply rewrite *javaAddLong*$(t1,t2)$ to *add*$(t1,t2)$. This semantics does obviously not model the real program semantics of Java and is hence unsound and incomplete w.r.t. to real-world Java programs. It is nevertheless useful for teaching purposes to avoid the complexities which stem from modulo operations.

Java integer semantics: Java integer semantics is modeled as specified by the JLS, i.e., some operations might cause an overflow. This means *javaAddLong* would be interpreted the same as *addJlong*. In this semantics the axiom rule for *javaAddLong* simply replaces the function symbol by *addJlong*. This semantics is sound and (relatively) complete, but comes with higher demands on the automation and requires in general more user interaction.

Integer prohibiting overflow semantics: This semantics provides a middle ground between the two previous semantics. Intuitively, when using this semantics one has to show that all arithmetic operations are safe in the sense that they do not overflow . In case of an overflow, the result is a fixed, but unspecified value. Verifying a program with this semantics ensures that either no overflow occurs, or in case of an overflow, the value of this operation does not affect the validity of the property under verification (i.e., the property is true for any outcome of the operation). This semantics is sound, but only complete for programs that do not rely on overflows.

The predicate symbols *inByte*, *inChar*, *inShort*, *inInt* and *inLong* which determine if the provided argument is in the value range of the named primitive type are also interpreted dependent on the chose integer semantics. While the ignoring overflow semantics always interprets these predicates as true, the two other semantics evaluate define them to be true if the given argument is within the bounds of the primitive type (for instance, *inInt*(x) is true in the latter semantics iff $x \geq -2^{31} \wedge x < 2^{31}$ is true).

Chapter 6
Abstract Interpretation

Nathan Wasser, Reiner Hähnle and Richard Bubel

6.1 Introduction

The previous chapters focused on the development of a *faithful* and *relatively complete* program logic for sequential Java. Consequently we obtain a formal language of high expressivity and a powerful calculus to prove the stated properties. Nevertheless expressivity comes with a cost, namely, an unpredictable degree of automation. This does not necessarily mean interaction with the theorem prover as such, but also the necessity to provide hand-crafted specifications like loop invariants or method contracts. The latter often needs to take idiosyncrasies of the theorem prover into account, at least, in regard of automation. This is also true in cases for which one is only interested in establishing simple properties like "No NullPointerExceptions are thrown."

Other techniques from static program analysis, like abstract interpretation as introduced by Cousot and Cousot [1977], utilize program abstraction to achieve full automation. But they pay with loss of precision that manifests itself in reduced expressivity (often only predefined properties can be expressed and ensured) and false positives.

In this chapter we show how to integrate abstract interpretation in JavaDL to achieve high automation while also maintaining high precision. Our approach has two main characteristics: i) abstraction of the state representation instead of the program, and ii) full precision until a loop or (recursive) method call is encountered. Only at those program points is abstraction applied and then only on the state region which might be modified by the loop or method. All other object fields or local variables keep their exact symbolic value.

© Springer International Publishing AG 2016
W. Ahrendt et al. (Eds.): Deductive Software Verification, LNCS 10001, pp. 167–189, 2016
DOI: 10.1007/978-3-319-49812-6_6

6.2 Integrating Abstract Interpretation

6.2.1 Abstract Domains

We introduce notions commonly used in abstract interpretation [Cousot and Cousot, 1977]. The core of abstract interpretation is abstract domains for the types occurring within the program. Each abstract domain forms a lattice and there is a mapping between each concrete domain D^T (i.e., the externalization of a concrete program type) and its corresponding abstract domain A^T. Their relationship is established by two total functions:

$$\alpha : 2^{D^T} \to A^T \qquad\qquad (abstraction\ function)$$

$$\gamma : A^T \to 2^{D^T} \qquad\qquad (concretization\ function)$$

The abstraction function maps a set of concrete domain elements onto an abstract domain element and the concretization function maps each abstract domain element onto a set of concrete domain elements, such that $\alpha(\gamma(a)) = a$ and $C \subseteq \gamma(\alpha(C))$ holds. A pair of functions with the latter two properties is a special case of a Galois connection called Galois insertion. Figure 6.1 illustrates such a mapping. The arrows represent the concretization (from wheel to vehicle) and abstraction function (from vehicle to wheel).

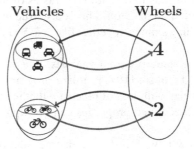

Figure 6.1 An example abstract domain: The concrete domain of vehicles is abstracted w.r.t. the number of wheels

We can now summarize the above into a formal definition of an abstract domain.

Definition 6.1 (Abstract Domain). Let D be a *concrete domain* (e.g., from a first-order structure). An *abstract domain* A is a complete lattice with partial order $\sqsubseteq$ and join operator $\sqcup$. It is connected to D with an *abstraction function* $\alpha : 2^D \to A$ and a *concretization function* $\gamma : A \to 2^D$ which form a Galois insertion [Cousot and Cousot, 1977], i.e. $\alpha(\gamma(a)) = a$ and $C \subseteq \gamma(\alpha(C))$. In this chapter we only deal with countable abstract domains.

Let $f : A \to A$ be any function. The monotonic function $f' : A \to A$ is defined as $f'(a) = a \sqcup f(a)$. If $\mathscr{A}$ satisfies the ascending chain condition (trivially the case if

$\mathscr{A}$ has finite height), then starting with any initial input $x \in A$ a least fixed point for f' on this input can be found by locating the stationary limit of the sequence $\langle x_i' \rangle$, where $x_0' = x$ and $x_{n+1}' = f'(x_n')$.

Abstract interpretation makes use of this when analyzing a program. Let p be a loop, x the only variable in p and $a \in A$ the abstract value of x before execution of the loop. Then we can see f as the abstract semantic function of a single loop iteration on the variable x. The fixed point for f' is an abstract value expressing an overapproximation of the set of all values of x before and after *each* iteration. Therefore it is sound to replace the loop with the assignment x $= a$.

If $\mathscr{A}$ does not satisfy the ascending chain condition, there may not be a stationary limit for $\langle x_i' \rangle$. In these cases a *widening operator* is required.

Definition 6.2 (Widening Operator $\cdot \nabla \cdot$). A widening operator for an abstract domain $\mathscr{A}$ is a function $\nabla : A \times A \to A$, where

1. $\forall a, b \in A. \ a \sqsubseteq a \nabla b$
2. $\forall a, b \in A. \ b \sqsubseteq a \nabla b$
3. for any sequence $\langle y_n' \rangle$ and initial value for x_0' the sequence $\langle x_n' \rangle$ is ultimately stationary, where $x_{n+1}' = x_n' \nabla y_n'$.

If $\mathscr{A}$ has a least element $\bot$, it suffices to use this as the initial value for x_0', rather than proving the property for all possible initial values.

Abstract domains come traditionally in two flavors *relational* and *nonrelational*. Advantages with relational abstract domains are expressiveness and the abilities to easily formulate often-occurring and helpful abstract notions such as $i \le a.\texttt{length}$. The advantage of nonrelational abstract domains is their ease of use from an implementation standpoint, as nonrelational abstract domains care only about the actual variable being updated, rather than having potential to change multiple values at once. We choose a third path: using nonrelational abstract domains but including invariant suggestions which can model certain relational-style expressions such as the example $i \le a.\texttt{length}$.

To achieve a seamless integration of abstract domains within JavaDL, we refrain from the introduction of abstract elements as first-class members. Instead we use a different approach to refer to the element of an abstract domain:

Definition 6.3 ($\gamma_{a,\mathbb{Z}}$-symbols). Given a countable abstract domain $A = \{a_1, a_2, \dots\}$. For each abstract element $a_i \in A - \{\bot\}$ there

- are infinitely many constant symbols $\gamma_{a,j} \in \text{FSym}$, $j \in \mathbb{N}$ and $\gamma_{a_i,j}^{\mathscr{M}} \in \gamma(a_i)$,
- is a unary predicate χ_{a_i} where $\chi_{a_i}^{\mathscr{M}}$ is the characteristic predicate of set $\gamma(a_i)$.

The interpretation of a symbol $\gamma_{a_i,j}$ is restricted to one of the concrete domain elements represented by a_i, but otherwise not fixed. In other words, the only guarantee about (restriction on) the actual value of $\gamma_{a_i,j}$ is to be an element of $\alpha(a_i)$.

6.2.2 Abstractions for Integers

In this subsection, we introduce a simple abstract domain for integers, which we use to illustrate our approach. This abstract domain is called *Sign Domain* and shown in Figure 6.2. As its naming suggests, it abstracts from the actual integer values and

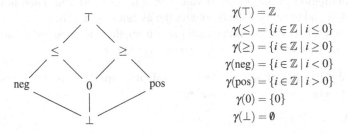

$$\gamma(\top) = \mathbb{Z}$$
$$\gamma(\leq) = \{i \in \mathbb{Z} \mid i \leq 0\}$$
$$\gamma(\geq) = \{i \in \mathbb{Z} \mid i \geq 0\}$$
$$\gamma(\mathrm{neg}) = \{i \in \mathbb{Z} \mid i < 0\}$$
$$\gamma(\mathrm{pos}) = \{i \in \mathbb{Z} \mid i > 0\}$$
$$\gamma(0) = \{0\}$$
$$\gamma(\bot) = \emptyset$$

Figure 6.2 Sign Domain: An abstract domain for integers

distinguishes them only w.r.t. their sign. The associated abstraction and concretization function obviously form a Galois connection.

The abstract domain is integrated into JavaDL by adding $\gamma_{a,\mathbb{Z}}$ symbols and their characteristic predicates χ_a for $a \in \{\mathrm{neg}, 0, \mathrm{pos}, \leq, \geq, \top\}$. The characteristic predicates are defined as follows:

$$\forall int\ x; (\chi_0(x) \leftrightarrow x \doteq 0) \qquad\qquad \forall int\ x; (\chi_\top(x) \leftrightarrow \mathrm{true})$$
$$\forall int\ x; (\chi_{\mathrm{neg}}(x) \leftrightarrow x < 0) \qquad\qquad \forall int\ x; (\chi_{\mathrm{pos}}(x) \leftrightarrow x > 0)$$
$$\forall int\ x; (\chi_\leq(x) \leftrightarrow x \leq 0) \qquad\qquad \forall int\ x; (\chi_\geq(x) \leftrightarrow x \geq 0)$$

6.2.3 Abstracting States

We now have all the parts together to explain how to abstract a given program state. We go further and embed the approach in a general notion of weakening, which provides us also with a natural soundness notion.

Given the following sequent:

$$c \geq 5 \Longrightarrow \{i := c+1\}\,[\texttt{i++;}]\,i > 0$$

The idea is to provide an *abstraction* rule that rewrites the above rule into:

$$c \geq 5 \Longrightarrow \{i := \gamma_{pos,1}\}\,[\texttt{i++;}]\,i > 0$$

where we replaced the 'more' complicated expression $c + 1$ on the right hand side of the update to i by a simpler gamma symbol. The latter sequent preserves the knowledge about the sign of i under which the box formula is evaluated (namely that it is strictly greater than 0), but we lose all knowledge about i's actual value. More formally, if the latter sequent is valid then also the first one is valid. We call the update $\mathtt{i} := \gamma_{pos,1}$ *weaker* than $\mathtt{i} := c + 1$ as the first one allows more reachable states: For the sequent to be true, the formula behind $\mathtt{i} := \gamma_{pos,1}$ must be true in all Kripke structures $\mathscr{K}$, i.e., for any positive value of i as $\gamma_{pos,1}$ does not occur anywhere else in the sequent. The original sequent only requires the formula behind the update to be true for all values strictly greater than 5.

We can formalize the weakening notion by introducing the update weakening rule from [Bubel et al., 2009]:

$$\text{weakenUpdate} \quad \frac{\Gamma, \mathscr{U}\,(\bar{\mathtt{x}} \doteq \bar{c}) \Longrightarrow \exists \bar{\gamma}.\mathscr{U}'(\bar{\mathtt{x}} \doteq \bar{c}), \Delta \qquad \Gamma \Longrightarrow \mathscr{U}'\varphi, \Delta}{\Gamma \Longrightarrow \mathscr{U}\varphi, \Delta}$$

where $\bar{\mathtt{x}}$ denotes a sequence of all program variables occurring as left-hand sides in $\mathscr{U}$ and $\bar{c}$ are fresh Skolem constants used to store the values of the variables $\bar{\mathtt{x}}$ under update $\mathscr{U}$. The formula $\exists \bar{\gamma}.\varphi$ is a shortcut for $\exists \bar{y}.(\chi_{\bar{a}}(\bar{y}) \wedge \psi[\bar{\gamma}/\bar{y}])$, where $\bar{y} = (y_1, \ldots, y_m)$ is a list of fresh first-order variables of the same length as $\bar{\gamma}$, and where $\psi[\bar{\gamma}/\bar{y}]$ stands for the formula obtained from ψ by replacing all occurrences of a symbol in $\bar{\gamma}$ with its counterpart in $\bar{y}$. This rule allows us to abstract any part of the state with a location-wise granularity.

Performing value-based abstraction becomes thus simply the replacement of an update by a weaker update. In particular, we do not perform abstraction on the program level, but on the *symbolic state* level. Thus abstraction needs to be defined only on symbolic states (updates) and not on programs.

6.3 Loop Invariant Generation

In this section we describe how to use update weakening to automatically infer loop invariants that allow us to verify unbounded loops without the need for a user provided loop invariant. To describe the approach we restrict ourselves to simple program variables of integer type. We discuss extensions for objects and in particular arrays in a later section.

As indicated earlier we intend to perform abstraction on demand when reaching a loop (or recursive method call), as those cases require user interaction in the form of loop specification or method contracts. Our aim is to avoid this tedious work. We solve this by two steps (i) an adapted loop invariant rule which allows one to integrate value abstraction as part of the anonymizing update, and (ii) a method to compute the abstracted state.

Assume a proof situation in which we encounter a loop. To reason about the loop's effect, we use the following rule:

invariantUpdate

$$\frac{\begin{array}{l}\Gamma, \mathscr{U}\,(\bar{x} \doteq \bar{c}) \Longrightarrow \exists \bar{\gamma}.\,\mathscr{U}'_{mod}(\bar{x} \doteq \bar{c}), \Delta \\ \Gamma, \mathscr{U}'_{mod}g,\ \mathscr{U}'_{mod}[\mathtt{p}](\bar{x} \doteq \bar{c}) \Longrightarrow \exists \bar{\gamma}.\,\mathscr{U}'_{mod}(\bar{x} \doteq \bar{c}), \Delta \\ \Gamma, \mathscr{U}'_{mod}\neg g \Longrightarrow \mathscr{U}'_{mod}[r]\varphi, \Delta\end{array}}{\Gamma \Longrightarrow \mathscr{U}\,[\mathtt{while}\ (g)\ \{p\};\ r]\varphi, \Delta}$$

With its three premisses and its basic structure, the invariantUpdate rule still resembles the classical loop invariant rule. The role of the loop invariant is taken over by the anonymizing update $\mathscr{U}'_{mod}$. The idea is to be smarter when anonymizing locations that might possibly be changed by the loop. Instead of anonymizing these locations by fresh Skolem constants, losing all information about their value and retroactively adding some knowledge back using a loop invariant, we use fresh $\gamma_{a,\mathbb{Z}}$ symbols. This way we keep some information about the value of these locations, namely, that their value remains within the concretization $\gamma(a)$ of the abstract element a. As we no longer have a traditional loop invariant, the lower bound of precision loss for the anonymized locations is given by the granularity of our abstract domain.

The rule's third premiss is the use case and represents the case where we have just exited the loop. The reachable states after the loop are contained in the set of all states reachable by update $\mathscr{U}'_{mod}$ strengthened by the fact that only those states need to be considered where the loop's guard evaluates to false. For all those states we have to show that after symbolic execution of the remaining program the property to prove holds. The second premise ensures that $\mathscr{U}'_{mod}$ is a sound approximation of all states reachable by any loop iteration. The first premiss ensures that the entry state is also contained in $\mathscr{U}'_{mod}$.

Example 6.4. Given the following sequent

$$\mathtt{i} \geq 0 \Longrightarrow \{\mathtt{n} := 0\}\,[\mathtt{while}\ (\mathtt{i>0})\ \{\mathtt{i--};\ \mathtt{n++};\}](\mathtt{i} \doteq 0 \wedge \mathtt{n} \geq 0)$$

To apply rule updateInvariant we need to provide $\mathscr{U}'_{mod}$. Intuitively, we see that the loop modifies both variables $\mathtt{i}$ and $\mathtt{n}$. About $\mathtt{n}$ we know that it is initially 0 and afterwards only increased. In case of $\mathtt{i}$ we know that its initial value is nonnegative and decreased by one with each loop iteration. Hence, we can conclude that both $\mathtt{i}$ and $\mathtt{n}$ are always covered by abstraction $\geq$. This gives us the following anonymizing update $\mathscr{U}'_{mod}$

$$\mathtt{i} := \gamma_{\geq,1} \,||\, \mathtt{n} := \gamma_{\geq,2}$$

The resulting proof goals after the rule application are: For the initial case

$$\mathtt{i} \geq 0, \{\mathtt{n} := 0\}(\mathtt{i} \doteq c_1 \wedge \mathtt{n} \doteq c_2) \Longrightarrow$$
$$\exists y_1, y_2.\big(\chi_{\geq}(y_1) \wedge \chi_{\geq}(y_2) \wedge \{\mathtt{i} := y_1 \,||\, \mathtt{n} := y_2\}(\mathtt{i} \doteq c_1 \wedge \mathtt{n} \doteq c_2)\big)$$

which can easily be proven valid by choosing $\mathtt{i}$ for y_1 and 0 for y_2 as instantiations of the existential formula on the right sequent side. The second branch proving that the update describes all possible values of $\mathtt{i}$ and $\mathtt{n}$ after any loop iteration is

$$i \geq 0, \{i := \gamma_{\geq,1} \,\|\, n := \gamma_{\geq,2}\}(i > 0),$$
$$\{i := \gamma_{\geq,1} \,\|\, n := \gamma_{\geq,2}\}[i--;n++;](i \doteq c_1 \wedge n \doteq c_2) \Longrightarrow$$
$$\exists y_1, y_2.(\chi_{\geq}(y_1) \wedge \chi_{\geq}(y_2) \wedge \{i := y_1 \,\|\, n := y_2\}(i \doteq c_1 \wedge n \doteq c_2))$$

This sequent can also be proven directly. After executing the loop body, applying the updates and some simplifications the above sequent becomes

$$i \geq 0, \ \gamma_{\geq,1} > 0, \ \gamma_{\geq,1} - 1 \doteq c_1, \ \gamma_{\geq,2} + 1 \doteq c_2 \Longrightarrow$$
$$\exists y_1, y_2.(\chi_{\geq}(y_1) \wedge \chi_{\geq}(y_2) \wedge \{i := y_1 \,\|\, n := y_2\}(i \doteq c_1 \wedge n \doteq c_2))$$

by choosing $\gamma_{\geq,1} - 1$ for y_1 and $\gamma_{\geq,2} + 1$ for y_2 we can prove the sequent as $\chi_{\geq}(\gamma_{\geq,2} + 1)$ is obviously true and the truth of $\chi_{\geq}(\gamma_{\geq,1} - 1)$ follows from the formula $\gamma_{\geq,1} > 0$ which is part of the antecedent (obtained from the knowledge that the loop guard is true).

Finally the last proof goal to be shown valid is

$$\{i := \gamma_{\geq,1} \,\|\, n := \gamma_{\geq,2}\}(\neg i > 0) \Longrightarrow \{i := \gamma_{\geq,1} \,\|\, n := \gamma_{\geq,2}\}[](i \doteq 0 \wedge n \geq 0)$$

which, once we derive that i is 0 from the antecedent, is trivial.

The question remains how to find a good candidate for $\mathcal{U}'_{mod}$ automatically. The solution is to start a side proof which unwinds the loop; once the loop body has been symbolically executed, we join the updates of all open branches by assigning each changed location the smallest abstract domain element that encompasses all of its potential values on the different branches. Repeat unwinding the loop until the update created by the join does not change any longer. The such obtained update is a sound candidate for $\mathcal{U}'_{mod}$.

Definition 6.5 (Joining Updates). The update join operation is defined as

$$\sqcup : (2^{\mathrm{Fml}} \times \mathrm{Upd}) \times (2^{\mathrm{Fml}} \times \mathrm{Upd}) \rightarrow (2^{\mathrm{Fml}} \times \mathrm{Upd})$$

and is defined by the property: Let $\mathcal{U}_1$ and $\mathcal{U}_2$ be arbitrary updates in a proof P and let C_1, C_2 be formula sets representing constraints on the update values. Then for $(C, \mathcal{U}) = (C_1, \mathcal{U}_1) \sqcup (C_2, \mathcal{U}_2)$ the following holds for $i \in \{1, 2\}$:

1. $\mathcal{U}$ is (P, C_i)-weaker than $\mathcal{U}_i$, and
2. $C_i \Longrightarrow \{\mathcal{U}_i\} \wedge C$

A concrete implementation $\sqcup_{abs}$ of $\sqcup$ for values can be computed as follows: For each update $x := v$ in $\mathcal{U}_1$ or $\mathcal{U}_2$ the generated update is $x := v$, if $\{\mathcal{U}_1\}x \doteq \{\mathcal{U}_2\}x$. Otherwise it is $x := \gamma_{\alpha_i, j}$ for some α_i where $\chi_{\alpha_i}(\{\mathcal{U}_1\}x)$ and $\chi_{\alpha_i}(\{\mathcal{U}_2\}x)$.

Example 6.6. We illustrate the described algorithm along the previous example: The sequent to prove was

$$i \geq 0 \Longrightarrow \{n := 0\} [\texttt{while (i>0) \{i--; n++;\}}](i \doteq 0 \wedge n \geq 0)$$

instead of 'guessing' the correct update, we sketch now how to find it automatically: Unrolling the loop once ends in two branches: one where the loop guard does not hold and the loop is exited (which we can ignore) and the second one where the loop body is executed. After finishing the symbolic execution of the loop body the sequent is

$$i > 0 \Longrightarrow \{i := i - 1 \,\|\, n := 1\} \,[\texttt{while (i>0) \{i--; n++;\}}](i \doteq 0 \wedge n \geq 0) \ .$$

We now compare the two sequents and observe that i and n has changed. Finding the minimal abstract element for n which covers both values 0 and 1 returns the abstract element $\geq$. For i we know that the previous value was greater-or-equal than the 0, after this iteration we know it has been decreased by one, but we also learned from the loop guard that on this branch the initial value of i was actually strictly greater than 0, hence, $i - 1$ is at least 0 and thus the abstract element covering both values is also $\geq$. We continue with the sequent

$$i > 0 \Longrightarrow \{i := \gamma_{\geq,1} \,\|\, n := \gamma_{\geq,2}\} \,[\texttt{while (i>0) \{i--; n++;\}}](i \doteq 0 \wedge n \geq 0)$$

where the update has been replaced by the 'abstracted' one. The result of unrolling the loop once more results in the sequent

$$\gamma_{\geq,1} > 0 \Longrightarrow \{i := \gamma_{\geq,1} - 1 \,\|\, n := \gamma_{\geq,2} + 1\} \,[\texttt{while (i>0) \{\dots\}}](i \doteq 0 \wedge n \geq 0) \ .$$

Joining this update with the previous one results in the update $i := \gamma_{\geq,4} \,\|\, n := \gamma_{\geq,4}$ which is (except for the numbering) identical to the previous one. This means we have reached a fixed point and we can use this update as the anonymizing update.

The approach of finding the update is sound, but we want to stress that this is actually not essential as the invariantUpdate rule checks the soundness of the provided updated.

6.4 Abstract Domains for Heaps

In KeY the program heap is modeled by the program variable heap of type *Heap*. Therefore any changes to the program heap will be expressed as an update to the program variable heap. Furthermore, the *program rules*, i.e., those calculus rules for dealing with program fragments, can only ever modify heap by *extension*. By this we mean that given an initial update heap $:= h$ the application of a program rule can produce an update heap $:= h'$ only if h is a subterm of h' and h' extends h only with *anon*, *create*, and/or *store* operations. *Heap simplification rules*, however, may reduce the heap term.

Our intentions for abstraction are to join multiple program states *originating from a single source program state*, such as the program state before execution of a loop, method call, if- or switch-statement. Therefore we can assume an initial value *old* for the program heap at the originating program point and based on this create the abstract domain as follows:

We define $LS \subset D^{LocSet}$ to contain all object/field pairs not containing the *created* field, i.e.:

$$LS = D^{Object} \times (D^{Field} \setminus \{created^{\mathscr{M}}\})$$

We define the family of abstract domains $\mathscr{A}_{old}^{Heap} = (A_{old}^{Heap}, \sqsubseteq_{old}, \sqcup_{old})$ for all initial well-formed heaps *old* as

$$A_{old}^{Heap} = \{\bot, \top\} \cup 2^{LS}$$

$$x \sqcup_{old} y = \begin{cases} x & \text{, if } y = \bot \\ y & \text{, if } x = \bot \\ \top & \text{, if } y = \top \\ \top & \text{, if } x = \top \\ x \cup y & \text{, otherwise} \end{cases}$$

$$x \sqsubseteq_{old} y = (y = x \sqcup_{old} y)$$

Abstraction and concretization functions are given as:

$$\alpha_{old} : 2^{D^{Heap}} \to A_{old}^{Heap}$$

$$heaps \mapsto \begin{cases} \bot & \text{, if } heaps = \emptyset \\ a & \text{, if } \forall h \in heaps, o \in D^{Object}. \\ & \quad wellFormed^{\mathscr{M}}(h) \wedge (old(o, created^{\mathscr{M}}) \to h(o, created^{\mathscr{M}})) \\ \top & \text{, otherwise} \end{cases}$$

$$\text{where } a = \{(o, f) \in D^{LS} \mid \exists h \in heaps.\ h(o, f) \neq old(o, f)\}$$

$$\gamma_{old} : A_{old}^{Heap} \to 2^{D^{Heap}}$$

$$\bot \mapsto \emptyset$$

$$\top \mapsto D^{Heap}$$

$$ls \subseteq LS \mapsto \{h \mid (\forall o \in D^{Object}.\ old(o, created^{\mathscr{M}}) \to h(o, created^{\mathscr{M}})) \wedge$$
$$(\forall (o, f) \in D^{LS \setminus ls}.\ h(o, f) = old(o, f))\}$$

As $\mathscr{A}_{old}^{Heap}$ contains infinite ascending chains due to both *Object* and *Field* being infinite, we require either a weakening or a subset of A_{old}^{Heap} for which no infinite ascending chains exist. We could, for example, reduce the set of available location sets from LS to the subset thereof for which no location set contains more than n elements, for some $n \in \mathbb{N}$. Anytime a larger location set were required, we would instead return $\top$. This works, but has the distinct disadvantage that the following infinite ascending chain $\langle x_i \rangle$ will wind up overapproximating not only for the cause of the infinite ascension (the field f), but also for all other fields as well:

$$x_0 = \emptyset \tag{6.1}$$
$$x_{i+1} = x_i \cup \{(o_i, f)\} \tag{6.2}$$

In order to keep the overapproximation as localized as possible, we consider the following points:

- *Field* can be separated into array indices $Arr = \{arr^{\mathscr{M}}(x) \mid x \in \mathbb{N}\}$ and non array indices $Field \setminus Arr$.
- For any Java program there is a finite subset $fs \subset (Field \setminus Arr)$ in a closed world determinable a priori which contains all non array index fields modifiable by the program.

We therefore introduce the family of abstract domains $\mathscr{A}_{old,fs,n,m,k}^{Heap}$ for all finite sets $fs \subset (Field \setminus Arr)$ and integers $n, m, k \in \mathbb{N}$, which contain no infinite ascending chains:

$$\mathscr{A}_{old,fs,n,m,k}^{Heap} = (A_{old,fs,n,m,k}^{Heap}, \sqsubseteq_{old,fs,n,m,k}, \sqcup_{old,fs,n,m,k})$$

$$A_{old,fs,n,m,k}^{Heap} = \{\bot, \top\} \cup \{W_{fs,n,m,k}(ls) \mid ls \subseteq LS\}$$

$$x \sqcup_{old,fs,n,m,k} y = \begin{cases} \top & \text{, if } x = \top \text{ or } y = \top \\ x & \text{, if } y = \bot \\ y & \text{, if } x = \bot \\ W_{fs,n,m,k}(x \cup y) & \text{, otherwise} \end{cases}$$

$$x \sqsubseteq_{old,fs,n,m,k} y = (y = x \sqcup_{old,fs,n,m,k} y)$$

where $W_{fs,n,m,k} : 2^{LS} \to 2^{LS}$ is defined as:

$$ls \mapsto \begin{cases} LS & \text{, if } \exists (o', f') \in ls. \ f' \notin (fs \cup Arr) \\ ls \cup W_{fs,n}^{N}(ls) \cup W_{m}^{M}(ls) \cup W_{k}^{K}(ls) & \text{, otherwise} \end{cases}$$

with $W_{fs,n}^{N}, W_{m}^{M}, W_{k}^{K}$ defined as:

$$W_{fs,n}^{N}(ls) = \{(o,f) \mid f \in fs \wedge |\{o' \mid (o',f) \in ls\}| > n\}$$

$$W_{m}^{M}(ls) = \{(o,f) \mid f \in Arr \wedge |\{f' \in Arr \mid (o,f') \in ls\}| > m\}$$

$$W_{k}^{K}(ls) = \begin{cases} D^{Object} \times Arr & \text{, if } |\{o \mid \exists f \in Arr. (o,f) \in ls\}| > k \\ \emptyset & \text{, otherwise} \end{cases}$$

The function $W_{fs,n,m,k}$ is the identity on any location set which:

- contains only pairs (o,f) where f is in fs or is an array index,
- contains no more than n pairs (o,f) for any fixed $f \in fs$,
- contains no more than m pairs $(o,arr^{\mathscr{M}}(x))$ for any fixed $o \in D^{Object}$, and
- contains pairs $(o,arr^{\mathscr{M}}(x))$ for no more than k different objects $o \in D^{Object}$.

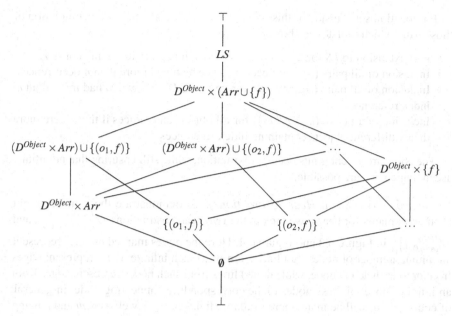

Figure 6.3 Abstract Domain $\mathscr{A}^{Heap}_{\text{heap},\{f\},1,0,0}$

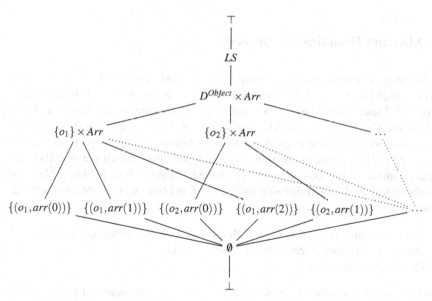

Figure 6.4 Abstract Domain $\mathscr{A}^{Heap}_{\text{heap},\emptyset,0,1,1}$

For location sets outside of this scope, $W_{fs,n,m,k}$ extends the set by completion of those pairs which violate the above rules, i.e.:

- Full extension to LS for any location set containing a field not in fs or Arr.
- Inclusion of all pairs (o, f) for each $f \in fs$ which had more than n occurrences.
- Inclusion of all pairs $(o, arr^{\mathcal{U}}(x))$ for each $o \in D^{Object}$ which had more than m index references.
- Inclusion of all pairs $(o, arr^{\mathcal{U}}(x))$ for all objects and indices if there were more than k different objects containing index references.

The above treatment limits overapproximation, while still ensuring that no infinite ascending chains are possible.

Example 6.7 (Two Small Heap Abstractions). To demonstrate these finite height abstract domains for heaps, we look at the two heap abstractions $\mathscr{A}_{\text{heap},\{f\},1,0,0}^{Heap}$ and $\mathscr{A}_{\text{heap},\emptyset,0,1,1}^{Heap}$ in Figure 6.3 and Figure 6.4. Here the nodes marked as "..." represent an infinite number of nodes, full lines from or to such infinite nodes represent edges from or to each actual node, while dotted lines from such nodes represent edges from an infinite subset of these nodes to the corresponding connecting node. In general, of course, there will be many more available fields in fs, as well as n, m and k being greater than 1.

6.5 Abstract Domains for Objects

In addition to an abstraction for the `heap` variable, there also exist local variables for objects which must be abstracted as well, therefore we require an abstract domain for D^{Object}. Most of the information about an object is actually only representable if the heap on which the object resides is also known. From an abstract domain point of view this would require a relational abstract domain linking objects and heaps. As our approach does not use relational abstract domains (at least not directly), our abstract domain for objects can only express the knowledge directly obtainable from only the object itself. The following attributes of an object can be obtained without knowledge of the heap:

- Reference equality of this object with any other object, in particular `null`.
- The `length` of this object (used only by arrays).
- The type of this object.

We therefore first introduce abstract domains for objects based on each of these points separately and can then combine them into one abstract domain for objects $\mathscr{A}^{Object}$.

6.5.1 Null/Not-null Abstract Domain

The abstract domain $\mathscr{A}_{null}^{Object}$ for objects based on reference equality to null is quite simple and at the same time incredibly useful, in that it can be used to check for possible NullPointerExceptions or prove the lack thereof in a piece of Java code. $\mathscr{A}_{null}^{Object}$ is shown in Figure 6.5 with abstraction and concretization functions.

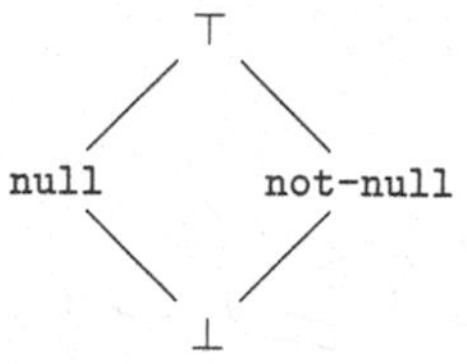

$$\alpha_{\mathscr{A}_{null}^{Object}}(X) = \begin{cases} \bot & \text{, if } X = \emptyset \\ \text{null} & \text{, if } X = \{\text{null}\cdot^{\mathcal{M}}\} \\ \text{not-null} & \text{, if null}\cdot^{\mathcal{M}} \notin X \\ \top & \text{, otherwise} \end{cases}$$

$$\gamma_{\mathscr{A}_{null}^{Object}}(x) = \begin{cases} \emptyset & \text{, if } x = \bot \\ \{null\} & \text{, if } x = \text{null} \\ D^{Object} \setminus \{null\} & \text{, if } x = \text{not-null} \\ D^{Object} & \text{, if } x = \top \end{cases}$$

Figure 6.5 Abstract Domain $\mathscr{A}_{null}^{Object}$

6.5.2 Length Abstract Domain

An abstract domain for objects based on their *length* is useful only for arrays. For all other object types the length is some arbitrary number which has no meaning. For arrays, however, abstracting these to their length can be quite helpful, for example one could conclude based on this abstraction whether a loop iterating over an array should be unrolled completely or a loop invariant generated for it.

We require an abstract domain $\mathscr{A}^{\mathbb{Z}}$ for the concrete domain $\mathbb{Z}$ and map each object's length to said abstract domain. We can then define the abstract domain for objects based on their *length* as $\mathscr{A}_{length}^{Object} := \mathscr{A}^{\mathbb{Z}}$ with abstraction and concretization functions as follows:

$$\alpha_{\mathscr{A}_{length}^{Object}}(X) = \alpha_{\mathscr{A}^{\mathbb{Z}}}(\{length^{\mathcal{M}}(x) \mid x \in X\})$$

$$\gamma_{\mathscr{A}_{length}^{Object}}(x) = \{o \in D^{Object} \mid length^{\mathcal{M}}(o) \in \gamma_{\mathscr{A}^{\mathbb{Z}}}(x)\}$$

We can use any abstract domain for $\mathbb{Z}$, for example the simple sign domain in Figure 6.2. However, using this abstract domain would not be very clever as the abstract elements neg and $\leq$ will never abstract valid array lengths, while the abstraction of both 1 and 10000 to the same abstract element pos is not very helpful. Instead, let us consider the following:

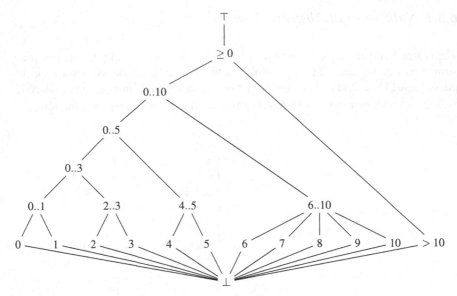

Figure 6.6 An Abstract Domain $\mathscr{A}_{\text{length}}^{Object}$

1. Iterating over an array of length 0 is trivial (do not enter loop) and therefore full precision should be kept, rather than abstracting by applying a loop invariant.
2. Iterating over an array of length 1 is similarly trivial (execute the loop body once) and therefore full precision should also be kept here by unrolling the loop, rather than applying a loop invariant. The loop invariant rule must still prove that the loop body preserves the invariant, thus execution of the loop body is always required once, even when applying a loop invariant.
3. Iterating over an array of length 2 or 3 can usually be done reasonably quickly by unrolling the loop a sufficient number of times, therefore unrolling should be favored over applying a loop invariant except in cases where symbolic execution of the loop body is extremely costly.
4. Iterating over an array of length 4 or 5 can often be done reasonably quickly by loop unrolling, therefore applying a loop invariant should only be done for somewhat complex loop bodies.
5. Iterating over an array of length 6 to 10, applying a loop invariant should be favored, except in cases where the loop body is trivial.
6. Iterating over an array of length greater than 10 should almost always be solved by applying a loop invariant.

   The above are reasonable guidelines (or in the case of lengths 0 and 1 simple fact), such that we can present the abstract domain in Figure 6.6 for the concrete domain $\mathbb{Z}$ and therefore also for objects based on their length.

6.5.2.1 Type Abstract Domain

Abstracting on object type requires knowledge of the type hierarchy. However, due to logical consequence of a formula requiring that the formula hold in all extensions of the type hierarchy, we must in essence create an abstract domain based on not just the type hierarchy given directly by the program, but any extension thereof.

For a set of objects X we offer abstractions for their types based on which exact types are present in X, i.e., a set of types such that each element in X is an exact instance of one of those types.

For any given type hierarchy $\mathscr{T}$ we must create an abstract domain, such that there exist abstraction and concretization functions for all type hierarchies $\mathscr{T}'$ which extend $\mathscr{T}$.

For a given type hierarchy $\mathscr{T} = (TSym, \sqsubseteq)$ we first define the set of all dynamic object types $O_d = \{d \in TSym \mid d \sqsubseteq Object$ and d is not marked abstract$\}$ and based on this define the abstract domain $\mathscr{A}_{O_d}^{Object}$, as shown in Figure 6.7. Then for any type hierarchy extension $\mathscr{T}' = (TSym', \sqsubseteq')$ of $\mathscr{T}$ the abstraction and concretization functions are given in Figure 6.8.

$$\mathscr{A}_{O_d}^{Object} = (A_{O_d}^{Object}, \sqsubseteq_{O_d}^{Object}, \sqcup_{O_d}^{Object})$$

$$A_{O_d}^{Object} = \{\top\} \cup (2^{O_d} \setminus O_d)$$

$$X \sqcup_{O_d}^{Object} Y = \begin{cases} \top & \text{, if } X = \top \text{ or } Y = \top \text{ or } X \cup Y = O_d \\ X \cup Y & \text{, otherwise} \end{cases}$$

$$X \sqsubseteq_{\mathscr{T}}^{Object} Y = \begin{cases} tt & \text{, if } Y = \top \\ f\!f & \text{, if } X = \top \text{ and } Y \neq \top \\ X \subseteq Y & \text{, otherwise} \end{cases}$$

Figure 6.7 Family of Abstract Domains $\mathscr{A}_{O_d}^{Object}$

$$\alpha_{O_d, \mathscr{T}'}^{Object}(X) = \begin{cases} \top & \text{, if } \exists x \in X. \ \delta'(x) \notin O_d \\ & \quad \text{or } \{d \in T_d \mid \exists x \in X. \ \delta'(x) = d\} = O_d \\ \{d \in T_d \mid \exists x \in X. \ \delta'(x) = d\} & \text{, otherwise} \end{cases}$$

$$\gamma_{O_d, \mathscr{T}'}^{Object}(X) = \begin{cases} \{o \in D' \mid \delta'(o) \sqsubseteq' Object\} & \text{, if } X = \top \\ \{o \in D' \mid \bigvee_{d \in X} \delta'(o) = d\} & \text{, otherwise} \end{cases}$$

Figure 6.8 Galois connection between $\mathscr{A}_{O_d}^{Object}$ and the Concrete Object Domain from $\mathscr{T}'$

Example 6.8. We can consider a simplified Java program containing only the types declared in Listing 6.1. Based on this we have the set of concrete object types

```
class Object {...}
abstract class A {...}
interface I {...}
class B extends A implements I {...}
```
Listing 6.1 Type declarations

$\{Object, B, Null\}$ and the abstract domain $\mathscr{A}^{Object}_{\{Object,B,Null\}}$ as shown in Figure 6.9.

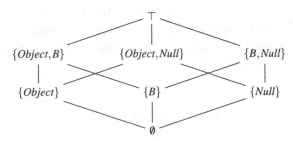

Figure 6.9 Abstract Domain $\mathscr{A}^{Object}_{\{Object,B,Null\}}$

The abstract domains $\mathscr{A}^{Object}_{O_d}$ can be used, for example, to:

- prove that casting of an object does not cause a `ClassCastException` to be thrown,
- prove that no `ArrayStoreException` is thrown when inserting an object into an array,
- prove that an `instanceof` check will be successful,
- prove that an `instanceof` check will be unsuccessful, and/or
- narrow the list of possible method body instantiations down which is created when unfolding a method call.

It is important to point out that although $\mathscr{A}^{Object}_{O_d}$ always has abstract elements $\{Null\}$ and $O_d \setminus \{Null\}$, it is not inherently stronger than the abstract domain $\mathscr{A}^{Object}_{null}$. This is because given a type hierarchy extension $\mathscr{T}'$ which introduces a new dynamic type $d' \sqsubseteq Object$, for which it holds for some o that $\delta'(o) = d'$ the following abstractions exist:

$$\alpha^{Object}_{O_d, \mathscr{T}'}(\{o\}) = \top$$
$$\alpha^{Object}_{null}(\{o\}) = \texttt{not-null}$$

6.5.2.2 Combining the Object Abstract Domains Into One

Of course, we would like just one abstract domain for objects encompassing all of the abstractions discussed in the previous subsections. The abstract domain $\mathscr{A}^{Object}$ for a given type hierarchy $\mathscr{T}$ is a partial cartesian product of the abstract domains $\mathscr{A}^{Object}_{null}$, $\mathscr{A}^{Object}_{length}$ and $\mathscr{A}^{Object}_{O_d}$ such that the abstraction and concretization functions for any type hierarchy extension $\mathscr{T}'$ can be given as in Figure 6.10. The reason why only a subset of the cartesian product is required is due to the following: As it must hold that $\alpha(\gamma(a)) = a$ for all abstract elements a, there can never be more than one abstract element representing the same set. We therefore cannot have both $(\bot, y, z)$ and $(x, \bot, z)$ as separate abstract elements, as intuitively both of these would have to represent the empty set. Additionally, while the abstraction for length is orthogonal to the abstractions for null and exact type (due to the function *length* being defined for all objects, including null and nonarray types), the abstractions for null and exact type are not. While it is true that in one abstraction we may know that null does not appear, while in the other abstraction we do not, it is nonetheless impossible for certain abstract elements to be combined without representing the empty set, for example the abstract elements null and $\{Object\}$.

The abstract domain $\mathscr{A}^{Object}$ is defined in Figure 6.11.

$$\alpha^{Object}(X) = (\alpha^{Object}_{null}(X), \alpha^{Object}_{length}(X), \alpha^{Object}_{O_d, \mathscr{T}'}(X))$$

$$\gamma^{Object}((a,b,c)) = \gamma^{Object}_{null}(a) \cap \gamma^{Object}_{length}(b) \cap \gamma^{Object}_{O_d, \mathscr{T}'}(c)$$

Figure 6.10 Abstraction and concretization Functions between $\mathscr{A}^{Object}$ and concrete objects in $\mathscr{T}'$

$$\mathscr{A}^{Object} - (A^{Object}, \sqsubseteq^{Object}, \sqcup^{Object})$$

$$A^{Object} \subseteq A^{Object}_{null} \times A^{Object}_{length} \times A^{Object}_{O_d}$$

$$(a,b,c) \sqsubseteq^{Object} (x,y,z) = a \sqsubseteq^{Object}_{null} x \wedge b \sqsubseteq^{Object}_{length} y \wedge c \sqsubseteq^{Object}_{O_d} z$$

$$(a,b,c) \sqcup^{Object} (x,y,z) = (a \sqcup^{Object}_{null} x, b \sqcup^{Object}_{length} y, c \sqcup^{Object}_{O_d} z)$$

Figure 6.11 Abstract Domain $\mathscr{A}^{Object}$

6.6 Extensions

In this section we briefly sketch how to add additional precision for arrays while staying fully automatic. For sake of presentation we use a simplified abstract domain for arrays (but which is included in the abstraction given in Section 6.4) and define a more specific notion to join heap values. Based on this we can then sketch how to automatically generate loop invariants for arrays that maintain a reasonable level of precision for many use cases. This section is basically a shortened version of [Hähnle et al., 2016] to which we refer the reader for details.

6.6.1 Abstractions for Arrays

We extend the abstract domain of the array elements to a range within the array. Given a set of indexes R, an abstract domain A for array elements can be extended to an abstract domain A_R for arrays by copying the structure of A and renaming each α_i to $\alpha_{R,i}$. The $\alpha_{R,i}$ are such that $\gamma_{\alpha_{R,i},j} \in \{arrObj \in \text{int}[] \mid \forall k \in R.\chi_{\alpha_i}(arrObj[k])\}$.

Example 6.9. As abstract domain A we use the sign domain for integers, producing for each $R \subseteq \mathbb{N}$ an abstract domain A_R:

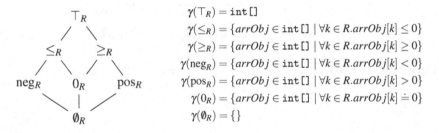

$$\gamma(\top_R) = \text{int}[]$$
$$\gamma(\leq_R) = \{arrObj \in \text{int}[] \mid \forall k \in R.arrObj[k] \leq 0\}$$
$$\gamma(\geq_R) = \{arrObj \in \text{int}[] \mid \forall k \in R.arrObj[k] \geq 0\}$$
$$\gamma(\text{neg}_R) = \{arrObj \in \text{int}[] \mid \forall k \in R.arrObj[k] < 0\}$$
$$\gamma(\text{pos}_R) = \{arrObj \in \text{int}[] \mid \forall k \in R.arrObj[k] > 0\}$$
$$\gamma(0_R) = \{arrObj \in \text{int}[] \mid \forall k \in R.arrObj[k] \doteq 0\}$$
$$\gamma(\emptyset_R) = \{\}$$

With $R = \{0,2\}$, we get $\gamma(\geq_{\{0,2\}}) = \{arrObj \in \text{int}[] \mid arrObj[0] \geq 0 \wedge arrObj[2] \geq 0\}$. Importantly, the array length itself is irrelevant, provided $arrObj[0]$ and $arrObj[2]$ have the required values. Therefore the arrays (we deviate from Java's array literal syntax for clarity) $[0,3,6,9]$ and $[5,-5,0]$ are both elements of $\gamma(\geq_{\{0,2\}})$.

Of particular interest are the ranges containing all elements modified within a loop. One such range is $[0..arrObj.\text{length})$. This range can always be taken as a fallback option if no more precise range can be found.

6.6.2 Loop Invariant Rule with Value and Array Abstraction

To be able to deal with arrays we extend the updateInvariant rule:

invariantUpdate

$$\Gamma, \mathcal{U} (\bar{x} \doteq \bar{c}) \Longrightarrow \exists \bar{\gamma}. \{\mathcal{U}'\}(\bar{x} \doteq \bar{c}), \Delta$$
$$\Gamma, \text{old} \doteq \mathcal{U} \text{heap} \Longrightarrow \mathcal{U} \mathit{Inv}, \Delta$$
$$\Gamma, \text{old} \doteq \mathcal{U} \text{heap}, \mathcal{U}'_{mod}(g \wedge \mathit{Inv}), \mathcal{U}'_{mod}[\text{p}](\bar{x} \doteq \bar{c}) \Longrightarrow$$
$$\exists \bar{\gamma}; \mathcal{U}'_{mod}(\bar{x} \doteq \bar{c}), \Delta$$
$$\Gamma, \text{old} \doteq \mathcal{U} \text{heap}, \mathcal{U}'_{mod}(g \wedge \mathit{Inv}) \Longrightarrow \mathcal{U}'_{mod}[\text{p}]\mathit{Inv}, \Delta$$
$$\Gamma, \text{old} \doteq \mathcal{U} \text{heap}, \mathcal{U}'_{mod}(\neg g \wedge \mathit{Inv}) \Longrightarrow \mathcal{U}'_{mod}[r]\varphi, \Delta$$

$$\overline{\Gamma \Longrightarrow \mathcal{U} [\text{while } (g) \ \{p\}; \ r]\varphi, \Delta}$$

where $\mathcal{U}'_{mod} := (\mathcal{U}' \parallel \mathcal{V}^{heap}_{mod})$ with $\mathcal{U}'$ being the $\mathcal{U}'_{mod}$ from the previous sections and $\mathcal{V}^{heap}_{mod}$ denotes the abstraction of the heap stored in program variable heap. The $\bar{x}, \bar{c}, \bar{\gamma}$ and $\exists \bar{\gamma}; \varphi$ are defined as previously. In addition to heap abstraction, we reintroduce the loop invariant formula Inv, which is subsequently used to express properties about the content of the heap. This includes explicit heap invariants of the form $\forall i \in S. \ C \rightarrow P(select_{int}(\text{heap}, \text{arrObj}, arr(i)))$ as well as invariants which further specify S or C. The program variable and old is a fresh constant used in Inv to refer to the heap before loop execution.

```
i = 0; j = 0;
while(i < a.length) {
  if (a[j] > 0) j++;
  b[i] = j;
  c[2*i] = 0;
  i++;
}
```

Listing 6.2 Example program for array abstraction

Most branches serve a similar approach as those in the previous version. The second and the third branch are new ensuring that the loop invariant formula is initially valid as well as preserved by the loop body. Given program p in Listing 6.2, applying the assignment rule to $\Gamma \Longrightarrow \mathcal{U} [\text{p}]\varphi, \Delta$ leads to $\Gamma \Longrightarrow \{\mathcal{U} \parallel \text{i} := 0 \parallel \text{j} := 0\}[\text{while} \ldots]\varphi, \Delta$. Now the invariantUpdate rule is applied with, e.g., the following values:

$$\mathcal{U}' = (\mathcal{U} \parallel \mathtt{i} := \gamma_{\geq,1} \parallel \mathtt{j} := \gamma_{\geq,2})$$

$$\mathcal{V}^{heap}_{mod} =$$

$$\qquad \mathtt{heap} := anon(anon(\mathtt{heap}, \mathtt{b}[0..i], anonHeap_1), \mathtt{c}[0..\mathtt{c}.\mathtt{length}], anonHeap_2)$$

$$Inv = \big(\forall k \in [0..\mathtt{j}); \; \chi_{>}(select_{int}(\mathtt{heap}, \mathtt{a}, arr(k)))\big)$$

$$\wedge \big(\forall k \in [0..\mathtt{i}); \; \chi_{\geq}(select_{int}(\mathtt{heap}, \mathtt{b}, k))\big)$$

$$\wedge \big(\forall m \in [0..\mathtt{c}.\mathtt{length});$$

$$\quad (m < 2 * i \wedge m\%2 \doteq 0) \rightarrow \chi_0(select_{int}(\mathtt{heap}, \mathtt{c}, arr(2*m))))\big)$$

$$\wedge \big(\forall m \in [0..\mathtt{c}.\mathtt{length}); \neg(m < 2*i \wedge m\%2 \doteq 0)$$

$$\quad \rightarrow (select_{int}(\mathtt{heap}, \mathtt{c}, arr(m)) \doteq select_{int}(\mathtt{old}, \mathtt{c}, arr(m))))\big)$$

The update $\mathcal{U}'_{mod}$ is equal to the original update $\mathcal{U}$ except for the values of i and j which can both be any nonnegative number. The arrays b and c have (partial) ranges anonymized. We use $arrObj[lower..upper]$ to express the set of locations consisting of all array elements of array $arrObj$ from *lower* (included) to *upper* (excluded).

Array a is not changed by the loop and thus not anonymized. The invariants in *Inv* express that

1. a contains positive values at all positions prior to the current value of j,
2. the anonymized values in b (cf. $\mathcal{V}^{heap}_{mod}$) are all nonnegative, and
3. the anonymized values in c are equal to their original values (if the loop does not or has not yet modified them) or are equal to 0.

6.6.3 Computation of the Abstract Update and Invariants

We generate $\mathcal{U}'$, $\mathcal{V}^{heap}_{mod}$ and *Inv* automatically in a side proof, by symbolic execution of single loop iterations until a fixed-point is found. The computation of $\mathcal{U}'$ is as in Section 6.3, but ignores the heap variable heap. We generate $\mathcal{V}^{heap}_{mod}$ and *Inv* by examining each array modification[1] and anonymizing the entire range within the array (expressed in $\mathcal{V}^{heap}_{mod}$) while adding a partial invariant to the set *Inv*. Once a fixed-point for $\mathcal{U}'$ is reached, we can refine $\mathcal{V}^{heap}_{mod}$ and *Inv* by performing in essence a second fixed-point iteration, this time anonymizing possibly smaller ranges and potentially adding more invariants.

To perform this we need to generalize our notion of joining updates to include heaps.

Definition 6.10 (Joining Heaps). Any operator with the signature

$$\sqcap : (2^{\mathrm{Fml}} \times \mathrm{DLTrm}_{Heap}) \times (2^{\mathrm{Fml}} \times \mathrm{DLTrm}_{Heap}) \rightarrow (2^{\mathrm{Fml}} \times \mathrm{DLTrm}_{Heap})$$

---

[1] Later we also examine each array access (read or write) in if-conditions to gain invariants such as $\forall k \in [0..\mathtt{j}). \; \chi_{>}(\mathtt{select}(\mathtt{heap}, \mathtt{a}, arr(k)))$ in the example above.

is a *heap join operator* if it satisfies the properties: Let h_1, h_2 be arbitrary heaps in a proof P, C_1, C_2 be formula sets representing constraints on the heaps (and possibly also on other update values) and let $\mathcal{U}$ be an arbitrary update. Then for $(C, h) = (C_1, h_1) \,\square\, (C_2, h_2)$ the following holds for $i \in \{1, 2\}$:

1. $(\mathcal{U} \parallel \text{heap} := h)$ is (P, C_i)-weaker than $(\mathcal{U} \parallel \text{heap} := h_i)$,
2. $C_i \implies \{\mathcal{U} \parallel \text{heap} := h_i\} \land C$, and
3. $\square$ is associative and commutative up to first-order reasoning.

We define the set of *normal form heaps* $Heap_{NF} \subset DLTrm_{heap}$ to be those heap terms that extend heap with an arbitrary number of preceding stores or anonymizations. For a heap term $h \in Heap_{NF}$ we define

$$writes(h) := \begin{cases} \emptyset & \text{if } h = \text{heap} \\ \{h\} \cup writes(h') & \text{if } h = store(h', a, arr(idx), v) \text{ or} \\ & h = anon(h', a[l..r], h'') \end{cases}$$

A concrete implementation $\square_{heap}$ of $\square$ is given as follows: We reduce the signature to $\square_{heap} : (2^{Fml} \times Heap_{NF}) \times (2^{Fml} \times Heap_{NF}) \to (2^{Fml} \times Heap_{NF})$. This ensures that all heaps we examine are based on heap and is a valid assumption when taking the program rules into account, as these maintain this normal form. As both heaps are in normal form, they must share a common subheap (at least heap). The largest common subheap of h_1, h_2 is defined as $lcs(h_1, h_2)$ and all writes performed on this subheap can be given as $writes_{lcs}(h_1, h_2) := writes(h_1) \cup writes(h_2) \setminus (writes(h_1) \cap writes(h_2))$. For the interested reader, the actual algorithms to compute the update abstractions are shown in [Hähnle et al., 2016].

6.6.4 Symbolic Pivots

Finally, we sketch briefly how to generate the loop invariant formula *Inv* capturing knowledge about the modified content of an array. In the previous section we computed the update $\mathcal{U}_{mod}$, which provides us the abstraction for primitive types as well as the heap, in particular, arrays. For the latter this information is relatively weak as it assumes any update to an array element could cause a change at any array index. With the generated $\mathcal{U}'$, however, we can now refine $\mathcal{V}_{mod}^{heap}$ and *Inv*. We try to keep the anonymizations in $\mathcal{V}_{mod}^{heap}$ to a minimum, while producing stronger invariants *Inv*.
    Consider the starting sequent

$$\Gamma \implies \mathcal{U}[\texttt{while } (g) \ \{p\}; \ r]\varphi, \Delta \ .$$

As $\mathcal{U}'$ is weaker than $\mathcal{U}$, the update $(\mathcal{U}' \parallel \text{heap} := \mathcal{U}\,\text{heap})$ remains weaker than $\mathcal{U}$. For the sequent

$$\Gamma \implies \{\mathcal{U}' \parallel \text{heap} := \mathcal{U}\,\text{heap}\}[\texttt{while } (g) \ \{p\}; \ r]\varphi, \Delta$$

while computing the heap join (by unrolling the loop) we reach open branches

$$\Gamma_i \Longrightarrow \{\mathscr{U}_i\}[\texttt{while (g) \{p\}; r}]\varphi,\Delta_i \ .$$

Aside from the values for heap, $\mathscr{U}'$ is weaker than $\mathscr{U}_i$, as $\mathscr{U}'$ is a fixed-point. We therefore do not have to join any nonheap variables when computing $(\mathscr{U}^*, Inv)$.

When joining constraint/heap pairs we distinguish between three types of $f_{m,n}$:

1. anonymizations, which are kept, as well as any invariants generated for them occurring in the constraints,
2. stores to concrete indexes, for which we create a store to the index either of the explicit value (if equal in both heaps) or of a fresh $\gamma_{i,j}$ of appropriate type, and
3. stores to variable indexes, for which we anonymize a (partial) range in the array and give stronger invariants.

Given a store to a variable index $store(h,a,arr(idx),v)$, the index idx is expressible as a function $index(\gamma_{i_0,j_0},\dots,\gamma_{i_n,j_n})$. These γ_{i_x,j_x} can be linked to program variables in the update $\mathscr{U}'$, which contains updates $\text{pv}_x := \gamma_{i_x,j_x}$.We can therefore express idx as the function $sp(\dots \text{pv}_x \dots)$.

We call $idx = sp(\dots \text{pv}_x \dots)$ a *symbolic pivot*, as it expresses what elements of the array can be changed based on which program variables and allows us to partition the array similar to pivot elements in array algorithms. Symbolic pivots split the array into an already modified partition and an unmodified partition, where (parts of) the unmodified partition may yet be modified in later iterations of the loop.

If $P(\mathscr{W}) = \forall k \in [\mathscr{U}\,sp..\mathscr{W}\,sp). \ \mathscr{W}\,\chi_{\alpha_j}(select_{int}(\texttt{heap},arrObj,arr(k)))$, for a symbolic pivot sp, $P(\mathscr{U})$ is trivially true, as we are quantifying over an empty set. Likewise, it is easy to show that the instance $Q(\mathscr{U})$ of the following is valid:

$$
\begin{aligned}
Q(\mathscr{W}) = \\
\forall k \notin [\mathscr{U}\,sp..\mathscr{W}\,sp); \\
select_{int}(\mathscr{W}\,\texttt{heap},\mathscr{W}\,arrObj,arr(k)) \doteq \\
select_{int}(\mathscr{U}\,\texttt{heap},\mathscr{W}\,arrObj,arr(k))
\end{aligned}
$$

Therefore, anonymizing an array $arrObj$ with

$$anon(h,arrObj[0..arrObj.\texttt{length}],anonHeap)$$

and adding invariants $P(\mathscr{U}^*)$ and $Q(\mathscr{U}^*)$ for the contiguous range $[\mathscr{U}\,sp..\{\mathscr{U}^*\}sp)$ is inductively sound, if $P(\mathscr{U}') \Longrightarrow P(\mathscr{U}_i)$ and $Q(\mathscr{U}') \Longrightarrow Q(\mathscr{U}_i)$.

Definition 6.11 (Iteration affine). Given a sequent $\Gamma \Longrightarrow \mathscr{U}\,[\texttt{p}]\varphi,\Delta$ where p starts with $\texttt{while}$, a term t is *iteration affine*, if there exists some $step \in \mathbb{Z}$ such that for any $n \in \mathbb{N}$, if we unroll and symbolically execute the loop n times, for each branch with sequent $\Gamma_i \Longrightarrow \mathscr{U}_i[\texttt{p}]\varphi,\Delta_i$ it holds that there is some value v, such that $\Gamma_i\cup!\Delta_i \Longrightarrow \mathscr{U}_i t \doteq v$ and $\Gamma\cup!\Delta \Longrightarrow \mathscr{U}\,t + n * step \doteq v$.

If the symbolic pivot is iteration affine, we know the exact elements that may be modified. We could anonymize only this range. However, as expressing the affine range as a location set is nontrivial, we anonymize the entire array and create the following invariants for the modified and unmodified partitions (using the symbols of Definition 6.11):

$$\forall k \in [0..arrObj.\texttt{length}). \; (k \geq \mathscr{U}\,sp \wedge k < sp \wedge (k - \mathscr{U}\,sp)\%step \doteq 0) \rightarrow P(k),$$
$$\text{and } \forall k \in [0..arrObj.\texttt{length}). \; \neg(k \geq \mathscr{U}\,sp \wedge k < sp \wedge (k - \mathscr{U}\,sp)\%step \doteq 0)$$
$$\rightarrow select_{int}(\texttt{heap}, arrObj, arr(k)) \doteq select_{int}(\mathscr{U}\,\texttt{heap}, arrObj, arr(k))$$

Finally, we can also add invariants (without anonymizations) for array accesses which influence control flow. For each open branch with a condition $C(select_{int}(h, arrObj, arr(idx)))$ not already present in the sequent leading to it, we determine the symbolic pivot for idx and create an iteration affine or contiguous invariant for it.

6.7 Conclusions

In this section we outlined how to integrate abstraction into JavaDL. We looked first into cases without a heap to explain the basic idea. We sketched then our approach to extend the approach to arrays. We explained the necessary extensions to maintain a reasonable amount of precision when abstracting arrays. The presented approach has also been used to cover method contracts and recursion [Wasser, 2015]. It has been applied in an eVoting case study [Do et al., 2016] to achieve full automation for the purpose of detecting information leaks.

Part II
Specification and Verification

Chapter 7
Formal Specification with the Java Modeling Language

Marieke Huisman, Wolfgang Ahrendt, Daniel Grahl, and Martin Hentschel

This text is a general, self contained, and tool independent introduction into the *Java Modeling Language*, JML. It appears in a book about the KeY approach and tool, because JML is the dominating starting point of KeY style Java verification. However, this chapter does not depend on KeY, nor any other specific tool, nor on any specific verification methodology. With this text, the authors aim to provide, for the time being, the definitive, general JML tutorial.

Other chapters in this book discuss the particular usage of JML in KeY style verification.[1] In this chapter, however, we only refer to KeY in very few places, without relying on it. This introduction is written for all readers with an interest in formal specification of software in general, and anyone who wants to learn about the JML approach to specification in particular. A preliminary version of this chapter appeared as a technical report [Huisman et al., 2014].

Introduction

The *Java Modeling Language*, JML, is an increasingly popular specification language for Java software, that has been developed as a community effort since 1999. The nature of such a project entails that language details change, sometimes rapidly, over time and there is no ultimate reference for JML. Fortunately, for the items that we address in this introduction, the syntax and semantics are for the greatest part already settled by Leavens et al. [2013]. Basic design decisions have been described in [Leavens et al., 2006b],[2] who outline these three overall goals:

- "JML must be able to document the interfaces and behavior of existing software, regardless of the analyses and design methods to create it. [...]

---

[1] Chapter 8 defines a translation of the JML variant supported by KeY into Java dynamic logic, and thereby defines a (translational) semantics of JML. Appendix A provides a language reference for the exact JML variant supported by KeY, presenting syntax, as well as more details on the semantics. Chapter 9 is entirely dedicated to *modular* specification and verification using JML and KeY. Chapter 16 is a tutorial on KeY, using JML in a very intuitive manner only.

[2] This 2006 journal publication is a revised version of a technical report that first appeared in 1998.

© Springer International Publishing AG 2016
W. Ahrendt et al. (Eds.): Deductive Software Verification, LNCS 10001, pp. 193–241, 2016
DOI: 10.1007/978-3-319-49812-6_7

- The notation used in JML should be readily understandable by Java programmers, including those with only standard mathematical training. [...]
- The language must be capable of being given a rigorous formal semantics, and must also be amenable to tool support."

This essentially means two things to the specification language: Firstly, it needs to express properties about the special aspects of the Java language, e.g., inheritance, object initialization, or abrupt termination. Secondly, the specification language itself heavily relies on Java; its syntax extends Java's syntax and its semantics extend Java's semantics. The former makes it convenient to talk about such features in a natural way, instead of defining auxiliary constructs or instrumenting the code as in other specification methodologies. The latter can also come in handy since, with a reasonable knowledge of Java, little theoretical background is needed in order to use JML. This has been one of the major aims in the design of JML. It however bears the problem that reasoning about specifications in a formal and abstract way becomes more difficult as even simple expressions are evaluated w.r.t. the complex semantics of Java.

History and Background

Assertions in source code to prove correctness of the implementation have already been proposed long time ago by Floyd [1967]. However, assertions were not widely used in practice—the `assert` statement in Java only first appeared in version 1.4, in 2002. Other programming languages adopted assertions earlier: Bertrand Meyer introduced the concept of *Design by Contract* (DbC) in 1986 with the Eiffel language [Meyer, 1992, 1997]. DbC is a programming methodology where the behavior of program components is described as a *contract* between the provider and the clients of the component. The client only has to study the component's contract, and this should tell him or her exactly what he or she can expect from the component. The provider is free to choose any implementation, as long as it respects the component's contract. Design by Contract has become a popular methodology for object-oriented languages. In this case, the components are the program's classes. Contracts naturally correspond with the object-oriented paradigm to hide (or encapsulate) the internal state of an object.

The Eiffel compiler came with a special option to check validity of a contract at runtime. Subsequently, the same ideas where applied to reason about other programming languages (including Modula-3, C++, and Smalltalk, that were all handled in the Larch project [Guttag and Horning, 1993, Leavens and Cheon, 1993]). With the growing popularity of Java, several people decided to develop a specification language for Java. Gary T. Leavens and his students at Iowa State University used their experience from the Larch project, and started work on a DbC specification language for Java in 1998. They proposed a specification language, and simultaneously developed a JML runtime assertion checker, that could be used to validate the contracts at runtime. At more or less the same time, K. Rustan M. Leino and his team at the DEC/Compaq research center started working on a tool for static code analysis. For the *Extended Static Checker for Java*, ESC/Java [Leino et al., 2000], they developed a specification language that was more or less a subset of JML. A successor, ESC/Java2 [Cok and Kiniry, 2005], finally adopted JML as it is now. Several projects have been targeting tool supported formal verification of Java programs: the LOOP project [van den Berg and Jacobs, 2001], the Krakatoa project [Marché et al., 2004], and of course KeY. While in KeY originally specifications had been written in the Object Constraint Language (OCL), that is part of UML, from version 0.99 (released in 2005) on, JML has been the primary input language.

Ever since, the community has worked on adopting a single JML language, with a single semantics—and this is still an ongoing process. Over the years, JML has become a very large language, containing many different specification constructs, some of which are only sensible in a single analysis technique. Because of the language being so large, not for all constructs the semantics is actually understood and agreed upon, and moreover all tools that support JML in fact only support a subset of it. There have been several suggestions of providing a formal semantics [Jacobs and Poll, 2001, Engel, 2005, Darvas and Müller, 2007, Bruns, 2009], but as of 2015, there is no final consensus. Moreover, JML suffers from the lack of support for current Java versions; currently there are no specifications for Java 5 features, such as enums or generic types. Dedicated expressions to deal with enhanced foreach loops have been proposed by Cok [2008].

How to Read this Chapter

When introducing JML, we mix a top-down and a bottom-up approach. At first, we introduce the probably most important concept of JML (and similar languages), method contracts, in a high-level manner (Section 7.1). We then jump to the most elementary building blocks of JML specifications, JML expressions (Section 7.2), which are needed to discuss method contracts in more detail (Section 7.3). Then, we lift the granularity of contracts from to the method to the class level (Section 7.4). After discussing the treatment of the `null` reference, and of exceptions (Sections 7.5, 7.6), we turn to measures for increasing the separation of specification and implementation, specification-only fields, methods, and variables (Section 7.7). Subtle complications of the integer semantics deserve their own, brief discussion (Section 7.8). Finally, we show that JML is not only used to specify desired behavior, but also to support the verification process through auxiliary assertions (Section 7.9). An overview of JML tools and a comparison with other specification languages (Section 7.10) conclude this tutorial.

During the course of this chapter, the reader may want to experiment with the examples (available from www.key-project.org/thebook2), using various tools, like KeY and OpenJML, among others. This is strongly encouraged. However, there are differences, unfortunately, concerning which language features and library methods are supported, and different restrictions on the way JML is written. Some of these difference are a bit arbitrary, others are more fundamental. For instance, runtime verification tools impose restrictions on JML which are not present in static verification tools, e.g., that invariants and postconditions have to be executable. The reader may therefore encounter examples that cannot be (without changes) processed by every JML tool.

7.1 Introduction to Method Contracts

Specifications, whether they are presented in natural language or some formalism, can express properties about system artifacts on various levels of granularity; like for instance the overall system, some intermediate level, like architectural components, or, on an even finer level of granularity, source code units. JML is designed for *unit* specification. In Java, those units are:

- methods, where JML specifies the effect of a single method invocation;
- classes, where JML merely specifies constraints on the internal structure of an object; and
- interfaces, where JML specifies the external behavior of an object.

Specifications of these units serve as *contracts* for their implementers, fixing what they can rely upon, and what they have to deliver in return, following the aforementioned Design by Contract paradigm.

We start by introducing method specifications in this section. While we go along, we will also introduce more general concepts, such as JML expressions, that are later used for class and interface specifications as well.

7.1.1 Clauses of a Contract

Contracts of methods are an agreement between the *caller* of the method and the *callee*, describing what guarantees they provide to each other. More specifically, it describes what is expected from the code that calls the method, and it provides guarantees about what the method will actually do. While in our terminology, 'contract' refers to the complete behavioral specification, written JML specifications usually consist of *specification cases*.[3] These specification cases are made up of several *clauses*.

The expectations on the caller are called the *preconditions* of the method. Typically, these will be conditions on the method's parameters, e.g., an argument should be a nonnull reference; but the precondition can also describe that the method should only be called when the object is in a particular state. In JML, each precondition is preceded by the keyword **requires**, and the conjunction of all requires clauses forms the method's precondition. We would like to emphasize that it is not the method

---

[3] In the context of KeY, what is called a *contract* approximately corresponds to a specification case in JML. What is called 'the contract' in JML (i.e., the complete specification) is considered as a set of multiple contracts for the same target in KeY. For details see Section 8.2.4.

implementer's responsibility to check or handle a violation of the precondition. Instead, this is the responsibility of the caller, and the whole point of contracts is to make this distribution of responsibilities explicit, and checkable. Having said that, it can be a difficult design decision when the caller should be responsible for 'good' parameters and prestates, and when the called method should check and handle this itself. We refer to Section 7.1.2 for a further discussion of *defensive* versus *offensive* specifications and implementations.

The guarantees provided by a method are called the *postcondition* of the method. They describe how the system state is changed by the method, or what the expected return value of the method is. A method only guarantees its postcondition to hold whenever it is called in a state that respects the precondition. If it is called in a state that does not satisfy the precondition, then no guarantee is made at all. In JML, every postcondition expression is preceded by the keyword **ensures**, and the conjunction of all ensures clauses forms the method's postcondition.

JML specifications are written as special comments in the Java code, starting with /*@ or //@. The @ symbol allows the JML parser to recognize that the comment contains a JML specification. Sometimes, JML specifications are also called *annotations*, because they annotate the program code. Preconditions and postconditions are basically just Java expressions (of Boolean type). This is done on purpose: if the specifications are written in a language that the programmer is already familiar with, they are easier for him or her to write and to read. JML extends Java's syntax; almost every side effect free Java expression, i.e., that does not modify the state and has no observable interaction with the outside world, (see [Gosling et al., 2013]) is also a valid JML expression. See Section 7.2 for a detailed discussion of JML expressions.

Example 7.1. Listing 7.1 contains an example of a basic JML specification. It contains specification cases for the methods in an interface Student, modeling a typical student at some university.

We discuss the different aspects of this example in full detail. To specify a certain method with JML, requires and ensures clauses are placed immediately before that method, within a JML comment, starting with /*@ or //@. For instance, the method changeStatus is specified in JML using two pre- and two postconditions.

The @ symbol is not only used at the beginning of a JML comment, but possibly also at the beginning of each line of the JML specification, and before the */. This is not necessary, but helps to highlight the JML specifications better. In general, an @ is ignored within a JML annotation if it is the first (nonwhite) character in the line, or if it is the last character before '*/.'

The requires and ensures clauses always consist of the keyword **requires** or **ensures**, respectively, followed by a Boolean expression. Note that a specification case must at least contain one **ensures** clause and that **requires** clauses may only appear at the beginning of a specification case.

For method getName, we specify that it is a **pure** method, i.e., it may not have any (visible) side effects. Also, it must terminate unconditionally (possibly with an exception). Only pure methods may be used in specification expressions, because these should not have side effects, and always terminate.

```
1  public interface Student {
2
3      public static final int bachelor = 0;
4      public static final int master = 1;
5
6      public /*@ pure @*/ String getName();
7
8      //@ ensures \result == bachelor || \result == master;
9      public /*@ pure @*/ int getStatus();
10
11     //@ ensures \result >= 0;
12     public /*@ pure @*/ int getCredits();
13
14     //@ ensures getName().equals(n);
15     public void setName(String n);
16
17     /*@ requires c >= 0;
18       @ ensures getCredits() == \old(getCredits()) + c;
19       @*/
20     public void addCredits(int c);
21
22     /*@ requires getCredits() >= 180;
23       @ requires getStatus() == bachelor;
24       @ ensures getCredits() == \old(getCredits());
25       @ ensures getStatus() == master;
26       @*/
27     public void changeStatus();
28
29
30 }
```

Listing 7.1 First JML example specification

Method `getStatus` is also specified as being pure. In addition, we specify that its result may only be one of two values: `bachelor` or `master`. To denote the return value of the method, the reserved JML keyword `\result` is used.

For method `getCredits` we also specify that it is pure, and in addition we specify that its return value must be nonnegative; a student thus never can have a negative amount of credits.

Method `setName` is nonpure, i.e., it may have side effects. Its postcondition is expressed in terms of the pure methods `getName` and `equals`: it ensures that after termination the result of `getName` is equal to the parameter n.

Method `addCredits`'s precondition states a condition on the method parameters, namely that only a positive number of credits can be added. The postcondition specifies how the credits change. Again, this postcondition is expressed in terms of a pure method, namely `getCredits`. Notice the use of the keyword `\old`. An expression `\old(E)` in the postcondition actually denotes the value of expression E in the state where the method call started, the *prestate* of the method. Thus the postcondition of `addCredits` expresses that the number of credits only increases:

after evaluation of the method, the value of `getCredits` is equal to the old value of `getCredits`, i.e., before the method was called, plus the parameter c.

Method `changeStatus`'s precondition specifies that this method only may be called when the student is in a particular state, namely when they have obtained a sufficient amount of credits to pass from the Bachelor status to the Master status. Moreover, the method may only be called when the student is still having a Bachelor status. The postcondition expresses that the number of credits is not changed by this operation, but the status is. Notice that the two preconditions and the two postconditions of `changeStatus` are written as separate **requires** and **ensures** clauses, respectively. Implicitly, these are each joined in conjunction, thus the specification is equivalent to the following specification:

```
/*@ requires getCredits() >= 180 &&
  @           getStatus() == bachelor;
  @ ensures getCredits() == \old(getCredits()) &&
  @           getStatus() == master;
  @*/
public void changeStatus();
```

The reader might have wondered why not all method specifications in `Student` have a pre- and a postcondition. Implicitly though, they have. For every specification clause, there is a default. For pre- and postconditions this is the predicate **true**, i.e., no constraints are placed on the caller of the method, or on the method's implementation.

Example 7.2. Thus for example the specification of method `getStatus` actually is the following:

—— Java + JML ——————————————————————————

```
/*@ requires true;
  @ ensures status == bachelor || status == master;
  @*/
public int getStatus() {
    return status;
}
```

———————————————————————————— Java + JML ——

7.1.2 Defensive Versus Offensive Method Implementations

An important point about method contracts is that they can be used to avoid *defensive* programming. Consider the specification of method `addCredits` in Listing 7.1,

This method assumes that its argument is nonnegative, and otherwise it is not going to function correctly. When one uses a defensive programming style, one would first test the value of the argument and throw an exception if this was negative. This clutters up the code, and in many cases it is not necessary. Instead, using specifications, one can use an 'offensive' coding style. The specification states what the method requires from its caller. It only guarantees to function correctly if the caller also fulfills its part of the contract. When validating the application, one checks that every call of the method is indeed within the bounds of its specification, and thus the explicit test in the code is not necessary. Thus, making good use of specifications can avoid adding many parameter checks in the code. Such checks are only necessary when the parameters cannot be controlled—for example, because they are given via an external user.

7.1.3 Specifications and Implementations

Method specifications are written independently of possible implementations. Classes that implement this interface may choose different implementations, as long as they respect the specification. Method specifications do not always have to specify the exact behavior of a method; they give minimal requirements that the implementation should respect.

Example 7.3. Considering the specification in Listing 7.1 again, the method specification for changeStatus prescribes that the credits may not be changed by this method. However, method addCredits is free to update the status of the student. So for example, an implementation that silently updates the status from Bachelor to Master is appropriate according to the specification. The specification case is repeated here for understandability and that it is not required and recommended to copy specifications of interfaces in classes that realize them.

```
—— Java + JML ————————————————————————————————
/*@ requires c >= 0;
  @ ensures getCredits() == \old(getCredits()) + c;
  @*/
public void addCredits(int c) {
    credits = credits + c;
    if (credits >= 180) {status = master;}
}
———————————————————————————————— Java + JML ——
```

According to the specification, both addCredits and changeStatus would be free to change the name of the student, even though we would typically not expect this to happen. A way to avoid this, is to add explicitly conditions getName()==\old(getName()) to all postconditions. Later, in Section 7.9.1, we will see how **assignable** clauses can be used to explicitly disallow these unwanted changes in a more convenient way.

7.2 Expressions

We have already seen that standard Java expressions can be used in JML specifications. These expressions have to be side effect free, thus for example assignments, or increment/decrement operators, are not allowed. As also mentioned above, JML expressions may contain method calls to pure methods.

In addition, JML defines several specification-specific constructs, to be used in expressions. The use of the \result and \old keywords has already been demonstrated in Listing 7.1, and the official language specification contains a few more of these. Besides Java's logical operators, such as conjunction &, disjunction |and negation !, also other logical operators are allowed in JML specifications, e.g., implication ==>, and logical equivalence <==>. Since expressions are not supposed to have side effects or terminate exceptionally, in JML in many cases the difference between logical operators such as & and |, and short circuit operators, such as &&, and || is not important. However, sometimes the short circuit operators have to be used to ensure an expression is well-defined. For instance, y != 0 & x/y == 5 may not be a well-defined expression, while y != 0 && x/y == 5 is.

7.2.1 Quantified Boolean Expressions

For specifying interesting properties, purely propositional Boolean expressions are too limited. How could one for instance express any of the following properties with just propositional connectors?

- An array arr is sorted.
- The variable m holds the maximum entry of array arr.
- All Account objects in an array allAccounts are stored at the index corresponding to their respective accountNumber field.

Given that the arrays in these examples have a statically unknown length, propositional connectives are not enough to express any of the above. What we need here is *quantification*. For that, Boolean JML expressions are extended by the following constructs.[4]

- (\forall T x; b)
  'for all x of type T, b holds'
- (\forall T x; a; b)
  'for all x of type T *fulfilling* a, b holds'
- (\exists T x; b)
  'there exists an x of type T such that b holds'
- (\exists T x; a; b)
  'there exists an x of type T *fulfilling* a, such that b holds'

---

[4] The JML keywords \forall and \exists correspond to $\forall$ and $\exists$ in textbook notation.

Here, T is a Java (primitive or reference) type, x is any name (hereby declared to be of type T), and a and b are Boolean JML expressions. The a is called *range predicate*. The two forms using a range predicate are not strictly needed, as they can be expressed without. (\forall T x; a; b) is logically equivalent to (\forall T x; a ==> b), and (\exists T x; a; b) is logically equivalent to (\exists T x; a && b). However, the range predicates have a certain pragmatics not shared by their logical counterparts. In (\forall T x; a; b), as well as in (\exists T x; a; b), the Boolean expression a is used intuitively to restrict range of x further than T does.

Example 7.4. Using quantifiers, we can specify that an array should be sorted, for instance in a precondition for a logarithmic `lookup` method that assumes sorting.

—— JML ————————————————————————————

```
//@ requires (\forall int i, j;
//@                     0 <= i & i < j & j < a.length;
//@                     a[i] <= a[j]);
public int lookup(int elem) {...
```
———————————————————————————————— JML ——

The first argument `int i,j` is the declaration of the variables over that the quantification ranges. The second argument `0 <= i & i < j & j < a.length` defines the range of the values for this variable, and the third argument is the actually universally quantified formula (`a[i] <= a[j]` in this case).

Example 7.5. An alternative, but less preferred, way to phrase the specification in Example 7.4 is the following:

—— JML ————————————————————————————

```
//@ requires (\forall int i, j;
//@               0 <= i & i < j & j < a.length ==> a[i] <= a[j]);
public int lookup(int elem) {...
```
———————————————————————————————— JML ——

Besides supporting readability, the range predicate form helps certain JML tools to 'execute' quantified formulas where possible. This is less important for theorem provers, like KeY. But a runtime verification tool would need to operationalize the precondition, by looping through all `i,j` fulfilling `0<=i & i<j & i<a.length`, instead of looping through all `i,j` between `Integer.MIN_VALUE` and `Integer.MAX_VALUE`.

Example 7.6. To specify that a method returns the index of an integer array `arr` holding the maximum entry, we can write the following postcondition.

—— JML ————————————————————————————

```
//@ ensures (\forall int i; 0 <= i &&
//@               i < arr.length; \result >= arr[i]);
```
———————————————————————————————— JML ——

But is that enough? (The reader may briefly reflect before reading on.) This single
line only specifies that the result is larger than any other element. An implementation
always returning `Integer.MAX_VALUE` would satisfy the above postcondition[5]. We
therefore need an additional postcondition that states that the result is actually an
element of the array:

—— JML ————————————————————————————
```
//@ ensures arr.length > 0 ==>
//@     (\exists int i; 0<=i && i<arr.length; \result==arr[i]);
```
———————————————————————————————— JML ——

Example 7.7. The following Boolean JML expressions say that all `Account` objects
in an array `allAccounts` are stored at the index corresponding to their respective
`accountNumber` field.

—— JML ————————————————————————————
```
(\forall int i; 0 <= i && i < allAccounts.length;
           allAccounts[i].accountNumber == i)
```
———————————————————————————————— JML ——

Such an expression could for instance be used in an invariant, see Section 7.4.1.

7.2.2 Numerical Comprehensions

In addition to the Boolean quantified expressions, JML offers so called *generalized quantifiers* `\sum`, `\product`, `\min`, `\max`, and `\num_of`. Those are actually
numerical comprehensions (or higher-order functions) with bound variables; see
Section 2.3.1. The postcondition in Example 7.6 can alternatively be given as:
```
//@ ensures \result ==
//@          (\max int i; 0 <= i && i < arr.length; arr[i]);
```
The above is syntactically similar to a quantified formula: the `\max` operator binds a
variable `i`, and a Boolean guard expression restricts it to be within the range of the
array's indices. The type of the `\max` expression is the type of its body; here it is `int`.
The intuitive semantics is obviously that the result is the maximum of all `arr[i]`
where `i` is in the array range. However, the `\max` construct is not total, i.e., it is not
always a well-defined expression. In case `arr` has zero length, for instance, there
is no maximum. A similar case appears with a noncompact range, e.g., the set of
all mathematical integers (represented by the JML type `\bigint`, see Section 7.8):
`(\max \bigint i; true; i)`.

Another comprehension operator is the summation operator `\sum`, of which we
make use in Example 7.9 on page 224 since the exact number of summands is not
known:

---
[5] See also Section 7.8 for a discussion on Java integers.

```
(\sum int i; 0 <= i && i < s1.length; s1[i].getCredits())
```

This expression corresponds to $\sum_{i=0}^{\text{s1.length}-1}$ s1[i].getCredits() in mathematical notation. More generally, sum comprehensions in JML can have several bound variables that range over sets of values. The general pattern is (\sum T x; P; Q) where T is a type, P a Boolean expression and Q an integer expression corresponds to $\sum_{x\in\{y\in T|P\}} Q$. Likewise the \product operator is used to express product comprehensions. Since addition (as multiplication) is commutative and associative, there is no particular order in which elements are summed up. Sums with empty ranges have value 0 by definition, empty products have value 1.

Expressions using the \num_of operator, that gives the cardinality of a finite set, can be expressed in terms of sums: (\num_of T x; P) is syntactic sugar for (\sum T x; P; 1).

However, like for maximum, sum comprehensions are not always well-defined. For instance, the expression (\sum \bigint i; 0 <= i; i) corresponds to $\sum_{i=0}^{\infty} i$, the value of which is undefined since it diverges. In some tools—including KeY— effective reasoning about these comprehensions is therefore restricted to closed integer intervals, for which sums, etc., are always defined. In particular, KeY only interprets sums of the shape (\sum int i; ℓ <= i && i < u; Q), where the lower bound ℓ is included and the upper bound u is excluded. This restricted form using intervals has the advantage of having a simple induction schema to define these comprehensions, that lays the foundation to reasoning about sums and products. More details about this are discussed in Section 8.1.

7.2.3 Evaluation in the Prestate

As indicated in the introductory example, JML allows us to mark any expression e in a postcondition with \old(e), which means that e is not evaluated in the current (post)state of the method, but in its prestate. In most cases, \old(e) is a subexpression of some bigger expression, and it is important to be aware that all parts of the expression not included in \old(...) construct are evaluated in the current (post)state. This is fairly obvious in many examples, like **ensures** getCredits() == \old(getCredits()) + c; in Listing 7.1. For a more subtle example, consider an ATM scenario, where an insertedCard (represented by an object with a Boolean field invalid) is 'confiscated' after too many failed attempts to enter the correct PIN, specified by

```
//@ ...
//@ ensures \old(insertedCard).invalid;
//@ ...
```

We encourage the reader, before reading on, to reflect on the difference between \old(insertedCard).invalid and \old(insertedCard.invalid).

Writing \old(insertedCard.invalid) would mean that the method implementation has to guarantee that the invalid field of the old insertedCard object was true *before* the method's execution. This makes no sense, as a method implementation can never influence its prestate. However, \old(insertedCard).invalid makes much more sense, as an implementation can, for instance, set the invalid field of the old insertedCard object to true. To demand the invalidation of the object insertedCard in the poststate, \old(insertedCard).invalid refers to the *current* field of the object *formerly* referred to by insertedCard.

7.3 Method Contracts in Detail

Now that the reader is familiar with the particular features of JML expressions, we are ready to continue the presentation of method contracts. Among other things, we will introduce specification visibility, much more structure, and more semantics, in contracts.

7.3.1 Visibility of Specifications

So far, the specifications have not specified anything about the values of an object's fields. Typically, these are declared private, which limits also their use within specifications. Basically JML uses the same access rules like Java which means that elements used within specifications have to be visible to it and that a specification itself also has a visibility. The access modifiers public, protected, and private are explicitly used to define specifications visibility. If none of these modifiers is used a specification has the default (package) visibility.

In addition to the Java access rules, JML forbids the usage of elements within specifications that are less visible than the specification itself. The reason of this restriction is to avoid to expose implementation details to the clients (information hiding). As a consequence, it is not possible to use private variables directly within protected or public specifications. However, it is possible to change their visibility only for the specification layer via spec_protected or spec_public. These modifiers have to be used with care and only if the adjusted field fits the abstraction level of the specification.

Example 7.8. If we specify the instance variables of CStudent to be spec_public, then its constructor can also be specified as in Listing 7.2.

A second restriction of specification visibility to keep in mind is that specifications that constrain a field must have at least the visibility of the field. The reason is that otherwise a user of a field would not see the constraints to maintain. This is especially important for invariants and constraints, discussed in Sections 7.4.1 and 7.4.3.

```
class CStudent implements Student {

    /*@ spec_public @*/ private String name;
    /*@ spec_public @*/ private int credits;
    /*@ spec_public @*/ private int status;

    :

    /*@ requires c >= 0;
      @ ensures credits == c;
      @ ensures status == bachelor;
      @ ensures name = n;
      @*/
    public CStudent (int c, String n) {
        credits = c;
        name = n;
        status = bachelor;
    }
}
```

Listing 7.2 Class CStudent with spec_public variables

7.3.2 Specification Cases

When specifying a method, it is often useful—and sometimes necessary—to describe the behavior separately for different parts of the prestate/input space. The structuring mechanism for that is the *specification case*, each of which is specific for a particular precondition. Specification cases are combined by the **also** keyword. The above method contracts consisted of only one specification case. We now give an example where two specification cases are given for one method.

Example 7.9. Listing 7.3 shows the specification of a class implementing a set of integers, with a limited capacity that is fixed at the time when the integer set object is constructed.

Here, method add is specified by two specification cases, one for the case, where the set is not full and the element to be added is not contained (size < limit && !contains(elem)); and one for the case, where the set is full or the element to be added is already contained (size == limit || contains(elem);). Note that it is possible to specify add with only one specification case. Refer to [Raghavan and Leavens, 2000] for a procedure to produce flat specifications.

Listing 7.3 is furthermore an example for extensive usage of quantification. Moreover, it demonstrates the power of pure methods. Without the ability to use contains in the specification of the other methods, all occurrences of contains would need to be replaced by the existentially quantified JML expression specifying contains, resulting in a much more complicated specification. We will extend on this example when discussing class invariants.

```
1  public class LimitedIntegerSet {
2    public final int limit;
3    /*@ spec_public @*/ private int arr[];
4    /*@ spec_public @*/ private int size = 0;
5
6    public LimitedIntegerSet(int limit) {
7      this.limit = limit;
8      this.arr = new int[limit];
9    }
10
11   /*@ requires size < limit && !contains(elem);
12    @ ensures \result == true;
13    @ ensures contains(elem);
14    @ ensures (\forall int e;
15    @                    e != elem;
16    @                    contains(e) <==> \old(contains(e)));
17    @ ensures size == \old(size) + 1;
18    @
19    @ also
20    @
21    @ requires size == limit || contains(elem);
22    @ ensures \result == false;
23    @ ensures (\forall int e;
24    @                    contains(e) <==> \old(contains(e)));
25    @ ensures size == \old(size);
26    @*/
27   public boolean add(int elem) {/*...*/}
28
29   /*@ ensures !contains(elem);
30    @ ensures (\forall int e;
31    @                    e != elem;
32    @                    contains(e) <==> \old(contains(e)));
33    @ ensures \old(contains(elem))
34    @            ==> size == \old(size) - 1;
35    @ ensures !\old(contains(elem))
36    @            ==> size == \old(size);
37    @*/
38   public void remove(int elem) {/*...*/}
39
40   /*@ ensures \result == (\exists int i;
41    @                              0 <= i && i < size;
42    @                              arr[i] == elem);
43    @*/
44   public /*@ pure @*/ boolean contains(int elem) {/*...*/}
45
46    :
47 }
```

Listing 7.3 Specifying limited size integer set

7.3.3 Semantics of Normal Behavior Specification Cases

An important question is when a method specification is actually satisfied. And in particular, if a method does not terminate, does it then satisfy its specification? The specifications as we have seen here implicitly state that the method must always terminate, i.e., they specify a *total correctness* condition, see [Hoare, 1969]. If method m is specified as follows:

```
/*@ requires P;
  @ ensures Q;
  @*/
public ... m(...) { ...
```

this means the following: If method m is executed in a prestate where P holds, *then* execution of method m from this prestate terminates, *and*—if it terminates normally[6]—in the final state the postcondition Q holds. Section 8.2 provides a more formal account on contract semantics.

Nontermination and Exceptions

To specify that a method may not terminate under some precondition, one can add an explicit `diverges` clause. A diverges clause specifies under which conditions a method may not terminate, for example to express that for certain parameters a method may not terminate. As we have seen above, the default is `false`, i.e., a method must always terminate. Like `requires`, `diverges` clauses are evaluated in the prestate; a `diverges` clause thus describes a precondition that is necessary for nontermination.

```
/*@ requires P;
  @ ensures Q;
  @ diverges x < 0;
  @*/
public ... m(int x) { ...
```

Sometimes we wish to exclude the case that a method may terminate because of an exception. In this case, the respective specification case is preceded by the keyword `normal_behavior`, which states that the method execution must terminate normally, and in the final state the postcondition must hold.

Lightweight and Heavyweight Specification

The JML reference manual [Leavens et al., 2013] further distinguishes between so called *lightweight* and *heavyweight* specifications. Heavyweight specification

---

[6] A method is said to terminate normally if either it reached the end of its body, in a normal state, or it terminated because of a `return` instruction. In Section 7.6 we discuss how we can specify methods that terminate because of an exception.

cases are preceded by one of the keywords **behavior**, **normal_behavior**, or **exceptional_behavior** (see Section 7.6); all others are lightweight. The difference is that, in lightweight specifications, there are no standardized defaults—except for **diverges** whose default is always **false**. Instead, every tool is free to choose its own semantics. KeY takes the choice of applying the same defaults as for heavyweight specifications. The visibility of a lightweight specification case in JML is always the one of the method they specify.

7.3.4 Specifications for Constructors

Constructors can be considered as special methods. In the prestate of a constructor, the object does not yet exist. Thus a precondition of a constructor can only put constraints on the constructor parameters, it cannot require anything about the internal state of the object—as the object does not exist yet when the constructor is called. However, the postcondition of the constructor can specify constraints on the state of the object. Typically, it will relate the object state to the constructor's parameters.

Example 7.10. Suppose we have a class **CStudent** implementing the **Student** interface. It could have the following constructor:

```
—— Java + JML ————————————————————————————————————————————
/*@ requires c >= 0;
  @ ensures getCredits() == c;
  @ ensures getStatus() == bachelor;
  @ ensures getName() == n;
  @*/
CStudent (int c, String n) {
    credits = c;
    name = n;
    status = bachelor;
}
————————————————————————————————————————————— Java + JML ——
```

Thus, it would be incorrect to specify **requires getCredits() >= 0;** or **requires getStatus() == bachelor;** these specifications are meaningless at the moment that the constructor is invoked.

7.3.5 Notions of Purity

Above in Section 7.1.1, we have said that only pure methods may be used in a method specification, and purity was defined as terminating unconditionally and having no visible side effects. 'No visible side effects' means that the state that was allocated on the heap before the method call may not be changed. Thus, this does not exclude that a method creates a new object and initializes it. In the same way, constructors are pure if they only operate on fields of the object they initialize, not touching the state that was allocated before the call to the constructor. If it, however, changes other parts of the state it is not pure. Later, in Section 9.4.4, we will see how purity annotations help to verify programs in a modular way. For clarity, this notion of purity in JML is sometimes known as *weak purity*. This is in contrast to *strict purity* that requires that the heap is not changed in any way. While weakly and strictly pure methods have the same observable behavior, reasoning about hidden changes in weakly pure methods can make a proof more complicated. In KeY's dialect of JML, strict purity is indicated by the modifier `strictly_pure`.

Apart from that, there are situations where methods are technically speaking not pure, but from a client point of view may be considered to be so. Consider for an example the function that computes a hash code. The first time this function is called on an object, a field of the object will be written, so that the next calls can be evaluated by looking up this field. Because of this, different notions of purity and *observational purity* exist in the literature [Barnett et al., 2004, 2005b, Darvas and Müller, 2006, Darvas and Leino, 2007, Naumann, 2007, Cok and Leavens, 2008].

For the scope of this chapter, it is sufficient to define purity simply as not having any observable side effects.

While pure methods must terminate under any circumstance, they may still raise exceptions or have a nontrivial precondition. In these cases, the value of a pure method invocation is not always well-defined. Therefore, it is a best practice to have **true** as precondition of pure methods and to rule out exceptions and not defined return values.

7.4 Class Level Specifications

Consider again the specification of `Student` in Listing 7.1. If we look carefully at the specifications and the description that we give about the student's credits, we notice that we implicitly assume some properties about the value of `getCredits` that hold throughout. For example, we wrote above:

"a student thus never can have a negative amount of credits"

and also

"the number of credits only increases."

But if we would like to make explicit that we assume that these properties always hold, we would have to add this to *all* specifications in `Student`, and thus in particular, also to all methods that do not relate at all to the number of credits. Thus for example, we would get the following specification:

```
——— Java + JML ———————————————————————————
/*@ requires getCredits() >= 0;
  @ ensures \result == bachelor || \result == master;
  @ ensures getCredits() >= 0;
  @*/
/*@ pure @*/ public int getStatus();
```
———————————————————————————— Java + JML ———

Clearly, this is not desired, because specifications would get very large, and besides describing the intended behavior of that particular method, they also describe properties over the lifetime of the object. Therefore, JML provides also class level specifications, such as invariants, history constraints, and initially clauses. These specify properties over the internal state of an object, and how the state can evolve during the object's lifetime.

7.4.1 Invariants

One of the most important and widely-used specification elements in object-orientation are type *invariants*[7], also called *class* or *interface invariants*, depending on where they are defined. An invariant is a Boolean (JML) expression over the object state, and can be seen as a condition to constrain the state an instance can be in. In addition, any constructor has to ensure that the invariant is established. Methods can be except from this scheme by adding the modifier **helper** to their declaration.

Example 7.11. Listing 7.4 shows three possible invariants that can be added to interface Student. These specify that credits are never nonnegative; a student's status is always either Bachelor or Master, and nothing else; and if a student's status is Master, he or she has earned more than 180 credits. The pure methods are used in the invariants.[8]

Of course, instead of specifying invariants, one could also add these specifications to all pre- and postconditions explicitly. However, this means that if you add a method to a class, you have to remember to add these pre- and postconditions yourself. Moreover, invariants are also inherited by subclasses (and by implementations of interfaces). Thus any method that overrides a method from a superclass still has to respect the invariants. And any method that is added to the subclass also has to respect the invariants from the superclass. This leads to a very nice separation of concerns.

---

[7] Not to be confused with loop invariants. Those will be discussed in Section 7.9.2.

[8] There is an unresolved discussion about whether methods that are used in invariants have to be helper, or how to otherwise avoid potential circularity between showing and assuming invariants. We choose to not mark public methods as helper, because helper methods are designed for local usage. Please note, though, that some tools, like OpenJML, require methods used in invariants to be helper.

```
interface Student {

    public static final int bachelor = 0;
    public static final int master = 1;

    /*@ instance invariant getCredits() >= 0;
      @ instance invariant getStatus() == bachelor ||
      @                     getStatus() == master;
      @ instance invariant getStatus() == master ==>
      @                     getCredits() >= 180;
      @
      @ instance initially getCredits() == 0;
      @ instance initially getStatus() == bachelor;
      @
      @ instance constraint getCredits() >= \old(getCredits());
      @ instance constraint \old(getStatus()) == master ==>
      @                     getStatus() == master;
      @ instance constraint \old(getName()) == getName();
      @*/

    public /*@ pure @*/ String getName();

    public /*@ pure @*/ int getStatus();

    public /*@ pure @*/ int getCredits();

    /*@ requires c >= 0;
      @ ensures getCredits() == \old(getCredits()) + c;
      @*/
    public void addCredits(int c);

    /*@ requires getCredits() >= 180;
      @ requires getStatus() == bachelor;
      @ ensures getCredits() == \old(getCredits());
      @ ensures getStatus() == master;
      @*/
    public void changeStatus();


}
```

Listing 7.4 Interface Student with class level specifications

An important point to realize is that invariants have to hold only in all states in which a method is called or terminates. Thus, inside the method, the invariant may be temporarily broken. Note that the kind of termination of a method does not matter. Regardless of terminating normally, exceptionally, or erroneously, a method has to meet the invariant.

Example 7.12. The following possible implementation of addCredits is correct, even though it breaks the invariant that a student can only be studying for a Master if they have earned more than 180 points inside the method: if `credits + c` is sufficiently high, the status is changed to Master. After this assignment the invariant does not hold, but because of the next assignment, the invariant is reestablished before the method terminates.

```
—— Java + JML ————————————————————————————
/*@ requires c >= 0;
  @ ensures getCredits() == \old(getCredits()) + c;
  @*/
public void addCredits(int c) {
  if (credits + c>= 180) {status = master;} // invariant broken
  credits = credits + c;
}
————————————————————————————— Java + JML ——
```

However, if a method calls another method on the same object, it has to ensure that the invariant holds before this callback. Why this is necessary, is best explained with an example.

```
interface CallBack {

    //@ instance invariant getX() > 0;
    //@ instance invariant getY() > 0;

    /*@ pure @*/ public int getX();
    /*@ pure @*/ public int getY();

    //@ ensures getX() == x;
    public void setX(int x);

    //@ ensures getY() == y;
    public void setY(int y);

    //@ ensures \result == getX() % getY();
    public int remainder();

    public int longComputation();

}
```

Listing 7.5 Interface `CallBack`

Example 7.13. Consider the interface `CallBack` in Listing 7.5. Typically, correctness of the method `remainder` crucially depends on the value of `getY` being greater than 0. Suppose we have an implementation of the `CallBack` interface, where the method `longComputation` is sketched in Listing 7.6.

```
public int longComputation(){
    ...
    if (getY() ...) {
        setY(0); // invariant broken
    }
    ...
    int r = remainder(); // callback
    ...
    setY(r + 1); // invariant reestablished
    ...
    return ...
}
```
Listing 7.6 Invariant broken during callback

Naively, one could think that the fact that the invariant about getY() is broken inside this method, is harmless, because the invariant is reestablished by the setY(r + 1) statement. However, the call to method remainder is a callback, and the invariant should hold at this point. In fact, correct functioning of this method call depends on the invariant holding. The invariant implicitly is part of remainder's precondition. If the invariant does not hold at the point of the callback, this means that remainder is called outside its precondition, and no assumption can be made about its result as well.

Although invariants are always specified within a class or interface, their effective scope is global. A method of some specific class is obliged to respect invariants of all other classes. There is a way to avoid the requirement that the invariant has to hold upon callback, by specifying that a method is a **helper** method. Such methods must not depend on the invariant to hold, and they do not guarantee that the invariant will hold afterwards. Typically, only private methods should be specified as helper methods, because one does not want that any other object can directly invoke a helper method. Finally we note that, while a *pure* helper method cannot assume the invariant to hold when it is called, it does *preserve* any invariant because of purity.

Where Do Invariants Come From?

Sometimes invariants are imposed by the domain which is modeled by the code. The interface Student in Listing 7.4 is such an example. Students can only have a positive number of credits, they must be either Master or Bachelor students, and so forth. Another common motivation for invariants is efficiency. Efficient computations often require to organize data in a specific way. One way is introducing redundancy, like for instance in an index of a book, mapping words to pages where they occur. Such an index is redundant (we can always search through the whole book to find the occurrences of a word), but it enables efficient look-up. On the downside, redundancy opens up for inconsistencies. The countermeasure is to use invariants, formalizing the consistency conditions (like each word in an index appearing in the text as well, at the page given by the index). Other ways to increase efficiency limit the organization of data to comply to certain restrictions. A prominent example of that is sortedness, which allows for quicker look-up. In the following, we demonstrate how sortedness can be expressed with an invariant.

Example 7.14. We turn the `LimitedIntegerSet` (Listing 7.3) into a sorted data structure, by adding the invariant

—— JML ——

```
/*@ public invariant (\forall int i;
  @                        0 < i && i < size;
  @                        arr[i-1] <= arr[i]) ;
  @*/
```

——— JML ——

to that class. With that, the implementer of each method can *rely* on sortedness in the prestate, and the implementer of each (impure) method has to *guarantee* sortedness in the poststate.

Static Invariants vs. Instance Invariants

Class invariants may or may not refer to the object `this` and its instance (i.e., nonstatic) fields or methods. For example, the class invariant in Example 7.14 refers to the instance field `arr`. Such invariants are also called *instance invariants*, and can be declared as such with the `instance` modifier. This is however not necessary, as class invariants are instance invariants per default. If, on the other hand, a class invariant does *not* refer to `this`, neither to any instance field or instance method, we can highlight that (and potentially help verification tools) by declaring the invariant as *static*, using the `static` modifier. Please note that, since instance methods might change static variables, static invariants have to be respected by instance methods as well.

Similarly, interface invariants may or may not refer to instance (i.e., nonstatic) methods. For example, all invariants in Listings 7.4 and 7.5 mention instance methods, and are therefore *instance* invariants. The reader may have noted that invariants in Listings 7.4 and 7.5 are explicitly declared as `instance invariant`. This is necessary because, for interfaces, the default is different from classes: invariants are static, if not declared otherwise.

Semantics of Invariants

Defining a precise semantics for invariants is still an active area of research, see, e.g., [Poetzsch-Heffter, 1997, Leino and Müller, 2004, Barnett et al., 2004, Müller et al., 2006, Bruns, 2009]. A complication is that, although invariants are declared in a particular class, not only instances of that class have to respect it, but all objects in the system. An alternative approach, that is used in the Spec# framework, is to explicitly add specification statements unpack and pack for invariants. An invariant may only be broken if it has been explicitly unpacked. When the invariant is reestablished, it has to be explicitly be packed again, and this only succeeds if the invariant indeed holds at this point. Every method can then specify explicitly whether it assumes invariants to hold (i.e., to be packed) or not. This approach is sometimes referred to as the *Boogie methodology* [Barnett et al., 2006].

Similar to the Boogie methodology, in the KeY system, invariants are not implicitly added to specifications. Instead, the specification must make explicit which specific invariants are included, and which are not. This specification may be more verbose, but it is clear from the given specification that invariants are assumed or established. See Section 9.2.1.3 for further discussion. The invariant for an object o can be referred to through \invariant_for(o). This allows fine-grained usage of invariants in specifications. Unlike in Boogie, explicit packing/unpacking instructions in the code are not necessary. Instead, the specifier has to specify a set of locations the invariant depends on at most (**accessible** clause). Usually, methods rely at least on the invariant of the current receiver. For convenience, this invariant is implicitly included for non**helper** methods (see Section 8.2 on proof obligations).

Finally, it is important to realize that the notion of invariants that we discussed here only makes sense in a sequential setting. In a multithreaded setting, there always may be another thread accessing the object simultaneously, and one cannot talk about initial and final states of a method invocation anymore. Instead, in a multithreaded setting, one sometimes specifies *strong invariants* that may never be broken. For instance, Zaharieva-Stojanovski and Huisman [2014] present a modular specification and verification technique for class invariants in a concurrent setting.

7.4.2 Initially Clauses

Sometimes, one explicitly wishes to specify the conditions that are satisfied by an object upon creation. Each (nonhelper) constructor[9] of the object has to establish the predicate specified by the *initially clause*. Another advantage of initially clauses is that they are inherited; that means that also constructors of subclasses have to fulfill them. Constructors in Java itself are not inherited. As a consequence, a constructor can rely on the guarantees provided by a called super constructor but does not have to maintain them.

Example 7.15. Listing 7.4 shows some possible initially clauses for the Student interface.

Again, it would be possible to specify this property as a postcondition of all constructors, instead of as a single initially clause. But in this way, any additional constructor has to respect the initially clause, and we ensure that also subclasses respect it.

---

[9] Again, typically only private constructors would be annotated as a helper constructor.

7.4.3 History Constraints

Invariants as we discussed above define a predicate that every state of the object should respect. However, sometimes one also wishes to specify how an object may evolve over time, i.e., the relationship that exists between the prestate and the poststate of a method call. This could be seen as a sort of general postcondition that has to be respected by every method, however the definition is actually more fine grained than that. For this, *history constraints* (usually *constraints* for short) have been introduced by Liskov and Wing [1993]. Constraints can be seen as implicit postconditions, but just as invariants and initially clauses, they have the advantage that they are inherited, and immediately are required to hold for any additional methods. Constraints may rely on syntactical features that are used to measure changes between states such as the \old operator. Assigning suitable semantics to history constraints is nontrivial; a possibility would be to see them as special two-state model methods (see Section 9.2.2). This is not yet implemented in KeY at the time of publishing this book.

Example 7.16. Listing 7.4 defines several constraints for the Student interface. The first constraint specifies that the amount of credits can never decrease. The second constraint specifies that if a student has obtained the Master status, he or she will remain a Master student, and cannot be downgraded to a Bachelor student again. Finally, the third constraint specifies that a student's name can never change.

When specifying constraints, it is important that they should denote a reflexive relation, i.e., it should be possible to respect a constraint without actually changing the state. In particular, any pure method should be able to respect the constraint. Therefore, one should not specify the following strict constraint:

```
constraint \old(getCredits()) < getCredits();
```

as it is impossible to respect this constraint with a pure method. Typically, constraints will also be transitive, so that when you consecutively call two methods from the same object, you also know the relationship that holds between the prestate of the first method, and the poststate of the second method.

Example 7.17. Consider the possible implementation of addCredits in Listing 7.7. To show that the constraint is respected, it has to hold for the following state pairs:

- (prestate, call-state changeStatus)
- (call-state changeStatus, return-state changeStatus)
- (return-state changeStatus, poststate)

Notice that if the constraint is transitive, the relationship also holds for the pair of prestate and poststate, which is indeed what we want.

Again, in a multithreaded setting, the meaning of constraints would become less clear. Because any interleaving is possible, all intermediate states must be assumed to be visible to other threads. However, a constraint such as that getName returns a constant value could still be meaningful also in a multithreaded setting (except

```
//@ constraint \old(getCredits()) <= getCredits();

/*@ requires c >= 0;
  @ ensures getCredits() == \old(getCredits()) + c;
  @*/
// prestate
public void addCredits(int c) {
    credits = credits + c;
    if (credits >= 180) {
        // call-state changeStatus
        changeStatus();
        // return-state changeStatus
    }
} // poststate
```

Listing 7.7 Checking history constraints

that the number of possible visible state pairs that have to be considered might grow exponentially). Therefore, in a concurrent setting one could imagine a notion of *strong history constraints*, i.e., a relationship that has to hold for any pair of consecutive states.

7.4.4 Initially Clauses and History Constraints: Static vs. Instance

Just as class invariants (see Section 7.4.1), also initially clauses and history constraints have instance as well as static versions, which can be declared with the `instance` and `static` modifier, respectively. The static variants cannot explicitly mention an instance (i.e., nonstatic) field or method, neither can they refer to `this` itself. The instance variants, on the other hand, have no such restriction.

In *classes*, the default for initially clauses and history constraints is `instance`, meaning this modifier can be omitted. For *interfaces*, the default for initially clauses and history constraints is `static`. Note that, in interface Student (Listing 7.4), all initially clauses and history constraints mention nonstatic methods or fields. They can therefore not be static (which is the default), and have to be marked as `instance` explicitly.

7.4.5 Inheritance of Specifications

Design by Contract allows one to impose the concept of *behavioral subtyping* [Liskov, 1988], that is usually defined by the *Liskov substitution principle*, or Liskov principle for short [Liskov and Wing, 1994]. A type T' is a behavioral subtype of type T if every observable behavior of T is also observable on T'. In an object-oriented program, this means that any subclass may be used wherever a superclass is expected. Behavioral subtyping expresses the idea that a subclass thus should behave as the superclass (at least, when it is used in a superclass context). Subclasses in Java do not always define behavioral subtypes. They can be used simply for the purpose of code reuse.

However, the substitution principle as originally stated by Liskov [1988] can sometimes be too strong in practice (see [Leavens, 1988]). For instance, what exactly is the refined behavior of a *linked* list, as compared to a list in general? Surely, there is no nondeterminism that can be refined. This means there cannot be strict behavioral subtypes regarding all behaviors. Instead, we focus on the client perspective again and define behavior subtypes regarding contracts (and invariants). This means that a class C' is a behavioral subtype of a super class C, if for every method m implemented in both C and C' (i.e., the implementation in C' is overriding), every specification case for $C :: m$ is also a specification case for $C' :: m$, and that the contract of $C :: m$ is refined by the contract of $C' :: m$. A full formalization of this definition of behavioral subtyping can be found in [Leavens and Naumann, 2006].

To ensure that a subclass indeed defines a behavioral subtype, specification inheritance can be used [Dhara and Leavens, 1995, Leavens and Dhara, 2000]: In JML, every (nonprivate) method in the subclass inherits the overridden method's specification cases defined in the superclass. And in addition, all invariants of the superclass are inherited by the subclass. Notice that this same approach applies for interfaces and implementing classes. An interface can be specified with its desired behavior. Every class that implements this interface should be a behavioral subtype of the interface, i.e., it should satisfy all the specifications of the interface. Concretely, this means the following:

- every method that overrides a method from a superclass, or implements from an interface, has to respect the method specification from the superclass;
- every class that implements an interface has to respect the specifications of the interface; and
- every class that extends another class has to respect the specifications of that class.

Still, it is possible to refine specifications in subclasses (or implementing classes), in addition to what is inherited. Any additional specification of an inherited method (whether or not the implementation is overridden) is added to the inherited specifications from the superclass, using the `also` keyword.

```
/*@ also
  @ <subclass-specific-spec-cases>
  @*/
public void method () { ...
```

Note that the JML annotation starts with `also`, not preceded by anything. This is because the inherited specification cases are still there, even if implicit, to be extended here by whatever is written after the `also`.

Invariants are also fully, and implicitly, inherited. Extending the set of inherited invariants by additional invariants specific for a subclass is easy, by simply writing them in the subclass, using the normal syntax for invariants. The same applies also to initially clauses and constraints.

The idea of behavioral subtypes is crucial for the correctness of object-oriented programs. We can specify the behavior of a class in an abstract way. For example, in class `Average` in Listing 7.8, we have an array of `Student` instances; the concrete instances that are stored in the array may have different implementations, but we know that they all implement the methods specified in the interface `Student` in Listing 7.1. This means that we can rely on the specification case of `Student#getCredits()` in Line 11 of `Average#averageCredits()`.

Respecting inherited specifications is a good practice, but it does not guarantee behavioral subtyping per se. JML allows us to make program elements more visible in the specification than they are in the implementation (through the `spec_public` modifier, see Section 7.3.1). In this way, specifications may expose implementation details. While it is also a good practice to declare those specifications private, in many cases, this would disable us from giving *any* meaningful specification. A solution to this dilemma is abstraction, that will be covered in Section 7.7.1 below.

7.5 Nonnull Versus Nullable Object References

In Java, the set of values of reference type include the null reference. (Note that the same is true for the values of array type, because each array type is also a subtype of `Object`.) But even if the type system always allows `null`, the specifier may want to exclude the null reference in many cases. Whether or not null is allowed can be expressed by means of simple (in)equations, like, for instance, o `!= null`, in pre/-postconditions or invariants. However, this issue is of so dominant importance that JML offers two special modifiers just for that, `non_null` and `nullable`. Class members (i.e., fields), method parameters, and method return values can be declared as `non_null` (meaning null is forbidden), or `nullable` (in which case null is allowed, but not enforced).

Here are some examples for forbidding null values.

`private /*@ non_null @*/ String name;`

adds the *implicit* invariant `invariant name != null;` to the class at hand.

`public void setName(/*@ non_null @*/ String n) {...`

adds the *implicit* precondition `requires n != null;` to each specification case of `setName`.

`public /*@ non_null @*/ String getName() {...`

adds the *implicit* postcondition `ensures \result != null;` to each specification case of `getName`.

The reader can imagine that `non_null` modifiers can easily bloat the specification. Therefore, JML has built-in `non_null` as the *default* for all fields, method parameters, and return types, such that all `non_null` modifiers in the above examples are actually redundant. By only writing the following, without any explicit `non_null`, we get *exactly* the same implicit invariants, preconditions, and postconditions as mentioned above.

```
private String name;

public void setName(String n) {...

public String getName() {...
```

But how can we allow null anyway? We can avoid the restrictive nonnull default by the aforementioned modifier `nullable`. In the above examples, we could allow null (and thereby avoid the implicit conditions), by writing

```
private /*@ nullable @*/ String name;

public void setName(/*@ nullable @*/ String n) {...

public /*@ nullable @*/ String getName() {...
```

Notice that the nonnull by default also can have some unwanted effects, as illustrated by the following example.

Example 7.18. Consider the following declaration of a `LinkedList`.

—— Java + JML ——————————————————————————————————

```
public class LinkedList {
    private Object elem;
    private LinkedList next;
    ...
}
```

——————————————————————————————————— Java + JML ——

Because of the nonnull by default behavior of JML, this means that all elements in the list are nonnull. Thus the list must be cyclic, or infinite.[10] This is usually not the intended behavior, and thus the `next` reference should be explicitly annotated as `nullable`.

—— Java + JML ——————————————————————————————————

```
public class LinkedList {
    private Object elem;
    private /*@ nullable @*/ LinkedList next;
    ....
}
```

——————————————————————————————————— Java + JML ——

In short, it is important to remember that for all class fields, method parameters, and method results, the null reference is forbidden wherever we do not state otherwise with the JML modifier `nullable`.

---

[10] A linked data structure having infinite length is indeed a contradiction. At runtime, there are only finitely many created objects on the heap.

In the context of allowing vs. forbidding the null reference, handling of arrays deserves special mentioning. The additional question here is whether, or not, the prohibition of null holds for the *elements* of the array. Without loss of generality, we consider the following array typed field declaration: `String[] arr;`. Because of nonnull being the default, this is equivalent to writing `/*@ non_null @*/ String[] arr;`. Now, in both cases, the prohibition of null references extends, in JML, to the elements of the array! In other words, both the above forms have the same meaning as if the following invariants were added:

—— Java + JML ——

```
//@ invariant arr != null;
//@ invariant (\forall int i;
//@                    i >= 0 && i < arr.length;
//@                    arr[i] != null);
```

————————————————————————————————————— Java + JML ——

Again, no such invariant is needed for disallowing null; writing `String[] arr;` is enough. We can, however, allow null for *both*, the whole array and its elements (at first), by writing `/*@ nullable @*/ String[] arr;`. To that, we can add further restrictions. For instance, if only the elements may be null, but not the whole array, we can write:

—— Java + JML ——

```
//@ invariant arr != null;
/*@ nullable @*/ String[] arr;
```

————————————————————————————————————— Java + JML ——

7.6 Exceptional Behavior

So far, we have only considered normal termination of methods. But in some cases, exceptions cannot be avoided. Therefore JML also allows one to specify explicitly under what conditions an exception may occur.

The **signals** and **signals_only** clauses are introduced to specify *exceptional postconditions*. In addition, one can give an **exceptional_behavior** method. Exceptional postconditions have the form **signals** $(E\ e)\ P$, where E is a subtype of `Throwable`, and the following meaning: *if* the method terminates because of an exception that is an instance of type E, then the predicate P has to hold. The variable name e can be used to refer to the exception in the predicate. Note the implication direction: a **signals** clause does *not* specify under which condition an exception may occur by itself, neither that it *must* occur. Such specification patterns can only be obtained in combination with **requires** and **ensures** clauses. The **signals** clause describes a necessary condition, but not a sufficient one. For a formal account on contract semantics, see Section 8.2 in the following chapter.

The `signals_only` clause is optional in a method specification. Its syntax is `signals_only` E_1, E_2, ..., E_n, meaning that if the method terminates because of an exception, the dynamic type of the exception has to be a subclass of E_1, E_2, ..., or E_n. If `signals_only` is left out, only the exception types that are declared in the method's **throws** clause and *unchecked exceptions*, i.e., instances of `Error` and `RuntimeException`, are permitted. These are exactly the exception types that are permitted by Java's type system.

```
1  class Average {
2
3      /*@ spec_public @*/ private Student[] sl;
4
5      /*@ signals_only ArithmeticException;
6        @ signals (ArithmeticException e) sl.length == 0;
7        @*/
8      public int averageCredits() {
9          int sum = 0;
10         for (int i = 0; i < sl.length; i++) {
11             sum = sum + sl[i].getCredits();
12         };
13         return sum/sl.length;
14     }
15 }
```

Listing 7.8 Class Average

Example 7.19. Consider for example class `Average` in Listing 7.8. The specification of method `averageCredits` states that the method may only terminate normally, or with an `ArithmeticException`—and thus, it will not throw an `ArrayIndexOutOfBoundsException`. Moreover, if an `ArithmeticException` occurs, then in this exceptional state the length of `sl` is 0.

Notice that it is incorrect in this case to use an **ensures** clause, instead of a **signals** clause: an **ensures** clause specifies a normal postcondition, that only holds upon normal termination of the method.

Above, in Section 7.1 we discussed **normal_behavior** specifications. Implicitly, these state that the method has to terminate normally. Similarly, JML also features an **exceptional_behavior** method specification. This specifies that, if the method terminates, then this must be due to an exception.[11] In contrast, a plain **behavior** specification may well contain both **ensures** clauses and **signals** or **signals_only** clauses, whereas a normal behavior specification may not contain these, and an exceptional behavior specification may not contain an **ensures** clause. As mentioned above in Section 7.3.2, a single method can be specified with several method specifications, joined with **also**. Exceptional behavior specifications are typically used in this case.

---

[11] Remember that an explicit **diverges** clause still permits nontermination.

Example 7.20. Consider the more detailed specification for `averageCredits` in Listing 7.9. This states that if `sl.length > 0`, i.e., there are students in the list,

```
class Average2 {

    /*@ spec_public @*/ private Student[] sl;

    /*@ normal_behavior
      @ requires sl.length > 0;
      @ ensures \result ==
      @           (\sum int i; 0 <= i && i < sl.length;
      @                        sl[i].getCredits())/sl.length;
      @ also
      @ exceptional_behavior
      @ requires sl.length == 0;
      @ signals_only ArithmeticException;
      @ signals (ArithmeticException e) true;
      @*/
    public int averageCredits() {
        int sum = 0;
        for (int i = 0; i < sl.length; i++) {
            sum = sum + sl[i].getCredits();
        };
        return sum/sl.length;
    }
}
```

Listing 7.9 Class `Average2`

then the method terminates and the result is the average value of the credits obtained by these students. If `sl.length == 0` then the method will terminate exceptionally, with an `ArithmeticException`.

In this example, the two preconditions together cover the complete state space for the value of `sl.length`. If `sl.length` could be less than 0, the method's behavior would not be specified.

Finally, it is important to realize that invariants and constraints also must hold when a method terminates exceptionally. This might seem strange at first: something goes wrong during the execution, so why would it be necessary that the object stays in a good state. But in many cases, the execution can recover from the exception, and normal execution can be resumed. But this means that it is necessary that also when an exception occurs, the object stays in a 'well-defined' state, i.e., a state in which the invariants hold, and that evolves according to the constraints.

A Note on `false`

The Boolean expression `false` is used frequently to exclude certain behaviors. For instance, the clause

```
signals (Throwable e) false;
```

states that the method at hand must not terminate exceptionally. Because, if it did, the property `false` would need to hold, which is never the case. Therefore, exceptional termination is never able to satisfy such a specification. Similarly, if one specifies a postcondition `ensures false`; this states that a method must not terminate normally. Thus a method specification:

```
ensures false;
signals (Throwable e) false;
diverges true;
```

implicitly says that a method must never terminate (neither normally, nor exceptionally). Finally, a method can also be specified with a precondition `requires false;`. This means that the method may not be invoked, as no caller can fulfill the precondition of the method.

7.7 Specification-Only Class Members

The previous sections shows how the behavior of code members is specified in JML. But sometimes it is easier or even required to introduce new members only for specification. Model fields, as discussed in Section 7.7.1, allow to provide abstraction from the concrete program state. For each abstract state, a relationship to the concrete program state can be defined. In addition to model fields, sometimes it is also useful to define model methods, i.e., methods that are used in specifications only.

This section also introduces ghost variables (Section 7.7.2). These can be used to extend the state space with specification-only information. They do not provide abstraction, but can record extra information. The use of model and ghost fields is often confused, and therefore Section 7.7.3 compares both approaches, and highlights their differences. For an in-depth account on model field and model method semantics, their encoding in KeY, and how to use them in verification, the reader is kindly referred to Section 9.2.

7.7.1 Model Fields and Model Methods

An important feature of specifications is that they provide abstraction over the concrete implementations. *Model fields* serve as an abstraction feature in a familiar guise. They are declared like regular fields, but within JML specifications and with the modifier keyword `model`. Model fields can be read from like regular fields, but there are no assignments to them since they do not have a state of their own. Instead, to make sure that the concrete implementation corresponds to the abstract specification, a link between the two has to be made. For this purpose, the *represents clause* defines how the value of the abstract variable is defined in terms of the values

of the concrete entities. In the so called functional form, the represents clause, that is
a class member, appears similar to an assignment, as can be seen in the following
example taken from [Breunesse et al., 2005].

Example 7.21. Class `Decimal` implements decimal variables using an `intPart` and
`decPart` variable, but the specification is given in terms of a single model field that
represents the value of the composed decimal number.

—— Java + JML ——

```
class Decimal {
    public static final short PRECISION = (short) 1000;
    /*@ spec_public @*/ private short intPart = (short) 0;
    /*@ spec_public @*/ private short decPart = (short) 0;

    //@ model int value;
    //@ represents value = intPart * PRECISION + decPart;
}
```

—— Java + JML ——

Sometimes, a represents clause cannot be defined directly as a translation into
concrete variables; sometimes a (nonfunctional) relation between the abstract and
the concrete state can be expressed, sometimes only a dependency relation. JML
provides a way to define nonfunctional represents clauses. Instead of the assignment
operator, they consist of the keyword `\such_that` followed by a Boolean expression.
It means that the model field points to some value such that this condition is satisfied.

Example 7.22. Consider class `MatrixImplem` in Listing 7.10. It implements a matrix
as a single array (on some platforms, like JavaCard, only one-dimensional arrays are
allowed). A model variable matrix is declared, that specifies the abstract representation of the matrix. Unfortunately, no functional represents clause can be specified for
this. Instead, the `such_that` keyword is used to define a relational represents clause,
that enables to write the specifications of the matrix methods in terms of the abstract
matrix variable.

Model fields are useful in many cases. Typical examples are specifications of
interfaces. The behavior of an interface is specified in terms of model variables, and
the classes implementing the interface define represents clauses for these model
variables, relating them to their own concrete implementation. Because of the flexible
connection between concrete and abstract state using the **represents** clause, this
does not impose any restriction on the internal state of a class implementing the
interface. Note that in interfaces, model field declarations are **static** by default,
nonstatic model field declarations must use the modifier **instance**.

Example 7.23. Listing 7.11 gives an alternative specification for interface `Student`
using model fields. It shows the specification for an implementing class `CCStudent`.
Note that it does not declare the model variables, but only defines the represents
clause.

```
public class MatrixImplem {

    //@ public model int[][] matrix;
    private int x;
    private int y;
    private int[] matrix_implem;
    /*@ represents matrix \such_that
      @ (\forall int i; i >= 0 && i < x;
      @    (\forall int j; j >= 0 && j < y;
      @       matrix[i][j] == matrix_implem[x * j + i]));
      @*/

    /*@ ensures
      @ (\forall int i; i >= 0 && i < x;
      @    (\forall int j; j >= 0 && j < y;
      @       matrix[i][j] == 0));
      @*/
    public MatrixImplem(int x, int y) {
        this.x = x;
        this.y = y;
        matrix_implem = new int [x * y];
    }

    //@ ensures \result == matrix[i][j];
    public /*@ pure @*/ int get (int i, int j) {
        return matrix_implem[x * j + i];
    }

    /*@ ensures \result >= 0 && \result < x
      @     ==> matrix[\result][coordY(elem)] == elem;
      @*/
    public /*@ pure @*/ int coordX (int elem) {
        for (int i = 0; i < matrix_implem.length; i++)
            if (matrix_implem[i] == elem)
                return i % x;
        return -1;
    }

    /*@ ensures \result >= 0 && \result < y
      @     ==> matrix[coordX(elem)][\result] == elem;
      @*/
    public /*@ pure @*/ int coordY (int elem) {
        for (int i = 0; i < matrix_implem.length; i++)
            if (matrix_implem[i] == elem)
                return i / x;
        return -1;
    }
}
```

Listing 7.10 Relational represents clause

```
public interface Student {

    /*@ public instance model int status;
      @ public instance model int credits;
      @ represents status = (credits < 180 ? bachelor : master);
      @*/

    /*@ public instance invariant status == bachelor || status == master;
      @ public instance invariant credits >= 0;
      @*/

    public static final int bachelor = 0;
    public static final int master = 1;

    /*@ pure @*/ public String getName();

    //@ ensures \result == status;
    /*@ pure @*/ public int getStatus();

    //@ ensures \result == credits;
    /*@ pure @*/ public int getCredits();

    //@ ensures getName().equals(n);
    public void setName(String n);

    /*@ requires c >= 0;
      @ ensures credits == \old(credits) + c;
      @*/
    public void addCredits(int c);

    /*@ requires credits >= 180;
      @ requires status == bachelor;
      @ ensures credits == \old(credits);
      @ ensures status == master;
      @*/
    public void changeStatus();
}

class CCStudent implements Student {

    private int[] creditList;

    /*@ private represents credits =
      @     (\sum int i; 0 <= i && i < creditList.length; creditList[i]);
      @*/

    // rest of class continued...
}
```

Listing 7.11 Interface Student with model fields and an implementation.

Sometimes, to complete a specification, one needs a method that only is intended for specification. To support this, JML provides *model methods*. A model method is defined as part of the specification. It can be implemented, but it may also be abstract. And the behavior of a model method is typically defined in terms of its pre- and postconditions again. Typical usages for model methods are:

- if the specification needs a method that is not related to the code, for example to sum all the elements in an array;
- if the specification needs a method that cannot be implemented easily, but that can be specified without any problem.

7.7.2 Ghost Variables

Sometimes the information needed in specifications is not provided by the source code itself. Typical examples are specifications that express something about the control flow, e.g., how often or in which order methods are called, or about the used resources, e.g., to limit the number of objects. This additional knowledge can be modeled with ghost variables.

A ghost variable in JML can be defined as a class/instance member or as a local variable. In both cases, it is declared like a normal Java variable, but inside a JML annotation preceded by the keyword **ghost**. The used type may be a specification-only type such as \bigint (see Section 7.8). The initial value of a ghost variable can be directly assigned at its declaration. Its value can be updated during method execution by a **set** statement. This is a JML annotation statement within a method body, consisting of a keyword **set** followed by an assignment. The left-hand side of the assignment has to be a ghost variable and the right sight can be any side-effect-free JML expression.

Example 7.24. Consider class LinkedList in Listing 7.12, that represents a linked data structure. In general, this structure could be circular. To specify that it really is a list, i.e., that it is finite and noncircular, we use a ghost field length to represent the length of a list. Since there may be more elements than Java's primitive int type can accommodate, we use the specification-only type \bigint. The invariant states that length is always positive and that the length of the tail is always smaller than the current one. From this, we may conclude the above property.

7.7.3 Ghost Variables Versus Model Fields

It is important to understand the difference between model and ghost variables. Both are variables that are used for specification purposes only, and they do not occur during the execution of the program.

```
1  public class LinkedList {
2      private /*@ spec_public @*/ int value;
3      private /*@ spec_public nullable @*/ LinkedList next;
4
5      //@ public ghost \bigint length;
6      //@ public invariant 0 < length;
7      //@ public invariant next == null || next.length+1 == length;
8  }
```

Listing 7.12 Using a ghost field to track recursion depth

However, model variables provide an abstract representation of the state. If the underlying state changes, implicitly the model variable also changes. Often it is possible to define this relationship explicitly as a translation, but sometimes it can only be given in a nonconstructive manner (or even as a dependency relation).

In contrast, ghost variables extend the state. They provide some additional information that cannot be directly related to the object state. Ghost variables are often used to keep track of the events that have happened on an object, e.g., which methods have been called, how often have these methods been called etc. There also exists work where ghost variables have been used to keep track of the resources used by the program: every time a new object is created, there is an associated **set** annotation that increases a resource counter, modeled as a ghost variable [Barthe et al., 2005]. In this way, the specification can state something about the number of objects that have been created by the program. This information allows then to define a resource analysis over the application.

7.8 Integer Semantics

Since JML incorporates Java expressions, specifications also adhere to the semantics of the Java numerical data types. This means in particular that always special care has to be taken regarding overflows in integer operations[12]. Undoubtedly, dealing with finite numerical data types is a very common source of programming errors. The most infamous example from the real world is the maiden flight of Ariane 5, where conversion of 64-bit floating-point data to 16-bit integers finally caused the spacecraft to be destroyed just seconds after lift off [Nuseibeh, 1997]. It is thus desirable to detect such errors and to not repeat them in the specification. We will show how to avoid this problem through the use of JML's \bigint data type, that represents the mathematical integers. This section does not discuss semantics of integral data types in general; those can be found in [Beckert et al., 2007, Chapter 12] or (more elaborate) in [Schlager, 2002].

---

[12] Similar issues arise with rounding in floating-point operations, which however will not be covered here.

Example 7.25. Regard the short method `mult()` below; it returns `a*b`, but this is not multiplication in the mathematical sense, since an overflow may occur.

```
public int mult (int a, int b) { return a*b; }
```

The naive specification **ensures** `\result == a*b;` would be trivially true since JML uses the very same overflow semantics as in Java.

This example shows a feature of Java that may be a large source of confusion. Integer operators in Java are often misunderstood to equal their mathematical counterparts, see, e.g., the survey by Chalin [2003]. But the actual mathematical functionality[13] represented by, e.g., `a*b` (where both are `int` expressions) is $((a+2^{31}) \cdot (b+2^{31}) \mod 2^{32}) - 2^{31})$. In addition, these operators are overloaded—the `*` operator has different semantics if one operand is of type `long` (64-bit integers). This means that, in many situations, naive specifications are just incorrect due to the presence of overflows. For instance, in Listing 7.4, the invariant that credits are nonnegative can be broken by method `addCredits()`, that does not check for overflows.

Example 7.26. To display even more obscure characteristics of overflow semantics, the following Boolean JML expression is trivially true. We leave it to the reader to find out with which element the quantifier would be instantiated.

—— JML ——————————————————————————————

```
(\exists int x; x-1 > x
                && (\forall int y; x <= y)
                && x == -x
                && x != 0 && x * 2 == 0);
```

————————————————————————————————— JML ——

Besides Java's bounded integer types (also known as *bit vector* types), JML offers the specification only primitive type `\bigint` that represents the mathematical integers $\mathbb{Z}$. 'Specification only' means that, besides variables bound by a quantifier, only ghost variables and ghost/model fields can be declared with type `\bigint`. The Java standard library also provides a type called `BigInteger`, that represents arbitrary precision integers. While `\bigint` is a primitive type with an infinite number of elements, `BigInteger` is just a regular Java object type. This means, in particular, that instances of `BigInteger` must be created through constructors and that quantification makes little sense since it only ranges over the (finitely many) created instances. It is therefore inadequate for specification purposes.

Let us come back to Example 7.25. How can we specify that there is no overflow? In Java, all arithmetic operations are *unchecked*, i.e., an overflow is not indicated in any way, e.g., by exceptions. A precondition like `a*b <= Integer.MAX_VALUE` is trivially true. Instead, we can apply numerical conversion to `\bigint` to expressions

---

[13] More mathematically speaking, the `int` data type with operators + and * forms a finite Abelian ring that is isomorphic to $\mathbb{Z}/\mathbb{Z}_{2^{32}}$. This means that addition and multiplication are commutative, associative, and distributive; but there are zero-dividers—as shown in Example 7.26.

of type `int`. Note that this kind of conversion, a widening, has no effect on the *values* of a and b, but on the semantics of the * operator. Under the preconditions that the (mathematical) product of *a* and *b* is within the bounds of `int`, we can ensures that the result is indeed the mathematical product:

—— Java + JML ————————————————————————————

```
//@ requires Integer.MIN_VALUE <= (\bigint) a * (\bigint) b;
//@ requires Integer.MAX_VALUE >= (\bigint) a * (\bigint) b;
//@ ensures \result == (\bigint) a * (\bigint) b;
public int mult (int a, int b) { return a*b; }
```

————————————————————————————— Java + JML ——

Because this specification is tedious to write and even more horrible to read, classes and methods can be annotated in JML with *math modifiers* [Chalin, 2004]. The default integer semantics in specifications can be changed by declaring the method `spec_bigint_math`, that achieves the above while saving to write down casts explicitly.

—— Java + JML ————————————————————————————

```
//@ requires Integer.MIN_VALUE <= a * b;
//@ requires Integer.MAX_VALUE >= a * b;
//@ ensures \result == a * b;
public /*@ spec_bigint_math @*/ int mult (int a, int b) {
    return a*b;
}
```

————————————————————————————— Java + JML ——

An even simpler way to express the absence of overflows is to change the semantics of the Java implementation through the `code_safe_math` modifier. It causes the program to be interpreted as if operations were checked, leading to an exception in case of overflow. The only thing left to show is that there are no exceptions:

—— Java + JML ————————————————————————————

```
//@ signals_only \nothing;
public /*@ code_safe_math @*/ int mult (int a, int b) {
    return a*b;
}
```

————————————————————————————— Java + JML ——

There are six math modifiers in total, declaring integer expressions in specifications or code to be interpreted as either Java integers with default operations, mathematical integers, or Java integers with checked operations. While these modifiers are currently not directly supported, the KeY prover offers to select different integer semantics with a similar effect; see Section 15.2.3 on page 531 and Section 5.4.

7.9 Auxiliary Specification for Verification

The previously discussed specification constructs are essential to the Design by Contract philosophy and relevant to all analysis techniques. However, for static verification of Java programs it is typically required to provide some additional information, like the locations a method might access (Section 7.9.1); guidance for the verification tool in the presence of loops via loop invariants (Section 7.9.2); or in general via assert statements (Section 7.9.3).

7.9.1 Framing

An important aspect of verification is modularity. Each method is verified in isolation, and any method call inside a body is abstracted by its method specification. To achieve this, it is not enough to specify what a method does; it is also required to specify what a method does *not* do. This is known as the *frame problem* [Borgida et al., 1995, Müller et al., 2003]. Basically, for modular verification one needs to know what is the *frame* of a method, i.e., what are the variables that may be changed at most by the method, and what is the *antiframe*, i.e., which variables must not be changed by the method.

To specify this, JML uses the *assignable clause*. This provides a set of variable locations that may be modified by a method (thus, it may be an over-approximation of the actual set of locations that are modified by the method). Location sets can be given through comma separated lists of single variables or one of the special keywords \nothing (only locations of newly allocated objects may be changed, corresponds to weak purity, see Section 7.3.5), \everything (any location may be changed), this.* (all locations provided by the current object), and array[*] or array[i..j] (all elements in the array or between indices i and j). Whereas assignable clauses are attached to single specification cases, pure methods are defined to have an empty frame under *any* precondition. The extension to JML that is used in KeY provides additional constructs to specify frames, offering more flexibility; see Section 9.3.2. Most importantly, the keyword \strictly_nothing denotes strictly the empty set of locations; strictly pure methods are annotated with strictly_pure, see Section 7.3.5.

JML also allows one to add an **accessible** clause to method specifications, Section 9.9.10 of the JML reference manual [Leavens et al., 2013]. This clause provides a set of variable locations on which the observable behavior of the method depends. The way this clause is used in KeY differs from and considerably goes beyond standard JML. We postpone explanation of **accessible** clauses to Sections 8.3.2 and 9.3.

Example 7.27. Listing 7.13 contains the specification of Listing 7.1, but with assignable clauses added. Method addCredits increases the achieved credits, which means that it may have to update the master flag to maintain the invariant. Therefore, the assignable clause of this method lists the instance variables `credits` and `master`. Even though the variables are not modified directly by the method, it is required to list them in the assignable clause, because they may be modified during the method execution. Methods `updateCredits`, `changeToMaster` and `setName` modify only one instance variable, that is listed in the assignable clause of their method specifications. Finally, method `getName` is specified as a pure method, that automatically implies that the assignable clause is `\nothing` by default.

Of course, it would be possible to add the information in the assignable clause to the postcondition, explicitly specifying that the variables not mentioned in the assignable clause are not changed. But this is not a satisfactory solution: a class might have many variables and only a few are typically changed by a method. Moreover, when a new variable is added, for every method that does not change it, an additional postcondition about this variable not being changed would have to be added. As one can imagine, this is error-prone, and leads to overly verbose specifications.

For readers who would like to dive further into the topic of modularity, Chapter 9 is entirely dedicated to aspects of modularity in specification and verification. In particular, it introduces a specification-only type `\locSet`, which represents sets of program locations as first class subjects.

7.9.2 Loop Invariants

A verification tool typically needs some guidance in presence of loops to verify that a method implementation complies to its specification. This is due to the general impossibility to statically evaluate the loop body repeatedly until the loop condition evaluates to false. The number of iterations is not static but depends on dynamic input parameters and initial states. In program verification, the dominating solution to this problem is the usage of a *loop invariant* [Floyd, 1967, Hoare, 1969]. This is a formula whose validity is preserved by the loop body (given the loop condition was true before). From this we can conclude that, if the entire loop starts in a state where the loop invariant holds, then it will still hold once the loop terminates in addition to the negated loop condition[14].

There exist approaches to automated invariant generation [German and Wegbreit, 1975, Karr, 1976] (see also Chapter 6), and the recent years saw a very dynamic development in this area. Yet, much more needs to be done to automatically find good invariants, and to integrate that into verification tools. (The bottleneck is currently not to generate formulas that are invariant over the loop body, but to identify those that contribute to the overall correctness proof.) For the time being, finding loop invariants that allow us to verify some code unit is still a largely manual task. Guidance on how to write loop invariants is beyond our scope here. But the reader can refer to Section 16.3 in this book.

---

[14] In fact, to reason about Java, it is required to also support abrupt loop termination, caused by an exception or programmatically by a `return`, `break` or `continue` statement.

```
 1 public class Student {
 2     private /*@ spec_public @*/ String name;
 3
 4     /*@ public invariant credits >= 0;
 5       @*/
 6     private /*@ spec_public @*/ int credits;
 7
 8     /*@ public invariant credits < 180 ==> !master &&
 9       @                   credits >= 180 ==> master;
10       @*/
11     private /*@ spec_public @*/ boolean master;
12
13     /*@ requires c >= 0;
14       @ ensures credits == \old(credits) + c;
15       @ assignable credits, master;
16       @*/
17     public void addCredits(int c) {
18         updateCredits(c);
19         if (credits >= 180) {
20             changeToMaster();
21         }
22     }
23
24     /*@ requires c >= 0;
25       @ ensures credits == \old(credits) + c;
26       @ assignable credits;
27       @*/
28     private void updateCredits(int c) {
29         credits += c;
30     }
31
32     /*@ requires credits >= 180;
33       @ ensures master;
34       @ assignable master;
35       @*/
36     private void changeToMaster() {
37         master = true;
38     }
39
40     /*@ ensures this.name == name;
41       @ assignable this.name;
42       @*/
43     public void setName(String name) {
44         this.name = name;
45     }
46
47     /*@ ensures \result == name;
48       @*/
49     public /*@ pure @*/ String getName() {
50         return name;
51     }
52 }
```

Listing 7.13 Full specification of Student with assignable clauses

In the first place, loop invariants are proof artifacts, comparable to induction hypotheses in inductive proofs. But JML offers the possibility to annotate loops, in the source code, with invariants, to be used by verification tools during the proof process. The corresponding keyword is `maintaining` or `loop_invariant`, followed by a Boolean JML expression. The JML comment that contains this must be placed directly in front of the loop. Notice that a loop invariant may contain an \old(E) expression. This refers to the value of the expression E before the method started, *not* to the value of E at the previous iteration of the loop.

As long as no `diverges` clause (see Section 7.3.3) is defined, it is required to prove that a method terminates. In presence of a loop this is only possible if a `decreasing` clause (also named *variant*) is provided together with the loop invariant. The decreasing term must be well-founded, which means that it cannot decrease forever. For the decreasing clause, it has to be shown that it is strictly decreasing for each loop iteration and that it evaluates to a nonnegative value in any state satisfying the invariant. Therefore, this is sufficient to conclude that the loop terminates. In JML the decreasing term is specified via keyword `decreasing`, followed by an expression of type integer.

Example 7.28. The loop invariant in method `search` in Listing 7.14 shows a very common loop invariant pattern for methods iterating over an array. All the elements that have been examined so far respect a certain property, and the loop terminates at least when all the elements in the array have been examined. Variable `found` indicates in this example whether the element to search is contained in the already examined elements or not. A loop invariant restricting the range of loop variables is typically always needed, but not sufficient alone. In this example, the range of loop variable i is limited to valid array indices (0 `<=` i `&&` i `<=` a.length). Finally, a well-founded decreasing clause is provided, that allows one to prove termination.

```
1  /*@ normal_behavior
2    @ requires a != null;
3    @ ensures \result == (\exists int i;
4    @                         0 <= i && i < a.length; a[i] == val);
5    @*/
6  public boolean search(int[] a, int val) {
7      int i = 0;
8      /*@ maintaining !(\exists int j;  0 <= j && j < i; a[j] == val);
9        @ maintaining 0 <= i && i <= a.length;
10       @ decreasing a.length - i;
11       @*/
12     while (i < a.length) {
13         if (a[i] == val)
14             return true;
15         i++;
16     }
17     return false;
18 }
```

Listing 7.14 Loop invariant example to search an element in an array

Loop invariants are sensitive to the frame problem as discussed for method calls in Section 7.9.1. Basically, it is necessary to specify which variable locations might be changed by a loop and which not. In KeY this is done with the assignable clause. Only locations have to be specified since local variables changed by the loop are computed automatically by KeY. Note that a loop assignable clause refers to all locations that are possibly changed by *any* loop iteration, not just a single one. For instance, if an array a is manipulated at a (variable) index i, it is not enough to specify `assignable a[i];` but instead `assignable a[*];` refers to any element.

Example 7.29. Method sum of Listing 7.15 computes the sum of the values provided by an array using a for-each loop. The assignable clause is explicitly set to `\strictly_nothing` to make sure that no objects are created during loop execution. Local variables are not listed in the assignable clause since they are automatically added by KeY.

```
1  /*@ requires array != null;
2   @ ensures \result == (\sum int i;
3   @                      0 <= i && i < array.length; array[i]);
4   @*/
5  public static int sum(int[] array) {
6      int sum = 0;
7      /*@ maintaining sum == (\sum int j;
8       @                      0 <= j && j < \index; array[j]);
9       @ maintaining \index >= 0 && \index <= array.length;
10      @ decreasing array.length - \index;
11      @ assignable \strictly_nothing;
12      @*/
13     for (int value : array) {
14         sum += value;
15     }
16     return sum;
17 }
```

Listing 7.15 Loop invariant example to compute the sum of an array

Java 1.5 introduced so called *enhanced for* loops (also called *foreach* loops, see [Gosling et al., 2013, Section 14.14]) that iterate over elements of an array or a collection. Here, the index variable is only implicit. As proposed by Cok [2008], the keyword `\index` refers to this value. An example is also shown in Listing 7.15.

7.9.3 Assertions and Block Contracts

Sometimes, the program verifier needs some additional guidance in proving a contract. This can be given as an intermediate *assertion*: `assert` P;[15] We have to prove that P is true in this intermediate state. Afterwards, we can use this additional knowledge to prove the overall proof obligation. In this way, assertions in the code are similar to cuts in proofs. JML also provides a dual `assume` statement. It is supposed to be assumed to be true without verifying it.

While the intuition behind these constructs is clear, they perturb the concept of design by contract. In particular, the statement `assume false;` would make any contract trivially satisfied. For this reason, in KeY `assert` and `assume` are replaced by the more flexible concept of *block contracts* [Wacker, 2012]. The behavior of any Java block can be specified in the same way as a method is specified (see Section 7.1) by placing the specification directly in front of the Java block. It can contain any clause that is available for method contracts. The only differences are: First, that `\old` represents the value before executing the block, and not the one before executing the method, and second, that the `\signals_only` definition must be explicitly specified, because a block has no throws definition from which it can be computed. Listing 7.16 shows the usage of a block contract within a longer method. The block itself swaps the value of the two variables x and y.

```
1  public void swapInBetween() {
2          :
3      /*@ ensures x == \old(y);
4        @ ensures y == \old(x);
5        @ assignable x, y;
6        @ signals_only \nothing;
7        @*/
8      {
9          y = x + y;
10         x = y - x;
11         y = y - x;
12     }
13         :
14 }
```

Listing 7.16 Usage of a block contract to swap two values

---

[15] JML `assert` statements are not to be confused with Java `assert` statements. The former are only present in specifications and meant to guide the prover. The latter is an actual program statement to be checked at runtime, that raises an exception upon failure.

7.10 Conclusion

This chapter has provided a short overview of the Java Modeling Language (JML), its main features and how it can be used to describe intended program behavior. More information about JML, including people involved in the community effort, the reference manual, tools supporting JML, teaching material, and relevant papers are available from the JML webpage jmlspecs.org.

To conclude, we briefly discuss other related program annotation languages, and the wide range of tool support that exists for JML.

7.10.1 Tool Support for JML

One of the strong points of JML is that many different kinds of tool support exist for it, covering the whole spectrum of formal methods. For an—unfortunately outdated— overview of JML tools, the reader may refer to [Burdy et al., 2003a]. We briefly describe a few, more information is available from the JML webpage. It should be noted that most recent tool development, including KeY, aims at combining different kinds of tool support within a single environment. In particular both the JMLEclipse [Chalin et al., 2010] and OpenJML [Cok, 2011] tool suites each include their own runtime checker, static analysis tool, and test case generator.

The original developers of JML started the work on JML with runtime checking in mind, i.e., JML should provide support to check pre- and postconditions *during* program execution. Many different tools exist that support this, for different subsets of JML, e.g., JMLRac [Cheon, 2003], AspectJML [Rebêlo et al., 2014], and as mentioned subtools of JMLEclipse and OpenJML. The runtime checking approach has also been the basis for model checking of JML annotated programs in Bogor: every program annotation is translated into an assertion, that is validated during the software model checking procedure [Robby et al., 2006].

JML is also used for test case generation. JMLunitNG [Zimmerman and Nagmoti, 2010] extends standard unit testing with knowledge derived from the program annotations. It is included in the OpenJML tool suite. The test case generation feature of KeY (see Chapter 12) uses information from the KeY prover to improve test case generation. As mentioned, also JMLEclipse provides support for test case generation, based on the JET tool [Cheon, 2007]. A recently developed test case generation tool is JMLOK2 [Milanez et al., 2014].

There are also several tools that support static checking of JML annotations, i.e., at compile time, without executing the program. These tools differ in the level of automation and the support they provide for manually constructing a proof. In general, the more user intervention is possible, the more complex properties can be verified. KeY is a typical example of a tool that can verify complex properties, but may require manual intervention. Other tools in this category are Krakatoa [Marché et al., 2004] and KIV [Balser et al., 2000, Stenzel, 2005].

ESC/Java [Leino et al., 2000] and its successor ESC/Java2 [Cok and Kiniry, 2005] follow the *auto-active verification* paradigm. They intend to provide automatic support for proving program correctness (if necessary, compromising soundness or completeness). Another tool that has been developed with automation in mind is JACK [Barthe et al., 2007], however it also provides support to fall back on interactive proving using Coq. Also the static verification subtools of JMLEclipse and OpenJML are developed with automation in mind. Finally, the VerCors tool set [Amighi et al., 2012] combines separation logic support for concurrent programs with JML annotations.

Last, it should be mentioned that there are also very different tools that support JML. There is a JMLdoc facility that allows one to generate web pages for JML annotations (similar to Javadoc). There also exist tools that generate JML annotations. These range from generating arbitrary JML specifications such as Daikon [Ernst et al., 2007], and Houdini [Flanagan and Leino, 2000] to tools that can generate one specific class of annotations, such as Chase [Cataño and Huisman, 2003]. The KeY project provides support for editing JML specifications in Eclipse. The Eclipse extension is called JML Editing and offers features such as syntax highlighting and refactoring. It is available at www.key-project.org/eclipse/JMLEditing.

7.10.2 Comparison to Other Program Annotation Languages

The JML language has been a pioneer in the area of *annotation based specification languages* dedicated to a single programming language. As explained above, in Section II, the intention of the developers was to provide a language to write assertions for Java programs. Its design has been inspired by earlier experiences of some of the developers on annotating Modula-3 [Leino and Nelson, 1998], and C++ (the Larch project) [Cheon and Leavens, 1994].

As a major difference to more abstract specification languages, such as Z [Spivey, 1992], VDM [Fitzgerald et al., 2008], Alloy [Jackson, 2003], the B method [Abrial, 1996], and UML [Rumbaugh et al., 2010], JML focuses solely on the phases of software development in which source code is written. It is also primarily intended to specify existing code, rather than to implement programs according to a preexisting specification. However, it should be noted that some work has been done on translating specifications in these high level languages into JML, e.g., for B [Cataño et al., 2012].

JML also has a number of similarities to the Object Constraint Language (OCL) [Warmer and Kleppe, 1999], a language for annotating UML class diagrams with constraints on object states. It is used for both meta modeling and application modeling. In the latter case, annotations are added to the fine design of the implementation, much like class and method specifications in JML. But unlike JML, OCL does not subscribe to any programming language, and therefore does not address language-specific concerns (like, e.g., exceptions). Earlier versions of KeY supported OCL as well [Beckert et al., 2007], but this has been discontinued.

JML has been an inspiration for many other program annotation languages that have emerged over the last years, such as the ANSI/ISO C Specification Language (ACSL) [Baudin et al., 2010], and the language of the VCC tool (formerly "Verifying C Compiler") [Cohen et al., 2009], Spec# for C# [Barnett et al., 2005a], and Dafny [Leino, 2010], that is an integrated annotation *and* programming language.

Recently, *separation logic* [O'Hearn et al., 2001, 2004] has become a popular alternative to Hoare logic to specify program behavior. Separation logic allows explicit reasoning about the heap, that makes it suitable for reasoning about pointer programs, and for concurrent programs. Several approaches exist that combine separation logic with JML (or JML like languages), to enable reasoning about pointers and/or concurrent programs, while maintaining the expressiveness of JML [Tuerk, 2009, Jacobs and Piessens, 2011, Amighi et al., 2012]. The *dynamic frame* approach [Kassios, 2011, Weiß, 2011] offers even more flexibility to specify and reason about complex heap modifications. KeY uses its own extension to JML, that makes use of dynamic frames; it is covered in Section 9.3.

Chapter 8
From Specification to Proof Obligations

Daniel Grahl and Mattias Ulbrich

Specification with the Java Modeling Language (JML) has been introduced by example in the previous chapter without giving formal definitions of the meaning of JML specifications. Unfortunately, the JML reference manual [Leavens et al., 2013] does not provide a *formal* semantics, but informal descriptions, often stated in operational terms of the Java language. This is a serious shortcoming since the primary use case of JML is formal specification. Some formal representations from within the JML community have been suggested before [Jacobs and Poll, 2001, Engel, 2005, Darvas and Müller, 2007, Bruns, 2009], but none of them prevailed. Furthermore, over the years several extensions or dialects to JML have emerged (e.g., the extension with dynamic frames by Weiß [2011] that is used in KeY).

In the present chapter, we provide a denotational formal semantics to JML by translating expressions and contracts to formulas in JavaDL. It thus links Chapter 3 on JavaDL with Chapter 7 on JML. We assume that the reader is familiar with JavaDL and with the basic syntax of JML, and that he or she has an intuitive sense of their semantics. This chapter gives a comprehensive definition of the semantics of JML, more specifically of the dialect of the specification language used in the KeY system. It is marked where the semantics presented in this chapter refines or deviates from that given in the reference manual.

The chapter is divided into three sections: In Section 8.1, we define a translation from JML expressions to JavaDL terms and formulas. In Section 8.2, we introduce JavaDL contracts to which JML specifications are translated. Finally, in Section 8.3, we give proof obligations for contracts, i.e., we explain which formulas need to be proven for a given program to be correct w.r.t. its contract. We distinguish three kinds of proof obligations: (1) functional correctness proof obligations (Section 8.3.1), (2) dependency proof obligations (Section 8.3.2), and (3) well-definedness proof obligations (Section 8.3.3). The full definition comprises many similar cases which we present exemplarily. A full account of the JML semantics can be found in Appendix A.

We focus on *local* correctness of a single method implementation. This means that we only cover the provider's side of a contract in the design by contract framework. Chapter 9 on modular specification and verification goes beyond this and defines

W. Ahrendt et al. (Eds.): Deductive Software Verification, LNCS 10001, pp. 243–287, 2016
DOI: 10.1007/978-3-319-49812-6_8

correctness of whole programs. Calculus rules that use contracts can be found there. Chapter 13 on information flow introduces yet another extension to JML, which is based on the semantics described in this chapter and generalizes the concept of dependency proof obligations from Section 8.3.2.

8.1 Formal Semantics of JML Expressions

We start by giving semantics to JML expressions by providing a translation to JavaDL terms or formulas (see Chapter 3). While JML has been designed to be intuitively understandable, in particular expression syntax being similar to first-order logic, a formal account is not always straightforward. On a closer look, the fact that JML semantics relies on the Java program that is being specified renders the whole issue more complex than expected. In particular, JML contains several implicit assumptions that are not contained per se in JavaDL.

A note on notation: We use typewriter font for terminal (program) syntax elements—such as local variables or operators—and math font for nonterminal JML expressions.

We fix a Java program Prg with JML annotations. Let JTypes$_{Prg}$ denote the set of JML types, including the reference types that are defined in Prg. Let JExp$_{Prg}$ denote the set of well-formed JML expressions w.r.t. Prg according to syntax and typing rules defined in the JML reference manual [Leavens et al., 2013].

JML expressions are statically typed such that for every operator the argument and result types can be inferred at compile-time. Thus the translation of overloaded operators distinguishes cases by types, e.g., the binary JML operator & is translated to either logical conjunction (if the operands are of type Boolean) or an appropriate bit vector operation (if the operands are of an integer type).

In JML, the concept 'formula' does not exist; its place is rather taken by Boolean expressions. JavaDL, on the other hand, distinguishes between Boolean terms and formulas. For a translation from JML to JavaDL we need to distinguish both cases and define the translation from JML expressions as a mapping to either terms or formulas in JavaDL.

Definition 8.1. Let $\mathcal{T}$ be a JavaDL type hierarchy for a Java program Prg. The translation function $\lfloor \cdot \rfloor : \text{JExp}_{Prg} \cup \text{JTypes}_{Prg} \to \text{Trm}_{Any} \cup \text{DLFml} \cup \mathcal{T}$ maps JML expressions and types to terms, formulas, or types in JavaDL. It is defined in Tables A.6–A.11 in Appendix A.2. Whether the result is a formula or a term depends on the context; if necessary, a Boolean term x can be converted to a formula $x \doteq TRUE$.

Logical symbols

The translated JavaDL terms may contain the predefined function symbols of the signature Σ_J (see Figure 2.4). In addition, they may contain the program variables and function symbols (i) self for the reference to the current receiver object (i.e., the equivalent to this in Java), (ii) heap for the current heap, (iii) heap^{pre} for the prestate heap, (iv) exc for an exception to be raised (and not caught) by the program, (v) res for the result of a method, as well as (vi) any local variables, parameters, and field identifiers defined by the Java program. The symbols heap^{pre}, exc, and res only appear in postconditions.

   In the remainder of this section, we discuss the translation for representative examples.

8.1.1 Types in JML

The type system of JML comprises the type system of Java and extends it with the specification-only types \bigint (mathematical integers), \real (real numbers), and \TYPE (the type of all types). The JML dialect used in KeY further introduces the types \seq (finite sequences), and \locset (location sets).[1] All Java/JML types that occur in the program under inspection (both primitive types and defined classes and interfaces) have a direct counterpart in JavaDL.

   In JML, the different integer data types (byte, short, char, int, long, and \bigint) refer to different ranges of mathematical integers while there is only one type *int* in JavaDL—representing the mathematical integers $\mathbb{Z}$. Note that these types are not subtypes of each other, but rather *retrenchments* [Schlager, 2002]. All JML integer types are translated to the same domain *int* in JavaDL. To account for the different value ranges, there exist restriction predicates *inInt*(x), *inByte*(x), etc. for each integral type except \bigint. The semantics of this type restriction depends on the choice of integer semantics in JavaDL; the resulting formulas will be different (see Section 5.4): For instance $I_{\text{Java}}(inInt) = [-2^{31}, 2^{31} - 1]$ while $I_{\text{math}}(inInt) = \mathbb{Z}$.

   All mentioned specification-only types (\real, \bigint, \TYPE, \seq and \locsec) are *primitive* data types, put in Java lingo. Note that the JML modeling classes, like JMLObjectSet, are not primitive but reference types. This chapter does not cover some of the available primitive data types: floating-point types (float and double) as well as the JML types \real and \TYPE are currently not supported in KeY. There is no translation into JavaDL for them. The interested reader can refer to [Bruns, 2009]. In contrast to the JML reference manual [Leavens et al., 2013], we do not allow array types such as \bigint []. Unlike all other array types, they are *not* subtypes of java.lang.Object and therefore expose some semantical irregularities.

   Reference types are mapped to their equally named Java correspondence. A distinction is made concerning whether or not the value null is included in the translation. By default, bound variables in JML do not include null as possible value. This default restriction is motivated by the observation that null dereference is a common

---

[1] For the underlying theories of finite sequences and location sets, see Sections 2.4 and 5.2, respectively. Usage of the \seq and \locset data types in JML specifications will be discussed in Sections 8.1.3 and 9.3.2, respectively.

source of programming errors. Chalin and Rioux [2005] reported on the observation that the majority of type references used in declarations in a Java program are designed to hold only values different from null. It is therefore natural to assume this constraint as the implicitly assumed default and have all situations in which null is an admissible value be annotated explicitly. This shortens specifications and enhances safety by making contracts stricter by default. Nonnull types are built into the Eiffel language [Meyer, 1989]. For Java, there are dedicated static checkers for nonnull annotated types (see [Chalin et al., 2008]).

We understand the JML type non_null $T \in$ JTypes (which excludes the null reference) as a subtype to the respective unrestricted type nullable T (i.e., the actual Java reference type). In JavaDL we represent both types as the same type T and encode the nonnullness as a constraint. We define a family of formulas inRange$_T(x)$ that represents the restrictions on term x to JML type $T \in$ JTypes. This type restriction formula is used anywhere in JavaDL formulas where range restriction is required, e.g., in preconditions or in quantifier ranges. Note that the symbol inRange() does not actually occur in formulas, but is merely an abbreviation used in this book.

For a reference type T that is not an array type, inRange$_T(x)$ is defined as the following formula:

$$x.created \doteq TRUE \wedge x \not\doteq \text{null}$$

For reference array types, e.g., Object[], there is a further restriction that all array entries $x[i]$ are different from null as well—even in depth in case of multidimensional arrays.[2] To encapsulate this 'deep nonnull,' we use the recursively defined predicate $nonNull(h, x, d)$ which means that in heap h reference x is not null for dimension d, see Section 8.2.1.2 for the formal definition.

Similar to the definition for reference types, the type \locset is restricted to location sets in which all members of the set belong to allocated objects. There is no JML expression denoting an unallocated object, and there is no way of constructing an expression that denotes a set that contains unallocated locations. In Section 9.3.4, we will encounter an example for why it is useful that dynamic frames in JML never contain unallocated locations.

8.1.2 Translating JML Expressions to JavaDL

This subsection explains the translation of selected, relevant operators. A comprehensive list can be found in Appendix A.2.

---

[2] The translation does not include that the entries must be created. It is an implicit axiom in JavaDL that all referenced objects are created. This is captured in the semantics of the *wellFormed* predicate, see Definition 3.5.

8.1.2.1 Boolean Logical Expressions

Boolean expressions are translated in a straightforward manner. For most JML operators, there is simply an alternative JavaDL syntax. E.g., all three expressions A != B, A <=!=> B, and A^B are translated to $\neg(\lfloor A \rfloor \leftrightarrow \lfloor B \rfloor)$. For quantified expressions, we add a type restriction to the range, as discussed above. E.g., (\forall int x; A; B) is translated to $\forall \; int \; x; (inInt(x) \wedge \lfloor A \rfloor \rightarrow \lfloor B \rfloor)$, where we assume the bound variable x in JML to be identified with the logical variable x. According to the JML reference manual [Leavens et al., 2013, Sect. 12.4.24.6], the range of quantification over reference types "may include references to objects that are not constructed by the program." Our translation deviates from this since in practice all nontrivial quantified expressions would not be well-defined.[3] This means that a JML expression (\forall Object o; B) is translated to $\forall \; Object \; o; (o.created \doteq TRUE \wedge o \not\doteq \texttt{null} \rightarrow \lfloor B \rfloor)$.

8.1.2.2 Integer Expressions

Operations on integers in JML are the same as in Java with two exceptions: Expressions with side effects such as x++ are not allowed in JML. The only addition is that expressions can be of type \bigint, on which arithmetic operators represent their mathematical counterparts. Depending on the promoted result type of the compound expression, there are up to three different translations: one each for types int, long, and \bigint. The promoted type is the least restrictive type of the subexpressions (see [Gosling et al., 2013, Sect. 5.1.2]). Other integral types do not occur; there is always an implicit promotion to int.

Arithmetic expressions of type \bigint are translated to their mathematical counterpart. E.g., n + m is translated to $\lfloor n \rfloor + \lfloor m \rfloor$ if at least one of n or m is of type \bigint. For the Java types int and long, the translation relies on dedicated functions which represent the respective modulo semantics; n + m is translated to either $javaAddInt(\lfloor n \rfloor, \lfloor m \rfloor)$ or $javaAddLong(\lfloor n \rfloor, \lfloor m \rfloor)$. As with the type restriction predicates above, these proxy functions have different semantics depending on the options in use. The division and modulo operators applied to \bigint are translated to the functions $jdiv$ and $jmod$,[4] respectively.

Bitwise operations are also translated for int and long (i.e., operations on the 32- and 64-bit vector types), but it is a type error to use them with \bigint. The full table of translations can be found in Table A.9 in the appendix. It is possible to use explicit conversions to enforce certain semantics; e.g., $-n$ where n is of type int is translated to $javaUnaryMinusInt(\lfloor n \rfloor)$ while -(\bigint)n is translated to $-\lfloor n \rfloor$.

---

[3] In JML, there is no way of expressing createdness of objects. At some point an explicit \created operator had been proposed and it was used in older versions of the KeY system, but it has never found its way into the reference manual.

[4] The functions $jdiv$ and $jmod$ represent division and remainder according to Java rules, albeit in the unbounded domain. They must not be confused with the / and % operators in JavaDL, which represent Euclidian division and modulo; see Section 5.4.

8.1.2.3 Generalized Quantifiers

JML features so-called generalized quantifiers,[5] which include sum and product comprehensions as well as minimum and maximum operators. Syntactically, all of them bind a (logic) variable of some type and consist of an optional Boolean guard expression and a body expression of type `int`, both of which the bound variable may appear in. Sum and product comprehensions are not always total functions—consider, e.g., $\sum_{i\in\mathbb{N}} i$. For this reason, JavaDL provides dedicated *bounded* comprehension operators over integer intervals, for which induction schemata can be given (see Section 5.4.2). For bounded comprehensions to be translated, we restrict them to conform to a shape like (`\sum T x; n <= x && x < m; t`) with only one bound variable and an interval which is closed to the left and open to the right, and where T is an integral type. Of course, this excludes certain (well-defined) comprehensions, because of their syntactical shape, such as (`\product Object o; false; 42`) or (`\sum \bigint i, j; 0 < i && i < j && j < 23; i*j`). Such comprehensions are translated to the unbounded sum and product operators sum and prod, for which only minimal reasoning support is available.

Bounded sum and product comprehensions in JavaDL represent iterated addition or multiplication in the mathematical integers. In JML, the type of a generalized quantifier is the type its body. For a faithful translation, an additional cast is applied to the bounded comprehensions. The expression (`\sum int x; n <= x && x < m; t`), for example, is translated to the following:

$$castToInt(bsum\{int\ x\}(\lfloor n \rfloor, \lfloor m \rfloor, \lfloor t \rfloor))$$

Minimum and maximum operators appear in the form (`\max T i; A; t`), which intuitively stands for 'the maximum of all $t(i)$ such that $A(i)$ holds.' However, maximum is not a total function either. Consider, e.g., (`\max \bigint i; i`), for which the above axiomatization would entail that there exists a largest integer. Minimum and maximum operators are translated to dedicated operators in JavaDL, for which there exists only minimal reasoning support at the time of writing;[6] using the `\min` and `\max` is discouraged. Minimum and maximum can instead be formalized in first-order logic with basic arithmetic. Since it allows for complete reasoning, this is the preferred way in practice.

8.1.2.4 Pure Method Calls

Methods declared as `pure` can be used as specification expressions. In JavaDL, pure methods are represented by observer symbols (see Definition 9.7). An instance method call o.m(p1, ..., pn) is thus translated to $C::m(\text{heap}, \lfloor o \rfloor, \lfloor p_1 \rfloor, \ldots, \lfloor p_n \rfloor)$

---

[5] See also [Mostowski, 1957] on the concept of *generalized quantifiers* in logic.

[6] In particular, the property described in the JML reference manual [Leavens et al., 2013, Sect. 12.4.24.2] is not provable, where the maximum over an empty range is defined as the minimum over the body type (which is also undefined for `\bigint`).

where C is the class of which $\lfloor o \rfloor$ is an instance containing the most specific method implementation for m according to the dynamic dispatch rules of the Java language. For static methods, the receiver parameter is `null`. Not all methods may be used in specifications: Since evaluating the specification must not change the execution context, only *pure* methods may be referred to from JML clauses. Note that in JML, methods that occur in specifications may also be *weakly pure*, i.e., they may create new objects on the heap and change their state, but do not have an influence on the existing part of the heap. The translation to JavaDL thus ignores possible side effects.

8.1.2.5 Referring to the Prestate

In postconditions of method contracts and in history constraints the expression `\old(x)` is used to denote the prestate value of x. There is no restriction on the type or syntactical structure of x in general; it may include pure method calls or object references. In JavaDL, this can be achieved by performing every heap access which appears in the scope of `\old` with the prestate heap $heap^{pre}$ instead of the default `heap`. This applies to both field accesses and observer symbols such as pure methods or model fields. E.g., the reference expression `\old(o.f.g)` is translated to $select_T(heap^{pre}, select_{T'}(heap^{pre}, o, f), g)$ and `\old(o.f).g` is translated to $select_T(heap, select_{T'}(heap^{pre}, o, f), g)$. A pure method call as in `\old(this.m())` is translated to $C::m(heap^{pre}, self)$.

This implementation is an improvement over older versions of KeY which did not use an explicit heap, but replaced occurrences of `\old` with fresh variables which were assigned prior to symbolic execution [Baar et al., 2001]. Neither was it allowed to access pure methods in the prestate.

Note that `\old` can only be applied to proper expressions. This means that JavaDL terms like $select_T(heap^{pre}, select_{T'}(heap, o, f), g)$ cannot be expressed in JML—at least not without jumping through hoops like adding model methods. The obvious `o.f.\old(g)` is not a well-formed JML expression because the reference suffix g is not an expression. The generalized version of `\old` with a label to refer to an arbitrary heap state (not just the prestate) is currently not supported in KeY.

Two Notions of the Past

Yi et al. [2013] propose another notion of referring to the prestate. While `\old` stands for a *value* (which may be of a reference type), the proposed `\past` operator represents a *pointer* into the prestate heap. This means that every expression using this pointer is implicitly evaluated in the prestate, e.g., `\past(o).f.g` or `\past(o.f).g` both mean the same as `\old(o.f.g)`. The main motivation for such an operator is to bridge a gap with `\old` which exposes implementation detail. Imagine o's static type to be an interface. How do we state that the object denoted by o in the poststate equals o in the prestate without exposing implementation details? Using \past, this can be expressed as o.equals(\past(o)), but there does not exist an equivalent expression using \old. Please note that the *value* of \past(o) is still the same as \old(o).

Even on the level of JavaDL, this is difficult to express. While not in standard JML, KeY's extension features two-state model methods (see Section 9.2.2). These represent observer functions which observe two heaps simultaneously. This allows the \old operator to appear in the implementation. We could give a two-state model method equalsOld() with the following implementation:

```
/*@ public two_state model boolean equalsOld ()
 @     { return this.f == \old(this.f); }
 @*/
```

However, we would have to implement such a model method for each concrete subtype because the implementation refers to the fields of the concrete type. Note that model methods are always *strictly* pure in our JML dialect.

The Boolean expression \fresh(o) also appears in postconditions and states that o points to a freshly allocated object, i.e., it was not created in the prestate and it is not a null reference:

$$\lfloor \texttt{\textbackslash fresh}(o) \rfloor = select_{boolean}(\texttt{heap}^{pre}, \lfloor o \rfloor, created) \doteq FALSE \land \lfloor o \rfloor \neq \texttt{null}$$

Note that the value of o is evaluated in the poststate. Please note that the \fresh operator is overloaded; there is an expression \fresh(s) where s is a location set expression in KeY's dialect of JML, which means that all locations in s belong to objects which were newly allocated.

8.1.2.6 Type Expressions

Standard JML features a type of types \TYPE, which is not present in KeY's JML since the underlying JavaDL assumes a finite type system. Type expressions as such are supported within certain contexts: Boolean expressions of the form \typeof(x) == \type(T) where x is an expression of any type and T is a type, are translated to $exactInstance_T(x)$ (introduced in Section 2.4.3). Only the syntax where a \typeof expression appears on the left hand side and \type(T) (denoting a fixed type) appears on the right hand side is supported. Any other occurrences of type equality are Skolemized.

To describe that an expression x evaluates to an instance of type T, but not necessarily to an exact instance of T, the Java operator instanceof can be used. The expression x instanceof T is translated to $instance_T(\lfloor x \rfloor)$.

8.1.2.7 Location Set Expressions

Weiß [2011] introduced dedicated location set expressions to JML. For some of them a translation is straightforward, as they have been designed to correspond to predicates and functions in JavaDL with obvious meaning, e.g., \intersect(s,t). But location set expressions also replace *reference set expressions* from standard JML. These are faithfully translated to terms in JavaDL. For instance, $\lfloor$\everything$\rfloor$ = *setMinus*(*allLocs*, *unusedLocs*(heap)), taking into account that JML only considers locations which belong to already *allocated* objects. Please note that the keyword \strictly_nothing (an extension introduced by KeY) is not an expression in this sense, but can be used to form a nonstandard **assignable** clause, see Definition 8.4 below.

The binary union operator is called \set_union for technical reasons. The JML language also features a set comprehension operator \infinite_union that binds a variable of any type and has a location set expression in the body. Optionally, a guard can be given. Like other comprehension operators, the translation from JML to JavaDL includes default guards. For instance, the JML expression \infinite_union(Object o; \singleton(o,f)) is translated to the following term:

$$infiniteUnion\{Object\ o\}(\text{if }(x.created \doteq TRUE \wedge x \neq \texttt{null})$$
$$\text{then }(\{(o,\texttt{f})\})\text{ else }(empty))$$

The set comprehension notation of standard JML is not supported in KeY.

8.1.2.8 Reachability

Both standard JML and the dialect used by KeY feature a \reach operator, but their syntax and semantics differ. Both serve the purpose of specifying properties on the set of objects (excluding null) which are reachable by subsequent field and array index references. In standard JML, \reach(o) intuitively stands for the set[7] of all objects transitively reachable through any instance field from the reference o.

By contrast, in KeY \reach is a predicate symbol that states whether an object is reachable from another one. It takes as a parameter the locations that are allowed in the reference chain—including static fields. The operator appears both as 3-place and 4-place, where \reach(ℓ, o_1, o_2) means '$\lfloor o_2 \rfloor$ is transitively reachable from $\lfloor o_1 \rfloor$ through any location in $\lfloor \ell \rfloor$,' where ℓ is a location set expression; and \reach(ℓ, o_1, o_2, n) stands for reachability in *exactly* $\lfloor n \rfloor$ steps. The former is equivalent to (\exists \bigint n; n >= 0; \reach(ℓ, o_1, o_2, n)).

Except for the fact that there is no explicit reasoning about sets of objects in KeY, its reachability operators are more expressive than those of standard JML. The standard JML expression \reach(o_1).contains(o_2) is equivalent to

---

[7] More precisely, it is an object of type JMLObjectSet since JML does have abstract data types.

\reach(o_1.*, o_1, o_2), while nontrivial location sets cannot be expressed in standard JML.

A similar operator is \reachLocs that denotes a location set consisting of all locations of reachable objects. Again, there are two versions of \reachLocs, one with an explicit number of steps and one with implicit quantification.

8.1.2.9 Escaping to JavaDL

It may happen that some properties cannot (or at least not without considerable effort) be represented in JML, but can be represented on the level of JavaDL. A typical case are user-defined functions or predicates which do not have a counterpart on the JML level.[8] For this purpose, KeY introduces escapes from JML into JavaDL. Within the delimiters (* *)+ (known as "informal predicate" in standard JML) any JavaDL term may appear, which is inserted verbatim during translation. Even more convenient is the function escape \dl_, which allows one to refer to a nonbinding JavaDL function (or predicate) while parameters are still given in JML. The escape sequence \dl_ must be immediately followed by a function name. Variable binding is not allowed.

For instance, \dl_add(a,\old(a)) refers to the function *add*, which represents addition in the mathematical integers. This function is not directly available in JML when the parameters have Java integer type. In case the JavaDL function has a heap parameter the base heap heap is implicitly added as the first parameter. Take a function $f : Heap \times Object \rightarrow Object$, for instance. \dl_f($o$) is translated into $f(\text{heap}, \lfloor o \rfloor)$. JML operators such as \old, whose translation to JavaDL can be tedious to express,may be used in parameters.

8.1.3 Abstract Data Types in JML

KeY's extension to JML additionally features the *abstract data type* [Reynolds, 1994] of finite sequences at the language level, referred to as \seq. This type is *primitive* in Java lingo, like the other specification-only types \bigint and \locset (see above). Reasoning about the underlying theory of finite sequences is well supported in KeY (see Section 5.2).

Algebraic data types can be defined *inductively*, i.e., their definition consists of a definition for each constructor. This kind of recursive definition is both well-founded and total due to the inductive nature of initial algebras [Jacobs and Rutten, 1997] that entails that every element of the carrier set can be uniquely described using a finite number of constructor applications (i.e., construction is invertible). As an example, in the List example above, we can model each state of the list using only the two

---

[8] Model methods (see 9.2.2) may instead be used for specification. However, in *reasoning*, model methods are treated similarly as (pure) Java methods, while functions or predicates can be given dedicated rules to reason about them efficiently.

constructors 'empty list' and 'appending an element,' which form a basic sequence data type. This principle also allows us to do proofs by induction. The length can be defined as an observer of these constructors. We can then perform induction over the length of a sequence.

The algebraic data type \seq of finite sequences is predefined in KeY-JML, its operations are displayed in Table 8.1. These operators are directly translated to their counterparts in JavaDL. Section 5.2 presents the underlying theory of finite sequences. In particular, we have a comprehension operator \seq_def where $(\texttt{\textbackslash seq\_def \textbackslash bigint } x;\ i;\ j;\ t)$ denotes the sequence $\langle t[x/i],\dots,t[x/j-1]\rangle$. Please note that \seq is not a parametric type; its elements are not typed. For this reason, sequence access always needs to be preceded by an (unsafe) type cast.[9]

Table 8.1 Defined operations on the \seq data type in JML (extension in KeY)

	syntax	signature
empty sequence	\seq_empty	$\rightarrow$ \seq
singleton sequence	\seq_singleton(e)	$T \rightarrow$ \seq
concatenation	\seq_concat($s1$, $s2$)	\seq$\times$\seq$\rightarrow$\seq
subsequence	$s[i..j]$	\seq$\times$\bigint$\times$\bigint$\rightarrow$\seq
comprehension	(\seq_def \bigint x; i; j; t)	\bigint$\times$\bigint$\times T \rightarrow$\seq
access	$(T)s[i]$	\seq$\times$\bigint$\rightarrow T$
length	s.length	\seq$\rightarrow$\bigint

Like \bigint or \locset, the type \seq counts as a primitive type in the Java sense. This means that all operations are side effect-free like mathematical functions, instances do not need to be created, and expressions can be compared using equality (==). In particular, it is allowed to quantify over all (infinitely many) sequences. Abstract data types must be distinguished from *model types* [Leavens et al., 2006b, Sect. 2.3] in standard JML, which are not supported by KeY. These model types—like JMLObjectSequence—still are Java reference types that may be used in specifications—with all their issues like createdness.

8.1.4 Well-Definedness of Expressions

Some functions or predicates are only partially defined. A standard example is the division function which is only defined for divisors other than zero. In the context of Java programs, illegal heap accesses are particularly important, e.g., the value of a field access on **null** is not defined, as is the value of a[5] where a is an array of length 5 or less. According to the JML reference manual [Leavens et al., 2013], a Boolean expression is valid in a state if it has the truth value true and "does not cause an exception to be raised."

---

[9] In JavaDL, the access function itself is type parametric. An access in JML (prefixed with a type cast) is translated to the appropriate typed access. See Table A.15 in Appendix A for details.

Our translation from JML to JavaDL ignores this dimension of undefinedness. KeY can generate well-definedness proof obligations (see Section 8.3.3 below) that establish well-definedness of JavaDL formulas as described by Kirsten [2013].

8.2 From JML Contract Annotations to JavaDL Contracts

In this section we introduce JavaDL contracts as the principal concept in the verification framework of KeY. First and foremost, JavaDL contracts serve as an intermediate layer between JML specifications and proof obligations in JavaDL. The largest part of this section is taken by defining a normalization of JML contracts comprising various steps (Section 8.2.1). Then the special cases of contracts for constructors (Section 8.2.4) and model methods and fields (Section 8.2.3) are covered and finally the formal definition of a JavaDL contract—and how it is derived from a JML contract—is given in Section 8.2.4. The subsequent Section 8.3 then describes how the JavaDL proof obligations for the correctness of a JML specification are constructed. It will be explained in Chapter 9 how contracts can be used in proofs for sound modular reasoning about Java programs.

The definition of a proof obligation encompasses more than a mere translation of the JML expressions in the clauses of the contract into JavaDL. Additional logical constructions are needed to model aspects of the Java world precisely in the first-order setting of JavaDL. We add constraints to confine the liberal model of general predicate logic to those system states which can be reached through the execution of Java code. For instance, in Java a field with a reference type can only point to either null or to an already created object, but in JavaDL, it could possibly also point to an object yet to be created. The proof obligations for methods use dynamic logic constructs of JavaDL as they need to talk about both the before- and the after-state of execution of methods.

We discuss in general how the contracts for a generic method are handled in KeY. For this sake we assume that a method m is defined in some class C as follows.

```
class C {
    public R m (final T₁ p₁, ..., final Tₙ pₙ) { ... }
      ⋮
}
```

We assume that all parameters p_i are declared final, i.e., they are not assigned a value in the method body.[10]

---

[10] This restriction is not present in the KeY system, but it eases the presentation.

8.2.1 Normalizing JML Contracts

JML is a feature-rich specification language in which the same specification intention can often be formulated in different ways. This eases the job for the specifier and makes specifications more concise and easier to understand.

For instance, JML allows the formulation of structured specifications. The behavior of a method does not need to be formulated as a single contract, but can be split up into multiple, possibly nested individual contracts (called *specification cases*) that model different parts of the behavior. Within a contract, multiple clauses of the same kind (e.g., several `ensures` clauses) can be used to express properties of the behavior; keywords like `normal_behavior` or `pure` can be used as abbreviations of frequently applied specification elements. Moreover, JML is designed as a redundant language in which many features have more than one associated keyword.

The syntactic richness of the specification language is a benefit when readability and understandability of specifications is desired. However, for the precise description of the translation of contracts, a small core language having the same expressiveness, is favorable. In the following, we consider such a core language[11] for JML in which additional specifications constructs are assumed *syntactic sugar* defined in terms of that core. The considered JML core language closely resembles the one presented by Raghavan and Leavens [2000], although we deliberately deviate in some respects.

We present a normalization process that translates a general JML method contract without syntactical restriction into a *normalized JML contract* in the core language. This 'desugaring' may yield one or more separate contracts[12] for the given method, of which it needs to satisfy all. Note that this transformation is only used as a concept for explanation; JML contracts are not implemented in this way in the KeY system.

The JML normalization process consists of the following steps:

1. Flattening of nested specifications
2. Making implicit specifications explicit
3. Processing of modifiers
4. Adding of default clauses, if not present
5. Contraction of multiple clauses
6. Separation of verification aspects

We consider two classes of normalized contracts: functional contracts and dependency contracts. Listing 8.1 displays the shape of a normalized functional method contract as we produce it in this section, while Listing 8.2 displays the shape of a normalized dependency contract. For details on JML clauses, see Section 7.1.1.

In the next paragraphs we outline the ideas behind the normalization steps. They may be skipped by readers familiar with the semantics of the desugared JML con-

---

[11] Our idea of a 'core' is to include a minimal syntax that has enough expressive means to accommodate the meaning of the entire language as we support it.

[12] We say here that a method can have more than one contract since that fits best the translation into JavaDL. Within the JML community it is more common to say that every method has *precisely one* contract with possibly several cases (including those inherited from supertypes). The difference is only terminological, not conceptual.

```
/*@ M behavior
  @ requires Pre;
  @ ensures Post;
  @ signals (Throwable e) ExPost;
  @ diverges [true|false];
  @ measured_by Var;
  @ assignable Ass;
  @ helper
  @*/
/*@nullable*/ RetType methodName(/*@nullable*/ T1 p1, ... )
```

Listing 8.1 JML functional method contract specification case template

```
/*@ M behavior
  @ requires Pre;
  @ measured_by Var;
  @ accessible Acc;
  @ helper
  @*/
/*@nullable*/ RetType methodName(/*@nullable*/ T1 p1, ... )
```

Listing 8.2 JML method dependency contract specification case template

structs and who are convinced that the shape of the normalized contract is general enough.

8.2.1.1 Flattening of Nested Specifications

JML allows the specification of nested cases (also called structured specifications) using the `{| ... |}` construct with opening and closing braces. It can be used to formulate specifications with some common clauses which are relevant for all cases, and with clauses for several separate and specific cases. The listing on the left of

```
before
{|      alt1
  also alt2  ...
  also altn  |}
```

```
  before
  alt1
also
  before
  alt2
...
also
  before
  altn
```

Figure 8.1 A nested JML specification (on the left) and the flattened contracts (on the right) after expansion

Figure 8.1 depicts the syntactical form of a nested specification where *before* is a (possibly empty) sequence of **requires** clauses and alt_i is a sequence of arbitrary JML clauses (possibly including further **requires** clauses). The intuitive meaning of the nested clauses is that *any one* of the clauses connected by **also** makes a valid contract (but not the 'outside' preconditions on their own). The nonnested specification cases can thus be derived by replacing {| ... |} by any one of the alternatives alt_i. The nested contract in the listing on the left of Figure 8.1 is, hence, equivalent to the list of the n separate specification cases (conjoined using the keyword **also**) that appears in the listing on the right. This expansion can be performed in the same manner when more than one nesting operator occurs, or if the nesting of cases is nested itself.

For the remaining desugaring steps, we consider the separated flat contracts individually.

8.2.1.2 Making Implicit Specifications Explicit

JML provides a number of modifiers and specific keywords for frequent specification scenarios. For the description of the translation, however, it is advisable to make their meaning explicit by means of other specification clauses to reduce the number of cases that need to be considered. Section 7.5 describes how the JML user can specify whether a method parameter or its return value may take the value **null**.

Making Nonnull Specifications Explicit

JML follows a 'nonnull by default' policy (see also Sections 7.5 and 8.1.1) which means that every reference type in a method declaration (type of a parameter or return type) which is not explicitly annotated with the JML modifier /*@nullable*/ is implicitly declared as nonnull. In a first normalization step, we make these implicit assumptions explicit by adding /*@non_null*/ in those places without explicit nullity annotation.[13]

Then we make the semantics of the nullity modifiers explicit by replacing every /*@non_null*/ modifier in front of a method parameter p by /*@nullable*/ and at the same time add the clause **requires** p != **null**; to every method contract for the method. If the return type of a method is /*@non_null*/, we also replace that modifier by /*@nullable*/ and add the clause **ensures** \result != **null**; to every contract for the method. These steps do not change the semantics of the contracts, but make it explicit.

In case the type of a method parameter (or the return type) is an array type over a reference type (e.g. Object[]), the nonnull annotation does not only specify that the value is always different from **null**, but also that all entries differ from **null**, too. For arrays of higher dimension this goes even deeper. To specify this, we introduce the JavaDL predicate *nonNull* : *Heap* × *Object* × *int*. The formula *nonNull*(h, x, d) is

---

[13] Unless the enclosing class has been annotated with /*@nullable_by_default*/, in which case /*@nullable*/ is the added modifier.

true if and only if x refers (on heap h) to an array of objects different from null that themselves are nonnull arrays of dimension $d - 1$. Formally, it is defined through the following axiom.

$$\forall Heap\ h,\ Object\ x;\ nonNull(h,x,0) \leftrightarrow x \neq \texttt{null} \wedge$$
$$\forall Heap\ h,\ Object\ x,\ int\ d;\ d > 0 \rightarrow (nonNull(h,x,d) \leftrightarrow x \neq \texttt{null} \wedge$$
$$(\forall int\ i;\ 0 \leq i \wedge i < x.length \rightarrow nonNull(h, select_{Object}(h,x,arr(i)),d-1))\ .$$

For a d-dimensional array parameter x declared as /*@non_null*/ Object[]^d x, the precondition then reads requires \dl_nonNull(x, d);.[14]

Making Object Invariant Specifications Explicit

Like the nonnullness of method parameters, receiver class invariants are also part of the specification without being explicitly written down.

In standard JML the objects for which the class invariants hold are determined by the so-called *visible state semantics*; in KeY's JML, all objects for which the class invariants hold must be stated explicitly using the operator \invariant_for. With one exemption: A nonstatic method is implicitly assuming (as a precondition) the invariant for the receiver object this before the method call and needs to assure it after the call (as a postcondition). This default specification can be explicitly deactivated by adding the modifier /*@helper*/ to the method specification.

To desugar the implicit invariant semantics for nonhelper methods, we add a helper modifier to the method and the clauses

- requires \invariant_for(this);
- ensures \invariant_for(this); and
- signals (Throwable e) \invariant_for(this);

to every specification case for the method. A static method has no receiver object, and thus cannot refer to an object invariant. Instead, the *static* class invariant is implicitly assumed and must be guaranteed. The translation as explicit clauses[15] reads requires \static_invariant_for(C); in which C is the enclosing class in which the static method defined.

The order of clauses plays an important role in the well-definedness of contracts (see Section 8.3.3). It is therefore important to mention that the newly added clauses are added *before* the first existing annotation.

---

[14] The first argument to \dl_nonNull of type *Heap* is added automatically by the translation as outlined in Section 8.1.2.9.

[15] The operator \static_invariant_for(C) referring to the static invariant of class C is a KeY extension to JML.

Making The Kind Of Behavior Explicit

JML supports specification not only of normally terminating program runs, but also for the case of abnormal termination (uncaught exceptions). When writing a specification, one can distinguish between specification of the normal and of the exceptional case by declaring them as `normal_behavior` and `exceptional_behavior`, respectively.

For a normalized contract, both keywords are reduced to the keyword `behavior` by which a contract is initiated. The normal behavior gets an additional clause `signals (Throwable t) false;` indicating that the method does not raise any exception or error. Likewise, exceptional behavior specifications get an additional postcondition `ensures false;` indicating that the method never terminates normally. Note that the declaration of either behavior does not specify divergence.

Desugaring `signals_only` Clauses

KeY supports `signals_only` clauses, which restrict the types of exceptions that can possibly be raised by a method. Unlike the `throws` declaration in the Java language, it does not only constrain *checked exception* types (subclasses of `Exception` which are not subclasses of `RuntimeException`), but all instances of class `Throwable`. For a discussion on exception types in Java, see the box on page 260.

The clause `signals_only` T_1, ..., T_p; lists one or more names T_i of classes extending `Throwable`. It can be replaced by the semantically equivalent clause:

`signals (Throwable e) (e instanceof` T_1 `||...||` `e instanceof` T_p`);`

8.2.1.3 Expanding Purity Modifiers

There are two more method modifiers `pure` and `strictly_pure` indicating that a method does not have (observable) side effects. They both mean that the method terminates unconditionally and that it does not modify existing heap locations. The modifier `pure` is hence translated into the two clauses `diverges false;` and `assignable \nothing;`. The modifier `strictly_pure` is an extension introduced to JML by KeY to indicate that the heap is not modified at all (neither existing nor freshly created locations; see also Section 7.9.1). It becomes `diverges false;` and `assignable \strictly_nothing;` when translated into JavaDL. The semantic differences between `pure`/`nothing` and `strictly_pure`/`strictly_nothing` are outlined in Section 8.2.4.

8.2.1.4 Adding Default Clauses

The clauses in the normalized contract in Listing 8.1 are not optional. If a contract does not have (at least) one clause for every keyword, clauses with default values

Table 8.2 Default values for absent clauses and operators used to contract two or more clauses with the same keyword

Clause	Default value	Contraction operator
requires	true	&&
ensures	true	&&
diverges	false	||
assignable	\everything	\set_union
accessible	\everything	\set_union
signals	(Throwable t) true	*see below*
signals_only	*see below*	*not allowed*
measured_by	*not specified*	*not allowed*

are added to make the contract complete. The second column in Table 8.2 lists the default values which are used for the clauses added in case a keyword does not occur.

Default values are designed in such a fashion that they match the user's expectations of an unconstrained method, known as the *principle of least surprise* [Leavens, 1988]. The default clauses express that the method may be called in any state and that it may terminate in any state. It may also terminate abnormally with any exception or error; it may read from or write to any location on the heap.

The default clause for **diverges** is a little different in this context since its default is to disallow nonterminating behavior. Instead, if nontermination is to be allowed for a specific method (e.g., for the event loop of a reactive system), it must be explicitly stated. In this respect, the default value is not the most liberal, but rather the most restrictive one. It matches user expectation, however, since more often than not *do* we want our code to terminate.

As described above, clauses of type **signals_only** are desugared. We define a default value in case no such clause is given, even though it will be translated into a **signals** clause. The default for **signals_only** clauses includes the *unchecked* exception types Error and RuntimeException as well as those *checked* exception types that are explicitly declared in the **throws** clause of the method signature. This is the most liberal specification possible in Java since these are all the exception types that the compiler permits to be thrown. For a method with the signature **void foo() throws IOException**, for instance, the default clause is

signals_only Error, RuntimeException, IOException; .

Exceptions and Errors

In Java methods one may throw exceptions and errors to indicate abnormal situations and to terminate execution abruptly. Java discriminates between *regular exceptions* (i.e., instances of java.lang.Exception) and *errors* (i.e., instances of java.lang.Throwable that are not instances of Exception). While the former are designed to be handled within the program (to recover from the abnormal

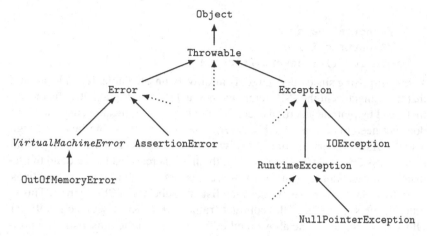

Figure 8.2 The type hierarchy of exceptions in Java

situation), the latter are reserved for severe, unexpected internal problems. Errors are not meant to be caught but to terminate the whole program abruptly. A typical example for an error is OutOfMemoryError that is thrown by the virtual machine if a memory allocation fails due to lack of (physical) memory.

Both, regular exceptions and errors, have *unchecked* exceptions as subtypes, that may be raised at any time during execution without the been to declare them at compile time. Unchecked regular exceptions are instances of java.lang.RuntimeException, unchecked errors are instances of java.lang.Error. All other exception types are *checked* exceptions. An excerpt from the Java type hierarchy is shown in Figure 8.2.

In the JML view of things, an execution which terminates abnormally by a thrown exception is still within the scope of the specification. JML distinguishes between normal postconditions (specified using **ensures**) and exceptional postconditions (specified using **signals**).

The situation is different for errors: The JML reference manual [Leavens et al., 2013, Sect. 9.6.2] defines any method contract to be fulfilled vacuously if the method terminates with an error. On the one hand, errors may appear at many occasions during execution and in an unpredictable (and in some sense nondeterministic) manner; hence, it may be justified to ignore them. On the other hand, an error represents a severe failure of the software system that must not be overlooked (see [Bloch, 2008, Item 57f.]).

One pathological example that shows that ignoring errors is problematic is the following method which employs the Java **assert** statement (not the JML equivalent in JML comments). If the asserted property is not met, an assertion in Java code raises an AssertionError. Hence, the following JML method contract is valid according to the JML reference manual [Leavens et al., 2013]:

```
//@ normal_behavior
//@ ensures false;
void foo () { assert false; }
```

This is surprising since the contract is intuitively unsatisfiable. It can be argued
that the semantics in the JML reference manual [Leavens et al., 2013]is mostly
motivated by runtime assertion checking, not by static verification, and therefore
does not need to be concerned with errors. Since, however, the Java language
actually allows the programmer to raise arbitrary instances of Throwable (and
its subclass Error)—and also to catch them—it is reasonable to extend the semantics of exceptional contracts to embrace errors as well as regular exceptions.

In KeY, JML `signals` clauses may list any subclass of Throwable. This is
vital for the soundness of the contract framework of KeY (see Section 9.1.3).
Otherwise, a caller of the above method could rely on the (unsatisfiable) postcondition after catching the error.

The actual causes of unpredictable errors (insufficient main memory, too
deeply nested recursions, incompatible class files, etc.) could be modeled in a
static analysis and be reasoned about. This would increase the verification cost
tremendously, however. In KeY, all such error causes are hence silently ignored.

The `measured_by` clauses do not have a default value. If it is not specified, that
aspect of the specification is left open. Unless the method calls itself recursively
(directly or indirectly via intermediate method calls), this clause is not required.

8.2.1.5 Contraction of Clauses

The normalized contracts of Listings 8.1, 8.2 not only require at least one clause
for every keyword, but also that there be *at most* one. Prior to normalization, there
may be several clauses of the same kind in a contract, which helps structuring the
specification. It is, for instance, considered good practice to specify each aspect of
the precondition in its own `requires` clause.

In cases where multiple clauses of the same kind have been specified, they must be
contracted to one single clause. The operator used to contract two or more clauses into
one clause depends on the kind of the clause. The operators used for the respective
clause types are listed in the right column of Table 8.2. Pre- and postconditions, for
instance, are both connected using the logical conjunction &&. Note that due to lazy
evaluation in Java, the order of clauses matters for well-definedness as we will point
out in Section 8.3.3.

The contraction of `signals` clauses is a little more delicate since they may give
postconditions for various exceptional situations. The two clauses

```
signals (ExcClass1 e) Post1;
signals (ExcClass2 e) Post2;
```

can be contracted to the semantically equivalent single `signals` clause

```
signals (Throwable e)   (e instanceof ExcClass1 ==> Post1)
                     && (e instanceof ExcClass2 ==> Post2) .
```

Depending on the type of the exception by which the method is terminated, the respective postcondition *must* hold.

For `signals_only` and `measured_by` clauses, multiple specifications do not make sense and are, hence, not allowed.

8.2.1.6 Separation of Verification Aspects

The contract language of JML is rich and the specifications may cover several behavioral aspects at the same time. We now describe how a single contract touching on more than one specification aspect is broken down into different single-aspect contracts.

Separation Of Functional And Dependency Contracts

A contract at this point may still have both functional clauses (that appear in Listing 8.1) and dependency clauses (that appear in Listing 8.2).

These are separated into the two categories: The functional clauses (`signals`, `diverges`, `ensures` and `assignable`) constitute the functional contract whereas the `accessible` clause makes up the dependency contract. The `requires` and `measured_by` clauses are shared by both.

If one of the functional or the dependency contract is trivially fulfilled (for instance if `accessible \everything` is specified), that trivial contract is dropped immediately.

Splitting Possibly Diverging Contracts

JavaDL can only handle either partial or total contracts and does not have a concept of contracts for conditional termination. Therefore, any contract with conditional termination is transformed into two unconditional contracts such that a contract that contains `diverges` d; becomes the two cases

```
requires d;        requires !d;
diverges true;     diverges false;
```

unless it is a constant (`true` or `false`) already. We will assume this shape of contract from now on.

8.2.1.7 Example

We illustrate with a small example the result of normalization. Listing 8.3 shows a method specified with a single method contract that contains both functional elements (like the **signals** or the **ensures** clauses) and dependency elements (the **accessible** clause).

```
class Example {
  /*@ public behavior
    @   requires to >= from;
    @   signals_only IndexOutOfBoundsException;
    @   signals (IndexOutOfBoundsException e) from < 0 || to >= a.length;
    @   ensures a[\result] >= a[from];
    @   accessible a[*];
    @*/
  /*@ pure */
  public int maxIntArray(int[] a, int from, int to) {
    // ...
  }
}
```

Listing 8.3 Example of a JML method contract prior to desugaring

Listing 8.4 shows the same method with the two contracts that are the result of the normalization process described above. Semantically, the two specifications are equivalent. It is easy to see that the original specification is much conciser. However, the normalized contracts have no implicit clauses and are easier to handle in logic.

8.2.2 Constructor Contracts

JML contracts can also be annotated to Java class constructors. The normalization process is almost the same as the one described above. But a few differences do exist:

- As the object has only been created just prior to the constructor call, assuming the instance invariant to hold already, is not sensible. Therefore, **\invariant_for(this)** is not an implicit precondition for constructors. It is, however, implicitly added to the (normal and exceptional) postconditions for constructors, because a constructor is obliged to establish initially the invariant of the created object. The static class invariant **\static_invariant_for**(C) is added to any nonhelper constructor of class C.
- In contrast to original JML, constructor contracts in KeY's variant of JML are attached to **new** invocations, i.e., the sequence of both instance allocation, field initialization, and the actual constructor execution (see Section 3.6.6).

```
class Example {
  /*@ public behavior
  @   requires a!= null
  @       && \invariant_for(this) && to >= from;
  @   signals (Throwable e)
  @          (e instanceof IndexOutOfBoundsException ==>
  @                        from < 0 || to >= a.length)
  @       && (e instanceof Throwable ==> \invariant_for(this))
  @       && (e instanceof IndexOutOfBoundsException);
  @   ensures a[\result] >= a[from] && \invariant_for(this);
  @   diverges false;
  @   assignable \nothing;
  @ also
  @   requires array != null
  @       && \invariant_for(this) && to >= from;
  @   accessible a[*];
  @*/
  /*@ helper */
  public int maxIntArray(/*@nullable*/int[] a, int from, int to) {
    // ...
  }
}
```

Listing 8.4 Example of the JML method contract from Listing 8.3 after desugaring

- As a consequence, the instance to be initialized is fresh, i.e., \fresh(this) is true in the poststate. Likewise, a (weakly) pure constructor may assign the fields of this.

8.2.3 Model Methods and Model Fields

JML supports methods which exist for verification purposes only: *model methods*. They reside, like all JML annotations, in special comments and may—as specification artifacts—make use of the language capabilities of JML. The types and expressions used in model methods need not be constrained to those of Java. Model methods can be subjected to contracts in exactly the same way as Java methods. When defining a model method, the modifier **model** must be used to indicate its nature as specification-only element (like for model fields).

A model method to compute the sum of the absolute values of a sequence of integers together with a method contract could thus read:

—— JML ——————————————————————————

```
/*@ public behavior
  @   requires seq.length > 0;
  @   ensures \result >= 0;
  @   assignable \strictly_nothing;
```

```
@ model int sumAbs(\seq seq) {
@     return (\sum int i;
@         0<=i && i<seq.length; Math.abs((int)seq[i]));
@ }
@*/
```

—————————— JML ——

Besides model methods, JML also supports the less general, but related, concept of *model fields* (motivated and introduced in Section 7.7.1). Conceptually, model fields can be considered as model methods without arguments. Thus, model fields are far more related to query *methods* than to ordinary Java *fields* since their value is not stored within the heap state space but is *computed* from the heap state. However, on the *syntactic* level model fields are declared like fields and quite differently than model methods. The expressive power of model methods is much higher than that of model fields and will be explained in detail in Section 9.2.2. To reduce the number of syntax elements in normalized annotations, this section reports on how model fields can be reduced to nullary model methods, and proceeds then with model methods.

Model fields have their definition fixed by a **represents** clause. Such clauses are implicitly private, in the sense that the definition given by them applies only to exact instances of the class with the clause; a redefinition (or a repetition of the original definition) is required in subclasses. Represents clauses have an unmodifiable implicit precondition \invariant_for(this); thus, the definition of a model field must only be expanded if the object invariant of the receiver object holds.

The general model field definition

```
/*@ model T modelField;
@   represents modelField = Repr;
@   accessible modelField : Acc
@               \measured_by Var;
@*/
```

hence is semantically equivalent[16] to the definition of the strictly pure model method

```
/*@ public behavior
@   accessible Acc;
@   measured_by Var;
@   requires \invariant_for(this);
@   assignable \strictly_nothing;
@ model T modelMethod() {
@   return Repr;
@ }
@*/
```

in which the represents clause *Repr* has become the value returned by the model method. All references to modelField must be replaced by a call modelMethod() to the method without arguments. The clause **requires** \invariant_for(this);

---

[16] See the box on page 267.

has been made explicit[17] to emphasize the fact that the invariant needs to hold when evaluating the model method.

If the value of a model field is not defined using a *functional* predicate `represents` but *relationally* using the more general `such_that` mechanism, the model field definition

```
/*@ model T modelField;
  @  represents modelField \such_that Cond;
  @*/
```

becomes as a model method with the semantically equivalent definition

```
/*@ public behavior
  @  requires \invariant_for(this);
  @  ensures Cond[this.modelField → \result];
  @  assignable \strictly_nothing;
  @ model T modelMethod();
  @*/
```

in which *Cond*[this.modelField → \result] denotes the JML expression *Cond* in which every reference to `this.modelField` has been replaced by the keyword `\result`.

A model method may—like an abstract method—be declared without specifying a method body. While an abstract method, however, must be refined in a concrete implementation class by a concrete method with a method body definition, a model method may remain underspecified without implementation. It is then the contract of the model method that characterizes the semantics of the symbol, see Section 9.2.2.

Subtle Differences Between Model Methods and Model Fields

Above we claimed that the model method replacement for a model field is semantically equivalent. This is the case when looking at the matter from a distance. Model methods possess some advanced features which make their semantics deviate slightly from model fields:

- *Model method bodies are inherited, but represents clauses of model fields are not.* As for an ordinary method, a model method definition is inherited by all subclasses unless they provide a new method definition. Thus, a subclass not mentioning a redefinition of the model method has the same definition as the superclass whereas the model field remains undefined for instances of the subclass.
- *Termination conditions are different between model methods and fields.* For recursive model fields, a variant must be specified using a `\measured_by` statement. Mutually dependent model fields need not provide evidence for termination and formulating inconsistent definitions is thus possible. Model

---

[17] It would also be assumed implicitly unless `modelMethod` were declared `helper`.

methods have a stricter termination model in the sense that there must never occur infinite recursion when evaluating them.

8.2.4 JavaDL Contracts

With normalized JML contracts at hand, it is time to bring the specification language artifacts into the logical context of JavaDL. In the following, we will see how JML contracts are translated into contracts on the level of JavaDL in such a fashion that most of the clauses in a normalized JML contract have a direct counterpart on the JavaDL side. Some of the clauses are contracted on the logical side, when they express aspects of common concern. As with normalized JML contracts, there are separate JavaDL contracts for the functionality of a method (describing the behavioral effects of a method) and contracts for the dependency of a query method (describing which part of the heap a computation may depend upon).

For the reader's convenience we repeat Definition 3.22 of functional method contracts here:

Definition 8.2 (Functional method contract). A functional JavaDL method contract for a method or constructor $R\,\mathtt{m}(T_1\;\mathtt{p}_1,\;\dots,\;T_n\;\mathtt{p}_n)$ declared in class C is a quadruple

$$(pre, post, mod, term)$$

that consists of

- a precondition $pre \in$ DLFml,
- a postcondition $post \in$ DLFml,
- a modifier set $mod \in \mathrm{Trm}_{LocSet} \cup \{\textsc{StrictlyNothing}\}$,
- and a termination witness $term \in \mathrm{Trm}_{Any} \cup \{\textsc{Partial}\}$.

All contract components may refer to the special program variables $\mathtt{self}$ (unless m is static), $\mathtt{heap}$ and to the program variables $\mathtt{p}_i$ $(1 \leq i \leq n)$ representing the method parameters. The postcondition may additionally refer to the program variables $\mathtt{heap}^{pre}$, $\mathtt{exc}$ and $\mathtt{res}$ (if the result type R of m is not $\mathtt{void}$).

The postcondition can access more program variables, because it talks about two program states (before and after the execution) while the other components of the contract are all evaluated in a single program state—the state before the execution.

The modifier set mod deviates a little from the other components since it may be either a term (describing the set of locations that may be changed) or the string $\textsc{StrictlyNothing}$ which does *not* stand for a term but is an indicator subject to special treatment when proving and applying the contract. The set mod denotes the set of *existing* memory locations that m may modify; hence, the empty location

set corresponds to `assignable \nothing`. A method with assignable STRICTLY-
NOTHING must not change *any* location, not even a freshly created one; this fact can
therefore not be expressed as a location set and requires the special indicator.

More on termination proofs for recursive methods can be found in Section 9.1.4,
specifically in the rule in Definition 9.14.

Ghostbusters

When we speak of a contract for a method then, more precisely, we mean the
complete program code consisting of the proper Java code and all JML annotations. That is not necessarily the same as the original Java code. Ideally, program
code and its specification are strictly separated: only the proper program is
executable, while its specification states a property on these executions. Unfortunately, that is not the case with *specification and annotation* languages like
JML. In addition to contracts and invariants, JML has annotations that are placed
as additional specification-only statements inside the code. These are assignments to ghost variables (i.e., `set` statements) or assertions (see Sections 7.7.2
and 7.9.3, respectively).

If contracts refer to the annotated code, then how can they make statements
about the *original* program? The principal idea is that a program augmentation
with JML statements must be a conservative extension w.r.t. program semantics,
i.e., JML statements must not have effects on the part of the state space accessible
by the Java program. Otherwise, the program executions which are considered
during verification would be different from the ones actually run by a Java
virtual machine, and the proofs worthless. The JML language rules forbid `set`
statements to assign to regular Java locations. However, `set` statements (and
even assertions) may still alter the control flow by raising exceptions. The
absence of such exceptions—typically runtime exceptions—needs to be proven
separately, see [Filliâtre et al., 2014].[18]

A dependency contract has fewer items:

Definition 8.3 (Dependency contract). A JavaDL method dependency contract
(pre, var, dep) for a method consists of

- a precondition $pre \in$ DLFml,
- a termination witness $term \in \text{Trm}_{Any}$,
- and a dependency set $dep \in \text{Trm}_{LocSet}$.

All components may refer to the program variables `self` (unless m is static), `heap`
and to the program variables p_i representing the method parameters.

---

[18] In KeY, not all checks have been implemented yet that are required to ensure JML statements are
conservative extension.

The preprocessing of contracts within JML laid out in Section 8.2.1 was designed to provide a quite direct translation into JavaDL contracts: Every normalized functional JML contract that adheres to the template in Listing 8.1 becomes a functional contract according to Definition 8.2, while every JML dependency contract adhering to Listing 8.2 becomes a dependency contract according to Definition 8.3. The elements of the contracts are extracted from their JML counterparts as follows:

- The precondition *pre* and the dependency set *dep* of a JavaDL contract are the direct translation of their JML counterpart: $pre := \lfloor Pre \rfloor$, $dep := \lfloor Acc \rfloor$.
- The JavaDL postcondition combines the postcondition for normal termination *Post* and the exceptional termination postcondition *Signals* into one formula:
  $post := (exc \doteq \texttt{null} \rightarrow \lfloor Post \rfloor) \land (exc \neq \texttt{null} \rightarrow \lfloor Signals \rfloor)$
- A special case exists for the modifier set. For most assignable clauses the modifier set *mod* is the JavaDL correspondent to the location set *Ass* specified as assignable clause. If the special symbol STRICTLYNOTHING has been used as assignable clause, however, the modifier set keeps this special symbol:
  $$mod := \begin{cases} \text{STRICTLYNOTHING} & \text{if } Ass = \text{STRICTLYNOTHING} \\ \lfloor Ass \rfloor & \text{otherwise} \end{cases}$$
  In Definition 8.4 and in equation (8.4) we will see that this case is treated specially in the construction of a proof obligation.
- The normalized JML contract allows only **true** or **false** as divergence clauses. The termination indicator *term* can be directly taken from the JML specification:
  $$term := \begin{cases} \text{PARTIAL} & \text{if } Diverges = \texttt{true} \\ \lfloor Var \rfloor & \text{if } Diverges = \texttt{false} \end{cases}$$

The Use of Contracts

In this chapter, a correctness proof for a method contract stands on its own. Whenever a contract has been proved sound, it has been ensured that the formal requirement laid out in the specification is fully met by the implementation. The use of method contracts as abstraction of method invocation has already been briefly covered in Section 3.7.1, but it is only in the next chapter on modular specification verification that we will learn how method contracts can be used to reason about Java programs in a *modular* fashion. There, the contracts give rise to new calculus rules applicable to method calls in programs. Those rules are only sound if the corresponding proof obligations have been discharged. They go hand in glove like *lemmas* in mathematical proof tradition: the claim of a lemma corresponds to the specification, its proof corresponds to the proofs conducted in this chapter, and using it within another proof corresponds to applying calculus rules that will be introduced in the next chapter.

8.2.5 Loop Specifications

Methods and model fields are not the only syntactical constructs that can be annotated with a specification. Loops can also be furnished with a formal specification.
Definition 3.23 introduced loop specifications as a triple $(inv, mod, term)$ of loop
invariant, modifier set and termination witness. Section 7.9.2 has already outlined
the syntax for loop specifications in JML:

```
/*@ maintaining maint;
  @ decreasing decr;
  @ assignable ass;
  @*/
```

JML allows the annotation of several loop invariants in one loop specification. If
more than one loop invariant clause is given, the clauses are combined into one using
&&. Table 8.3 lists the clauses allowed in loop specifications and their default values
in case they are omitted. JML has synonyms for the loop specification keywords
which are also listed in the table.

Table 8.3 Clauses in JML loop specifications

JML keyword	synonyms	default value
maintaining	maintains, loop_invariant	true
decreasing	decreases	PARTIAL
assignable		\everything

The translation from a JML loop specification as above into a JavaDL loop
specification $(inv, mod, term)$ is straightforward and works as follows:

$$inv = \lfloor maint \rfloor$$
$$mod = \lfloor ass \rfloor$$
$$term = \lfloor decr \rfloor$$

The translation of JML expressions in loop invariants that make use of the \old
operator requires a little attention: The old state refers to the state in which the
enclosing method has been invoked; it does *not* refer to the state directly prior to
loop entry, and it does *not* refer to the state after the last iteration.

The translation of heap expressions in \old refers to the heap variable heap^{pre}
which has then been set to the according heap at method entry, a method parameter
p is mapped to special purpose program variable p^{pre} in which p's value at method
entry is stored. Local variables are not affected by \old.

8.3 Proof Obligations for JavaDL Contracts

JML and JavaDL method contracts capture requirements on the behavior of Java methods in a formal manner. For the verification of method implementations, formulas will be introduced in the following that encode their correctness into JavaDL. Their validity is equivalent[19] to the correctness of the method implementation with respect to the contract of the method. On the other hand, if the formula can be falsified, the counterexample is a proof that the contract is not correct. Proof obligations thus define a semantics for JavaDL contracts: A method implementation fulfills its formal contract if and only if the corresponding JavaDL proof obligation is universally valid.

While proof obligations for methods can already be used to prove programs correct, the specification and verification of individual methods of a Java program is part of a greater task: the modularization of verification process. In Section 9.4.3 we will encounter inference rules that replace method invocations by instances of their JavaDL method contracts. These rules tie in with the proof obligations presented here in the sense that the correctness of the latter imply the soundness of the former rules presented in Chapter 9.

By the way: A method contract relevant for a method needs not be annotated with the method implementation under verification: Recall that JML features inheritance of contracts in order to implement the concept of behavioral subtyping (see Section 7.4.5). Therefore, if a method implementation overrides an implementation from a superclass or if it implements a signature declared in an interface, the implementation inherits all (nonprivate) specifications from the supertype.

8.3.1 Proof Obligations for Functional Correctness

Below we define a JavaDL formula whose validity is equivalent to the correctness of a function method contract. Unlike in other verification frameworks (e.g., earlier versions of KeY [Beckert et al., 2007]), we do not encode the verification condition into various assertions to be proved, but construct one single formula per contract. The general idea of this proof obligation is to show that the precondition implies that the postcondition holds after the execution of the method. But the postcondition is not the only guarantee that we are interested in: the assignable clause specified in JML (respectively the *mod* set in the JavaDL functional contract) states the locations that may be modified by the method; and this also needs to be checked. If $Contract = (pre, post, mod, term)$ with $term \neq$ PARTIAL is a functional contract for total correctness of method m according to Definition 8.2, both proof objectives can be expressed together as the formula

$$pre \rightarrow \langle \text{res} = \text{self.m}(\text{p}_1, \ldots, \text{p}_n); \rangle post \land frame \qquad (8.1)$$

---

[19] As a matter of fact, these formulas actually *define* the notion of correctness in KeY.

in JavaDL. The formula *frame* capturing the framing condition will be defined in (8.4) and (8.5) below. In Section 9.5, a concrete example for a functional contract proof obligation is examined more closely.

Free Preconditions

Since Java is a real-world programming language whose rich feature set has to be modeled logically in JavaDL, the above proof obligation is too simple. A number of adaptations need to be made to the proof obligation (8.1) to accommodate the idiosyncrasies of the Java language and its encoding in JavaDL. One point is that (8.1) is too strong since the initial state is only constrained by the precondition. The state space that JavaDL spans for all possibly definable interpretations of the logical symbols contains a lot more states than are reachable by the execution of Java programs. This includes the range of values that are admissible for programs. A typical example is that the `this` pointer (i.e., the program variable `self`) must not hold the `null` reference. From the logic's perspective, nothing speaks against this particular value; it must be ruled out explicitly: Additional assumptions must be made that constrain the states to those that can actually be reached by a Java program, thus weakening the proof obligation, e.g., by assuming $\texttt{self} \neq \texttt{null}$.

This weakening improves precision of the proof obligation, yet it does not compromise its correctness since we are only interested in proving the contract correct w.r.t. all states reachable by a Java program. This additional assumption is called the *free precondition*:

$$
\begin{aligned}
\mathit{freePre} := \quad & \mathit{wellFormed}(\mathit{heap}) \\
& \wedge \texttt{self} \neq \texttt{null} \\
& \wedge \texttt{self}.\mathit{created} \doteq \mathit{TRUE} \\
& \wedge \mathit{exactInstance}_C(\texttt{self}) \\
& \wedge \mathit{paramsInRange}
\end{aligned}
\tag{8.2}
$$

The free precondition contains the assumption that the heap is well-formed (e.g., there are no dangling references, see Figure 2.7 in Section 2.4.3 on page 42), that the receiver object is of exact type C, and that the values of all parameters are within the bounds defined by their type:

$$
\mathit{paramsInRange} := \bigwedge_{i=1}^{n}
\begin{cases}
p_i \doteq \texttt{null} \vee p_i.\mathit{created} \doteq \mathit{TRUE} \\
\qquad \text{if the parameter is of reference type} \\
\mathit{inInt}(p_i) \quad \text{if the parameter is declared } \texttt{int } p_i \\
\mathit{inByte}(p_i) \quad \text{if the parameter is declared } \texttt{byte } p_i \\
\vdots \\
\qquad \text{likewise for } \texttt{short}, \texttt{long}, \texttt{char} \\
\mathit{true} \qquad \text{otherwise}
\end{cases}
\tag{8.3}
$$

The predicates *inInt*, etc., are true if the argument is within the bounds of that type (int for *inInt*). See Section 5.4.3 for the semantics of the predicates in the various integer semantics available in KeY.

Also method $m(p_1, \ldots, p_n)$ in (8.1) is subject to a change: The method call needs to be wrapped in a try-catch statement to capture an exception that might be thrown during the execution of m in the dedicated program variable exc—thus making thrown exceptions accessible to the postcondition. In the method call, it is also made specific which implementation of the method is to be used (dynamic binding is switched off) by using the method body statement (see Section 3.6.5) instead of the method call. Finally, an update is added to provide access to values from before the method execution.

Definition 8.4 (Proof obligation for functional contracts). Consider a functional method contract *Contract* = (*pre*, *post*, *mod*, *term*) for the method $m(p_1, \ldots, p_n)$ declared in class or interface C. The implementation of m in a class $C' \sqsubseteq C$ is called correct with respect to *Contract* if the following JavaDL formula, called the *contract proof obligation* for *Contract*,

$$pre \wedge freePre \rightarrow \{\text{heap}^{pre} := \text{heap} \| \text{exc} := \text{null} \| \text{mby} := term\}$$

$$\left[\!\!\left[\begin{array}{l} \texttt{try \{ res=self.m(}p_1,\ldots,p_n\texttt{)@C'; \}} \\ \texttt{catch(Throwable e) \{ exc = e; \}} \end{array}\right]\!\!\right] (post \wedge frame)$$

is valid. The modality $[\![\cdot]\!]$ is instantiated by $[\cdot]$ if *term* = PARTIAL and by $\langle\cdot\rangle$ otherwise. The assignment to res is omitted if m is declared void. The update mby := *term* is left out if *term* = PARTIAL.

This definition makes use of a formula *frame* (called the *framing condition*) encoding the proof obligation that the method does not change locations outside the modifier set *mod*. If *mod* = STRICTLYNOTHING, then the framing condition is

$$frame := \forall o \forall f;\ o.f \doteq o.f@\text{heap}^{pre} \tag{8.4}$$

requiring that every location on the heap that is reached after the method invocation holds the same value as before that invocation. If *mod* differs from STRICTLYNOTH-ING, the condition is more sophisticated and reads as follows:

$$frame := \forall o \forall f;\quad o.created@\text{heap}^{pre} \doteq FALSE$$
$$\vee\, o.f \doteq o.f@\text{heap}^{pre} \tag{8.5}$$
$$\vee\, (o,f) \in \{\text{heap} := \text{heap}^{pre}\}mod$$

This condition states that any heap location (o, f) either

- belongs to an object o which has not (yet) been created before the method invocation, or
- holds the same value after the invocation as before the invocation, or
- belongs to the modifier set described by *mod* (evaluated in the prestate).

The framing problem will be topic of a larger discussion in Section 9.3.

The modality in the contract proof obligation is prefixed with an update which prepares a few program variables:

$heap^{pre} := heap$ the heap state before the method execution is stored in the program variable $heap^{pre}$ to have it available for evaluation of the postcondition.

$exc := null$ There is no exception observed initially. Unless an exception is raised, this variable will remain `null`.

$mby := term$ The value of the termination witness at the beginning of the method is stored in mby. In Definition 9.18 in Section 9.4.3, we will see that when invoking a method n, its variant expression $term_n$ must be proved smaller[20] than mby to guarantee that there is no infinite recursion.

'Assignable' Semantics Versus 'Modifies' Semantics

There is a subtle difference in the understanding of `assignable` clauses between what JML defines and how KeY implements it in form of the proof obligation from Definition 8.4. In standard JML, a heap location may only ever be assigned to if it is contained in the assignable clause. That means that it must not occur on the left hand side of any Java assignment operator unless included in the assignable set (hence the name 'assignable').

KeY's dialect of JML, however, sees this a little more liberal: The assignable clause specifies the set of locations that may have a modified content after the method has finished. This semantics considers a location unchanged if it has the original value at the end of the method call. It may change its value throughout the course of the method as long it regains the old value at the end of the method. We called this set the 'modifies' set for that reason. It is evident that the assignable semantics is stricter than the modifies semantics. Every program that is correct with respect to former is correct with respect to the latter.

The opposite direction does not hold. Listing 8.5 shows a small example of a program that is correct w.r.t. modifies semantics, but not w.r.t. to the assignable semantics: The method must not 'change' any existing location on the heap (`assignable \nothing;`). The value of `this.f` is temporarily changed in line 9 but restored directly afterwards to the original value such that at the end of the method, the original value is in `this.f` again (at least in sequential, single-threaded programs). For sequential programs, in which only the initial and terminal state are relevant, nothing speaks against the more liberal understanding since intermediate violations cannot be observed. The 'modifies' semantics admits more programs in which locations may have their values changed during the run. The choice of semantics does make a difference, however, for multithreaded

---

[20] w.r.t. a well-founded ordering

programs where threads may rely upon the fact that a parallelly executed thread
keeps the heap state untainted.

```
1  class Assignable {
2      int f;
3
4      /*@ normal_behavior
5        @  assignable \nothing;
6        @*/
7      void pureMethod() {
8          int old = this.f;
9          this.f = 0;
10         this.f = old;
11     }
12 }
```

Listing 8.5 The two semantics of `assignable` clauses

The general proof obligation as it has been introduced in Definition 8.4 applies to
normal Java methods. The general idea for the proof obligation applies as well to
special types of methods and to model methods. However, there are cases that differ
from the above pattern and we will in the following list the proof obligations for
constructors, abstract classes and model methods.

8.3.1.1 Constructors

The proof obligations for constructor contracts are a little different from the proof
obligations presented in Definition 8.4 for ordinary Java methods. It is the Java block
within the modality which has to be modified; for a constructor $A(T_1\ p_1, \ldots, T_n\ p_n)$
for a class A it reads:

```
try {
  A self = A.<createObject>();
  self.<init>(p1, ..., p_n);
  self.<initialized> = true;
} catch(Throwable e) { exc = e; }
```

The Java code fragment makes use of the synthetic methods `<createObject>` and
`<init>` and the synthetic Boolean field `<initialized>` which are not part of the
Java language but additions introduced in the context of symbolic execution and
object creation in KeY. See Section 3.6.6.3 for an introduction to these synthetic
symbols and on how they are used during symbolic execution of object creation.

Note that the contract for a constructor does not only span over the initializing
code in the constructor's body but also includes the creation of the object. This has

as an implication that the `this` reference (which points to a created object after the constructor) is a not-yet-created object in the prestate: `\fresh(this)` is a valid postcondition for any constructor.

8.3.1.2 Methods in Abstract Classes

If the class C is declared `abstract`, there cannot be objects that are exactly of that type. The predicate $exactInstance_C(\texttt{self})$ can thus never hold, the free precondition is always false, and the condition in Definition 8.4 is trivially valid. This seems against the semantics of method contracts, but since proof obligations exist also for inherited methods, it is ensured that every running implementation is verified against their contracts.

The KeY system treats abstract classes specially in that it suppresses the creation of the corresponding trivial proof obligations altogether to allow the user to focus on the relevant proof obligations.

8.3.1.3 Model Methods

For a strictly pure model method with a single side-effect-free return statement, the Java modality can be replaced by an update. Let the body of a model method be `return` $Expr$ for some JML expression $Expr$.

The proof obligation for a such model method is thus

$$pre \wedge freePre \rightarrow \{\texttt{exc} := \texttt{null} \| \texttt{mby} := term\}\{\texttt{res} := \lfloor Expr \rfloor\}post \ .$$

in which a simple update takes the place of the Java modality.

Since $Expr$ is side-effect-free, exceptions need not be considered here. An advantage of this formulation of the model method proof obligation is that JML-expressions (going beyond the Java language) can be used in the return statement as they need not go through symbolic execution.

For model methods which are not strictly pure or which have a nontrivial method body, a modality like in Definition 8.4 must be used. If the body additionally makes use of JML-only expressions or statements, a more liberal modality operator which allows for JML constructs in Java programs is needed. Currently, this is not supported in the KeY system.

8.3.1.4 Static Methods

Static methods differ from instance methods essentially in one respect: They do not have a "`this`" reference pointing to receiver object. For a static method the proof obligation of Definition 8.4 therefore needs to be adapted by

1. dropping the conjuncts in the free precondition *freePre* which refer to the program variable `self` and by
2. changing the method body statement such that it refers to the class rather than to the receiver object self. (The assignment in the modality then reads $res = C.m(p_1, \ldots, p_n) @C.$)

8.3.2 Dependency Proof Obligations

We are not solely interested in verifying that the result of a method invocation adheres to a given postcondition, but we are also interested in formalizing, specifying and verifying that the result of a method depends at most on a given set of locations on the heap.

This question is closely related to the noninterference problem examined in the light of information flow properties in Chapter 13, and dependency checking can be regarded as a special case of noninterference checking.

In Section 8.3.1, we discussed that for assignable clauses we do not check that every write operation affects a location in the set of modifiable locations, but rather look at the locations' contents in the end. A similar situation arises now for checking read accesses to heap locations. One approach would be to check (by adding assertions during symbolic execution) that every read access is to an admissible location.

Like for checking assignable clauses, we take a more liberal approach that requires checking an assertion only after the execution of the method has finished: We assert that the result of the method is *semantically* independent from all locations from which it must not read. This is more liberal than read access checking in that it allows a location to be read as long as the value does not have any influence on the method's result. In the expression `o.f*0`, for instance, it not necessary that `o.f` is in the dependency set since the result of the operation is constant and does not depend on the location's value though that occurs syntactically in the evaluation.

Now, the task is to come up with a JavaDL proof obligation for this independence. One technique to formalize that the result of a method *m* depends at most on a set of inputs specified in *dep* is to prove the following: Invoking the method in two memory states that agree on memory locations in *dep* (but may disagree on all other locations) must yield the same result. This formalization of noninterference is called *self-composition* (see [Darvas et al., 2003, 2005]), and a variation of it is also used for noninterference proofs with KeY, see Section 13.5.1 for details.

Definition 8.5 (Proof obligation for dependency contracts). Consider a method dependency contract $Contract = (pre, term, dep)$ for the method $T \ m(p_1, ..., p_n)$ declared in class C with $T \neq$ void. The implementation is called correct with respect to *Contract* if the following JavaDL formula, called the *dependency contract proof obligation*,

$$pre \wedge freePre \wedge wellFormed(h) \wedge \mathtt{mby} \doteq term$$
$$\wedge\, \mathtt{heap_2} \doteq anon(\mathtt{heap}, setMinus(allLocs, dep), h)$$
$$\wedge \qquad\qquad [\mathtt{res\ =\ self.m(p_1,\ \ldots,\ p_n)@C;}]\mathtt{res} \doteq r_1$$
$$\wedge\, \{\mathtt{heap := heap_2}\}[\mathtt{res\ =\ self.m(p_1,\ \ldots,\ p_n)@C;}]\mathtt{res} \doteq r_2$$
$$\rightarrow\ r_1 \doteq r_2$$

is valid. In this formula additional constants $h, \mathtt{heap_2} : Heap$ and $r_1, r_2 : \lfloor T \rfloor$ are used.

The rule is implemented slightly differently (yet equivalently) in the KeY system where the proof obligation coincides with the one for dependency contracts for general observer symbols as introduced in Definition 9.12 in Section 9.3.3.

Our interpretation of accessible clauses requires only that the result value of a method must depend at most on the locations in *dep* while any heap location may be modified without restriction. This deviates from the semantics defined for JML where every effect (on result or heap state) may depend at most on the part of the heap specified in a `accessible` clause.

In the course of Chapter 9 we will see that dependency contracts play an important role for modular reasoning within the KeY approach. Their primary use case is to specify in which cases pure methods used within specifications return the same result. For this purpose it is natural to only analyze dependency of the method return value disregarding all effects on heap locations. The reader who is interested in more accurate and general specification and more powerful verification of information flow properties using KeY is referred to Chapter 13.

8.3.3 Well-Definedness Proof Obligations

Some operators of the expression language have a canonical semantics only for a subset of possible inputs, and the meaning of expressions in which such operators are applied outside this set—called the operator's *domain*—is yet to be defined. As an example, consider the following method specification

—— Java + JML ——————————————————————————————

```
/*@ public normal_behavior
  @  ensures \result >= 1000 / n;
  @*/
int m(int n) { ... }
```

———————————————————————————————— Java + JML ——

which postulates that 1000/n is a lower bound for the result value. If somewhere in the program the method is invoked via m(0), the problem of the specification becomes apparent: To evaluate the postcondition, the expression 1000/0 would also have to be evaluated—but what is the result of this operation?

Since the expression language of JML is an extension of the side effect-free expressions in Java, it is desirable that the semantics of Java expressions should be retained if they are used in JML context. This is problematic since evaluating 1/0 in Java does not give a value but raises a `DivisionByZeroException`. Exception handling is a concept for managing program control flow and not for expression evaluation: If an exception is raised during expression evaluation, control flow is transferred abruptly and the according expression does not give any value.

In JavaDL, all functions and predicates are total such that every expression always yields a value in its co-domain. The expression 1/0 evaluates to an integer value—however, we cannot assume anything about this value, except that it is an integer. This approach is called *underspecification*; see Section 2.3.2 and [Schmitt, 2011, Sect. 2] for more details. It has the advantages of being easily definable and that axioms of classical logic are still valid. If a function symbol is applied to argument values which are not in its domain, then the function symbol is left uninterpreted for these input values. For a formula to be valid, it is required to be satisfied for all possible results in the undefined places; i.e., it must be valid in all structures which lift the places of partiality with an arbitrary value. For example, two interpretations that map 1/0 to 0 and 1/0 to 42, respectively, both need to be taken into consideration when proving the validity of a formula. The property $\exists int\, x;\ x \doteq 1/0$ is valid since JavaDL's division is a total function and in any model there is one integer (albeit unknown) value which is equal to 1/0. The equality $1/0 \doteq 1/0$ is also valid due to the reflexivity of $\doteq$. However, neither of the statements $1/0 > 0$ nor $\neg(1/0 > 0)$ is valid since 1/0 is positive in some interpretations and is nonpositive in the others. Likewise, the equality $1/0 \doteq 2/0$ is neither valid nor unsatisfiable; it also depends on the semantics of the underspecified parts of integer division.

There are several concepts to model undefinedness logically. Besides underspecification, the issue of undefined function applications can be modeled using a dedicated error element, three-valued logics, dependent types, or partial functions to name a few concepts. For an extensive comparison refer to [Hähnle, 2005].

In the following, proof obligations will be introduced that show that an expression does not depend on the semantics of undefined function applications. Hence, the concept by which function applications outside domains are modeled becomes irrelevant since the valuation of expressions is guaranteed not to be influenced by external valuations.

The analysis presented in the following is targeted at JML specifications. This raises the question: What are the admissible argument values for the JML operators? According to the JML reference manual [Leavens et al., 2013], a Boolean expression is satisfied in a state if it has the truth value true and "does not cause an exception to be raised." Raising an exception is thus the Java/JML indication for applying a function outside its domain. We capture this in the following definition which cannot be entirely formal since we have not formally defined the concepts of memory state (being program execution contexts with local variables, heap, method call stack, ...).

Definition 8.6 (Well-definedness). Given a JML expression e and a memory state s, the expression e is called *well-behaving* in s if the from-left-to-right short-circuit evaluation of e in s does not raise an exception. The expression e is called *well-defined* if it is well-behaving in all memory states.

A JML method contract is called well-defined if

1. its precondition is well-defined, and
2. all clauses evaluated in the prestate are well-behaving in all states that satisfy the precondition, and
3. all clauses evaluated in the poststate (i.e., **signals** and **ensures** clauses) are well-behaving in all states which are reachable by executing the method in a state satisfying the precondition.

The intuition behind this exception-based definition becomes more natural when considering another use case of JML specifications (besides deductive verification): During runtime assertion checking, a specification is to be refused and to be considered ill-defined if its evaluation causes an exception.

When checking JML contracts, it is always the precondition which is checked before anything else. Hence, all other specification elements are only ever evaluated if the precondition holds (and is well-behaving). Hence for the well-definedness of contracts, the fact that the precondition holds[21] can be safely assumed when investigating the well-definedness of other specification elements. We say that the precondition *guards* the other specification elements. The idea of a conservative formulation of specifications in which the precondition guards the postcondition has been brought forward by Leavens and Wing [1998].

Example 8.7. The method contract for method m introduced at the beginning of the section is not well-defined since there is a memory state (namely, if $n = 0$) in which the postcondition is not well-behaving.

The situation can be remedied by adding the precondition **requires n != 0;** to the contract. Under assumption of this precondition, the division 1000/x does not raise an exception; the postcondition is well-defined.

It is not only the precondition that guards other parts of a specification. Since expressions are evaluated from left to right in Java (and, hence, also in JML), it is possible to guard subexpressions which occur 'further to the right' from within the same specification element. As soon as the result of certain Boolean operations is inevitable in the evaluation of a Java expression, the remainder of the expression is no longer considered for evaluation. This is called *short-circuit* or *lazy* evaluation. When the JVM computes the value of A && B for the short-circuited conjunction &&, it first evaluates A and if that is false, the conjunction is falsified and B needs not be evaluated for the result. In the logic we can formulate this as

$$val(\lfloor A \ \&\& \ B \rfloor) = \begin{cases} f\!f & \text{if } val(\lfloor A \rfloor) = f\!f \\ val(\lfloor B \rfloor) & \text{if } val(\lfloor A \rfloor) = tt \end{cases}$$

---

[21] *nota bene*: we assume that the precondition holds, not that it is well-behaving or well-defined.

The value $val(\lfloor B\rfloor)$ is only referred to if A evaluates to true. Hence, It suffices when B is well-behaving in states where A is satisfied. In classical (two-valued) logics, this definition is not different from the usual definition of conjunction. It *is* different if one allows *val* to fail, for instance, by giving a special error truth value different from *tt* and *ff*.

Example 8.8. The class invariants of the following class are well-defined since all possibly not well-behaving operations are guarded.

—— Java + JML ————————————————————————————————

```
1  class GuardExample {
2    int[] values;
3    int length;
4    /*@ nullable @*/ GuardExample next;
5
6    //@ invariant next != null ==> length == next.length+1;
7    //@ invariant (\forall int i;
8    //@    0<=i && i < values.length; values[i] > 0);
9  }
```

————————————————————————————————————— Java + JML ——

The first invariant in line 6 aligns the values of the `length` fields of nodes in a singly linked list. In the expression `next.length`, the operand `next` may be `null` and the field access locally ill-behaving. But when evaluating the entire invariant, it cannot raise an exception since the implication operator `==>` has short-circuit semantics. If `this.next` is different from the `null` reference, the equality can be evaluated without raising an exception; and if `this.next` is `null`, then the left hand side of the implication evaluates to false and the expression is already true without evaluation of the equality.

The second invariant in line 7 is also well-defined since for every possible value for `i`, the range check `0<=i && i<values.length` guards the array access `values[i]` which can thus not cause an `ArrayIndexOutOfBoundsException`.

8.3.3.1 Well-Definedness of JML Expressions

In order to be able to describe the proof obligations which come up for JML expressions, we introduce a new transformation function ω which takes a JML expression and produces a JavaDL formula from it.

Definition 8.9. The well-definedness term transformation operator $\omega : \text{JExp} \to \text{DLFml}$ assigns to every JML expression a JavaDL formula. It is defined in Appendix A.3. For its evaluation, it makes use of the translation function $\lfloor \cdot \rfloor$ from Definition 8.1.

The intention behind ω is that whenever $\omega(e)$ is true then e is well-behaving. This logical notion of a well-definedness condition refines the informal Definition 8.6 and leads to

Proposition 8.10. *Let s be a memory state and $\lfloor s \rfloor$ the corresponding JavaDL struc-ture. and $e \in$ JExp. If $\lfloor s \rfloor \models \omega(e)$, then e is well-behaving in s. If $\omega(e)$ is universally valid, then e is well-defined.*

A formal proof is omitted mainly since it would require the formalization of left-to-right short-circuit evaluation for the entire JML language, which we do not want to provide here.

Instead, we focus on central items of ω's definition, the full definition can be found in Appendix A.3. For many JML function and operator applications, well-definedness of the application reduces to well-definedness of all arguments. Only if the function's domain is restricted, additional requirements are to be met. For the arithmetic expressions we have, for instance,

$$\omega(A + B) = \omega(A) \wedge \omega(B) \quad \text{(accordingly for } *, +, -, <, ==, \dots)$$
$$\text{but} \quad \omega(A \; / \; B) = \omega(A) \wedge \omega(B) \wedge \lfloor B \rfloor \neq 0 \quad \text{(accordingly for \%)} \; .$$

Note that the well-definedness transformation ω refers to the evaluation transforma-tion $\lfloor \cdot \rfloor$. Boolean expressions support short-circuit evaluation as mentioned above:

$$\omega(A \; \&\& \; B) = \omega(A) \wedge (\lfloor A \rfloor \to \omega(B))$$
$$\omega(A \; ==> \; B) = \omega(A) \wedge (\lfloor A \rfloor \to \omega(B))$$
$$\omega(A \; || \; B) = \omega(A) \wedge (\neg \lfloor A \rfloor \to \omega(B))$$
$$\text{but} \quad \omega(A \; \& \; B) = \omega(A) \wedge \omega(B)$$

An interesting question for short-circuit evaluation is the extension of the concept to quantifiers. One can argue that the existentially quantified formula (\exists int x; 1/(x+1) == 1) is well-defined since there exists a witness (the value 0) that makes the statement true such that all other evaluations are irrele-vant and can be omitted due to short-circuit evaluation. That would require, however, that in a left-to-right evaluation the matrix of the quantifier is evaluated at 0 before it is evaluated at -1 (which would raise an exception). To do so, a (well-)ordering of the values of the quantified domain must be fixed such that in the sequence of valuations those coming later are guarded by those ordered before. In the case of integers, a natural order might be suggested, but for other domains (like Object), no canonical, intuitive order comes to mind. For that reason, we opt for a conservative approach for the well-definedness of quantifiers: The valuation of one instantiation cannot guard another instantiation, and we have

$$\omega((\backslash Q \; T \; v; \; A; \; B)) = \forall \lfloor T \rfloor \; v; \; \big(\omega(A) \wedge (\lfloor A \rfloor \to \omega(B))\big)$$

for a generalized quantifier $Q \in \{\texttt{forall}, \texttt{exists}, \texttt{sum}, \texttt{infinte\_union}, \texttt{product}, \texttt{min}, \texttt{max}\}$, where a missing guard A defaults to **true** as usual.

Another important issue of well-definedness is null dereferencing. The operator $o.f$ for a field access is only well-behaving if the receiver object is different form the null reference. The same applies to array accesses, where the index must additionally lie within the array bounds such that we have

$$\omega(A.\texttt{f}) = \omega(A) \land \lfloor A \rfloor \neq \texttt{null} \qquad \text{for a field access}$$

$$\text{and} \quad \omega(A\,[B]) = \omega(A) \land \omega(B) \land \lfloor A \rfloor \neq \texttt{null} \land 0 \leq \lfloor B \rfloor \land \lfloor B \rfloor < \mathit{length}(\lfloor A \rfloor)$$

for an array access.

For references to method invocations within specifications, the design-by-contract principle persists: A method invocation must satisfy the precondition of the contract. Let $\texttt{Pre}_m$ be the functional precondition[22] of method m (compare Listing 8.1). The precondition refers to the formal receiver this and parameters $\texttt{p}_1, \ldots, \texttt{p}_n$ which have to be replaced by the concrete receiver o and the arguments a_i:

$$\omega(o.\texttt{m}(a_1,\ldots,a_n)) = \omega(o) \land \lfloor o \rfloor \neq \texttt{null} \land \bigwedge_{i=1}^{n} \omega(a_i) \land$$

$$\left\lfloor \texttt{Pre}_m[\texttt{p}_1/a_1,\ldots,\texttt{p}_n/a_n,\texttt{this}/o] \right\rfloor$$

8.3.3.2 Well-Definedness of Method Contracts

Using the well-definedness term transformation ω, we can now also define a condition for the well-definedness of method contracts. According to Definition 8.6, well-definedness of contract clauses other than the precondition is only required conditionally under assumption of the precondition being satisfied (the precondition guards the other clauses).

Definition 8.11 (Method contract well-definedness). Let the normalized method contract according to Listing 8.1 for method m be given. The well-definedness proof obligation for the contract for m is

$$\omega(\texttt{m}) = \omega(\mathit{Pre}) \land$$
$$(\lfloor \mathit{Pre} \rfloor \to \omega(\mathit{Var}) \land \omega(\mathit{Ass}) \land$$
$$\{\texttt{heap} := \mathit{anon}(\texttt{heap}, \lfloor \mathit{Ass} \rfloor, \texttt{heap}') \| \texttt{heap}^{\mathit{pre}} := \texttt{heap}\}$$
$$(\omega(\mathit{Post}) \land (\lfloor e \rfloor \neq \texttt{null} \to \omega(\mathit{ExPost})))))$$

and the well-definedness proof obligation for the dependency contract in Listing 8.2 reads

$$\omega(\texttt{m}) = \omega(\mathit{Pre}) \land (\lfloor \mathit{Pre} \rfloor \to \omega(\mathit{Var}) \land \omega(\mathit{Acc})) \ .$$

While the precondition *Pre*, the variant *Var*, the accessible clause *Acc*, and the assignable clause *Ass* are all evaluated in the prestate of the method invocation, the postcondition *Post* and the exceptional postcondition *ExPost* are evaluated in the poststate. Since the specification should be consistent in itself without reference to the implementation, the poststate should not be considered as the state after the

---

[22] If m has more than one contract, it suffices to satisfy one of the preconditions. Then $\texttt{Pre}_m$ refers to the disjunction of the preconditions of all functional method contracts which guarantee absence of exceptions (e.g., by being annotated normal_behavior).

execution of the implementation. Instead a most general poststate is assumed in which all assignable locations on the heap are assigned an unknown value using the anonymizing function *anon* (see Figure 2.11 in Section 2.4.5).

For well-definedness, the order of clauses is important. During normalization, if several clauses of a kind are present, they are combined into one (see Section 8.2.1.5). Two preconditions are conjoined into one using the short-circuit conjunction && such that preconditions mentioned earlier in a contract guard preconditions which are mentioned afterwards. Nonnullness among other implicit assumptions is made explicit during normalization (see Section 8.2.1.2). The explicit clauses which result from this normalization are added *before* the explicit preconditions such that they can guard them.

Example 8.12. Consider the following method contract with two preconditions.

—— Java + JML ————————————————————————————
```
//@ requires a.length > 0;
//@ requires a[0] == 0;
void m(/*@non_null*/ int[] a);
```
———————————————————————————————— Java + JML ——

A desugaring normalization of this contract results in the following contract with a single precondition

—— Java + JML ————————————————————————————
```
//@ requires a != null && a.length > 0 && a[0] == 0;
void m(/*@nullable*/ int[] a);
```
———————————————————————————————— Java + JML ——

in which a!=null and a.length > 0 together guard the array access a[0] such that this contract is well-defined.

8.3.3.3 Observations Concerning Well-Definedness

Modularity of Well-Definedness Proof Obligations

A remark on the precision of well-definedness for well-behaving specifications: It may be that a specification behaves well for all runs of a program, but that expressions—when inspected in isolation—are not well-defined. If x is a variable whose value is set to 1 initially, and never changed later, then the expression $1/x$ is well-behaving within the context of this program. However, if the context (i.e., the concrete program) is removed and the expression is considered in isolation, $1/x$ needs to be considered ill-defined. This is the view that KeY takes.

It is a deliberate choice: Specifications should be checked modularly for well-definedness ignoring the concrete program which they annotate. Well-definedness should *not* be a property depending on the behavior of the program. This has the benefit that if the program context changes (modification or extension of the program text), the well-definedness of the specification is not compromised.

Method contracts can always be made well-defined by adding the necessary assumptions guaranteed by the code explicitly to the specification. Making the guards explicit also clarifies specifications since it explicitly points out corner cases which are often the reason behind misunderstood specifications.

On The Evaluation Of Ill-Behaving Contracts

Up to this point, we have defined when a contract is or is not well-defined and found proof obligations to show its well-definedness. But, what happens if a clause of a contract is evaluated despite being ill-defined?

JML answers this by saying that any ill-behaving Boolean expression evaluates to false. This is called *strong validity* by Chalin and Rioux [2008]. It can be rephrased as 'an expression in which undefined subexpressions occur syntactically is not satisfied.' This is a very restrictive definition; occurrences of undefined expressions have an effect on satisfiability even if they do not matter in the classical logic sense.

Originally, JML propagated underspecification for the semantics of ill-defined expressions; the JML expression $1/0$ == $1/0$ would have been evaluated to true, now it evaluates to false. Chalin [2007] demonstrated through empirical studies that this semantics for function application outside of definition domain operations did not match programmers' expectations. For a software engineer, the expression $1/0$ does not have a value but raises an exception which has to be dealt with.

Left-to-Right Versus Bidirectional Evaluation

JML defines the evaluation of expressions from left to right with short-circuiting as shown above. This is owed to the fact that JML semantics is based on the semantics of the Java programming language.

However, when discussing the issue of well-definedness of logical formulas, there is no reason why the formula $x \neq 0 \wedge 1/x > 0$ should be treated any differently from $1/x > 0 \wedge x \neq 0$—the conjunction is commutative after all.

And it *is* possible to define well-definedness symmetrically such that both conjuncts guard each other and the order of arguments to connectives does not play a role for their semantics. If done naively, the bi-directional guarding produces well-definedness proof obligations which are exponential in the length of the original formula. However, Darvas et al. [2008] proposed an efficient encoding that produces well-defined conditions with bidirectional guarding with linear effort.

However, it was not the complexity of the proof-obligation that was the rationale for the choice of JML semantics, but its heritage from Java semantics. The expression $1/x > 0$ && x != 0 *may* throw an exception in Java even if its truth value does not depend on the value of $1/x$.

The well-definedness proof mechanism implemented in KeY (see [Kirsten, 2013]) supports both left-to-right and efficient bidirectional short-circuiting semantics.

Well-Definedness Is An Issue Of Pragmatics

Is well-definedness an issue of the syntax or the semantics of the specification language? There are aspects of well-formedness at the syntactic level: the adherence of programs and specifications to the languages' grammars and their well-typedness. The syntax and type checking for JML and JavaDL can be done efficiently on a syntactical level. However, well-definedness following Definition 8.6 is not a syntactic property that can be checked automatically by an efficient static analysis in all cases; it is not decidable. At the same time, it is wise to separate the concerns of well-definedness of a specification from its meaning. From a language designer's point of view, well-definedness is neither a syntactic nor a semantic problem but answers to the question whether a statement is sensible (in its context). Linguists call the field of interpretation of statements beyond that of its bare (model-theoretic) evaluation the *pragmatics* of a language. The statement $1/x > 0$, for instance, might invoke in the reader the *implicature* "x cannot be 0 since it occurs as denominator in a division." Doing well-definedness checking ensures that pragmatic issues outside the semantic truth value evaluation do not arise.

Auxiliary JML statements that may occur within the code (such as the set statement to assign to ghost variables/fields or loop invariants) have not been considered here, and neither have been class or loop invariants. For details on their treatment in KeY, see [Kirsten, 2013]. The implementation in KeY is slightly different from the current presententation, because it operates on JavaDL, where well-definedness of heap and field expressions is checked in addition.

Chapter 9
Modular Specification and Verification

Daniel Grahl, Richard Bubel, Wojciech Mostowski, Peter H. Schmitt, Mattias Ulbrich, and Benjamin Weiß

Software systems can grow large and complex, and various programming disciplines have been developed addressing the problem how programmers can cope with such complex systems. We focus in this book on the paradigm of object-orientation which seems to be the widely adopted mainstream approach.

In parallel to these development in software engineering, formal verification needs complementary techniques for dealing with large software systems and increased complexity. Yet, achieving complete functional verification of a complex piece of software still poses a grand challenge to current research ([Leino, 1995, Hoare and Misra, 2005, Leavens et al., 2006a, 2007, Klebanov et al., 2011, Huisman et al., 2015]). In this chapter we will present which support the KeY system offers in this direction and review the research background it is based on. In most subsections we will come back to concepts already presented in earlier chapters, but now with special emphasis on modularization. We will take extra pain to precisely delineate these dependencies.

It is common wisdom that the keys to scale up a technique for large applications are *modularization* and *abstraction*. In our case, the deductive verification of object-oriented software, the central pillar for modularization and abstraction is the *Design by Contract* principle as pioneered by Meyer [1992]. Once the contract for a method has been separately verified we need not at every call to this method inspect its code again but use its contract instead. In Chapter 7 method contracts have already been introduced as a central concept of the behavioral specification language JML (Java Modeling Language). Syntax and semantics of JML method contracts have been thoroughly explained there. Chapter 8 explained how JML method contracts are translated into proof obligations in JavaDL whose validity entails the correctness of the method w.r.t. the contract. In this chapter, we explain what needs to be considered when *using* a contract instead of the code of a method on the caller side and present logical calculus rules implementing this. A separate subsection is devoted to recursive methods. They are a special case since the contract to be verified is used itself at every recursive call of the method.

Method contracts can only play out their advantages if they do not themselves make use of implementation details. To achieve this it is necessary to have means

© Springer International Publishing AG 2016
W. Ahrendt et al. (Eds.): Deductive Software Verification, LNCS 10001, pp. 289–351, 2016
DOI: 10.1007/978-3-319-49812-6_9

available that abstract away from the code. To this end JML offers *model fields* and *model methods*, syntax elements that only occur in specifications and are not part of the code. These have already been addressed Section 7.7.1. Here we present in great detail the semantics of these concepts at the level of JavaDL and also show and discuss calculus rules.

Object invariants have already been addressed in Section 7.4.1. Here we present technical details, the representation of invariants as implicit model fields and how they are handled in KeY. In modular specification and verification, knowing which memory locations a method does *not* change is almost as important as knowing the effects of it. How to formalize and utilize this information is known as the *frame problem*. There is a long history of verification techniques that deal with the frame problem. Our approach, see [Weiß, 2011], is inspired by the *dynamic frames* technique from [Kassios, 2011] that aims at providing modular reasoning in the presence of abstractions as they occur in object oriented programs. In Section 7.9 we encountered already the `assignable` clause in JML specifications that provides a set of locations that a method might at most assign to. In Section 8.2 we saw how the JML `assignable` clause is translated into the mod part of a JavaDL loop or method contract. The calculus rules for proving these contracts were already covered in Section 3.7. In this chapter rules will be presented (1) for a more fine grained treatment of anonymization in loop verification and (2) for *using* method contracts.

In a way complementary to the information which locations a method may write to is the information which locations a method may read from. How this information is formulated was already explained (1) on the JML level via `accessible` clauses in Section 7.9, (2) as a JavaDL dependency contract in Definition 8.3 and, (3) as a JavaDL proof obligation in Definition 8.5. In this chapter `accessible` clauses for model methods are introduced. The previous proof obligation for dependency contracts has to be revised to cover this extension.

Although we use Java and JML as technological basis in this chapter, we expect all mentioned concepts to be adaptable to other object-oriented programming languages and their associated specification languages.

Chapter Overview

We start off this chapter with introducing the basic concepts of modular specification in Section 9.1. This will explain in general method contracts, behavioral subtyping, and lead up to our formalization of modular code correctness. A running example that will be used throughout this chapter will make its first appearance in Section 9.1.2. The special case of unbounded recursion is discussed in Section 9.1.4.

We present model fields as they appear in standard JML and their role in the KeY system in Section 9.2.1, as well as the more advanced concept of model methods in Section 9.2.2. The *frame problem* is the topic of Section 9.3.

Section 9.4 takes us to the second theme in the title of this chapter—verification. Building on the calculus for JavaDL from Section 3.5, we introduce additional rules for modular reasoning. This includes 1. an improved loop invariant rule, that retains most of the execution context and that caters for unbounded recursion depth (Section 9.4.2); 2. a rule for applying functional methods contracts (Section 9.4.3); 3. a rule for dependency contracts, based on the dynamic frame theory (Section 9.4.4); and 4. rules for inserting class invariants into the proof (Section 9.4.5).

In Section 9.5 we will verify the example from Section 9.1.2 putting to work the techniques that will have been introduced by then.

In Section 9.6 we give a quick glimpse of related work and the chapter closes with a summarizing look back on what has been covered in Section 9.7.

9.1 Modular Verification with Contracts

Method contracts are a central pillar of modular program verification. When combined with behavioral subtyping, they provide means for both abstraction and modularization. In this section, we will, after a review of the general background and the presentation of the chapter's running example, discuss the notion of modularity employed in JavaDL and how it can be used for the verification of recursive methods.

9.1.1 Historical and Conceptual Background

The concept of modules in programming languages can be traced back to early examples such as Simula 67 [Nygaard and Dahl, 1981] or Modula [Wirth, 1977]. Single modules (i.e., method implementations or classes containing them) may be added, removed, or changed with only minimal changes to their clients; programs can be reused or evolved in a reliable way. Modular analysis of a module can be based on the module itself in isolation—without a concrete representation of its environment. This allows one to adapt modules to other environments without losing previously established guarantees.

These ideas were put forth with the development of object-oriented programming: "The cornerstone of object-oriented technology is reuse." [Meyer, 1997] In object-oriented programming (OOP), methods (or procedures) consist of declarations and implementations. Declarations are visible to clients while implementations are hidden. One important addition in OOP to the base concept of modularity is that classes (i.e., modules) are meant to define types—and subclasses define subtypes. And, in particular, different classes may implement a method in different ways (*overriding*), including covariant and contravariant type refinement. A client never knows which implementation is actually used. Any call to a (nonprivate) method is subject to *dynamic dispatch*, i.e., the appropriate implementation is chosen at runtime from the context. This concept is also known as *virtual* method invocation.

The concept of a *contract* between software modules was first proposed by Lamport [1983] and later popularized by Meyer [1992] under the trademark *Design by Contract*. It allows one to abstract from those concrete implementations and to approximately predict module behavior statically.[1] The metaphor of a legal contract gives an intuition: A client (method caller) and a provider (method implementer) agree on a contract that states that, under given resources (preconditions), a product with certain properties (postconditions) is provided. This is a separation of duties; the provider can rely on the preconditions, otherwise he or she is free to do anything. Given the preconditions, he or she is only obliged to ensure the postconditions, no matter *how* they are established. On the other hand side, the client is obliged to ensure the preconditions and can only assume a product to the given specifications. In the basic setup, a method contract just consists of such a pair of pre- and postcondition. As it has already been explained in Chapter 7, state of the art specification languages as JML feature contracts with several clauses (of which all can be seen as specialized, functional or nonfunctional pre- or postconditions).

Contracts do not only play an important role in software design, but also in verification. In verifying a method that calls another method, there are two possibilities to deal with that case. Either, the implementation can be inserted or a contract can be used. The former is intriguingly simple; this is what would happen in an actual execution. But it carries three disadvantages:

1. It transgresses the concept of information hiding.
2. The concrete implementation of the callee must be known. This cannot always guaranteed in static verification techniques as in many cases the actual type of objects is not known at verification time. When verifying extensible programs, the implementation code may not even be available at verification time.
3. In the case of recursive implementations (with an unbounded recursion depth), inserting the same implementation again would let the proof run in circles.

This leaves contracts as a good choice to deal with method calls in most cases. In Subsection 16.4 the reader is guided through a tutorial example of using simple contracts.

Behavioral Subtyping

In a completely modular context, the concrete method implementations generally are not known. Nevertheless, a client will assume that all implementations of a common public interface (i.e., a method declaration) behave in a uniform way. This concept is known as *behavioral subtyping, Liskov's substitution principle*, or the *Liskov-Leavens-Wing principle* [Liskov, 1988, Leavens, 1988, Liskov and Wing, 1993, 1994].[2,3] It can be formulated as follows: A type T' is a behavioral subtype of a type T if instances of T' can be used in any context where an instance of T is expected by an observer. In other words, behavioral "subtyping prevents surprising

---

[1] Note that contracts give semantical properties about modules and are in some sense orthogonal to design documents such as class diagrams, that are mostly syntactical.

[2] Liskov and Wing themselves use the term "constraint rule."

[3] Despite first appearing in Leavens' thesis, it has been attributed to Liskov because of her widely influential keynote talk at the OOPSLA conference 1988.

behavior" [Leavens, 1988]. Note that this notion of a 'type' is different to both types in logic (see Section 2.2) and types in Java (i.e., classes and interfaces).

Behavioral subtyping is a semantical property of implementations. Although the concept is tightly associated with design by contract, it cannot be statically enforced by programming languages. It is not uncommon to see—especially in undergraduate exercises—that subclasses in object-oriented programs are misused in a nonbehavioral way. Imagine, for instance, a class `Rectangle` being implemented as a subclass of `Square` because it adds a length to `Square`'s width. This kind of data-centric reuse is a typical pattern for modular programming languages without inheritance. Not all rectangles are squares, so intuitively, this should not define a behavioral subtype. But whether it actually does, depends on the public interface (i.e., the possible observations). If the class signature of `Square` allows one to set the width to a and to observe the area as a^2, then the subclass `Rectangle` is not a behavioral subtype.

For modular reasoning about programs, we may only assume contracts for a dynamically dispatched method that are associated with the receiver's static type, since the precise dynamic type depends on the context. This technique is known as *supertype abstraction* [Leavens and Weihl, 1995]. Behavioral subtyping is essential to sound supertype abstraction.[4] To (partially) enforce it, in the Java Modeling Language, method contracts are inherited to overriding implementations [Leavens and Dhara, 2000]; see also Section 7.4.5. We can provide additional specifications in subclasses, which are conjoined with the inherited specification. This means, whatever the subclass specification states locally, it can only *refine* the superclass specification, effectively. This leads us to a slightly relaxed version of behavioral subtyping: instead of congruence w.r.t. *any* observable behavior, we restrict it to the *specified* behavior.[5] This relaxation renders behavioral subtyping more feasible in practice, as it allows more freedom in implementing unspecified behavior, in particular regarding exceptional cases. Consider, for instance, a class that implements a collection of integers. Is a collection of nonnegative integers a behavioral subtype?—The correct answer is 'maybe;' it depends on whether the operations that add members to the collection are sufficiently abstract to be implemented differently.

This notion of behavioral subtyping w.r.t. specified behavior also enables us to regard interfaces and abstract classes as behavioral supertypes of their implementations. While they do not provide a (complete) implementation themselves, they can be given a specification that is inherited to the implementing classes.

---

[4] Leavens and Naumann [2006] present a language-independent formalization of behavioral subtyping and prove that it is actually equivalent to supertype abstraction.

[5] Still, it is possible to explicitly specify the observable behavior in its entirety. On the other hand side, specification is slightly more expressive than program constructs. The reason for this is that specification can refer to the entire heap. For instance, the notions of weak purity and strong purity differ in whether objects may be freshly allocated. This difference is not observable programmatically. Yet, JML allows one to declare a method strictly pure or—more generally—to express the number of created objects. While strict purity annotations may simplify modular verification, it cannot be included in a behavioral interface specification since it reveals an implementation detail.

9.1.2 Example: Implementing a List

Consider we want to implement a mutable list of integers in Java. It should support the following operations: (i) adding an element at the front, (ii) removing the first entry, (iii) indicating whether it is empty, (iv) returning its size, (v) retrieving an element at a given position (random access).

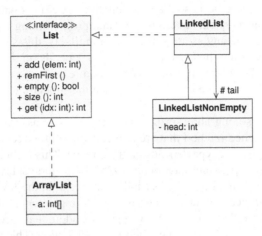

Figure 9.1 A list interface and its implementations

Figure 9.1 shows a UML class diagram with the interface List that provides the intended signature as public methods. There are multiple ways to implement this interface. The figure shows two possibilities attached via dashed triangle-headed arrows: firstly simply as an ArrayList and secondly using a variant of the *composite* design pattern by the classes LinkedList and LinkedListNonEmpty. The annotation on the association from LinkedList to LinkedListNonEmpty signifies that LinkedList contains a protected field of type LinkedListNonEmpty.

The list $[1, 2, 3]$ is represented in this design as follows (with squares for instances of class LinkedList and circles for instances of LinkedListNonEmpty):

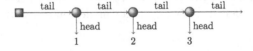

Note how the empty list is represented. This approach is called the *sentinel* pattern and prevents the **null** reference to be exposed.

An common alternative pattern for linked lists uses two classes Nil and Cons, where Nil is a singleton representing the empty list and Cons is a *sentinel*, that plays the same role as LinkedListNonEmpty in our example. This pattern is appropriate to implement *immutable* list objects. The disadvantage is that Nil and Cons are not (behavioral) subtypes of one or another.

Before looking at an implementation, let us briefly discuss contracts in natural language. The operation 'removing the first element' only makes sense when there is at least one element—this would make a precondition. Similarly, 'retrieving an element at position *n*' only makes sense if *n* is nonnegative and there are at least *n* elements in the list. Again, implementations are free to do anything if they are called in a context where these preconditions do not hold. Listing 9.1 shows an implementation of class `LinkedList`. Here, we see two different styles of method implementations. In Lines 11ff., method `remFirst()` silently returns directly if it is called on an empty list, i.e., the precondition is violated. Alternatively, we could first check for such violations and then throw a more precise exception explicitly. This style is known as *defensive* implementation, where the implementing code checks for and handles abnormal situations. In lines 24ff., method `get()` is implemented in an *offensive* manner. It does not check for abnormal situations, but optimistically calls `tail.get(idx)` where `tail` may be a `null` reference. In case the precondition is violated, an instance of `NullPointerException` will be thrown. Design by contract itself does not advertise either style, but in practice the latter is usually preferred.

```
 1 public class LinkedList implements List {
 2
 3     protected LinkedListNonEmpty tail;
 4
 5     public void add (int elem) {
 6         LinkedListNonEmpty tmp = new LinkedListNonEmpty(elem);
 7         tmp.tail = this.tail;
 8         this.tail = tmp;
 9     }
10
11     public void remFirst () {
12         if (empty()) return;
13         else tail = tail.tail;
14     }
15
16     public boolean empty () {
17         return tail == null;
18     }
19
20     public int size () {
21         return empty()? 0: tail.size();
22     }
23
24     public int get (int idx) {
25         return tail.get(idx);
26     }
27 }
```

Listing 9.1 An implementation to the `List` interface using a linked data structure

It is instructive to observe that most methods in `LinkedList` delegate to an element of the subclass `LinkedListNonEmpty`. This is possible since every (nonnull)

object in `LinkedListNonEmpty` represents a non empty list, while objects in the supertype `LinkedList` represent—*possibly empty* lists. This ensures that we have a behavioral subtype relation here. A nonempty linked list exposes at least the expected behavior of a possibly empty linked list. This allows for a maximum of reuse in class `LinkedListNonEmpty`, which is shown in Listing 9.2; only three methods need to be overridden.

Note that the default constructor of `LinkedList` returns a (nonunique) empty list.

```
1 class LinkedListNonEmpty extends LinkedList {
2
3     private int head;
4
5     LinkedListNonEmpty (int elem) { head = elem; }
6
7     public boolean empty () { return false; }
8
9     public int size () {
10        return 1+(tail==null? 0: tail.size());
11    }
12
13    public int get (int idx) {
14        if (idx == 0) return head;
15        else return tail.get(idx-1);
16    }
17 }
```

Listing 9.2 Nonempty lists is a behavioral subtype to lists

The implementation of `size` in lines 9ff in Figure 9.2 does not work for lists of length greater than $2^{31} - 1$. We will live with this imperfection rather than resort to using `BigInteger`.

The above list example will be used throughout the rest of this chapter. Notable other case studies covering single linked lists can be found in the literature [Zee et al., 2008, Gladisch and Tyszberowicz, 2013]. In [Bruns, 2011] the more general data type of maps is considered. Its specification uses model fields and dynamic frames and its implementation is based on red/black trees. This has been proposed as one of the challenges in [Leino and Moskal, 2010].

9.1.3 Modular Program Correctness

In this section we explain our understanding of modular program correctness in a spirit similar to and inspired by Müller [2002], Roth [2006]. Müller [2002] defines the concept of modular correctness by distinguishing *open programs* and *closed programs*. Open programs are intended to be used in different (not a priori known) contexts, like, for instance, library code. Closed programs are self-contained and not meant to be extended. When analyzing the correctness of a closed program, stronger assumptions can be made than for the analysis open programs; in particular, every object must be an instance of one of the types declared in the program under test which may not be a safe assumption if the program is used in an extending context.

We will define modular correctness by the portability of correctness proofs to program extensions. Before we can look at modular correctness, we need to fix the notion of a program extension. Remember that for the purposes of this book, a Java program is a collection of class and interface declarations.

Definition 9.1 (Program Extension). A Java program p' is called an extension of the Java program p, denoted by $p' \supseteq p$, if

1. p' is obtained from p by adding new class or interface declarations, *and*
2. the declarations obtained from p are in no way modified.

We stress that in passing from p to p' no field, method, **extends** or **implements** declarations of existing classes or interfaces may be added, modified or removed. On the other hand, classes in which are new in p' may implement interfaces or extend classes from p, and methods introduced in p may be overridden in new subclasses in p'.

The soundness of logical inferences in JavaDL may depend on the type system and thus on the investigated program. For example: it is sound to deduce from $instance_B(x) \doteq TRUE$ that $instance_A(x) \doteq TRUE$ if and only if the type hierarchy contains $B \sqsubseteq A$. However, there are also inference rules that are either independent of the program or resilient to a program extension.

Definition 9.2 (Modular soundness). Let p be a Java program.

A logical inference rule is called *modularly sound* for p if it is a sound inference rule for every program extension p' with $p' \supseteq p$.

A proof is called *modularly correct* for p if it has been conducted with only modularly sound inference rules.

Most rules in the JavaDL sequent calculus in KeY are independent of the type hierarchy of the program (rules of propositional logic, rules dealing with numbers, sequences, ...). Some rules depend on the type hierarchy but are modularly sound (like the removal of unnecessary type cast operations). Only very few rules of the calculus are *not* modularly sound. In their core, all of them rely on the principle of enumeration of all subtypes of a type declaration:

Let T be a type declaration in p and furthermore $\{U_1, \dots, U_k\} = \{U \mid U \sqsubseteq T$ and U is not abstract.$\}$ denote the set of nonabstract class declarations which extend T (directly or indirectly). The rule typeDist allows replacing an instance predicate $instance_T(x)$ by the disjunction over all possible exact instance predicates $exactInstance_{U_i}(x)$ of the subtypes.

$$instance_T(x) \rightsquigarrow exactInstance_{U_1}(x) \vee \dots \vee exactInstance_{U_k}(x) \qquad \text{typeDist}$$

In an extension, a new subclass U_{k+1} of T may be added rendering this rule unsound.

The rule methodCall defined in Section 3.6.5.5 is another rule that is not modularly sound based on the same principle of type enumeration. With it, a method call $o.\mathtt{m}()$ can be replaced by a type distinction over the dynamic type of o during symbolic execution, resulting in method-body statements $o.\mathtt{m}()@U_i$ enumerating the different overriding implementations of $\mathtt{m}()$. Again a new subclass with a new implementation breaks the rule's soundness.

It is evident from Definition 9.2 that a proof which is modularly correct for p can also be conducted in $p' \supseteq p$ without adaptation.

Definition 9.3 (Modular Correctness). Let p be a program and C a set of contracts (functional or dependency) for the declarations in p.

A program p is called *modular correct* if there exists a proof modularly correct for p for every proof obligation for $c \in C$.

Lemma 9.4. *Let $p, p' \supseteq p$ be programs and C a set of contracts for p and $C' \supseteq C$ a set of contracts for p' with $C'\big|_p = C$.*

If p is modularly correct and there exist proofs for all proof obligations in $p' \setminus p$ against C', then p' is correct.

This means that once a library has been proved modularly correct, it can be used in any context, and it suffices to prove the context correct against its contracts and the contracts of the library to obtain a correct composed program.

As a consequence of definition 9.3, modular correctness proofs may only contain method inlining for private or final methods which cannot be overridden. For general method inlining, it is up to the verifying person to decide if they want to conduct a proof for an open or for a closed program.

9.1.4 Verification of Recursive Methods

We turn now to the verification of recursive methods. The simplest version of a recursive method is a method that calls itself, a pattern often found in implementations of divide-and-conquer algorithms. Method get() in Listing 9.2, which retrieves the n-th element of a list, is a typical example.

The issue which sets recursive methods apart from normal methods is that when verifying their correctness, we are confronted with a situation that results in a circular proof dependency. Assume we are verifying the correctness of the previously mentioned get() method. During the verification we end up at the recursive method invocation tail.get(idx-1). How can we proceed now (and also maintain modular correctness)? Obviously applying the contract for this call of get introduces a circular proof dependency, we use a contract whose correctness depends on the contract currently been proven. Closely related, but not identical, is the topic of termination. Next to loops, recursive methods are the other source for nonterminating programs.

One note of caution, in KeY we are oblivious to the method frame stack size. Hence, for instance, a partial correctness proof for a contract requiring a method not to terminate with an exception may succeed even though a StackOverflowError would be thrown in real life. In other words, when verifying a Java program, *we are only correct under the assumption that no concrete run of the program causes a StackOverflowError to be thrown by the virtual machine.*

In case of partial correctness the introduced proof dependency does not pose any problem and we can apply the contract for the method, as already observed by Hoare [1971]. Intuitively, that is sound for the following reason: When symbolically executing the method, we explore all paths that do not lead to a recursive call, i.e., all base cases are covered. Paths with recursive calls can then simply use the contract performing the step cases from $n + 1$ recursive invocations to n invocations. The only problem is when the recursion is not well-founded, which would lead to an infinite recursion. But in case of partial correctness, the validity of the contract is then a triviality.

Let us turn to the case of total correctness. Its solution is similar to the treatment of termination in loops: the user has to supply an expression as part of the method contract which we call a *termination witness*. A termination witness is always nonnegative and strictly decreasing with each call. In JML a termination witness is specified using the keyword measured_by, see also Section 8.2.

Example 9.5. A call get(idx) of the get() method from Listing 9.2 retrieves the idx-th element of the list as follows: if the argument's idx value is 0 then the value at the current list element is returned otherwise the method recursively retrieves the (idx-1)-th element of the tail of the list. A reasonable choice for the termination witness is the argument itself, namely,

     @ measured_by idx;

which is obviously strictly decreased at each recursive call together with the precondition that the value of idx must be nonnegative it follows directly that at each recursive call site the value is strictly decreased and nonnegative.

In the process of verifying a recursive method the value of the termination witness is captured by an equation in the prestate. When we then apply the contract we are just about to prove, we have as part of the precondition to show that the value of the termination witness is nonnegative and less than the captured value of the prestate. This additional preconditions ensures well-foundedness w.r.t. the proof dependencies.

When the user or the system applies a method contract it should be clear if it is a recursive method or not. How is this checked? The detection is trivial for the examples above as we have a direct recursion. But what about mutual recursions or what if an extension adds an (indirect) recursion—how do we maintain correctness in such situations? The solutions is to track the contracts used in a proof. When applying the method contract rule, the system checks if there exists a proof for the contract depending (directly or indirectly) on the proof obligation we are currently verifying. If a dependency is detected, the system allows the application of the contract rule only if the contract in question is equipped with a measured_by clause and upon contract application we require to show that the value of that expression is strictly less than in the initial state of the current method. Thus, circular reasoning is avoided:

Either the dependency is unidirectional or the termination witness guarantees well-foundedness.

We conclude this section with some words on the expressiveness of termination witnesses and loop variants. In the above examples the termination witnesses are always strictly decreasing integer expressions with lower bound 0. The KeY system also allows the declaration of termination witnesses and loop variants of other data types. The binary JavaDL predicate symbol $\prec: \top \times \top$ used in termination proofs is axiomatized as a well-founded (Noetherian) relation. Besides supporting integers, KeY comes with built-in axioms for lexicographic ordering of pairs and finite sequences. One may, e.g., use the declaration `measured_by i, j;` with integer expressions `i` and `j`. This will be interpreted as the lexicographical ordering of pairs (i, j). In this case the definition of $\prec$ requires to show that either i has decreased strictly (while remaining nonnegative) or that i did not change and instead j has been strictly decreased, i.e., $(i_1, j_1) \prec (i_2, j_2)$ iff $i_1 \prec i_2 \vee (i_1 = i_2 \wedge j_1 \prec j_2)$. The relation $\prec$ can be extended to other data types, but it is then the user's responsibility that the axiomatization guarantees that $\prec$ is well-founded.

9.2 Abstract Specification

Specifications in JML are relatively close to the implementation in comparison to other specification mechanisms like OCL or Z that operate on abstract data. But even if specification refer to implementation entities at source code level, abstraction and modularization are indispensable for handling larger programs. Consider, for instance, the interface `List` again. We have not yet stated specifications for its methods. Our goal is to provide an interface specification that is amenable to *modular* specification and verification, i.e., one which is robust to extensions of the implementation. This puts us in a dilemma since such a specification must speak for parts of the software which are not yet there but may be added in an extension. Therefore, it must not expose implementation details.

A common approach is to use *pure methods* in specifications, see [Gladisch and Tyszberowicz, 2013]. Listing 9.3 shows the example of the `List` interface, specified using pure query methods. We can specify the behavior of all methods using the two pure methods `size()` and `get()`. The query `empty()` checks is a list is empty, which is true if its size (returned by the query `size()`) is zero. In the same way, the specification of `add()` uses the pure method `get()`: The observable effect of adding an element is that it can be retrieved again at the last position of the list, and that the elements at all other positions of the list remain unchanged. Using queries in specifications requires that every impure method lists the changes to all relevant queries in its postcondition. The abstract value of a `List` object is thus 'distributed' over the two queries `get()` and `size()`.

Often it is more convenient for the specifier, however, if the abstract object state is not only available through these methods but as an explicit artifact that can be handled effectively.

```
1  public interface List {
2
3      //@ public invariant size() >= 0;
4
5      /*@ public normal_behavior
6        @ ensures size() == \old(size()) + 1;
7        @ ensures get(\old(size)) == elem;
8        @ ensures (\forall int i; 1 <= i && i < size()-1;
9        @                          get(i) == \old(get(i-1)));
10       @*/
11      public void add (int elem);
12
13      /*@ public normal_behavior
14        @ requires !empty();
15        @ ensures size() == \old(size()) - 1;
16        @ ensures (\forall int i; 0 <= i && i < size();
17        @                          get(i) == \old(get(i+1)));
18       @*/
19      public void remFirst ();
20
21      /*@ public normal_behavior
22        @ ensures \result == (size() == 0);
23        @*/
24      public /*@ pure @*/ boolean empty ();
25
26      /*@ public normal_behavior
27        @ requires 0 <= idx && idx < size();
28        @*/
29      public /*@ pure @*/ int get (int idx);
30
31      public /*@ pure @*/ int size ();
32  }
```

Listing 9.3 Java interface List specified using pure methods

To this end, JML offers model fields and model methods as specification-only abstract representations of concrete implementation data; they have already been introduced briefly in Section 7.7.1, These mechanisms enable implementation hiding: the requirement specification only refers to model fields while the abstraction relation is part of the (hidden) implementation details. We will discuss model fields in Section 9.2.1 and the more general concept of model methods in Section 9.2.2 below in depth. Both concepts are deliberately close to actual Java (both syntactically and semantically), which makes them more comprehensible for Java programmers.

It is natural to represent the abstract state of an instance of the interface List as a finite sequence, and we will use the abstract data type (ADT) \seq introduced in Section 8.1.3 for this purpose. \seq is an algebraic data type (a primitive data type in Java terms). It comprises constructors for 1. empty sequence, 2. singleton sequences, 3. sequence concatenation, 4. subsequences, and 5. comprehension, and has random access and length observer functions. See Section 5.2 for details on the corresponding theory in JavaDL.

Example 9.6. Assume that the contents of a list can be abstracted to a \seq representation of the list and that the entity theList holds this abstract value. Then we can describe the addition of an element (as new first element of the list) as a concatenation of a singleton sequence and the prestate sequence:

—— JML ——————————————————————————————

```
/*@ public normal_behavior
  @ ensures theList ==
  @       \seq_concat(\seq_singleton(elem),\old(theList));
  @*/
public void add (int elem);
```

—————————————————————————————————— JML ——

Analogously, the other modification methods can be specified using sequence operations. The remaining question is: what type of program entity does the identifier theList refer to in this example? Or, how does this ADT representation integrate into the specification? One solution is to use model fields, as explained in the following.

9.2.1 Model Fields

Based on the idea of *abstract variables* by Hoare [1972], JML provides model fields [Leino and Nelson, 2002] as a means of abstraction from the concrete program state in a syntactically convenient form (i.e., as fields in a class; see also Section 7.7.1). Together with modeling-only types such as sequences, model fields allow us to give abstract interface specifications.

It is not possible to assign values to model fields, they do not have a proper, modifiable state space of their own, but they *observe* the state space spanned by heap memory by *computing* a value from values on the heap. The relation between a model field and the state, i.e., the abstraction relation, is specified through *represents clauses*. A model field can be defined by a functional relation where the field's name is followed by the assignment operator = and an expression compatible with the type of the model field. A more general relational form is also available and uses the keyword \such_that followed by a Boolean expression. Model field definitions may refer to Java entities as well as to other specification-only entities like other model fields. In general, the abstraction relation needs not be total, i.e., not every concrete object needs to possess an abstract value. For instance, the model field x defined via represents x = x+1 has an empty abstraction relation; no instance has an abstract value.

We will use the term *concrete field* to denote both Java fields and JML ghost fields (see Section 7.7.2) in order to distinguish them from model fields. Even though model fields syntactically resemble concrete fields, their semantics is closer to methods. The model field declaration corresponds to a method declaration as the public interface and the represents clause corresponds to an implementation. If model fields have publicly observable properties, they need to be specified in class invariants. In contrast, ghost fields behave like 'real' Java fields that can only be used within the specification.

9.2.1.1 Example: List Specification with Model Fields

To specify the abstract behavior of the List interface, we introduce a model field theList as shown in Listing 9.4. It is a member of this interface and can be referred to in specifications like a concrete Java field Model fields declared in classes are instance members by default as for concrete fields. Model fields declared in interfaces are class members by default. This can be overridden by the modifier instance.

Now all operations declared on lists can be specified in terms of this model field. For instance, the postcondition to method add() on line 4 in Listing 9.4 states that an element is added to the front of the sequence, or more precisely that the sequence in the poststate is a concatenation of the singleton sequence containing the element with the sequence in the prestate.

Note that the two queries get() and size() which were basic operations in the query-based specification in Listing 9.3 are now also specified in terms of the model field. Thanks to the abstract data type, this specification is very concise and intuitive.

In the concrete implementations of the interface, a represents clause specifies the abstraction relation. Listing 9.5 shows an implementation of ArrayList, which internally uses an array to store the list elements. The add and remFirst methods increase/decrease the size every time and copy all elements one place to the right/left. This is not very efficient, but serves its demonstrative purpose here. The model field is represented by the elements of the array (as a sequence):

```
represents theList = (\seq_def int i; 0; size; a[i]);
```

Now that we have a working implementation for List, we can verify the methods in ArrayList against the abstract contracts given in List and linked through the represents clause for theList. Given adequate loop invariants for add/remFirst, all method implementations can be verified completely automatically with KeY. We turn our attention to the second implementation of the List interface through the class LinkedList in Listing 9.1. Here we need a *recursive* represents clause i.e., a represents clause that refers to the same model field theList again.

A list's abstract value is defined by the tail's model field's value—or the empty sequence if tail is a null reference. This leads to the following represents clause in class LinkedList

```
represents theList = tail==null? \seq_empty: tail.theList;
```

```
1  public interface List {
2      //@ public instance model \seq theList;
3
4      /*@ public normal_behavior {}
5      @ ensures theList == \seq_concat(\seq_singleton(elem),
6      @                                \old(theList));
7      @*/
8      public void add (int elem);
9
10     /*@ public normal_behavior
11     @ requires !empty();
12     @ ensures theList == \old(theList[1..theList.length]);
13     @*/
14     public void remFirst ();
15
16     /*@ public normal_behavior
17     @ ensures \result == (size() == 0);
18     @*/
19     public /*@ pure @*/ boolean empty ();
20
21     /*@ public normal_behavior
22     @ ensures \result == theList.length;
23     @*/
24     public /*@ pure @*/ int size ();
25
26     /*@ public normal_behavior
27     @ requires 0 <= idx && idx < size();
28     @ ensures \result == (int)theList[idx];
29     @*/
30     public /*@ pure @*/ int get (int idx);
31 }
```

Listing 9.4 Interface specification using a model field

This is *overridden* by

—— Java + JML ————————————————————————————————————

```
class LinkedListNonEmpty {
    ⋮
    /*@ private represents theList =
    @        \seq_concat( \seq_singleton(head),
    @                     tail==null? \seq_empty: tail.theList);
    @*/
}
```

————————————————————————————————————— Java + JML ——

in the subclass LinkedListNonEmpty. It is here that the head attribute is available.

```
1  public final class ArrayList implements List {
2
3      private int[] a = new int[0];
4      /*@ private represents theList =
5       @      (\seq_def int i; 0; a.length; a[i]);
6       @*/
7
8      public void add (int elem) {
9          int[] tmp = new int[a.length+1];
10         /*@ maintaining 0 <= i && i <= a.length;
11          @ maintaining (\forall int j; i < j && j <= a.length;
12          @                     tmp[j] == \old(a[j-1]));
13          @ decreasing i;
14          @ assignable tmp[*];
15          @*/
16         for (int i= a.length; i > 0; i--)
17             tmp[i] = a[i-1];
18         a = tmp;
19         a[0] = elem;
20     }
21
22     public void remFirst () {
23         int[] tmp = new int[a.length-1];
24         /*@ maintaining 0 < i && i <= a.length;
25          @ maintaining (\forall int j; 0 < j && j < i;
26          @                     tmp[j-1] == \old(a[j]));
27          @ decreasing a.length - i;
28          @ assignable tmp[*];
29          @*/
30         for (int i= 1; i < a.length; i++)
31             tmp[i-1] = a[i];
32         a = tmp;
33     }
34
35     public boolean empty () {
36         return size() == 0;
37     }
38
39     public int size () {
40         return a.length;
41     }
42
43     public int get (int idx) {
44         return a[idx];
45     }
46 }
```

Listing 9.5 ArrayList implementation of the List interface

9.2.1.2 Semantics of Model Fields

The semantics of model field is given by a set of logical axioms that arise canonically from the represents clauses [Weiß, 2011]. In JavaDL terms, model fields (as well as calls to pure methods) are represented by *observer symbols* (called *location dependent symbols* by Beckert et al. [2007], Bubel [2007]). The intuition is that they 'observe' a set of locations on the heap and compute a value from them. The parameters differ between the different kinds of observer symbols; model fields have the heap and the receiver object as sole arguments[6]. Boolean model fields are translated to observer predicates, model fields of all other types become observer functions.

Definition 9.7 (Observer symbol). An *observer symbol* is either a function symbol $f : Heap^k \times T \times A_1 \times \cdots \times A_n \to A' \in \text{FSym}$ or a predicate symbol $p : Heap^k \times T \times A_1 \times \cdots \times A_n \in \text{PSym}$ where $T \sqsubseteq \text{Object}$ and $k, n \in \mathbb{N}$, $k \geq 1$.

Observer symbols formalize heap-dependent functions, hence, all have in common that they take one or more parameters of type *Heap* .

The fundamental difference between regular Java fields and JML model fields becomes apparent when their translations to JavaDL are compared; which will be done here by an illustrative example:

Example 9.8. Consider the class fragment

—— Java + JML ——————————————————————————————————————

```
class C {
  int f;
  //@ model int mf;
}
```
——————————————————————————————————————— Java + JML ——

in which a regular Java field f and a model field mf are declared. If c is a variable of type C, then the field references are translated to JavaDL as follows (remember from Section 8.1 that $\lfloor \cdot \rfloor$ is the translation from JML to JavaDL):

$$\lfloor \texttt{c.f} \rfloor = select_{int}(\texttt{heap}, \lfloor \texttt{c} \rfloor, \texttt{C::f})$$
$$\lfloor \texttt{c.mf} \rfloor = \texttt{C::mf}(\texttt{heap}, \lfloor \texttt{c} \rfloor)$$

While the one access c.f becomes a heap read access, the other c.mf is translated into an application of the according observer symbol. We silently omit the class prefix from the verbose symbol names C::f and C::mf and use f and mf in the following if the context is clear.

Do not confuse concrete fields and model fields: To make proof obligations more legible in KeY, the pretty printing mechanisms are the same for both expressions, yielding the seemingly structurally equal terms $c.f$ and $c.mf$ in the logic. If the heap in which the fields are evaluated is not the default heap, but a term h, then the accesses read $c.f@h$ and $c.mf@h$.

---

[6] Without loss of generality, we only cover *instance* observers here. The static case is similar, only lacking the receiver object parameter.

Observer symbols are the entities that carry the value of model fields, however the value returned by them is not constrained yet. It is the represents clause for the model field which provides this constraint on the side of JML. Two types of represents clauses were introduced in Section 9.2.1, functional and relational. To ease the presentation in this section, we regard a functional clause `represents mf = def` as a shorthand for the general relational form `represents mf \such_that mf == def`. The defining represents clauses give rise to JavaDL axioms thus fixing the meaning of the observer symbols.

Definition 9.9 (Represents axiom). Let $m : Heap \times C \to A \in$ FSym be an observer function[7] symbol representing a model field m defined in type T. Let `represents` m `\such_that` rep be the definition of m in type $T' \sqsubseteq T$. The *represents axiom* is the formula

$$\forall Heap\ h; \forall T'\ o; \big(exactInstance_{T'}(o) \doteq TRUE \to$$
$$\{\texttt{self} := o \,\|\, \texttt{heap} := h\}(\text{inRange}_A(m(h,o)) \land \lfloor rep \rfloor)\big) \quad (9.1)$$

where `self` $\in$ PVar is the program variable to which `this` is translated in JavaDL.

The type restriction $\text{inRange}_A(m(h,o))$ ensures that the model field's value is always valid and not an unallocated object or an integer out of range.

Example 9.10. Consider the class fragment of Example 9.8; now augmented by the JML clause

```
//@ represents mf = f;
```

which binds the value of the model field `mf` directly to that of the Java field f. Whenever $c.f$ changes for an object c of type C, the value $c.mf$ silently changes as well. In the logic, this coupling is fixed in a represents axiom which is equivalent to

$$\forall Heap\ h; \forall C\ c;\ exactInstance_C(c) \doteq TRUE \to mf(h,c) \doteq select_{int}(h,c,\texttt{f})\ .$$

This axiom cannot compromise consistency of the logic since it provides a definition for the symbol *mf* in form of a conservative extension.

In general, represents axioms need not be conservative extensions and may introduce inconsistencies. Keep in mind that with an unsatisfiable axiom any statement— even "false"—can be proved valid.

KeY provides some measures to prevent the introduction of most obvious contradictory represent axioms. As a first measure against unsatisfiability, Weiß [2011] proposes to restrict the represent axiom to situations where $\lfloor rep \rfloor$ is satisfiable, i.e., axiom (9.1) is replaced by the conditional formula

---

[7] If m is a Boolean model field, it is represented by a observer predicate symbol $m : Heap \times T \in$ PSym instead of a function symbol. The definition remains the same.

$\forall Heap\ h; \forall T'\ o;\ \big(exactInstance_{T'}(o) \doteq TRUE\ \wedge$

$$(\exists R\ r; \{\texttt{self} := o \,\|\, \texttt{heap} := h\} \lfloor rep[\texttt{self}.\texttt{m}/r]\rfloor) \rightarrow$$

$$\{\texttt{self} := o \,\|\, \texttt{heap} := h\}(\text{inRange}_A(m(h,o)) \wedge m(h,o) \doteq \lfloor rep\rfloor)\big) \quad (9.2)$$

in which $rep[\texttt{self}.\texttt{m}/r]$ denotes the represents clause in which every occurrence of the model field m is replaced by the quantified variable r of type R which is the value type of the model field. This prevents that represents clauses like **represents** m \such_that m!=m lead to immediate inconsistencies. The value of $m(h,o)$ is defined only if the represents clause is satisfiable—and it remains underspecified if rep is not satisfiable.

Not only relational represents clauses can be unsatisfiable, also a functional clause can be unsatisfiable if it employs nonprimitive recursion, like, e.g., in **represents** m = m+1. However, the guard introduced in (9.2) can only guarantee *local satisfiability* for individual clauses. It may still occur that multiple represents clauses contradict each other. In particular, a contradiction may arise from mutually recursive represents clauses. Consider, e.g., a case with two int fields x and y with the two represents clauses **represents** x \such_that x > y and **represents** y \such_that y > x, in which the values of x and y mutually depend on each other. Both are obviously satisfiable on their own, but their conjunction is not. Later in this chapter, we will explain how to deal with recursive represents clauses in order to further mitigate the issue of unsatisfiability.

If inconsistencies are brought into the system through represents clauses, this is not a soundness issue of the calculus. The axioms are part of the specification and thus reflect the intention of the specifier to whom it is up to account for his or her axioms. This is a very liberal view on the matter with one important consequence: When reviewing the specification of a program, it is vital to inspect *all* represents clauses annotated to the program since they may introduce inconsistencies into the specification rendering it entirely worthless. As we will see later in Section 9.2.2.3 a different decision has been taken for the semantics of model methods: Their (possible recursive) computation must always terminate, the functions they define are thus always consistent conservative extensions.

9.2.1.3 A Model Field for Class Invariants

There is one model field which receives special treatment and is considered "built in" by the KeY system: It is called \inv, of type **boolean**, and declared in class Object. This model field is used to model class invariants (also called object invariants, see also Section 7.4.1 on how to use them in JML). The KeY dialect of JML deliberately deviates from standard JML semantics in this respect because the model field formalization integrates better with the dynamic frames approach taken by KeY (which is explained in the upcoming Section 9.3).

Standard JML implements the *visible state semantics* for class invariants which requires that the invariants of an object o must hold in a state s if s is a poststate of a constructor call on o, if s is a pre- or poststate of a method call on o, or if no call on

o is in progress. This allows invariants to be broken temporarily, as long as a method is in the process of being executed on the object for which the invariant is broken.

The problem with this definition is that the set of methods being executed when entering m is not a property of m itself, or the current heap state. Rather, it is a property of a particular call to m. A modular verification attempt of m independently of the rest of the program is not able to know which other methods are already on the call stack when entering m. Thus, the only invariants that can safely be assumed to hold in the beginning are the invariants of the receiver object **this** which is a very weak, often insufficient assumption. This problem can be mitigated by means of combining visible states with ownership approaches, a few of which are listed in Section 9.6.

In KeY-JML specifications have to state explicitly which object invariants are expected to be satisfied using the (standard JML) keyword \invariant_for. Only the invariant for the receiver object **this** of a method is by default implied by both precondition and postcondition of a method (see Section 8.2.1.2).

Note that, to formulate that the invariant of object o holds, two equivalent notations can be used: o.\inv is the same as \invariant_for(o) (while only the latter is defined in standard JML).

All calculus rules which are applicable to model field apply to \inv as well. However, the definition of invariants works differently and this allows more modular inference rules. Both advanced aspects are explained in Section 9.4.5.

9.2.1.4 Calculus Rules for Model Fields

Like the other kinds of axiom, the axioms generated from represents clauses can also be expressed as rules instead of as formulas. For every class D that declares a represents clause *rep* for a model field m the following rule $rep_{D,m}$ is available.

$$\frac{\Gamma,\ exactInstance_D(d) \doteq TRUE,\ \{heap := h \,\|\, self := d\}rep \implies \Delta}{\Gamma,\ exactInstance_D(d) \doteq TRUE \implies \Delta}\ rep_{D,m}$$

Even though rule $rep_{D,m}$ can be applied to any sequents with $exactInstance_D(d) \doteq TRUE$ in the antecedent, the application in KeY is triggered by an occurrence of an application $m(h,d)$ of the observer symbol m on either side of the sequent. Because the rule matches against d being an *exact* instance of class D, there is at most one applicable rule. The rule is an obvious adaptation of the represents axiom (9.3) in Definition 9.9.

For functional clauses of the form **represents** m = *def*, we can also use the conditional rewriting rule repSimple$_{D,m}$

$$m(h,d) \rightsquigarrow \{heap := h \,\|\, self := d\}def$$
$$\text{if } exactInstance_D(d) \doteq TRUE \implies \text{on the sequent.}$$

The rule repSimple$_{D,m}$ allows replacing references to a model field by its definition *def* directly. This is more efficient in practice than adding an equation to the antecedent. Applying repSimple$_{D,m}$ repeatedly to a recursively defined model field would result in a infinite expansion of the proof sequent. The proof strategy in KeY is designed to apply recursive definitions very sparsely and only up to a certain depth to avoid infinite recursion expansion.

The type restriction from Definition 9.9 is not represented in these rules. Instead, there is a separate rule

$$\frac{\Gamma, \mathsf{inRange}_A(m(h,d)) \Longrightarrow \Delta}{\Gamma \Longrightarrow \Delta} \;\; \mathsf{OnlyCreatedObjectsObserved}$$

that can be applied whenever the observer symbol $\mathsf{m}(h,d)$ of type A appears in the sequent $\Gamma \Longrightarrow \Delta$.

KeY offers a taclet option modelFields : showSatisfiability (see p. 530 for details on taclet options) to control whether local satisfiability is to be checked upon using a represents clause. If this option is activated, the rules rep/repSimple have an additional premiss implementing the existential quantifier from (9.2). Proving local satisfiability usually makes proofs more complicated. Moreover, as mentioned earlier, local satisfiability is only an heuristic measure that cannot always guarantee consistency.

9.2.1.5 Discussion

Model fields are a powerful and often welcome specification instrument. It is however debatable whether general nonfunctional model fields may not create more problems than they solve.

For consistency one would have to prove simultaneous satisfiability of all represents clauses in the system. This is currently not enforced in KeY, it is not modular, and one may doubt whether that will ever be practical. Thus, the responsibility to work with a consistent set of axioms rests on the specifier. A theoretical alternative is presented in [Beckert and Bruns, 2012] that evaluates all model fields simultaneously and checks for *global* satisfiability of represents clauses. It avoids inconsistencies in the logic through underspecification. The practicality of this approach is under investigation. For model methods consistency must always be shown by means of termination witnesses (see Section 9.2.2.3).

In case of generalized relational \such_that represent clauses, there may be more than one possible value. But, since model fields are represented by functions in the logic, evaluation is deterministic and only depends on the heap and the receiver. to a model field. When the model field is evaluated several times in the same heap, it has the same value. In particular, classical logic equations like $m(heap, o) \doteq m(heap, o)$ are still valid. If the heap changes slightly, the model field value may be different. Dependency contract rules (see Section 9.4.4) can be used to prove that its value stays the same if it does not depend on the changed fields.

Using objects of reference type for abstract object states is problematic since they must point to objects that exist on the concrete heap. This means that represents axioms may postulate the existence of such object, which is another source of potential inconsistency.

From our experience, we recommend to use functional represents clauses only.

9.2.2 Model Methods

In JML expressions, one can not only refer to fields but also to invocations of pure methods. Moreover, JML allows the definition of model methods which are—quite analogous to model fields—method declarations to be used in specifications only. Like model fields, model methods do not reside in locations on the heap but compute a value which *depends* on the values of locations on the heap—they are observer symbols.

As pointed out by Mostowski and Ulbrich [2015, 2016], JML model methods are a generalization of JML model *fields* and go beyond them in several respects:

1. They are parametric, i.e., they can take arguments like Java methods.
2. Method contracts can be specified for model methods like for Java methods.
3. Model methods can be used to abstract from expressions which are evaluated in more than one state (so called *two-state predicates*).
4. Model methods always define conservative extensions. Their definition is given by a constructive method body, and they are required to always terminate (`diverges false`). This implies that their definitions are well-founded and no inconsistencies are introduced.

A JML model method and its contract are stated like all other JML constructs within special JML comments. A model method definition in KeY follows the following general schema (all clauses in [...] are optional)

```
class C {
  /*@ model_behavior8
    @    [requires pre;]
    @    [ensures post;]
    @    [accessible acc;]
    @    [measured_by mby;]
    @    [two_state] [no_state]
    @ model R m(T1 p1, ..., Tn pn) {
    @       return exp;
    @ }
    @*/
}
```

This pattern allows only for those model methods whose body consists of a single return statement, a restriction which simplifies the treatment of a model method in the logical context as it avoids the evaluation of the method body using a JavaDL modality. Later in this section, we will see that the concept of model methods can be generalized to method bodies with real control flow, but the presentation in this section and the implementation in KeY follow the above pattern.

As for pure Java methods and for JML model fields, a model method declaration gives rise to an observer symbol (see Definition 9.7) in JavaDL. For the above declaration, a observer function symbol C::m is introduced to represent the model

---

[8] The keyword `model_behavior` is not strictly required but the specifier is encouraged to use it.

method in JavaDL. Leaving aside the two-state modifier for the moment, its signature is C::m : $Heap \times C \times T_1 \times \ldots \times T_n \to R$.

Semantically, the evaluation of a model method invocation is coupled to the expression *exp* in the **return** statement by the following definition axiom which refines the general represents axiom (9.1) for observer symbols from Definition 9.9:

$$\forall Heap \text{ heap}, C \text{ self}, T_1 \ p_1, \ldots, T_n \ p_n;$$
$$exactInstance_C(\text{self}) \doteq TRUE \wedge \lfloor pre \rfloor \to$$
$$\text{C::m}(\text{heap}, \text{self}, p_1, \ldots, p_n) \doteq \lfloor exp \rfloor) \quad (9.3)$$

The formula, as shown, violates the JavaDL restriction that program variables, in this case heap and self, cannot be quantified. But, to make formulas in this section more readable, we take the liberty to write $\forall Heap \text{ heap}; \varphi$ as an abbreviation for the formula $\forall Heap \ h; \{\text{heap} := h\}\varphi$.

The function symbol C::m is determined by the class (or interface) C in which the method m has been first declared. All method definitions overriding that initial declaration refer to the same function symbol (and not to a new symbol). Constraining the same function symbol thus realizes the dynamic dispatch of model methods. That is, the function symbol is always the same, while its meaning is implied by the exact type of self changes.

For a subclass C' of C overriding m, another axiom of shape (9.3) is added for C::m, with the typing guard changed to $exactInstance_{C'}(c) \doteq TRUE$. If C' chooses not to override m, an axiom is added as if the definition with the body of the superclass-method had been repeated, which matches programmers' expectations as it is the same behavior as for Java method declarations. The guards $exactInstance_{C'}(\text{self}) \doteq TRUE$ ensure that the definition only applies if the receiver object self is *exactly* of the defining type. These typing guards make sure that (possibly contradicting) definitions of C::m constrain different parts of its domain and that definitions are not automatically inherited. Unlike model fields, the definition of model methods may be additionally constrained by a precondition. It is not strictly necessary to restrict the domain in which C::m can be applied, but we decided that it is better to allow a specifier to say when a model method is defined. Also to deal with the well-definedness and well-foundedness (see Section 9.2.2.3), it is important to limit the definition to those situations for which it is well-defined.

Since our model method body (see above) consists only of a single side-effect-free **return** statement, definition (9.3) can make use of its expression directly. If a one-state model method *did* have a nontrivial method body, the above axiom would need to involve a dynamic logic operator and read

$$\forall Heap \text{ heap}, C \text{ self}, T_1 \ p_1, \ldots, T_n \ p_n;$$
$$\left(exactInstance_C(\text{self}) \doteq TRUE \wedge \lfloor pre \rfloor \to \right.$$
$$\left. [\text{res} = \text{self.m}(p_1, \ldots, p_n);] (\text{C::m}(\text{heap}, \text{self}, p_1, \ldots, p_n) \doteq \text{res}) \right) ,$$

ensuring that the value of the function symbol is the same as the result value of the method call. This formula points out a crucial advantage of dynamic logic in comparison to other program logics like wp-calculus or Hoare calculus: dynamic logic is closed under all its operators which allows us to state the quantified program formula directly in JavaDL, and not on a meta-level. The dynamic logic thus also allows us to seamlessly extend the presented approach to nonmodel queries.

Besides its method body, a model method may also have a functional contract (in its postcondition). Unlike the body which *defines* the value of the function symbol, the contract *describes a property* of the symbol and is not an axiom, but a theorem. To establish the correctness of the contract theorem, it suffices to prove that the definition makes the postcondition true, i.e., that

$$\forall Heap\ \mathtt{heap}, C\ \mathtt{self}, T_1\ p_1, \ldots, T_n\ p_n;$$
$$(exactInstance_C(\mathtt{self}) \doteq TRUE \wedge \lfloor pre \rfloor \rightarrow$$
$$\{\mathtt{res} := C\mathtt{::m}(\mathtt{heap}, \mathtt{self}, p_1, \ldots, p_n)\} \lfloor post \rfloor) . \quad (9.4)$$

follows from axiom (9.3). If (9.4) is shown for every class C' extending C (with a corresponding type guard), the statement is shown for all conceivable instances of C. Therefore, when using the proved contract as additional assumption, it is save to omit the type guard $exactInstance_C(\mathtt{self}) \doteq TRUE$ from (9.4). This approach is still modular, however: The verification of C happens independently of that of its subclasses. At the time of verification, one can even be oblivious to the existence of subtypes.

The properties of model fields cannot be specified in contracts, they need to be captured in class invariants. Model method contracts have one crucial modularization advantage over formalizing properties in invariants: While the former are proved once and for all in a separate proof obligation, the latter need to be reproved whenever the invariant needs to be reestablished.

9.2.2.1 Two-State Model Methods

As has been mentioned before, the expressive power of model methods goes beyond that of Java methods and model fields in that more than one state can be referred to from a method body or contract. The number of accessible heaps is not limited in theory, but in practice three types of model methods have proved useful:

- *No-state model methods* can be used to formalize mathematical statements which are not heap-dependent at all. A query which checks if a sequence (of type `\seq`) is duplicate-free would be an example for a no-state model method. In KeY the JML modifier `no_state` can be used to mark a model method heap-independent.
- *One-state model methods* are like regular Java methods or model fields bound to a single evaluation context. This is the default if no state modifier is annotated to the method

- *Two-state model methods* are evaluated in two evaluation contexts. They are valuable where two-state predicates need to be specified which formalize the relationship between the before- and the after-state of an operation. In KeY-JML, two state. methods are annotated with the modifier `two_state`.

No-state model methods are not really observer functions since they do explicitly not dependent on the heap. Two-state model methods, however, are observers that receive *two* heap arguments ($k = 2$ in Definition 9.7). We show how the representation axiom (9.3) needs to be adapted to the two-state case; the other conditions are analogous.

$$\forall Heap \text{ heap}, Heap \text{ heap}_2, C \text{ self}, T_1 \ p_1, \ldots, T_n \ p_n;$$
$$(exactInstance_C(\texttt{self}) \doteq TRUE \wedge \lfloor pre \rfloor \rightarrow$$
$$\texttt{C::m(heap,heap}_2,\texttt{self},p_1,\ldots,p_n) \doteq \{\text{heap}^{pre} := \text{heap}_2\} \lfloor exp \rfloor) \quad (9.5)$$

The second heap heap_2 is thus automatically mapped to the prestate heap which is accessed from JML via the `\old` operator.

The translation of a reference to a two-state model method in JML to JavaDL remains to be defined. This extends the translation outlined in Section 8.1.2.4 such that we have for a one-state model method *osm* and a two-state model method *tsm* defined in class C that

$$\lfloor o.\texttt{osm}(p_1,\ldots,p_n) \rfloor = \texttt{C::osm(heap}, \lfloor o \rfloor, \lfloor p_1 \rfloor, \ldots, \lfloor p_n \rfloor)$$
$$\lfloor o.\texttt{tsm}(p_1,\ldots,p_n) \rfloor = \texttt{C::tsm(heap,heap}^{pre}, \lfloor o \rfloor, \lfloor p_1 \rfloor, \ldots, \lfloor p_n \rfloor) \ .$$

Note how the heap arguments need not be specified in the JML specification but are added during the translation. The second heap heap_2 is automatically mapped to the prestate heap heap^{pre}.

Example 9.11. Consider the program given in Listing 9.4 once more. To showcase a very simple application scenario for two-state model methods, assume that the specifier wants to capture the difference in the length of the abstraction between before and after an operation into a model method `sizeDiff()`:

```
—— JML ————————————————————————————————————
  /*@ model two_state int sizeDiff() {
  @    return theList.length - \old(theList.length);
  @ }
  @*/


  /*@ normal_behavior
  @ ensures sizeDiff() == 1;
  @*/
  void add(Object o);
————————————————————————————————————— JML ——
```

```
class Cell {                          class Recell extends Cell {
  int val;                              int oval;

  /*@ ensures \result == val; @*/       /*@ ensures val == oval; @*/
  int /*@ pure @*/ get() {              void undo() {
    return val;                           val = oval;
  }                                     }

  /*@ ensures val == v; @*/             /*@ ensures oval==\old(val); @*/
  void set(int v) {                     void set(int v) {
    val = v;                              oval = val;
  }                                       super.set(v);
}                                       }

class Client {                        }
  /*@ ensures c.val == v; @*/
  static void callSet(Cell c,int v){
    c.set(v);
  }
}
```

Figure 9.2 Listings of Cell/Recell example

Note how \old is used to refer canonically to the second heap.

Using such two-state model methods makes obviously only sense when the model method is only invoked (referred to) in places where two states are imminently present: for instance in postconditions of method contracts (but also signals clauses or history constraints)

9.2.2.2 Dynamic Dispatch for Contracts using Model Methods

The possibility to override the implementation of a method defined in a super-type is the essential polymorphism feature of the object orientation paradigm. The mechanism which chooses at runtime the implementation to be taken for a method invocation is called *dynamic dispatch*. Also in the context of design-by-contractand behavioral subtyping, different implementations for the same operation can coexist— if they adhere to a common specification. It is most natural that not only the *implementations* but also the *specifications* vary from subtype to subtype, for instance by adding implementation-dependent aspects. This dynamic dispatch mechanism should, hence, also be available for the formulation of *formal* specifications in an equally flexible way.

Instead of spelling out the definition of this specification element, it should be possible to refer to it *symbolically*. Only when the dynamic type of the object is known, one also knows the actual contract definition.

We motivate and explain our specification approach by means of a small Java example, shown in the listings in Figure 9.2. Another example (modeling the visitor pattern) and a larger case study (modeling symbolic permissions) can be found in [Mostowski and Ulbrich, 2015].

The challenge presented here has originally been proposed by Distefano and Parkinson [2008] and has been dealt with by Bengtson et al. [2011] using a higher-order separation logic. The listings in Figure 9.2 show the program annotated with traditional specification means. Cell objects encapsulate integer values which can be set using a method set and be retrieved using get. The class Recell, which extends Cell, allows an additional one level undo operation which restores the cell value to the state before the most recent call to set. The class Client provides a method callSet which indirectly calls the set method of the Cell argument it receives. This particular indirection may seem artificial, but indirection is a very natural phenomenon in object orientation, e.g., in a situation where this operation is done only conditionally or after some locks have been acquired or in combination with other operations.

The contract of callSet copies the postcondition of Cell.set literally. It does not guarantee the stronger postcondition of Recell.set if the argument is of type Recell. The present contract does not suffice to verify the following test case:

—— Java ———
```
Recell rc = new Recell();
rc.set(4);
Client.callSet(rc, 5);
rc.undo();
assert rc.get() == 4;
```
——————————————————————————————————————— Java ——

While this program would not fail its assertion, the proof for that would not succeed as the abstraction of callSet by its contract neglects the additional postcondition oval == \old(val) introduced in Recell and only ensures the weaker postcondition of Cell.

This could be amended by introducing case distinctions on the type of the argument in the postcondition of Cell.set. This could be achieved by an additional clause c instanceof Recell ==> ((Recell)c).oval == \old(c.val)s. However, it has significant limitations regarding the modularity of the specification: (1) Details on the implementation of Recell are revealed where it is not necessary and should be kept under the hood and, more severely, (2) the implementation of Recell might not yet be known at the time that Cell is implemented or specified. Assume Cell and Client are part of a library and Recell is a user-written extension. How can the library account for all potential extensions?

This is precisely where abstract predicates in the form of model methods can be used to solve the issue. In the listings of Figure 9.3, the example has been reformulated using a model method post_set (lines 4–8) formalizing the postcondition of the method set (used in line 15). The model method has a body which defines its value.

```
   class Cell {                            class Recell extends Cell {
2    int val;                                int oval;

4    /*@ ensures \result ==> get()==x;       /*@ model two_state
     @ model two_state                       boolean post_set(int x) {
6    boolean post_set(int x) {                 return super.post_set(x) &&
       return val == x;                          oval == \old(get());
8    } @*/                                   } @*/

10   /*@ ensures \result == val; @*/         /*@ ensures get()==\old(oval); @*/
     int /*@ pure @*/ get() {                void undo() {
12     return val;                             val = oval;
     }                                       }
14
     /*@ ensures post_set(v); @*/            void set(int x) {
16   void set(int v) {                         oval = get(); super.set(x);
       val = v;                              }
18   }                                     }
   }
```

Figure 9.3 Listings of Cell/Recell example annotated with model methods

In this case, it returns true if and only if its argument x is equal to the value stored in field val. Looking at class Cell alone, no semantic change has been done.

Things change when the class Recell is again added to the scenario. In Recell, the model method post_set is overridden and adds a condition to the result obtained by Cell.post_set. By redefining the predicate locally for all instances of class Recell, the semantics of the contract Cell.set has now also changed, although syntactically it is the same. As the contract refers to the postcondition only *symbolically*, its semantics is left open and can be redefined by an implementing class. Furthermore, post_set makes use of its **two_state** declaration in class Recell as the definition relates values from two execution states, namely \old(get()) and oval. The two states that this definition refers to are the pre- and poststate of the method **set**.

The redefinition of post_set in Recell cannot be arbitrary, however. The model method has got a contract (line 4) saying that whenever its result is true, the condition val == x needs to hold. All overriding implementations need to obey that contract, but may add to it. This ensures behavioral subtyping.

The above example test case can be proved correct if the model method invocation c.post_set(v) is used as postcondition for Client.callSet abstracting away from the actual definition of the postcondition.

Model methods can also be used to modularly specify framing conditions (using dynamic frames, which will be discussed in Section 9.3.2 below). Listing 9.6 shows the scenario including frame conditions where the frame has been abstracted by a single state model method footprint().

Note how this method is used to specify the part of the heap on which the cell operates. The actual shape of this set of locations is different in the two classes; this can be addressed by giving the exact definition for footprint() in the corresponding classes. To provide global constraints on the footprint we can specify a contract for this model method. In the example we added an upper and a lower bound for the location set.

```
class Cell {
    int val;

    /*@ accessible \nothing;
      @ ensures \subset(\result, this.*) &&
                 \subset(\singleton(this.val), \result);
    model \locset footprint() {
        return \singleton(this.val);
    } @*/

    /*@ accessible footprint();
      @ ensures \result ==> get()==x;
    model two_state boolean post_set(int x) {
        return get() == x;
    } @*/

    /*@ accessible footprint();
      @ ensures \result == val; @*/
    int /*@ pure @*/ get() { return val; }

    /*@ ensures post_set(v);
      @ assignable footprint(); @*/
    void set(int v) { val = v; }
}

class Recell extends Cell {
    int oval;

    /*@ model \locset footprint() {
        return \set_union(this.val, this.oval);
    } @*/

    /*@ model two_state
    boolean post_set(int x) {
        return super.post_set(x) &&
               oval == \old(get());
    } @*/

    /*@ ensures get() == \old(oval);
      @ assignable footprint(); @*/
    void undo() { val = oval; }

    void set(int x) {
        oval = get(); super.set(x);
    }
}
```

Listing 9.6 Cell/Recell annotated with footprint specifications

9.2.2.3 Model Methods and Termination

Showing termination for *programs* is optional; analyzing the partial correctness problem alone can be a challenge already. For the definition of model methods, however, termination is a central point that must *not* be omitted. A model method definition gives rise to a universally quantified axiom claiming that the function has certain properties even if it may be unsatisfiable. Consider for instance the problematic declaration

```
class X { /*@ model int bad() { return this.bad() + 1; } @*/ }
```

for which the model method would be translated into the axiom

$$\forall Heap\ \texttt{heap}, X\ \texttt{self}; (exactInstance_X(\texttt{self}) \rightarrow$$
$$\texttt{X::bad}(h, \texttt{self}) \doteq \texttt{X::bad}(h, \texttt{self}) + 1),$$

which is obviously inconsistent. Consistency can be guaranteed if termination (or *well-foundedness*) of all recursive method references is checked. Here, the **measured_by** clauses are employed to avoid such unsatisfiable recursive definitions. We require that all definitions are primitive recursive. The termination witness *mby* specifies for each method a termination measurement which must be decreased in all referenced (model) method invocations in *exp*. To this end, an additional proof obligation per model method is generated to ensure this. Assuming that the termination witness of a model method referenced in *exp* is *mby'*, it has to be shown that *mby'* is a strict nonnegative predecessor of *mby*, i.e., $0 \le mby' < mby$.

In practice, one may also encounter mutually recursive definitions of model methods. In this case simple integer expressions as termination clauses are in general not sufficient. For that reason, we additionally allow tuples of integer expressions with a standard lexicographic order to serve as termination clauses and the above mechanism is modified accordingly to check the lexicographic ordering of the expressions instead, see also the last paragraph of Section 9.1.4 on page 300. Furthermore, to weaken the resulting proof obligations, we use left-to-right evaluation similar to that of well-definedness checking described in Section 8.3.2. Thus, expressions in return statements only need to decrease the termination witness if a prefixing guard is true.

9.3 The Frame Problem

For *modular* static verification, where we assume that the program may be extended, even the goal to check the correctness of individual program parts locally—that is, without considering the program as a whole—puts higher demands both on specifications and on the specification language itself than for approaches working under a closed program assumption. This sets modular verification apart from runtime checking. JML pledged to satisfy the additional demands of modular verification, but the classical static frame annotations fall short of this goal. Weiß [2011] presents a solution with an extension to the framing concept of JML, based on the *dynamic frames* approach by Kassios [2006, 2011]. Dynamic frames is a flexible approach for framing in the presence of dynamic data structures and data abstraction. Compared with alternative solutions, such as data groups [Leino, 1998], the advantages of this approach are its simplicity and generality.

9.3.1 Motivation

In object-oriented programming, data is organized in pointer-based data structures in which references from one object reach out to other objects in the memory, thus combining individual parts of the memory to complex compound data networks. The structure built up by the references is usually not limited by the programming language. In particular, the Java programming language does not pose any restrictions (other than by its type system) on how objects may refer to one another. There are many reasons to employ references between objects: They may point to objects which constitute a separate subpart of a larger structure. References may be used for efficiency reasons like in caches, to point into areas which are shared between various components. One direct consequence of the ability to have arbitrary pointer chains leading from one to another object is that effects of a piece of code cannot be assumed to be local to some object. The code may follow references on the heap and may potentially modify parts of the memory which are seemingly 'far away' from the original starting point. If an item is added to a collection that is kept as a heap data structure, for instance, it seems natural to assume that the content of a second, different list, would not be affected by such an action. But there are implementations which deliberately share data between collection instances to save memory. A glitch in such an implementation may indeed result in the modification of more objects than intended and their independence may not always silently be assumed.

It is thus an obligation of formal specification and verification to name the places in memory to which a piece of code has read or write access. An alternative to stating which part of the memory a program may look at or modify is to explicitly state what a program must *not* touch. While this seems like a viable alternative at first glance, it bears many issues concerning modularity: A specification cannot be local since it would have to include that a very distant part of the memory remains unchanged by the code. It may also not be open to extensions of the program because a specification cannot possibly talk about memory entities which are only to be included in an extension of the program.

We will now demonstrate these general concerns by an example. We consider in Listing 9.7 a simple client to our running List class example. A client object holds references to two list instances. The m() method adds an element to one of them. The question is how to prove the postcondition that states that the other list has not changed in size. We have to add the precondition that a and b do not *alias*, otherwise the postcondition could never be valid.

```
class Client {
    List a, b;

    //@ requires a != b;
    //@ ensures b.size() == \old(b.size());
    void m() { a.add(23); }
}
```

Listing 9.7 Client code using two instances of the List interface (from Listing 9.9)

As we have seen above in Section 9.1.2, a correct implementation of add() must satisfy the postcondition that the passed element has been added to the list. This is an impartial description of the method's behavior. For our particular situation here, however, we aim for the property that a.add() does *not* do anything harmful to b—that, besides the given functional property, "nothing else changes" [Borgida et al., 1995]. Such a property is usually expressed as a set of locations to which the method may write at most, called the *frame* of the method and a set of locations on which the result of a query depends at most, called the *footprint*.

Listing 9.8 shows the client specification with framing. One problem we encounter when trying to specify its frame, is that we need to address the concrete locations on which the method depends and to which it writes. This means that we have to expose the nature of the contained list, i.e., which implementation of the List interface is used. Here, we chose the LinkedList implementation and fixed it using a class invariant. Its **accessible** clause defines the footprint, i.e., the program locations it reads and on which its functionality depends. The **accessible** clause defines the locations that might be changed by the method.

```
class Client {
    List a, b;
    //@ invariant a instanceof LinkedList && b instanceof LinkedList;

    //@ requires a != b;
    //@ requires ((LinkedList)a).tail != ((LinkedList)b).tail;
    //@ ensures b.size() == \old(b.size());
    //@ accessible a, ((LinkedList)a).tail;
    //@ assignable ((LinkedList)a).tail;
    void m() { a.add(23); }
}
```

Listing 9.8 Client code using framing (exposing implementation details)

But what if we do want to keep the nature of the used list open? We answer this question in the following section by providing a solution on how to frames elegantly and without exposing (or even fixing) implementation details.

9.3.2 Dynamic Frames

The *dynamic frame* theory [Kassios, 2011] aims at solving the frame problem in the presence of data abstraction. The essence of the dynamic frames approach is to leverage the ubiquitous location sets to first-class citizens of the specification language: specification expressions are enabled to talk about such location sets directly. In particular, this allows us to explicitly specify that two such sets do not overlap, or that a particular concrete location is not part of a particular set. This is an important property for pointer-based programs, which is called the absence of *abstract aliasing* (also known as *deep aliasing*) [Leino and Nelson, 2002, Kassios, 2006]. For example, this property is what is missing in the specification of Listing 9.7. The knowledge that the location sets represented by a.footprint and b.footprint are disjoint allows us to conclude that the postcondition is actually satisfied.

What is called a *dynamic frame* is an abstract set of locations. A dynamic frame is 'dynamic' in the sense that the set of locations to which it evaluates can change during program execution, just like the value of a model field can change.

Dynamic Frames in JML

Weiß [2011] presented an implementation of the dynamic frames approach in KeY, using an extension of JML that includes high-level specification elements for location set expressions. The type \locset has already been briefly introduced in Chapter 8, with the underlying JavaDL data type introduced in Section 2.4. Semantically, expressions of type \locset stand for sets of memory locations. These expressions replace the *store ref* expressions from the JML reference manual [Leavens et al., 2013]as the expressions that are used to write **assignable** and **accessible** clauses. The primary difference between store ref expressions and \locset expressions is that \locset is a proper type. This for example allows us to declare model and ghost fields of this type.

The singleton set consisting of the (Java or ghost) field f of the reference expression o can be denoted in JML as \singleton(o.f), and the singleton set consisting of the *i*-th component of the array reference a as \singleton(a[i]). The set consisting of a range of array components and the set consisting of all components of an array are written as a[i..j] and a[*], and the set of all fields of an object is written as o.*. The keywords \nothing and \everything refer to the empty set and the set of all locations, respectively.More precisely, \everything refers to the set of all locations belonging to created objects. In the same spirit, \nothing is used to denote the set of locations that belong to freshly allocated objects. Intuitively, they denote the set of 'observably all' locations and 'observably none.' The actual empty set (in the mathematical sense) is denoted by \strictly_nothing similar to the difference between the **pure** and **strictly_pure** annotations.

In addition, JML features the following basic set operations on expressions of type \locset, with the standard mathematical meaning: the set intersection \intersect,

the set difference \set_minus, the set union \set_union, the subset predicate
\subset, and the disjointness predicate \disjoint.

The notations o.f and a[i] can be used as short-hands for the singleton sets
\singleton(o.f) and \singleton(a[i]), but only in contexts where understanding them as representing the *value* of o.f or a[i] is syntactically forbidden. For
example, on the top level of a modifies clause, the expression o.f is equivalent to
\singleton(o.f) if f is a Java or ghost field of type int, but it denotes the value
of the field if the f is of type \locset. As another familiar shorthand, a comma separated list $s_1, \ldots, s_n$ can be used to abbreviate the union of the \locset expressions
s_i where this does not lead to syntactical ambiguity.

Frames and Dependencies

Depend clauses have already been the topic of Subsection 8.3.2 and Definition 8.3
with the emphasis on their representation in JavaDL and the translation from JML.
Here, we place dependency contracts in the context of modular verification.

While depends clauses for pure methods are already part of standard JML, we
generalize the mechanism of depends clauses to model fields here. A depends clause
for a model field is declared as a class member, using the syntax accessible m: f;
where m is a model field (defined for the class containing the depends clause) and
where f is an expression of type \locset. Such a depends clause means that m
may depend at most on the locations in f (in other words, 'f frames m'), provided that the invariants of the this object hold in the current state. More formally,
accessible m: f is true in a state s if any state change (starting in s) that preserves the values of the locations in the evaluation of f in s also preserves the value
of m. This is a contract that all represents clauses for m must satisfy (in the current class or interface and in its subclasses), just like a depends clause for a pure
method is a contractual obligation on all implementations of the method. As dynamic
frames may be model fields themselves, they may also occur on the right hand side
of a depends clause. It is a common pattern for a dynamic frame to frame itself:
accessible f: f means that, if the values of the *locations* in the value of f are
not changed, then the value of f *itself* also remains the same.

We extend the \fresh operator so that it can be applied to location sets, in addition
to applying it to objects. An expression \fresh(f), where f is an expression of type
\locset, is satisfied in a postcondition if and only if all the locations in the poststate
interpretation of f belong to an object that was not yet allocated in the prestate. More
formally, it is $\lfloor\fresh(f)\rfloor = subset(\lfloor f\rfloor, unusedLocs(\text{heap}^{pre}))$; see Figure 2.11
for the semantics of *unusedLocs*.

The so-called *swinging pivots* operator \new_elems_fresh can be applied to a
dynamic frame f within a postcondition. The meaning of \new_elems_fresh(f)
is that if there are any locations in the set f in the poststate that have not been
there in the prestate, then these must belong to objects that have been freshly allocated in between (in the sense of \fresh). It is thus equivalent to the expression \fresh(\set_minus(f,\old(f))). Intuitively, a swinging pivot indicates a

change on the heap that is benign—in the sense that no previous separation properties can be invalidated. In combination with `assignable` and `accessible` clauses, the swinging pivots operator is useful to specify preservation of the absence of abstract aliasing. For example, if for some method execution we know that

1. the dynamic frames f and g do not contain any unallocated locations in the prestate,
2. f and g are disjoint in the prestate,
3. g frames itself in the prestate (`accessible` $g:g$),
4. only the values of the locations in f may be different in the poststate (i.e., `assignable` f), and that
5. the modification respects `\new_elems_fresh(`f`)`,

then we can conclude that f and g are still disjoint in the poststate. The reasoning behind this is as follows: `assignable` f and the disjointness of f and g together imply that the values of the locations in g are not changed. Combined with g being self-framing, this implies that the location set referred to by g itself also remains the same. The set f may change, but `\new_elems_fresh(`f`)` guarantees that if this change adds to f any additional locations, then these locations were previously unallocated. As the set g is unchanged and did not contain any unallocated locations in the prestate, the locations added to f cannot be members of g, and so the sets must still be disjoint. We see a concrete application of this chain of reasoning in Section 9.3.4.

9.3.3 Proof Obligations for Dynamic Frames Specifications

Section 8.3.2 presented a proof obligation which, if proven valid, ensures that the dependency contract of a pure method is correct. The formula presented in Definition 8.5 uses modalities for the evaluation of the method under examination.

In the previous section, we showed how to specify dynamic frames for model fields using `accessible` clauses, and Section 9.2.2 showed that model methods can also be specified with such clauses. But the proof obligation in Definition 8.5 from Chapter 8 cannot be applied in this situation: The rule embeds the method call into a JavaDL modality which is not possible for model fields and model methods.

To this end, we generalize this proof obligation to one which applies to arbitrary observer symbols.

Definition 9.12 (Proof obligation for dependency contracts of observers). Given an observer symbol $obs : Heap \times E \times T_1 \times \ldots \times T_n$ together with its dependency contract $(pre, term, dep)$. The definition of obs is called correct w.r.t. the dependency contract if the following JavaDL formula

$$pre \wedge freePre \wedge wellFormed(h) \wedge mby \doteq term$$
$$\rightarrow \quad obs(\texttt{heap},\texttt{self},\texttt{p}_1,\ldots,\texttt{p}_n)$$
$$\equiv obs(anon(\texttt{heap}, setMinus(allLocs, dep), h), \texttt{self}, \texttt{p}_1, \ldots, \texttt{p}_n)$$

is valid for the fresh constant $h : Heap$ and parameter variables $p_1 : T_1, \ldots, p_n : T_n$. The symbol $\equiv$ is interpreted as $\doteq$ if obs is a function symbol and as $\leftrightarrow$ if it is a predicate symbol.

For a model field, there are no arguments to the observer (i.e., $n = 0$), but a model method may possess additional arguments besides the receiver `self`.

9.3.4 Example Specification with Dynamic Frames

A version of the `List` interface from Section 9.1.2 this time specified using dynamic frames, is shown in Listing 9.9. As in Listing 9.3, the specification of the interface is based on the pure methods `get()` and `size()`. It also includes a dynamic frame `footprint`, that abstracts from the concrete memory locations that represent the list in possible subclasses. This dynamic frame is used in the modifies clause of the `add()` method, and in the depends clauses of the pure methods of `List`. In lines 3 and 6 of Listing 9.9, depends clauses are additionally given for the model fields `footprint` and (implicitly) `\inv`: their values, too, may depend at most on the locations in `footprint`.

As none of the methods of `List` are annotated as **helper** methods, all contracts contain implicit pre- and postconditions that assert that `\invariant_for(this)` is true before and after method execution. No other objects have to satisfy their invariants before calling the methods of the interface.

The additional postcondition for `add()` in line 12 demands that, even though the set `footprint` may change, all locations that are added to it must be fresh. This grants an implementation of `add()` the license to discard old data structures in `footprint` and to add fresh ones as needed. The same holds for `remFirst()`, where the footprint is even strictly smaller in the poststate. For the other methods of `List`, there is no need for a postcondition that describes their effect on `footprint`. Roughly, this is because these methods are pure, and thus we expect that they cannot affect `footprint` at all. This expectation is correct, but the precise justification for this is more complex than it may seem at first sight, because pure methods *are* allowed to allocate and initialize new objects, and because without further knowledge, such a state change *might* affect the interpretation of a model field such as `footprint`. Fortunately, the semantics of JML guarantees that dynamic frames like `footprint` never contain any unallocated locations. We know from the depends clause in line 6 that `footprint` frames itself, i.e., that a change to locations that are not in the value of `footprint` cannot affect the value of `footprint`. Thus, any change to previously unallocated locations in a pure method is guaranteed to leave the value of `footprint` untouched.

```
1 public interface List {
2     //@ public model instance \locset footprint;
3     //@ public accessible footprint: footprint;
4
5     //@ public instance invariant size() >= 0;
6     //@ public instance accessible \inv: footprint;
7
8     /*@ public normal_behavior
9       @ ensures size() == \old(size()) + 1 && get(size()-1) == elem;
10      @ ensures (\forall int i;0 <= i &&
11      @   i < size()-1;get(i) == \old(get(i)));
12      @ ensures \new_elems_fresh(footprint);
13      @ assignable footprint;
14      @*/
15     public void add (int elem);
16
17     /*@ public normal_behavior
18      @ requires !empty();
19      @ ensures size() == \old(size()) - 1;
20      @ ensures (\forall int i;0 <= i &&
21      @   i < size();get(i) == \old(get(i+1)));
22      @ ensures \new_elems_fresh(footprint);
23      @ assignable footprint;
24      @*/
25     public void remFirst ();
26
27     /*@ public normal_behavior
28      @ ensures \result == (size() == 0);
29      @ accessible footprint;
30      @*/
31     public /*@ pure @*/ boolean empty ();
32
33     /*@ public normal_behavior
34      @ ensures \result == size();
35      @ accessible footprint;
36      @*/
37     public /*@ pure @*/ int size ();
38
39     /*@ public normal_behavior
40      @ requires 0 <= idx && idx < size();
41      @ ensures \result == get(idx);
42      @ accessible footprint;
43      @*/
44     public /*@ pure @*/ int get (int idx);
45 }
```

Listing 9.9 Interface List specification using pure methods and a dynamic frame footprint

9.3.4.1 Specifying the List Client

Listing 9.10 shows the Client class from Listing 9.7 with dynamic frame specifications. We have only inserted the additional preconditions in lines 7f.: when entering method m() of class Client, the invariants of a and b must hold, and there must not be abstract aliasing between a.footprint and b.footprint. Given this specification, we are now able to conclude that the postcondition in Line 9 holds, by using only the code and specifications in Listings 9.9 and 9.10.

```
1  class Client {
2      List a, b;
3      static int x;
4
5      /*@ normal_behavior
6        @ requires a != b;
7        @ requires \invariant_for(a) && \invariant_for(b);
8        @ requires \disjoint(a.footprint, b.footprint);
9        @ ensures b.size() == \old(b.size());
10       @ ensures \invariant_for(a) && \invariant_for(b);
11       @*/
12      void m() { a.add(23); }
13 }
```

Listing 9.10 The client from Listing 9.9 specified with dynamic frames

We reach this conclusion as follows. The disjointness of a.footprint and b.footprint implies that there is no abstract aliasing between a and b before calling a.add(). Thus, the depends clause of size() guarantees that changing the locations *in the prestate value* of a.footprint would not affect b.size(). But calling a.add() may have an effect on the model field a.footprint itself. But we know that a.footprint is only changed in an benign way; this is what the swinging pivots predicate states in line 12 of Listing 9.9. From this we can deduce that both footprints are still disjoint in the poststate. Overall, we can conclude that the postcondition in line 9 holds.

Analogously, the depends clause for the class invariant in List guarantees that \invariant_for(b) still holds after the change, as asserted in line 10. Listing 9.10. This property holds independently of the concrete implementations of List that may occur as the dynamic type of List, as long as all these implementations satisfy the specifications given in the interface.

9.3.4.2 Specifying the ArrayList Implementation

A particular implementation of the List interface is shown in Listing 9.11, which already appeared earlier. We have now added specifications based on dynamic frames and made the default constructor explicit. The contents of the dynamic frame `footprint` are defined for objects of dynamic type `ArrayList` through the represents clause in line 3. This represents clause satisfies the depends clause for `footprint` in Listing 9.9, because all locations that its right hand side depends on are themselves part of the right hand side. If we would omit `a` in the represents clause, then the depends clause would be violated: the location `this.a` would then not be a member of the value of `this.footprint`, but changing the value of this location would still affect the value of the expression `this.a[*]` and thereby the value of `this.footprint`.

The **invariant** declarations of `ArrayList` (the implicit clause `this.a!=null` plus the one inherited from `List`) define the represents clause for the implicit mode field `\inv`. This represents clause satisfies the depends clause for `\inv` specified in Listing 9.9, because it only accesses locations that are part of `footprint` as defined in the applicable represents clause for `footprint`. We do not consider `a.length` to be a location here, because it is unmodifiable.

Line 9 of Listing 9.11 gives a postcondition `\fresh(footprint)` for the constructor of `ArrayList`. This postcondition is satisfied by the implementation of the constructor: in deviation from the JML reference manual [Leavens et al., 2013], the `this` object is considered to be fresh in the postcondition of a constructor,[9] and consequently the location `this.a` is also fresh. By the represents clause of `footprint`, its other members are the locations of the array that is stored in `a`. This array is freshly allocated.

9.4 Calculus Rules for Modular Reasoning

In Chapter 3, an extensive sequent calculus for JavaDL has been introduced, and Section 3.7 gives a brief introduction to the concept of abstraction and presents rules that deal with the two kinds of abstraction relevant for our purposes, loop invariants and method contracts. In this section, we present advanced rules that go beyond those shown in Chapter 3. We begin with invariant rules for loops in Section 9.4.2 and a contract-rule for method calls in Section 9.4.3. These rules incorporate the concept of dynamic frames outlined in Section 9.3.2. Another central rule for frame-aware reasoning are dependency rules which allow deducing if two applications of an observer symbol have the same value by inspection of their footprints. JavaDL dependency contracts have been introduced in Section 8.2.4, according proof obligations in Section 8.3.2. This chapter will present in Section 9.4.4 rules that *use* proved dependency contracts to infer that observer invocations must have the same value. Finally rules will be stated that allow the expansion of model field and method definitions in Section 9.4.5.

---

[9] This means, the constructor contract is considered a contract for the entire `new` call, that includes object allocation, initialization, and the constructor; see Section 3.6.6.

```
1  public final class ArrayList implements List {
2
3      //@ private represents footprint = a, a[*];
4
5      private int[] a;
6
7      /*@ public normal_behavior
8        @ ensures size() == 0;
9        @ ensures \fresh(footprint);
10       @*/
11     public /*@ pure @*/ ArrayList() {
12         a = new int[0];
13     }
14
15     public void add (int elem) {
16         int[] tmp = new int[a.length+1];
17         for (int i= a.length; i > 0; i--)
18             tmp[i] = a[i-1];
19         a = tmp;
20         a[0] = elem;
21     }
22
23     public void remFirst () {
24         int[] tmp = new int[a.length-1];
25         for (int i= 1; i < a.length; i++)
26             tmp[i-1] = a[i];
27         a = tmp;
28     }
29
30     public /*@ strictly_pure @*/ boolean empty () {
31         return size() == 0;
32     }
33
34     public /*@ strictly_pure @*/ int size () {
35         return a.length;
36     }
37
38     public /*@ strictly_pure @*/ int get (int idx) {
39         return a[idx];
40     }
41 }
```

Listing 9.11 Java class ArrayList implementing the List interface of Listing 9.9

9.4.1 Anonymizing Updates

When modeling abstraction, it is important that the concrete memory state at a point during execution can be replaced with a fresh unconstrained state. This is needed in particular when dealing with unbounded loops or with method invocations—both of which are abstraction by means of an overapproximation (the contract or the loop invariant).

In order to be able to continue execution with "any value for x satisfying the invariant," for instance, we need to forget the value of x and assume then the invariant holds. This is done by assigning an unconstrained new value to x in an update. Harel et al. [2000] suggest to incorporate the notation x :=? into dynamic logic with the semantics $[x :=?]\varphi \leftrightarrow \forall x; \varphi$ for such a forgetting assignment. In JavaDL, we employ updates and assign to x a fresh unconstrained Skolem constant x' (of the same type as x) that may hold any value. We call such updates *anonymizing updates*. They are also called *random assignment* or *wildcard assignments* in literature.

Heap anonymization, i.e., anonymization of the program variable heap is particularly interesting in the face of dynamic frames: In the abstraction rules in Chapter 3, we treated heap like any other program variable and anonymized it with a fresh Skolem variable h'. But having dynamic frames at hand, we can do better now and only assign fresh values to those locations inside a frame, leaving all locations outside the frame untouched.

To this end, we use the function $anon : Heap \times LocSet \times Heap \rightarrow Heap$ (whose semantics was introduced in Figure 2.11 in Section 2.4.5) which does precisely that. The heap update

$$\{heap := anon(heap, mod, h')\}$$

ensures that in its scope, the heap coincides with $h' : Heap$ on all locations in mod and all not yet created locations and coincides with heap before the update elsewhere.

9.4.2 An Improved Loop Invariant Rule

Other parts of this book describe how a JavaDL loop specification is obtained: Section 16.3 provides guidelines for the user to find useful loop invariants, Section 7.9.2 explains how loop specifications can be formulated in JML and Section 8.2.5 describes how JavaDL loop specification are obtained from the JML specifications.

Here, we assume that a JavaDL loop specification $(inv, mod, term)$ according to Definition 3.23 is given with loop invariant inv, modifier set mod and termination witness $term$. A first rule for dealing with JavaDL loop specification has already been presented in Section 3.7.2 ignoring the mod and $term$ parts. Here we will remedy this omission.

The general structure of a loop invariant rule looks like this:

$$
\begin{array}{ll}
\text{Invariant Initially Valid} & \text{(INIT)} \\
\text{Body Preserves Invariant} & \text{(STEP)} \\
\text{Use Case} & \text{(USE)} \\
\hline
\end{array}
$$
$$\Gamma \Longrightarrow \mathcal{U}[\pi \text{ while}(se)p;\ \omega]\varphi, \Delta$$

We assume that the loop condition se is a simple expression and that the loop body p always terminates normally. How to deal with the general case, that se may not be simple and p may contain return, continue, or break statements if explained in Subsections 3.7.2.3 and 3.7.2.4.

We will comment in detail on the three premisses:

1. In the *base case* INIT, it is to be proved that the invariant holds in the initial state of the loop execution;
2. in the *step case* STEP, it is to be proven that execution of the loop body p in a state which satisfies the loop invariant reestablishes the invariant; if *term* $\neq$ PARTIAL then it has also to be shown that the termination witness *term* strictly decreases;
3. in the *use case* USE we may assume that the invariant holds after the loop has finished and continue symbolic execution with the remainder program ω.

and end up with the rules loopInvariant and termLoopInvariant in Definitions 9.13 and 9.14.

The base case requires that the invariant is true in the current context spanned by Γ, Δ and $\mathcal{U}$.

$$\Gamma \Longrightarrow \mathcal{U}\, inv,\ \Delta \qquad\qquad \text{(INIT)}$$

The information about the execution context encoded in the update $\mathcal{U}$ and the formula sets Γ and Δ is retrieved by matching the calculus rule against the a sequent it is applied to.

The step and use cases are to be proved in symbolic states where an arbitrary number of loop iterations have already been executed, potentially invalidating all information in the context. The necessary *masking* of the context can be formalized by anonymizing as introduced in the last section. This led to the introduction of the anonymizing update $\mathcal{V}$ in the simple loop invariant rule in Section 3.7.2. For the convenience of the reader we repeat its step case

$$\Gamma \Longrightarrow \mathcal{U}\,\mathcal{V}\left(inv \wedge se \doteq TRUE \rightarrow [p]inv\right), \Delta\ . \qquad\qquad (\text{STEP}_0)$$

In this condition, $\mathcal{V}$ anonymizes the variable heap and all local variables which are potentially modified in the loop body p. As far as the heap is concerned, this is a very coarse approximation because *all* locations on the heap are assigned a fresh unconstrained value. This implies a burden for the specifying person as he or she must encode into the loop invariant which memory locations the loop does *not* change. Therefore, we will now go one step further and incorporate the modifier set of the loop specification into the rule to limit the anonymization of the heap.

Remember that the loop specification contains a modifier set term $mod : LocSet \cup \{\text{STRICTLYNOTHING}\}$ which models the locations which can be modified by the loop. If $mod \neq \text{STRICTLYNOTHING}$, we replace the coarse anonymizing update $\mathcal{V}$ in (STEP_0) by the more precise anonymizing update

$$\mathcal{W} := \{\text{heap} := anon(\text{heap}, mod, h') \,\|\, \mathtt{b}_1 := b'_1 \,\|\, \ldots \,\|\, \mathtt{b}_n := b'_n\} \qquad (9.6)$$

in which $\mathtt{b}_1, \ldots, \mathtt{b}_n$ enumerate the local variables that can be modified by the loop body, and $b'_1, \ldots, b'_n$ are fresh anonymization constants of appropriate type. The heap is partially anonymized with the fresh values taken from a fresh unconstrained heap object $h' : Heap$.

The set of locations affected by the anonymizing update cannot be statically determined, it is the value of the term *mod* which determines the extension of the location set. This is why the frames featuring in this approach are called *dynamic frames*: The location sets may differ between different states.

Let us have a closer look at the case $mod = \emptyset$. Unraveling the semantics definition of *anon* from Figure 2.11, we see that (despite *mod* being empty) all fields of objects not yet created in heap are anonymized. This models that in the code block abstracted by the anonymization, new objects may be created. This may put a considerable burden on the verification. In case it is known that the code block does not change anything and does not create new objects, the according `assignable` clause of the method contract or loop specification may be set to `\strictly_nothing` which will be translated to the special indicator $mod = \text{STRICTLYNOTHING}$. The corresponding update then is

$$\mathscr{W} := \{b_1 := b_1' \| \ldots \| b_n := b_n'\}$$

which is (9.6) without the assignment to heap.

On the other hand, no matter what locations occur in *mod* the semantics definition of *anon* guarantees that no created object may be deleted.

The loop specification $(inv, mod, term)$ guarantees that after an arbitrary number of loop iterations at most the locations in *mod* have changed. We have exploited this fact in the anonymizing update $\mathscr{W}$ just described. On the other hand, we have to prove that after the next loop iteration still at most the location in *mod* may change. To this end, we add the formula *frame* to the postcondition in the step case premiss. We have encountered *frame* already in (8.5) in Section 8.3.1 when the method contract proof obligation was presented. It serves the same purpose there and here: to ensure that at most the locations in M are modified:

$$frame(M) := \forall o \forall f; \quad o.created@\text{heap}^{pre} \doteq FALSE$$
$$\lor o.f \doteq o.f@\text{heap}^{pre} \tag{9.7}$$
$$\lor (o, f) \in M$$

Since the modifies clause *mod* is to be evaluated in the state *before* the loop execution and not in the current state, mod cannot be used directly. Instead, a new program variable $M : LocSet$ is introduced that captures the modifies set in the prestate by means of an update $\mathscr{M} := \{M := mod\}$

At this intermediate point the step case thus reads:

$$\Gamma \Longrightarrow \mathscr{U}\mathscr{M}\mathscr{W}\,(inv \land se \doteq TRUE \to [p](inv \land frame(M))),\,\Delta \qquad (\text{STEP}_1)$$

The corresponding use case that goes with this step case is the same as the one already introduced with the simple rule in Chapter 3—but with the refined anonymizing update $\mathscr{W}$ that only masks out *mod*.

$$\Gamma \Longrightarrow \mathscr{U}\mathscr{W}\,(inv \land se \doteq FALSE \to [\pi\,\omega]\varphi),\,\Delta \qquad (\text{USE}_1)$$

One more addition is needed, concerning what we might call *free invariants* in parallel to the *free preconditions* explained in Section 8.2.4. These are well-formedness statements that we need not verify since they are automatically maintained by the semantics of the Java language. But it is helpful, and in many cases vital, to have them explicitly available at the beginning of each loop iteration. For the local variables $a_1, \ldots, a_m$ in whose scopes the loop lies we define:

$$
locVarInRange := \bigwedge_{i=1}^{m} \begin{cases} a_i \doteq \texttt{null} \lor a.created \doteq TRUE \\ \qquad \text{if } a_i \text{ is of reference type} \\ inInt(a_i) \quad \text{if } a_i \text{ is of type int} \\ inByte(a_i) \quad \text{if } a_i \text{ is of type byte} \\ \vdots \qquad \text{likewise for short, long, char} \\ disjoint(a_i, unusedLocs(\texttt{heap})) \\ \qquad \text{if } a_i \text{ is a ghost variable of type } LocSet \\ true \qquad \text{otherwise} \end{cases} \tag{9.8}
$$

This definition of *locVarInRange* parallels (8.3) where the same is assumed about method arguments in a method invocation.

locVarInRange formalizes that all variables a_i must have reachable values, i.e., they must not refer to noncreated objects, their value must be in range, and they must not hold location sets that contain locations belonging to noncreated objects. We add *locVarInRange* to the INIT premiss to be shown next to the invariant. If this property holds in the initial state of the loop, then the semantics of Java guarantees that it is preserved by arbitrary loop iterations. It may thus be used as an assumption in the second and third premiss.

We have now assembled all we need to formulate the loop invariant rules. We mention once again that the rules are presented under the assumption that the loop condition is a simple expression, and that loop body does not throw exceptions and does not use `return`, `break` and `continue` statements. The rule can be extended to handle these technicalities in the same way as in Section 3.7.2.

Since the sequent context $(\Gamma, \Delta, \mathcal{U})$ is maintained by this invariant rule, we omit it in the following rule schema as explained in Section 3.5.1.

Definition 9.13 (Rule loopInvariant without Termination). Let $(inv, mod, term)$ be a loop specification (see Definition 3.23) with $term = \text{PARTIAL}$, se a simple expression (see Table 3.2) and p_{norm} a program fragment (see Definition 3.2) that does never throw an exception and does not contain break, continue, return statements.

The rule loopInvariant is defined as

$$
\begin{array}{c} \Longrightarrow inv \land wellFormed(\texttt{heap}) \land locVarInRange \\ \Longrightarrow \mathcal{M}\mathcal{W}\big(inv \land wellFormed(h') \land locVarInRange \land se \doteq TRUE \to \\ [p_{norm}](inv \land frame)\big) \\ \Longrightarrow \mathcal{W}\big(inv \land wellFormed(h') \land locVarInRange \land se \doteq FALSE \to [\pi\ \omega]\varphi\big) \\ \hline \Longrightarrow [\pi \texttt{ while}(se) \texttt{ \{ } p_{norm} \texttt{ \} } \omega]\varphi \end{array}
$$

where:
- *locVarInRange* is defined in (9.8),
- *frame* is defined in (9.7),
- $a_1, \ldots, a_m \in$ ProgVSym are the local program variables in whose scopes the loop lies (except for heap),
- $b_1, \ldots, b_n \in$ ProgVSym are the program variables that are potentially modified by the loop body p (except for heap),
- h', $b'_1, \ldots, b'_n$ are fresh constant symbols of appropriate type,
- $\mathcal{M} = \{M := mod\}$,
- $\mathcal{W} = \begin{cases} \{b_1 := b'_1 \parallel \ldots \parallel b_n := b_n\} & \text{if } mod = \text{STRICTLYNOTHING} \\ \{\text{heap} := anon(\text{heap}, mod, h') \parallel b_1 := b'_1 \parallel \ldots \parallel b_n := b'_n\} & \text{otherwise.} \end{cases}$

For the heap, assuming *wellFormed*(heap) in the scope of the update $\mathcal{W}$ would amount to assuming *wellFormed*(*anon*(heap, *mod*, *h*)). Assuming *wellFormed*(h') is shorter and simpler, in particular because this term does not depend on heap.

We have not considered termination so far. Rule loopInvariant is one for the 'box' modality. In the corresponding invariant rule for the 'diamond' modality, we are required to ensure that the loop terminates. This incorporates two things: (1) every loop iteration terminates, and (2) there is no program execution with infinitely many loop iterations. The first goal can be ensures by using the diamond modality in the step case and the second is established through a well-founded relation and the *term* component of the loop specification. The well-founded relation $\prec: Any \times Any$ has already been introduced in Section 9.1.4 and can be reused here. If every loop iteration makes the variant term smaller, no infinite repetitions are possible.

Definition 9.14 (Rule termLoopInvariant**).** Let $(inv, mod, term)$ be a loop specification (see Definition 3.23) with *term* $\neq$ PARTIAL, *se* a simple expression (see Table 3.2) and p_{norm} a program fragment (see Definition 3.2) that does never throw an exception and does not contain break, continue, return statements.

The rule termLoopInvariant is defined as

$$\frac{\begin{array}{l} \Longrightarrow inv \wedge wellFormed(\text{heap}) \wedge locVarInRange \\ \Longrightarrow \mathcal{T}\mathcal{M}\mathcal{W}\big(inv \wedge wellFormed(h') \wedge locVarInRange \wedge se \doteq TRUE \rightarrow \\ \qquad \langle p_{norm} \rangle (inv \wedge frame \wedge term \prec term^{\text{pre}})\big) \\ \Longrightarrow \mathcal{W}\big(inv \wedge wellFormed(h') \wedge locVarInRange \wedge se \doteq FALSE \rightarrow \langle \pi\ \omega \rangle \varphi\big) \end{array}}{\Longrightarrow \langle \pi\, \texttt{while(se) \{ } p_{norm}\texttt{ \} }\omega \rangle \varphi}$$

where:
- all conditions from Definition 6 apply,
- $term^{\text{pre}} : Any$ is a fresh program variable,
- $\mathcal{T} = \{term^{\text{pre}} := term\}$ is the update that stores the value of *term* before the loop body into variable $term^{\text{pre}}$.

One may wonder why in Definitions 9.13 and 9.14 *wellFormed*(heap) has been added to the proof obligations in the INIT case. After all this can never be violated by a Java program. The explanation is that a user might inadvertently produce a proof state e.g., by the cut rule, where $wellFormed(\text{heap})$ might not hold.

Lemma 9.15 below establishes a formal connection between the two framing formalisms using *frame* and *anon* respectively. This connection is the reason why it is admissible to use *anon* for anonymizing the locations in the modifies clause, while using *frame* in the proof obligation for verifying the correctness of the modifies clause in the second premiss.

Lemma 9.15 (Connection between *frame* and *anon*). *Let mod* $\in \text{Trm}_{LocSet}$ *and frame be as in* (9.7).

Let furthermore noDeallocs(h_1, h_2) be the formula

$$unusedLocs(h_2) \subseteq unusedLocs(h_1)$$
$$\wedge\, select_{Any}(h_1, \texttt{null}, created) \doteq select_{Any}(h_2, \texttt{null}, created)\ .$$

Then the following holds:

$$\models \quad (frame(mod) \wedge noDeallocs(\text{heap}^{pre}, \text{heap}))$$
$$\leftrightarrow \text{heap} \doteq anon(\text{heap}^{pre}, \{\text{heap} := \text{heap}^{pre}\}mod, \text{heap})$$

A proof of Lemma 9.15, an easy comparison of the semantic definition of *anon* and the *frame* formula—though with many case distinctions—can be found in [Weiß, 2011, Appendix A.5]. Roughly speaking, the lemma gives a necessary and sufficient condition for the equation $h_2 = anon(h_1, M, h_2)$. This equation describes a situation where for all locations that h_2 does not overwrite h_2 and h_1 coincide.

The formula $noDeallocs(\text{heap}^{pre}, \text{heap})$ expresses that all objects created in the prestate heap array are still created in the current heap array (and that createdness of *null* does not change). Obviously, this is a very essential property of the Java memory model. The impossibility of deallocating created objects is also built into the semantics definition of *anon*, see Figure 2.11. Lemma 9.15 is a main ingredient in the proof of Theorem 9.17, which establishes that the loop invariant rules are sound.

But why are there two mechanisms for formalizing the framing condition in the first place? One is used where framing needs to be shown, and the other one is used in the use case. The loop invariant rules uses both mechanisms. The reason is that having an explicit function symbol to refer to the updated state allows us to formulate heap anonymization as an update.

The following lemma shows that both notions are semantically equivalent: heap anonymization using *anon* is as good as total anonymization together with assuming the condition *frame*.

Lemma 9.16. *Let noDeallocs be like in Lemma 9.15, frame as defined in* (9.7) *and $\varphi \in$ DLFml a formula in which M does not occur. Then the following formula is universally valid.*

$$(\forall Heap\; h;\, (noDeallocs(\text{heap}, h) \rightarrow$$

$$\{\text{heap}^{pre} := \text{heap} \,\|\, \text{heap} := anon(\text{heap}, mod, h)\}\varphi))$$

$$\leftrightarrow \quad (\forall Heap\; h;\, (noDeallocs(\text{heap}, h) \rightarrow$$

$$\{\text{heap}^{pre} := \text{heap} \,\|\, \text{heap} := h \,\|\, M := mod\}(frame(M) \rightarrow \varphi)))$$

We have formalized this lemma as a JavaDL formula and proved it using the KeY system.

Theorem 9.17. *Rule* termLoopInvariant *is sound.*

A variant of Theorem 9.17 for the 'box' modality is proven by Weiß [2011, Appendix A.6].

9.4.3 A Rule for Method Contracts

In Section 8.3.1 we came across proof obligation formulas whose validity implies the correctness of a method contract. In this section, we will encounter rules which make use of method contracts essentially by abstracting away from the method invocation by assuming its contract's postcondition instead.

These two concepts go hand in glove: The rule useMethodContract shown in the following is sound if the corresponding method contract proof obligation is a valid formula.

A rule that makes use of a functional method contract is defined in Definition 9.18 below. We show the general case of a nonstatic method whose return type is not **void**. The rules for **void** or static methods are similar, but lack the assignment to x or the references to **self** and *se*, respectively. The presented rule is a refinement of the rule simpleContract presented in Section 3.7.1. It incorporates the issues of framing and termination which had been factored out in Chapter 3.

Like there, the rule makes a few assumptions about the receiver and the arguments of the method call: They are assumed to be simple expressions (see Table 3.2 for a listing of simple expressions), requiring no further symbolic execution. The symbolic execution rules methodCallUnfoldTarget and methodCallUnfoldArguments establishing this property have been presented in Section 3.6.5.4.

Definition 9.18 (Rule useMethodContract**).** Let $R\; m(T_1\; p_1, \ldots, T_n\; p_n)$ be a method defined in class or interface C, $se \in \text{DLTrm}_{C'}$ a simple expression of type C', $a_1 \in \text{DLTrm}_{T_1}, \ldots, a_n \in \text{DLTrm}_{T_n}$ simple expressions, x : R a program variable. Let $(pre, post, mod, term)$ be a functional method contract for m stated in a class C'' such that $C' \sqsubseteq C'' \sqsubseteq C$ with $term \neq \text{PARTIAL}$.

The rule useMethodContractTotal is defined as follows:

$$\Longrightarrow \mathscr{V}\,(pre \wedge wellFormed(\texttt{heap}) \wedge paramsInRange)$$
$$\Longrightarrow \mathscr{V}\,(term \prec \texttt{mby})$$
$$\Longrightarrow \mathscr{V}\,(\texttt{self} \neq \texttt{null} \wedge \texttt{self}\,.\,created \doteq TRUE)$$
$$\Longrightarrow \mathscr{V}\,\mathscr{W}\,(post \wedge wellFormed(h) \wedge reachableRes \wedge \texttt{exc} \doteq \texttt{null} \rightarrow$$
$$\langle \pi\ \texttt{x=res; }\ \omega\rangle\varphi)$$
$$\Longrightarrow \mathscr{V}\,\mathscr{W}\,(post \wedge wellFormed(h) \wedge reachableRes \wedge \texttt{exc} \neq \texttt{null} \rightarrow$$
$$\langle \pi\ \texttt{throw exc; }\ \omega\rangle\varphi)$$

$$\rule{6cm}{0.4pt}$$

$$\Longrightarrow \langle \pi\ \texttt{x = }se\texttt{.m}(a_1,\ldots,a_m)\texttt{; }\ \omega\rangle\varphi$$

where:

- $paramsInRange \in$ DLFml is defined in (8.3),
- $reachableRes = \texttt{inRange}_R(\texttt{res}) \wedge \texttt{inRange}_{\texttt{Throwable}}(\texttt{exc})$,
- $\mathscr{V} = \{\texttt{self} := se \,\|\, \texttt{p}_1 := a_1 \,\|\, \ldots \,\|\, \texttt{p}_n := a_n\}$,
- $\mathscr{W} = \{\texttt{heap}^{pre} := \texttt{heap} \,\|\, \texttt{heap} := anon(\texttt{heap}, mod, h) \,\|\, \texttt{res} := r \,\|\, \texttt{exc} := e)$ is an anoymizing update with $h : Heap, r : R, e : \texttt{Throwable} \in$ FSym fresh symbols. If $mod =$ STRICTLYNOTHING, then the heap content is not modified by the method, and the assignment to heap is removed.

The formulas $paramsInRange$ and $reachableRes$ play the same roles as the formula $locVarInRange$ in the loopInvariant rule of Definition 9.13. Similar to that, the update $\mathscr{W}$ anonymizes the locations that may be changed by the call to m by setting them to unknown values with the help of the fresh constant symbol h. It also sets the variables res and exc to unknown values denoted by the fresh constant symbols r and e, respectively. As before, an empty modifies clause still gives rise to anonymization. Specifying the method as strictly pure, however, leads to the update $\mathscr{W}$ leaving the heap untouched. The update $\mathscr{V}$ instantiates the variables used in the contract with the corresponding terms in the method call statement.

In the first premiss, the precondition has to be established. According to our understanding of a contract this is a necessary requirement to use the postcondition as an approximation of the method call. In addition the proof obligations $wellFormed(\texttt{heap})$ and $paramsInRange$ have to been dispatched. The reason is the same as in Rule 9.13: to save-guard against inadvertent violation of these conditions by the user, e.g., by the cut rule.

Termination is addressed in the second premiss; the termination witness of the called method must be smaller than the termination witness of the current method context stored in the program variable mby (which is set in the correctness proof obligations, see Definition 8.4). The next premiss requires establishing that the receiver object se is created and different from null.

Unlike the rule methodContractPartial presented in Figure 3.7 in Section 3.7.1 handling the case of a null receiver by throwing an exception, this rule strictly requires nonnull receiver and is thus weaker but proves way more efficient in practice. There is a taclet option to control which behavior is taken.

The last two cases effect that method invocation is replaced by using the postcondition. In the fourth premiss, the method call is replaced by an assignment of the result to x, under the assumption that no exception has been thrown ($\texttt{exc} \doteq \texttt{null}$). If the call raises an exception ($\texttt{exc} \neq \texttt{null}$) in the last premiss, the control flow of the program continues with raising this exception (see Section 3.6.7). In both cases, the control flow continues in the context of $\pi...\omega$. Unlike the postcondition *post* the formulas *wellFormed*(h) and *reachableRes* need not be proved. The semantics of Java guarantees that they are true after termination of any program.

In the KeY implementation, the first two premises have been combined into one.

Theorem 9.19. *Rule* useMethodContract *is sound, provided that for all subtypes $C' \sqsubseteq C$ of the type C in which method m has been declared, the proof obligation for functional correctness from Definition 8.4 is valid.*

A proof of Theorem 9.19 can be found in [Weiß, 2011, Appendix A.7]. The proof is similar to the proof of Theorem 9.17 in many respects. In particular, it also makes use of Lemma 9.15, which states that the heap is unaffected in all locations outside *mod* if and only if frame condition (9.7) is valid for *mod*.

Using contracts for constructors works essentially the same as in Definition 9.18, except that (1) the first active statement in the conclusion is a constructor invocation of the form x = new $C(a'_1, ..., a'_m)$; (2) the propositions about self in the first premiss are omitted, (3) in the update $\mathcal{V}$ the subupdate self $:= se$ is replaced with self $:= x$, and (4) the second premiss contains an additional assumption besides *post* $\wedge$ *wellFormed*(h) $\wedge$ *reachableRes*, namely the formula (9.9) below, which states (i) that the dynamic type of the created object is C, (ii) that the object was not created previously, and (iii) that it is created in the current heap.

$$exactInstance_C(\mathbf{x}) \doteq TRUE$$
$$\wedge\, \mathbf{x}.created@\mathtt{heap}^{pre} \doteq FALSE \tag{9.9}$$
$$\wedge\, \mathbf{x}.created \doteq TRUE$$

When a method contract is attached to a constructor, the subject of this *constructor contract* is the entire object allocation and initialization, see Section 3.6.6. This means, it refers to an allocation statement of the form **new** $C(...)$. It does not constrain the behavior of nested constructor invocations via **this**(...); nor **super**(...); statements. For this reason, there are no contracts available for calls to **this**() or **super**().

Using the contract of a recursive method *mr* is in no way different from using the contract of a nonrecursive method. This is, however, not true when in the course of proving the contract of *mr* this contract is used for one of the recursive calls. The KeY system will detect this circularity and only allow it if the contract contains a **measured_by** clause. See Section 9.1.4 for details on dealing with recursion.

Traditionally, the concept of a contract applies to methods (and constructors) only, which represent natural software modules. However, the concept can be used to modularize the target program further by providing a contract to an arbitrary code block within a method body. Rule useBlockContract in Section 13.5.1.3 is an adaptation of the method contract rule.

9.4.4 A Rule for Dependency Contracts

Dually to method contracts which describe the effects of a method, *dependency contracts* describe what *affects* the value of observer expressions. The concept of a JavaDL dependency contract $(pre, term, dep)$ has already been introduced in Definition 8.3, its associated correctness proof obligation in Section 8.3.2. Intuitively, this formula establishes that under assumption of a precondition *pre*, the value of an observer depends at most on the locations in the location set *dep*. Recursive definitions for *dep* are allowed. In this case the termination witness *term* is used to provide well-foundedness of the definition.

In this section, we show how dependency contracts can be used to show that observer terms are equal even if examined in different heap contexts. In contrast to useMethodContract, the rule useDependencyContract is applied on a term or formula in the logic, not on a program modality with a method call as the active statement.

The underlying logical idea behind the dependency contract boils down to the following implication which should give you an intuition of its semantics.

$$frame(\overline{dep}) \wedge \{\mathtt{heap} := \mathtt{heap}^{pre}\}pre \wedge well \wedge noDeallocs(\mathtt{heap}^{pre}, \mathtt{heap}) \rightarrow$$
$$obs(\mathtt{heap}^{pre}, \mathtt{p}_1, \ldots, \mathtt{p}_n) \doteq obs(\mathtt{heap}, \mathtt{p}_1, \ldots, \mathtt{p}_n)$$

$$(9.10)$$

The implication states that an observer symbol *obs* yields the same value if evaluated in two heaps $\mathtt{heap}^{pre}$ and $\mathtt{heap}$ if the two heaps and the arguments $\mathtt{p}_i$ of the observer satisfy the following conditions in the premiss of (9.10):

1. $\mathtt{heap}^{pre}$ and $\mathtt{heap}$ must coincide on the dependency set *dep*, see (9.11) below,
2. the precondition *pre* of the observer must be satisfied,
3. the two heaps and all arguments must be well-formed, see (9.12) below,
4. there is no deallocation; all objects allocated in $\mathtt{heap}^{pre}$ are still allocated in $\mathtt{heap}$.

We have encountered the formula *frame* which captures the equality of the locations in *dep* already in (9.7). We need to formalize here that everything but the locations in *dep* may change, hence we use the complement $\overline{dep}$ of *dep*:

$$frame(\overline{dep}) = \forall o \forall f; (\quad o.created@\mathtt{heap}^{pre} \doteq FALSE$$
$$\vee o.f \doteq o.f@\mathtt{heap}^{pre}$$
$$\vee \neg(o, f) \in \{\mathtt{heap} := \mathtt{heap}^{pre}\}dep)$$

$$(9.11)$$

The well-formedness condition *well* includes the two heaps and all parameters and reuses the predicate *paramsInRange* introduced in (8.3):

$$well = wellFormed(\mathtt{heap}^{pre}) \wedge wellFormed(\mathtt{heap}) \wedge paramsInRange \quad (9.12)$$

The property *noDeallocs* that no objects are ever deleted from the heap has been introduced in Lemma 9.15.

We now introduce the rule useDependencyContract which formalizes the informal semantics explanation outlined in (9.10). It adds an assumption to the sequent that is itself an implication with left-hand side *guard*. The right-hand side relates the value of an observer symbol *obs* for the heaps denoted by the terms $h^{pre}, h^{post} \in \text{Trm}_{Heap}$, where h^{post} results from h^{pre} through a cascade of applications of the function symbols *store*, *create*, and *anon*. Such cascades are the result of symbolic execution of heap manipulating programs with successive update simplification. It is instructive to compare the rule useDependencyContract with the proof obligation of Definition 8.5.

Definition 9.20 (Rule useDependencyContract).

$$\frac{\Gamma, guard \rightarrow obs(h^{pre}, o, a_1, \ldots, a_n) \equiv obs(h^{post}, o, a_1, \ldots, a_n) \Longrightarrow \Delta}{\Gamma \Longrightarrow \Delta}$$

where:

- $obs \in \text{FSym}$ (or $obs \in \text{PSym}$) is an observer symbol $obs : Heap \times E \times T_1 \times \ldots \times T_n \rightarrow T$ (or $obs : Heap \times E \times T_1 \times \ldots \times T_n$, respectively) with $n \in \mathbb{N}$
- $(pre, dep, term)$ is a dependency contract for *obs*,
- $o \in \text{Trm}_E, a_1 \in \text{Trm}_{T_1}, \ldots, a_n \in \text{Trm}_{T_n}$ are valid arguments for *obs*.
- $h^{post} = f_k(f_{k-1}(\ldots(f_1(h^{pre}, \ldots))))$ with $f_1, \ldots, f_k \in \{store, create, anon\}$
- $\equiv$ stands for $\doteq$ if $obs \in \text{FSym}$ and for $\leftrightarrow$ if $obs \in \text{PSym}$
- *guard* is the formula

$$\mathscr{P}\{\text{heap}^{pre} := h^{pre} \,\|\, \text{heap} := h^{post}\} frame(\overline{dep})$$
$$\wedge \mathscr{P}\{\text{heap} := h^{pre}\} pre$$
$$\wedge wellFormed(h^{pre}) \wedge wellFormed(h^{post})$$
$$\wedge \mathscr{P} paramsInRange \wedge o \not\doteq \text{null} \wedge o.created \doteq TRUE$$

in which the update $\mathscr{P} = \{\text{p}_1 := a_1 \,\|\, \ldots \,\|\, \text{p}_n := a_n\}$ assigns the concrete arguments to the formal parameters of *obs*.

Besides the property that only certain locations change, the equality of the observer applications in (9.10) requires the heap evolution does not deallocate previously created objects; as for instance formalized in Lemma 9.15. For the state change from h^{pre} to h^{post}, the absence of deallocations is guaranteed by the fact that the latter is derived from the former by invocations of the function *store*, *create* and *anon*. Their semantics ensure that no object is ever deallocated. This is formalized in the following lemma.

Lemma 9.21 (No deallocations). *Let* $h^{post} \in \text{Trm}_{Heap}$ *with*

$$h^{post} = f_k(f_{k-1}(\ldots(f_1(h^{pre}, \ldots))))$$

for some $f_1, \ldots, f_k \in \{store, create, anon\}$ *with* $1 \leq k$ *and for some* $h^{pre} \in \text{Trm}_{Heap}$. *Then the following holds:*

$$\models noDeallocs(h^{pre}, h^{post})$$

The lemma—is also needed for the proof of Theorem 9.22 below—is the reason why *noDeallocs* can be excluded from the condition *guard* in Definition 9.20.

Theorem 9.22. *Rule* useDependencyContract *is sound, provided that for all subtypes $E' \sqsubseteq E$ of the static receiver type E of obs, the proof obligation for dependency contracts from Definition 8.5 for pure methods and the obligation from Definition 9.12 for general observer symbols, respectively, is valid.*

Proofs for this theorem and for Lemma 9.21 can be found in [Weiß, 2011, Appendix A].

This is plausible since the proof obligation for dependency contracts (Definition 8.5) expresses that the observer *obs* does not depend on locations outside *dep*. If the formula *guard* in (9.12) is valid, i.e., the difference between the heaps h^{pre} and h^{post} lies only in *dep*, then we can conclude that the value of *obs* is the same for both heaps.

Automatic application of the useDependencyContract rule is not as straightforward as for other rules. The rule can be applied to many different combinations of h^{pre} and h^{post} which increases the search space considerably. To avoid a large number of 'unsuccessful' applications where *guard* cannot be proven and where the application thus does not contribute to the proof, a strategy that proves to work well in practice is to apply the rule only lazily (once all other means of advancing the proof have been exhausted), and only for choices of h^{pre} that already occur on the sequent. Best results for an automatic rule application are obtained whenever h^{pre} is a constant and appears in an equation together with h^{post} in the antecedent.

An application of the useDependencyContract rule will be demonstrated in the course of verifying the List example in Section 9.5.

9.4.5 Rules for Class Invariants

As outlined in Section 9.2.1.3, in JavaDL, class invariants are realized by means of a special model field \inv whose counterpart in JavaDL is the implicit observer symbol Object::*inv* $\in$ PSym.

The definition of the class invariant of a type T collects all class invariant declarations in T and the public invariants of T's supertypes, their combination is essentially the represents clauses for the model field \inv. If more than one object invariant declaration is relevant, e.g., **invariant** e_1; ... **invariant** e_n, the collection of the individual invariant declarations stands for a single represents clause

$$\text{represents } \texttt{\textbackslash inv} = e_1 \text{ \&\& } \dots \text{ \&\& } e_n \ . \tag{9.13}$$

This represents clause defines the meaning of the observer Object::*inv* : *Heap* × Object for objects exactly of type T. The rules for expanding represents clauses ($\text{rep}_{D,m}$ from Section 9.2.1.4) and for dependency contracts (useDependencyContract from the last section) can be used in proofs like for any other model field.

One property sets class invariants aside from arbitrary model fields: While for general model fields, the definition may change arbitrarily in subclasses, public class invariants are inherited to subtypes according to the principle of behavioral subtyping. The invariant can only be changed by adding further clauses. The implicit represents clause from (9.13) thus enumerates all clauses in the current class and all clauses inherited from its super types.

The following classInv$_T^j$ rule allows inferring an individual invariant clause **invariant** e_j present in type T if the invariant Object::$inv(h,o)$ is known to hold for the object $o \in \mathrm{Trm}_T$.

$$\frac{\texttt{Object::}inv(h,o),\ \{\texttt{heap} := h \,\|\, \texttt{self} := o\}\lfloor e_j \rfloor \implies}{\texttt{Object::}inv(h,o) \implies} \text{ classInv}_T^j$$

Note that this rule[10] can only be applied if Object::$inv(h,o)$ occurs in the antecedent, i.e., under the assumption that the invariant holds. It can be applied for any object $o \in \mathrm{Trm}_T$ of type T also if it belongs to one of T's subtypes. Unlike the represents axiom rep$_{D,m}$, it does not require that o is exactly of type T.

Rule classInv$_T^j$ only adds a *consequence* of the invariant to the sequent, not its definition. The entire invariant can only be soundly added when the dynamic type T of the 'receiver' object o is known. In these cases, the rewrite rule repSimple$_{D,m}$ for represents clauses can be used to replace an invariant by its definition:

$$\texttt{Object::}inv(h,o) \rightsquigarrow \bigwedge_{j=1}^{n} \lfloor e_j \rfloor$$

if exactInstance_T(o) ≐ TRUE occurs in the antecedent

if $exactInstance_T(o) \doteq TRUE$ occurs in the antecedent

In many cases, in particular when conducting modular proofs, the definition of the invariant cannot be fully expanded because its actual definition is unknown to the current context. When modularly reasoning that an invariant still holds after a modification of the heap, dependency contracts can be valuable. When both the formulas Object::$inv(h,o)$ and Object::$inv(h',o)$ appear in the sequent, rule useDependencyContract can be applied to reduce one to the other.

Example 9.23. Let us turn back to the List interface outline in Listing 9.9 whose sole class invariant in line 5 states that the size of a list is nonnegative. Assume we have a program variable al of type ArrayList (Listing 9.11), and we know that the invariant for the list al is satisfied, i.e., that Object::$inv(\texttt{heap},\texttt{al})$ is true.

Then the rule classInv$_{\texttt{List}}^1$ allows us to deduce that List::$size(\texttt{heap},\texttt{al}) \geq 0$ since the invariant clause is inherited from List to ArrayList.

However, to establish that the invariant for al holds, it does not suffice to show this property. The array list class has an additional (implicit) invariant $\neg\texttt{self.a} \doteq \texttt{null}$ which also needs to be proved. If $exactInstance_{\texttt{ArrayList}}(\texttt{al}) \doteq TRUE$ is known, then these two properties make up the definition of the invariant.

When reasoning modularly, on the other hand, there might exist a further subtype of ArrayList (which is not declared **final**) which has an invariant definition which

---

[10] The actual rule name used in the KeY prover fits the template Partial_inv_axiom_for_JML_class_invariant_nr_j_in_T.

differs from the one in `ArrayList`. This prohibits the calculus from replacing the invariant symbol by the collection of known invariant clauses—there might be more, yet unknown, clauses.

There are few situations in which a specifier wants to constrain implementation details to the enclosing class. In such cases, a class invariant declaration intentionally should not be inherited by the refining subclasses. To distinguish between class invariant declarations subject to inheritance and local declarations, the former can be declared as `public invariant` and the latter as `private invariant`. By default, class invariants are private.

9.5 Verifying the List Example

This section is a continuation of Section 9.3.4. We assume a list implementation according to the structure shown in the class diagram in Figure 9.1. The program that we consider contains the interface `List` from Listing 9.9 annotated with dynamic frames and a class `Client`. In this modular proof scenario, we do not consider specific implementations of the `List` interface, such as `LinkedList` or `ArrayList`, that were presented above. All reasoning can be based on the interface specification alone. As an example for the verification of JML specifications with dynamic frames, we consider a proof for the method m of the `Client` class:

```
/*@ normal_behavior
  @ requires \invariant_for(list);
  @ requires \disjoint(list.footprint, ((Client)null).*);
  @ requires 0 < list.size();
  @*/
static void m(List list) {
    x++;
    list.get(0);
}
```

The JML method contract is translated to a JavaDL method contract where the precondition *pre*, the postcondition *post* and the modifies clause *mod* are:

$$pre = \texttt{list}.\mathit{inv} \land \mathit{disjoint}\big(\texttt{list.footprint}, \mathit{allFields}((\texttt{Client})\texttt{null})\big)$$
$$\land 0 < \texttt{list.size()} \land \texttt{list} \neq \texttt{null}$$
$$post = \texttt{exc} \doteq \texttt{null}$$
$$mod = \mathit{allLocs} \setminus \mathit{unusedLocs}(\texttt{heap})$$

To ease the presentation of the more bulky formulas of the concrete example, we employ a few self-explanatory abbreviations in this subsection and write $\in, \cap, \setminus, \ldots$ instead of *elementOf*, *union*, *setMinus*, ...

The corresponding proof obligation from Definition 8.4 is:

$\textsf{list}.\textit{inv} \wedge \textit{disjoint}(\textsf{list}.\textsf{footprint}, \textit{allFields}((\textsf{Client})\textsf{null}))$

$\wedge\, 0 < \textsf{list.size}() \wedge \textsf{list} \not\doteq \textsf{null}$

$\wedge\, \textit{wellFormed}(\textsf{heap}) \wedge (\textsf{list} \doteq \textsf{null} \vee \textsf{list}.\textit{created} \doteq \textit{TRUE})$

$\rightarrow \{\textsf{heap}^{pre} := \textsf{heap}\}\langle\textsf{exc = null};$

$\qquad\qquad\qquad\quad \textsf{try \{ self.m(list); \}}$

$\qquad\qquad\qquad\quad \textsf{catch(Exception e) \{ exc = e; \}}\rangle$ $\qquad$ (9.14)

$\big(\textsf{exc} \doteq \textsf{null}$

$\quad \wedge\, \forall \textit{Object}\, o; \forall \textit{Field}\, f;$

$\qquad ((o, f) \in \{\textsf{heap} := \textsf{heap}^{pre}\}(\textit{allLocs} \setminus \textit{unusedLocs}(\textsf{heap}))$

$\qquad\qquad \cup\, \textit{unusedLocs}(\textsf{heap}^{pre})$

$\qquad \vee\, \textit{select}_{Any}(\textsf{heap}, o, f) \doteq \textit{select}_{Any}(\textsf{heap}^{pre}, o, f))))$

Note that the method does not return a value, and that thus the assignment of the returned value to the program variable res is omitted. The following invariant axiom rule of Section 9.4.5 is visible when proving the validity of formula (9.14)

- The object invariant declaration 'public invariant 0 <= size()' in List gives rise to an inv axiom for *inv* on objects of type List, as discussed in Section 9.4.5 and in particular in Example 9.23:

$$\frac{\Gamma,\ \textit{inv}(h, \textit{list}),\ \{\textsf{heap} := h \,\|\, \textsf{self} := \textit{list}\}(0 \leq \textsf{self.size}()) \implies \Delta}{\Gamma,\ \textit{inv}(h, \textit{list}) \implies \Delta}$$

where *list* is a placeholder for a term of type List (or of a subtype). The axiom is visible in the context of Client because of the public visibility of the underlying invariant declaration.

The structure of a proof for the proof obligation is shown in Figure 9.4. Starting from the root sequent '$\implies formula(9.14)$,' the first steps are simplifying the sequent and applying nonsplitting first-order rules (indicated as 'FOL' in the figure), which leads to the following sequent:

$$\left.\begin{aligned}
&\textsf{list}.\textit{inv}, \\
&\textit{allFields}(\textsf{null}) \cap \textsf{list}.\textsf{footprint} \doteq \textit{empty}, \\
&0 < \textsf{list.size}(), \\
&\textit{wellFormed}(\textsf{heap}), \\
&\textsf{list}.\textit{created} \doteq \textit{TRUE}, \\
&\textsf{self}.\textit{created} \doteq \textit{TRUE}
\end{aligned}\right\}\Gamma$$

$\qquad\qquad \implies$

$\qquad\qquad \textsf{list} \doteq \textsf{null},$

$\qquad\qquad \langle\textsf{exc = null};$

$\qquad\qquad\ \ \textsf{try \{ Client.m(list); \}}$

$\qquad\qquad\ \ \textsf{catch(Exception e) \{ exc = e; \}}\rangle(\textsf{exc} \doteq \textsf{null})$

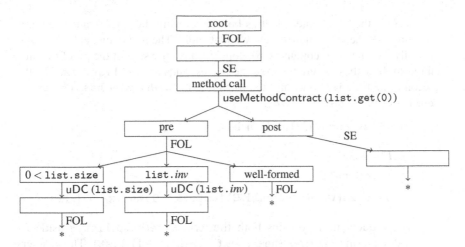

Figure 9.4 Structure of proof for the method contract of method m in class `Client`

The formula *disjoint*(`list.footprint`, *allFields*(`self`)) has been reduced to the formula *allFields*(`null`) ∩ `list.footprint` $\doteq$ *empty*. The negated occurrence of the formula `list` $\doteq$ `null` in the antecedent has been replaced by the nonnegated occurrence in the succedent via the notLeft rule. The formula *frame* below the modality has vanished entirely, because it holds trivially due to the modifies clause being `everything`. Subsequently, the update $heap^{pre}$:= `heap` has been eliminated using the dropUpdate$_2$ rule of Table 3.1, because $heap^{pre}$ no longer occurred in its scope.

Next, we start symbolic execution of the program inside the diamond modality, indicated as 'SE' in Figure 9.4. As one of the first steps of symbolic execution, the body of the method m being verified is inlined as described in Section 3.6.5. Eventually, symbolic execution reaches the method call '`list.get(0)`' inside `m()`. This call is dispatched using its **normal_behavior** JML contract by applying the useMethodContract rule of Section 9.4.3. The application of useMethodContract splits the proof into four branches. We consider here only the two branches for 1. proving the precondition ('pre' branch) valid and 2. continuing after normal termination using the method's postcondition ('post' branch). The other branches close trivially.

- After applying the update w to the formula below it, the 'pre' branch is:

$$\Gamma \implies$$

`list` $\doteq$ `null`,

$$\{exc := \text{null} \,\|\, \text{heap} := store(\text{heap}, \text{null}, \texttt{Client::\$x}, \texttt{Client.x} + 1)\}$$

$$\left(0 \le 0 \wedge 0 < \texttt{list.size()} \wedge \texttt{list}.inv \wedge wellFormed(\text{heap})\right.$$

$$\left.\wedge \texttt{list} \ne \text{null} \wedge \texttt{list}.created \doteq TRUE\right)$$

where Γ is the same antecedent as before. Closing the 'pre' branch requires showing that the six conjuncts below update hold. The first conjunct $0 \leq 0$ holds trivially. For the other conjuncts, we consider a further split of the proof tree into three subbranches, where the first one corresponds to '$0 < \text{list.size()}$,' the second one to '$\text{list.}inv$,' and the third one to '$wellFormed(\text{heap}) \wedge \text{list} \neq \text{null} \wedge \text{list.}created \doteq TRUE$):'

– "$0 < \text{list.size()}$." This branch is:

$$\Gamma \implies$$
$$\text{list} \doteq \text{null},$$
$$0 < \text{size}\big(store(\text{heap}, \text{null}, \text{Client::\$x}, \text{Client.x}+1)\}, \text{list}\big)$$

The sequent now contains both the term $\text{size}(\text{heap}, \text{list})$ (inside Γ) and the term $\text{size}\big(store(\text{heap}, \text{self}, \text{x}, \text{self.x}+1), \text{list}\big)$. This triggers an application of the useDependencyContract rule of Section 9.4.4 (indicated as uDC in Figure 9.4), where we choose $h^{pre} = \text{heap}$ and $h^{post} = store(\text{heap}, \text{null}, \text{Client::\$x}, \text{Client.x}+1)\}$. The rule uses the dependency contract for size generated out of the JML depends clause 'accessible footprint' in line 9 of Listing 9.9. It adds the formula $guard \rightarrow equal$ to antecedent, where the subformula $guard$ (after some simplification) is:

$$wellFormed(\text{heap})$$
$$\wedge\, wellFormed\big(store(\text{heap}, \text{null}, \text{Client::\$x}, \text{Client.x}+1)\big)$$
$$\wedge\, \text{list.}inv \wedge \text{list} \neq \text{null} \wedge \text{list.}created \doteq TRUE$$
$$\wedge\, \big(allFields(\text{null}) \cap \text{list.footprint} \doteq empty\big)$$

All conjuncts of $guard$ follow directly from the rest of the sequent. The formula $equal$ is:

$$\text{size}(\text{heap}, \text{list}) \doteq$$
$$\text{size}\big(store(\text{heap}, \text{null}, \text{Client::\$x}, \text{Client.x}+1), \text{list}\big)$$

Because Γ demands that $0 < \text{size}(\text{heap}, \text{list})$ and the succedent contains $0 < \text{size}\big(store(\text{heap}, \text{null}, \text{Client::\$x}, \text{Client.x}+1), \text{list}\big)$, the information given by $equal$ is enough to close this branch of the proof.

– "$\text{list.}inv$." The branch is:

$$\Gamma \implies$$
$$\text{list} \doteq \text{null},$$
$$inv\big(store(\text{heap}, \text{null}, \text{Client::\$x}, \text{Client.x}+1), \text{list}\big)$$

The sequent now contains the formulas $inv(\texttt{heap},\texttt{list})$ (inside Γ) and $inv\big(store(\texttt{heap},\texttt{null},\texttt{Client::\$x},\texttt{Client.x}+1),\texttt{list}\big)$. The proof continues as on the "$0 < \texttt{list.size()}$" branch above, except that we apply the useDependencyContract rule for inv instead of for $\texttt{size()}$.

- '$wellFormed(\texttt{heap}) \wedge \texttt{list} \neq \texttt{null} \wedge \texttt{list}.created \doteq TRUE$.' This branch is easy to close, using propositional reasoning only.

- After some simplification, the "post" branch is:

$$\Gamma \implies$$
$$\texttt{list} \doteq \texttt{null},$$
$$\{\texttt{exc} := \texttt{null} \,\|\, \texttt{heap} := store(\texttt{heap},\texttt{null},\texttt{Client::\$x},\texttt{Client.x}+1)\}$$
$$\{\texttt{heap} := anon(\texttt{heap},,h) \,\|\, \texttt{exc}' := e\}$$
$$(\texttt{exc}' \doteq \texttt{null} \wedge (\texttt{exc}' \doteq \texttt{null} \rightarrow \texttt{list}.inv)$$
$$\wedge (instance_{\texttt{Exception}}(\texttt{exc}') \rightarrow (false \wedge \texttt{list}.inv))$$
$$\wedge wellFormed(h)$$
$$\rightarrow \langle\texttt{try \{ method-frame(source=m(List)@Client):\{\} \}}$$
$$\texttt{catch(Exception e) \{ exc = e; \}}\rangle(\texttt{exc} \doteq \texttt{null}))$$

where $\texttt{exc}' : \texttt{Exception} \in \text{ProgVSym}$ is the variable used in the applied contract for $\texttt{get}$, and where the constant symbol $e : \texttt{Exception} \in \text{FSym}$ are fresh. The remaining program is basically a **try-catch** with an empty **try** body. Symbolic execution finishes without entering the **catch** block, and hence, excis still **null** afterwards, which allows us to close the branch.

This concludes the example proof for the method contract mct_m. The proof shows that the implementation of method m in **Client** satisfies the contract mct_m, provided that all implementations of get in subclasses of List satisfy the **normal_behavior** method contract for get, and provided that all implementations of size() and inv in subclasses of List satisfy the respective dependency contracts.

9.6 Related Methodologies for Modular Verification

Data Groups

KeY's dialect of JML uses dynamic frames whereas standard JML supports *data groups*. Data groups enable the specification of modifies and depends clauses while leaving a certain amount of freedom to implementations about the actual locations that are modified or read. Inclusion of a location into a data group can either be *static* (using data group inclusions [Leino, 1998] via **in**) or *dynamic* (via **maps ... \into** clauses). Static inclusion of a field adds the locations of the field of all instances to the data group. This makes membership checking easy, but is little suited for dynamic structures. Dynamic inclusion allows a data group of an object to contain locations of other objects and is suitable for dynamic data structures.

Due to dynamic inclusion, the usage of JML's data groups is unsuitable for modular verification as it cannot be known locally whether a location belongs to a data group or not. This may depend on the subclasses. Solutions by imposing global restrictions on the usage of data groups in programs have been proposed by Leino et al. [2002], but are not part of the standard.

Techniques Related to Dynamic Frames

KeY-JML has been inspired by and is very closely related to the dynamic frames based version of the Spec# specification language [Barnett et al., 2005a] that has been proposed by Smans, Jacobs, Piessens, and Schulte [2008]. The main difference is that their language operates on pure functions (and does not support model fields). The advantage is uniformity, but pure method bodies are not allowed to contain specification-only features like quantifiers.

As an extension of their language, Smans et al. propose an implicit framing field footprint which is used as default value in modifies and depends clauses. This approach could be adopted in KeY and JML as well.

Another relative of dynamic frames in JML is the programming and verification language *Dafny* by Leino [2010]. In Dafny specifications, dynamic frame footprints usually occur as ghost fields of type 'set of objects'. Frame specifications in Dafny are thus coarser (all locations of an object are considered), but reasoning is simpler than with arbitrary location sets. Much like with the model field \inv in KeY-JML, Dafny specifications encode invariants by introducing a Boolean pure function Valid.

Ownership

Müller et al. [2003] describe a version of JML that features abstraction dependencies in place of data groups. *Ownership types* [Clarke et al., 1998], more precisely, the *universe types* of Müller [2002], can be used to make dependency specifications modular. Roughly, the idea of *ownership* is to structure the domain of objects hierarchically into a tree of disjoint *contexts*. An ownership *type system* guarantees statically that, at run-time, every object is only ever referenced from within its context or from its owner object. Ownership can thus prevent unwanted aliasing and abstract aliasing.

A widely used ownership based approach to object invariants is the *Spec# methodology* of Barnett et al. [2004], also known as the *Boogie methodology*. Here, objects are furnished with a ghost field st representing their state concerning the invariants. The value of st is either 'valid' or 'invalid'. If an object o is valid, all objects owned by o are valid, and the invariants of o is guaranteed to hold. If it is invalid, its owner must have been invalidated, too. Invariants may refer only to locations of this and of owned objects, and object fields can only be modified when the object has been put in the 'invalid' state.

The methodology also addresses the frame problem: Code cannot compromise the invariant of valid objects. Even if classes may be unknown at verification time, objects are guaranteed to be valid unless they are in the process of being worked on.

A more recent development is the ownership-related invariant protocol *semantic collaboration* by [Polikarpova et al., 2014]. It is a generalization which weakens the hierarchical principle of ownership and allows for more liberal structures. This is achieved by introducing new relationships subjects and observers: the objects in subjects may be used in invariants even if they are not strictly below in the ownership hierarchy. Conversely, the subjects must require that all its observers are invalidated when modified. Semantic collaboration can be used to specify and verify design patterns like the observer or visitor pattern which are difficult to treat with ownership alone.

The authors of Spec# report that the Spec# methodology proved too restrictive for some programs they encountered [Barnett et al., 2011]. On the other hand, the *VCC* project turned back to an ownership based approach, after reportedly encountering limiting performance problems with an approach based on dynamic frames [Cohen et al., 2009].

An advantage of ownership based specification and verification techniques over the very liberal technique of dynamic frames is that the framework clearly fixes which invariants can be expected to hold and need to be established. This results in clearer and shorter specifications. Dynamic frames, on the other hand, are not restricted to strictly hierarchical structures but their liberal framework allows for any kind of interaction and interdependencies between objects and their invariants. While this relieves a burden as far as the layout of data structures is concerned, it requires the specifier to write more extensive specifications.

Separation Logic

Separation logic [Reynolds, 2002, O'Hearn et al., 2001, 2009] is a nonclassical extension to Hoare logic. Similar to the dynamic frames approach, it allows explicit reasoning about the heap, which makes it suitable for reasoning about pointer programs and about concurrent programs. Separation properties are however not formulated explicitly using location sets. They are rather blended with functional specifications, using special 'separating' logical connectives. Instead of modifies clauses and depends clauses, framing information is inferred from a method's precondition: only locations mentioned by the precondition may be read or written by the method. This leads to specifications that tend to be shorter, but perhaps less intuitive, than dynamic frames specifications.

Abstraction in separation logic is achieved by abstraction predicates [Parkinson and Bierman, 2005] which serve a similar purpose as object invariants with model fields. Parkinson [2007] makes the case that class invariants may be obsolete as a fundamental concept in specifying object-oriented programs, pointing out the restrictions of the existing modular global invariant protocols and arguing that a concept like abstract predicates can provide a more flexible foundation for expressing consistency properties of object structures. A defense of invariants as an independent concept controlled by a global invariant protocol has been put forward by Summers et al. [2009].

The VerCors system by Amighi et al. [2014a] features a high-level specification language inspired by JML. It uses separating conjunctions and implications, a built-in permission predicate, and abstract specification predicates [Parkinson and Bierman, 2005] (which are similar to Boolean model methods). Programs and specifications are translated to the Chalice tool [Leino et al., 2009] for verification.

Implicit Dynamic Frames

Implicit dynamic frames [Smans et al., 2012] is an approach inspired both by dynamic frames and by separation logic. Instead of using location sets explicitly, the technique centers around a concept of *permissions*: a method may read or write a location only if it has acquired the permission to do so, and these permissions are passed around between method calls by mentioning them in pre- and postconditions. The C and Java verifier VeriFast [Jacobs et al., 2011c] is based on implicit dynamic frames.

Region Logic

Specifications in region logic [Banerjee et al., 2008b] are closely related to dynamic frames specifications, more so than specifications in the implicit dynamic frames approach. There, modifies and depends clauses are expressed with the help of *regions*, that are expressions that evaluate to sets of object references. Region logic is an extension of Hoare logic for reasoning about such specifications [Banerjee et al., 2008a, Rosenberg et al., 2012].

Model Fields

Although model fields are an important element of specifications in JML, there is not yet a common understanding of their semantics. There are several proposed semantics implicitly given through their implementation in actual verification and runtime checking tools. These are sometimes restricted to 'functional' represents clauses [Müller, 2002, Cok, 2005], to model fields of a primitive type, or by restricting the syntax of represents clauses [Breunesse and Poll, 2003, Leino and Müller, 2006]. A detailed discussion can be found in [Bruns, 2009, Sect. 3.1.5].

9.7 Conclusion

This chapter presented a framework for composing and verifying modular design-by-contract specifications. One of its core features is the introduction of a type \locset, elevating sets of memory locations to first-class citizens of the language, thus allowing the specification of memory dependency constraints using *dynamic frames*. A feature of this framework is the flexibility in writing specifications without assumptions on the heap structure: Almost any memory dependency pattern can be formulated using dynamic frames, and it allows for a remarkably simple and uniform treatment of model fields and methods, pure methods, and class invariants. Specifications can not only determine the dependencies of methods but also of model fields. The absence of abstract aliasing can be specified explicitly in contracts and invariants, using operators such as \disjoint and \new_elems_fresh. The downside of this simplicity is that specifications may get more verbose, and that their verification may be computationally more expensive.

Furthermore, modularity is also achieved by means of *abstraction*. The framework has a variety of means for abstraction in specifications which can be used to formulate and verify specifications modularly; modular correctness proofs are still valid if the program is extended.

To achieve these modularity goals in the verification system addressed in this book, the chapter presented advanced calculus rules.

Outlook

KeY's contributions to specification and verification of concurrent programs have not reached a state to warrant inclusion in this book. One of the most promising lines of attack is the use of permissions as outlined in Section 10.7.2. There is ongoing research also with respect to modularity. Grahl [2015] describes a modular approach to the verification of concurrent programs based on the *rely/guarantee* technique from [Jones, 1983]. Grahl extends the specification concepts by dynamic frames. The classical rely/guarantee approach is not entirely modular since it considers programs that are closed under parallel composition. This issue is solved by Grahl [2015] through the addition of frame annotations.

Chapter 10
Verifying Java Card Programs

Wojciech Mostowski

10.1 Introduction

One of the fundamental assumptions of the KeY project at its beginning was that it
should support verification of an actual programming language and handle realistic
programs. Back then, complete handling of arbitrary Java programs was still considered an unreachable goal in source code based interactive verification. For that reason
a simpler, yet actually existing and officially developed, Java technology was chosen
as our verification target, namely Java Card—a considerably stripped down version
of Java for programming smart cards [Chen, 2000]. The additional motivation for
choosing this particular technology were the corresponding application areas that are
subject to strict security requirements. Nowadays, smart cards are widely used in the
financial sector (bank cards), telecommunications (SIM cards), identity (electronic
passports and identity cards), and transportation (electronic tickets). Many of the
products are indeed developed on the Java Card platform, in particular, the Dutch
biometric passport is based on the Java Card technology. The security requirements
of such applications and, sadly, still often occurring security problems in this area[1]
highly justify the use formal verification.

In fact, other verification tools back in the days have chosen the Java Card dialect
for similar reasons. The KIV [Balser et al., 2000], Krakatoa [Marché et al., 2004], or
Jack [Burdy et al., 2003b] tools all explicitly mention Java Card as a target language
in the corresponding publications. Furthermore, Java Card was also in the center of
the EU VerifiCard project started in 2001 [Jacobs et al., 2001], that consolidated the
efforts to provide verification techniques for Java based smart cards.

Many research teams targeted their effort towards Java Card, but the KeY system was the first tool to implement extensions to support an initially *overseen* by
researchers feature of Java Card, the atomic transaction mechanism [JavaCardRTE,
Chap. 7]. This *extension* of the Java Card Virtual Machine allows one to group

---

[1] Two recent high profile cases of security flaws in smart card based applications are the Dutch
OV-chipcard [Garcia et al., 2008] and one of the smart card based payment authentication protocol
for Internet banking [Blom et al., 2012].

© Springer International Publishing AG 2016
W. Ahrendt et al. (Eds.): Deductive Software Verification, LNCS 10001, pp. 353–380, 2016
DOI: 10.1007/978-3-319-49812-6_10

assignments into atomic blocks in the context of two types of writable memory on smart card chips: volatile RAM and persistent EEPROM. From the point of view of a formal verification system, the most complicating factor of the transaction mechanism is the possibility of a programmatic abort of an on-going transaction. The result of such an abort is a program that continues its execution, but with *selected* variable assignments reverted according to the complex Java Card Virtual Machine transaction rules.

Our formalization of Java Card transactions for the previous generation of the KeY system [Beckert and Mostowski, 2003, Mostowski, 2006] was admittedly rather heavyweight with deep changes in the implementation of KeY. Nevertheless, the formalization provided a complete and sound verification framework for Java Card programs. This was illustrated with realistically sized case studies described by Mostowski [2005, 2007].

In this chapter, we discuss a new solution tailored to the explicit heap model of KeY as described in detail in Chapter 3. The core of the new solution is the *simultaneous* use of two heaps during the verification. The first heap is used as usual, and keeps track of the current reachable state of the program for the purpose of evaluating properties to be verified. The second additional heap is used to keep a backup copy of the main heap for the purpose of transaction roll-back in case of an abort. The resulting solution turns out to be very simple and clean, and most importantly, is very modular with respect to the rest of the JavaDL. Further simplifications of our new formalization come from a more pragmatic approach to the notion of a verifiable Java Card program. Following our practical experience with Java Card technology [Mostowski and Poll, 2008], rather than to support every possible and contrived use of transaction related constructs, we opted to support only patterns commonly agreed as safe by security experts [Pallec et al., 2012]. Programs not adhering to these patterns cannot be verified because of the design of the formalization. Furthermore, apart from supporting Java Card, the idea of using more than one heap, in general arbitrary many heaps, provides solutions for other areas of research in Java verification, in particular for permission-based reasoning about concurrent programs.

The chapter starts with introducing the Java Card technology in more detail in the next section, and then continues with explaining the details of our current formalization of transactions based on two heaps in Section 10.3. In Section 10.5 we discuss the (transparent) extensions to JML to accommodate multiple heap references also on the specification level. Section 10.6 discusses the verification of several Java Card example programs. Finally, in Section 10.7 we discuss the applications of reasoning based in multiple heaps in other areas of verification.

10.2 Java Card Technology

In the following, we concentrate on features of Java Card relevant for this chapter. A comprehensive overview of the Java Card technology is described by Chen [2000], and [JavaCardRTE, JavaCardVM] provide a technical reference.

The Java Card technology is now at version 3.0 and divided into two editions: *Classic* and *Connected*. In this chapter, we refer to the classic edition which is still the established standard in the smart card industry and is essentially the same as previous Java Card versions that were only released as one edition. The connected edition is a feature-rich regular Java edition and no longer a subset of Java like the classic edition. However, the connected edition remains still to be fully accepted as it is not widely used by the industry, yet. Also, Java Card devices actually implementing the 3.0 connected version are still scarce, despite the fact that the connected variant of Java Card was proposed more than 8 years ago.

The Java Card technology in general provides means to program smart cards with Java. The classic edition of Java Card consists of a language specification, which defines the subset of permissible Java in the context of smart cards, a Java Card Virtual Machine specification, which defines the semantics of the Java byte-code when run on a smart card, and finally the Java Card API, which provides access to the specific routines usually found on smart cards, in particular the transaction mechanism. What makes Java Card easier for verification is the lack of concurrency, floating-point numbers, or dynamic class loading, and a very small API (less than 100 classes). The important feature that adds complexity to the Java Card environment compared to Java is that programs can directly operate on two memories built into the card chip. Any data allocated in the EEPROM memory is *persistent* and kept between card sessions, the data that resides in RAM is *transient* and always lost at the end of a card session. That is, EEPROM provides storage facilities to the card, and RAM provides computation space. The following are the memory allocation rules:

- all local variables are transient,
- all newly created objects and arrays are by default persistent, and
- when allocated with a dedicated API call, an array (but not an object) can be made transient.

Note the important difference between a reference to an object and the actual object contents. While the object fields are stored in the persistent memory, the object reference can be kept in a local variable and be transient itself. A garbage collector is not obligatory in Java Card either. Thus, careless handling of allocated references leads to memory leaks, something that is often addressed in Java Card programming guidelines [Pallec et al., 2012]. Any Java reference, once allocated in its target memory, is transparent to the programmer from the syntax point of view, and it is only the underlying Java Card virtual machine that takes appropriate actions according to the memory type associated with a given reference.

Example 10.1. Suppose the following program would be run in a Java Card execution environment:

—— Java Card ————————————————————————————————

```
class MyClass {
  int persistentField;
```

```
void method(int parameter) {
  int localVariable = parameter * 2;
  this.persistentField = localVariable;
  if(persistentField < 0) {
    MyClass mc = new MyClass();
    mc.method(persistentField);
  }
}
}
```
——————————————————————————————————————— Java Card ——

Being an instance field of a class, the value of persistentField is stored in a permanent chip memory location. The local variables parameter and localVariable are stored in the transient RAM memory and are forgotten upon method exit. The assignment this.persistentField = localVariable; effectively copies data from one type of memory to another type, but this transfer between different memory types is not explicit in the program. The mc variable is also local and hence transient, however, the contents of the freshly created object of class MyClass to which mc refers is part of the persistent storage, and so are all of its fields. Upon return from method, a memory leak occurs—the reference to the freshly created object that was stored only in the local variable is lost. On Java Card devices without garbage collection, such leaked memory is irrecoverable.

Additionally, this particular program would very likely cause a memory overuse problem on an actual device. The continuous allocations of MyClass would quickly exhaust the limited amount of available persistent memory (which is usually in the range of 64kB to 128kB), but even sooner the RAM memory (in the range of 4kB) would be filled with the call stack caused by the recursion and cause a stack overflow exception. Hence, it is often advisable not to use recursive method calls on Java Card, and not to do postinitialization object allocation. We come back to the issue of object allocation later in Section 10.3.3.

Objects allocated in EEPROM, like in the example above, provide the only permanent storage to an application. To maintain consistent updates of this persistent data, Java Card offers the atomic transaction mechanism accessible through the API. The following is a brief, but complete summary of the semantics of transactions: Updating a single field or array element is always atomic. Updates can be grouped into transaction blocks, an API call to the static method JCSystem.beginTransaction() opens such a block; it is ended by a commitTransaction() call, an explicit abortTransaction() call, or an implicit abort caused by an unexpected program termination (e.g., card power loss). A commit guarantees that all the updates in the block are executed in one atomic step. An abort reverts the contents of the *persistent memory* to the state before the transaction was entered. Note that an explicit abort does not terminate the whole application, only cancels out persistent updates from the corresponding transaction. The program continues execution with the persistent updates reverted but all the transient updates are still in effect.

Example 10.2. The following program uses a transaction to ensure consistent update
of persistent fields a and b:

—— Java Card ————————————————————————————————————

```
class MyClass {
  int a, b;

  void transferFromAtoB(int num) {
    JCSystem.beginTransaction();
    a = a - num;
    b = b + num;
    if(a < 0 || b < 0) {
      // Too much transfered / overflow
      JCSystem.abortTransaction();
    } else {
      JCSystem.commitTransaction();
    }
  }
}
```

————————————————————————————————————— Java Card ——

In case that either of the two fields goes beyond its assumed bound (they are supposed
to be nonnegative), the transaction is aborted, and the values of both fields are reverted
to their respective values when the transaction was started. Regardless of the outcome
of the transaction, the program could continue its execution and, e.g., try to update
a and b with a smaller value, say num/2. Finally, had the local num variable itself
been updated in any way within the transaction, it would maintain its updated value
regardless of the transaction outcome.

Finally, the API provides so-called *nonatomic* methods to bypass the transaction
mechanism. A nonatomic update of a *persistent* array element is never reverted by an
abort, provided the same array was not manipulated with regular assignments earlier
in the same transaction. We postpone illustrative examples of nonatomic updates to
the next section when we explain the details of the formalization of such updates.

10.3 Java Card Transactions on Explicit Heaps

In the following, driven by examples, we gradually present the complete formalization
of the Java Card transaction semantics in JavaDL using two heap variables. To start
with, we introduce synthetic transaction statements to the Java syntax. That is,
the calculus should allow for symbolic execution of #beginTr, #commitTr, and
#abortTr synthetic statements that define the transaction boundaries in the verified
program. Bridging the actual API transaction calls from the JCSystem discussed
in Section 10.2 to these logic-only statements is a straightforward extension of the

verification system. Then, consider the following snapshot of a more realistic Java Card program, where the fields `balance` and `opCount` are persistent, permanently storing the current balance and operation count of some payment application. The local variables `change` and `newBalance` are transient:

—— Java Card ——

```
int newBalance = 0;
#beginTr;
  this.opCount++;
  newBalance = this.balance + change;
  if(newBalance < 0) {
    #abortTr;
  } else {
    this.balance = newBalance;
    #commitTr;
  }
```

—— Java Card ——

Following the rules from Chapter 3, symbolic execution of this program piece results in the following sequence of state updates to the heap and local variables—ignoring the transaction statements for now:

$$\{newBalace := 0\}$$
$$\{heap := store(heap, self, opCount, select_{int}(heap, self, opCount) + 1)\}$$
$$\{newBalance := select_{int}(heap, self, balance) + change\}$$
$$\{heap := store(heap, self, balance, newBalance)\}$$

The symbolic execution of the `if` statement causes proof splitting, and the last update only appears on the `else` proof branch where `newBalance` is assumed to be nonnegative.

After further simplification, these state updates can be applied to evaluate a postcondition. It could, e.g., query the new value of operation count, i.e., the term $select_{int}(heap, self, opCount)$. The evaluation of this term would indicate a one unit increase with respect to the value stored on the heap before this code is executed.

10.3.1 Basic Transaction Roll-Back

Now let us consider what is required to model the basic semantics of an abort, first under the assumption of a simplified Java Card definition, in which updates to local variables should be kept while updates to persistent locations should be rolled back to the state before the transaction. Up till now, data in these persistent locations are synonymous with the data stored on the heap in the logic. Hence, under the above assumption, it is sufficient to roll back the value of the whole heap. This can be done by introducing two simple symbolic execution rules for transaction statements

#beginTr and #abortTr that respectively store and restore the value of the heap to and from a temporary heap variable *savedHeap* (the $\langle\!\langle \cdot \rangle\!\rangle$ operator indicates that the rule is applicable to both the box and the diamond modality):

$$\text{beginTransaction} \quad \frac{\Longrightarrow \mathcal{U}\,\{savedHeap := heap\}\langle\!\langle[\pi\,\omega]\rangle\!\rangle\phi}{\Longrightarrow \mathcal{U}\,\langle\!\langle[\pi\,\texttt{\#beginTr};\,\omega]\rangle\!\rangle\phi}$$

$$\text{abortTransaction} \quad \frac{\Longrightarrow \mathcal{U}\,\{heap := savedHeap\}\langle\!\langle[\pi\,\omega]\rangle\!\rangle\phi}{\Longrightarrow \mathcal{U}\,\langle\!\langle[\pi\,\texttt{\#abortTr};\,\omega]\rangle\!\rangle\phi}$$

This can be done and works as expected because the *heap* variable has the *call-by-value* characteristics. Now the state updates (on the negative newBalance branch) of our example program are the following:

$\{newBalace := 0\}$
$\{savedHeap := heap\}$
$\{heap := store(heap, self, opCount, select_{int}(heap, self, opCount) + 1)\}$
$\{newBalance := select_{int}(heap, self, balance) + change\}$
$\{heap := savedHeap\}$

Whatever terms referring to heap contents are to be evaluated with these updates, the result are the values on the heap at the point where it was saved in the *savedHeap* variable. The commit statement needs no special handling apart from silent stepping over this statement. In this case, the saved value of the *heap* in the *savedHeap* variable is simply forgotten until a possible subsequent new transaction where *savedHeap* is freshly overwritten with a more recent *heap*.

These rules are sufficient for superficial treatment of transactions in JavaDL under the assumption made at the beginning of this section. Note that, so far, no new or modified assignment rules of any kind were introduced, yet assignments can be canceled.

10.3.2 Transaction Marking and Balancing

The two rules we just introduced do not enforce any order on the transaction statements. Indeed, they allow to successfully verify programs:

    #abortTr; #beginTr;   or   #commitTr; #commitTr;

One solution to enforce balancing of transactions is to keep track of a transaction depth counter and make additional checks upon transaction statements. In fact, this is how the Java Card API methods enforce balancing. In Java Card, transactions cannot be nested, i.e., the maximum allowed depth is always 1. However, by the same specification, an open transaction does not have to be terminated within the same syntactical block of a program, it is only required that the transaction is eventually terminated within the same card session, if not, the transaction is aborted by the system itself. Thus, in principle, a transaction can be initiated in one method, and terminated in another.

In the logic we opt for a more restrictive use of transactions, with the following rationale. Java Card security guidelines [Pallec et al., 2012] ban programs with large transaction blocks spanning over several methods (due to the high risk of overrunning the transaction buffer). A logic calculus allowing for such arbitrary "spreading" of transaction statements would need to carry around complete information about the state of a transaction across method invocations, a complication that would make proofs unnecessarily more cluttered and difficult.

Following this rationale, our formalization not only relies on this transaction use restricted to one method, but also enforces it, in the following way. A transaction marker $_{TR}$ attached to any modality indicates that the current execution context of the verified program is an open transaction. In practice, such a marked modality is simply a separate modality $\langle _{TR}\cdot \rangle$ (or $[_{TR}\cdot]$ as the case may be). Rules for handling transaction opening and closing statements defined only for the adequate modalities automatically enforce correct transaction balancing. Similarly, the absence of a logic rule for an empty transaction modality prevents closing proof goals with open transactions. Overall this forces a complete transaction block to appear in a single verification context, i.e., one method. Furthermore, special array assignment rules (which we introduce shortly) are also defined for the transaction context only, without cluttering any nontransaction context. This keeps regular Java verification efforts clear of any transaction artifacts in the logic without the need to introduce any special Java Card modes or switches in the prover or similar mechanisms.

The new rules for the transaction statements are the following, now with an explicit rule for the commit statement, in which nothing happens to the *heap* variable, but the transaction context is canceled out by changing the transaction modality $\langle [_{TR}\cdot] \rangle$ back to $\langle [\cdot] \rangle$:

$$\text{beginTransaction} \quad \frac{\Gamma \Longrightarrow \mathcal{U}\{savedHeap := heap\}\langle [_{TR}\pi\,\omega] \rangle \phi, \Delta}{\Gamma \Longrightarrow \mathcal{U}\langle [\pi\,\texttt{\#beginTr};\,\omega] \rangle \phi, \Delta}$$

$$\text{abortTransaction} \quad \frac{\Gamma \Longrightarrow \mathcal{U}\{heap := savedHeap\}\langle [\pi\,\omega] \rangle \phi, \Delta}{\Gamma \Longrightarrow \mathcal{U}\langle [_{TR}\pi\,\texttt{\#abortTr};\,\omega] \rangle \phi, \Delta}$$

$$\text{commitTransaction} \quad \frac{\Gamma \Longrightarrow \mathcal{U}\langle [\pi\,\omega] \rangle \phi, \Delta}{\Gamma \Longrightarrow \mathcal{U}\langle [_{TR}\pi\,\texttt{\#commitTr};\,\omega] \rangle \phi, \Delta}$$

10.3.3 Object Creation and Deletion

In Section 10.2 we already mentioned that object allocation on Java Card requires special attention due to limited memory of a smart card and absence of a garbage collector. Because of this, according to the Java Card specification, objects created inside transactions require detailed consideration. In short, when aborting a transaction all objects created in that transaction need to be deallocated, regardless of whether these objects are still referenced from objects outside of the transaction. To prevent

dangling references, all such references to the deleted objects must be replaced with
null by the Java Card virtual machine. In other words, the Java Card virtual machine
should perform an explicit, *forced* garbage collection upon transaction abort.

This causes problems for our logic, which, being a logic for garbage-collected
Java, was never designed to do any object allocation back-tracking (probably, none
of the logics for Java are). However, this is also problematic in the actual Java Card
virtual machine implementations. It is not uncommon for the implementations to be
buggy and lead to serious security issues, as reported by Mostowski and Poll [2008].
Because of that, both security guidelines and newer Java Card specifications strongly
discourage object allocation inside transactions altogether.

In our formalization of transactions, we take the same approach, we do not allow
objects to be allocated in transaction contexts. This is simply done by *not* providing
any object allocation rules for the transaction modalities.

10.3.4 Persistent and Transient Arrays

By default, in Java Card new objects and arrays are allocated in the persistent memory.
For scenarios where an object needs to be allocated in transient memory, the Java
Card API offers special static methods that redirect allocation to the transient memory,
namely:

- makeTransientBooleanArray(short size, byte transientType),
- makeTransientByteArray(short size, byte transientType),
- makeTransientShortArray(short size, byte transientType),
- makeTransientObjectArray(short size, byte transientType).

Hence, only arrays can be allocated in transient memory, contents of other objects
are always persistent. When allocating transient arrays, one also specifies, through
the transientType argument, the moment when the transient memory is cleared.
In Java Card the transient memory can be cleared either upon card reset, i.e., when
the card session is terminated, or already upon application termination. The latter is
useful in practice when, e.g., one application does not wish for any other application
to access the data it worked on for security reasons. However, for our formalization,
this is irrelevant. But, to be consistent with the API philosophy, in the following we
keep using a number to describe the different types of Java Card memory, rather than
just a Boolean differentiating between transient and persistent memory types.

In the next step we need to address the issue of separate transaction treatment for
persistent and transient arrays in Java Card. Our solution is general enough to also
consider the possibility of regular objects to be transient, but we refer only to arrays
in our explanations.

So far in our formalization, we roll back the whole contents of the heap. The
actual Java Card transaction semantics require that the contents of transient arrays,
allocated by the above API methods, are never rolled back. Since in JavaDL all
arrays are stored on the heap, we somehow need to introduce a *selective* roll-back

mechanism. We achieve this with the following. Whenever an array element is updated in a transaction we check for the persistency type of the array. The check itself is simply done by introducing an additional implicit integer field to all objects, called `<transient>`, that maintains the information about the persistency type of an object. Standard JavaDL allocation rules set this field to 0 that denotes persistent objects, while the dedicated API methods for creating transient arrays specify this field to reflect the `transientType` argument discussed above.

Then, when handling assignments, for persistent arrays we take no additional action, for transient arrays we update the value on the heap and additionally update the value on the backup heap *savedHeap*. During an abort, the regular heap is restored to the contents of the backup heap that now also includes updates to transient arrays that were not supposed to be rolled back. The resulting assignment rule for arrays is the following (for simplicity we skip array bounds checks and similar here, these are no different from the rules discussed in Section 3.6.2):

arrayAssignTransaction

$$
\frac{
\begin{array}{l}
\mathcal{U}\,(a.\texttt{<transient>} \doteq 0) \Longrightarrow \{heap := store(heap,a,i,se)\}\langle\!\langle_{TR}\pi\,\omega]\!\rangle\phi \\
\mathcal{U}\,(a.\texttt{<transient>} > 0) \Longrightarrow \{savedHeap := store(savedHeap,a,i,se)\} \\
\qquad\qquad\qquad\qquad \{heap := store(heap,a,i,se)\}\langle\!\langle_{TR}\pi\,\omega]\!\rangle\phi
\end{array}
}{
\Longrightarrow \mathcal{U}\,\langle\!\langle_{TR}\pi\,\texttt{a[i]=se;}\,\omega]\!\rangle\phi
}
$$

Assuming that arrays `tr` and `ps` are, respectively, transient and persistent, the symbolic execution of this program:

```
tr[0] = 0;
ps[0] = 0;
#beginTr;
   tr[0] = 1;
   ps[0] = 1;
#abortTr;
```

results in the following sequence of state updates:

$$
\begin{array}{l}
\{heap := store(heap,tr,0,0)\}\{heap := store(heap,ps,0,0)\} \\
\{savedHeap := heap\} \\
\{heap := store(heap,tr,0,1)\}\{savedHeap := store(savedHeap,tr,0,1)\} \\
\{heap := store(heap,ps,0,1)\} \\
\{heap := savedHeap\}
\end{array}
$$

With these updates, the evaluation of terms $select_{int}(heap,ps,0)$ and $select_{int}(heap,tr,0)$ results in 0 and 1, respectively, as required by the Java Card transaction semantics.

10.3.5 Nonatomic Updates

The last quirk in the semantics of Java Card transactions are the so-called *nonatomic* updates of persistent array elements. Such updates are invoked by dedicated API calls and they bypass transaction handling, i.e., no roll-back of data updated nonatomically is ever performed, similarly to local variables and transient array updates, even though the data is persistent. By this definition updates to transient arrays as defined by Java Card are in fact nonatomic, as they are indeed never rolled back either. We have just introduced a mechanism that prevents the roll-back of transient arrays, by checking the <transient> field of the array and providing corresponding state updates. To extend this behavior to persistent arrays, we allow for the implicit <transient> field of an array to be mutable in our logic. In turn, we can temporarily change the assignment semantics for an array by manipulating the <transient> field. Concretely, a nonatomic assignment to a persistent array element can be modeled by first setting the <transient> field to a positive value, then performing the actual assignment, and then changing the value of <transient> back to 0. Hence, a nonatomic assignment a[i] = se, where a is a persistent array, is simply modeled as:

a.<transient> = 1; a[i] = se; a.<transient> = 0;

Then, the array assignment rule we provided above introduces the necessary updates to the regular and backup heaps to achieve transaction bypass, i.e., a nonatomic assignment.

Similarly to transient memory allocation, in Java Card the nonatomic updates are delegated to dedicated API methods. Hence, the manipulation of the <transient> field is delegated to the reference implementation of these API methods, and this *emulation* of nonatomic assignments is easily achieved in the actual Java Card programs to be verified by KeY.

Unfortunately, there is one more additional condition that Java Card defines for nonatomic updates that we need to check. A request for a nonatomic update becomes effective only if the persistent array in question has not been already updated atomically (i.e., with a regular assignment) within the same transaction. If such an update has been performed, any subsequent updates to the array are always atomic within the same transaction and rolled back upon transaction abort. We illustrate this with the following two simple programs operating on a persistent array a, for simplicity we mark a nonatomic assignment with #=, which would otherwise require a lengthy call to a static API method:

```
a[0] = 0;                      a[0] = 0;
#beginTr;                      #beginTr;
  a[0] #= 1;                     a[0] = 2;
  a[0] = 2;                      a[0] #= 1;
#abortTr;                      #abortTr;
assert a[0] == 1;             assert a[0] == 0;
```

The program on the left results in a[0] equal to 1 (a nonatomic update is in effect), the program on the right rolls a[0] back to 0, as the regular assignment a[0] = 2; disables any subsequent nonatomic assignments, and hence all transaction updates are reverted.

To introduce this additional check in the logic, we employ one more implicit field for array objects, <transactionUpdated>, that maintains information about atomic updates. Set to true, it indicates that the array was already updated with a regular assignment, false indicates no such updates and allows for nonatomic updates in the same transaction still to be effective. The new assignment rule for arrays needs to be altered to handle all these conditions and also to record the changes to the <transactionUpdated> field itself. Without quoting the complete assignment rule again, the complete state updates to be introduced for an assignment a[i] = se is the following:

$$\{heap := store(heap, a, i, se)\}$$
$$\{savedHeap :=$$
$$\quad \text{if } select_{int}(heap, a, \texttt{<transient>}) \doteq 0 \text{ then}$$
$$\quad\quad store(savedHeap, a, \texttt{<transactionUpdated>}, TRUE)$$
$$\quad \text{else}$$
$$\quad\quad \text{if } select_{int}(savedHeap, a, \texttt{<transactionUpdated>}) \doteq FALSE \text{ then}$$
$$\quad\quad\quad store(savedHeap, a, i, se)$$
$$\quad\quad \text{else } savedHeap\}$$

The updates to the <transactionUpdated> field are purposely stored on the backup heap *savedHeap* to ease the resetting of this field with each new transaction. On transaction abort, the heap reverting update filters out any updates to this field on the backup heap using the anonymization function (see Section 3.3.1) of the logic:

$$\{heap := anon(savedHeap, allObjects(\texttt{<transactionUpdated>}), heap)\}$$

This expresses the operation of copying the contents of heap *savedHeap* to *heap*, but retaining the value of the <transactionUpdated> field in all objects in *heap*. Thus all manipulations of <transactionUpdated> in proofs are local to a single transaction.

10.4 Taclets for the New Rules

The implementation of the new logic rules to handle Java Card transactions that we have just presented is almost trivial. Only a handful of new taclets (see Chapter 4) have to be added to the KeY rule base, most of them very simple. Only the rule for assigning array elements within transactions is considerably more complicated because of the cascade update that needs to be introduced. Yet it only involves changing one kind of rule for array assignments. The only nontaclet extensions, i.e. *internal* to KeY, are:

- the introduction of the additional modalities $\langle\!\langle_{TR}\cdot]\rangle$ in the KeY data structures. With the help of schematic modal operators these new modalities are easily added to the existing rules for Java constructs that are not affected by transaction semantics,
- the addition of the built-in Java statements for transaction boundaries #beginTr, #commitTr, and #abortTr to the Java syntax. In the implementation they received fully descriptive names;
- the addition of two new implicit fields to objects, <transient> and <transactionUpdated>.

Below we give the essential taclets that implement the new rules.

The two additional modalities $\langle_{TR}\cdot\rangle$ and $[_{TR}\cdot]$ are denoted with

```
\diamond_transaction{ ... }\endmodality
```

and

```
\box_transaction{ ... }\endmodality
```

in the taclet language, respectively. The existing rules for all Java constructs are extended to handle these new modalities by including them in the schematic modal operator #allmodal:

```
\modalOperator { diamond, box,
        diamond_transaction, box_transaction } #allmodal;
```

Then, the rules for entering and exiting the transactions for the diamond operator are given with the following three taclets:

—— KeY ——————————————————————————————————

```
beginJavaCardTransactionDiamond {
  \find (==> \<{.. #beginJavaCardTransaction; ...}\> post)
  \replacewith(==> {savedHeap := heap}
      \diamond_transaction{.. ...}\endmodality post)
  \heuristics(simplify_prog)
  \displayname "beginJavaCardTransaction"
};


commitJavaCardTransactionDiamond {
  \find (==> \diamond_transaction{..
                #commitJavaCardTransaction;
                ...}\endmodality post)
  \replacewith(==> \<{.. ...}\> post)
  \heuristics(simplify_prog)
  \displayname "commitJavaCardTransaction"
};


abortJavaCardTransactionDiamond {
  \find (==> \diamond_transaction{..
                #abortJavaCardTransaction;
                ...}\endmodality post)
```

```
\replacewith(==> {heap := anon(savedHeap,
  allObjects(java.lang.Object::<transactionUpdated>),
  heap)} \<{.. ...}\> post)
\heuristics(simplify_prog)
\displayname "abortJavaCardTransaction"
};
```

—— KeY ——

The rule for the abort also includes the heap update necessary to reset all transaction-updated flags for arrays as described at the end of Section 10.3.5.

Then, the rule for new instance allocations of arrays (see Section 3.6.6.3) needs to be amended to include the initialization of the new implicit fields for transaction handling:

—— KeY ———

```
allocateInstanceWithLength {
  \find (==> \modality{#allmodal}{.#pm@#t2()..
              #lhs = #t.#allocate(#len)@#t;
           ...}\endmodality post)
  \replacewith (==> { heap :=
     store(store(create(heap, #lhs),
       #lhs, java.lang.Object::<transient>, 0),
       #lhs, java.lang.Object::<transactionUpdated>, FALSE) }
     \modality{#allmodal}{.. ...}\endmodality post)
  ...
};
```

—— KeY ——

Finally, the rule for assigning array elements is now the following. We skip the null object reference, array index bounds, and array store validity checks for clarity, as they are exactly the same as described in Section 3.6.2:

—— KeY ———

```
assignment_to_array_component_transaction {
  \schemaVar \modalOperator { diamond_transaction,
    box_transaction } #transaction;
  \find (\modality{#transaction}{..
          #v[#se] = #se0;
          ...}\endmodality post)
  \sameUpdateLevel
  "Normal␣Execution␣(#v␣!=␣null)": \replacewith(
    {heap := store(heap, #v, arr(#se), #se0)}
    {savedHeap :=
      \if(int::select(heap, #v,
          java.lang.Object::<transient>) = 0)
      \then(store(savedHeap, #v,
```

```
            java.lang.Object::<transactionUpdated>, TRUE))
      \else(
          \if(boolean::select(savedHeap, #v,
              java.lang.Object::<transactionUpdated>) = FALSE)
          \then(store(savedHeap, #v, arr(#se), #se0))
          \else(savedHeap)) }
      \modality{#transaction}{.. ...}\endmodality post)
  \add (!(#v=null) & lt(#se, length(#v)) &
      geq(#se,0) & arrayStoreValid(#v, #se0) ==> );
  ...Other proof branches to check for exceptions...
  \heuristics(simplify_prog, simplify_prog_subset)
};
```

—— KeY ——

10.5 Modular Reasoning with Multiple Heaps

The taclets that we have just discussed cover the implementation of the new logic rules to handle Java Card transactions. This makes the core JavaDL calculus and the associated proving engine of KeY aware of transactions. It does not yet, however, handle modular reasoning with contracts in the presence of multiple, simultaneously evolving heap data structures. This issue of modularity for multiple heaps is entirely orthogonal to the transaction semantics. That is, other possible extensions to KeY that involve the use of more than one heap face the same problem. Such additional heaps can be used to model some concrete execution artifact, like the transaction handling described here or different physical memories present on some device. Alternatively, additional heaps can be used to introduce additional abstractions to the logic, for example, permission accounting for thread-local concurrent reasoning. We discuss these possible scenarios in a bit more detail in the concluding Section 10.7.

From the point of view of KeY, heap variables are simply program variables, only that they require special handing when proof obligations are generated and when contract or loop rules are applied (see Chapter 9). In particular, location sets declared in **assignable** clauses are used to properly handle framing. In the presence of multiple, simultaneously changing heaps, the framing conditions, and hence the **assignable** clauses, have to take into account the additional heaps.

To lift this up to the specification layer of JML, we now allow the assignable clauses to take an additional (and optional) argument that declares the heap that the subsequently listed locations refer to. When no heap argument is given, the default memory heap represented with the **heap** variable, is assumed. In this extension of JML, the heap argument is given in angle brackets following immediately the **assignable** keyword. Hence, the following are all valid assignable clauses:

`assignable o.f;`	*refers to the default heap*
`assignable<heap> o.f;`	*the same, but explicit*

`assignable<savedHeap> o.f, o.g;`   *locations that can change*
                                     on the backup heap

`assignable<heap><savedHeap> o.f;`   *location that can change*
                                     on both heaps simultaneously

For such specifications (for methods and/or loops), KeY can now generate and use appropriate framing conditions over all defined heaps. On the implementation side KeY can handle any arbitrary, but fixed, number of additional heaps. We give more realistic examples of how this is used in practice in the next section.

The idea of making heaps explicit parameters in assignable clauses is further extended to other specification constructs to allow even more flexible reasoning. In principle, not all of the additional heaps are *active* in all verification and/or proof contexts. In particular, `savedHeap` is only relevant in proof contexts where there is an active Java Card transaction, i.e., only within the scope of transaction modalities $\langle\![_{TR}\cdot]\!\rangle$. In other contexts, all specification expressions relating to the `savedHeap` can be just ignored. Since we allow all of the specification elements, in particular **requires** and **ensures** clauses, to declare the heaps they relate to, KeY can selectively create method contracts that filter out the correspondingly unused heaps for the different verification and proof contexts. Conversely, the presence of additional heaps in the specification give the KeY system an indication whether the given contract is applicable in a given context. In particular, contracts that are not listing assignable locations for the `savedHeap` are not considered applicable in transaction contexts.

Apart from assignable and other specification clauses, the user has to be able to refer to locations on different heaps in regular JML expressions. To this end, the operator `\backup` can be applied to any field or array element access expression to indicate that the backup heap `savedHeap` should be accessed rather than the regular one, exactly in the same way as the `\old` operator accesses the heap prior to the method call. Other additional heaps would introduce their own corresponding access keywords, for example, `\perm` to specify concurrent access permissions stored a separate heap (again, see the end of the concluding Section 10.7).

The final extension for JML to fully access the Java Card transaction extensions is the ability to access the implicit fields `<transient>` and `<transactionUp-dated>` from specifications. Both can be simply accessed directly as field references. Additionally, for any object o, the former can be access with a proper Java Card API call, `JCSystem.isTransient(o)`, the latter can be accessed with the JML keyword `\transactionUpdated(o)`.

10.6 Java Card Verification Samples

This section is devoted to a handful of examples that make use of the presented formalization of Java Card transactions. We start with the JML specified version of the balance updating method that we used as a running example in Section 10.3, then we discuss how the actual reference implementation of the native transaction-*sensitive* array manipulation routines of the Java Card API can be specified and verified with KeY. Finally, we show a short example of Java Card code implementing a pin counter update routine using one of these API methods. It illustrates the verifiability of the effects of nonatomic updates to ensure the routine's security. All of the presented examples are verified with KeY fully automatically, hence we discuss mostly the specifications.

10.6.1 Conditional Balance Updating

Below we list the updateBalance example we used earlier in Section 10.3 with full JML specifications. The method has two specification cases to reflect the two possible outcomes of the method: either both object fields are updated or none of them is. Additionally, we specify that both fields should never be negative:

—— Java + JML ——————————————————————————

```
public class PurseApplet {

  short balance = 0; //@ invariant balance >= 0;
  short operationCount = 0; //@ invariant operationCount >= 0;

  /*@ public normal_behavior
        requires JCSystem.getTransactionDepth() == 0;
        requires balance + change >= 0;
        ensures balance == \old(balance) + change;
        ensures operationCount == \old(operationCount) + 1;
        ensures \result == \old(balance) + change;
      also
      public normal_behavior
        requires JCSystem.getTransactionDepth() == 0;
        requires balance + change < 0;
        ensures balance == \old(balance);
        ensures operationCount == \old(operationCount);
        ensures \result == \old(balance) + change;
    @*/
  public short updateBalance(short change) {
    short newBalance = 0;
    JCSystem.beginTransaction();
    this.operationCount++;
    newBalance = (short)(this.balance + change);
    if(newBalance < 0) {
    JCSystem.abortTransaction();
      return newBalance;
    }
```

```
    this.balance = newBalance;
    JCSystem.commitTransaction();
    return newBalance;
}
...
}
```
———————————————————————————————— Java + JML ——

The newly calculated balance is returned by the method, regardless of the actual outcome of the balance updating, i.e., the method also returns a possibly negative would-be balance. This is to illustrate that updates to local variables are not at all affected by transactions. In both specification cases, the method's result is the same, i.e., equal to the sum of the initial balance and the requested change. Also, both specification cases require that there is not any on-going transaction when this method is called. That is, the transaction depth recorded by the API should be 0. The remaining parts of the two specification cases spell out the property that the two object fields are updated simultaneously. If the new requested balance is not negative, the operation count is increased and the new balance is stored. Otherwise, both fields remain unchanged.

10.6.2 Reference Implementation of a Library Method

As mentioned in Section 10.2, the Java Card API is a substantially cut-down version of the regular Java API. The classic edition Java Card API consists of less than 100 classes, moreover, a lot of the methods in the API are not implemented in Java Card themselves, but as native code. This is because most of the API is an interface to the smart card hardware: an Application Protocol Data Unit (APDU) buffer that is used for communication with the host, the transaction facilities that we have been discussing here, or the cryptographic facilities usually supported by a dedicated CPU.

One particular part of this API is responsible for efficient handling of bulk memory updates, i.e., complete array updating or copying. These *native* array methods not only improve the performance, but also offer transaction specific handling of the arrays. That is, one class of array methods ensure atomic update of the given array (as if the whole operation were included in a transaction block), the second class allow for nonatomic updates of array elements. Such nonatomic updates, as discussed in Section 10.3.5, allow by-passing an on-going transaction to effectively enforce unconditional update of persistent memory that would otherwise be reverted by a transaction abort.

From the point of view of the reference implementation, these nonatomic methods are the most interesting and the most challenging. Here we discuss one that fills an array with data, the arrayFillNonAtomic method from the Util class with the following signature:

```
public static final short arrayFillNonAtomic(
      byte[] bArray, short bOffset, short length, byte value)
    throws NullPointerException, ArrayIndexOutOfBoundsException;
```

In regular execution contexts, i.e., outside of any transaction, this method does what one would expect: It fills the range of array elements from bOffset to bOffset+length-1 incl. with the value byte. The return value is the first offset index right after the modified elements. The specification is straightforward with JML, our specification also requires conditions for normal termination:

—— Java + JML ——————————————————————————————

```
public normal_behavior
  requires JCSystem.getTransactionDepth() == 0;
  requires bArray != null && length >= 0;
  requires bOffset >= 0 && bOffset+length <= bArray.length;
  ensures (\forall short i; i >= 0 && i < length;
                  bArray[bOffset+i] == value);
  ensures \result == bOffset + length;
  assignable bArray[bOffset..bOffset+length-1];
```
————————————————————————————————— Java + JML ——

The first precondition limits the use of the method to nontransaction contexts only. The code to achieve this behavior is also straightforward, this is done with a simple loop specified with JML:

—— Java + JML ——————————————————————————————

```
/*@ loop_invariant i >= 0 && i <= length &&
      (\forall short j; j>=0 && j<length;
        bArray[bOffset + j] == (j < i ?
            value : \old(bArray[bOffset + j]))
    );
    decreases length - i;
    assignable bArray[bOffset..bOffset+length-1]; @*/
for(short i=0; i<length; i++) {
  bArray[bOffset + i] = value;
}
return (short)(bOffset + length);
```
————————————————————————————————— Java + JML ——

The verification of this poses KeY no problems whatsoever.

Extending both the specification and the reference implementation to the transactional behavior makes things a little bit more complicated. First of, our top-level specification needs to state what the effects on the contents of the savedHeap are going to be. This is specified with the following and reflects the semantics of nonatomic updates described in Section 10.3.5 above.

—— JML ——————————————————————————————————

```
public normal_behavior
```

```
requires JCSystem.getTransactionDepth() == 1;
requires !\transactionUpdated(bArray);
requires JCSystem.isTransient(bArray) ==
    JCSystem.NOT_A_TRANSIENT_OBJECT;
requires bArray != null && length >= 0;
requires bOffset >= 0 && bOffset+length <= bArray.length;
ensures (\forall short i; i >= 0 && i < length;
    bArray[bOffset+i] == value);
ensures \result == bOffset + length;
ensures (\forall short i; i>=0 && i<length;
    \backup(bArray[bOffset + i]) == value);
assignable<heap><savedHeap>
    bArray[bOffset..bOffset+length-1];
```
── JML ──

The presence of the savedHeap reference in the assignable clause makes this specification applicable to transaction contexts, the first precondition narrows this to transaction contexts only. Then, we limit ourselves only to persistent arrays and require that the array has not been updated with regular assignments in the same transaction, i.e., to execution contexts where the update caused by the method is indeed nonatomic. The remaining preconditions are as before to ensure nonexceptional behavior of the method. The first two postconditions are the same as before and specify the effects of the method on the state of the regular heap. The third postcondition states that the contents of bArray is also changed on the backup heap. Effectively this means that the method bypasses the transaction and updates the array unconditionally.

The implementation of the method and the specification of the loop also need to be changed accordingly. First, to emulate the nonatomic update in the code we need to temporarily change the persistency type of the array, following the schema described in Section 10.3.5 above. This should only be done in case the array is not already transient. Thus, we surround the loop with the following:

── Java Card ───

```
final boolean changeTransient = (JCSystem.isTransient(bArray)
    == JCSystem.NOT_A_TRANSIENT_OBJECT);
if(changeTransient) {
    JCSystem.nativeKeYSetTransient(bArray,
        JCSystem.CLEAR_ON_RESET);
}

// The update loop...

if(changeTransient) {
    JCSystem.nativeKeYSetTransient(bArray,
        JCSystem.NOT_A_TRANSIENT_OBJECT);
```

```
}
```

———————————————————————————————— Java Card ——

The method nativeKeYSetTransient is a built-in KeY method that can change the
<transient> field of objects, something that is not normally possible with regular
Java syntax.[2]

Finally, we add specifications to our update loop to also account for changes
on the savedHeap. The loop invariant quoted before stays the same, as does the
decreases clause. We add a new loop invariant that states the effects of the loop on
the backup heap and adds this heap to the assignable clause:

—— JML ————————————————————————————————————

```
// Previous loop invariant and decreases clause
loop_invariant (\forall short j; j >= 0 && j < length;
    \backup(bArray[bOffset + j]) == value);
assignable<heap><savedHeap>
    bArray[bOffset..bOffset+length-1];
```

————————————————————————————————————— JML ——

KeY also has no problems verifying this modified method automatically. The
final remark for this method is that it is clear that we introduced redundancy in the
specification. The first, nontransactional specification is practically a subset of the
second specification. This was done purposely for the clarity of the presentation.
However, it is possible to combine the two specifications (both the method contract
and the loop specification) into one and make KeY construct a contract that is
applicable in both nontransactional and transactional contexts. This is done by also
annotating the **requires** and **ensures** clauses with the corresponding heap variable.
Then, in a nontransaction context only the clauses *not* annotated with savedHeap are
used, in transaction contexts both clauses are used. In particular, the postconditions
that specify quantifier expressing the new state of the array would now be specified
in one contract with:

—— JML ————————————————————————————————————

```
ensures (\forall short i; i >= 0 && i < length;
    bArray[bOffset+i] == value);
ensures<savedHeap> (\forall short i; i >= 0 && i < length;
    \backup(bArray[bOffset+i]) == value);
```

————————————————————————————————————— JML ——

---

[2] One can consider the <transient> field purposely hidden, so that only the API is allowed to
make changes of this field that are legal in terms of Java Card specification.

10.6.3 *Transaction Resistant PIN Try Counter*

We can now use the method `arrayFillNonAtomic` to implement a transaction-safe
PIN (Personal Identification Number) try counter [Hubbers et al., 2006]. A try counter
is a simple one variable counter that gets decreased with every authentication event,
i.e., entering the PIN. Only when the entered PIN is correct, the try counter gets reset
to its predefined maximum value (typically 3). Once the counter reaches zero, no
further authentication attempts should be possible, and resetting the PIN back to a
usable state requires some sort of a administrative procedure, for example, entering a
PUK (Personal Unlocking Key) code or simply getting a new card.

   This describes the security of the PIN try counter on the functional level, and up
to this point such a try counter is trivial to implement. On top of this functionality,
one needs to ensure that the try counter is resistant to all sorts of attacks. Using
the transaction mechanism, one of the possible attacks on a PIN is the following.
The try counter of the PIN is stored in the persistent memory of the card so that
the PIN state is not reset during every new card session. Then, one could use an
aborting transaction to revert the try counter. The PIN checking routine is enclosed
in a transaction. The attacker guesses a PIN code and in case the PIN is not correct
the transaction is aborted, which in effect reverts all the updates to the persistent
memory, and that would include the try counter. Effectively this gives the attacker an
infinite number of possible guesses to break the PIN code. And, given the usually
short PIN numbers (4 or 6 decimal digits), this breaks the security of the card wide
open. Such an attack is realistically possible if an attacker is able to upload such an
exploiting applet that would attempt to break the global PIN of the card, normally
accessible through one of the security APIs of Java Card.

   To tackle this problem, the try counter needs to be updated in a nonatomic fashion,
so that no transaction aborts would ever affect its value. Although the Java Card
API provides nonatomic updates for arrays only, it is still possible to implement a
try counter using these methods. Instead of storing the counter in a single variable
(object field), we store the counter in a one element array. Then we simply always
use a nonatomic method from the API to update the try counter.[3] For this we provide
the following Java Card class:

—— Java Card ——

```
final public class TryCounter {
  private byte[] counter = new byte[1];
  private final byte max;

  public TryCounter(byte max) {
    this.max = max;
    reset();
  }
```

---

[3] To prevent denial-of-service attacks, also resetting the counter to its maximum value should be
done in a nonatomic ways. Otherwise, a correct PIN may not be able to reset the counter properly
when any possible on-going transaction gets aborted or interrupted.

```
  public void reset() {
    Util.arrayFillNonAtomic(counter, (short)0, (short)1, max);
  }

  public boolean decrease() {
    if(counter[0] == (byte)0) return false;
    byte nv = (byte)(counter[0] - 1);
    Util.arrayFillNonAtomic(counter, (short)0, (short)1, nv);
    return true;
  }

  public byte get() {
    return counter[0];
  }
}
```
—— Java Card ——

For verification we shall also provide a handful of JML annotations. We concentrate
here on the decrease method. The invariants that we need are the following:

—— JML ——
```
invariant counter != null && counter.length == 1 &&
  JCSystem.isTransient(counter) ==
    JCSystem.NOT_A_TRANSIENT_OBJECT;
invariant !\transactionUpdated(counter) && counter[0] >= 0;
```
——— JML ——

Then the contract for decrease in most part reflects the contract for arrayFill-
NonAtomic as decrease essentially just calls arrayFillNonAtomic:

—— JML ——
```
public normal_behavior
  ensures \result <==> (\old(counter[0]) != 0);
  ensures counter[0] == \old(counter[0]) - (\result ? 1 : 0);
  ensures<savedHeap> \backup(counter[0]) ==
    \old(counter[0]) - (\result ? 1 : 0);
  assignable<heap><savedHeap> counter[0];
```
——— JML ——

We are now ready to specify and verify our security property, i.e., that the counter
is decreased regardless of any on-going (and aborting) transaction. We do this by
writing an auxiliary test method with the following specification:

—— Java + JML ——————————————————————————————————
```
/*@ normal_behavior
    requires \invariant_for(c) && c.get() > 0;
```

```
     ensures \invariant_for(c) && c.get() == \old(c.get()) - 1;
   @*/
void testCounter(TryCounter c, boolean abort) {
  JCSystem.beginTransaction();
  c.decrease();
  if(abort) {
    JCSystem.abortTransaction();
  } else {
    JCSystem.commitTransaction();
  }
}
```

———————————————————————————————— Java + JML ——

The unspecified Boolean parameter `abort` makes KeY consider both transaction cases and effectively verifies that the counter is always decreased. Similar specifications and additions to the `TryCounter`'s invariant are required to also verify the `reset()` method's resistance to transactions, we leave this is as an exercise for the reader.

10.7 Summary and Discussion

This chapter discussed a complete solution to reason about Java Card transactions in JavaDL using KeY. The base of the solution is the manipulation of two memory heaps to model the effects of selective transaction roll-backs. This formalization is fully implemented in KeY, and we presented complete relevant verification examples of realistic Java Card programs.

In its previous instance [Beckert et al., 2007], the KeY system was the first verification system to fully handle Java Card platform intricacies. The current formalization presented in this chapter improves considerably over the previous one discussed in detail in [Beckert and Mostowski, 2003] and [Mostowski, 2006], while considerably sized Java Card verification case studies done with the previous version of KeY are discussed in [Mostowski, 2005] and [Mostowski, 2007]. In the new formalization, there is no need to introduce new semantics for state updates of KeY and the number of additional (transaction marked) modalities is smaller. Also the number of logic rules that extend the basic KeY logic is very low compared to our previous work. As for efficiency, there is not much to discuss—all the examples from this chapter verify fully automatically with KeY in a matter of seconds. The simplicity of our current solution also underlines the good choice of modeling the memory with explicit heap variables—explicit manipulation of these variables makes our Java Card reasoning model very compact.

10.7.1 Related Work

We are only aware of one more verification system that formalized Java Card transactions with similar success to KeY, namely the Krakatoa tool [Marché and Rousset, 2006]. There, a complete solution is also provided with corresponding extensions to JML and implemented in the Why verification platform. When it comes to simplicity and reusability of their solution, we would place it somewhere in between our old and our new solution. In particular, the notion of backup heap locations is used there, however, each single memory location has its own corresponding backup cell on the same heap as the original memory locations, instead of the whole heap being copied/mirrored like in our solution. A support for Java Card transactions has been also reported for the VeriFast platform [Jacobs et al., 2011a,b], however, it is not clear how and if the semantics of the transactions has been formalized there. Finally, Java Card transactions have been considered to be formalized in the LOOP tool using program transformation to explicitly model transaction recovery directly in the Java code, but the ideas where never implemented in the tool [Hubbers and Poll, 2004].

10.7.2 On-going and Future Research

The use of multiple heaps is a generic feature of our formalization. That is, the same methodology of simultaneous manipulation of several heaps can be used to model other specific features of (Java) programs or to add new elements to the verification model. In particular, in distributed systems one can consider the local and remote memories as separate heaps. Similarly, multi-level caches can be treated by assigning separate heap to each cache. Going further, multi-core systems (like GPUs) could be also modeled using multiple explicit heaps, each heap representing the local memory of a single core. Finally, real-time Java can be also considered in this context, where programs access memories with different physical characteristics on one embedded device.[4]

10.7.3 Multiple Heaps for Concurrent Reasoning

In the context of the VerCors project[5] [Amighi et al., 2012], we concentrate on extending the KeY logic with permission accounting to enable thread-local verification of concurrent Java programs. The VerCors project is concerned with the verification of concurrent data structures, both from the point of view of possible thread interfer-

---

[4] Admittedly, in the last two examples the different memories are likely to be disjoint and not sharing any heap locations, hence not really utilizing the full power of reasoning with multiple heaps.

[5] www.utwente.nl/vercors/.

ence and with respect to meaningful functional properties. Permission accounting [Boyland, 2003] is a specification oriented methodology for ensuring noninterference of threads. Single threads verified with respect to permission annotations (specifying rights to read and/or write memory locations) are guaranteed to be data-race free. This approach is very popular in verification methods based on Separation Logic or similar concepts [Reynolds, 2002]. In particular, the VeriFast [Jacobs et al., 2011b] system implements fractional permission accounting, and the Chalice [Leino et al., 2009] verifier also uses permission annotations to verify concurrent programs specified with implicit dynamic frames style specifications [Smans et al., 2012]. The VerCors project also employs permission accounting in its own version of Separation Logic [Amighi et al., 2014b] and its corresponding automated tool set [Blom and Huisman, 2014]. Adapting KeY to incorporate permission accounting is a step in providing also interactive verification support in the VerCors project [Huisman and Mostowski, 2015, Mostowski, 2015].

The essential part of adding permission accounting to KeY is the addition of the parallel permission heap to the logic, simply represented with the `permissions` heap variable. This heap stores access permissions to object locations while the corresponding location values are stored on the regular heap like before.[6] Each access to the regular heap is guarded by checking the corresponding access right on the permission heap. Locations on the permission heap can also change like on the regular heap. Namely, permissions to single object locations are mutated when permission transfer occurs in the verified program, that is, upon new object creation, forking and joining of threads, and acquiring/releasing synchronization locks (either through the `synchronized` blocks or through dedicated Java concurrency API classes). As with the Java Card transaction treatment the `permissions` heap is explicit in the specifications. In particular, locations listed in the assignable clause for permission indicate possible permission transfer. Conversely, locations not listed in such an assignable clause are guaranteed to preserve their permissions.

Example 10.3. At the time of the writing of this chapter, the current official version of KeY already implements permission accounting as an experimental feature. For example, the three following (admittedly artificial) methods annotated with permission specifications are easily verifiable with KeY:

——— Java + JML ————————————————————————————————

```
public class MyClass {

    int a, b;
    Object o;

    /*@ public normal_behavior
        requires<permissions> \writePerm(\perm(this.o));
```

---

[6] In fact, this is the same way of treating permissions as in the Chalice verifier [Leino et al., 2009]. In Chalice memory locations are stored on the regular heap denoted with H, while permissions reside in the permission mask denoted with P. In Chalice, however, these variables are hidden from the user in the depth of the module translating the specifications and programs to the SMT solver.

```
      ensures<permissions>
        \perm(this.o) == \old(\perm(this.o));
      ensures \fresh(this.o);
      assignable<heap><permissions> this.o;
   @*/
  public void method1() {
    o = new Object();
  }


  /*@ public normal_behavior
       requires<permissions> \writePerm(\perm(this.o));
       ensures \fresh(this.o);
       assignable<heap> this.o;
       assignable<permissions> \nothing;
    @*/
  public void method2() {
    o = new Object();
  }


  /*@ public normal_behavior
       requires<permissions>
         \writePerm(\perm(this.a)) && \readPerm(\perm(this.b));
       ensures this.a == this.b;
       assignable this.a;
       assignable<permissions> \nothing; @*/
  public MyClass method3() {
    this.a = this.b;
    MyClass tmp = new MyClass();
    tmp.a = 1;
    tmp.b = 1;
    return tmp;
  }
}
```

—— Java + JML ——

The references to the `permissions` heap in the specification clauses follow the
same pattern as described in Section 10.5 in the context of the `savedHeap` variable.
The additional JML keywords present in the specifications are \perm, \readPerm,
and \writePerm. The first one is analogous to the \backup operator, and it redirects
object location look-up to the permission heap instead of the regular heap. The other
two keywords are operators to interface JML with the corresponding predicates
in the logic that evaluate the underlying permission expressions to establish the
resulting access rights. Permission expressions as such are an orthogonal issue to
heap handling. Many verification systems use fractional permissions in the range
$(0, 1]$ represented with rational numbers [Boyland, 2003], where 1 denotes a full

access (write) permission, and any positive number strictly less than 1 a partial access (read) permission. In KeY, we are using fully symbolic permission expressions that are described in detail in [Huisman and Mostowski, 2015]. However, in the specification that we present here the permission values are abstracted away to be simply read or write permissions, and they could be anything, including the classical fractional permissions.

The first two methods are identical in code, but they differ in the specifications. For `method1()` we state that the permission to `this.o` might be changed by this method, and in the postcondition we specify what this change is going to be, simply that the permission stays the same. Thus, the specification can be optimized to what is stated for `method2()`, i.e., that the permission to `this.o` does not change at all. For `method3()` we need to require that there is a read permission to `this.b` and a write permission to `this.a`. This ensures that the first assignment in the method is valid. Then a new object is created and both its fields are assigned with new values. None of these remaining statements require any additional access permissions. This is because local variables are always fully accessible, and new objects are always allocated with full access permission to the current thread. As in the other two methods, apart from creating new objects, `method3()` does not do any permission transfers, hence the assignable `\nothing` for the permission heap. Note that because of the object creation, we cannot specify `\strictly_nothing` for any of these methods as this would exclude new object creation, which also affects the permission heap.

At the time of writing this, the full support for permission accounting is not yet finished in the KeY system and should be considered experimental. The crucial missing element is the verification of specifications themselves. That is, in permission-based concurrent reasoning, it is only sound to express properties about object locations to which the specification has at least a read access. That is, similarly to the accessible condition checking for self-framed footprints described in Section 9.3, all permission-based specifications need to frame themselves in terms of read access permissions. The details of the self-framing of permission-based specification in KeY are described in [Mostowski, 2015], where we also discuss modular specifications for API synchronization classes using JML model methods (see Section 8.2.3).

Part III
From Verification to Analysis

Chapter 11
Debugging and Visualization

Martin Hentschel, Reiner Hähnle, and Richard Bubel

11.1 Introduction

Out of the four papers ([Burstall, 1974, Boyer et al., 1975, Katz and Manna, 1975, King, 1976]) that independently introduced symbolic execution as a program analysis technique during the mid 1970s, no less than three mention debugging as a motivation. Indeed, symbolic execution has a number of natural properties that make it attractive in helping to debug programs:

- A time-consuming task for users of classical interactive debuggers is to set up a (small) initial program state which leads to an execution that exhibits the failure. It is usually nontrivial to build the required, complex data structures. Symbolic program execution, on the other hand, permits to execute any method or any statement directly without setting up an initial state. This is possible by using symbolic values instead of concrete ones. The capability to start debugging from any code location makes it also easy to debug incomplete programs.
- Not only is it time-consuming to build concrete initial states, it is often also difficult to determine under which exact conditions a failure will occur. This can be addressed by symbolic execution, which allows one to specify initial states only partially (or not at all) and which generates *all* reachable symbolic states up to a chosen depth.
- Classical debuggers typically pass through a vast number of program states with possibly large data structures before interactive debugging mode is entered. Once this happens, it is often necessary to visit previous states, which requires to implement reverse (or omniscient) debugging, which is nontrivial to do efficiently, see [Pothier et al., 2007]. In a symbolic execution environment reverse debugging causes only little overhead, because (a) symbolic execution can be started immediately in the code area where the defect is suspected and (b) symbolic states are small and contain only program variables encountered during symbolic execution.
- The code instrumentation typically required by standard debuggers can make it impossible to observe a failure that shows up in the unaltered program (so-called

© Springer International Publishing AG 2016
W. Ahrendt et al. (Eds.): Deductive Software Verification, LNCS 10001, pp. 383–413, 2016
DOI: 10.1007/978-3-319-49812-6_11

"Heisenbugs," see [Gray, 1985]). This can be avoided by symbolic execution of the unchanged code.

The question is then why—given these advantages of symbolic execution, plus the fact that the idea to combine it with debugging has been around for 40 years—all widely used debuggers are still based on interpretation of programs with concrete start states. Stable Mainstream debugging tools evolved slowly and their feature set remained more or less stable in the last decades, providing mainly the standard functionality for step-wise execution, inspection of the current program state, and suspension of the execution before a marked statement is executed. This is all the more puzzling, since debugging is a central, unavoidable, and time-consuming task in software development with an accordingly huge saving potential.

The probable answer is that, until relatively recently, standard hardware simply was insufficient to realize a debugger based on symbolic execution for real-world programming languages. On a closer look, there are three aspects to this. First, symbolic execution itself: reasonably efficient symbolic execution engines for interesting fragments of real-world programming languages are available only since ca. 2006 (for example, [Beckert et al., 2007, Grieskamp et al., 2006, Jacobs and Piessens, 2008]). Second, and this is less obvious, to make good use of the advantages of symbolic execution pointed out above, it is essential to *visualize* symbolic execution paths and symbolic states and navigate through them. Otherwise, the sheer amount and the symbolic character of the generated information make it impossible to understand what is happening. Again, high-quality visual rendering and layout of complex information was not possible on standard hardware in real-time until a few years ago. The third obstacle to adoption of symbolic execution as a debugging technology is lack of integration. Developers expect that a debugger is smoothly integrated into the development environment of their choice, so that debugging, editing, testing, and documenting activities can be part of a single workflow without breaking the tool chain.

These issues were for the first time addressed in a prototypic symbolic state debugger by Hähnle et al. [2010]. However, that tool was not very stable and its architecture was tightly integrated into the KeY system. As a consequence, the *Symbolic Execution Debugger* (SED) [Hentschel et al., 2014a] presented in this chapter was completely rewritten, much extended and realized as a reusable Eclipse extension.

The SED extends the Eclipse debug platform by symbolic execution and visualization capabilities. Although different symbolic execution engines can be integrated into the SED platform, we will consider in the following only the integration of KeY as symbolic execution engine. In contrast to the KeY verifier, the SED can be used without any specialist knowledge, exactly like a standard debugger. To make full usage of its capabilities, however, it is of advantage to know the basic concepts of symbolic execution. To make the chapter self-contained we give a short introduction into symbolic execution and to our notion of a symbolic execution tree in Section 11.2. The debugging and visualization capabilities of SED are explained in tutorial style in Section 11.3. We show how to employ the SED profitably in various use cases, including tracking the origin of failures, help in program understanding, and even actual program verification. We also explain its architecture, which has a highly modular design and allows other symbolic execution engines than KeY to be integrated into SED. How KeY is employed in the SED, and which technical features are necessary, is the topic of the final Section 11.4.

The reader who only wants to know how the SED is used and is not interested in its realization can safely skip Section 11.3.7 and Section 11.4.

11.2 Symbolic Execution

In this section we explain symbolic execution and our notion of a symbolic execution tree by way of examples.

Listing 11.1 shows Java method `min`, which computes the minimum of two given integers. When the method is called during a concrete execution, the variables x and y have defined values. The `if` statement can compare these values and decide to execute either the then or the else block. Concrete execution always follows exactly one path trough a (sequential) program. To explore different paths it is required to execute the program multiple times with different input values.

```java
1  public static int min(int x, int y) {
2      if (x < y) {
3          return x;
4      }
5      else {
6          return y;
7      }
8  }
```

Listing 11.1 Minimum of two integers

Symbolic execution uses symbolic in lieu of concrete values, so that when method `min` is called, variables x and y are assigned symbolic values x and y. As long as nothing is known about the relation of x and y, the `if` statement cannot decide whether to follow the then or the else branch. Consequently, symbolic execution has to split to follow both branches, resulting in a symbolic execution tree. One branch continues the execution in case that the *branch condition* $x < y$ is fulfilled and the other in case that $!(x < y)$ holds instead. The conjunction over all parent branch conditions is named *path condition* and defines a constraint on the input values that ensures this path to be taken. The knowledge gained from branch conditions is used in subsequent symbolic execution steps to prune infeasible execution paths. If method `min` is called a second time with the same symbolic values x and y and with one of the possible branch conditions from the first call, then symbolic execution will not split again. In this way symbolic execution discovers all feasible execution paths and each symbolic path may represent infinitely many concrete executions.

The complete symbolic execution tree of method `min` is shown in Figure 11.1. The root of each symbolic execution tree in our notion of symbolic execution is a *start node*, usually followed by a call of the method to execute.

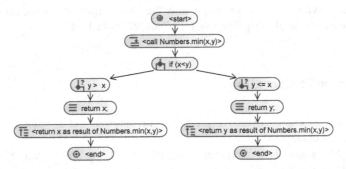

Figure 11.1 Symbolic execution tree of static method `min` defined in class `Numbers`

Typically, an `if` statement splits execution. For this reason it is represented as a *branch statement*. Its child nodes are *branch conditions* representing the condition when a branch is taken. Branch conditions occur after branch statements if and only if execution splits. If a branch statement does not split, then its child is the next statement to execute. But also other statements than explicit branch statements can split execution, for instance, an object access that may throw a `NullPointerException`. Whenever a statement splits execution, its children show the relevant branch conditions and continue execution.

In the example, on each branch a return statement is executed which causes a method return and lets the program terminate normally (without an uncaught exception).

Loop statements are unwound by default, similar to a concrete program execution. The first time when a loop is entered it is represented as a *loop statement* in the symbolic execution tree. Whenever the loop guard is executed, it will be represented as a *loop condition* node and may split execution into two branches. One where the guard is false and the execution is continued after the loop and one where it is true and the loop body is executed once and the loop guard is checked again. As a consequence, unwinding a loop can result in symbolic execution trees of unbounded depth. As an illustration we use the method in Listing 11.2 which computes sum of array elements.

The beginning of a symbolic execution tree resulting from execution of `sum` with precondition `array != null` is shown in Figure 11.2. The left branch stops before the loop guard is evaluated the second time, whereas the right branch terminates after the computed sum is returned. When symbolic execution is continued on the left branch, similar child branches will be created until `Integer.MAX_VALUE` is reached.

To render symbolic execution trees finite in presence of loops, optionally, a loop invariant can be supplied [Hentschel et al., 2014b]. In this case a *loop invariant* node is shown in the symbolic execution tree splitting execution into two branches. The

```
1  public static int sum(int[] array) {
2      int sum = 0;
3      for (int i = 0; i < array.length; i++) {
4          sum += array[i];
5      }
6      return sum;
7  }
```

Listing 11.2 Sum of all array elements

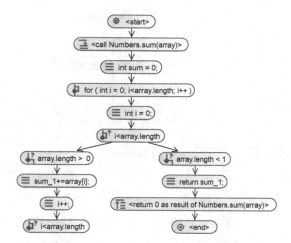

Figure 11.2 Symbolic execution tree of static method sum defined in class Numbers

first *body preserves invariant* branch represents all possible loop iterations ending in *loop body termination* nodes.[1] The second *use case* branch continues execution after the loop. It is possible that the invariant was initially not valid or that it is not preserved by the loop body. This would be a problem in a verification scenario, but a violated loop invariant should not stop one from debugging a program. Therefore, different icons indicate whether the loop invariant holds initially and in a *loop body termination* node.

The sum example in Listing 11.2 is extended by a weak (and wrong) loop invariant in Listing 11.3. A correct loop invariant would treat the case that i can be zero. For verification it is also required to specify how the value of sum is changed by the loop.

The resulting symbolic execution tree using the loop invariant and precondition array != null is shown in Figure 11.3. The icon of the loop invariant indicates that it is initially not fulfilled.

Method calls are handled by default by inlining the body of the called method. In case of inheritance, symbolic execution splits to cover all possible implementations indicated by *branch condition* nodes in front of the *method call* node.

---

[1] In case an exception is thrown or a jump outside of the loop is initiated by a return, break or continue statement, execution is continued directly in the *body preserves invariant* branch.

```
1 /*@ loop_invariant i > 0 && i <= array.length;
2   @ decreasing array.length - i;
3   @ assignable \strictly_nothing;
4   @*/
5 for (int i = 0; i < array.length; i++) { /* ... */ }
```

Listing 11.3 Wrong and weak loop invariant of loop from Listing 11.2

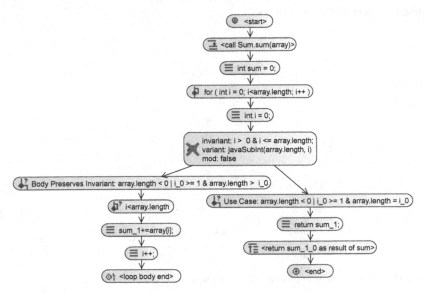

Figure 11.3 Symbolic execution tree of static method sum using a loop invariant

The usage of inlined methods is explained with help of the example in Listing 11.4 which executes in method run of class Main the run method of an IOperation. Two different IOperation implementations are available.

The resulting symbolic execution tree under precondition operation != null is shown in Figure 11.4. The target method is inlined first and its body is executed between the *method call* and the corresponding *method return* node. The only statement calls method run on the argument operation. As the concrete implementation is unknown, symbolic execution has to split to consider both of them, shown by the child *branch condition* nodes. The left branch continues execution in case that operation is an instance of BarOperation and the right one in the other case. Both branches inline the target method next, execute the return statement, return from the called method, and finally terminate normally.

As in the case of loops, recursive method calls can lead to unbounded symbolic execution trees. But even unfolding nonrecursive calls can quickly lead to infeasibly large symbolic execution trees. To address this issue, instead of inlining the method body, it is possible to replace a method call by a *method contract* (see Chapter 7). This can also be useful when the source code of a method implementation is not available (for example, if it is proprietary code or simply unfinished).

```
 1 public class Main {
 2    public static String run(IOperation operation) {
 3       return operation.run();
 4    }
 5 }
 6
 7 interface IOperation {
 8    public String run();
 9 }
10
11 class FooOperation implements IOperation {
12    public String run() {
13       return "foo";
14    }
15 }
16
17 class BarOperation implements IOperation {
18    public String run() {
19       return "bar";
20    }
21 }
```

Listing 11.4 Method call with inheritance

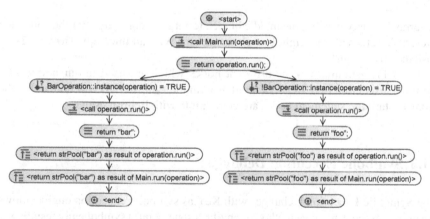

Figure 11.4 Symbolic execution tree of static method `run`

Upon application of a method contract, symbolic execution is continued separately for the specification cases corresponding to normal and to exceptional behavior. As in the case of loop invariants, node icons are used to indicate if certain conditions like preconditions or that the callee is not **null** could not be established.

Listing 11.5 shows the contract of method sum from Listing 11.2. The sum method is used to compute the average of all array elements in Listing 11.6.

The symbolic execution tree resulting from the execution of method average, where the contract of sum is used to handle the call to sum, is shown in Figure 11.5. The left branch terminates with an uncaught ArithmeticException in case that

```
1  /*@ normal_behavior
2   @ requires array != null;
3   @ ensures \result == (\sum int i; i >= 0 && i < array.length; array[i]);
4   @
5   @ also
6   @
7   @ exceptional_behavior
8   @ requires array == null;
9   @ signals_only NullPointerException;
10  @ signals (NullPointerException) true;
11  @*/
12 public static /*@ pure @*/ int sum(/*@ nullable @*/ int[] array) {
13     // ...
14 }
```

Listing 11.5 Method contract of method sum from Listing 11.2

```
1 public static int average(/*@ nullable @*/ int[] array) {
2    return sum(array) / array.length;
3 }
```

Listing 11.6 Average of all array elements

the array is empty whereas the middle branch terminates normally after the computed average is returned. The right branch terminates with an uncaught Throwable in case the array is null.

Table 11.1 summarizes the different nodes which are used in our notion of a symbolic execution tree. Readers familiar with the Eclipse IDE will notice that the icons in start and statement nodes are compatible with Eclipse usage.

11.3 Symbolic Execution Debugger

The Symbolic Execution Debugger with KeY as symbolic execution engine allows the user to execute any Java method or any Java statement(s) symbolically resulting in a symbolic execution tree as discussed in Section 11.2. The main goal of the tool is to help program understanding. Like a traditional debugger it allows the user to control the execution, to inspect states and to suspend execution at defined breakpoints.

11.3.1 Installation

The Symbolic Execution Debugger and other Eclipse extensions provided by the KeY project can be added to an existing Eclipse installation via an update-site. The supported Eclipse versions and the concrete update-site URLs are available on the

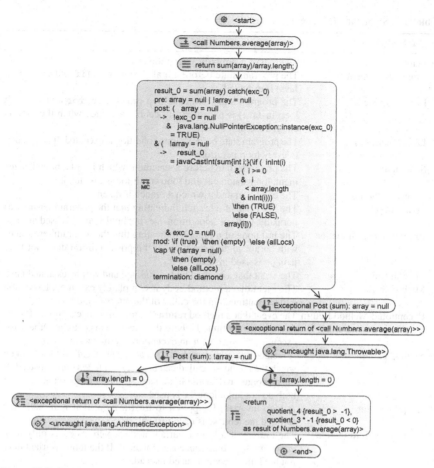

Figure 11.5 Symbolic execution tree of method `average` using a contract for the called method

KeY website (www.key-project.org). When reading the following sections for the first time, we strongly recommend to have a running Eclipse installation with the SED extension at hand, so that the various features can be tried out immediately. We assume that the reader is familiar with the Java perspective of the Eclipse IDE.

11.3.2 Basic Usage

The main use case of the SED using KeY is to execute a Java method symbolically. It can be achieved by opening the context menu of a method and by selecting **Debug As, Symbolic Execution Debugger (SED)**. Alternatively, it is possible to execute individual Java statements by selecting them first in the Java text editor and then by selecting the same context menu entry. Additional knowledge to limit feasible execution paths

Table 11.1 Symbolic execution tree nodes

Icon & Node Type	Description
◉ Start	The root of a symbolic execution tree.
⑂ Branch Statement	The program state before a branch statement (`if` and `switch` in Java) is executed.
♩ Loop Statement	The program state before a loop (`while`, `do`, `for` and for-each loop in Java) is executed. It occurs only once when the loop is entered the first time.
♩? Loop Condition	The program state before a loop condition is executed. It is repeated in every loop iteration.
≡ Statement	The program state before a statement which is not a branch statement, loop statement and loop condition is executed.
⑂² Branch Condition	The condition under which a branch is taken.
⊕ Termination	The last node of a branch indicating that the program terminates normally. If the postcondition does not hold icon ⊗ is used instead.
⊘⸮ Exceptional Termination	The last node of a branch indicating that the program terminates with an uncaught exception. If the postcondition does not hold icon ⊗⸮ is used instead.
⎓ Method Call	The event that a method body is inlined and will be executed next.
⊤≡ Method Return	The event that a method body is completely executed. Execution will be continued in the caller of the returned method.
�≡ Exceptional Method Return	The event that a method returns by throwing an exception. Execution will be continued where the exception is caught. Otherwise, execution finishes with an exceptional termination node.
▩ₘc Method Contract	A method contract is applied to treat a method call. If the object on which the method is called can be `null`, icon ▩ is used instead. If the precondtion does not hold, icon ▩ shows this circumstance. If both do not hold, icon ▩ is used.
♩ᵢ Loop Invariant	A loop invariant is applied to treat a loop. If it is initially not fulfilled the icon ♩ is used instead.
⊕ᵢ Loop Body Termination	The branch of a loop invariant node which executes only loop guard and loop body once is completed. If the loop invariant does not hold, the icon ⊗ᵢ is used instead.

can be supplied as a precondition in the *Debug Configuration*. Also a full method contract can be selected instead of specifying a precondition.[2] In this case icons of termination nodes will indicate whenever the postcondition is not fulfilled. After starting execution, it is recommend to switch to the perspective **Symbolic Debug** which contains all relevant views explained in Table 11.2.

Figure 11.6 shows a screenshot of the **Symbolic Debug** perspective in which the symbolic execution tree of method `equals`, whose implementation is shown in the bottom right editor, is visualized. The method checks whether its Number argument instance has the same content as `this`, which is named `self` in KeY. The left branch represents the case when both instances have the same content, whereas the content is different in the middle branch. The right branch terminates with an uncaught `NullPointerException`, because the argument is `null`.

---

[2] The use of a method contract activates full JML support including `non_null` defaults.

Table 11.2 Views of perspective Symbolic Debug

View	Description
Debug	Shows symbolic execution trees of all launches, as well as to switch between them and to control execution.
Symbolic Execution Tree	Visualizes symbolic execution tree of selected launch.
Symbolic Execution Tree (Thumbnail)	Miniature view of the symbolic execution tree for navigation purposes.
Variables	Shows the visible variables and their symbolic values.
Breakpoints	Manages the breakpoints.
Properties	Shows all information of the currently selected element.
Symbolic Execution Settings	Customizes symbolic execution, e.g., defines how to treat method calls and loops.

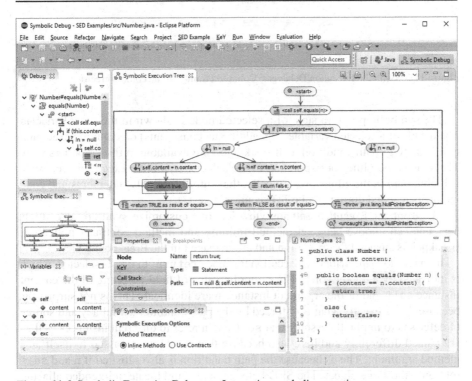

Figure 11.6 Symbolic Execution Debugger: Interactive symbolic execution

The additional frames (rectangles) displayed in view **Symbolic Execution Tree** of Figure 11.6 represent the bounds of code blocks. Such frames can be independently collapsed and expanded to abstract away from the inner structure of code blocks, thus achieving a cleaner representation of the overall code structure by providing only as much detail as required for the task at hand. A collapsed frame contains only one branch condition node per path (namely the conjunction of all branch

conditions of that particular path), displaying the constraint under which the end of
the corresponding code block is reached. In Figure 11.7, the method call node is
collapsed. Collapsed frames are colored green, if all execution paths reached the end
of the frame. Otherwise they are colored orange. Expanded frames are colored blue.

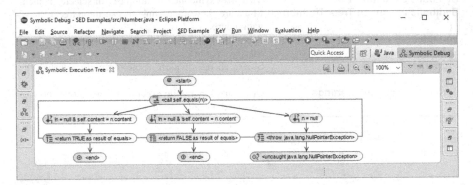

Figure 11.7 Symbolic Execution Debugger: Collapsed frame (frame color is green)

The symbolic program state of a selected node is shown in the view **Variables**.
The details of a selected variable (e.g. additional constraints) or symbolic execution
tree node (e.g. path condition, call stack, etc.) are available in the **Properties** view.
The source code line corresponding to the selected symbolic execution tree node
is highlighted in the editor. Additionally, the editor highlights statements and code
members reached during symbolic execution.

The **Symbolic Execution Settings** view lets one customize symbolic execution,
e.g., one can choose between method inlining and method contract application.
Breakpoints suspend the execution and are managed in the **Breakpoints** view.

In Figure 11.6 the symbolic execution tree node `return true;` is selected, which
is indicated by a darker color. The symbolic value of field `content` of the current
instance `self` and of the argument instance n are identical. This is not surprising,
because this is exactly what is enforced by the path condition. A fallacy and source
of defects is to implicitly assume that `self` and n refer to different instances as they
are named differently and here also because that an object is passed to itself as a
method argument. This is because the path condition is also satisfied if n and `self`
reference the same object. The SED helps to detect and locate unintended aliasing
by determining and visualizing all possible memory layouts w.r.t. the current path
condition.

Selecting context menu item **Visualize Memory Layouts** of a symbolic execution
tree node creates a visualization of possible memory layouts as a *symbolic object
diagram*, see Figure 11.8. It resembles a UML object diagram and shows (i) the
dependencies between objects, (ii) the symbolic values of object fields and (iii) the
symbolic values of local variables of the current state.

The root of the symbolic object diagram is visualized as a rounded rectangle
and shows all local variables visible at the current node. In Figure 11.8, the local

variables n and self refer to objects visualized as rectangles. The symbolic value of the instance field content is shown in the lower compartment of each object. The local variable exc is used by KeY to distinguish among normal and exceptional termination.

The scrollbar of the toolbar (near the origin of the callout) allows one to select different possible layouts and to switch between the current and the initial state of each layout. The initial state shows how the memory layout looked before the execution started resulting in the current state. Figure 11.8 shows both possible layouts of the selected node return true; in the current state. The second memory layout (inside the callout) represents the situation, where n and self are aliased.

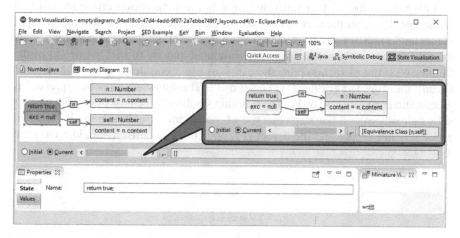

Figure 11.8 Symbolic Execution Debugger: Possible memory layouts of a symbolic state

11.3.3 Debugging with Symbolic Execution Trees

The Symbolic Execution Debugger allows one to control execution like a traditional debugger and can be used in a similar way. A major advantage of symbolic execution is that it is not required to start at a predefined program entry point and to run the program until the point of interest is reached. Instead, the debug session can start directly at the point of interest. This avoids building up large data structures and the memory will contain only the variables used by the code of interest. If knowledge about the conditions under which a failure can be observed is available, it can be given as a precondition to limit the number of explored execution paths.

The main task of the user is, like in a traditional debugger, to control execution and to comprehend each performed step. It is helpful to focus on a single branch where the execution is expected to reach a faulty state. If this is not the case, the focus can be changed to a different branch. There is no need for a new debugging session or to find new input values resulting in a different execution path. It is always possible to go back to previous steps, because each node in the symbolic execution tree provides the full symbolic state.

Of special interest are splits, because their explicit rendering in the symbolic execution tree constitutes a major advantage of the SED over traditional debuggers. Unexpected splits or missing expected splits are good candidates for possible sources of defects. This is explained by example. Listing 11.7 shows a defective part of a *Mergesort* implementation for sorting an array called `intArr`. The exception shown in Listing 11.8 was thrown during a concrete execution of a large application that contained a call to `sort`. It seems that method `sortRange` calls itself infinitely often in line 9 until the call stack is full, which happened in line 7.

Either the value of `l` or the value of `r` is the termination criterion. Using a traditional debugger the user has to execute the whole program with suitable input values until method `sort` is executed. From this point onward, she may control the execution, observe how the `r` value is computed and try to find the origin of the failure. With the SED, however, she can start execution directly at method `sort`. Clearly, the array `intArr` needs to be not **null**. This knowledge can be expressed as precondition `intArr != null`. The resulting symbolic execution tree in Figure 11.9 shows already after a few steps that the `if`-statement is not branching in case that `intArr` is not empty and the defect is found (the comparison should have been `l < r`).

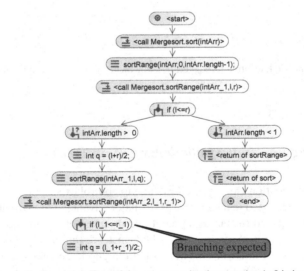

Figure 11.9 Symbolic Execution Tree of the mergesort implementation in Listing 11.7

---

[3] Modified version of the Mergesort implementation by Jörg Czeschla,
see javabeginners.de/Algorithmen/Sortieralgorithmen/Mergesort.php

```
1  public class Mergesort {
2      public static void sort(int[] intArr) {
3          sortRange(intArr, 0, intArr.length - 1);
4      }
5
6      public static void sortRange(int[] intArr, int l, int r) {
7          if (l <= r) {
8              int q = (l + r) / 2;
9              sortRange(intArr, l, q);
10             sortRange(intArr, q + 1, r);
11             merge(intArr, l, q, r);
12         }
13     }
14
15     private static void merge(int[] intArr, int l, int q, int r) {
16         int[] arr = new int[intArr.length];
17         int i, j;
18         for (i = l; i <= q; i++) {
19             arr[i] = intArr[i];
20         }
21         for (j = q + 1; j <= r; j++) {
22             arr[r + q + 1 - j] = intArr[j];
23         }
24         i = l;
25         j = r;
26         for (int k = l; k <= r; k++) {
27             if (arr[i] <= arr[j]) {
28                 intArr[k] = arr[i];
29                 i++;
30             }
31             else {
32                 intArr[k] = arr[j];
33                 j--;
34             }
35         }
36     }
37 }
```

Listing 11.7 Defective part of a mergesort implementation[3]

11.3.4 Debugging with Memory Layouts

It is easy to make careless mistakes in operations which modify data structures. To find them with a traditional debugger can be time consuming, because large data structures have to be inspected after each execution step. A complication is that a program state contains not only the data structure of interest, but all information computed before the state of interest is reached. Traditional debuggers present the current state typically as variable-value pairs in a list or tree. This representation makes it very hard to figure out object type data structures.

```
Exception in thread "main" java.lang.StackOverflowError
        at Mergesort.sortRange(Mergesort.java:7)
        at Mergesort.sortRange(Mergesort.java:9)
        at Mergesort.sortRange(Mergesort.java:9)
        at Mergesort.sortRange(Mergesort.java:9)
        ...
```

Listing 11.8 Exception thrown by the mergesort implementation of Listing 11.7

With the Symbolic Execution Debugger it is possible to visualize the current state as well as the initial state from which the execution started in the form of a symbolic object diagram. As an example, consider the rotate left operation of an AVL tree. Each node in such a tree has a left and a right child and it knows its parent as well. Again, symbolic execution is started directly in the method of interest, here the `rotateLeft` method and we let the SED compute all memory layouts for one of its return nodes.

Consider the initial state in Figure 11.10. The node to rotate is named `current` and it is the root of the tree because its parent is `null`. It has a right child, which in turn has a left child. The AVL tree itself is named `self`. Additionally, precondition `current != null && current.right != null` is used to ensure that the nodes to rotate exist.

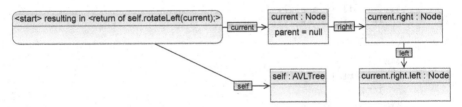

Figure 11.10 Initial symbolic object diagram of an AVL Tree rotate left operation

The symbolic state automatically computed and visualized by the SED after performing the rotation is shown in Figure 11.11. It shows the initial objects with all performed changes. By inspecting this diagram it is obvious that the parent of object `current.right.left` was not correctly updated because its parent is now the node itself.

11.3.5 Help Program and Specification Understanding

An important feature of symbolic execution trees is that they show control and data flow at the same time. Thus they can be used to help understanding programs and specifications just by inspecting them. This can be useful during code reviews or in early prototyping phases, where the full implementation is not yet available. It

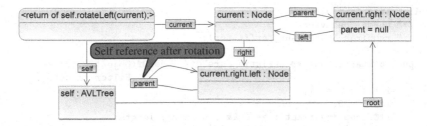

Figure 11.11 Current symbolic object diagram of an AVL Tree rotate left operation

works best, when some method contracts and/or invariants are available to achieve compact and finite symbolic execution trees. However, useful specifications can be much weaker than would be required for verification.

For example, Listing 11.9 shows a defective implementation of method indexOf which should return the first array index excepted by the given Filter or -1 in case none of the array elements were accepted. The method is specified by a basic method contract limiting the expected input values. In addition, a very simple loop invariant is given.

The corresponding symbolic execution tree is shown in Figure 11.12. It captures the full behavior of indexOf. Without checking any details, one can see that the left-most branch terminates in a state where the loop invariant is not preserved. Now, closer inspection shows the reason to be that, when the array element is found, the variable i is not increased, hence the **decreasing** clause of the invariant is violated. The two branches below the *use case* branch correspond to the code after the loop has terminated. In one case an element was found, in the other not. Looking at the return node, however, we find that in both cases instead of the index computed in the loop, the value of i is returned.

As this example demonstrates, symbolic execution trees can be used to answer questions, for example, about thrown exceptions (none in the example) or returned values. Within the SED the full state of each node is available and can be visualized. Thus it is easily possible to see whether and where new objects are created and which fields are changed when (comparison between initial and current layout). Using breakpoints, symbolic execution is continued until a breakpoint is hit on any branch. Thus it can be used to find execution paths (i) throwing a specified exception, (ii) accessing or modifying a specified field, (iii) calling or returning a specified method or (iv) causing a specified state.

11.3.6 Debugging Meets Verification

As the SED is based on symbolic execution it actually *verifies* the target program for the contract specified in the debug configuration. The program was proven correct if and only if each branch in the symbolic execution tree ends with a termination

```
1  public class ArrayUtil {
2      /*@ normal_behavior
3       @ requires \invariant_for(filter);
4       @*/
5      public static int /*@ strictly_pure @*/ indexOf(Object[] array,
6                                                      Filter filter) {
7          int index = -1;
8          int i = 0;
9          /*@ loop_invariant i >= 0 && i <= array.length;
10          @ decreasing array.length - i;
11          @ assignable \strictly_nothing;
12          @*/
13         while (index < 0 && i < array.length) {
14             if (filter.accept(array[i])) {
15                 index = i;
16             }
17             else {
18                 i++;
19             }
20         }
21         return i;
22     }
23
24     public static interface Filter {
25         /*@ normal_behavior
26          @ requires true;
27          @ ensures true;
28          @*/
29         public boolean /*@ strictly_pure @*/ accept(/*@ nullable @*/
30                                                     Object object);
31     }
32 }
```

Listing 11.9 A defective and only partially specified implementation

node and no warning icons are raised in the whole tree. This means that all branches terminate in a state where the specified postcondition is fulfilled. If a method call is approximated by a method contract, the precondition- and caller-no-null checks must have been successful, too. Likewise, all applied loop invariants are valid at the start of their loop and are preserved by the loop body.

Whereas a proof tree in KeY shows all performed steps during the proof, including intermediate steps of symbolic execution and proofs of first-order verification conditions, a symbolic execution tree contains only nodes that correspond to reachable program states. Hence, the debugger provides a view on a KeY proof from the developer's perspective, hiding intermediate and nonprogram related steps. Program states are visualized in a user-friendly way and are not encoded into side formulas of sequents.

Another advantage of SED over the KeY system is that insufficient or wrong specifications are directly highlighted. Whenever a symbolic execution tree node

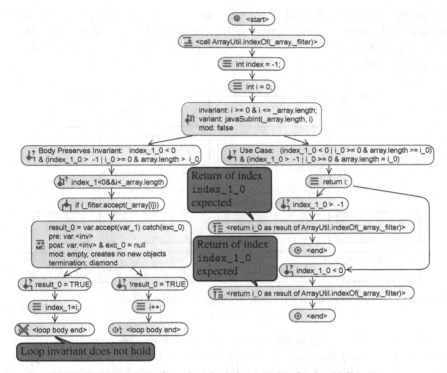

Figure 11.12 Symbolic execution tree of method `indexOf` (see Listing 11.9)

is crossed out, then something went wrong in proving the verification conditions for that path. The user can then inspect the parent nodes and check whether the implementation or the specifications contain a defect. More specifically, if the post-condition in a termination node is not fulfilled, then the symbolic program state at that point should be inspected. Wrong values relative to the specified behavior indicate a defect in the implementation. Values that have been changed as expected, but which are not mentioned in the specification indicate that the specification has to be extended. Moreover, crossed out method call and loop invariant nodes indicate that the precondition of the proven method contract is too weak or that something went wrong during execution. If a loop invariant is not preserved, the state of the loop body at the termination nodes gives hints on how to adjust the loop invariant.

11.3.7 Architecture

The Symbolic Execution Debugger (SED) is an Eclipse extension and can be added to existing Eclipse-based products. In particular, SED is compatible with the Java Development Tools (JDT) that provide the functionality to develop Java applications in Eclipse. To achieve this and also a user interface that seamlessly integrates with Eclipse, SED needs to obey a certain architecture, which is shown in Figure 11.13. The gray-colored components are part of the Eclipse IDE, whereas the remaining components are part of the SED extension.

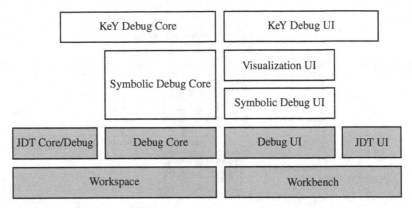

Figure 11.13 Architecture of the Symbolic Execution Debugger (SED)

The foundation is the Eclipse Workspace which provides resources such as projects, files and folders, and the Eclipse Workbench which provides the typical Eclipse user interface with perspectives, views and editors. Eclipse implements on top of these the debug platform which defines language-independent features and mechanisms for debugging. Specifically, Debug Core provides a language-independent model to represent the program state of a suspended execution. This includes threads, stack frames, variables, etc. Debug UI is the user interface to visualize the state defined by the debug model and to control execution. JDT Core defines the functionality to develop Java applications, including the Java compiler and a model to represent source code, whereas JDT Debug uses the debug platform to realize the Java debugger. Finally, JDT UI provides the user interface which includes the editor for Java source files.

The Symbolic Execution Debugger is based on the components provided by Eclipse. First, it extends the debug platform for symbolic execution in general. Second, it provides a specific implementation based on KeY's symbolic execution engine, described in Section 11.4.

Symbolic Debug Core extends the debug model to represent symbolic execution trees. This is done in a way that is independent of the target programming language and of the used symbolic execution engine.[4] It is also necessary to extend the debugger user interface, which is realized in Symbolic Debug UI. It contains in particular the tree-based representation of the symbolic execution tree that is displayed in the **Debug** view. The graphical representation of the symbolic execution tree shown in

---

[4] Each implementation of the symbolic debug model can define new node types to represent additional language constructs not covered by Table 11.1.

the **Symbolic Execution Tree** view as well as the visualization of memory layouts is provided language-independently by Visualization UI. Finally, KeY Debug Core implements the symbolic debug model with help of KeY's symbolic execution engine (implemented as pure Java API without any dependency to Eclipse). The functionality to debug selected code and to customize the debug configuration is provided by KeY Debug UI.

The extendable architecture of SED allows one to reuse the symbolic debug model for symbolic execution to implement alternative symbolic debuggers while profiting from the visualization functionality. All that needs to be done is to provide an implementation of the symbolic debug model for the target symbolic execution engine. KeY's symbolic execution API itself is part of the KeY framework and has no dependencies to the Symbolic Execution Debugger or to Eclipse. This makes it possible to use it like any other Java API.

11.4 A Symbolic Execution Engine based on KeY

The KeY verification system (see Chapter 15) is based on symbolic execution, but it is not directly a symbolic execution engine. In this section we describe how to realize a symbolic execution engine as API based on the KeY system. It is used for instance by the Symbolic Execution Debugger (see Section 11.3). We attempted to make this section self-contained, but it is certainly useful to have read Chapter 3 in order to appreciate the details.

11.4.1 Symbolic Execution Tree Generation

All the required functionality is implemented by KeY, because it already performs symbolic execution to verify programs. The simplified[5] schema of proof obligations to verify a piece of Java code looks as follows in KeY:

$$\Longrightarrow pre \rightarrow \mathcal{U} \left\langle \begin{array}{l} \texttt{try \{codeOfInterest\}} \\ \texttt{catch (Exception e) \{exc = e\}} \end{array} \right\rangle post$$

The meaning is as follows: assuming precondition *pre* holds and we are in a symbolic state given by $\mathcal{U}$, then the execution of the code between the angle brackets terminates, and afterwards postcondition *post* holds. The catch-block around *codeOfInterest* is used to assign the caught exception to variable exc which can be used by the post condition to separate normal from exceptional termination. The code of interest is usually the initial method call but can be also a block of statements.

Rules applied on a ⟨code⟩*post* modality rewrite the first (active) statement in code and then continue symbolic execution. Symbolic execution is performed at

---

[5] The proof obligation is explained in detail in Section 8.3.1

the level of atomic expressions, such that complex Java statements and expressions have to be decomposed before they can be executed. For example, the method call even(2 + 3) requires a simple argument expression, so that the sum must be computed before the method call can be performed. As a consequence, many intermediate steps might be required to execute a single statement of source code. An empty modality $\langle\rangle$ *post* can be removed, and the next step will be to show that the postcondition is fulfilled in the current proof context.

All symbolic execution rules have in common that, if necessary, they will split the proof tree to cover all conceivable execution paths. This means that the rules themselves do not prune infeasible paths. It is the task of the automatic proof strategy (or the user) to check the infeasibility of new proof premises before execution is continued.

We realize a symbolic execution engine on top of the proof search in KeY by extracting the symbolic execution tree for a program from the proof tree for the corresponding proof obligation. The main tasks to be performed are:

- Define a 'normal form' for proof trees that makes them suitable for generation of a symbolic execution tree.
- Design a proof strategy that ensures proof trees to be of the expected shape.
- Separate feasible and infeasible execution paths.
- Identify intermediate proof steps stemming from decomposition of complex statements into atomic ones. Such intermediate steps are not represented in the symbolic execution tree.
- Realize support for using specifications as an alternative to unwind loops and to inline method bodies.

It is important to postpone any splits of the proof tree caused by an attempt to show the postcondition until symbolic execution has completely finished. Otherwise, multiple proof branches representing the same symbolic execution path might be created. Whereas this does not affect the validity of a proof, it would cause redundant branches in a symbolic execution tree.

We also want to have at most one modality formula (of the form $\langle\text{code}\rangle\textit{post}$) per sequent, otherwise it is not clear what the target of symbolic execution is. Later, we will see that to support the use of specifications, this condition has to be relaxed.

The standard proof strategy used by KeY for verification almost ensures proof trees of the required shape. It is easy to modify this strategy: first, we forbid for the moment symbolic execution rules that introduce multiple modalities; second, we stipulate that all rules not pertaining to symbolic execution and that cause splitting are only applied after finishing symbolic execution. Even with these restrictions the proof strategy is often powerful enough to close infeasible execution paths immediately.

After the strategy stops, symbolic execution tree generation takes place. During this it is required to separate proof branches representing a feasible execution path from infeasible ones. This information is not available in the proof itself, because it is not needed for proving. Complicating is also the fact that KeY throws information away that is not needed for verification, however, it might later be needed for symbolic execution tree generation. This can be easily solved with the following trick.

The uninterpreted predicate *SET* is added to the postcondition of the initial proof obligation:

$$\Longrightarrow pre \rightarrow \mathcal{U} \left\langle \begin{array}{l} \texttt{try } \{codeOfInterest\} \\ \texttt{catch (Exception e) } \{\texttt{exc = e}\} \end{array} \right\rangle post \land SET(\texttt{exc})$$

The effect is that infeasible paths will be closed as before and feasible paths remain open since no rules exist for the predicate *SET*. Variables of interest are listed as parameters, so KeY is not able to remove them for efficiency if no longer needed.

To separate statements that occur in the source code from statements that are introduced by decomposition we use meta data in the form of suitable tags. Each statement occurring in the source code contains position information about its source file as well as the line and column where it was parsed. Statements introduced during a proof have no such tags.

The mechanisms described above are sufficient to generate a symbolic execution tree by iterating over a given proof tree. Each node in a proof tree is classified according to the criteria in Table 11.3 and added to the symbolic execution tree. Java API methods can optionally be excluded. In this case only method calls to non-API methods are added and statement nodes are only included if they are contained in non-API methods.

Table 11.3 Classification of proof nodes for symbolic execution tree nodes (excluding specifications)

SET node type	Criterion in KeY proof tree
Start	The root of the proof tree.
Method Call	The active statement is a method body statement.
Branch Statement	The active statement is a branch statement and the position information is defined.
Loop Statement	The active statement is a loop statement, the position information is defined, and it is the first loop iteration.
Loop Condition	The active statement is a loop statement and the position information is defined.
Statement	The active statement is not a branch, loop, or loop condition statement and the position information is defined.
Branch Condition	The parent of proof tree node has at least two open children and at least one child symbolic execution tree node exist (otherwise split is not related to symbolic execution).
Normal Termination	The emptyModality rule is applied and `exc` variable has value `null`.
Exceptional Termination	The emptyModality rule is applied and `exc` variable has not value `null`.
Method Return	A rule which performs a method return by removing the current method frame is applied and the related method call is part of the symbolic execution tree.

To detect the use of specifications in the form of method contracts and loop invariants it is sufficient to check whether one of the rules UseOperationContract or LoopInvariant was applied. The problem is that specifications may contain method

calls, as long as these are side effect-free (so-called query methods). During the KeY
proof these give rise to additional modalities in a sequent. Hence, we must separate
such 'side executions' from the target of symbolic execution. This is again done with
the help of meta information. We add a so-called *term label SE* to the modality of
the proof obligation, such as in:

$$\Longrightarrow pre \to \mathcal{U} \left\langle \begin{array}{l} \texttt{try \{}codeOfInterest\texttt{\}} \\ \texttt{catch (Exception e) \{exc = e\}} \end{array} \right\rangle (post \wedge SET(\text{exc})) \,\text{«}SE\text{»}$$

A term label is a noncorrectness relevant information attached to a term and maintained during a proof. When symbolic execution encounters a modality with an *SE*
label, it will be inherited to any child modalities. It is easy to modify the KeY proof
strategy to ensure that modalities without an *SE* label are executed first, because their
results are required for the ongoing symbolic execution. Finally, during symbolic
execution tree generation only nodes with an *SE* label are considered.

A complication is that symbolic execution of modalities without an *SE* label may
cause splits in the proof tree, but the knowledge gained from their execution is used in
symbolic execution of the target code. Such splits have to be reflected in the symbolic
execution tree. We will discuss later in Section 11.4.3 how they can be avoided.

When a method contract is applied, two branches continue symbolic execution,
one for normal and one for exceptional method return. Two additional branches
check whether the precondition is fulfilled in the current state and whether the caller
object is `null`. The latter two are proven without symbolic execution and their proof
branches will be closed if successful. Boolean flags (represented as crossed out icons
in the SED) on a method contract node indicate their verified status as described in
Section 11.2.

The situation is similar for loop invariant application: one proof branch checks
whether the loop invariant is initially (at the start of the loop) fulfilled. A Boolean flag
(icon in the SED) on the loop invariant node indicates its verified status. A second
branch continues symbolic execution after the loop and a third branch is used to
show that the loop invariant is preserved by the loop guard and the loop body. The
latter is complex, because in case an exception is thrown or that the loop terminates
abnormally via a `return`, `break` or `continue`, the loop invariant does not need to
hold. The loop invariant rule (see Section 3.7.2) of KeY solves this issue by first
executing loop guard and loop body in a separate modality. If this modality terminates
normally, then the proof that the loop invariant holds is initiated. Otherwise, symbolic
execution is continued in the original modality, without assuming that the invariant
holds. As above, the problem of multiple modalities is solved by term labels. We add
a (proof global) counter to each *SE* label. The label of the original proof obligation is
$SE(0)$ and it is incremented whenever needed. KeY's proof strategy is modified to
ensure that symbolic execution is continued in the modality with the highest counter
first.

The loop invariant rule encodes in the preserves branch whether a loop iteration
terminated abnormally or normally. Depending on the kind of termination different
properties have to be shown. The different cases are distinct subformulas of the form

$$reasonForTermination \rightarrow propertyToHold$$

We label the subformula *reasonForTermination* which characterizes the normal termination case with a *LoopInvariantNormalBehaviorTermLabel* term label[6]. If this labeled formula could be simplified to true, then a loop body termination node is added to the corresponding branch of the symbolic execution tree.

There is one special case we have not covered yet. The proof branches that check whether a loop invariant holds initially, whether a precondition holds, and whether the caller object is `null`, each can be proven without symbolic execution, as they contain no modality. This does not hold, however, when a loop invariant or a method contract is applied on the branch that shows the invariant to be preserved by loop condition and loop body. The reason is that in this case the modality which continues symbolic execution in case of an abnormal loop exit is still present and the proof strategy is free to continue symbolic execution on it. We are not interested in this execution, because it does not contribute to the verification of the actual proof obligation. Consequently, all term labels have to be removed from proof branches that only check the conditions listed above.

11.4.2 Branch and Path Conditions

Applicability of a proof rule in KeY generally depends only on the sequent it is applied to, not on other nodes in the proof tree. Consequently, KeY does not maintain branch and path conditions during proof construction, because the full knowledge gained by a split is encoded in the child nodes. A branch condition can be seen as the logical difference between the current node and its parent and the path condition is simply the conjunction over all parent branch conditions or, in other words, the logical difference between the current node and the root node.

In the case of symbolic execution rules, branch conditions are not generated from modalities to avoid a proliferation of modality formulas. Instead, splitting symbolic execution rules rewrite the active statement contained in their modality and add knowledge gained by the split in the succedent of the premises. Consequently, branch conditions in symbolic execution trees are defined by:

$$\left(\bigwedge added\ antecedent\ formula \right) \wedge \neg \left(\bigvee added\ succedent\ formula \right)$$

Method contract and loop invariant rules are so complex that they cannot be expressed schematically in KeY with the help of taclets (see Chapter 4), but are computed. After applying a method contract the branch conditions contain the knowledge that the caller object is not `null` and that the conjunction of all preconditions (both for normal and exceptional termination) hold. The branch condition on the proof branch ensuring that an invariant is preserved is the conjunction of the loop invariant

---

[6] For technical reasons the label is currently around the whole implication and the analysis checks the evaluation of the left subformula (*reasonForTermination*).

and the loop guard. The branch condition on the branch that continues symbolic execution after the loop is the conjunction of the loop invariant and the negated loop guard.

11.4.3 Hiding the Execution of Query Methods

As pointed out above, the presence of query methods in specifications or in loop guards may spawn modalities that have nothing to do with the target code. These are used to compute a single value, such as a method return value or a Boolean flag. Even though their execution is hidden in the symbolic execution tree, possible splits in the proof tree caused by them are visible, because the knowledge gained from them is used during subsequent symbolic execution. Such splits complicate symbolic execution trees, so we want to get rid of them.

These modalities have in common the fact that they are top level formulas in a sequent that compute a single value *const* in the current symbolic state $\mathcal{U}$:

$$\mathcal{U} \langle \texttt{tmp} = \ldots \rangle const \doteq \texttt{tmp}$$

This computation is 'outsourced' from the main proof via a built-in rule that executes the modality in a side proof. The initial proof obligation of the side proof is:

$$\Gamma \Longrightarrow \mathcal{U} \langle \texttt{tmp} = \ldots \rangle ResultPredicate(\texttt{tmp}), \Delta$$

It executes the modality in state $\mathcal{U}$ with an uninterpreted predicate *ResultPredicate* as postcondition. That predicate is parameterized with variable tmp, which will be replaced during the proof by its computed value. Γ and Δ are all first-order top-level formulas of the original sequent, representing the context knowledge[7].

The standard KeY verification strategy is used in the side proof. If it stops with open goals, where no rule is applicable, the results can be used in the original sequent.[8] Each open branch in the side proof contains a result *res* as parameter of the predicate *ResultPredicate(res)* that is valid relative to a path condition *pc* (Section 11.4.2). Now for each such open branch a new top-level formula is added to the sequent from which the side proof was outsourced. If the modality with the query method was originally in the antecedent, then $pc \rightarrow const \doteq res$ is added to the antecedent, otherwise, $pc \wedge const \doteq res$ is added to the succedent. The last step is to clean up the sequent and to remove the now redundant modality of the query.

---

[7] In the context of this chapter, formulas containing a modality or a query are excluded from the context knowledge. Otherwise, a side proof would reason about the original proof obligation as well.

[8] The side proof is never closed, because the predicate in the postcondition is not provable. If the proof terminates, because the maximal number of rule applications has been reached, then the side proof is abandoned.

11.4.4 Symbolic Call Stack

KeY encodes the method call stack with help of method frames directly in the Java program of a modality. For each inlined method, a new method frame is added that contains the code of the method body to execute. For more details, we refer to Section 3.6.5.

During symbolic execution tree generation the symbolic call stack has to be maintained. Whenever a method call node is detected, it is pushed onto the call stack. All other nodes remove entries from the maintained call stack until its size is equal to the number of method frames in their modality.

The branch of the loop invariant rule that checks whether the loop body preserves the invariant contains multiple modalities with different call stacks. The modality that executes only the loop guard and the loop body contains only the current method frame. All parent method frames are removed. This requires to maintain a separate call stack for each counter used in *SE* term labels. Whenever a modality with a new counter is introduced, its call stack is initialized with the top entry from the call stack of the modality where the loop invariant was applied.

11.4.5 Method Return Values

Method return nodes in a symbolic execution tree that return from a method declared as nonvoid allow one to access return values.

Several proof rules are involved in a method return. Assuming that the argument of the **return** statement has been decomposed into a simple expression, the methodCallReturn rule executes the return statement. For this, the rule adds an assignment statement that assigns the returned value to the result variable given in the current method frame. As the result variable is then no longer needed, it is removed from the method frame. A subsequent rule executes that assignment and yet another rule completes the method return by removing the, by now, empty method frame.

According to Table 11.3 a method return node is the proof tree node that removes the current method frame, say cmf. At this point, however, the name of the result variable is no longer available. This requires to go back to the parent proof tree node r, where rule methodCallReturn which assigns the returned value to the result variable of cmf was applied.

A side proof, similar to the one in Section 11.4.3, can be performed to compute returned values and the conditions under which they are valid. The proof obligation is:

$$\Gamma \Longrightarrow \mathcal{U} \left\langle \begin{array}{l} \text{cmf (result->resVar, } \dots \text{):} \\ \text{return resExp;} \end{array} \right\rangle ResultPredicate(\text{resVar}), \Delta$$

The symbolic state $\mathcal{U}$ is that of the return node r. Only the return statement is executed in the current method frame cmf. Postcondition is the uninterpreted predicate

ResultPredicate that collects the computed result. Γ and Δ are all first-order top-level formulas of the sequent of *r* representing the context knowledge. After applying the standard verification strategy, each open branch represents a return value valid under its path condition.

11.4.6 Current State

The values of visible variables in each symbolic execution tree node can be inspected. Visible variables are the current **this** reference, method parameters, and variables changed by assignments. This includes local variables and static fields, but highlights also two differences as compared to Java:

- KeY does not maintain local variables on the call stack. If a name is already in use it is renamed instead. As a consequence, the current state contains also local variables from all previous methods in the call stack.
- For efficiency, KeY removes variables from symbolic states as soon as they are no longer needed. This means that a previously modified local variable may get removed if it is not used in the remaining method body.

Each visible variable can have multiple values caused by, for instance, aliasing, or because nothing is known about it yet. The values for a variable **loc**, together with the conditions under which they are valid, are computed in a side proof, similar as in Section 11.4.3. The proof obligation is $\Gamma \implies \mathcal{U} ResultPredicate(\text{var}), \Delta$ using the same notation as above.

If a value is an object, then it is possible to query its fields in the same way. This brings the problem that it is possible to query fields about which no information is contained in the current sequent. Imagine, for instance, class **LinkedList** with instance variable **LinkedList next** and a sequent which says that **obj.next** is not **null**. When **obj.next** is now queried, its value will be a symbolic object. Since the value is not **null** we can query **obj.next.next**. But this time, the sequent says nothing about **obj.next.next**, consequently it could be **null** or not. In case it is not **null**, the query **obj.next.next.next** can be asked, etc. To avoid states with unbounded depth, the symbolic execution engine returns simply < **unknown value** > in case a field is not mentioned in the queried sequent.

Defining the current state by visible variables offers a view related to the source code. Alternatively, the current state could be defined as all locations and objects contained in the update (ignoring visibility). This offers a view related to verification with JavaDL.

11.4.7 Controlled Execution

A proof strategy not only decides which rule is applied next, but also selects the branch on which the next rule is applied and it decides when to stop rule application. The strategy used for verification performs a depth first proof search. It applies rules on one branch until it is closed or no more rules are applicable. It continues then with another branch in the same way until the whole proof is closed or a preset maximal number of rule applications is reached.

This behavior is not suitable for symbolic execution because a single path may never terminate. Instead, the symbolic execution strategy applies rules on a branch as long as the next rule application would generate a new symbolic execution tree node. Before that rule is applied, the strategy continues on another branch. When the next rule on all branches would cause a new symbolic execution tree node, the cycle starts over on the first branch. This ensures that one symbolic execution step at a time is performed on all branches. A preset number m of maximally executed symbolic execution tree nodes per branch is used as a stop condition in case that a symbolic execution tree has an unbounded depth.

If m is set to one, this corresponds to a *step into* instruction in an interactive debugger. A *step over* can be realized by stopping when a node with the same or lower stack trace size than the current one is encountered. The instruction *step return* is even more strict and requires that the stack trace size is indeed lower. More advanced stop conditions are available for each supported breakpoint type (e.g., line or exceptional breakpoints).

11.4.8 Memory Layouts

Aliased references do not necessarily result in different execution paths. One single symbolic execution path can represent many concrete execution paths with differently aliased references, corresponding to different data structures in memory. The symbolic execution engine allows one to compute for each node in the symbolic execution tree all possible aliasing structures and the resulting data structures in memory. Each equivalence class of variables referring to the same object, together with the resulting memory structure, is named a *memory layout*.

Memory layouts can be computed for the current state as well as for the initial state where the current computation started. The first step in doing this is to compute all possible equivalence classes of the current state. Based on this, it is then possible to compute the specific values resulting in the memory structure.

To compute the equivalence classes, the used objects occurring in the current sequent must be known. These are all terms with a reference type, meaning that they represent an object in Java, except those objects created during symbolic execution, and the variable exc in the proof obligation (11.4.1). Symbolic states $\mathcal{U}$ in KeY explicitly list objects created during symbolic execution, so they can be easily filtered out. The constant `null` is also added to the used objects because we want to check whether an object can be `null`.

After the used objects are identified, a side proof checks which of them can be aliases. The initial proof obligation is simply the current context knowledge

$$\Gamma \Longrightarrow \Delta$$

where Γ and Δ are all first-order top-level formulas of the original sequent.

For each possible combination of two used objects o_1 and o_2 (ignoring symmetry), first a case distinction on $\mathcal{U}_{root}(o_1 \doteq o_2)$ is applied to all open goals of the side proof, then the automatic proof strategy is started. The updates $\mathcal{U}_{root}$ of the proof tree root is considered because it backups the initial state and thus provide additional equality constraints.

This will close all branches representing impossible equivalence classes. The branch conditions from the case distinctions on each open branch of the side proof represent the equivalence classes of a memory layout m. The symbolic values of variables $\text{var}_1, \ldots, \text{var}_n$ can be queried as shown in Section 11.4.6, but with the slightly modified initial sequent $\Gamma, cbc \Longrightarrow \mathcal{U} \mathit{ResultPredicate}(\text{var}_1, \ldots, \text{var}_n), \Delta$, where cbc is the conjunction of the branch conditions from case distinctions on the path specifying m. As the case distinctions were exhaustive on all used objects, only a single value can be computed from this query. The side proof can be based either on the current node or on the root of the proof to inspect how the memory was before symbolic execution started.

The symbolic execution API does not query field by field to compute the full data structures of the memory. Instead, all variables used in the sequent are queried at once, which is achieved by adding them as parameters $\text{var}_1, \ldots, \text{var}_n$ to predicate *ResultPredicate*.

11.5 Conclusion And Future Work

Recent years witnessed a renewed dynamics in research devoted to debugging. To a considerable degree this is based on breakthroughs in static analysis of software, see [Ayewah et al., 2008]. The book by Zeller [2006] presents a systematic approach to debugging and an overview of currently developed and researched debugging techniques.

The Symbolic Execution Debugger is the first debugging tool that is (a) based on symbolic execution and first-order automated deduction, (b) visualizes complex control and data structures, including reference types, (c) can render unbounded loops and method calls with the help of specifications, and (d) is seamlessly integrated into a mainstream IDE (Eclipse). Other tools have capabilities (b) and (d), but to the best of our knowledge, the SED is the first tool to realize (a) and (c). A prototype of the SED was presented by Hähnle et al. [2010], however, it lacked (c).

The SED can also be used as alternative GUI for the KeY prover. It is possible to use the SED for formal verification (see Section 11.3.6) and in addition to switch into interactive mode when KeY's proof strategy was not powerful enough to close a goal automatically. The advantages are obvious: the SED-like interface for the KeY prover inherits properties (b) and (d) from above. In addition it is not only attractive to software developers unfamiliar with formal methods, but it also constitutes a continuous transition from the world of software developers into the world of formal verification.

In future work we plan to develop the SED further into a software analysis tool that supports *code reviews*, as pioneered by Fagan [1976]. For this it is necessary to increase the coverage of Java beyond what is currently supported by the KeY verifier. The most important gaps are floating-point types and concurrent programs. Both areas constitute open research problems for formal verification, however, it is not at all unrealistic to implement support of these features in the context of debugging. The reason is that for debugging purposes often an approximation of the program semantics is already useful. For example, floating-point types might be approximated by fixed point representations or by confidence intervals, whereas symbolic execution of multithreaded Java would simply concentrate on the thread from which execution is started.

Chapter 12
Proof-based Test Case Generation

Wolfgang Ahrendt, Christoph Gladisch, Mihai Herda

12.1 Introduction

Even though the area of formal verification made tremendous progress, other validation techniques remain very important. In particular, software testing has been, and will be, one of the dominating techniques for building up confidence in software. Formal verification on the one hand, and testing on the other hand, are complementary techniques, with different characteristics in terms of the achieved level of confidence, required user competence, and scalability, among others.

The fundamental complementarity between verification and testing is thus: on one hand, as Dijkstra famously remarked, it is generally impossible to guarantee the absence of errors merely by testing, i.e., testing is necessarily incomplete. But formal verification suffers from a different kind of incompleteness: it applies only to those aspects of a system that are formally modeled, while testing can exhibit errors in any part of the system under test. Therefore, testing and verification need to address different goals. One of the main challenges of testing is the creation of good *test suites*, i.e., sets of *test cases*. The meaning of 'good' is generally fuzzy, but there exist criteria, some of which we discuss in Section 12.3.

Beyond the complementary nature of formal verification and testing, the former can even contribute to the latter. The ability of the verification machinery to analyze programs very thoroughly can be reused for the automated creation of test suites which enjoy certain quality criteria by construction. This goal is achieved also by KeYTestGen, the verification based test case generation facility of KeY. To explain the basic principle, let us first recapitulate the 'standard' usage of KeY as a formal verification tool.

From source code augmented with JML specifications (see Chapter 7), KeY generates proof obligations (see Chapter 8) in dynamic logic (DL, see Chapter 3). During verification with the KeY prover, the proof branches over case distinctions, largely triggered by Boolean decisions in the source code (see below, Section 12.6). On each proof branch, a certain path through the program is executed symbolically. It turns out that for test case generation, one can use the same machinery. The idea is

© Springer International Publishing AG 2016
W. Ahrendt et al. (Eds.): Deductive Software Verification, LNCS 10001, pp. 415–451, 2016
DOI: 10.1007/978-3-319-49812-6_12

to let the prover construct a (possibly partial) proof tree (with a bounded number of loop unwindings), to then read off a *path condition* from each proof branch, i.e., a constraint on the input parameters and initial state for a certain path to be taken. If we generate concrete test input data satisfying each of these constraints, we can achieve strong code coverage criteria by construction, like for instance MC/DC (Modified Condition/Decision Criterion, see Definition 12.6). KeYTestGen implements these principles [Engel and Hähnle, 2007, Beckert and Gladisch, 2007, Gladisch, 2011]. It is integrated into the KeY GUI, and offers the automated generation of test cases in the popular JUnit [Beck, 2004] format.

In addition to the source code, KeY's test generation facility employs formal specifications, for two purposes. First, specifications are needed to complete the test cases with *oracles* to check the test's pass/fail status. The second role of specifications is to allow symbolic execution of method calls within the code under test. The prover can use the specification, rather than the implementation, of called methods to continue symbolic execution.

```
1  public class ArrayUtils {
2      /*@ public normal_behavior
3        @ ensures (\forall int i; 0<=i && i<a.length; a[i]==b[i]);
4        @*/
5      public void arrCopy(int[] a, int[] b) {
6          for(int i=0; i<a.length; i++) {
7              b[i]=a[i];
8          }
9      }
10 }
```

Listing 12.1 Method `arrCopy` violates its contract

As an example, Listing 12.1 shows the method `arrCopy` which is supposed to copy the contents of array a to array b. This is clearly not the case since the length of the array b may be smaller than that of array a, in which case a is only partially copied and an exception is thrown. We will show in the rest of this chapter how the user can find errors, like also this one, using KeYTestGen. Throughout the chapter we will explain what effects different settings and options have on the generated tests and give advice which of them should be used for different purposes.

12.2 A Quick Tutorial

This section contains instructions for the set-up and basic usage of KeYTestGen. Naturally, some of the artifacts and concepts that appear in this section will be clarified only in the latter sections.

12.2.1 Setup

The minimal software requirement that is needed in order to run KeYTestGen is the KeY system and the Z3 SMT solver. Version 4.3.1 (or higher) of Z3 is required which can be downloaded from github.com/Z3Prover/z3.[1] If the Z3 command is available in the environment in which KeY is running, then KeYTestGen will run out of the box. The SMT solver is needed for the test data generation. This is the only requirement necessary for test case generation, the other two libraries mentioned in this section are merely required for running the test cases when certain options have been selected during the test case generation phase.

OpenJML is a library which contains various tools for the JML specification language. Among them there is a runtime assertion checker (RAC) which can be used to check at runtime whether the code fulfills the JML specification. This library is needed for compiling and running the generated test cases with OpenJML. Note, however, that OpenJML as of this moment is not compatible with Java 8, such that it must be compiled and executed with Java 7. The library can be downloaded from www.openjml.org. KeYTestGen requires OpenJML version 0.7.2 or higher.

Objenesis is a library which allows the initialization of private class fields and the instantiation of classes which do not have a default constructor. When the Objenesis option is selected, then the generated test cases use functions from this library when initializing object fields of the test data. This library can be downloaded from objenesis.org. KeYTestGen requires Objenesis version 2.2 or higher.

12.2.2 Usage

Generating test cases for the method `arrCopy` in Listing 12.1 consists of the following steps[2]:

1. First download the examples for this chapter from this book's web page, www.key-project.org/thebook2.
2. Start KeY. (See also Section 15.2.)
3. We open the file browser by selecting **File** → **Load** (or selecting ▦ in the tool bar), and navigate to the examples directory for this chapter.
4. Preselect the **arrCopy** folder and press the **Open** button.
5. The **Proof Management** window will open. In its **Contract Targets** pane, we make sure that **ArrayUtils** is expanded, and therein select the method **arrCopy()**. We are asked to select a contract (in this case, there is only one), and press the **Start Proof** button.
6. Press ✿ in the main window which opens the **Test Suite Generation** window.

---

[1] In addition, Z3 is offered as a package for various Linux distributions.

[2] Here it is assumed that KeY is configured with the default settings and that the environment has been setup according to Section 12.2.1. Default settings of KeY can be enforced by deleting the .key directory in the user's home directory and restarting KeY.

7. Select the settings as shown in Figure 12.1 (adjusting the paths to your environment) and press the **Start** button.
8. Browse to the directory where the tests have been generated. The path is displayed in the notification panel of the **Test Suite Generation** window. Compile and execute the tests.

In the following, we describe these steps in more detail and describe also alternative steps.

Concerning the Java code under test, two technicalities should be noted. First, the generation of test inputs is based on symbolic execution of the source code. This requires either the entire source code under test, or source code stubs (method signatures) of all called library methods. The imported files can be placed in the same directory as the file that is loaded: KeY will load all files from that directory. Second, KeY can load only methods annotated with *Java Modeling Language* (JML) contracts (or specifications). This issue can be easily solved by placing the trivial JML contract

```
/*@ public normal_behavior  requires true; ensures true; @*/
```

in the source code line above the method that is called in the code under test (similar as in Listing 12.1). The keyword `normal_behavior` specifies that no exception is thrown, `requires` specifies the precondition, and `ensures` specifies the postcondition of the method. Since the precondition is true, all inputs and initial states of the method are permitted; since the postcondition is true as well, all outputs and final states of the method satisfy the postcondition, thus the JML contract is trivial.[3]

KeYTestGen bases test generation on the analysis of (possibly partial) proofs. Any partial or completed proof in KeY for a Java program can be used. If no such proof is available, KeYTestGen will generate one. To open the **Test Suite Generation** window, the user needs to press the ✪ button. From the **Test Suite Generation** window, shown in Figure 12.1, the user can start the test case generation process by pressing the **Start** button. The process can be forcefully stopped by using the **Stop** button.

The left side of the **Test Suite Generation** window consists of a notification panel. It notifies the user about the progress of the test case generation process, about any errors which may have occurred during the process, and the directory in which the generated test files are stored. In Figure 12.1, the output reports on the symbolic execution and test case generation for the *arrCopy* example shown in Listing 12.1, after loading the specified program into KeY. After the program is symbolically executed, path conditions are extracted for the resulting open goals.

Since the option to include postconditions is checked, the postconditions are not removed from the proof obligation. In this case, KeYTestGen will try to avoid generating test cases that satisfy the postcondition. To prepare the checking, a preprocessing step called "Semantic Blasting" is applied to each of the goals, replacing the occurrence of certain KeY functions by an axiomatization of their semantics, as explained in Section 12.7. The resulting goals are then translated to bounded SMT format and

---

[3] While such trivial contracts of called methods satisfy the technical requirement for test generation, more informative specifications may be needed in some cases to produce good test cases.

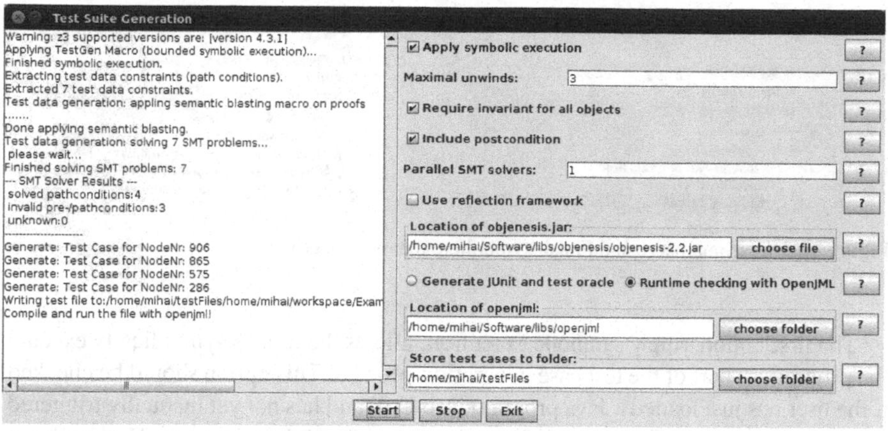

Figure 12.1 The Test Suite Generation window

handed over to an SMT solver, here Z3. In the example, not all path conditions lead to counterexamples, only four paths can be solved. For the remaining three conditions, where the postcondition is satisfied, no test data is generated. The four test cases are then generated and written to a file. The final lines in the notification panel tell the user into which directory the test cases and supplementary files were stored. The user may browse this directory, compile and run the tests.

Two possibilities are offered for compiling and executing the generated tests. When the option **Use JUnit and test oracle** is enabled, KeYTestGen generates test cases in JUnit format, featuring test oracles that are translated from the JML specification of the currently loaded Java program. The generated files are located in the directory specified in the text area **Store test cases to folder** and can be compiled using a Java compiler. OpenJML does not support the JUnit API and uses its own runtime checker as test oracle. When using OpenJML, the former option must be disabled and the path of the folder containing the OpenJML library should be specified in the text field at the bottom. For convenience, KeYTestGen generates in this case the shell scripts compileWithOpenJML.sh and executeWithOpenJML.sh in the test output directory. These scripts can be used for compiling and running the tests on Linux systems. The usage of these scripts is explained in Section 12.8.2. (Also, the scripts contain instructions as comments.) On other systems the user can manually compile and run the tests as instructed in the OpenJML's user manual.

12.2.3 Options and Settings

Here we summarize the remaining options and settings of the **Test Suite Generation** window. Some of the options and settings are described in more detail throughout the chapter where the respective techniques are explained.

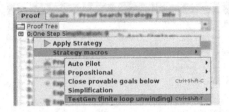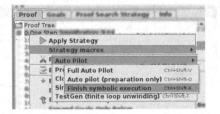

Figure 12.2 TestGen macro and Finish symbolic execution macro

The first option, **Apply symbolic execution**, allows the user to symbolically execute the program as part of the test case generation process. This option should be checked if the user has just loaded a Java program into KeY and has not yet manually triggered proof tree generation, i.e., the proof tree consists only of the root node. The symbolic execution performed here is based on the **TestGen** macro provided by KeY. Macros (see Section 15.3) are proof search strategies that a user can manually trigger by a right-click on a proof node in the proof tab of the main KeY window and selecting **Strategy macros** (see Figure 12.2).

The only difference between the **Apply symbolic execution** option in the **Test Suite Generation** window and the **Finish Symbolic Execution** macro of the main window is that loop invariants and method contracts for methods called inside the method under test are not needed. Instead, loops are unwound and method calls inlined finitely often as specified by the second option **Maximal Unwinds**. The number given in this option is the maximum number of allowed occurrences of loop unwinding or method inlining rule applications from the root of the proof tree to a leaf. After reaching it on a given path, symbolic execution will stop on that path. KeYTestGen will then use the resulting proof tree for generating a test suite.

The **Require invariant for all objects** option needs to be checked if the user wants the generated test data objects to fulfill their respective class invariants. The default semantics of KeY requires only the class invariants of the `this` object. The **Include postcondition** option allows the user to choose whether test data should be generated for all leaf nodes in the proof tree, or whether KeYTestGen should only generate test data that does not satisfy the postcondition of the method under test (see Section 12.6 for more details). The first type of test data is useful if the user is interested in a high coverage test suite, while the second type is useful when looking for counterexamples only, i.e., inputs that violate the postcondition. It should be noted that activating **Include postcondition** only affects the open proof goals where symbolic execution is finished.[4]

The option **Concurrent Processes** determines how many instances of the Z3 SMT solver will run in parallel when looking for test data.

When the method under test uses classes without a default constructor, or if private or protected object fields must be initialized by the test, then the option **Use reflection framework** should be activated. When activated, the Objenesis library

---

[4] There is no modality containing a program in the sequent.

is used to instantiate classes without default constructors and the Java reflection framework is used to initialize private and protected fields. The text field below the option allows the user to set the path of the location the Objenesis library file. It should be noted that the runtime checker OpenJML is not capable of handling code using the reflection framework. In this case, it is recommended to also activate the option **Generate JUnit and test oracle**.

12.3 Test Cases, Test Suites, and Test Criteria

This section is a brief introduction into some testing concepts and criteria. It is neither complete nor general, but aims to give the reader a lightweight introduction to the testing-related taxonomy that matters in the present context. For an in-depth treatment see, for example, [Ammann and Offutt, 2008]. Here, our particular focus is automation of testing activities.

In general, the two major activities in a testing process are the *creation* and the *execution* of sets of test cases. Traditionally, both activities were manual, whereas modern testing methods automate the execution of test cases. For Java, the pioneering framework for automated test execution is JUnit, developed by Kent Beck and Erich Gamma [Beck, 2004]. Automated test case creation, however, is less common, even though in the past decade a considerable number of test generation tools have been proposed. Several of them are, like KeYTestGen, based on symbolic execution and can automatically generate test cases in the JUnit format. As a result, both the creation and the execution of test cases are automated. What sets KeYTestGen apart from most other approaches is its embedding into a program logic for formal verification. As a consequence, KeYTestGen can interleave test generation and advanced logical simplification, for example, when filtering out test cases that do not meet preconditions. It is also possible to formulate and satisfy strong coverage criteria and to generate test oracles from postconditions, as will be shown below. Related work is discussed in Section 12.10 below.

A *test case* can formally be described as a tuple $\langle D, Or \rangle$ consisting of *test data* D and *oracle Or*, where D is a tuple $\langle P_D, S_D \rangle$ of input parameters P_D and initial state S_D before the execution of the test case. The oracle is a function $Or(R, S_f) \mapsto \{pass, fail\}$, telling for each combination of return value R and final state S_f whether those are the expected results of executing this test case.

A *test suite* TS^m for a (Java) method m consists of n test cases for that method:

$$TS^m = \{\langle D_1, Or_1 \rangle, \ldots, \langle D_n, Or_n \rangle\} \tag{12.1}$$

In the simplest cases Or_i compares the result with a single expected value unique for D_i, but in general, Or_i may accept a whole set of results. This definition reflects the fact that the oracle is *specific* for each and every test case in testing theory as well as in most testing frameworks, such as JUnit. In the KeYTestGen approach, however, we aim at having a single, *generic* oracle, Or^m, for each method m, to be computed from the JML specification of m. Then, a test suite TS^m, looks like

$$TS^m = \{\langle D_1, Or^m \rangle, \ldots, \langle D_n, Or^m \rangle\} \ . \tag{12.2}$$

Accordingly, in our usage of JUnit, we place a call to the same oracle method in each test case. Conceptually, as the oracle is the same for all D_j in TS^m, we can omit Or^m from the representation of test cases, and keep it separate. Thus, we finally define a test suite TS^m as:

$$TS^m = \langle \{D_1, \ldots, D_n\}, Or^m \rangle \tag{12.3}$$

where $\{D_1, \ldots, D_n\}$ is the set of test data, which we now can identify with the set of test cases, and Or^m is the, now single, oracle for m. Assuming a test suite TS^m is given in any of the forms (12.1), (12.2), or (12.3), we write $\mathscr{D}(TS^m)$ to denote the *test data set* $\{D_1, \ldots, D_n\}$ of the test suite.

Automation of test suite generation should relieve the developers from

- identifying and manually writing test data sets,
- identifying and manually writing oracles,
- using additional tools to assess coverage properties of test suites.

The KeYTestGen tool presented in this chapter automates and merges these items. It computes a test suite (12.3), and from that (provided the JUnit option is checked) assembles a JUnit test suite which is closer to the form (12.2). The generated test suite is formally guaranteed to satisfy certain coverage criteria which are explained below. From the user's perspective, the generated test suite does not need further investigation to check what kind of coverage it achieves.

Approaches used for deriving test data can be roughly divided in two main categories:

White-box testing: when derivation of test data sets is based on analyses of source code.

Black-box testing: when derivation of test data sets is based on external descriptions of the software (specification, design documents, requirements, probability distributions).

KeYTestGen is actually a hybrid of these two categories. Its generation of the test data set $\mathscr{D}(TS^m)$ is mainly white-box, with elements of black-box. It is mainly based on a thorough analysis of the source code, but also on the preconditions from the specification. It is its white-box nature which allows KeYTestGen to generate test suites featuring strong code based coverage criteria by construction (including MC/DC, see below). In general, the view of a clear cut between white-box and black-box methods is somewhat old-fashioned. Several approaches combine the two, in which case we can call the method *gray-box*. Moreover, used artifacts, like, e.g., software models, can be positioned in between the internal and external descriptions. In any case, the value of these notions is that they mark the extreme points of the design space.

Please note that, regardless of the test data, most methods treat the generation of oracles entirely in black-box fashion. The same is true for KeYTestGen. Otherwise, the oracles would be in danger of inheriting errors from the implementation.

Let us turn to coverage criteria which may, or may not, be fulfilled by test suites, or, more precisely, by their test data sets. Two important groups of code based coverage criteria are classified as *graph coverage criteria* and *logical coverage criteria*. Each graph coverage criterion defines a specific way in which a test data set may, or may not, cover the control flow graph.

Definition 12.1 (Control flow graph). A Control Flow Graph represents the code of a program unit as a graph, where every statement is represented by a node and edges describe control flow between statements. Edges can be constrained by conditions.

On the other hand, when coverage criteria are defined with reference to the set of logical expressions occurring in the source code, they are referred to as logical coverage criteria. These criteria talk about the values logical (sub)expressions take during the execution of different test cases, and the way they are exercised. There is a rich body of results on subsumptions between different coverage criteria (see [Zhu et al., 1997] for an extended comparison). A testing criterion C_1 *subsumes* C_2 if, for any test suite TS fulfilling C_1, it is true that TS fulfills C_2.

Definition 12.2 (Branch, Path, Path condition). A (program) *branch* is a pair of program locations (a, b) where a is followed by b in the control flow, with the restriction that a is also followed by a location other than b in the control flow. A (program) *path* is a consecutive sequence of program positions that may be visited in one execution of a program unit. A *path condition* is a condition on the inputs and the initial state of a program unit that must be met in order for a particular path through the unit to be executed.

For example, the program

```Java
if (x>0) { A } else { B };
x = x - 1;
if (x<0) { C } else { D }
```

has four branches: (if(x>0), A), (if(x>0), B), (if(x<0), C), and (if(x<0), D). And it contains four paths, within which AC, AD, BC, and BD are executed, respectively. These correspond to path conditions x>0 && (x-1)<0, x>0 && !(x-1)<0, !x>0 && (x-1)<0, and !x>0 && !(x-1)<0, respectively. After simplification, they become x>0 && x<1, x>0 && x>=1, x<=0 && x<1, and x<=0 && x>=1. Note that in general the guards may be complex statements with side effects, in which case they must be considered as part of the branch or path.

Definition 12.3 (Feasible/infeasible path condition). If a path cannot be executed because its path condition is contradictory (i.e., it is equivalent to false), then the path, respectively the path condition, is called *infeasible*. Otherwise, the path, respectively the path condition, is *feasible*. A feasible or infeasible program branch is defined analogously.

In the above program the paths AC and BD are infeasible because the path conditions x>0 && x<1 and x<=0 && x>=1 are infeasible, i.e., unsatisfiable. (We assume x to be of type int.)

Definition 12.4 (Full feasible bounded path coverage). Let BP be the set of paths of a method or a sequence of statements P which are bound by a given number of method invocations and loop iterations. A test suite T satisfies *full feasible bounded path coverage* for P if every feasible path of BP is executed by at least one test of T.

For example, a test suite satisfying full feasible bounded path coverage with bound 2 for the program

```
while (i<n) { if (cond) { A } else { B } }
```

must execute the feasible paths from the set {AA, AB, BA, BB}.

Definition 12.5 (Full feasible branch coverage). Let BB be the set of branches of a method or a sequence of statements P. A test suite T satisfies *full feasible branch coverage* for P if every feasible branch of BB is executed by at least one test of T.

Full feasible branch coverage requires that in the above loop the two branches (if(cond), A) and (if(cond), B) are executed if feasible paths exists containing these branches. We will see in Section 12.6 that achieving full feasible branch coverage can be very challenging in certain cases (e.g., Listings 12.2 and 12.3), but due to the theorem proving capabilities of KeY it can be achieved also for difficult cases.

The MC/DC coverage criteria is in particular interesting for industrial applications, because it is required in the aviation domain for certification of critical software by the DO-178C/ED-12C standard [RTCA] and it is highly recommended in the automotive domain by the standard ISO 26262. Its interest lies in providing relatively strong coverage while its complexity (the size of test suites) grows linearly with the number of atomic conditions in a program. In the following, we give no formal definition for *conditions* and *decisions*, but explain those terms by the example following the definition.

Definition 12.6 (Modified Condition / Decision Coverage (MC/DC) [RTCA]). Every point of entry and exit in the program has been invoked at least once, every condition in a decision in the program has been taken on all possible outcomes at least once, and each condition has been shown to independently affect the decision's outcome. A condition is shown to independently affect a decision's outcome by varying just that condition while holding fixed all other possible conditions.

In [Vilkomir and Bowen, 2001] the MC/DC coverage criterion is illustrated by the following example:

Table 12.1 MC/DC coverage example as illustrated in [Vilkomir and Bowen, 2001]

combination number	values				variations			MC/DC
	A	B	C	d	A	B	C	
1	1	1	1	1				
2	1	1	0	1	*	*		+
3	1	0	1	1			*	+
4	0	1	1	1				
5	1	0	0	0	*	*		+
6	0	1	0	0	*			+
7	0	0	1	0				
8	0	0	0	0				

```
d = (A && B) || (A && C) || (B && C)
```

The decision is the entire expression denoted by d. The conditions are the three subexpressions (A && B), (A && C), and (B && C). A test suite satisfying the MC/DC criterion is shown in Table 12.1. The pair satisfying each condition is marked '*'. The subset of combinations marked '+' satisfies the criterion.

KeYTestGen can satisfy different coverage criteria. Which coverage criterion is satisfied depends on the selected settings in the **Proof Strategy Settings** tab of the KeY GUI. These settings determine among others how the program is analyzed. If **Loop treatment** is set to **Expand**, then the resulting test suite achieves *full feasible bounded path coverage* (Definition 12.4). The bound for expanding (or unrolling) loops can be set in the **Test Suite Generation** dialogue (by pressing the ⊙ button). If **Loop treatment** is set to **Invariant** and sufficiently strong loop invariants are provided by the user for loops in the program, then *full feasible branch coverage* (Definition 12.5) can be achieved. To fully satisfy either of the coverage criteria it is necessary that symbolic execution of the program is executed to the end on every execution branch, i.e., the maximum number of rule applications must be set sufficiently high in the **Proof Search Strategy** tab. A description of how the symbolic program analysis works and how test cases are selected is provided in Section 12.6.

In order to obtain MC/DC coverage using KeYTestGen, it is necessary to set **Proof splitting** to **Free** in the **Proof strategy settings** tab when KeY performs symbolic program analysis (symbolic execution, see Section 12.6). The complexity of the program analysis and the number of test cases may grow rapidly. This is because in addition to MC/DC coverage also the coverage criteria defined in Definition 12.4 or 12.5 will be fulfilled when the symbolic program analysis is performed with the respective settings.

12.4 Application Scenarios and Variations of the Test Generator

12.4.1 KeYTestGen for Test Case Generation

KeYTestGen is designed to generate unit tests for one method at a time, hereafter method under test (MUT). Within this scenario it can be used in a variety of ways. For example, it can be used as a stand-alone test generation tool with or without the use of formal specifications, or it can be used to support or complement the formal verification process with KeY. It covers a spectrum of automation possibilities from interactively selected tests for specific branches of a proof tree up to fully automatic generation of test suites. KeYTestGen can generate JUnit tests suites and test oracles from JML specifications, or it can generate a set of test methods that simply execute the MUT without any additional features (see Section 12.2.2). The user may choose to use his own test oracle. For instance, the generated test suites can be compiled and executed with the runtime assertion checker of OpenJML [Cok, 2011] as shown in Section 12.8.2.

In the simplest usage scenario, KeYTestGen performs symbolic execution (as described in Section 12.6) of the MUT and generates a test suite that executes all the paths of the MUT up to a given bound on loop unwindings and recursive method calls. The generated tests not only can initialize the parameters P_D of the MUT but also the fields of objects S_D (using the notation in Section 12.3). A generated JUnit test may create objects, possibly with a complex linked data structure, to exercise a particular path through the MUT.

In an advanced usage of KeYTestGen, the user may provide formal specifications, possibly with quantified formulas, as they are also used in formal verification. The formal specifications can be used in two ways: (a) to restrict test generation such that the precondition of the MUT is satisfied and to generate a test oracle from the postcondition, and (b) to reduce the number of test cases that arise from method and loop unwindings. An example of case (a) is:

```
/*@ requires 0<=i && i<b.length; @*/
... b[i]=x; ...
```

where the precondition prevents an array overflow that may be caused by the expression b[i]. For an example of case (b) consider the program:

```
arrCopy(a,b);
x=b[i];
```

which calls the method from Listing 12.1. Before the statement x=b[i] can be analyzed via symbolic execution, the symbolic execution engine must first analyze the call arrCopy(a,b). One possibility is that symbolic execution enters the method and executes its body as described in Section 12.6.4 below. Generally, this may create many test cases from case distinctions in the called method. The other possibility is to—loosely speaking—replace the method call by its postcondition which specifies the result of all possible executions in one expression, hence reducing the number of test cases. The same principle applies to loops that may be annotated with loop

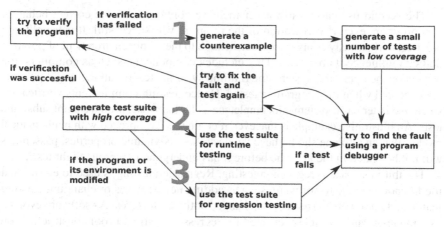

Figure 12.3 Three use-cases of KeYTestGen when used in connection with formal verification.

invariants. We elaborate on this technique in Section 12.6.5. When using method contracts, the generated tests are white-box tests with respect the MUT, but they are black-box tests with respect to methods called by the MUT. To take advantage of method contracts or loop invariants the user must select the respective options in the **Proof Search Strategy** tab of the KeY GUI.

12.4.2 KeYTestGen for Formal Verification

When using KeYTestGen in the context of formal verification, we consider three use cases. These are summarized in Figure 12.3.

The first use case is finding, i.e. locating, software faults. Tests are helpful to find software faults because when a program is executed in its runtime environment, i.e. not symbolically, then a standard program debugger can be utilized.[5] Program debuggers are powerful tools that enable the user to follow the program control flow at different levels of granularity and they enable the inspection of the program state. A strength of program debuggers is also that the user reads the source code as it is executed, which is helpful for understanding it. When a proof attempt fails, either due to a timeout[6] or because no more rules are applicable, it is difficult to read the program (execution) from the open proof branches. Even if a counterexample is generated which represents the initial state of the program revealing the fault it maybe hardly readable by an inexperienced user. However, this information can be used to initialize a program in its runtime environment, enabling to use a program debugger.

---

[5] It is also possible to use the KeY system as a debugger based on symbolic execution, rather than concrete execution. This is described in Chapter 11 of this book.

[6] Maximum number of rule applications reached.

The second use case is to further increase confidence in the correct behavior of a program, even if verification of the program was successful. It is usually not practical to rigorously apply formal verification to the whole environment of program that can influence its behavior. This includes components, such as compilers, the hardware, the operating system, the runtime system, etc. But all these components are executed when the program is tested. Hence, testing complements verification where the latter has a systemic incompleteness. In this sense, proofs cannot substitute tests. An illustrative example is that even if engineers have proved with mathematical models that an airplane should have the desired aerodynamic properties, passengers will not be seated in the airplane before it has undergone numerous flight tests.

The third use case is regression testing. Regression testing is used to ensure that modifications made to software, such as adding new features or changing existing features, do not worsen (regress) unchanged software features. As software evolves, existing tests can be quickly repeated for regression testing. Proof construction, on the other hand, is more expensive and therefore it is reasonable to run a set of tests before proceeding to a verification attempt after the software has been modified. More on regression verification with KeY can be found in [Beckert et al., 2015].

Hence, in the first use case a single test or a small number of focused tests is generated if the verification has failed. A successful verification attempt on the other hand leads to the second and third use cases. Contrary to the first use case, in the other use cases a high code coverage test suite is desired.

12.5 Architecture of KeYTestGen

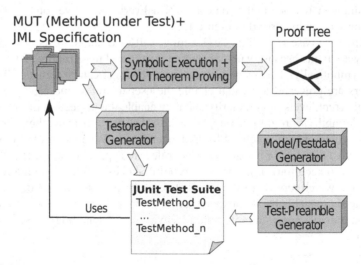

Figure 12.4 Main components and test generation procedure of KeYTestGen

Figure 12.4 depicts the test generation process and its main components. The input to KeYTestGen is a Java method under test (MUT), with its JML requirement specification. The KeYTestGen approach starts with the creation of a *proof tree*. The branches of the proof tree mimic the execution of the program with symbolic values.[7] Case distinctions (including implicit distinctions like, e.g., whether or not an exception is thrown) in the program are reflected as branches of the proof tree. The different branches are used for deriving different test cases.

A *path condition*, together with the *precondition* from the specification, constitute a *test data constraint*, which has to be satisfied by the test data of a test case for this path. For example, to generate a test that creates an *ArrayIndexOutOfBoundsException* when executing the statement b[i]=a[i] in method *arrCopy* (Listing 12.1), the test data constraint b.length>=0 && b.length < a.length may be generated. The extraction of test data constraints from the proof tree is described in Section 12.6.

To create a test, concrete *test (input) data D* must be generated which satisfies the test data constraint obtained from the first phase. For example, we may use the concrete array lengths b.length==1 && a.length==2 to satisfy the above test data constraint. This task is handled by the *model generator* (Section 12.7). Here the term *model* means the first-order logic interpretation that satisfies the test data constraint. The challenge of model generation in the context of KeYTestGen is to generate models for quantified formulas which may stem from the requirement specification, loop invariants, other JML annotations, or from the logical modeling of the object heap in the KeY framework.

The *test suite* consists of a set of *test methods* (*test drivers*). The generation of the test driver is discussed in Section 12.9. It prepares the initial state of the test, executes the MUT, and checks the final state after the execution of the MUT with a *test oracle* (*Or*). The first part executed by each test driver (test method) is the *test preamble*. The test preamble prepares the initial state in which the MUT is executed by creating Java objects and initializing program variables and fields with test data. The model which is generated by the model generator is therefore the input to the test preamble generator. For example, given the test data b.length==1 && a.length==2, the test preamble may generate the statements int[] a=new int[2]; int[] b=new int[1];. Additional test data is required to initialize the array elements, but in this example no specific values were defined by the test data constraint. The final part of the test driver is the *test oracle*. The test oracle can be either an external runtime assertion checker (e.g. OpenJML), or generated by KeYTestGen from the requirement specification when the user chooses the option Generate JUnit and test oracle in the Test Suite Generation window (see Figure 12.1). The generation of the test oracle is explained in Section 12.8.

---

[7] Symbolic values are expressions over variables.

12.6 Proof-based Constraint Construction for Test Input Data

When KeY reads source code and its specification, it translates these entities to a Dynamic Logic (DL) formula, representing the various properties to be verified, see Chapter 8. DL (see Chapter 3) is a superset of first-order logic (FOL, see Chapter 2). It includes all FOL operators, e.g., $\wedge$ (and), $\vee$ (or), $\neg$ (not), $\rightarrow$ (implication); predicates such as $<$ (less than), $\doteq$ (equality), as well as named predicates and functions; and quantifiers $\exists$ (exists) and $\forall$ (forall). Additionally, in DL one can write $\langle p \rangle \phi$ to express that formula ϕ is true in the state after executing the program p. Thus, the formula PRE $\rightarrow \langle p \rangle$POST means that if p is executed from a state where the precondition PRE is true, then in the final state after executing p the postcondition POST must be true as well. *Update operators* $\{x := e \,|| \, \ldots\}$ are used to collect assignments from a program which have been simplified such that the expressions e has no side-effects. Since KeY uses Java programs and defines Java-specific predicates we refer to KeYFOL and JavaDL. In the following we use the *sequent* notation $A \Rightarrow B$ which is an implication where A is a conjunction of formulas and B is a disjunction of formulas.

12.6.1 Symbolic Execution for Test Constraint Generation

A proof in KeY is essentially inference on DL formulas, using a proof strategy called symbolic execution. It is exactly this principle which makes the KeY prover an excellent basis for code coverage-oriented test generation. Therefore, we briefly demonstrate the principle of KeY-style symbolic execution on an example.

Consider the DL formula (12.4), where we abstract away from the concrete pre- and postcondition PRE and POST, and from the program fragments p_1 and p_2. The program swaps the values stored in x and y, using arithmetic, and continues with an if statement branching over 2x>y.

$$\text{PRE} \Rightarrow \langle \texttt{x=x+y; y=x-y; x=x-y; if (2x>y) \{p_1\} else \{p_2\}} \rangle \text{POST}$$
$$(12.4)$$

When proving this formula, KeY symbolically executes one statement after the other, turning Java code into a compact representation of the *effect* of the statements. This representation is called *update*, which essentially is an explicit substitution, to be applied at some later point. In our example, symbolic execution of x=x+y; y=x-y; x=x-y; will, in several steps, arrive at the DL formula given in (12.5).

$$\text{PRE} \Rightarrow \{x := y \,||\, y := x\} \langle \texttt{if (2x>y) \{p_1\} else \{p_2\}} \rangle \text{POST} \qquad (12.5)$$

The '$x := y \,||\, y := x$' is the update, where the $||$ symbol indicates its parallel nature; that is, the substitutions of x and y will be simultaneous once the update gets applied.

The next step in the proof is a branching caused by the if statement. Essentially, we branch over the if condition 2x>y, but not without applying the update on the condition. This leads to the two proof branches for proving the following formulas:

$$\text{PRE} \land (\{x := y \,\|\, y := x\}2x > y) \Rightarrow \{x := y \,\|\, y := x\}\langle p_1 \rangle \, \text{POST}$$
$$\text{PRE} \land (\{x := y \,\|\, y := x\}2x \leq y) \Rightarrow \{x := y \,\|\, y := x\}\langle p_2 \rangle \, \text{POST}$$

Next, we apply the update (i.e., the substitution) on $2x > y$ and $2x \leq y$, resulting in:

$$\text{PRE} \land 2y > x \Rightarrow \{x := y \,\|\, y := x\}\langle p_1 \rangle \, \text{POST} \qquad (12.6)$$

$$\text{PRE} \land 2y \leq x \Rightarrow \{x := y \,\|\, y := x\}\langle p_2 \rangle \, \text{POST} \qquad (12.7)$$

Note that the update application has exchanged x and y on the left side of $\Rightarrow$, translating the condition on the intermediate state into a *condition on the initial state* for the path p_1 or p_2 to be taken, respectively. And indeed, the original program (see 12.4) will, for instance, execute p_1 if $2y > x$ holds in the initial state. If we choose to create tests from the proof branches 12.6 and 12.7, then two test cases will be created, where the formulas $\text{PRE} \land 2y > x$ and $\text{PRE} \land 2y \leq x$ are used as the test data constraints, respectively.

When the proof continues on 12.6 and 12.7, p_1 and p_2 will be executed symbolically in a similar fashion. When symbolic execution is finished, all proof branches will have accumulated *conditions on the initial state* for one particular program path being taken. If we now generate test data satisfying these conditions, we arrive at test cases covering all paths the program can take (up to the used limit of loop unwindings and recursion inlining).

Updates are extremely useful not only for verification, but also from the logic testing criteria perspective, as they solve the *inner variable problem*, i.e., the problem of inferring initial conditions on variables from intermediate conditions on variables. Applying an update on a branching condition means to compute the *weakest precondition* of the branching condition with respect to the symbolically executed program up to this point.

It is worth noting that KeY may generate more than two proof branches for an if statement, as the guard could be a complex Boolean formula. All the possible combinations (with respect to lazy evaluation) are evaluated.

12.6.2 Implicit Case Distinctions

KeY can create proof branches also for implicit conditions that check whether an exception should be raised. To enable this feature, the user must select the option **runtimeExceptions:allow** in the **Options → Taclet Options** menu. When this option is activated, then, for example, symbolic execution of the code:

$$\text{PRE} \Rightarrow \langle \text{u.v = a[i]; p} \rangle \, \text{POST}$$

will result in the following five proof branches:

$\text{PRE} \land \mathtt{a} \doteq \mathtt{null}$
$\Rightarrow \langle \mathtt{throw\ new\ NullPointerException();\ p} \rangle\ \text{POST}$

$\text{PRE} \land \mathtt{u} \doteq \mathtt{null}$
$\Rightarrow \langle \mathtt{throw\ new\ NullPointerException();\ p} \rangle\ \text{POST}$

$\text{PRE} \land \mathtt{a} \not\doteq \mathtt{null} \land \mathtt{i} < 0$
$\Rightarrow \langle \mathtt{throw\ new\ ArrayIndexOutOfBoundsException();p} \rangle\ \text{POST}$ (12.8)

$\text{PRE} \land \mathtt{a} \not\doteq \mathtt{null} \land \mathtt{i} \geq \mathtt{a.length}$
$\Rightarrow \langle \mathtt{throw\ new\ ArrayIndexOutOfBoundsException();p} \rangle\ \text{POST}$ (12.9)

$\text{PRE} \land \mathtt{u} \not\doteq \mathtt{null} \land 0 \leq \mathtt{i} \land \mathtt{i} \leq \mathtt{a.length}$
$\Rightarrow \langle \mathtt{p} \rangle\ \text{POST}$

Hence, the test data constraints are in this case the formulas:

$$\text{PRE} \land \mathtt{a} \doteq \mathtt{null}$$

$$\vdots$$

$$\text{PRE} \land \mathtt{u} \not\doteq \mathtt{null} \land 0 \leq \mathtt{i} \land \mathtt{i} \leq \mathtt{a.length}$$

It should be noted that in the **Proof Search Strategy** settings **Proof splitting** must not be set **off**. If proof splitting is deactivated, then the proof branches 12.8 and 12.9 will be subsumed by one proof branch:

$\text{PRE} \land \mathtt{a} \not\doteq \mathtt{null} \land (\mathtt{i} < 0 \lor \mathtt{i} \geq \mathtt{a.length})$
$\Rightarrow \langle \mathtt{throw\ new\ ArrayIndexOutOfBoundsException();p} \rangle\ \text{POST}$ (12.10)

When generating a test from the proof branch 12.10, one test will be created satisfying only one of the subconditions in $(\mathtt{i} < 0 \lor \mathtt{i} \geq \mathtt{a.length})$. Hence, activating **Proof splitting** is needed to ensure MC/DC coverage.

12.6.3 Infeasible Path Filtering

It is possible that some paths through a program cannot be taken, because the conditions to execute the path may contradict each other. Consider for instance the program:

$$\mathtt{if\ (x<y)\ \{if\ (x>y)\ \{\ s\ \}\ \}}$$

The statement s cannot be executed because it is not possible that both conditions, $x < y$ and $x > y$, are satisfied. The path to s is an *infeasible path* (see Definition 12.3). When constructing the proof tree and applying the $\mathtt{if}$-rule twice, we obtain two proof branches in which s is not reached and the following proof branch, where s is reached:

$$\text{PRE} \land x < y \land x > y \Rightarrow \langle \mathtt{s} \rangle\ \text{POST}$$

If KeY continues proof tree construction, it will infer that $x < y \wedge x > y$ is unsatisfiable and create the proof branch:

$$PRE \wedge \mathit{false} \Rightarrow \langle s \rangle \, POST$$

Since *false* appears in the assumption, the implication (sequent) is *true* and the proof branch is immediately closed by KeY. During symbolic execution KeY detects most of the infeasible paths and filters them out from further inspection. Since no state can satisfy the test data constraint $PRE \wedge \mathit{false}$ no test will be generated for this path.

12.6.4 Using Loop Unwinding and Method Inlining

The simplest way of dealing with a loop is by unwinding it. Consider the sequent:

$$PRE \Rightarrow \langle \texttt{while (i<n) \{i++;\}} \; p \rangle \, POST$$

When the loopUnwind rule is applied once, then the following sequent is obtained:

$$PRE \Rightarrow \langle \texttt{if (i<n) \{i++; while (i<n) \{i++;\}\}} \; p \rangle \, POST \qquad (12.11)$$

The rule introduces an `if`-statement whose guard is the loop condition (here `i<n`). Its branch consists of the loop body (`i++;`) followed by the original loop statement. Application of the rule for the `if`-statement yields the two proof branches:

$$PRE \wedge i \geq n \Rightarrow \langle p \rangle \, POST \qquad (12.12)$$
$$PRE \wedge i < n \Rightarrow \langle \texttt{i++; while (i<n) \{i++;\}} \; p \rangle \, POST \qquad (12.13)$$

A test that is based on (12.12) satisfies the condition $PRE \wedge i \geq n$ and triggers program behavior where the loop is not entered. A test that derived from (12.13) satisfies the condition $PRE \wedge i < n$ which ensures that the loop is executed at least once. After symbolic execution of the statement `i++` the loopUnwind rule can be applied again. When the loopUnwind rule is applied m times, proof branches are generated with test data constraints which ensure that the loop iterates exactly $0, 1, 2, \ldots, m-1$ times, and the final test ensures that the loop iterates *at least m* times. Loop unwinding is explained in detail in Section 3.6.4.

Loop unwinding can be activated in the **Proof Search Strategy** settings tab by selecting **Loop treatment** to **Expand**. When using the play button of KeY, the number of loop unwindings is indirectly controlled by the maximum number of rule applications. Another possibility is to explicitly set the number of loop unwindings in the **Test Suite Generation** window and then use the **TestGen** strategy macro (see Figure 12.2). The macro applies symbolic execution rules and limits the number of rule applications of the **loopUnwind** rule. The limit of loop unwinding is applied to each proof branch individually. For example, if the number of loop unwindings is limited to 3 (default value) and the proof tree is fully expanded, then tests will be generated which execute 0, 1, or 2 loop iterations and some tests will iterate loops at least 3 times.

Method inlining works in a similar fashion as loop unwinding, where method calls are replaced by the body of the called method (see Section 3.6.5). When a method call is replaced by its body, symbolic execution can continue until the next method call is encountered and method inlining can be applied again. Each method that is symbolically executed is then also executed by a test, if the path to the method is feasible.

The advantage of using loop unwinding and method inlining is that no interaction is required by the user. The problem is that the size of the proof tree can become too large so that symbolic execution of the program may not finish. No coverage guarantees can be given for program parts which were not symbolically executed. Another problem is that the source code of methods (e.g., library methods) may not be available.

12.6.5 Using Loop Invariants and Method Contracts

When finite unwinding of method calls and loops is used during symbolic execution, the user does not have to provide method contracts or loop invariants. This technique is also known as bounded symbolic execution. When using KeYTestGen as an extension to verification (see Figure 12.3), method contracts and loop invariants are typically available. Method contracts and loop invariants provide an alternative approach to symbolically executing the body of a method or loop. Loosely speaking, a method contract can replace a method call and a loop invariant can replace a loop during symbolic execution. Furthermore, the proof tree generated by the verification attempt can be directly reused for test case derivation. A short example of using a method contract is shown in Section 12.4. For a detailed explanation of the method contract and loop invariant rules, see Section 3.7.

Method contracts and loop invariants, hereafter contracts, can be used to create test cases that are likely to be missed by bounded symbolic execution [Gladisch, 2008]. In some cases the latter requires an exhaustive inspection of all execution paths which is impractical in the presence of complex methods and impossible in the presence of loops, because loops and recursive methods may represent unboundedly many paths.

Listings 12.2 and 12.3 show examples of programs for which branch coverage is hard to achieve with bounded symbolic execution. In order to execute A() in Listing 12.2, the loop body has to be entered at least 11 times, and in order to execute C(), it has to be executed exactly 20 times. These numbers could be arbitrarily large and the result of complex computations, hence requiring exhaustive inspection of all paths in order to find the case where the branch guards are satisfied. A similar situation occurs in Listing 12.3. Before symbolic execution can process the statement if (i==20) { C(); } it must first symbolically execute the method call D(). When the method call is treated by method inlining an exhaustive inspection of D(),

```
1  /*@ public normal_behavior
2        requires 0<=n;
3        ensures true;
4  @*/
5  public void foo1(int n) {
6    int i=0;
7    /*@ loop_invariant 0<=i && i<=n;
8          decreases n-i;
9    @*/
10   while(i < n) {
11        if (i==10) { A(); }
12        B();
13        i++;
14   }
15   if (i==20) { C(); }
16 }
```

Listing 12.2 First example where branch coverage is difficult to achieve

```
1  int i;
2  /*@ public normal_behavior
3        requires i<=n;
4        ensures i==n;
5        modifies i;
6  @*/
7  public void D(int n) {
8        while (i < n) { i++; A(); }
9  }
10
11 /*@ public normal_behavior
12        requires i<=n;
13        ensures i==n;
14        modifies i;
15 @*/
16 public void foo2(int n) {
17        D(n);
18        if (i==20) { C(); }
19 }
```

Listing 12.3 Second example where branch coverage is difficult to achieve

which consists of a loop, may be required to find a path such that after the execution of D() the branch condition i==20 holds. Hence, achieving *full feasible branch coverage* (Definition 12.5) is challenging.

When using the loop invariant and method contract rules during proof construction, test data constraints can be derived from the proof tree solving the described problem. If the contracts are strong enough, the test data constraints ensure the execution of desired feasible paths (a) after loops and method calls or (b) within loops. Intuitively, a loop invariant or a method contract is strong enough if it does not over-approximate the behavior of the loop or method with regard to the program variables which are critical to enter a desired program position; details can be found in [Gladisch, 2011, 2008].

The loop invariant rule creates three proof branches with the following proof obligations: (a) the loop invariant holds before the loop is entered, (b) the loop invariant is preserved by the loop body, and (c) from the loop invariant and the program after the loop the postcondition follows. When applying the loop invariant rule in the analysis of Listing 12.2, then from (b), i.e.,

$$\{i := 0\}\{i := i_0\}\overbrace{(0 \le i \wedge i \le n \wedge i < n)}^{I} \quad \Rightarrow \quad \langle \text{if } (\text{i==10}) \ \{\text{A}();\} \ldots \rangle \, I$$

the following proof obligation is derived (among other proof branches):

$$\{i := 0\}\{i := i_0\}\overbrace{(0 \le i \wedge i \le n \wedge i < n \wedge i \doteq 10)}^{I} \quad \Rightarrow \quad \langle \text{A}(); \ldots \rangle \, I \quad (12.14)$$

The first update $\{i := 0\}$ stems from the assignment `int i=0;` before the loop and the second update $\{i := i_0\}$ replaces the program variable i with a fresh symbol i_0 because it can be modified by the loop and must be distinct from i. The constraint $0 \le i \wedge i \le n$ is the loop invariant, followed by the loop guard $i < n$ and the guard $i \doteq 10$ of the if-statement `if (i==10) {A();}`. Simplification of 12.14 yields:

$$i_0 < n \wedge i_0 \doteq 10 \Rightarrow \langle \text{A}(); \ldots \rangle \, I$$

Therefore, the test data constraint for this path, as extracted by KeYTestGen, is $i_0 < n \wedge i_0 \doteq 10$, which implies that $n > 10$ must be satisfied before the loop in order to execute the method call A() inside the loop.

From premiss (c) of the loop invariant rule with subsequent symbolic execution of the conditional statement the following test data constraint is derived:

$$\{i := 0\}\{i := i_{sk}\}\overbrace{(0 \le i \wedge i \le n \wedge i \ge n \wedge i \doteq 20)}^{I}$$

It simplifies to

$$(i_{sk} \doteq n \wedge i_{sk} \doteq 20)$$

which implies that if $n \doteq 20$, then C() will be executed in Listing 12.2. Similarly, test data constraints can be obtain in order to execute C() in Listing 12.3.

The programs shown in Listings 12.2 and 12.3 can be found in the example directory **coverage/**. Since these examples do not use bounded expansion of loops and methods, the user should not use the **TestGen** macro. Instead, the user should set in the **Proof Search Strategy** tab, **Loop treatment** to **Invariant** and **Method treatment** to **Contract**. When pressing the play button, the method foo1() or foo2(), respectively, is verified and a closed proof tree is obtained. Using the **Test Suite Generation** window, a test suite can be generated. However, the resulting tests will not be "correct"—when executing the tests and monitoring the execution using, e.g., OpenJML, the precondition will be violated. The reason is that using the standard settings of the model generator (Section 12.7) the test data constraints such as $n > 10$ or $n \doteq 20$ cannot be satisfied, because the model generator uses bounded integers. To generate correct test cases it is necessary to set the **Integer Bound** of the model generator to 6 bits instead of the default 3 bits. The **Integer Bound** as well as other bounds can be adjusted in **Options → SMT Solver Options → General SMT Options** (see Figure 12.5).

Verification-based test case generation is a flexible technique with respect to the complexity of the test generation and the resulting quality of the tests. The quality and number of the tests depends on the scope of the proof tree construction and on the selection of test data constraints from the proof tree. For instance, the simplest test is a random test that is generated when the test data is derived from a proof tree which consists only of the root sequent. In this case, the test data constraint is empty, i.e., true, and is satisfied by any generated test data. On the other end of the spectrum, the most sophisticated kind of test is the one which is derived from an open proof branch of a failed verification attempt. Open proof branches of a fully expanded proof tree indicate cases with a high probability of a software fault with respect to the MUT's specification. In an extreme case a single very specific test may be generated that reveals a fault. Closed proof branches, on the other hand, correspond to program paths and conditions that have been already verified and are filtered out from test generation. However, the user may choose to generate test cases also from closed branches to get a high test coverage of the MUT (e.g., for testing the environment or for regression testing).

The branches of the proof tree represent different test cases. Any formula in the proof tree can be used as a test data constraint. However, depending on which formulas are chosen for the test data constraints, different specification conditions, program branches, or paths are tested.

Soundness of the verification system ensures that all paths through the MUT are analyzed, except for parts where the user chooses to use abstraction, e.g., through method contracts or loop invariants. Creating tests for proof branches that were created using bounded symbolic execution ensures full feasible bounded path coverage of the regarded program part of the MUT, i.e., all paths of the symbolically executed program parts will be tested.

12.7 From Constraints to Test Input Data

After extracting the test data constraints from the proof tree, as shown in the previous section, we need to find test data satisfying either constraint. The test data is used as input to the method under test (MUT) in the test suite (see Section 12.5). In order to find such inputs we search for models of the test data constraints. A model is a first-order logic interpretation satisfying a formula. In terms of testing, the model is an assignment of concrete values to object fields and parameters, that constitute the initial state S_D and input parameters P_D, following Section 12.3. For example, if a model is found for the path condition of an execution path p, and the program is

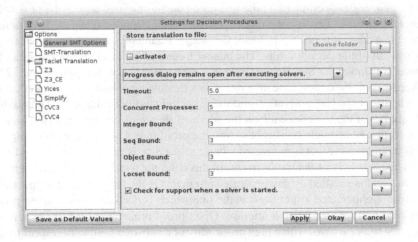

Figure 12.5 SMT solver options. Settings of the bounded model generator that are used for counter example generation as well as for test data generation.

executed using the input resulting from this model, path *p* will be executed. If no model is found, then the path may be infeasible.

We currently use the third party SMT solver Z3 to find models for test data constraints (see Section 12.2.1). Constraints are translated from KeY's Java first-order logic (JFOL, see Chapter 2) to the SMT-LIB 2 language which is supported by most SMT solvers.

The translation from JFOL to SMT-LIB poses two main challenges. First, we need to ensure that the models found by the SMT solver are also models for the original JFOL formula. Second, we need to make sure that the SMT solver is able to find a model within a reasonable amount of time. Unfortunately, the current state-of-the-art does not allow us to fully address both objectives. For this reason we have decided to use bounded data types, i.e., each data type can have only a bounded number of instances. As a consequence, the SMT solver can find models a lot faster, but at the same time some models may be missed because the bounds might be too small and some models may be spurious for the same reason. For the missing models problem, we would argue in favor of the small scope hypothesis [Jackson, 2002], claiming that, in practice, most bugs in a program can be found by testing all inputs within a small scope. As for the problem regarding the spurious models, it hardly occurs when KeY is used within its normal use case of verifying Java code specified by JML. Usually—but not necessarily—such cases occur if fixed constant values are used in the MUT which cannot be represented by the bounded data type. An example of such a case was shown in Listings 12.2 and 12.3. The user has the possibility to adjust the bounds using the following menu item **Options → SMT Solver Options → General SMT Options** which will open the window shown in Figure 12.5.

The rest of this section presents some of the more interesting details of the translation from JFOL to SMT-LIB. Where it is clear from the context we write 'SMT' as an abbreviation for 'SMT-LIB language'. The model generator presented in this section is largely based on KeY's counterexample generator described in [Herda, 2014].

12.7.1 The Type System

The SMT-LIB language does not support subtyping, all declared SMT sorts represent disjoint data type domains. This section explains how we specify in SMT the KeY type hierarchy, which includes the Java type hierarchy. The KeY type hierarchy is described in Section 2.4.1. It should be noted that the global program state that constitutes also the initial state S_D of the test input is stored in a logical constant[8] of type *Heap*. Input parameters P_D and all local program variables of the MUT are stored as logical constants of type *Any* or subtypes of it.

In the SMT-LIB data language, types are called *sorts*. The KeY type system is specified in SMT using the following eight SMT sorts: *Bool, IntB, Heap, Object, Field, LocSet, SeqB,* and *Any*. All KeY reference types are translated to the sort *Object*.

The KeYTestGen translation interprets the bit-vector values representing bounded integers as signed integers with values ranging from $-|IntB|/2$ to $(|IntB|/2) - 1$. In the **SMT Solver Options** window (see Figure 12.5) the user can specify different bit sizes for the *IntB, Object, LocSet* and *SeqB* sorts. The bit sizes for the *Heap* and *Field* sorts are calculated by considering the number of constants of the respective type in the proof obligation. The *Field* sort has to support all field names and also all possible array positions determined by the size of the *IntB* sort. The bit size of the *Any* sort is computed automatically and depends on the largest size of the other SMT sorts.

For each SMT sort S (except *Any, Heap,* and *Field*) membership predicates and cast functions are declared. The functions are used to check if an instance of *Any* is of type S and the enable casts between S and *Any*. We declare the following functions for each SMT sort S except *Any*:

1. $isS : Any \rightarrow Bool$
2. $Any2S : Any \rightarrow S$
3. $S2Any : S \rightarrow Any$

In order to specify Java reference types we define the following two predicates for each reference type T:

1. $instance_T : Object \rightarrow Bool$
2. $exactInstance_T : Object \rightarrow Bool$

---

[8] A logical constant is a function of arity 0. The value of a logical constant is given by its first-order logic interpretation, which can change due to the dynamic nature of *dynamic* logic.

For an Object o and a reference type T, $instance_T(o)$ is true iff o is of type T and $exactInstance_T(o)$ is true iff o is of type T and neither a subtype of T nor *null*. We also add the necessary assertions to the SMT translation to ensure that the SMT specification models the Java type hierarchy while respecting the modularity principle of KeY, i.e., existing proofs will not be affected if new class and interface declarations are added to the program (see Section 9.1.3). For this, the SMT solver will take not yet declared reference types into consideration when searching for models.

12.7.2 Preserving the Semantics of Interpreted Functions

JFOL defines several interpreted functions, i.e., functions that are axiomatized and, therefore, have a fixed semantics (e.g., $+$). When talking about program states, two important interpreted functions are *store* and *select* (see Section 2.4.1 and p. 527). The function *store* is needed to store values to object fields on the heap and the function *select* is needed to read values of object fields from the heap.

We need to preserve the semantics for all interpreted functions which appear in the proof obligation, otherwise the SMT solver will make use of incorrect interpretations when generating models. For example, if no semantics is specified for the *store* function, the solver could generate a model in which the store function returns the heap it received as an input, which would be incorrect.

We can translate the relevant KeY rules to SMT as follows. KeY already provides a translation from taclets into JFOL (see Section 4.4). From there we translate into SMT assertions. For assertions to be satisfiable the size of the *Heap* sort has to be carefully set. It needs to be large enough to contain all possible heaps that may result from the *store* function. We can consider the heap sort a two dimensional array of size $|Object| \times |Field|$ which contains values of type *Any*. The number of heaps $|Heap|$ which we need to support is $|Any|^{|Object| \cdot |Field|}$. This number is huge, even for examples with few objects and fields, and would severely affect the performance of the SMT solver.

But to obtain a correct model it is not always necessary to specify the semantics of interpreted functions for all possible inputs. We can provide a specification merely for those inputs that actually appear in the proof obligation. This is achieved by syntactically replacing all interpreted function calls with their semantics. We call this approach *semantic blasting*.

Semantic blasting of functions and predicates that are defined constructively, i.e., not in terms of observer functions, is straightforward: they are replaced by their definition. One example is the replacement the *subset* predicate by using (the translation of) the *subsetToElementOf* rule (see Section 2.4.4).

The functions dealing with heaps, location sets, and sequences, however, do not have a constructive (or inductive) definition. Their semantics is specified in a co-inductive manner using observer functions such as *select*, *elementOf*, *get*, and *length*. For these we can perform a straightforward replacement only if they appear as an argument of an observer function. For example, for the *store* function we can apply the *selectOfStore* rule only if we encounter a term of the form $select(store(h, o, f, v), o', f')$.

For the remaining case, when an interpreted function call f with a co-inductive definition is not an argument of an observer function, semantic blasting is performed in three steps:

1. The pullout taclet replaces an occurrence of f with a constant and adds a defining equality to the antecedent., see Example 4.10.
2. A suitable extensionality rule (equalityToSelect for heaps, equalityToElementOf for location sets, and equalityToSeqGetAndSeqLenRight for sequences) is applied to the equality added to the antecedent. The extensionality rule states that two terms t_1 and t_2, both of type Heap, LocSet or Seq, respectively, are equal if for all observer functions *obs* of that type and for all appropriate lists of parameters P for the observer function *obs* the following holds: $obs(t_1, P) \doteq obs(t_2, P)$.
3. On the right hand side of the defining equation f appears now as the argument of an observer function and we proceed as above.

Example 12.7. Given the sequent $\Rightarrow p(store(h, o, f, v))$ the semantic blasting steps are as follows:

1. Apply pullout:
$$c \doteq store(h, o, f, v) \Rightarrow p(c)$$

2. Apply the equalityToSelect:
$$\forall o' \forall f'\, select(c, o', f') \doteq select(store(h, o, f, v).o', f') \Rightarrow p(c)$$

3. We can now apply selectOfStore:
$$\forall o' \forall f'\, select(c, o', f') \doteq$$
$$if\,(o \doteq o' \wedge f \doteq f' \wedge f \not\doteq created)\; v\; else\; select(h, o, f)$$
$$\Rightarrow p(c)$$

12.7.3 Preventing Integer Overflows

When dealing with integer constraints, the solver may find models which are correct under the semantics of bounded integers (with modulo arithmetic). Such a model could be wrong when in KeY the default integer semantics of mathematical integers was set. In such cases a spurious counter example or a false positive test would be generated. To prevent this, we identify the terms which can cause an overflow and generate new terms from them which have the same operator but the operands have an increased bit-size. From $a + b$, if a and b are bit-vectors of size n, we generate the term $incr(a) + incr(b)$, where the function *incr* takes a bit-vector of size n and returns a bit-vector of size $n + 1$ with identical lower n bits.

Additionally we add assertions ensuring that the result of the same arithmetic operation on the increased bit-vectors is not greater than *max_int* or smaller than *min_int* . For the previous example we add the assertions $incr(a) + incr(b) \leq max\_int$ and $incr(a) + incr(b) \geq min\_int$. The multiplication operation is handled similarly, however, we double the bit-vector size of the operands instead of increasing it by one.

12.7.4 Model Extraction

If the given path condition is satisfiable (under the bounded data type semantics), then the SMT solver will provide a model of it, if no timeout occurs. In the case of the Z3 solver, the model consists of function definitions. To initialize the test inputs we extract the required test data from the model by using the *get-value* SMT command. This command takes a ground term as an argument and returns the result of its evaluation. If the SMT solver found a model, then KeY sends a sequence of *get-value* queries to the solver and in this way determines the values of constants and the contents of heaps, locations sets, and sequences in the model.

12.8 Specification-based Test Oracle Generation

The purpose of a test oracle is to decide whether a test case was successful or not (see Section 12.3). It is executed right after the MUT and it inspects the return value R and final state S_f of the MUT. In KeY, the JML specification of the MUT determines whether the tuple $\langle R, S_f \rangle$ is an error state or not. Hence, the specification which is provided in a declarative form must be translated into an executable test oracle. For this purpose two possibilities are supported by KeYTestGen. Section 12.8.1 describes how KeYTestGen generates a test oracle from a JML specification. Section 12.8.2 describes the usage of a JML runtime assertion checker instead.

12.8.1 Generating a Test Oracle from the Postcondition

KeYTestGen generates an oracle when the option **Use JUnit and test oracle** is enabled in the **Test Suite Generation** window (Figure 12.1). The test oracle is a Boolean Java method which returns true if the test case satisfies the JML specification of the MUT and false otherwise. It is generated from the postcondition and checks whether the postcondition holds after the code under test was executed. We do not generate the postcondition directly from JML, but rather from its JavaDL translation in KeY (see Chapter 8). In this way we ascertain to maintain the exact semantics of the postcondition as in KeY. For example, KeY may include class invariants and termination conditions as part of the postcondition. The precondition does not need

to be checked, because it is part of the test data constraint and is always satisfied by
the process of test input data generation (see Sections 12.6 and 12.7).

Each test suite contains only one oracle method which is used in all test cases. In
each test case, after running the MUT, we assert that the test oracle method returns
true by using the JUnit method `assertTrue`. Listing 12.4 shows an abridged version
of the test oracle generated for the `arrCopy` example presented in Listing 12.1. In the
full definition of the method, the parameters include all program variables evaluated
in the MUT's final state of execution (e.g., a) as well as in the state before the
execution (e.g., `_prea`), the information whether an exception was thrown (`exc`), as
well as the sets of bounded data types (e.g., `allInts`). Method `testOracle` returns
true if the generated test data satisfies the postcondition of `arrCopy` in Listing 12.1
and false otherwise. The test oracle in this case checks whether all entries in arrays a
and b are equal, whether the implicit invariant for the `self` object holds and whether
an exception is thrown.

```
1  public boolean testOracle(int[] a, int[] _prea, ...){
2      return ((sub1(a, _prea, ...) &&
3          inv_javalangObject(self, a, _prea, ...) && (exc == null));
4  }
5
6  public boolean sub1(int[] a, int[] _prea, ...){
7      for(int i : allInts) {
8          if (!(!((0 <= i) && (i < a.length)) || (a[i] == b[i]))) {
9              return false;
10         }
11     }
12     return true;
13 }
14
15 public boolean inv_javalangObject(java.lang.Object o, ...) {
16     return true;
17 }
```

Listing 12.4 The test oracle generated for the example in Listing 12.1

Translating Simple Operators

Propositional and arithmetic operators in JavaDL are translated using Boolean and
arithmetic Java operators. For example, $\tau(F_1 \wedge F_2)$ is translated as $\tau(F_1)$ && $\tau(F_2)$,
where τ denotes the translation function from JFOL to Java.

Translating Quantified Formulas

Since the translation of test data constraints to SMT-LIB uses bounded data types (see Section 12.7.1), the model returned by the SMT solver contains only a finite number of instances of each type. We restrict the quantification domain of unbounded quantifiers in the postcondition to these bounded domains. This approach is not correct in general, as the result of a test case may be a false positive or a false negative. However, it is a reasonable approach since evaluating quantified formulas over arithmetic expressions in unbounded domains is not feasible.

Concretely, in the test preamble (see Section 12.5) we create a `java.util.Set` for each of `boolean`, `int`, and `Object`. Then we add to each of these sets all instances of the corresponding bounded data type to support bounded quantified formulas over these three types. For each quantified formula we create an additional Boolean Java method whose body contains a loop. This loop iterates over the set of instances of the variable type. An example is the method `sub1` in Listing 12.4, where `allInts` is the bounded set of integers.

Translating Heap Terms

The global program state is modeled in KeY using a heap data type (see Section 12.7.1). The heap can be thought of as a mapping from object fields to their values. The JFOL functions *select* and *store* are used for reading and writing object fields on the heap (see Section 2.4.1). In the postcondition no changes are made to the heap, hence, we only need to concern ourselves with *select* function calls. Generally we translate a *select* term of the form $select(h, o, f)$ simply as the Java expression $o.f$ except for the cases when f is an array field or when h is the initial heap. The two latter cases are treated as follows:

- Array fields are modeled in KeY with the *arr* function, which takes an integer, representing the index, and returns a field. The translation of a *select* function call with an array field as an argument, $\tau(select(h, o, arr(i)))$ is then the Java array expression $o[\tau(i)]$, where o is an object of array type and i a term of integer type.
- The translation of *select* terms is handled differently when the heap argument is the initial heap. In this case we need to evaluate the expression in the prestate. This happens when a parameter[9] or the JML keyword `\old` is used in the postcondition. We store the prestate in the test preamble by creating and initializing a duplicate instance of each object we would normally create. An example is shown in Listing 12.5, where variables that store the initial state have the prefix *_pre*. The duplicate objects form a structure isomorphic to the original object structure in the initial state. The execution of the MUT affects the original objects but it does not affect the duplicate objects. Thus, when we wish to evaluate an expression in the initial state, we use these duplicates instead of the original

---

[9] In JML method parameters are evaluated always in the prestate.

object. If the expression is of reference type, the result will be one of the duplicate objects. To maintain the semantics we have to return the original object associated with the isomorphic duplicate.

Translating Class Invariants

We translate the class invariants that are possibly included in the postcondition by generating a Boolean Java method for each reference type T. This method takes an argument of type T and returns *true* if the instance fulfills the class invariant of that reference type and false otherwise. The body of the invariant method is the translation of the JavaDL formula representing the class invariant of T. The same translation is used as for the postcondition.

12.8.2 Using a Runtime Assertion Checker

As an alternative to generating a test oracle, KeYTestGen integrates a runtime assertion checker supplied by OpenJML to check at runtime whether the postcondition is fulfilled. In this case test cases consist only of the test preamble and MUT. The generated code must be compiled and executed with OpenJML. For this purpose we generate two bash scripts to be executed by the user. These scripts can be used for compiling and running the tests on Linux systems. The scripts are created in the same folder as the generated test suite. The first, `compileWithOpenJML.sh` does not need any arguments. However, the paths to the OpenJML and Objenesis libraries must be set as explained in Section 12.2.3. Running this script will compile the Java files of the code under test and of the test suite in such a way to enable run time assertion checking. The second script, `executeWithOpenJML.sh` must be called with the name of the generated test suite class. The script runs all test cases and each time a JML assertion is violated an error message is displayed.

Figure 12.6 shows the output OpenJML runtime assertion checker for the example in Listing 12.1. (The exact output may vary, as it depends on the exact versions and configurations of all tools in the tool chain.) The error messages show that the code violates the normal behavior JML clause, meaning that the code under test throws an exception.

12.9 Synthesizing Executable Test Cases

In this section we show how the output of KeYTestGen looks like. After generating the test input data (see Section 12.7) we can use it to synthesize an executable test driver for each test (see Section 12.5). A test driver consist of three parts:

1. Test preamble

Figure 12.6 OpenJML output for example in Listing 12.1

2. Code under test
3. Test oracle

Generating the test oracle is optional. The user can use a runtime assertion checker as explained in Section 12.8.2. The settings are described in Section 12.2.3.

Listing 12.5 shows one of the generated test cases for the example in Listing 12.1. The test preamble (lines 4–37) is generated from the model that is obtained by SMT solving as described in Section 12.7. The model contains values for constants along with the contents of all heaps which appear in the test data constraint (see Section 12.6). The goal of the test preamble is to reproduce the initial state from the model in the executable environment, so we focus on the contents of the initial heap from the model.

In the first part (lines 4–12) of the test preamble all constants and objects of the model are declared and initialized. The test driver is optimized in the sense that only objects are created which are potentially reachable by the MUT and the test oracle. Solving this reachability problem is possible because it is sufficient to analyze a bounded number of concrete objects and the relations (field references) between them. This optimization reduces the code size. Thus, it improves not only the compile and execution times, but most importantly it improves readability of the source code when using a program debugger (see Section 12.4). In the second part, fields/components of the created objects/arrays are initialized with the values that they have in the model (lines 13–25).

When objects must be created from classes without a default constructor, or when private or protected fields must be initialized, the user can activate the option **Use reflection framework** in the **Test Suite Generation** window (see Section 12.2). In this case, object creation using the Java keyword 'new' as well as expressions with read and write access to fields are replaced by equivalent methods from RFL.java. This

```
1   //Test Case for NodeNr: 917
2   @org.junit.Test
3   public void testcode1(){
4     //Test preamble: creating objects and intializing test data
5       java.lang.ArrayIndexOutOfBoundsException _o3 =
6           new java.lang.ArrayIndexOutOfBoundsException();
7       java.lang.ArrayIndexOutOfBoundsException _pre_o3 =
8           new java.lang.ArrayIndexOutOfBoundsException();
9     int[] _o2 = new int[1];  int[] _pre_o2 = new int[1];
10    int[] _o4 = new int[2];  int[] _pre_o4 = new int[2];
11    ArrayUtils     _o1 = new ArrayUtils();
12    ArrayUtils _pre_o1 = new ArrayUtils();
13    /*@ nullable */ int[]      a = (int[])_o4;
14    /*@ nullable */ int[] _prea = (int[])_pre_o4;
15    /*@ nullable */ int[]      b = (int[])_o2;
16    /*@ nullable */ int[] _preb = (int[])_pre_o2;
17    boolean measuredByEmpty = (boolean)true;
18    /*@ nullable */ ArrayUtils       self = (ArrayUtils)_o1;
19    /*@ nullable */ ArrayUtils _preself = (ArrayUtils)_pre_o1;
20    /*@ nullable */ java.lang.ArrayIndexOutOfBoundsException a_8 =
21        (java.lang.ArrayIndexOutOfBoundsException)_o3;
22    /*@ nullable */ java.lang.ArrayIndexOutOfBoundsException _prea_8 =
23        (java.lang.ArrayIndexOutOfBoundsException)_pre_o3;
24    _o2[0] = -4; _pre_o2[0] = -4;
25    _o4[0] = 0;  _pre_o4[0] = 0;  _o4[1] = 0;  _pre_o4[1] = 0;
26    Map<Object,Object> old = new HashMap<Object,Object>();
27      old.put(_pre_o1,_o1);  old.put(_pre_o3,_o3);
28      old.put(_pre_o2,_o2);  old.put(_pre_o4,_o4);
29    Set<Boolean> allBools = new HashSet<Boolean>();
30      allBools.add(true);       allBools.add(false);
31    Set<Integer> allInts  = new HashSet<Integer>();
32      allInts.add(-4); allInts.add(-3); allInts.add(-2);
33      allInts.add(-1); allInts.add(0);  allInts.add(1);
34      allInts.add(2);  allInts.add(3);
35    Set<Object> allObjects= new HashSet<Object>();
36      allObjects.add(_o3); allObjects.add(_o2);
37      allObjects.add(_o1); allObjects.add(_o4);
38    //Other variables
39    /*@ nullable */ java.lang.Throwable      exc = null;
40    /*@ nullable */ java.lang.Throwable _preexc = null;
41    //Calling the method under test
42    int[] _a = a;  int[] _b = b;
43    {
44      exc=null;
45      try   { self.arrCopy(_a,_b); }
46      catch (java.lang.Throwable e) { exc=e; }
47    }
48    //calling the test oracle
49    assertTrue(testOracle( exc, _preexc, self, _preself, a, _prea,
50                  b, _preb, allBools, allInts, allObjects, old));
51  }
```

Listing 12.5 A test case generated for the example in Listing 12.1

file is generated together with the test suite and provides wrapper methods for the Java reflection framework and the Objenesis library.

In lines 29–37, some Java containers are created which are needed by the test oracle to check quantified formulas (see paragraph *Translating Quantified Formulas* in Section 12.8.1). For the *Boolean*, *integer*, and reference types a `java.util.Set` is created containing all instances of these types that exist in the model. Also, as described in Section 12.8.1, the test oracle may have to read the values of object fields and program variables as they were in the prestate of the MUT while being executed in the poststate of the MUT. For this purpose the test driver has duplicate variables with the prefix `_pre` for every object. These objects have an isomorphic structure to the original objects. The connection between the original and duplicate objects is preserved by the map defined in lines 26–28.

The MUT and the code surrounding it (lines 41–47) is taken from the JavaDL modality in KeY in the root node of the proof tree. Using the surrounding code, and not just the invocation of the MUT, is important to ensure that actual execution of the code has the same semantics as symbolic execution of the code. The surrounding code typically consists of a *try/catch* block allowing the specification (or test oracle) to decide what to do if an exception was thrown. Since the modality contains Java code, we can usually simply copy it. However, the code may contain variables that do not appear in the generated model (see Section 12.7). These variables are declared and initialized in lines 38–40.

The test oracle is called in line 49 and is generated as explained in Section 12.8.1.

12.10 Perspectives and Related Work

Traditionally test data generation tools have been classified as black-box and white-box generation tools, see for instance [Ammann and Offutt, 2008]. Black-box approaches base test data generation on noncode artifacts such as abstract execution models or specifications, whereas white-box approaches base test data generation on the code under test. Gray-box techniques combine these two approaches and use both code and noncode artifacts. KeYTestGen is a gray-box approach because it uses both the code and the JML specification for generating the tests. In a recent survey by Galler and Aichernig [2014], several test case generation tools from industry and academia are classified according to this distinction, and evaluated.

Another possible classification of test case generation approaches is by the technique used for the test data generation. In a survey by Anand et al. [2013], the following techniques are identified:

1. Techniques using *symbolic execution* to obtain high coverage. The authors identify the path explosion problem (i.e., the number of paths in the symbolic execution tree grows too large) as the main obstacle for tools using this technique and present possible solutions for it. Dynamic symbolic execution, also called concolic execution, which combines symbolic and dynamic execution,

is a widespread approach adopted by numerous other tools. Techniques using symbolic execution are considered to be part of the white-box category.

2. The *model-based* testing approach derives test cases from an executable model representing an abstraction of the software. Different kinds of models can be used, examples include finite state machines and labeled transition systems. In a first phase abstract test cases are derived from the model and in the second phase these test cases are concretized in order to make them applicable on the original software. Online model-based testing techniques run each test case after generating it and use the information from the result when generating the next test cases. Offline model-based testing techniques generate the entire test suite before running the test cases. Model-based testing is a black-box technique.

3. *Combinatorial* testing is a technique which is used for testing different configurations of a software (for example parameters of a method, command line parameters, or options on a graphical user interface). It focuses on finding bugs that arise when a certain configuration is chosen by the user. To achieve full coverage all combinations of all options need to be tested, which is usually infeasible due to the large number of necessary test cases. Combinatorial testing proposes the choosing of a limited number of sample values for each option and then only tests all n-combinations of the options using the chosen values. The goal is to provide satisfactory coverage with a limited test budget. For $n = 2$ the approach is called all-pairs testing. This is also a black-box technique.

4. *Adaptive random* testing improves upon random resting, which is a test case generation technique that generates the test data randomly. The empirically founded assumption on which the adaptive random testing approach is based says that inputs which do not cause a failure are contiguous, and consequently the inputs causing a failure are contiguous as well. For this reason different algorithms are used to spread the generated test data evenly on the input domain. Thus, the chances of finding a failure-inducing input are higher than in the case of random testing. (Adaptive) random testing is a black-box technique.

KeYTestGen falls in the category of tools based on symbolic execution. In the rest of this section, we give a selection of tools using that technique. A survey of popular test generation tools based on symbolic execution is described by Cadar et al. [2011]. A recent evaluation of symbolic execution-based test generation tools is done in [Cseppento and Micskei, 2015].

StaDy, a recent extension of a deductive verification tool with test generation capabilities, is based on Frama-C [Petiot et al., 2014]. Frama-C is a platform for analyzing C code specified with the ANSII C Specification Language (ACSL). Only an executable subset of ACSL is supported for test generation. StaDy translates the specified C code and adds code for checking errors, similarly to compiling the specified Java code with OpenJML RAC (see 12.8.2). PathCrawler [Botella et al., 2009], a concolic test case generator, is then used to generate inputs for the instrumented code.

Symbolic PathFinder [Păsăreanu et al., 2013] also uses symbolic execution and constraint solving to generate test cases for Java programs. It is an extension of Java PathFinder, a model checker for Java, and uses its functionality to explore the paths of the symbolic execution tree. The advantage of this approach is that the model checker can handle comparatively large symbolic execution trees and supports advanced features of Java such as multithreading. Symbolic PathFinder supports only simple assertions, without quantifiers.

KLEE [Cadar et al., 2008a] is a symbolic execution test generation tool for C programs built on top of the LLVM framework. It is a redesign from scratch of the EXE [Cadar et al., 2008b] tool, with the main goal of improved performance and scalability. KLEE was able to generate tests for the GNU coreutils utility suite, which contains the implementations of many utilities (e.g., cat, cp, ls) of UNIX-like operating systems. It found bugs that were missed for as long as fifteen years. In 90 hours KLEE was able to generate a test suite with a higher statement coverage than the developers' own test suite which was written over a period of fifteen years.

Pex [Tillmann and de Halleux, 2008] uses dynamic symbolic execution to generate unit tests for .NET programs. It supports simple assertions and assumptions without quantifiers. Pex was used to generate tests for a core .NET component, and found some serious bugs therein. Microsoft's Visual Studio 2015 Enterprise Edition contains a test case generation feature, IntelliTest, which is based on Pex.

CREST [Burnim and Sen, 2008] uses concolic execution to generate unit tests for C programs. It provides some novel heuristics for exploring the symbolic execution tree, achieving significantly higher branch coverage in the generated test suite than traditional tools based on concolic execution when only a limited number of test cases can be generated.

LCT [Kähkönen et al., 2011] is a concolic test case generator for Java programs. Both test case generation and the execution of the test cases can be done in parallel, thus increasing the scalability of the tool.

SAGE [Godefroid et al., 2012] uses dynamic symbolic execution for generating test cases for x86 binaries. It is used at Microsoft for testing large programs such as image processors or media players which are shipped with the Windows operating system. A distinguishing feature of SAGE is the heuristics used for exploring the symbolic execution tree, thus generating a high coverage test suite with a small number of test cases.

MergePoint [Avgerinos et al., 2014] combines static and dynamic symbolic execution in order to generate test cases for binaries. It has been used to test Debian binaries.

12.11 Summary and Conclusion

KeYTestGen shows how KeY's formal verification engine can be used for test case generation. It demonstrates that proving and testing can be usefully combined. Proving and testing have a lot in common. Proving can be thought of as a virtual or symbolic testing approach, where the tests are first-order logic interpretations. In essence, KeYTestGen turns these interpretations into executable test cases which execute the code under test in the same way as if it was symbolically executed.

Proving and testing are complementary techniques. Symbolic execution considers infinitely many values for variables, such that one can prove that a program satisfies a specification for an unbounded number of inputs. However, finding a proof is generally difficult and if a proof attempt does not succeed due to a timeout or because no more rules are applicable on a proof branch, one cannot conclude that a fault exists in a program. Vice versa, during testing only a bounded number of program behaviors can be considered. However, testing has many important advantages. It can be fully automated, a target program *and* its entire runtime environment (including hardware) are tested, and if a test fails we know that a fault exists. The user has the possibility to follow the execution of a test using a program debugger, to obtain intuition about why the program does not satisfy its specification. In contrast to proofs, tests can be easily repeated for regression testing when the program under test has been modified in a nontrivial way.

We discussed variations of the test generator with different features and options. The main configuration options and features of KeYTestGen are:

- test generation for individual Java methods with JML specifications;
- support for JUnit;
- unwinding/inlining loops and methods, or utilizing abstractions in form of loop invariants and method contracts;
- support for different coverage criteria such as *full feasible bounded path coverage*, *full feasible branch coverage*, and *Modified Condition/Decision Coverage*;
- testing of implicit conditions and corner cases such as *NullPointerExceptions*, *ArrayIndexOutOfBoundsExceptions*, and arithmetic under- and overflows;
- support for specifications with quantified formulas through bounded quantification domain approximation;
- generation of a test oracle or using the third party runtime checker OpenJML;
- the possibility to create objects from classes without default constructor and initialization of private and protected fields.

KeYTestGen provides a variety of ways how it can be used. A new user may start with very simple test case generation, to then gradually add specifications and try out the more sophisticated features of the tool. In this way, the approach allows a smooth learning curve. Overall, KeYTestGen allows the software developer to profit from the very powerful analysis KeY performs on source code, by letting it create good test suites, in a highly automated fashion.

Chapter 13
Information Flow Analysis

Christoph Scheben and Simon Greiner

13.1 Introduction

Software systems are becoming increasingly trusted to handle sensitive information, though they have the potential to abuse this trust with serious consequences. in particular if they are connected to the internet. We allow web browsers to access our bank accounts, but also allow them to send usage reports to the browser's developers. A mainstream smartphone application has permissions to read our digital photo albums, contact lists and calendar, while at the same time it is free to use the phone's internet connection in every way possible. This chapter discusses how the KeY System can be used to address the increasingly important question of *information flow control*: does a program introduce information flows between resources in a way which is in violation of our security policy?

As a concrete example consider an electronic voting system: an important property of voting systems is the preservation of privacy of votes. Information on votes may not be published directly nor indirectly.

```
for (int i = 0; i < votes.lengh; i++) {
  publish(votes[i]);
}
```
Listing 13.1 Example for an explicit leak

In Listing 13.1, the secret value of a vote is directly written to the output channel `publish`. Therefore, this kind of information leak is called *explicit*. In Listing 13.2, the information is leaked indirectly via the control flow of the program. By observing the output, it is possible to decide whether the first vote was cast for candidate 0 or not. This is called an *implicit* leak. In complex programs, these leaks can be much more subtle.

© Springer International Publishing AG 2016
W. Ahrendt et al. (Eds.): Deductive Software Verification, LNCS 10001, pp. 453–471, 2016
DOI: 10.1007/978-3-319-49812-6_13

```
if (votes[0] == candidates[0])
  publish("The␣result␣is␣");
  publish(calculateResult(votes, candidates));
} else {
  publish("The␣outcome␣is␣");
  publish(calculateResult(votes, candidates));
}
```

Listing 13.2 Example for an implicit leak

Information can also be leaked via *side channels*, such as execution time, power consumption, heat generation, and others. These kinds of information flow are not considered here. Instead, we focus on explicit and implicit leaks.

In order to verify a program for secure information flow, we need a general notion on what *secure information flow* means. Intuitively, a program has this property, if the observable output is not influenced by secret input, i.e., the observable output does not depend on the secret input. This is obviously the case, if for all program executions with the same nonsecret input, the public output is equal. Darvas et al. [2005] phrase this for a program α the following way: A program α has secure information flow if "Running two instances of α with equal low-security values and arbitrary high-security values, the resulting low-security values are equal, too." Here, low-security values are values which can be observed by potential attackers whereas all other values are called high-security values. This policy is called *noninterference* [Lampson, 1973, Denning, 1976, Cohen, 1977, Goguen and Meseguer, 1982].

For instance, let the observable output be the variable l, while all other variables are not observable. Then, the program l = h + 1; is insecure: Two runs of l = h + 1; with different values of h result in states with different values for l. If, on the other hand, neither l nor h are observable, the program has secure information flow. The program also has secure information flow, if h and l are observable. The program l = 0; if (h) { l = 1; } is insecure if solely the value of l is observable, because l has the value 0 if, and only if, h has the value false. The program h = 0; if (l) { h = 1; } on the other hand has secure information flow in thiscase. Indeed, l is not changed at all.

In the past, a variety of sophisticated information flow analysis techniques and tools have been developed. As in functional verification, the proposed techniques can be divided into lightweight (that is, automatic but approximate) and heavyweight (that is, semiautomatic but precise approaches.

Popular lightweight approaches are security type systems (a prominent example in this field is the Java Information Flow (JIF) system by Myers [1999]), the analysis of program dependence graphs for graph-theoretical reachability properties [Hammer et al., 2006], specialized approximate information flow calculi based on Hoare like logics [Amtoft et al., 2006, Scheben, 2014] and the usage of abstraction and ghost code for explicit tracking of dependencies [Bubel et al., 2009]. A popular heavyweight approach is to state information flow properties by self-composition [Barthe et al., 2004, Darvas et al., 2005] and use off-the-shelf software verification systems to check for them. An alternative is to formalize information flow properties in higher-order logic and use higher-order theorem provers for the verification of those properties, as presented for instance by Nanevski et al. [2011].

Lightweight approaches are usually efficient and scale well on large programs, but do not have the necessary precision to express and verify complex information flow-properties of programs with controlled release of information. An instance of programs with controlled release of information are electronic voting systems. In those systems, secrecy of votes is an important property which could not be proven by approximate approaches so far. Heavyweight approaches on the other hand were, until recently, applicable to artificially small examples only.

This chapter discusses deductive verification of complex information flow-properties of open programs with controlled release of information. This approach allows analysis of Java programs by comparing two symbolic executions of the program, a variation of self-composition [Scheben and Schmitt, 2012, Scheben, 2014]. The feasibility of the approach has been proven by a case study on a simplified electronic voting system (Chapter 18), carried out in cooperation with the research group of Prof. Ralf Küsters from the University of Trier. The approach has also been used in [Dörre and Klebanov, 2015] to analyze information flow in the Android pseudo-random number generator.

In the following section we give an intuitive understanding of an information flow specification and its relation to a possible attacker model. In Section 13.3 we formally define noninterference. In Section 13.4, JML specifications for information flow properties for Java programs are defined, and used in Section 13.5 to formalize noninterference in JavaDL to gain proof obligations for the KeY prover. Directly proving the resulting proof obligation with the KeY tool may not be feasible for realistic programs, we therefore also present optimizations of the proof process for information flow properties in KeY in this section. Finally, we conclude in Section 13.6 and point to alternative approaches for verification of information flow properties in KeY.

The presentation (including the introduction) is based on [Scheben and Schmitt, 2012, 2014, Scheben, 2014].

We assume the reader to be familiar with some topics presented in earlier chapters. For understanding the details of the following presentation, it might be helpful to read the chapters on JavaDL (Chapter 3), theories used in the KeY framework (Chapter 5), specifications in JML (Chapter 7), and modular specification and verification (Chapter 9) first.

13.2 Specification and the Attacker Model

Information flow is a property of a program, and thus can be analyzed and verified. In order to verify the flow of information in a program, we need a specification describing the intended flow of information. The examples in the introduction separate the input and output of a program into an observable and a secret part. The input is the state and the parameters before execution of the program, the output is the state after execution and possibly the return value. The specification describes the observable part of these states, and thus implicitly specifies the secret parts as everything else.

To describe the observable part of a state, we use *observation expressions*. In the simplest case, an observation expression is a list (or sequence) of program variables. The sequence $\langle x, y \rangle$ of program variables x and y, for instance, describes that x and y are observable.

Restricting observation expressions to program variables is often too coarse-grained. It may be necessary to specify that only parts of the information contained in a program variable or the aggregation of several variables is observable. Therefore, we allow arbitrary JavaDL terms or JML expressions to appear in observation expressions. To specify, for example that only the last bit of x and the sum of y and z is observable, the observation expression $\langle$ x%2, (y + z) $\rangle$ can be used.[1] In general, it is possible to combine two observations described by two observation expressions R_1 and R_2 of sequence type by concatenation. We denote their concatenation by $R_1; R_2$. Since any observation expression R can be embedded into a singleton sequence, we extend the concatenation of observation expressions to any type in the obvious way.

This very flexible way of specification has two major advantages. For one, it allows us to express very precisely the information which actually may be seen by a possible attacker. In Chapter 18, we present the verification of information flow in an e-voting system. In this context, we specify that the result of an election may be observable, while other information, for example who voted for which candidate is not. Second, the approach allows a precise specification of method contracts and loop invariants, which is helpful when a modular analysis for realistic programs is necessary.

Typically in literature, information flow is used to verify the security of a program with respect to an attacker. The attacker is able to see the low part of the input and output of a program, which we call observations. It is counterintuitive to specify that an attacker is able to observe only the last bit of a parameter or only some elements of the heap but not others. Therefore we want to point out that the motivation behind our approach for specification is mainly driven by a precise specification of information flow, not by a realistic attacker model. Usually, an attacker is able to observe certain outputs of a program, for example the return value of a method or calls to logging methods. Observation expressions do not describe the ability of a realistic attacker, but the parts of inputs and outputs of a program which may influence each other. A program that has a specified information flow is secure against all attackers who are able to see only a subset of the information described by observation expressions.

Given the specification of observable parts of states, we can now give a formal definition of what it means for a program to have secure information flow.

---

[1] For a precise definition of observation expressions see [Scheben, 2014].

13.3 Formal Definition of Secure Information Flow

Intuitively, a program is noninterferent, i.e., it has secure information flow, if two runs of the program with equal low-security input have equal low-security output. Observation expressions describe the low part of states, while states are the input and output of programs. We can formally define what it means for states to have equal low-security values.

Definition 13.1 (Agreement of states). Let R be an observation expression.

Two states s and s' agree on R, abbreviated by $\mathrm{agree}(R, s, s')$, if and only if $eval_s(R) = eval_{s'}(R)$.

With the agreement of states we can define noninterference formally.

Definition 13.2 (Unconditional Noninterference). Let α be a program and R_1, R_2 observation expressions.

Program α allows information to flow only from R_1 to R_2, denoted by the predicate $\mathrm{flow}(\alpha, R_1, R_2)$, if and only if for all states s_1, s_1', s_2, s_2' such that $eval_{s_1}(\alpha) = \{s_2\}$ and $eval_{s_1'}(\alpha) = \{s_2'\}$, we have

$$\text{if } \mathrm{agree}(R_1, s_1, s_1') \quad \text{then} \quad \mathrm{agree}(R_2, s_2, s_2').$$

The observation expressions R_1 and R_2 describe the publicly available information of a pre- and a poststate of the system respectively. For all states which agree on the publicly available information, the states resulting from an execution of α agree on the part of the state described by R_2. Of course, this only holds if both runs of α actually terminate. If one run does not terminate, its poststate is undefined and therefore $\mathrm{agree}(R_2, s_2, s_2')$ is undefined. Therefore this notion of noninterference is *termination insensitive*.

In the simplest case, R_i expresses explicit declarations of program variables and fields which are considered low. In more sophisticated scenarios the R_i may be inferred from a multi-level security lattice (see for instance [Scheben, 2014]). Usually we will have $R_1 = R_2$. But, there are other cases: to declassify an expression e_{decl}, for instance, one would choose $R_1 = R_2; e_{decl}$.

As seen in Chapter 9, method contracts are useful in order to provide abstract knowledge about parts of a program, for example the states in which a method may be called. We would like to have a notion of noninterference which also respects knowledge about these states. In contract-based specifications, this condition is given by the precondition. The following definition of *conditional noninterference* allows us to use this knowledge.

Definition 13.3 (Conditional Noninterference). Let α be a program, R_1, R_2 observation expressions and ϕ a formula.

Program α allows information to flow only from R_1 to R_2 under condition ϕ, denoted by $\mathrm{flow}(\alpha, R_1, R_2, \phi)$, if and only if for all states s_1, s_1', s_2, s_2' such that $eval_{s_1}(\alpha) = \{s_2\}$ and $eval_{s_1'}(\alpha) = \{s_2'\}$ we have

$$\text{if} \quad s_1 \vDash \phi, s_1' \vDash \phi \text{ and } \mathrm{agree}(R_1, s_1, s_1') \quad \text{then} \quad \mathrm{agree}(R_2, s_2, s_2').$$

The idea behind this generalization is that in many cases a method in isolation has secure information flow only in case a precondition holds, for instance, if a parameter is not `null`. In such a situation, it is necessary to use the precondition within the information flow proof and show in a different proof that the precondition holds whenever the method is called. For details about modular specification and verification, please refer to Chapter 9.

Conditional noninterference enjoys the following compositionality property.

Lemma 13.4 (Compositionality of *flow*). *Let α_1, α_2 be programs, and $\alpha_1;\alpha_2$ their sequential composition. If $flow(\alpha_1,R_1,R_2,\phi_1)$, $flow(\alpha_2,R_2,R_3,\phi_2)$ and $s_1 \vDash (\phi_1 \rightarrow \langle\alpha_1\rangle\phi_2) = true$ hold for all states s_1, s_2, s_3 such that α_1 started in s_1 and terminates in s_2, and α_2 started in s_2 and terminates in s_3, then $flow(\alpha_1;\alpha_2,R_1,R_3,\phi_1)$ holds.*

Now that conditional noninterference has been defined formally, we show how it can be specified on program level with the help of JML. Finally, we present how noninterference can be verified using the KeY System.

13.4 Specifying Information Flow in JML

In Chapter 7 JML was introduced as a specification language, mainly for functional properties of Java programs. In this section, we want to show how JML can be extended to allow the specification of noninterference properties for Java programs. The presentation follows [Scheben and Schmitt, 2012] and [Scheben, 2014].

JML is built according to the *design by contract* (DBC) concept. To achieve a natural integration of information flow and functional specifications, the JML extension uses DBC for the specification of noninterference as well. Conditional noninterference with declassification is specified by information flow method contracts. Similar to functional method contracts, which specify the functional behavior of methods, information flow method contracts specify the information flow behavior of methods.

Information flow contracts augment functional JML contracts by **determines** clauses. Each **determines** clause defines a restriction on the information flow. The clause defines two lists of JML expressions, one expressing the observation expression for the poststate, the other list expressing the observation expression for the prestate. The **determines** clause

```
//@ determines l \by l;
void m();
```

specifies for the method `m()` that attackers may observe the value of the program variable `l` before and after the execution of `m()`.

It is possible to define different observation expressions for the pre- and the poststate of a method:

```
//@ determines l \by l, x;
void m();
```

specifies that the observation expression in the prestate of method m() contains the locations 1 and x, while in the poststate, it contains 1 only. This is useful for declassification as the method sum() in Figure 13.1 illustrates. The method calculates

```
class C {
  private int[] values;

  /*@ determines \result \by
    @        (\sum int i; 0 <= i && i < values.length; values[i]);
    @*/
  int sum() {
    int s = 0;
    for (int value : values) {
      s += value;
    }
    return s;
  }
}
```

Figure 13.1 Program declassifying the sum of an array

the sum of the entries of the array `values` and returns the result. Accordingly, the specification allows a declassification of the sum to the result.

A contract may contain several **determines** clauses. This is useful if a program run is observed by different parties with different abilities. For instance, there might be a party which may observe the unrestricted information stored in the field unrestricted and another party which may observe the information in unrestricted as well as the restricted information stored in the field restricted. Both parties may not access the information in secret1 and secret2. This situation can be specified naturally with the help of two **determines** clauses as shown in Figure 13.2.

```
class C {
  private int unrestricted, restricted, secret1;

  /*@ determines unrestricted              \by unrestricted;
    @ determines unrestricted, restricted  \by unrestricted,
    @                                          restricted;
    @*/
  void m(int secret2) {
    unrestricted++;
    restricted = restricted + unrestricted;
    secret1 = secret1 * (restricted + secret2);
  }
}
```

Figure 13.2 Program with multiple information flow contracts

The semantics of the `determines` clauses is defined with the help of conditional noninterference (see Definition 13.3): Let R_{post} be defined as the concatenation of the expressions behind the `determines` keyword. Let R_{pre} be defined as the concatenation of the expressions behind the `\by` keyword and the expressions behind an optional `\declassifies` keyword. Let further ϕ_{pre} be the precondition of the contract defined as usual by `requires`-clauses and class invariants. A method m fulfills a `determines` clause if and only if flow($m, R_{pre}, R_{post}, \phi_{pre}$) is valid.

Similar to method contracts, we extend JML loop invariants by `determines` clauses. We omit a detailed presentation for loop invariants here, the interested reader may refer to [Scheben, 2014] for a complete discussion.

13.5   Information Flow Verification with KeY

We have a formalization of information flow and a specification method as an extension of JML. In this section we explain how these two parts can be translated into JavaDL, providing us with a proof obligation which can naturally be verified in KeY. Since performing proofs in KeY efficiently depends, among others, on the number of branches a proof has, we also introduce an optimization which neither limits expressiveness nor precision, but reduces the number of branches an information flow proof consists of.

When considering information flow in object-oriented languages like Java, some special cases arise when it comes to object creation. KeY makes the assumption that the identity of an object created by calling a constructor is nondeterministic. This means, for one, it is not guaranteed that two runs of a program with the same initial heap generate the same object. And second, it is not possible to judge the order of creation for two new objects. We do not discuss this special issue here, but refer the interested reader to the related work [Beckert et al., 2014, Scheben, 2014]. The implementation in the KeY system however does consider this.

First, we define the JavaDL equivalent for the semantic *agree* predicate.

Definition 13.5 (Observation Equivalence). The formulas $\bar{x}_1$, $\bar{x}_2$ and the heaps h_1, h_2 are *observationally equivalent* with respect to observation expression R, written $obsEq(\bar{x}_1, h_1, \bar{x}_2, h_2, R)$, iff $\{\mathtt{heap} := h_1 \mathbin{\|} \bar{\mathtt{x}} := \bar{x}_1\}R \doteq \{\mathtt{heap} := h_2 \mathbin{\|} \bar{\mathtt{x}} := \bar{x}_2\}R$ evaluates to *true*.

Observational equivalence and the *agree* predicate are indeed equivalent.

Lemma 13.6. *Let s_1, s_2 be two states described by the formulas $\bar{x}_1$, h_1 and $\bar{x}_2$, h_2, respectively. Let R be an observation expression.*
The formula $obsEq(\bar{x}_1, h_1, \bar{x}_2, h_2, R)$ is valid if and only if $agree(R, s_1, s_2)$ holds.

Now we are ready to formulate conditional noninterference (Definition 13.3) in JavaDL.

Lemma 13.7. *Let α be a program with local variables $\bar{x}$ of types $\bar{X}$, let R_1, R_2 be observation expressions and let ϕ be a formula.*

The formula

$$\Psi_{\alpha,\bar{x},R_1,R_2,\phi} \equiv \forall Heap\, h_1, h_1', h_2, h_2'\, \forall \bar{X}\, \bar{x}_1, \bar{x}_1', \bar{x}_2, \bar{x}_2'$$
$$\{\mathtt{heap} := h_1 \mid\mid \bar{x} := \bar{x}_1\}(\phi \wedge \langle \alpha \rangle (\mathtt{heap} \doteq h_2 \wedge \bar{x} \doteq \bar{x}_2)) \wedge$$
$$\{\mathtt{heap} := h_1' \mid\mid \bar{x} := \bar{x}_1'\}(\phi \wedge \langle \alpha \rangle (\mathtt{heap} \doteq h_2' \wedge \bar{x} \doteq \bar{x}_2'))$$
$$\rightarrow \big(obsEq(\bar{x}_1, h_1, \bar{x}_1', h_1', R_1) \rightarrow obsEq(\bar{x}_2, h_2, \bar{x}_2', h_2', R_2)\big)$$

is valid if and only if $flow(\alpha, R_1, R_2, \phi)$ holds.

The formula shown in Lemma 13.7 is a direct formalization of information flow in JavaDL. This direct formalization expresses the intended property very precisely, however, containing two modalities and requiring two symbolic program executions comes at a price during verification. In the following we show some inefficiencies of this approach and introduce some optimization of the proof process which takes these inefficiencies into consideration and allows proving noninterference for larger programs.

13.5.1 Efficient Double Symbolic Execution

We use the example in Figure 13.3 to show several points for improvement when performing noninterference proofs.

The first point becomes obvious, when we have a closer look at the symbolic execution of the program. In the proof obligation as defined in Lemma 13.7 the program, which is executed first only differs in the name of the heap variable in the update and some renaming of parameters and return values from the second execution. Nevertheless, all rules necessary for symbolic execution are applied twice, once for each modality containing the program. Especially for larger programs and more complicated programs, this additional effort can become relevant. We can reduce the costs of calculating the weakest precondition by performing this calculation only once and then reuse the result for the noninterference proof.

Second, the poststate of one program execution is compared to all possible poststates of the second program execution. If the program has n possible execution paths, the symbolic execution yields n branches. Combining both program executions

```
/*@ public normal_behavior
  @ determines l \by l;
  @*/
public void m() {
  l = l+h;
  if (h!=0) {l = l-h;}
  if (l>0) {l--;}
}
```

Figure 13.3 Example of a secure program

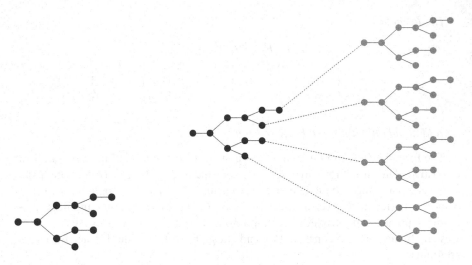

Figure 13.4 Sketch of the control flow graphs of (a) the original program and (b) the program with double symbolic execution

results in $O(n^2)$ branches for which the observation expressions have to be compared. In contrast, specialized information flow calculi, which consider the program only once, have to check only the outcome of the n paths through the program.

Let again α be the program as shown in Figure 13.3. The control flow graph of α is sketched in Figure 13.4(a). After combining both executions we have to perform a proof on the proof tree according to Figure 13.4(b).

In the following sections, we introduce optimizations, first regarding the calculation of the weakest precondition. This is followed by a discussion how the number of comparisons can be reduced. Finally, we show how block contracts can be used to further increase scalability and present how these optimizations can be used in the KeY system. The following argumentations are based on Dynamic Logic. Readers which are more familiar with weakest precondition calculi might prefer the presentation in [Scheben and Schmitt, 2014].

13.5.1.1 Reducing the Cost for the Weakest Precondition Calculation

First, we show that it is possible to prove noninterference in our setting with the help of only one symbolic execution of α.

Lemma 13.8. *Let* heap *and* $\bar{x}$ *be the program variables of* α *and let* h_1, $\bar{x}_1$, h_2, $\bar{x}_2$, h_1', $\bar{x}_1'$, h_2' *and* $\bar{x}_2'$ *be variables of appropriate type.*
There exist formulas ψ *and* ψ' *without modalities, which replace* $\{$heap $:=$ $h_1 \parallel \bar{x} := \bar{x}_1\}\langle\alpha\rangle$(heap $\doteq h_2 \wedge \bar{x} \doteq \bar{x}_2$) *and* $\{$heap $:= h_1' \parallel \bar{x} := \bar{x}_1'\}\langle\alpha\rangle$(heap $\doteq$ $h_2' \wedge \bar{x} \doteq \bar{x}_2'$) *in Lemma 13.7.*
The formulas ψ *and* ψ' *can be calculated with a single symbolic execution of* α.

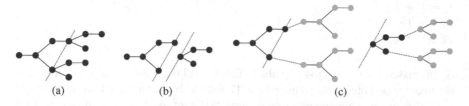

(a)   (b)   (c)

Figure 13.5 Reducing the verification overhead by compositional reasoning

Proof. Let $\mathcal{K}$ be a Kripke structure, s a state and β a variable assignment. The main step is finding a formula ψ—by symbolic execution of α—such that $(\mathcal{K}, s, \beta) \vDash \{\text{heap} := h_1 \mid\mid \bar{x} := \bar{x}_1\}\langle\alpha\rangle(\text{heap} \doteq h_2 \wedge \bar{x} \doteq \bar{x}_2)$ implies $(\mathcal{K}_{ext}, s, \beta) \vDash \psi$ for an extension $\mathcal{K}_{ext}$ of $\mathcal{K}$ by new Skolem symbols. (We need to consider extensions of $\mathcal{K}$, because the symbolic execution of α might introduce new Skolem symbols.) Note that the application of the JavaDL calculus—which contains all necessary rules for the symbolic execution of α—on $\{\text{heap} := h_1 \mid\mid \bar{x} := \bar{x}_1\}\langle\alpha\rangle(\text{heap} \doteq h_2 \wedge \bar{x} \doteq \bar{x}_2)$ does not deliver the desired implication: it approximates $\{\text{heap} := h_1 \mid\mid \bar{x} := \bar{x}_1\}\langle\alpha\rangle(\text{heap} \doteq h_2 \wedge \bar{x} \doteq \bar{x}_2)$ in the wrong direction. We have to take an indirection.

Intuitively, the formula $\{\text{heap} := h_1 \mid\mid \bar{x} := \bar{x}_1\}\langle\alpha\rangle(\text{heap} \doteq h_2 \wedge \bar{x} \doteq \bar{x}_2)$ is valid in $(\mathcal{K}, s, \beta)$ if α started in state $s_1 : \text{heap} \mapsto h_1^\beta, \bar{x} \mapsto \bar{x}_1^\beta$ terminates in state $s_2 : \text{heap} \mapsto h_2^\beta, \bar{x} \mapsto \bar{x}_2^\beta$. We calculate a formula ψ_{not} which is *at most* true if α started in $s_1 : \text{heap} \mapsto h_1^\beta, \bar{x} \mapsto \bar{x}_1^\beta$ does *not* terminate in $s_2 : \text{heap} \mapsto h_2^\beta, \bar{x} \mapsto \bar{x}_2^\beta$. Then $\psi = \neg\psi_{not}$ is *at least* true if α started in s_1 terminates in s_2. We obtain ψ_{not} by symbolic execution of $\{\text{heap} := h_1 \mid\mid \bar{x} := \bar{x}_1\}\langle\alpha\rangle(\text{heap} \neq h_2 \vee \bar{x} \neq \bar{x}_2)$: application of the JavaDL calculus on the sequent $\Longrightarrow \{\text{heap} := h_1 \mid\mid \bar{x} := \bar{x}_1\}\langle\alpha\rangle(\text{heap} \neq h_2 \vee \bar{x} \neq \bar{x}_2)$ results in a set of sequents F_{seq}, where each $f_{seq} \in F_{seq}$ does not contain modalities any more. Let F be the set of meaning formulas for F_{seq}. We set $\psi_{not} = \bigwedge_{f \in F} f$.

Given ψ, we observe that we obtain a formula ψ' such that $(\mathcal{K}, s, \beta) \vDash \{\text{heap} := h_1' \mid\mid \bar{x} := \bar{x}_1'\}\langle\alpha\rangle(\text{heap} \doteq h_2' \wedge \bar{x} \doteq \bar{x}_2')$ implies $(\mathcal{K}, s, \beta) \vDash \psi'$ by a simple renaming of the variables $h_1, \bar{x}_1, h_2, \bar{x}_2$ to $h_1', \bar{x}_1', h_2', \bar{x}_2'$ and by the renaming of the new Skolem symbols $\bar{c}$ to new primed Skolem symbols $\bar{c}'$. The thus obtained formulas ψ and ψ' can be used to replace $\{\text{heap} := h_1 \mid\mid \bar{x} := \bar{x}_1\}\langle\alpha\rangle(\text{heap} \doteq h_2 \wedge \bar{x} \doteq \bar{x}_2)$ and $\{\text{heap} := h_1' \mid\mid \bar{x} := \bar{x}_1'\}\langle\alpha\rangle(\text{heap} \doteq h_2' \wedge \bar{x} \doteq \bar{x}_2')$ in Lemma 13.7. Their calculation involves only one symbolic execution.

The full correctness proof of the approach can by found in [Scheben, 2014].

13.5.1.2 Reducing the Number of Comparisons

The second problem, the quadratic growth of the number of necessary comparisons in the number of program paths, can be tackled with the help of compositional reasoning if the structure of the program allows for it. Reconsider the initial example:

```
l = l + h;
if (h != 0) { l = l - h; }
if (l > 0) { l--; }
```

As discussed above, the first part above the dashed line, and the second part below the line, are noninterferent on their own. Therefore, by Lemma 13.4 on compositionality of *flow*, the complete program is noninterferent. As illustrated in Figure 13.5, checking the two parts independently from each other results in less verification effort: When splitting the control flow graph of the entire program along the dashed line (Figure 13.5(a)), each subprogram has only two paths as shown in (b). When symbolically executing both of the subprograms twice, we gain four paths each (c and d).

Thus, altogether only eight comparisons of post states have to be made to prove noninterference of the complete program. Checking the complete program at once would require (about) 12 comparisons.[2] We summarize the above observation in the following lemma.

Lemma 13.9. *Let α be a program with m branching statements.*

If α can be divided into m noninterferent blocks with at most one branching statement per block, then noninterference of α can be shown with the help of double symbolic execution with $3m$ comparisons.

Since a program with m branching statements has at least $n = m + 1$ paths, Lemma 13.9 shows that the verification effort of double symbolic execution approaches can be reduced from $O(n^2)$ to $O(n)$ comparisons, if the program under consideration is compositional with respect to information flow. In the best case, a program with m branching statements has $\Omega(2^m)$ paths. In this case, the verification effort reduces to $O(\log(n))$ comparisons, if the program under consideration is compositional with respect to information flow.

Unfortunately, the separation is not always as nice as in the example above. Consider for instance the following program:

```
if (l > 0) { if (l % 2 == 1) { l--; } }
```

The program can be divided into blocks

$b_1 = $ `if (l % 2 == 1) { l--; }`

and

$b_2 = $ `if (l > 0) { $b_1$ }`.

To conclude that b_2 is noninterferent, it is necessary to use the fact that b_1 is noninterferent in the proof of b_2. Unfortunately, the double execution approach does not easily lend itself to such compositional verification. In the next section, the problem of compositional reasoning will be discussed.

---

[2] By symmetry, the number of comparisons can be reduced further in both cases: in the first case $2 \cdot (2 + 1) = 6$ comparisons are sufficient, in the second case $4 + 3 + 2 + 1 = 10$ comparisons are enough.

13.5.1.3 Compositional Double Symbolic Execution

If a program α calls a block b, one (sometimes) does not want to look at its code but rather use a software contract for b, a contract that had previously been established by looking only at the code of b. This kind of compositionality can also be applied to methods instead of blocks and is essential for the scalability of all deductive software verification approaches. With double symbolic execution, the block b is not only called in the first execution of α, but also in the second execution. This poses the technical problem of somehow synchronizing the first and second call of b for contract application.

In this paragraph, we show how software contracts can be applied in proofs using double symbolic execution. An important feature of our approach is the seamless integration of information flow and functional reasoning allowing us to take advantage of the precision of functional contracts also for information flow contracts, if necessary.

In the context of functional verification, compositionality is achieved through method contracts. We extend this approach to the verification of information flow properties. We define *information flow contracts* as a tuple of a precondition and observation expressions for the pre- and the poststate.

Definition 13.10 (Information Flow Contract). An information flow contract (in short: flow contract) to a block (or method) b with local variables $\bar{x} := (x_1, \ldots, x_n)$ of types $\bar{A} := (A_1, \ldots, A_n)$ is a tuple $\mathscr{C}_{b,\bar{x}::\bar{A}} = (pre, R_1, R_2)$, where (1) *pre* is a formula which represents a precondition and (2) R_1, R_2 are observation expressions which represent the low expressions in the pre- and poststate.

A flow contract $\mathscr{C}_{b,\bar{x}::\bar{A}} = (pre, R_1, R_2)$ is valid if and only if the predicate flow(b, R_1, R_2, pre) is valid.

The difficulty in the application of flow contracts arises from the fact that flow contracts refer to two invocations of a block b in different contexts.

Example 13.11. Consider

```Java
if (1>0) { l++; if (l%2 == 1) {l--;} }
```

again, with blocks $b_1 = $ `if (l%2 == 1) {l--;}` and $b_2 = $ `if (1>0) {l++; `b_1`}`. Let $\mathscr{C}_{b_1,\bar{x}::\bar{A}} = \mathscr{C}_{b_2,\bar{x}::\bar{A}} = (true, 1, 1)$ be flow contracts for b_1 and b_2. To prove $\mathscr{C}_{b_2,\bar{x}::\bar{A}}$ by double symbolic execution,

$$l \doteq l' \rightarrow (\langle \text{if } (1>0) \text{ \{l++; } b_1\}; \text{ if } (1'>0) \text{ \{l'++; } b_1\}\rangle l \doteq l')$$

has to be shown. (For presentation purposes, we ignore the heap in this example.) Symbolic execution of the program, as far as possible, yields:

$$\text{apply-} \atop \text{Equality +} \atop \text{close}$$

$$\cfrac{1 \doteq 1', 1 > 0}{\Longrightarrow \{1 := 1+1\}} \atop {\langle b_1; \atop \text{if } (1'>0)\{ \atop 1'++; \atop b_1 \atop \} \atop \rangle 1 \doteq 1'}} \quad (13.1)$$

$$\text{close} \cfrac{*}{\cfrac{1 \doteq 1'}{1' > 0}} \atop \Longrightarrow 1 > 0, \atop \{1' := 1'+1\} \atop \langle b_1' \rangle 1 \doteq 1'$$

$$\text{close} \cfrac{*}{1 \doteq 1'} \atop \Longrightarrow 1 > 0, \atop 1' > 0, \atop 1 \doteq 1'$$

$$\vdots \ \textit{symbolic execution}$$

$$\Longrightarrow 1 \doteq 1' \to (\langle \texttt{if (1>0) \{1++; } b_1\texttt{\}; if (1'>0) \{1'++; } b_1'\texttt{\}} \rangle 1 \doteq 1')$$

To close branch (13.1), $\mathcal{C}_{b_1, \bar{x}::\bar{A}}$ needs to be used—but it is not obvious how this can be done, because $\mathcal{C}_{b_1, \bar{x}::\bar{A}}$ refers to the invocation of b_1 in the first and the second execution at the same time. A similar problem occurs if $\mathcal{C}_{b_2, \bar{x}::\bar{A}}$ is proved with the help of the optimizations discussed above.

The main idea of the solution is a coordinated delay of the application of flow contracts. The solution is compatible with the optimizations discussed above and additionally allows the combination of flow contracts with functional contracts.

Let b be a block with the functional contract $\mathcal{F}_{b, \bar{x}::\bar{A}} = (pre, post, Mod)$ where (1) the formula *pre* represents the precondition; (2) the formula *post* represents the postcondition; and (3) the term *Mod* represents the assignable clause for b. In functional verification, block contracts are applied by the rule useBlockContract, introduced by Wacker [2012]. The rule is an adaptation of the rule useMethodContract from Section 9.4.3 for blocks. For presentation purposes, we consider a simplified version of the rule only:

$$\text{useBlockContract} \cfrac{pre \qquad \qquad \qquad \Gamma \Longrightarrow \{u\}pre, \Delta \atop post \ \ \Gamma \Longrightarrow \{u; u_{anon}\}(post \to [\pi\ \omega]\phi), \Delta}{\Gamma \Longrightarrow \{u\}[\pi\ \texttt{b};\ \omega]\phi, \Delta}$$

Here, u is an arbitrary update; $u_{anon} = (\texttt{heap} := anon(\texttt{heap}, Mod, h), \bar{x} := \bar{x}')$ is an anonymizing update setting the locations of *Mod* (which might be modified by b) and the local variables which might be modified to unknown values; h of type *Heap* and $\bar{x}'$ of appropriate types are fresh symbols. We require *pre* to entail equations $\texttt{heap}_{pre} \doteq \texttt{heap}$ and $\bar{x}_{pre} \doteq \bar{x}$ which store the values of the program variables of the initial state in program variables $\texttt{heap}_{pre}$ and $\bar{x}_{pre}$ such that the initial values can be referred to in the postcondition. Additionally, we require that *pre* and *post* entail a formula which expresses that the heap is well-formed.

The plan is to use an extended version of the rule useBlockContract during symbolic execution—in many cases for the trivial functional contract $\mathcal{F}_{b, \bar{x}::\bar{A}} = (true, true, allLocs)$—which adds some extra information to the sequent allowing a delayed application of information flow contracts. The extra information is encapsulated in a new two-state predicate $C_b(\bar{x}, h, \bar{x}', h')$ with the intended meaning that b started in state s_1 : heap $\mapsto h, \bar{x} \mapsto \bar{x}$ and terminates in state s_2 : heap $\mapsto h', \bar{x} \mapsto \bar{x}'$. This predicate can be integrated into the rule useBlockContract as follows:

useBlockContract2

$$
\frac{
\begin{array}{ll}
\textit{pre} & \Gamma \Longrightarrow \{u\}\textit{pre}, \Delta \\
\textit{post} & \Gamma, \{u\}C_b(\bar{x}, \text{heap}, \bar{x}', h'), \{u; u_{anon}\}(\text{heap} \doteq h' \wedge \bar{x} \doteq \bar{x}') \\
& \qquad \Longrightarrow \{u; u_{anon}\}(\textit{post} \rightarrow [\pi \; \omega]\phi), \Delta
\end{array}
}{
\Gamma \Longrightarrow \{u\}[\pi \; b; \; \omega]\phi, \Delta
}
$$

where h' and $\bar{x}'$ are fresh function symbols. By [Scheben, 2014], useBlockContract2 is sound. The introduction of $C_b(\bar{x}, h, \bar{x}', h')$ to the post branch allows us to store the initial and the final state of b for a delayed application of information flow contracts: the two predicates $C_b(\bar{x}_1, h_1, \bar{x}'_1, h'_1)$ and $C_b(\bar{x}_2, h_2, \bar{x}'_2, h'_2)$ appearing on the antecedent of a sequent can be approximated by an instantiation of a flow contract $\mathscr{C}_{b,\bar{x}::\bar{A}} = (\textit{pre}, R_1, R_2)$ for b by

$$
\begin{array}{l}
\{\text{heap} := h_1 \; || \; \bar{x} := \bar{x}_1\}\textit{pre} \wedge \{\text{heap} := h_2 \; || \; \bar{x} := \bar{x}_2\}\textit{pre} \\
\rightarrow \left(obsEq(\bar{x}_1, h_1, \bar{x}'_1, h'_1, R_1) \rightarrow obsEq(\bar{x}_2, h_2, \bar{x}'_2, h'_2, R_2) \right) \quad.
\end{array}
$$

This approximation is applied by the rule useFlowContract:

useFlowContract

$$
\frac{
\begin{array}{l}
\Gamma, C_b(\bar{x}_1, h_1, \bar{x}'_1, h'_1), C_b(\bar{x}_2, h_2, \bar{x}'_2, h'_2), \\
\qquad \{\text{heap} := h_1 \; || \; \bar{x} := \bar{x}_1\}\textit{pre} \wedge \{\text{heap} := h_2 \; || \; \bar{x} := \bar{x}_2\}\textit{pre} \\
\qquad \rightarrow \left(obsEq(\bar{x}_1, h_1, \bar{x}'_1, h'_1, R_1) \rightarrow obsEq(\bar{x}_2, h_2, \bar{x}'_2, h'_2, R_2) \right) \\
\Longrightarrow \Delta
\end{array}
}{
\Gamma, C_b(\bar{x}_1, h_1, \bar{x}'_1, h'_1), C_b(\bar{x}_2, h_2, \bar{x}'_2, h'_2) \Longrightarrow \Delta
}
$$

Formally, a flow contract $C_b(\bar{x}, h, \bar{x}', h')$ is valid in a Kripke structure $\mathscr{K}$ and a state s if and only if

$$
\{\bar{x} := \bar{x} \; || \; \text{heap} := h\}\langle b \rangle(\text{heap} \doteq h' \wedge \bar{x} \doteq \bar{x}')
$$

is valid in $(\mathscr{K}, s)$. Note that the usage of the rule useBlockContract2 during symbolic execution allows the application of arbitrary functional contracts in addition to flow contracts. This allows for taking advantage of the precision of functional contracts within information flow proofs, if necessary. The default, however, is using the trivial functional contract $\mathscr{F}_{b,\bar{x}::\bar{A}} = (true, true, allLocs)$ as in the presented example. The soundness proof for the above approach can be found in [Scheben, 2014].

Example 13.12. Let $\mathscr{F}_{b_1,\bar{x}::\bar{A}} = (true, true, allLocs)$ be the trivial functional contract for b_1. Applied on the example from above, (13.1) can be simplified as shown in Figure 13.6. For presentation purposes, all heap symbols have been removed from the example. Therefore, C_{b_1} takes only two parameters and $obsEq$ only three parameters. Adding the heap results in essentially the same proof but with more complex formulas.

The proof uses the following abbreviations of rule names:

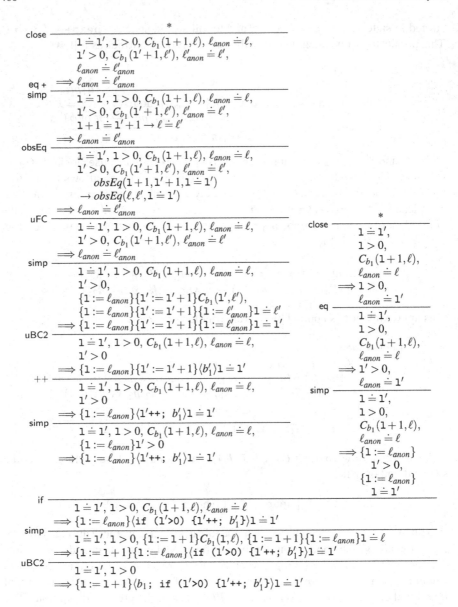

Figure 13.6 Proof tree of Example 13.12.

Abbreviation	Full name	Abbreviation	Full name
uBC2	useBlockContract2	eq	applyEquality
uFC	useFlowContract	if	conditional
obsEq	replaces $obsEq(\cdot)$ by its definition (Lemma 13.6)	simp	combination of all update simplification rules
++	plusPlus	close	close
eq + simp	repeated application of the rules eq and simp		

Firstly, the symbolic execution is continued by the rule useBlockContract2 and (after several simplifications) by the rule conditional. The conditional rule splits the proof into two branches. The right branch, which represents the case that the condition $1' > 0$ evaluates to false, can be closed after further simplifications and the application of equalities. On the other branch, the remaining program is executed symbolically by the rule plusPlus and another application of useBlockContract2, now on the block b_1'. After some further simplifications, we are in the position to apply the flow contract for b_1: the antecedent of the sequent contains the two predicates $C_{b_1}(1 + 1, \ell)$ and $C_{b_1}(1' + 1, \ell')$ on which the rule useFlowContract can be applied. With the help of the guarantees from the flow contract for b_1, the proof closes after some final simplifications.

13.5.2 Using Efficient Double Symbolic Execution in KeY

In this section, we show how efficient double execution proofs can be performed in the KeY system. Readers not familiar with the KeY system may find it helpful to read Chapter 15 on using the KeY prover first.

Efficient double execution is implemented in KeY with the help of strategy macros. The simplest way to use the optimizations is by application of the macro **Full Information Flow Auto Pilot**. It can be selected by highlighting an arbitrary term, left-clicking, choosing the menu item **Strategy macros** and then **Full Information Flow Auto Pilot**. KeY should be able to prove most of the information flow examples delivered with KeY (under **examples** → **firstTouch** → **InformationFlow**) automatically this way.

On complicated examples, the auto pilot might fail. In this case, we can gain better control of the proof by application of the following steps.

As discussed in Section 13.5.1, double execution considers the same program twice, but it suffices to calculate only one weakest precondition. Therefore we start a side-proof for the weakest precondition calculation. This is done as follows:

1. We highlight an arbitrary term and left-click. We then choose the menu item **Strategy macros** and in the upcoming menu the item **Auxiliary Computation Auto Pilot**. A side proof opens and KeY tries to automatically calculate the weakest precondition.

    KeY succeeded in the calculation if the open goals of the side proof do not contain modalities any more. If a goal still contains a modality, then one can either simply try to increase the number of auto-mode steps or one can remove the modalities by interactive steps.

If one of the open goals contains an information flow proof obligation from a block contract or from an information flow loop invariant, then this goal has to be closed by going through steps (1) to (3) again before continuing with step (2).

2. We choose an open goal, highlight an arbitrary term in the sequent and left-click. We choose the menu item **Strategy macros** and in the upcoming menu the item **Finish auxiliary computation**. The side-proof closes and a new taclet (rule) is introduced to the main proof. The new taclet is able to replace the double execution term (the shortest term which contains both modalities) by two instantiations of the calculated formula.

3. On simple examples, it suffices to activate the auto mode by choosing the menu item **Continue** from the menu **Proof**. On more complex examples it is helpful to run the strategy macro **self-composition state expansion with inf flow contracts** first. The latter macro applies the new rule and afterwards tries to systematically apply information flow contracts.

The macro **Full Information Flow Auto Pilot** applies steps (1)–(3) automatically.

13.6 Summary and Conclusion

We have presented how information flow properties can be specified in JML and that KeY can analyze whether Java programs satisfy the specification. The approach implemented in the KeY prover allows for a very precise specification of information flows which is important especially in a real-world object-oriented programming language. Information flow is represented in JavaDL directly by the semantic meaning of the property: We directly compare two executions of a program only differing in the secret input. While this allows for precise reasoning with KeY, the pairwise comparison of all execution paths leads to quadratic growth of proof obligations. Therefore, we also show how the proof process can be optimized such that verifying real-world programs becomes feasible.

The approach as presented here was applied for the verification of a simplified e-voting case study. Experiences of this work can be found in Chapter 18.

Another approach for precise information flow analysis has been developed by Klebanov [2014]. The approach is based on symbolic execution in KeY, combined with an external quantifier elimination procedure and a model counting procedure. The method and tool chain not only identify information leaks in programs but quantify them using a number of information-theoretical metrics.

Very popular enforcement methods for information flow properties in the literature are type systems. These approaches are usually less precise than the approach presented here, however only a single execution of a program has to be considered during analysis. So-called *dependent types* allow to further improve precision of type-based analysis. Here, dependencies between variables and partial and aggregated information is tracked during symbolic execution. Using theorem provers for the analysis of programs with dependent types, it is possible to track the semantics of information during a program run. An extension for KeY supporting a type-based reasoning of information flow in programs can be found in [Bubel et al., 2009, van Delft and Bubel, 2015].

Chapter 14
Program Transformation and Compilation

Ran Ji and Richard Bubel

The main purpose of the KeY system is to ensure program correctness w.r.t. a formal specification on the level of source code. However, a flawed(?) compiler may invalidate correctness properties that have been formally verified for the program's source code. Hence, we additionally need to guarantee the correctness of the compilation result w.r.t. its source code.

Compiler verification, as a widely used technique to prove the correctness of compilers, has been a research topic for more than 40 years [McCarthy and Painter, 1967, Milner and Weyhrauch, 1972]. Previous works [Leroy, 2006, 2009, Leinenbach, 2008] have shown that compiler verification is an expensive task requiring nontrivial user interactions in proof-assistants like Coq [Leroy, 2009]. Maintaining these proofs for changes to the compiler back-end (e.g., support of new language features or optimization techniques) is not yet counted into that effort.

In this chapter, instead of verifying a compiler, we use the verification engine of KeY to prove a correct bytecode generation through a sound program transformation approach. Thus program correctness on source code level is inherited to the bytecode level. The presented approach guarantees that the behavior of the compiled program coincides with that of the source program in the sense that both programs terminate in states in which the values of a user specified region of the heap are equivalent.

Moreover, we often want the generated program to be more optimized than the original program. If the source and the target programs are in the same language, this program translation process is also known as *program specialization* or *partial evaluation*.

The correctness of the source program (w.r.t. its specification) entails correctness of the generated program. No further verification on the level of bytecode is needed, though verification of Java programs on the bytecode level, even if interaction is needed, is also possible using dynamic logic [Ulbrich, 2011, 2013].

When constructing the symbolic execution tree (see Section 11.2) the program is analyzed by decomposing complex statements into a succession of simpler statements. Information about the heap and local program variables is accumulated and added in the form of formulas and/or updates. This information can be used to deem certain execution paths as unfeasible.

© Springer International Publishing AG 2016
W. Ahrendt et al. (Eds.): Deductive Software Verification, LNCS 10001, pp. 473–492, 2016
DOI: 10.1007/978-3-319-49812-6_14

Technically, we implemented symbolic execution as part of the sequent calculus (see Section 3.5.6), whose rules are applied analytically from bottom-to-up. For the program generation part, the idea is to apply the sequent calculus rules reversely (i.e., top-down) and to generate the target program step-by-step.

This chapter is structured as follows: Section 14.1 introduces partial evaluation and how it can be interleaved with symbolic execution to boost the performance of automatic verification. We discuss how to achieve verified correct compilation in Section 14.2 and discuss a prototypical implementation in Section 14.3.

14.1 Interleaving Symbolic Execution and Partial Evaluation

We first motivate the general idea for interleaving symbolic execution and partial evaluation (Section 14.1.1). Then we show how to integrate a program transformer soundly into a program calculus in Section 14.1.2 and conclude with a short evaluation of the results.

14.1.1 General Idea

To motivate our approach of interleaving partial evaluation and symbolic execution, we first take a look at the program shown in Figure 14.1(a). The program adapts the value of variable y to a given threshold with an accuracy of eps by repeatedly increasing or decreasing y as appropriate. The function abs(·) computes the absolute value of an integer.

Symbolically executing the program results in the symbolic execution tree (introduced in Section 11.2) shown in Figure 14.2, which is significantly more complex than the program's control flow graph (CFG) in Figure 14.1(b). The reason is that symbolic execution unwinds the program's CFG producing a tree structure. As a consequence, identical code is repeated on many branches, however, under different path conditions and in different symbolic states. Merging back different nodes of the tree is usually not possible without approximation or abstraction [Bubel et al., 2009, Weiß, 2009].

During symbolic execution, there are occasions in which fields or parameters have a value which is fixed a priori, for instance, because certain values are fixed for some call sites, the program is an instantiation of a product family or contracts exclude certain program paths. In our case, the program from Figure 14.1(a) is run with a fixed initial value (80) for y and the threshold is fixed to 100.

To exploit this knowledge about constant values and to derive more efficient programs, partial evaluation has been used since the mid 1960s, for instance as part of optimizing compilers. The first efforts were targeted towards Lisp. Due to the rise in popularity of functional and logic programming languages, the 1980s saw a large

```
y = 80;
threshold = 100;

if (y > threshold) {
    decrease = true;
} else {
    decrease = false;
}

while (abs(y-threshold) > eps) {
    if (decrease) {
        y = y-1;
    } else {
        y = y+1;
    }
}
```

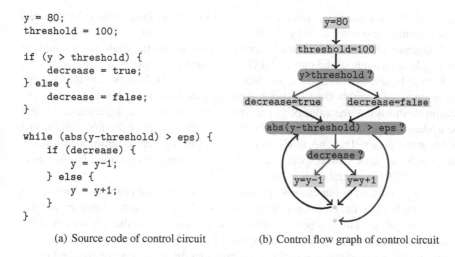

(a) Source code of control circuit   (b) Control flow graph of control circuit

Figure 14.1 A simple control circuit *Java* program and its control flow graph

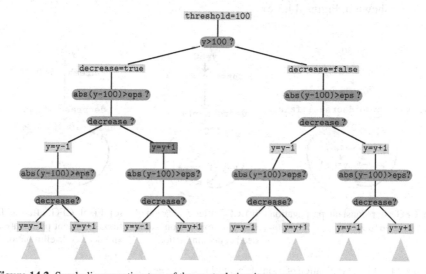

Figure 14.2 Symbolic execution tree of the control circuit program

amount of research in partial evaluation of such languages. A seminal text on partial evaluation is the book by Jones et al. [1993].

In contrast to symbolic execution, the result of a partial evaluator, also called *program specializer* (or short mix), is not the symbolic value of output variables, but another, equivalent program. The known fixed input is also called *static input* while the part of the input that is not known at compile time is called *dynamic input*.

Partial evaluation traverses the CFG (e.g., the one of Figure 14.1(b)) with a partial evaluator, while maintaining a table of concrete (i.e., constant) values for the program locations. In our example, that table is empty at first. After processing the two initial assignments, it contains $\mathcal{U} = \{y := 80 \| \mathtt{threshold} := 100\}$.

Whenever a new constant value becomes known, the partial evaluator attempts to propagate it throughout the current CFG. This *constant propagation* transforms the CFG from Figure 14.1(b) into the one depicted in Figure 14.3(a). We can observe that occurrences of y within the loop (incl. the loop guard) have *not* been replaced. The reason for this is that the value of y at these occurrences is not static, because it might be updated in the loop. Likewise, the value of decrease after the first conditional is not static either. The check whether the value of a given program location can be considered static with respect to a given node in the CFG is called *binding time analysis* (BTA) in partial evaluation.

Partial evaluation of our example proceeds now to the guard of the first conditional. This guard became the *constant expression* 80>100 which can be evaluated to *false*. As a consequence, one can perform *dead code elimination* on the left branch of the conditional. The result is depicted in Figure 14.3(b). Now the value of decrease is static and can be propagated into the loop (note that decrease is not changed inside the loop). After further dead code elimination, the final result of partial evaluation is the CFG shown in Figure 14.3(c).

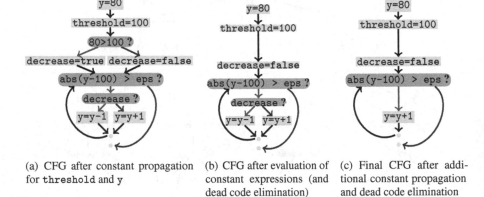

(a) CFG after constant propagation for threshold and y

(b) CFG after evaluation of constant expressions (and dead code elimination)

(c) Final CFG after additional constant propagation and dead code elimination

Figure 14.3 Partial evaluation of a simple control circuit program

The hope with employing partial evaluation is that it is possible to factor out common parts of computations in different branches by evaluating them partially *before* symbolic execution takes place. The naïve approach, however, to *first* evaluate partially and *then* perform symbolic execution fails miserably. The reason is that for partial evaluation to work well, the input space dimension of a program must be significantly reducible by identifying certain input variables to have static values (i.e., fixed values at compile time).

Typical usage scenarios for symbolic execution like program verification are not of this kind. For example, in the program shown in Figure 14.1, it is unrealistic to classify the value of y as static. If we redo the example without the initial assignment y=80, then partial evaluation can only perform one trivial constant propagation. The fact that input values for variables are not required to be static can even be considered to be one of the main advantages of symbolic execution and is the source of its generality: it is possible to cover all finite execution paths simultaneously, and one can start execution at any given source code position without the need for initialization code.

The central observation that makes partial evaluation work in this context is that *during* symbolic execution, static values are accumulated continuously as path conditions added to the current symbolic execution path. This suggests to perform partial evaluation *interleaved* with symbolic execution.

To be specific, we reconsider the example shown in Figure 14.1(a), but we remove the first statement, which assign y the value 80. As observed above, no noteworthy simplification of the program's CFG can be any longer achieved by partial evaluation. The CFG's structure after partial evaluation remains exactly the same and only the occurrences of variable threshold are replaced by the constant value 100. If we symbolically execute this program, then the resulting execution tree spanned by unrolling the loop twice is shown in Figure 14.2. The first conditional divides the execution tree in two subtrees. The left subtree deals with the case that the value of y is too high and needs to be decreased, the right subtree with the complementary case.

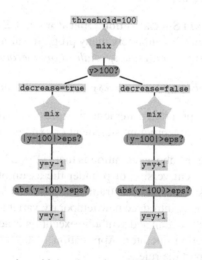

Figure 14.4 Symbolic execution with interleaved partial evaluation

All subsequent branches result from either the loop condition (omitted in Figure 14.2) or the conditional expression inside the loop body testing the value of decrease. As decrease is not modified within the loop, some of these branches are infeasible. For example the branch below the boxed occurrence of y=y+1 (filled in red) is infeasible, because the value of decrease is true in that branch. Symbolic execution will not continue on these infeasible branches, but abandon them by *proving* that the path condition is contradictory. Since the value of `decrease` is only tested *inside* the loop, however, the loop must still be unwound first and the proof that the current path condition is contradictory must be repeated. Partial evaluation can replace this potentially expensive proof search by *computation* which is drastically cheaper.

In the example, specializing the remaining program in each of the two subtrees after the first assignment to `decrease` eliminates the inner-loop conditional, see Figure 14.4 (the partial evaluation steps are labeled with `mix`). Hence, interleaving symbolic execution and partial evaluation promises to achieve a significant speed-up by removing redundancy from subsequent symbolic execution.

14.1.2 The Program Specialization Operator

We define a program specialization operator suitable for interleaving partial evaluation with symbolic execution in JavaDL. The operator implements a program transformer which issues correctness conditions as side-proofs that are 'easy' to proof directly and can thus be safely integrated into the sequent calculus. This approach avoids formalizing the partial evaluator in the program logic itself which would be tedious and inefficient.

Definition 14.1 (Program Specialization Operator). Let Σ be a sufficiently large signature containing countably infinitely many program variables and function symbols for any type and arity. A *program specialization operator*

$$\downarrow_\Sigma: ProgramElement \times Updates_\Sigma \times For_\Sigma \to ProgramElement$$

takes as arguments a (i) program statement or expression, (ii) an update and (iii) a formula; and maps these to a program statement or expression.

The intention behind the above definition is that $p \downarrow_\Sigma (\mathscr{U}, \phi)$ denotes a "simpler" but semantically equivalent version of p under the assumption that both are executed in a state which satisfies the constrained imposed by $\mathscr{U}$ and ϕ. The program specialization operator may introduce new temporary variables or function symbols.

Interleaving partial evaluation and symbolic execution is achieved by introduction rules for the specialization operator. Application of the program transformer is triggered by application of the rule

$$\text{introPE} \ \frac{\Gamma \implies \mathscr{U}[(p) \downarrow (\mathscr{U}, true)]\phi, \Delta}{\Gamma \implies \mathscr{U}[p]\phi, \Delta}$$

where $(p) \downarrow (\mathscr{U}, true)$ returns a semantically equivalent program w.r.t. initial state $\mathscr{U}$ and condition ϕ. The program transformer is usually defined recursively over the program structure. We discuss a selection of program transformation rules that can be used to define the specialization operator in the next section.

14.1.3 Specific Specialization Actions

We instantiate the generic program specialization operator of Definition 14.1 with some possible actions. In each case we derive soundness conditions.

Specialization Operator Propagation

The specialization operator needs to be propagated through the program as most of the different specialization operations work locally on single statements or expressions. During propagation of the operator, its knowledge base, the pair $(\mathcal{U}, \phi)$, needs to be updated by additional knowledge learned from executed statements or by erasing invalid knowledge about variables altered by the previous statement. Propagation of the specialization operator as well as updating the knowledge base is realized by the following program transformation (read $p \rightsquigarrow p'$ as program p is transformed into program p')

$$(\texttt{p};\texttt{q}) \downarrow (\mathcal{U}, \phi) \quad \rightsquigarrow \quad \texttt{p} \downarrow (\mathcal{U}, \phi); \texttt{q} \downarrow (\mathcal{U}', \phi') \;.$$

This rule is unsound for arbitrary $\mathcal{U}'$, ϕ'. Soundness is ensured under a number of restrictions:

1. Let *mod* be a collection that contains all program locations possibly changed by p including local variables. This can be proven similar to framing in case of loop invariants (see Section 8.2.5).
2. Let $\mathcal{V}_{mod}$ be the anonymizing update for *mod*, which assigns each local program variable contained in *mod* a new constant and performs the heap anonymization using the *anon* function. By fixing $\mathcal{U}' := \mathcal{U}\,\mathcal{V}_{mod}$, we ensure that the program state reached by executing p is covered by at least one interpretation and variable assignment over the extended signature.
3. ϕ' must be chosen in such a way that $\models \mathcal{U}(\phi \to \langle p \rangle \phi')$ holds. This ensures that the postcondition of p is correctly represented by ϕ'. Computation of such a ϕ' can be arbitrarily complex. The actual complexity depends on the concrete realization of the program specialization operator. Usually, ϕ' is a relatively cheaply computed safe approximation (abstraction) of p's postcondition.

Constant propagation

Constant propagation is one of the most basic operations in partial evaluation and often a prerequisite for more complex rewrite operations. Constant propagation entails that if the value of a variable v is known to have a constant value c within a certain program region (typically, until the variable is potentially reassigned) then usages of v can be replaced by c. The rewrite rule

$$(v) \downarrow (\mathcal{U}, \phi) \rightsquigarrow c$$

models the replacement operation. To ensure soundness the rather obvious condition $\models \mathcal{U}(\phi \to v \doteq c)$ has to be proved where c is an interpreted constant (e.g., a compile-time constant or literal).

Dead-Code Elimination

Constant propagation and constant expression evaluation often result in specializations where the guard of a conditional (or loop) becomes constant. In this case, unreachable code in the current state and path condition can be easily located and pruned.

A typical example for a specialization operation eliminating an infeasible symbolic execution branch is the rule

$$(\texttt{if (b) \{p\} else \{q\})} \downarrow (\mathcal{U}, \phi) \quad \rightsquigarrow \quad \texttt{p} \downarrow (\mathcal{U}, \phi) \ ,$$

which eliminates the **else** branch of a conditional, if the guard can be proved true. The soundness condition of the rule is straightforward and self-explaining: $\models \mathcal{U}(\phi \to \texttt{b} \doteq TRUE)$.

Another case is

$$(\texttt{if (b) \{p\} else \{q\})} \downarrow (\mathcal{U}, \phi) \quad \rightsquigarrow \quad \texttt{q} \downarrow (\mathcal{U}, \phi)$$

where the soundness condition is: $\models \mathcal{U}(\phi \to \texttt{b} \doteq FALSE)$.

Safe Field Access

Partial evaluation can be used to mark expressions as safe that contain field accesses or casts that may otherwise cause abrupt termination. We use the notation @(e) to mark an expression e as safe, for example, if we can ensure that o $\neq$ null, then we can derive the annotation @(o.a) for any field a in the type of o. The advantage of safe annotations is that symbolic execution can assume that safe expressions terminate normally and needs not to spawn side proofs that ensure it. The rewrite rule for safe field accesses is

$$\texttt{o.a} \downarrow (\mathcal{U}, \phi) \quad \rightsquigarrow \quad \texttt{@(o.a)} \downarrow (\mathcal{U}, \phi) \ .$$

Its soundness condition is $\models \mathcal{U}(\phi \to \neg(\texttt{o} \doteq \texttt{null}))$.

Type Inference

For deep type hierarchies dynamic dispatch of method invocations may cause serious performance issues in symbolic execution, because a long cascade of method calls is created by the method invocation rule (Section 3.7.1). To reduce the number of implementation candidates we use information from preceding symbolic execution to narrow the static type of the callee as far as possible and to (safely) cast the reference to that type. The method invocation rule can then determine the implementation candidates more precisely:

$$\mathtt{res} = \mathtt{o}.m(\mathtt{a}_1,\dots,\mathtt{a}_n); \downarrow (\mathscr{U},\phi) \quad \rightsquigarrow$$
$$\mathtt{res} = @((Cl)\mathtt{o} \downarrow (\mathscr{U},\phi)).m(\mathtt{a}_1 \downarrow (\mathscr{U},\phi),\dots,\mathtt{a}_n \downarrow (\mathscr{U},\phi));$$

The accompanying soundness condition $\models \mathscr{U}(\phi \rightarrow instance_{Cl}(x) \doteq TRUE)$ ensures that the type of o is compatible with Cl in any state specified by $\mathscr{U}$, ϕ.

A note to the side conditions: The side conditions are in general full-blown first-order proofs and the needed effort to discharge them could eliminate any positive effects of the specialization. But in practice, these side conditions can be (i) proven very easily as the accumulated information is already directly contained in the formula ϕ without the need of full first-order reasoning; and (ii) the conditions can be proven in separate side-proofs and hence, do not pollute the actual proof tree. This results in a shorter and more human-readable proof object.

14.1.4 Example

As an application of interleaving symbolic execution and partial evaluation, consider the verification of a GUI library. It includes standard visual elements such as `Window`, `Icon`, `Menu` and `Pointer`. An element has different implementations for different platforms or operating systems. Consider the following program snippet involving dynamic method dispatch:

—— Java ——
```
framework.ui.Button button = radiobuttonX11;
button.paint();
```
—— Java ——

The element `Button` is implemented in one way for Max OS X while it is implemented differently for the X Window System. The class `Button`, which is extended by the classes `CheckBox`, `Component`, and `Dialog`, defines the method `paint()`. Altogether, `paint()` is implemented in 16 different classes including `ButtonX11`, `ButtonMPC`, `RadioButtonX11`, `MenuItemX11`, etc. The type hierarchy is outlined in Figure 14.5. In the code fragment above, `button` is assigned an object of type `RadioButtonX11` which implements `paint()`. We want to prove that it always terminates, and hence, the formula $\langle \mathtt{gui} \rangle true$ should be provable where `gui` abbreviates the code above.

First, we employ symbolic execution alone to do the proof. During this process, `button.paint()` is unfolded into 16 different cases by the method invocation rule (see Section 3.6.5.5), each corresponding to a possible implementation of `button`

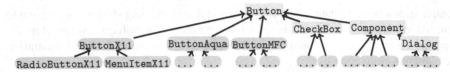

Figure 14.5 Type hierarchy for the GUI example

in one of the subclasses of `Button`. The proof is constructed automatically using an experimental version of KeY; the proof consists of 161 nodes on ten branches.

In a second experiment, we interleave symbolic execution and partial evaluation to prove the same claim. The partial evaluator propagates with the help of the TypeInference rule presented in the previous section the information that the run-time type of `button` is `RadioButtonX11` (known from the declared type of variable `radiobuttonX11` and the type hierarchy) and the only possible implementation of `button.paint()` is `RadioButtonX11.paint()`. All other possible implementations are pruned. Only 24 nodes and two branches occur in the proof tree when running KeY integrated with a partial evaluator.

The reduction in the size of the proof tree is in particular important for human readability and increases the efficiency of the interactive proving process. A thorough evaluation and more details can be found in Ji [2014].

14.2 Verified Correct Compilation

The previous section was concerned with the interleaving of partial evaluation and symbolic execution. In this section, we go one step further and discuss how to employ JavaDL and symbolic execution calculus to support more semantics-preserving program transformations. One interesting use case is the compilation of a program into a target language that the compiled program behaves verifiably equivalent w.r.t. to its source code version. For ease of presentation, we describe the approach here for a source-to-source transformation of a while language. But the presented approach can be extended to all sorts of source and target languages. A detailed description including bytecode compilation can be found in [Ji, 2014].

Equivalence checking between code and compilation result is important in compiler correctness checking. General equivalence checking of programs of the same abstraction level is also an active field of research.

The simplified language for this presentation is a while-language (with a Java-like syntax) that operates on integer variables and comes without intricacies like abrupt termination. The verifiably correct output is a simplified (and possibly specialized) variant of the original one.

Semantic equivalence is a relational property of the two compared programs. In order to accommodate such relational problems on the syntactical level in JavaDL, a new modality, called the *weak bisimulation modality*, is introduced that contains not one but two programs. The two programs in the modality are meant to be equivalent, but need not reach fully equivalent poststates. A criterion can be given which decides about the equivalence of states. This criterion is the set of observable variables *obs* on which the termination states have to coincide.

Definition 14.2 (Weak bisimulation modality—syntax). Let p, q be two while-language programs, $obs, use \subseteq$ ProgVSym sets of program variables and $\phi \in$ DLFml a first-order formula.

We extend the definition of JavaDL formulas: Under the above conditions $[\, p \,\between\, q \,]@(obs, use)\phi$ is also a JavaDL formula.

This modality is closely related to the relational Hoare calculus by Benton [2004], the notion of product programs by Barthe et al. [2011] and similar to the two-program weakest-precondition calculus in [Felsing et al., 2014, Kiefer et al., 2016]. The principle idea behind the modality is that $[\, p \,\between\, q \,]@(obs, use)\phi$ holds if the programs p, q behave equivalently w.r.t. the program variables in *obs*. The formula ϕ is used as postcondition for program p such that the weak bisimulation modality implies the 'ordinary' modality $[p]\phi$. Initially, formula ϕ is chosen as *true*. Only when handling loops, to increase precision by means of a loop invariant, other formulas can appear for ϕ.

In the verification-based compilation process outlined in the following, the bisimulation modality serves two purposes:

1. It guides the generation of compiled code after symbolic execution.
2. It allows the formal equivalence verification between source code and compilation result afterwards.

Before looking at the formal semantics of the modality and stating the calculus rules performing these tasks, we will give a brief overview over the compilation process. The initial input is the source program p and the equivalence criterion *obs*; this can, for example, be the set that only contains the variable holding the returned value if the result-equivalence is the target property.

The process follows a two-step protocol. In the first step, the source program is symbolically executed. This can be done using rules corresponding to ones of the calculus presented in Chapter 3, in a fashion similar to the symbolic execution debugger outlined in Section 11.2. It starts from the modality $[\, p \,\between\, Q_1 \,]@(obs, U_1)true$ with Q_1 and U_1 placeholder meta variable symbols which have no impact in the first phase. In the second phase, a compilation algorithm will fill these gaps starting from the leaves of the symbolic execution tree such that every step is one for which the calculus for the bisimulation modality has a rule.

The result is a closed proof tree with root $[\, p \,\between\, q \,]@(obs, use)true$ for some program q synthesized during the second phase. The proof guarantees us that q is equivalent to the input program p as far as the observations in *obs* are concerned.

To explain the meaning of the likewise synthesized *use*, we first introduce the set $usedVar(s, p, obs)$ capturing precisely those program variables whose value influences the final value of an observable location $l \in obs$ after executing p in a state s.

Definition 14.3 (Used program variable). Let s be a (Kripke) state (see Section 3.3.1).

A variable $v \in \mathrm{ProgVSym}$ is *used by program p from s* with respect to variable set *obs* if there is a program variable $l \in obs$ such that

$$s \models \forall v_l; \left((\langle \mathrm{p} \rangle l \doteq v_l) \rightarrow \exists v_0; \{v := v_0\} \langle \mathrm{p} \rangle l \neq v_l \right) .$$

The set $usedVar(s, \mathrm{p}, obs)$ of used program variables is defined as the smallest set containing all program variables in s by p with respect to *obs*.

A program variable v is used if and only if there is an interference with a location contained in *obs*, i.e., the value of v influences at least the value of one observed variable. Conversely, this means that if two states coincide on the variables in *use*, then the result states after the execution of p coincide on the variables in *obs*.

If two states s, s' coincide on the variables in a set $set \subseteq \mathrm{ProgVSym}$, we write $s \approx_{set} s'$.

Definition 14.4 (Weak bisimulation modality—semantics). Let p, q be while-programs, $obs, use \in \mathrm{ProgVSym}$, s a Kripke state. Then $s \models [\,\mathrm{p} \,\slashed{0}\, \mathrm{q}\,]\,@(obs, use)\phi$ if and only if

1. $s \models [\mathrm{p}]\phi$
2. $use \supseteq usedVar(s, \mathrm{q}, obs)$
3. for all $s \approx_{use} s'$ and $(s, t) \in \rho(\mathrm{p})$, $(s', t') \in \rho(\mathrm{q})$, we have $t \approx_{obs} t'$.

The formula $[\,\mathrm{p} \,\slashed{0}\, \mathrm{q}\,]\,@(obs, use)\phi$ holds if the behaviors of p and q are equivalent w.r.t. the program variables contained in the set *obs*, and the set *use* contains all program locations and variables that may influence the value of any program variable or location contained in *obs* or the truth value of ϕ.

In the compilation scenario, p is the source program and q the created target program, hence validity of the formula ensures that the compilation is correct w.r.t. the equivalence criterion *obs*.

Bisimulation modalities can be embedded into sequents like $\Gamma \Longrightarrow \mathcal{U}[\,\mathrm{p} \,\slashed{0}\, \mathrm{q}\,]\,@(obs, use)\phi, \Delta$, and the sequent calculus rules for the bisimulation modality are of the following form:

$$\Gamma_1 \Longrightarrow \mathcal{U}_1[\,\mathrm{p}_1 \,\slashed{0}\, \mathrm{q}_1\,]\,@(obs_1, use_1)\phi_1, \Delta_1$$

$$\vdots$$

$$\text{ruleName} \;\; \frac{\Gamma_n \Longrightarrow \mathcal{U}_n[\,\mathrm{p}_n \,\slashed{0}\, \mathrm{q}_n\,]\,@(obs_n, use_n)\phi_n, \Delta_n}{\Gamma \Longrightarrow \mathcal{U}[\,\mathrm{p} \,\slashed{0}\, \mathrm{q}\,]\,@(obs, use)\phi, \Delta}$$

As mentioned earlier, application of the bisimulation rules is a two step process:

Step 1: Symbolic execution of source program p as usual using rules obtained from the ones in Chapter 3. The equivalence criterion *obs* is propagated from one modality to its children in the proof tree. In every arising modality, the second program parameter and the use set are filled with distinct meta-level placeholder symbols. The observable location sets obs_i are propagated and contain those variables on which the two programs have to coincide. Intuitively, the variables mentioned here are protected in the sense that information about the value of these variables must not be thrown away during the symbolic execution step as the synthesized program will have to maintain their value.

Step 2:   Synthesis of the target program q and used variable set *use* from q_i and use_i by applying the rules in a leave-to-root manner. Thus the placeholder symbols are instantiated. Starting with a leaf node, the program is generated until branching node is reached where the generation stops. The synthesis continues in the same fashion with the remaining leaves until programs for all subtrees of a branching node have been generated. Then these programs are combined according to the rule applied on the branching node.

For instance, in case of an if-then-else statement, first the then-branch and then else-branch are generated before synthesizing the corresponding conditional statement in the target program (see rule ifElse). Note that, in general, the order of processing the different branches of a node matters, for instance, in case of the loopInvariant the program for the branch that deals with program after the loop has to be synthesized before the loop body (as the latter's set of observable variable depends on those used on the other branch).

We explain some of the rules in details.

$$\text{emptyBox } \frac{\Gamma \Longrightarrow \mathscr{U}\phi,\Delta}{\Gamma \Longrightarrow \mathscr{U}[\, \{\} \,\, \rangle\!\langle \,\, \{\} \,]@(obs,obs)\phi,\Delta}$$

The emptyBox rule is the starting point of program transformation in each sequential block. The location set *use* is set to *obs*.

$$\text{assignment}$$
$$\frac{\Gamma \Longrightarrow \mathscr{U}\{\mathtt{l} := \mathtt{r}\}[\, \omega \,\, \rangle\!\langle \,\, \overline{\omega} \,]@(obs,use)\phi,\Delta}{\left(\begin{array}{ll} \Gamma \Longrightarrow \mathscr{U}[\, \mathtt{l}{=}\mathtt{r};\omega \,\, \rangle\!\langle \,\, \mathtt{l}{=}\mathtt{r};\overline{\omega} \,]@(obs,use \setminus \{\mathtt{l}\} \cup \{\mathtt{r}\})\phi,\Delta & \text{if } \mathtt{l} \in use \\ \Gamma \Longrightarrow \mathscr{U}[\, \mathtt{l}{=}\mathtt{r};\omega \,\, \rangle\!\langle \,\, \overline{\omega} \,]@(obs,use)\phi,\Delta & \text{otherwise} \end{array}\right)}$$

The assignment rule above comes in two variants. In the symbolic execution phase (first step) both are identical. The difference between both comes to play in the program synthesis phase (second step), i.e., when we instantiate the meta variables for the program and the used variable set.

In the second step, we check if the program variable $\mathtt{l}$ is contained in the *use* set of the premiss, i.e., the variable has been potentially read by the original program after the assignment. If $\mathtt{l}$ is read later-on, then the assignment of the original program (left compartment of the bisimulation modality) is generated for the specialized program. Otherwise the assignment is not generated for the specialized program.

In addition, the used variable set has to be updated, if the assignment was generated. The update used variable set removes first the variable on the left-hand side ($\mathtt{l}$) as it is assigned a new value, and hence, the old value of l is unimportant from that time on. Thereafter, the variable $\mathtt{r}$ on the right-hand side is added to the used variable set (as we read from it) which ensures that the following program syntheses steps will ensure that the correct value of r is computed. The order of the removal and addition is of importance as can be seen for the assignment l=1; where the computed used variable set must contain variable l.

$$\text{ifElse} \quad \frac{\begin{array}{c} \Gamma, \mathcal{U}\, \mathtt{b} \Longrightarrow \mathcal{U}\, [\, \mathtt{p}; \omega \,\,\langle\,\, \overline{\mathtt{p}}; \overline{\omega}\,]\, @\, (obs, use_{\mathtt{p};\omega})\phi, \Delta \\ \Gamma, \mathcal{U}\, \neg\mathtt{b} \Longrightarrow \mathcal{U}\, [\, \mathtt{q}; \omega \,\,\langle\,\, \overline{\mathtt{q}}; \overline{\omega}\,]\, @\, (obs, use_{\mathtt{q};\omega})\phi, \Delta \end{array}}{\begin{array}{c} \Gamma \Longrightarrow \mathcal{U}\, [\, \mathtt{if\ (b)\ \{p\}\ else\ \{q\}}\ \omega \,\,\langle \\ \mathtt{if\ (b)\ \{\overline{p}; \overline{\omega}\}\ else\ \{\overline{q}; \overline{\omega}\}}\,]\, @\, (obs, use_{\mathtt{p};\omega} \cup use_{\mathtt{q};\omega} \cup \{\mathtt{b}\})\phi, \Delta \end{array}}$$

(with b Boolean variable)

On encountering a conditional statement, symbolic execution splits into two branches, namely the then branch and else branch. The generation of the conditional statement will result in a conditional. The guard is the same as used in the original program, the then branch is the generated version of the source then branch continued with the rest of the program after the conditional, and the else branch is analogous to the then branch.

Note that the statements following the conditional statement are symbolically executed on both branches. This leads to duplicated code in the generated program, and, potentially to code size duplication at each occurrence of a conditional statement. One note in advance: code duplication can be avoided when applying a similar technique as presented later in connection with the loop translation rule. However, it is noteworthy that the application of this rule might have also advantages: as discussed in Section 14.1, symbolic execution and partial evaluation can be interleaved resulting in (considerably) smaller execution traces. Interleaving symbolic execution and partial evaluation is orthogonal to the approach presented here and can be combined easily. In several cases this can lead to different and drastically specialized and therefore smaller versions of the remainder program ω and $\overline{\omega}$. The *use* set is extended canonically by joining the *use* sets of the different branches and the guard variable.

loopInvariant

$$\frac{\begin{array}{c} \Gamma \Longrightarrow \mathcal{U}\, inv, \Delta \\ \Gamma, \mathcal{U}\, \mathcal{V}_{mod}(\mathtt{b} \wedge inv) \Longrightarrow \mathcal{U}\, \mathcal{V}_{mod} \\ [\, \mathtt{p} \,\,\langle\,\, \overline{\mathtt{p}}\,]\, @\, (use_1 \cup \{\mathtt{b}\}, use_2)inv, \Delta \\ \Gamma, \mathcal{U}\, \mathcal{V}_{mod}(\neg\mathtt{b} \wedge inv) \Longrightarrow \mathcal{U}\, \mathcal{V}_{mod}[\, \omega \,\,\langle\,\, \overline{\omega}\,]\, @\, (obs, use_1)\phi, \Delta \end{array}}{\Gamma \Longrightarrow \mathcal{U}\, [\, \mathtt{while(b)\{p\}}\ \omega \,\,\langle\,\, \mathtt{while(b)\{\overline{p}\}}\ \overline{\omega}\,]\, @\, (obs, use_1 \cup use_2 \cup \{\mathtt{b}\})\phi, \Delta}$$

(with b a Boolean program variable and *inv* a first-order formula)

The loop invariant rule has, as expected, three premises like in other appearances in this book. Here we are interested in compilation of the analyzed program rather than in proving its correctness. Therefore, it would be sufficient to use *true* as a trivial loop invariant. In this case, the first premise ensuring that the loop invariant is initially valid contributes nothing to the program compilation process and can be ignored (if *true* is used as invariant then it holds trivially).

Using a stronger loop variant allows the synthesis algorithm to be more precise since the context on the sequent then contains more information which can be exploited during program synthesis.

Two things are of importance: the third premise (`use case`) executes only the program following the loop. Furthermore, this code fragment is not executed by any of the other branches and, hence, we avoid unnecessary code duplication. The second observation is that variables read by the program in the third premise may be assigned in the loop body, but not read in the loop body. Obviously, we have to prevent that the assignment rule discards those assignments when compiling the loop body. Therefore, in the *obs* for the second premise (`preserves`), we must include the used variables of the `use case` premise and, for similar reasons, the program variable(s) read by the loop guard. In practice, this is achieved by first executing the `use case` premise of the loop invariant rule and then including the resulting use_1 set in the *obs* of the `preserves` premise. The work flow of the synthesizing loop is shown in Figure 14.6.

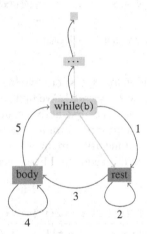

Figure 14.6 Work flow of synthesizing loop

Now we show the program transformation in action.

Example 14.5. Given observable locations *obs*={x}, we perform program transformation for the following program.

```Java
y = y + z;
if (b) {
    y = z++;
    x = z;
} else {
    z = 1;
```

```
    x = y + z;
    y = x;
    x = y + 2;
}
```
—— Java ——

In the first phase, we do symbolic execution using the extended sequent calculus from above We use placeholders sp_i to denote the program to be generated, and placeholders use_i to denote the used variable set. To ease the presentation, we omit postcondition ϕ, as well as the context formulas Γ and Δ. The first active statement is an assignment, so the assignment rule is applied. A conditional is encountered. After the application of ifElse rule, the result is the symbolic execution tree shown in Figure 14.7.

$$\dfrac{\mathcal{U}_1 b \Longrightarrow \mathcal{U}_1[\, \texttt{y=z++;} \ldots \rangle\ sp_2\,]@(\{\texttt{x}\}, use_2) \quad \mathcal{U}_1 \neg b \Longrightarrow \mathcal{U}_1[\, \texttt{z=1;} \ldots \rangle\ sp_3\,]@(\{\texttt{x}\}, use_3)}{\dfrac{\Longrightarrow \{\texttt{y := y+z}\}[\,\texttt{if(b)\{...\}else\{...\}}\ \rangle\ sp_1\,]@(\{\texttt{x}\}, use_1)}{\Longrightarrow [\,\texttt{y = y + z;} \ldots \rangle\ sp_0\,]@(\{\texttt{x}\}, use_0)}}$$

Figure 14.7 Symbolic execution tree until conditional

Now the symbolic execution tree splits into two branches. $\mathcal{U}_1$ denotes the update computed in the previous steps: $\{\texttt{y := y+z}\}$. We first concentrate on the then branch, where the condition b is *True*. The first active statement y=z++; is a complex statement. We decompose it into three simple statements using the postInc rule. Then after a few applications of the assignment rule followed by the emptyBox rule, the symbolic execution tree in this sequential block is shown in Figure 14.8.

$$\dfrac{\mathcal{U}_1 b \Longrightarrow \mathcal{U}_1\{\texttt{t := z}\}\{\texttt{z := z+1}\}\{\texttt{y := t}\}\{\texttt{x := z}\}\phi}{\dfrac{\mathcal{U}_1 b \Longrightarrow \mathcal{U}_1\{\texttt{t := z}\}\{\texttt{z := z+1}\}\{\texttt{y := t}\}\{\texttt{x := z}\}[\, \{\} \ \rangle\ sp_8\,]@(\{\texttt{x}\}, use_8)}{\dfrac{\mathcal{U}_1 b \Longrightarrow \mathcal{U}_1\{\texttt{t := z}\}\{\texttt{z := z+1}\}\{\texttt{y := t}\}[\, \texttt{x=z;} \ \rangle\ sp_7\,]@(\{\texttt{x}\}, use_7)}{\dfrac{\mathcal{U}_1 b \Longrightarrow \mathcal{U}_1\{\texttt{t := z}\}\{\texttt{z := z+1}\}[\, \texttt{y=t;} \ldots \rangle\ sp_6\,]@(\{\texttt{x}\}, use_6)}{\dfrac{\mathcal{U}_1 b \Longrightarrow \mathcal{U}_1\{\texttt{t := z}\}[\, \texttt{z=z+1; y=t;} \ldots \rangle\ sp_5\,]@(\{\texttt{x}\}, use_5)}{\dfrac{\mathcal{U}_1 b \Longrightarrow \mathcal{U}_1[\, \texttt{int t=z; z=z+1; y=t;} \ldots \rangle\ sp_4\,]@(\{\texttt{x}\}, use_4)}{\mathcal{U}_1 b \Longrightarrow \mathcal{U}_1[\, \texttt{y=z++;} \ldots \rangle\ sp_2\,]@(\{\texttt{x}\}, use_2)}}}}}$$

Figure 14.8 Symbolic execution tree of then branch

Now the source program is empty, so we can start generating a program at this node. By applying the emptyBox rule in the other direction, we get sp_8 as {}

(empty program) and $use_8=\{x\}$. The next rule application is assignment. Because $x \in use_8$, the assignment $x = z$; is generated and the used variable set is updated by removing x but adding z. So we have sp_7: $x = z$; and $use_7=\{z\}$. In the next step, despite another assignment rule application, no statement is generated because $y \notin use_7$, and sp_6 and use_6 are identical to sp_7 and use_7. Following 3 more assignment rule applications, in the end we get sp_2: $z = z + 1$; $x = z$; and $use_2=\{z\}$. So $z = z + 1$; $x = z$; is the program synthesized for the then branch.

Analogous to this, we can generate the program for the else branch. After the first phase of symbolic execution, the symbolic execution tree is built as shown in Figure 14.9. In the second phase, the program is synthesized after applying a sequence of assignment rules. The else branch is sp_3:

$$z = 1; \ x = y + z; \ y = x; \ x = y + 2; \ ,$$

with $use_3=\{y\}$.

$$\mathcal{U}_1 \neg b \Longrightarrow \mathcal{U}_1\{z := 1\}\{x := y+z\}\{y := x\}\{x := y+2\}\phi$$

$$\overline{\mathcal{U}_1 \neg b \Longrightarrow \mathcal{U}_1\{z := 1\}\{x := y+z\}\{y := x\}\{x := y+2\}[\ \{\} \ \emptyset \ sp_{12}\ ]@(\{x\}, use_{12})}$$

$$\overline{\mathcal{U}_1 \neg b \Longrightarrow \mathcal{U}_1\{z := 1\}\{x := y+z\}\{y := x\}[\ x=y+2; \ \emptyset \ sp_{11}\ ]@(\{x\}, use_{11})}$$

$$\overline{\mathcal{U}_1 \neg b \Longrightarrow \mathcal{U}_1\{z := 1\}\{x := y+z\}[\ y=x; \ldots \ \emptyset \ sp_{10}\ ]@(\{x\}, use_{10})}$$

$$\overline{\mathcal{U}_1 \neg b \Longrightarrow \mathcal{U}_1\{z := 1\}[\ x=y+z; \ldots \ \emptyset \ sp_9\ ]@(\{x\}, use_9)}$$

$$\overline{\mathcal{U}_1 \neg b \Longrightarrow \mathcal{U}_1[\ z=1; \ldots \ \emptyset \ sp_3\ ]@(\{x\}, use_3)}$$

Figure 14.9 Symbolic execution tree of else branch

Now we have synthesized the program for both branches of the if-then-else statement. Back to the symbolic execution tree shown in Figure 14.7, we can build a conditional by applying the ifElse rule. The result is sp_1:

$$if(b) \ \{ \ z=z+1; \ x=z; \ \} \ else \ \{ \ z=1; \ x=y+z; \ y=x; \ x=y+2; \ \} \ ,$$

and $use_1=\{b,z,y\}$. After a final assignment rule application, the program generated is shown in Listing 14.1.

Remark 14.6. Our approach to program transformation will generate a program that only consists of simple statements. The generated program is optimized to a certain degree, because the used variable set avoids generating unnecessary statements. In this sense, our program transformation framework can be considered as *program specialization*. In fact, during the symbolic execution phase, we can interleave partial evaluation actions, i.e., constant propagation, dead-code elimination, safe field access and type inference (Section 14.1.2). It will result in a more optimized program.

Example 14.7. We specialize the program shown in Example 14.5. In the first phase, symbolic execution is interleaved with simple partial evaluation actions.

```
y = y + z;
if (b) {
  z = z + 1;
  x = z;
} else {
  z = 1;
  x = y + z;
  y = x;
  x = y + 2;
}
```

Listing 14.1 The generated program for Example 14.5

In the first two steps of symbolic execution until conditional, no partial evaluation is involved. The resulting symbolic execution tree is identical to that shown in Figure 14.7.

There are 2 branches in the symbolic execution tree. Symbolical execution of the then branch is the same as in Example 14.5. It builds the same symbolic execution tree (Figure 14.8).

Notice that after executing the statement t = z;, we did not propagate this information to the statement y = t; and rewrite it to y = z;. The reason being z is reassigned in the statement z = z + 1; before y = t;, thus z is not a "constant" and we cannot apply constant propagation. In the program generation phase, we also get sp_2: z = z + 1; x = z; and $use_2 = \{z\}$ for this sequential block.

The first step of symbolic execution of the else branch is the application of the assignment rule on z = 1;. Now we can perform constant propagation and rewrite the following statement x = y + z; into x = y + 1;. The next step is a normal application of the assignment rule on x = y + 1;. Now we apply the assignment rule on y = x;. Since neither x nor y is reassigned before the statement x = y + 2;, x is considered as a "constant" and we do another step of constant propagation. The statement x = y + 2; is rewritten into x = x + 2;. After final application of the assignment rule and emptyBox rule, we get the symbolic execution tree:

$$\mathcal{U}_1 \neg b \Longrightarrow \mathcal{U}_1 \{z := 1\}\{x := y+1\}\{y := x\}\{x := x+2\} @ (\{x\}, \_)$$

$$\mathcal{U}_1 \neg b \Longrightarrow \mathcal{U}_1 \{z := 1\}\{x := y+1\}\{y := x\}\{x := x+2\} [\; \lozenge\; sp_{12}\;] @ (\{x\}, use_{12})$$

$$\mathcal{U}_1 \neg b \Longrightarrow \mathcal{U}_1 \{z := 1\}\{x := y+1\}\{y := x\} [\; x=x+2;\; \lozenge\; sp_{11}\;] @ (\{x\}, use_{11})$$

$$\mathcal{U}_1 \neg b \Longrightarrow \mathcal{U}_1 \{z := 1\}\{x := y+1\} [\; y=x;\ldots\; \lozenge\; sp_{10}\;] @ (\{x\}, use_{10})$$

$$\mathcal{U}_1 \neg b \Longrightarrow \mathcal{U}_1 \{z := 1\} [\; x=y+1;\ldots\; \lozenge\; sp_9\;] @ (\{x\}, use_9)$$

$$\mathcal{U}_1 \neg b \Longrightarrow \mathcal{U}_1 [\; z=1;\ldots\; \lozenge\; sp_3\;] @ (\{x\}, use_3)$$

In the second phase of program generation, after applying the emptyBox rule and 4 times assignment rules, we get sp_3: x = y + 1; x = x + 2; and $use_3 = \{y\}$.

Combining both branches, we finally get the specialized version of the original, shown in Listing 14.2.

```
y = y + z;
if (b) {
  z = z + 1;
  x = z;
}
else {
  x = y + 1;
  x = x + 2;
}
```

Listing 14.2 The generated program for Example 14.7

Compared to the result shown in Listing 14.1, we generated a more optimized program by interleaving partial evaluation actions during symbolic execution phase. Further optimizations can be achieved by involving updates during program generation, which are discussed in [Ji, 2014].

14.3 Implementation and Evaluation

We have a prototype implementation of the program transformation framework named PE-KeY introduced in this chapter.

We applied our prototype partial evaluator also on some examples stemming from the JSpec test suite [Schultz et al., 2003]. One of them is concerned with the computation of the power of an arithmetic expression, as shown in Figure 14.10.

The interesting part is that the arithmetic expression is represented as an abstract syntax tree (AST) structure. The abstract class Binary is the superclass of the two concrete binary operators Add and Mult (the strategies). The Power class can be used to apply a Binary operator op and a neutral value for y times to a base value x, as illustrated by the following expression:

power = new Power(y, new op(), neutral).raise(x)

The actual computation for concrete values is performed on the AST representation. To be more precise, the task was to specialize the program

power = new Power(y, new Mult(), 1).raise(x);

The ac under the assumption that the value of y is constant and equal to 16.

As input formula for PE-KeY we use:

$y \doteq 16 \rightarrow$
   [power=new Power(y,new Mult(),1).raise(x); $\langle$ sp$_{res}$]@$(obs, use)post$

with *post* denoting an unspecified predicate which can neither be proven nor disproved. PE-KeY then executes the program symbolically and extracts the specialized program sp$_{res}$ as power = (...((x*x)*x)*...)*x; (or power = x^{16}). The

```
class Power extends Object{
 int exp;
 Binary op;
 int neutral;

 Power(int exp, Binary op,
        int neutral) {
   super();
   this.exp = exp;
   this.op = op;
   this.neutral = neutral;
 }

 int raise(int base) {
   int res = neutral;
   for (int i=0; i<exp; i++) {
     res = op.eval( base, res );
   }
   return res;
 }
}
```

```
class Binary extends Object {
  Binary() { super(); }
  int eval(int x, int y) {
    return this.eval(x, y);
  }
}

class Add extends Binary {
  Add() { super(); }
  int eval(int x, int y) {
    return x+y;
  }
}

class Mult extends Binary {
  Mult() { super(); }
  int eval(int x, int y) {
    return x*y;
  }
}
```

Figure 14.10 Source code of the Power example as found in the JSpec suite

achieved result is a simple int-typed expression without the intermediate creation of the abstract syntax tree and should provide a significantly better performance than executing the original program.

14.4 Conclusion

In this chapter we described how symbolic execution and thus verification can benefit from interleaving partial evaluation and symbolic execution steps. This interleaving results in smaller, less redundant proof and symbolic execution trees making these easier to comprehend. This is advantageous for both manual interaction with the prover itself and for code reviews/debugging using the symbolic execution debugger (see Chapter 11).

We also presented how to integrate verifiably correct compilation of programs within our verification framework based on JavaDL. We showcased our application along the implementation of a partial evaluator that produces verifiably correct specialized programs. Our approach can make use of the full power of our verifier and thus produce optimized [Ji, 2014] programs. [Ji and Hähnle, 2014] adapt the approach to implement an information flow analysis.

Part IV
The KeY System in Action

Chapter 15
Using the KeY Prover

Wolfgang Ahrendt and Sarah Grebing

15.1 Introduction

This whole book is about the KeY *approach* and *framework*. This chapter now focuses on the KeY *prover*, and that entirely from the user's perspective. Naturally, the graphical user interface (GUI) will play an important role here. However, the chapter is not all about that. Via the GUI, the system and the user communicate, and interactively manipulate, several artifacts of the framework, like formulas of the used logic, proofs within the used calculus, elements of the used specification languages, among others. Therefore, these artifacts are (in parts) very important when using the system. Even if all of them have their own chapter/section in this book, they will appear here as well, in a somewhat superficial manner, with pointers given to in-depth discussions in other parts.

We aim at a largely self-contained presentation, allowing the reader to follow the chapter, and to *start* using the KeY prover, without necessarily having to read other chapters of the book before. The reader, however, can gain a better understanding by following the references we give to other parts of the book. In any case, we do recommend to read Chapter 1 beforehand, where the reader can get a picture of what KeY is all about. The other chapters are *not* treated as prerequisites to this one, which of course imposes limitations on how far we can go here. Had we built on the knowledge and understanding provided by the other chapters, we would be able to guide the user much further into the application of KeY to larger as well as more difficult scenarios. However, this would raise the threshold for getting started with the prover.

The KeY framework was designed from the beginning to be usable *without* having to read a thick book first. Software verification is a difficult task anyhow. Neither the system nor the used artifacts (like the logic) should add to that difficulty, and are designed to instead lower the threshold for the user. The used logic, *dynamic logic* (DL), features transparency w.r.t. the programs to be verified, such that the code literally appears in the formulas, allowing the user to relate back to the program when proving properties about it.

© Springer International Publishing AG 2016
W. Ahrendt et al. (Eds.): Deductive Software Verification, LNCS 10001, pp. 495–539, 2016
DOI: 10.1007/978-3-319-49812-6_15

The *taclet* language for the declarative implementation of both, rules and lemmas, is kept so simple that we can well use a rule's declaration as a tooltip when the user is about to select the rule. The calculus itself is, however, complicated, as it captures the complicated semantics of Java. Still, most of these complications do not concern the user, as they are handled in a fully automated way. Powerful strategies relieve the user from tedious, time consuming tasks, particularly when performing *symbolic execution*.

In spite of a high degree of automation, in many cases there are significant, nontrivial tasks left for the user. It is the very purpose of the GUI to support those tasks well.

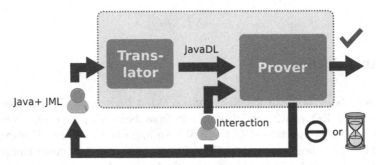

Figure 15.1 Verification process using the KeY system

The general proof process using the KeY system is illustrated in Figure 15.1. The user provides Java source code with annotations written in JML and passes them to the KeY system, which translates these artifacts into a proof obligation in Java Dynamic Logic. Now the user is left with the choice of trying to let the prover verify the problem fully automatically or of starting interactively by applying calculus rules to the proof obligation. If the user chooses to start the automated proof search strategy offered by the prover, the result can be one of the two: either the prover succeeds in finding a proof or the prover stops, because it was not able to apply more rules automatically (either because the maximal number of proof steps has been reached or the prover cannot find anymore applicable rules). This is the point in the proof process, where the user gets involved. The user now has to decide whether to guide the prover in finding a proof by applying certain rules (or proof steps) by hand or whether the look for mistakes in the annotation or the corresponding source code, which is one reason why the prover is not able to apply rules automatically anymore. Observing a wrong program behavior or specification leads the user to the correction of the mistake in the source code or annotation and to start the whole proof process over again.

When proving a property which is too involved to be handled fully automatically, certain steps need to be performed in an interactive manner. This is the case when either the automated strategies are exhausted, or else when the user deliberately performs a strategic step (like a case distinction) manually, *before* automated strategies are invoked (again). In the case of human-guided proof steps, the user is asked to solve tasks like: *selecting a proof rule* to be applied, *providing instantiations for* the proof rule's *schema variables*, or *providing instantiations for quantified variables* of the logic. The system, and its advanced GUI, are designed to support these steps well. For instance, the selection of the right rule, out of over 1500(!), is greatly simplified by allowing the user to highlight any syntactical subentity of the proof goal simply by positioning the mouse. A dynamic context menu will offer only the few proof rules which apply to this entity. Furthermore, these menus feature tooltips for each rule pointed to. These tooltips will be described in 15.2.1. When it comes to interactive variable instantiation, *drag-and-drop* mechanisms greatly simplify the usage of the instantiation dialogues, and in some cases even allow to omit explicit rule selection. Other supported forms of interaction in the context of proof construction are the inspection of proof trees, the pruning of proof branches, and arbitrary undoing of proof steps.

Performing interactive proof steps is, however, only one of the many functionalities offered by the KeY system. Also, these features play their role relatively late in the process of verifying programs. Other functionalities are (we go backwards in the verification process): controlling the automated strategies, customizing the calculus (for instance by choosing either of the mathematical or the Java semantics for integers), and generating proof obligations from specifications. Working with the KeY system has therefore many aspects, and there are many ways to give an introduction into those. In the following, we focus on the KeY prover only, taking an 'inside out' approach, describing *how* the prover and the user communicate *which artifacts* for *which purpose* with each other. In addition hints for the user are provided on how to proceed in the verification process interactively, when automation stops.

In general, we will discuss the usage of the system by means of rather (in some cases extremely) simple examples. Thereby, we try to provide a good understanding of the various ingredients before their combination (seemingly) complicates things. Also, the usage of the prover will sometimes be illustrated by at first performing basic steps manually, and demonstrating automation thereafter. Please note that the toy examples used all over this chapter serve the purpose of a step by step introduction of the concepts and usage of the KeY system. They are not suitable for giving any indication of the capabilities of the system. (See Chapter 16 instead.)

Before we start, there is one last basic issue to discuss at this point. The evolution of both, the KeY *project* in general, and the KeY *system* in particular, has been very dynamic up to now, and will continue to be so. As far as the *system* and its GUI is concerned, it has been constantly improved and will be modified in the future as well. The author faces the difficult task of not letting the description of the tool's usage depend too much on its current appearance. The grouping of menus, the visual placement of panes and tabs, the naming of operations or options, all those can potentially change. Also, on the more conceptual level, things like the configuration policy for strategies and rule sets, among others, cannot be assumed to be frozen for all times. Even the theoretical grounds will develop further, as KeY is indeed a research project. A lot of ongoing research does not yet show in the current public release of the KeY system. The problem of describing a dynamic system is approached from three sides. First, we will continue to keep available the book release of the system, 2.6, on the KeY book's web page. Second, in order to not restrict the reader to that release only, we will try to minimize the dependency of the material on the current version of the system and its GUI. Third, whenever we talk about the specific location of a pane, tab, or menu item, or about key/mouse combinations, we stress the dynamic nature of such information in this way.

For instance, we might say that "one can trigger the run of the automated proof search strategy which is restricted to a highlighted term/formula by $\boxed{\texttt{Shift}}$ + click on it." There is a separate document shipped with the KeY system, the *Quicktour*[1] which is updated more often and describes the current GUI and features of the KeY system.

Menu navigation will be displayed by connecting the cascaded menu entries with "→", e.g., **Options** → **SMT Solvers Options**. Note that menu navigation is release dependent as well. Most functionalities in the KeY system can also be activated by keystrokes in order to be more efficient while performing proof tasks.

This chapter is meant for being read with the KeY system up and running. We want to explore the system *together* with the reader, and reflect on whatever shows up along the path. Downloads of KeY, particularly 2.6, the release version related to this book, are available on the project page, www.key-project.org. The example input files, which the reader frequently is asked to load, can be found on the web page for this book, www.key-project.org/thebook2. The example files can also be accessed via the **File** → **Load examples** as well. However, for this chapter we assume the reader to have downloaded the example files from the web-page and extracted them to a folder in the reader's system.

15.2 Exploring KeY Artifacts and Prover Simultaneously

Together with the reader, we want to open, for the first time, the KeY system, in order to perform first steps and understand the basic structure of the interface. There are two ways to start the stand-alone KeY prover. Either you download the archive of KeY 2.6, unpack it, and in the key directory execute the key.jar file, in the standard way .jar files are executed in your system and setup. Or you execute KeY directly from your browser, by navigating to the **webstart** link of KeY 2.6, and simply click it.

In both cases, the **KeY–Prover** main window pops up. Like many window-based GUIs, the main window offers several menus, a toolbar, and a few panes, partly tabbed. Instead of enumerating those components one after another, we immediately load an example to demonstrate some basic interaction with the prover. Please note that most of the GUI components are labeled with tooltips, which are visible when hovering over that component. They give useful information about the features of the system.

---

[1] Available from the Download pages at www.key-project.org.

15.2.1 *Exploring Basic Notions And Usage: Building A Propositional Proof*

In general, the KeY prover is made for proving formulas in *dynamic logic* (DL), an extension of *first-order logic*, which in turn is an extension of *propositional logic*. We start with a very simple propositional formula, when introducing the usage of the KeY prover, because a lot of key concepts can already be discussed when proving the most simple theorem.

Loading the First Problem

The formula we prove first is contained in the file andCommutes.key. In general, .key is the suffix for what we call *problem files*, which may, among other things, contain a formula to be proven. (The general format of .key files is documented in Appendix B.) For now, we look into the file andCommutes.key itself (using your favorite text editor):

```
——— KeY Problem File ————————————————————————————————————————————
\predicates {
        p;
        q;
}
\problem {
        (p & q) -> (q & p)
}
————————————————————————————————————————————— KeY Problem File ———
```

The \problem block contains the formula to be proven (with -> denoting the logical implication and & denoting the logical and). In general, all functions, predicates, and variables appearing in a problem formula are to be declared beforehand, which, in our case here, is done in the \predicates block. We load this file by selecting **File** → **Load** (or selecting 📁 in the tool bar) and navigating through the opened file browser. The system not only loads the selected .key file, but also the whole calculus, i.e., its rules, as well as locations referenced by the file. This includes the source folder and its subdirectories.

Reading the Initial Sequent

Afterwards, we see the text ==> p & q -> q & p displayed in the **Current Goal** pane. This seems to be merely the \problem formula, but actually, the arrow ==> turns it into a *sequent*. KeY uses a sequent calculus, meaning that sequents are the basic artifact on which the calculus operates. Sequents have the form

$$\phi_1, \ldots, \phi_n \Longrightarrow \phi_{n+1}, \ldots, \phi_m$$

with $\phi_1, \ldots, \phi_n$ and $\phi_{n+1}, \ldots, \phi_m$ being two (possibly empty) comma-separated lists of formulas, distinguished by the sequent arrow $\Longrightarrow$ (written as ==> in both input and output of the KeY system). The intuitive meaning of a sequent is: if we assume all formulas $\phi_1, \ldots, \phi_n$ to hold, then *at least one* of the formulas $\phi_{n+1}, \ldots, \phi_m$ holds. In our particular calculus, the order of formulas within $\phi_1, \ldots, \phi_n$ and within $\phi_{n+1}, \ldots, \phi_m$ does not matter. Therefore, we can for instance write $\Gamma \Longrightarrow \phi \rightarrow \psi, \Delta$ to refer to sequents where *any* of the right-hand side formulas is an implication. Γ and Δ are both used to refer to arbitrary, and sometimes empty, lists of formulas. We refer to Chapter 2, Section 2.2.2, for a proper introduction of a (simple first-order) sequent calculus. The example used there is exactly the one we use here. We recommend to double-check the following steps with the on paper proof given there.

We start proving the given sequent with the KeY system, however in a very interactive manner, step by step introducing and explaining the different aspects of the calculus and system. This purpose is really the *only* excuse to *not* let KeY prove this automatically.

Even if we perform all steps manually for now, we want the system to minimize interaction, e.g., by not asking the user for an instantiation if the system can find one itself. For this, please make sure that the menu item **Minimize interaction** option (at **Options** → **Minimize interaction**) is checked for the whole course of this chapter.

Applying the First Rule

The sequent ==> p & q -> q & p displayed in the **Current Goal** pane states that the formula p & q -> q & p holds *unconditionally* (no formula left of ==>), and *without alternatives* (no other formula right of ==>). This is an often encountered pattern for proof obligations when starting a proof: sequents with empty left-hand sides, and only the single formula we want to prove on the right-hand side. It is the duty of the *sequent calculus* to take such formulas apart, step by step, while collecting assumptions on the left-hand side, or alternatives on the right-hand side, until the sheer shape of a sequent makes it trivially true, which is the case when *both sides have a formula in common*[2]. (For instance, the sequent $\phi_1, \phi_2 \Longrightarrow \phi_3, \phi_1$ is trivially true. Assuming both, ϕ_1 and ϕ_2, indeed implies that "at least one of ϕ_3 and ϕ_1" holds, namely ϕ_1.) It is such primitive shapes which we aim at when proving.

'Taking apart' a formula refers to breaking it up at its top-level operator. The displayed formula p & q -> q & p does not anymore show the brackets of the formula in the problem file. Still, for identifying the leading operator it is not required to memorize the built in operator precedences. Instead, the term structure gets clear by moving the mouse pointer back and forth over the symbols in the formula area, as the subformula (or subterm) under the symbol currently pointed at always gets highlighted. In general to get the whole sequent highlighted, the user needs to point to the sequent arrow ==>. To get the whole formula highlighted in our example, the

---

[2] There are two more cases, which are covered in Section 15.2.2 on page 513.

user needs to point to the implication symbol ->, so this is where we can break up
the formula.

Next we want to *select a rule* which is meant specifically to break up an implication
on the right-hand side. A left mouse-click on -> will open a context menu for rule
selection, offering several rules applicable to this sequent, among them **impRight**,
which in the usual text book presentation looks like this:

$$\text{impRight} \quad \frac{\Gamma, \phi \Longrightarrow \psi, \Delta}{\Gamma \Longrightarrow \phi \to \psi, \Delta}$$

The conclusion of the rule, $\Gamma \Longrightarrow \phi \to \psi, \Delta$, is not simply a sequent, but a sequent
schema. In particular, ϕ and ψ are *schema variables* for formulas, to be instantiated
with the two subformulas of the implication formula appearing on the right-hand
side of the current sequent. (Γ and Δ denote the sets of all formulas on the left- and
right-hand side, respectively, which the rule is *not* concerned with. In this rule, Γ
are all formulas on the left-hand side, and Δ are all formulas on the right-hand side
except the matching implication formula.)

As for any other rule, the *logical meaning* of this rule is downwards (concerning
validity): if a sequent matching the premiss $\Gamma, \phi \Longrightarrow \psi, \Delta$ is valid, we can conclude
that the corresponding instance of the conclusion $\Gamma \Longrightarrow \phi \to \psi, \Delta$ is valid as well.
On the other hand, the *operational meaning* during proof construction goes upwards:
the problem of proving a sequent which matches $\Gamma \Longrightarrow \phi \to \psi, \Delta$ is reduced to
the problem of proving the corresponding instance of $\Gamma, \phi \Longrightarrow \psi, \Delta$. During proof
construction, a rule is therefore applicable only to situations where the current goal
matches the rule's conclusion. The proof will then be extended by the new sequent
resulting from the rule's premiss. (This will be generalized to rules with multiple
premisses later on.)

To see this in action, we click at **impRight** in order to apply the rule to the current
goal. This produces the new sequent p & q ==> q & p, which becomes the new
current goal. By *goal*, we mean a sequent to which no rule is yet applied. By *current
goal* we mean the goal in focus, to which rules can be applied currently (the node
selected in the proof tree in the **Proof** tab).

Inspecting the Emerging Proof

The user may have noticed the **Proof** tab as part of the tabbed pane in the lower left
corner. It displays the structure of the current (unfinished) proof as a tree. All nodes
of the current proof are numbered consecutively, and labeled either by the name of
the rule which was applied to that node, or by **OPEN GOAL** in case of a goal. The
selected and highlighted node is always the one which is detailed in the **Current Goal**
or **inner node** pane in the right part of the window. So far, this was always a goal,
such that the pane was called **Current Goal**. But if the user clicks at an *inner node*, in
our case on the one labeled with **impRight**, that node gets detailed in the right pane

now called **Inner Node**. It can not only show the sequent of that node, but also, if the checkbox **Show taclet info** is selected, the upcoming rule application.

Please observe that the (so far linear) proof tree displayed in the **Proof** tab has its root on the top, and grows downwards, as it is common for trees displayed in GUIs. On paper, however, the traditional way to depict sequent proofs is bottom-up, as is done all over in this book. In that view, the structure of the current proof (with the upper sequent being the current goal) is:

$$\frac{p \wedge q \Longrightarrow q \wedge p}{\Longrightarrow p \wedge q \rightarrow q \wedge p}$$

For the on-paper presentation of the proof to be developed, we refer to Chapter 2.

Understanding the First Taclet

With the inner node still highlighted in the **Proof** tab, we click onto the checkbox **Show taclet info (Inner Nodes only)** in the left lower corner of the **Proof** tab. We now obtain the rule information in the **Inner Node** pane, saying (simplified):

—— KeY Output ————————————————————————
```
impRight {
  \find ( ==> b -> c )
  \replacewith ( b ==> c )
  \heuristics ( alpha )
}
```
————————————————————————— KeY Output ——

What we see here is what is called a *taclet*. Taclets are a domain specific language for programming sequent calculus rules, developed as part of the KeY project. The depicted taclet is the one which in the KeY system *defines* the rule **impRight**. In this chapter, we give just a hands-on explanation of the few taclets we come across. For a good introduction and discussion of the taclet framework, we refer to Chapter 4.

The taclet **impRight** corresponds to the traditional sequent calculus style presentation of **impRight** we gave earlier. The schema b -> c in the \find clause indicates that the taclet is applicable to sequents if one of its formulas is an implication, with b and c being schema variables matching the two subformulas of the implication. Further down the **Inner Node** pane, we see that b and c are indeed of kind \formula:

—— KeY Output ————————————————————————
```
\schemaVariables {
  \formula b;
  \formula c;
}
```
————————————————————————— KeY Output ——

The sequent arrow ==> in \find(==> b -> c) further restricts the applicability of the taclet to the *top-level*[3] of the sequent only. For this example the taclet is only applicable to implications on the *right-hand side* of the sequent (as b -> c appears right of ==>). The \replacewith clause describes how to construct the *new* sequent from the current one: first the matching implication (here p & q -> q & p) gets deleted, and then the subformulas matching b and c (here p & q and q & p) are added to the sequent. To which side of the sequent p & q or q & p, respectively, are added is indicated by the relative position of b and c w.r.t. ==> in the argument of \replacewith. The result is the new sequent p & q ==> q & p. It is a very special case here that \find(==> b -> c) matches the whole old sequent, and \replacewith(b ==> c) matches the whole new sequent. Other formulas could appear in the old sequent. Those would remain unchanged in the new sequent. In other words, the Γ and Δ traditionally appearing in on-paper presentations of sequent rules are omitted in the taclet formalism. (Finally, with \heuristics clause the taclet declares itself to be part of some heuristics, here the alpha heuristics which defines the priority with which the rule is applied during the execution of the automated strategies.) The discussed taclet is the complete definition of the **impRight** rule in KeY, and all the system knows about the rule. The complete list of available taclets can be viewed in the **Info** tab as part of the tabbed pane in the lower left corner, within the **Rules** →**Taclet Base** folder. To test this, we click that folder and scroll down the list of taclets, until **impRight**, on which we can click to be shown the same taclet we have just discussed. It might feel scary to see the sheer mass of taclets available. Please note, however, that the vast majority of taclets is never in the picture when *interactively* applying a rule in any practical usage of the KeY system. Instead, most taclets, especially those related to symbolic execution, are usually applied automatically.

Backtracking the Proof

So far, we performed only one tiny little step in the proof. Our aim was, however, to introduce some very basic elements of the framework and system. In fact, we even go one step back, with the help of the system. For that, we make sure that the **OPEN GOAL** is selected (by clicking on it in the **Proof** tab). We now *undo* the proof step which led to this goal, by clicking at ⟲ (Goal Back) in the task bar or using the short cut Ctrl + Z. In this example, this action will put us back in the situation we started in, which is confirmed by both the **Current Goal** pane and the **Proof** tab. Please observe that **Goal Back** reverts always only the last rule application and not for instance, all rules applied automatically by the proof search strategy.

---

[3] Modulo leading updates, see Section 15.2.3.

Viewing and Customizing Taclet Tooltips

Before performing the next steps in our proof, we take a closer look at the *tooltips* for rule selection. (The reader may already have noticed those tooltips earlier.) If we again click at the implication symbol -> appearing in the current goal, and *pre*select the **impRight** rule in the opened context menu simply by placing the mouse at **impRight**, without clicking yet, we get to see a tooltip, displaying something similar to the **impRight** taclet discussed above.

The exact tooltip text depends on option settings which the user can configure. Depending on those settings, what is shown in the tooltip is just the taclet as is, or a certain 'significant' part of it. Note that, in either case, schema variables can be already instantiated in what is shown in tooltips, also depending on the settings. For this chapter we control the options actively here, and discuss the respective outcome. We open the tooltip options window by **View → ToolTip options**, and make sure that all parts of taclets are displayed by making sure the **pretty-print whole taclet ...** checkbox is checked.

The effect of a taclet to the current proof situation is captured by tooltips where the schema variables from the \find argument are already instantiated by their respective matching formula or term. We achieve this by setting the **Maximum size ... of tooltips ... with schema variable instantiations displayed ...** to, say, 40 and have the **show uninstantiated taclet** checkbox unchecked. When trying the tooltip for **impRight** with this, we see something like the original taclet, however with b and c already being instantiated with p & q and q & p, respectively:

—— Tooltip ——

```
impRight {
  \find ( ==> p & q -> q & p )
  \replacewith ( p & q ==> q & p )
  \heuristics ( alpha )
}
```

——— Tooltip ——

This instantiated taclet-tooltip tells us the following: if we clicked on the rule name, the formula p & q -> q & p, which we \find somewhere on the *right-hand side* of the sequent (see the formula's relative position compared to ==> in the \find argument), would be \replace(d)with the two formulas p & q and q & p, where the former would be added to the *left-hand side*, and the latter to the *right-hand side* of the sequent (see their relative position compared to ==> in the \replacewith argument). Please observe that, in this particular case, where the sequent only contains the matched formula, the arguments of \find and \replacewith which are displayed in the tooltip happen to be the *entire* old, respectively new, sequent. This is not the case in general. The same tooltip would show up when preselecting **impRight** on the sequent: r ==> p & q -> q & p, s.

A closer look at the tooltip text in its current form, reveals that the whole \find clause actually is redundant information for the user, as it is essentially identical with the anyhow highlighted text within the **Current Goal** pane. Also, the taclet's name is already clear from the preselected rule name in the context menu. On top of that, the \heuristics clause is actually irrelevant for the *interactive* selection of the rule. The only nonredundant piece of information in this case is therefore the \replacewith clause. Accordingly, the tooltips can be reduced to the minimum which is relevant for supporting the selection of the appropriate rule by unchecking **pretty-print whole taclet ...** option again. The whole tooltip for **impRight** is the one-liner:

```
—— Tooltip ——————————————————————————————
\replacewith ( p & q ==> q & p )
——————————————————————————————— Tooltip ——
```

In general, the user might play around with different tooltip options in order to see which settings are most helpful. However, for the course of this chapter, please open again the **View → ToolTip options** again, set the "Maximum size ... of tooltips ... with schema variable instantiations displayed ..." to 50 and check both checkboxes, "pretty-print whole taclet ..." as well as "show uninstantiated taclet." Nevertheless, we will not print the \heuristics part of taclets in this text further on.

Splitting Up the Proof

We apply **impRight** and consider the new goal p & q ==> q & p. For further decomposition we could break up the conjunctions on either sides of the sequent. By first selecting q & p on the right-hand side, we are offered the rule **andRight**, among others. The corresponding tooltip shows the following taclet:

```
—— Tooltip ——————————————————————————————
andRight {
  \find ( ==> b & c )
  \replacewith ( ==> b );
  \replacewith ( ==> c )
}
——————————————————————————————— Tooltip ——
```

Here we see *two* \replacewiths, telling us that this taclet will construct *two* new goals from the old one, meaning that this is a *branching rule*. Written as a sequent calculus rule, it looks like this:

$$\text{andRight} \; \frac{\Gamma \Longrightarrow \phi, \Delta \qquad \Gamma \Longrightarrow \psi, \Delta}{\Gamma \Longrightarrow \phi \land \psi, \Delta}$$

We now generalize the earlier description of the meaning of rules, to also cover branching rules. The *logical meaning* of a rule is downwards: if a certain instantiation of the rule's schema variables makes *all* premises valid, then the corresponding instantiation of the conclusion is valid as well. Accordingly, the *operational meaning* during proof construction goes upwards. The problem of proving a goal which matches the conclusion is reduced to the problem of proving *all* the (accordingly instantiated) premises. If we apply **andRight** in the system, the **Proof** tab shows the proof branching into two different **Cases**. In fact, both branches feature an **OPEN GOAL**. At least one of them is currently visible in the **Proof** tab, and highlighted to indicate that this is the new current goal, being detailed in the **Current Goal** pane as usual. The other **OPEN GOAL** might be hidden in the **Proof** tab, as the branches *not* leading to the current goal appear *collapsed* in the **Proof** tab by default. A collapsed/expanded branch can however be expanded/collapsed by clicking on ⊞/⊟.[4] If we expand the yet collapsed branch, we see the full structure of the proof, with both **OPEN GOAL**s being displayed. We can even switch the current goal by clicking on any of the **OPEN GOAL**s.[5]

An on-paper presentation of the current proof would look like this:

$$\frac{\dfrac{p \wedge q \Longrightarrow q \qquad p \wedge q \Longrightarrow p}{p \wedge q \Longrightarrow q \wedge p}}{\Longrightarrow p \wedge q \to q \wedge p}$$

The reader might compare this presentation with the proof presented in the **Proof** tab by again clicking on the different nodes (or by clicking just anywhere within the **Proof** tab, and browsing the proof using the arrow keys).

There are also several other mechanisms in the KeY system which help inspecting the current proof state. Instead of expanding/collapsing whole branches, it is also possible to hide intermediate proof steps in the current proof tree. This can be done by right-clicking onto the proof tree in the **Proof** tab and selecting the context menu entry **Hide Intermediate Proofsteps**. This results in a more top-level view on the proof tree – only branching nodes, closed and open goals are displayed. Still, some proof trees tend to get quite large with a lot of open and closed goals. For a better overview over the open goals, there is also an option to hide closed goals in the **Proof** tab. It can be accessed similar to the **Hide Intermediate Proofsteps** option. The KeY system incorporates another feature supporting the comprehension of the proof, allowing for textual comments to the proof nodes. This feature is accessible by right clicking onto the proof node in the proof tree and choosing the menu entry **Edit Notes**. A dialog appears in which the user can enter a note which is then attached to the chosen proof node. This note can later be read when hovering with the mouse over the chosen proof node.

Closing the First Branch

To continue, we select **OPEN GOAL** p & q ==> q again. Please recall that we want to reach a sequent where identical formulas appear on both sides (as such sequents are trivially true). We are already very close to that, just that p & q remains to be

---

[4] Bulk expansion, and bulk collapsing, of proof branches is offered by a context menu via right click on any node in the **Proof** tab.

[5] Another way of getting an overview over the open goals, and switch the current goal, is offered by the **Goals** tab.

decomposed. Clicking at & offers the rule **andLeft**, as usual with the tooltip showing the taclet, here:

```
—— Tooltip ——————————————————————————————
andLeft {
  \find ( b & c ==> )
  \replacewith ( b, c ==> )
}
——————————————————————————————— Tooltip ——
```

which corresponds to the sequent calculus rule:

$$\text{andLeft } \frac{\Gamma, \phi, \psi \Longrightarrow \Delta}{\Gamma, \phi \wedge \psi \Longrightarrow \Delta}$$

We apply this rule, and arrive at the sequent `p, q ==> q`. We have arrived where we wanted to be, at a goal which is *trivially true* by the plain fact that one formula appears on both sides, *regardless* of how that formula looks like. (Of course, the sequents we were coming across in this example were all trivially true in an intuitive sense, but always only because of the particular form of the involved formulas.) In the sequent calculus, sequents of the form $\Gamma, \phi \Longrightarrow \phi, \Delta$ are considered valid *without any need of further reduction.*

This argument is also represented by a rule, namely:

$$\text{close } \frac{*}{\Gamma, \phi \Longrightarrow \phi, \Delta}$$

Rules with no premiss *close* the branch leading to the goal they are applied to, or, as we say in short (and a little imprecise), *close the goal* they are applied to.

The representation of this rule as a taclet calls for two new keywords which we have not seen so far. One is \closegoal, having the effect that taclet application does not produce any new goal, but instead closes the current proof branch. The other keyword is \assumes, which is meant for expressing assumptions on formulas *other than* the one matching the \find clause. Note that, so far, the applicability of rules always depended on *one* formula only. The applicability of **close**, however, depends on *two* formulas (or, more precisely, on two formula occurrences). The second formula is taken care of by the \assumes clause in the **close** taclet:

```
—— Taclet ————————————————————————————————
close {
  \assumes ( b ==> )
  \find ( ==> b )
  \closegoal
}
——————————————————————————————— Taclet ——
```

Note that this taclet is not symmetric (as opposed to the **close** sequent rule given above). To apply it interactively on our **Current Goal** p, q ==> q, we have to put the *right-hand side* q into focus (cf. \find(==> b)). But the \assumes clause makes the taclet applicable only in the presence of further formulas, in this case the identical formula on the *left-hand side* (cf. \assumes(b ==>)).

This discussion of the **close** sequent rule and the corresponding **close** taclet shows that taclets are more fine grained than rules. They contain more information, and consequently there is more than one way to represent a sequent rule as a taclet. To see another way of representing the above sequent rule **close** by a taclet, the reader might click on the q on the *left-hand side* of p, q ==> q, and preselect the taclet **close**.

The tooltip will show the taclet:

—— Tooltip ——

```
closeAntec {
  \assumes ( ==> b )
  \find ( b ==> )
  \closegoal
}
```

—— Tooltip ——

We, however, proceed by applying the taclet **close** on the right-hand side formula q. After this step, the **Proof** pane tells us that the proof branch that has just been under consideration is closed, which is indicated by that branch ending with a **Closed goal** node colored green. The system has automatically changed focus to the next **OPEN GOAL**, which is detailed in the **Current Goal** pane as the sequent p & q ==> p.

Pruning the Proof Tree

We apply **andLeft** to the & on the left, in the same fashion as we did on the other branch. Afterwards, we *could* close the new goal p, q ==> p, but we refrain from doing so. Instead, we compare the two branches, the closed and the open one, which both have a node labeled with **andLeft**. When inspecting these two nodes again (by simply clicking on them), we see that we broke up the same formula, the left-hand side formula p & q, on both branches. It appears that we branched the proof too early. Instead, we should have applied the (nonbranching) **andLeft**, once and for all, before the (branching) **andRight**. *In general it is a good strategy to delay proof branching as much as possible and thereby avoiding double work on the different branches.* Without this strategy, more realistic examples with hundreds or thousands of proof steps would become completely unfeasible.

In our tiny example here, it seems not to matter much, but it is instructive to apply the late splitting also here. We want to redo the proof from the point where we split too early. Instead of reloading the problem file, we can *prune* the proof at the node labeled with **andRight** by right-click on that node, and selecting the context menu entry **Prune Proof**. As a result, large parts of the proof are pruned away, and the second node, with the sequent p & q ==> q & p, becomes the **Current Goal** again.

Closing the First Proof

This time, we apply **andLeft** *before* we split the proof via **andRight**. We close the two remaining goals, p, q ==> q and p, q ==> p by applying **close** to the right-hand q and p, respectively. By closing all branches, we have actually closed the entire proof, as we can see from the **Proof closed** window popping up now.

Altogether, we have proven the validity of the *sequent* at the root of the proof tree, here ==> p & q -> q & p. As this sequent has only one formula, placed on the right-hand side, we have actually proven validity of that formula p & q -> q & p, the one stated as the \problem in the file we loaded.

Proving the Same Formula Automatically

As noted earlier, the reason for doing all the steps in the above proof manually was that we wanted to learn about the system and the used artifacts. Of course, one would otherwise prove such a formula automatically, which is what we do in the following.

Before loading the same problem again, we can choose whether we abandon the current proof, or alternatively keep it in the system. Abandoning a proof would be achieved via the main menu entry: **Proof** → **Abandon** or the shortcut $\boxed{\texttt{Ctrl}}$ + $\boxed{\texttt{W}}$. It is however possible to keep several (finished or unfinished) proofs in the system, so we suggest to start the new proof while keeping the old one. This will allow us to compare the proofs more easily.

Loading the file andCommutes.key again can be done in the same fashion as before or alternatively via the menu entry **Reload**, the toolbar button ↻ or the shortcut $\boxed{\texttt{Ctrl}}$ + $\boxed{\texttt{R}}$. Afterwards, we see a second *'proof task'* being displayed in the **Proofs** pane. One can even switch between the different tasks by clicking in that pane. The newly opened proof shows the **Current Goal** ==> p & q -> q & p, just as last time. For the automated proof process with KeY, we are able to set options in the **Proof Search Strategy** tab. One option is the slider controlling the maximal number of automated rule applications. It should be at least **1000**, which will suffice for all examples in this chapter.

By pressing the "Start/Stop automated proof search" button ▷ in the toolbar, we start the automated proof search strategy. A complete proof is constructed immediately. Its shape (see **Proof** tab) depends heavily on the current implementation of the proof search strategy and the use of the *One Step Simplifier* ➡. One step simplification in the KeY system means that the automated prover performs several simplification rules applicable at once by a single rule application. One example for such a simplification rule is the rule **eq_and** which simplifies the formula true & true to true. Which rules the prover has used can be found in the proof tree in a node labeled with **One Step Simplification**. This option comes in very handy when proofs tend to get large. Because of the summarization of simplification rules, the proof tree is more readable. For the following examples we assume that the *One Step Simplifier* is turned off (the toolbar icon ▤ is unselected) and we point out to the reader when to toggle it to on. However, the automatically created proof will most likely look different from the proof we constructed interactively before. For a comparison, we switch between the tasks in the **Proofs** pane.

Rewrite Rules

With the current implementation of the proof search strategy, only the first steps of the automatically constructed proof, **impRight** and **andLeft**, are identical with the interactively constructed proof from above, leading to the sequent p, q ==> q & p. After that, the proof does *not* branch, but instead uses the rule **replace_known_left**:

—— Taclet ——
```
replace_known_left {
   \assumes ( b ==>  )
   \find ( b )
   \sameUpdateLevel
   \replacewith ( true )
}
```
—— Taclet ——

It has the effect that any formula (\find(b)) which has *another appearance* on the left side of the sequent (\assumes(b ==>)) can be replaced by true. Note that the \find clause does not contain ==>, and therefore does not specify where the formula to be replaced shall appear. However, only one formula at a time gets replaced.

Taclets with a \find clause not containing the sequent arrow ==> are called *rewrite taclets* or *rewrite rules*. The argument of \find is a schema variable of kind \formula or \term, matching formulas or terms, respectively, at *arbitrary* positions, which may even be nested. The position can be further restricted. The restriction \sameUpdateLevel in this taclet is however not relevant for the current example. When we look at how the taclet was used in our proof, we see that indeed the *subformula* p of the formula q & p has been rewritten to true, resulting in the sequent p, q ==> true & p. The following rule application simplifies the true away, after which **close** is applicable again.

Saving and Loading Proofs

Before we leave the discussion of the current example, we save the just accomplished proof (admittedly for no other reason than practicing the saving of proofs). For that, we either use the shortcut $\boxed{\texttt{Ctrl}}$ + $\boxed{\texttt{S}}$, or select the main menu item **File → Save**, or the button ▤ in the toolbar. The opened file browser dialogue allows us to locate and name the proof file. A sensible name would be andCommutes.proof, but any name would do, *as long as the file extension is* .proof. It is completely legal for a proof file to have a different naming than the corresponding problem file. This way, it is possible to save several proofs for the same problem. Proofs can actually be saved regardless of whether they are finished or not. An unfinished proof can be continued when loaded again. Loading a proof (finished or unfinished) is done in exactly the same way as loading a problem file, with the only difference that a .proof file is selected instead of a .key file.

15.2.2 Exploring Terms, Quantification, and Instantiation: Building First-Order Proofs

After having looked at the basic usage of the KeY prover, we want to extend the discussion to more advanced features of the logic. The example of the previous section did only use propositional connectives. Here, we discuss the basic handling of first-order formulas, containing terms, variables, quantifiers, and equality. As an example, we prove a \problem which we load from the file projection.key:

—— KeY Problem File ————————————————————————————

```
\sorts {
        s;
}
\functions {
        s f(s);
        s c;
}
\problem {
        ( \forall s x; f(f(x)) = f(x) )   ->   f(c) = f(f(f(c)))
}
```

————————————————————————————— KeY Problem File ——

The file declares a function f (of type s → s) and a constant c (of sort s). The first part of the \problem formula, \forall s x; f(f(x)) = f(x), says that f is a *projection*: For all x, applying f twice is the same as applying f once. The whole \problem formula then states that f(c) and f(f(f(c))) are equal, given f is a projection.

Instantiating Quantified Formulas

We prove this simple formula interactively, for now. After loading the problem file, and applying **impRight** to the initial sequent, the **Current Goal** is:
\forall s x; f(f(x)) = f(x) ==> f(c) = f(f(f(c))).

We proceed by deriving an additional assumption (i.e., left-hand side formula) f(f(c)) = f(c), by instantiating x with c. For the interactive instantiation of quantifiers, KeY supports *drag and drop* of terms over quantifiers (whenever the instantiation is textually present in the current sequent). In the situation at hand, we can drag any of the two c onto the quantifier \forall by clicking at c, holding and moving the mouse, to release it over the \forall. As a result of this action, the new **Current Goal** features the *additional* assumption f(f(c)) = f(c).

There is something special to this proof step: even if it was triggered interactively, we have not been specific about which taclet to apply. The **Proof** pane, however, tells us that we just applied the taclet **instAll**. To see the very taclet, we can click at the previous proof node, marked with **instAll**. We then make sure, that the checkbox **Show taclet info (Inner Nodes only)** at the bottom of the **Proof** tab is checked, such that the **Inner Node** pane displays (simplified):

```
—— KeY Output ————————————————————————————
instAll {
  \assumes ( \forall u; b ==>  )
  \find ( t )
  \add ( {\subst u; t}b ==>  )
}
————————————————————————————— KeY Output ——
```

{\subst u; t}b means that (the match of) u is substituted by (the match of) t in (the match of) b, during taclet application.

Making Use of Equations

We can use the equation f(f(c)) = f(c) to simplify the term f(f(f(c))), meaning we *apply* the equation to the f(f(c)) subterm of f(f(f(c))). This action can again be performed via drag and drop, here by dragging the equation on the left side of the sequent, and dropping it over the f(f(c)) subterm of f(f(f(c))).[6] In the current system, there opens a context menu, allowing to select a taclet with the display name **applyEq**.[7]

Afterwards, the right-hand side equation has changed to f(c) = f(f(c)), which looks almost like the left-hand side equation. We can proceed either by swapping one equation, or by again applying the left-hand side equation on a right-hand side term. It is instructive to discuss both alternatives here.

First, we select f(c) = f(f(c)), and apply **eqSymm**. The resulting goal has two identical formulas on both sides of the sequent, so we *could* apply **close**. Just to demonstrate the other possibility, we undo the last rule application using **Goal Back** , leading us back to the **Current Goal** f(f(c)) = f(c),...==> f(c) = f(f(c)).

---

[6] More detailed, we move the mouse over the "=" symbol, such that the whole of f(f(c)) = f(c) is highlighted. We click, hold, and move the mouse, over the second "f" in f(f(f(c))), such that exactly the subterm f(f(c)) gets highlighted. Then, we release the mouse.

[7] Possibly, there are more than one offered; for our example, it does not matter which one is selected.

The other option is to apply the left-hand equation to `f(f(c))` on the right (via drag and drop). Afterwards, we have the *tautology* `f(c) = f(c)` on the right. By selecting that formula, we get offered the taclet **eqClose**, which transforms the equation into `true`. (If the reader's system does not offer **eqClose** in the above step, please make sure that **One Step Simplification** is unchecked in the **Options** menu, and try again.)

Closing 'by True' and 'by False'

So far, all goals we ever closed featured identical formulas on both sides of the sequent. We have arrived at the second type of closable sequents: one with `true` on the *right* side. We close it by highlighting `true`, and selecting the taclet **closeTrue**, which is defined as:

```
— Taclet —————————————————————————————————————————
closeTrue {
  \find ( ==> true )
  \closegoal
}
——————————————————————————————————————— Taclet —
```

This finishes our proof.

Without giving an example, we mention here the third type of closable sequents, namely those with `false` on the *left* side, to be closed by:

```
— Taclet —————————————————————————————————————————
closeFalse {
  \find ( false ==> )
  \closegoal
}
——————————————————————————————————————— Taclet —
```

This is actually a very important type of closable sequent. In many examples, a sequent can be proven by showing that the assumptions (i.e., the left-hand side formulas) are contradictory, meaning that `false` can be derived on the left side.

Using Taclet Instantiation Dialogues

In our previous proof, we used the "drag-and-drop" feature offered by the KeY prover to instantiate schema variables needed to apply a rule. This kind of user interaction can be seen as a shortcut to another kind of user interaction: the usage of *taclet instantiation dialogues*. While the former is most convenient, the latter is more general and should be familiar to each KeY user. Therefore, we reconstruct the (in spirit) same proof, this time using such a dialogue explicitly.

After again loading the problem file `projection.key`, we apply **impRight** to the initial sequent, just like before. Next, to instantiate the quantified formula `\forall s x; f(f(x)) = f(x)`, we highlight that formula, and apply the taclet **allLeft**, which is defined as:

```
───── Taclet ─────────────────────────────────────────────
allLeft {
  \find ( \forall u; b ==> )
  \add ( {\subst u; t}b ==> )
}
─────────────────────────────────────────────── Taclet ───
```

This opens a **Choose Taclet Instantiation** dialogue, allowing the user to choose the (not yet determined) instantiations of the taclet's schema variables. The taclet at hand has three schema variables, b, u, and t. The instantiations of b and u are already determined to be `f(f(x)) = f(x)` and x, respectively, just by matching the highlighted sequent formula `\forall s x; f(f(x)) = f(x)` with the `\find` argument `\forall u; b`. The instantiation of t is, however, left open, to be chosen by the user. We can type c in the corresponding input field of the dialogue,[8] and click **Apply**. As a result, the `f(f(c)) = f(c)` is added to the left side of the sequent. The rest of the proof goes exactly as discussed before. The reader may finish it herself.

Skolemizing Quantified Formulas

We will now consider a slight generalization of the theorem we have just proved. Again assuming that f is a projection, instead of showing `f(c) = f(f(f(c)))` for a particular c, we show `f(y) = f(f(f(y)))` *for all* y. For this we load `generalProjection.key`, and apply **impRight**, which results in the sequent:

```
───── KeY Output ─────────────────────────────────────────
\forall s x; f(f(x)) = f(x) ==> \forall s y; f(y) = f(f(f(y)))
─────────────────────────────────────────── KeY Output ───
```

As in the previous proof, we will have to instantiate the quantified formula on the left. But this time we also have to deal with the quantifier on the right. Luckily, that quantifier can be eliminated altogether, by applying the rule **allRight**, which results in:[9]

```
───── KeY Output ─────────────────────────────────────────
\forall s x;  f(f(x)) = f(x) ==> f(y_0) = f(f(f(y_0)))
─────────────────────────────────────────── KeY Output ───
```

---

[8] Alternatively, one can also drag and drop syntactic entities from the **Current Goal** pane into the input fields of such a dialogue, and possibly edit them afterwards.

[9] Note that the particular name y_0 can differ.

We see that the quantifier disappeared, and the variable y got replaced. The replacement, y_0, is a *constant*, which we can see from the fact that y_0 is not quantified. Note that in our logic each logical variable appears in the scope of a quantifier binding it. Therefore, y_0 can be nothing but a constant. Moreover, y_0 is a *new* symbol.

Eliminating quantifiers by introducing new constants is called *Skolemization* (after the logician Thoralf Skolem). In a sequent calculus, universal quantifiers (\forall) on the right, and existential quantifiers (\exists) on the left side, can be eliminated this way, leading to sequents which are equivalent (concerning provability), but simpler. This should not be confused with quantifier *instantiation*, which applies to the complementary cases: (\exists) on the right, and (\forall) on the left, see our discussion of **allLeft** above. (It is instructive to look at all four cases in combination, see Chapter 2, Figure 2.1.)

Skolemization is a simple proof step, and is normally done fully automatically. We only discuss it here to give the user some understanding about new constants that might show up during proving.

To see the taclet we have just applied, we select the inner node labeled with **allRight**. The **Inner Node** pane reveals the taclet:

—— KeY Output ——————————————————————————————
```
allRight {
  \find ( ==> \forall u; b )
  \varcond ( \new(sk, \dependingOn(b)) )
  \replacewith ( ==> {\subst u; sk}b )
}
```
———————————————————————————————— KeY Output ——

It tells us that the rule removes the quantifier matching \forall u;, and that (the match of) u is \substituted by the \newly generated Skolem constant sk in the remaining formula (matching b).

The rest of our current proof goes exactly like for the previous problem formula. Instead of further discussing it here, we simply run the proof search strategy to resume and close the proof.

15.2.3 Exploring Programs in Formulas: Building Dynamic Logic Proofs

Not first-order logic, and certainly not propositional logic, is the real target of the KeY prover. Instead, the prover is designed to handle proof obligations formulated in a substantial extension of first-order logic, *dynamic logic* (DL). What is dynamic about this logic is the notion of the world, i.e., the interpretation (of function/predicate symbols) in which formulas (and subformulas) are evaluated. In particular, a formula and its subformulas can be interpreted in *different* worlds.

The other distinguished feature of DL is that descriptions of how to construct one world from another are explicit in the logic, in the form of *programs*. Accordingly, the worlds represent computation *states*. (In the following, we take 'state' as a synonym for 'world'.) This allows us to, for instance, talk about the states both *before* and *after* executing a certain program, *within the same formula*.

Compared to first-order logic, DL employs two additional (mixfix) operators: $\langle . \rangle$. (diamond) and $[.]$. (box). In both cases, the first argument is a *program*, whereas the second argument is another DL formula. With $\langle p \rangle \varphi$ and $[p]\varphi$ being DL formulas, $\langle p \rangle$ and $[p]$ are called the *modalities* of the respective formula.

A formula $\langle p \rangle \varphi$ is valid in a state if, from there, an execution of p terminates normally and results in a state where φ is valid. As for the other operator, a formula $[p]\varphi$ is valid in a state from where execution of p does *either* not terminate normally *or* results in a state where φ is valid.[10] For our applications the diamond operator is way more important than the box operator, so we restrict attention to that.

One frequent pattern of DL formulas is $\varphi \rightarrow \langle p \rangle \psi$, stating that the program p, when started from a state where φ is valid, terminates, with ψ being valid in the post state. (Here, φ and ψ often are pure first-order formulas, but they can very well be proper DL formulas, containing programs themselves.)

Each variant of DL has to commit to a formalism used to describe the programs (i.e., the p) in the modalities. Unlike most other variants of DL, the KeY project's DL variant employs a real programming language, namely Java. Concretely, p is a sequence of (zero, one, or more) Java statements. Accordingly, the logic is called JavaDL.

The following is an example of a JavaDL formula:

$$x < y \rightarrow \langle t = x; \ x = y; \ y = t; \rangle \ y < x \qquad (15.1)$$

It says that in each state where the program variable x has a value smaller than that of the program variable y, the sequence of Java statements t = x; x = y; y = t; terminates, and afterwards the value of y is smaller than that of x. It is important to note that x and y are *program* variables, not to be confused with *logical* variables. In our logic, there is a strict distinction between both. Logical variables must appear in the scope of a quantifier binding them, whereas program variables cannot be quantified over. This formula (15.1) has no quantifier because it does not contain any logical variables.

As we will see in the following examples, both program variables and logical variables can appear mixed in terms and formulas, also together with logical constants, functions, and predicate symbols. However, inside the modalities, there can be nothing but (sequents of) *pure* Java statements. For a more thorough discussion of JavaDL, please refer to Chapter 3.

---

[10] These descriptions have to be generalized when nondeterministic programs are considered, which is not the case here.

Feeding the Prover with a DL Problem File

The file `exchange.key` contains the JavaDL formula (15.1), in the concrete syntax used in the KeY system:[11]

——— KeY Problem File ————————————————————————————————

```
\programVariables { int x, y, t; }
\problem {
        x < y
     -> \<{ t=x;
            x=y;
            y=t;
          }\> y < x
}
```

——————————————————————————————————————— KeY Problem File ———

When comparing this syntax with the notation used in (15.1), we see that diamond modality brackets ⟨ and ⟩ are written as \<{ and }\> within the KeY system. What we can also observe from the file is that all program variables which are *not* declared in the Java code inside the modality (like t here) must appear within a \programVariables declaration of the file (like x and y here).

Instead of loading this file, and proving the problem, we try out other examples first, which are meant to slowly introduce the principles of proving JavaDL formulas with KeY.

Using the Prover as an Interpreter

We consider the file `executeByProving.key`:

——— KeY Problem File ————————————————————————————————

```
\predicates { p(int,int); }
\programVariables { int i, j; }
\problem {
        \<{ i=2;
            j=(i=i+1)+4;
          }\> p(i,j)
}
```

——————————————————————————————————————— KeY Problem File ———

As the reader might guess, the \problem formula is not valid, as there are no assumptions made about the predicate p. Anyhow, we let the system try to prove this formula. By doing so, we will see that the KeY prover will essentially *execute* our (rather obscure) program i=2; j=(i=i+1)+4;, which is possible because all

---

[11] Here as in all .key files, line breaks and indentation do not matter other than supporting readability.

values the program deals with are *concrete*. The execution of Java programs is of course not the purpose of the KeY prover, but it serves us here as a first step towards the method for handling symbolic values, *symbolic execution*, to be discussed later.

We load the file `executeByProving.key` into the system. Then, we run the automated JavaDL strategy (by clicking the play button ▶). The strategy stops with `==> p(3,7)` being the (only) **OPEN GOAL**, see also the **Proof** tab. This means that the proof *could* be closed *if* `p(3,7)` was provable, which it is not. But that is fine, because all we wanted is letting the KeY system compute the values of i and j after execution of `i=2; j=(i=i+1)+4;`. And indeed, the fact that proving `p(3,7)` would be sufficient to prove the original formula tells us that 3 and 7 are the final values of i and j.

We now want to inspect the (unfinished) proof itself. For this, we select the first inner node, labeled with number **0:**, which contains the original sequent. By using the down-arrow key, we can scroll down the proof. The reader is encouraged to do so, before reading on, all the way down to the **OPEN GOAL**, to get an impression on how the calculus executes the Java statements at hand. This way, one can observe that one of the main principles in building a proof for a DL formula is to perform *program transformation* within the modality(s). In the current example, the complex second assignment `j=(i=i+1)+4;` was transformed into a sequence of simpler assignments. Once a leading assignment is simple enough, it moves out from the modality, into other parts of the formula (see below). This process continues until the modality is empty (`\<{}\>`). That empty modality gets eventually removed by the taclet **emptyModality**.

Discovering Updates

Our next observation is that the formulas which appear in inner nodes of this proof contain a syntactical element which is not yet covered by the above explanations of DL. We see that already in the second inner node (number **1:**), which looks like:

```
—— KeY Output ——————————————————————————————
==>
  {i:=2}
    \<{ j=(i=i+1)+4;
      }\> p(i,j)
——————————————————————————————————— KeY Output ——
```

The `i:=2` within the curly brackets is an example of what is called *updates*. When scrolling down the proof, we can see that leading assignments turn into updates when they move out from the modality. The updates somehow accumulate, and are simplified, in front of a "shrinking" modality. Finally, they get applied to the remaining formula once the modality is gone.

Updates are part of the version of dynamic logic invented within the KeY project. Their main intention is to represent the effect of some (Java) code they replace. This effect can be accumulated, manipulated, simplified, and applied to other parts of the formula, in a way which is disentangled from the manipulation of the program in the modality. This enables the calculus to perform *symbolic execution* in a natural way, and has been very fruitful contribution of the KeY project. First of all, updates allow proofs to symbolically execute programs in their natural direction, which is useful for proof inspection and proof interaction. Moreover, the update mechanism is heavily exploited when using the prover for other purposes, like test generation (Chapter 12), symbolic debugging (Chapter 11), as well as various analyzes for security (Chapter 13) or runtime verification [Ahrendt et al., 2015], to name a few.

Elementary updates in essence are a restricted kind of assignment, where the right-hand side must be a *simple* expression, which in particular is *free of side effects*. Examples are `i:=2`, or `i:=i + 1` (which we find further down in the proof). From elementary updates, more complex updates can be constructed (see Definition 3.8, Chapter 3). Here, we only mention the most important kind of compound updates, *parallel updates*, an example of which is `i:=3 || j:=7` further down in the proof. Updates can further be considered as *explicit substitutions* that are yet to be applied. This viewpoint will get clearer further-on.

Updates extend traditional DL in the following way: if φ is a DL formula and u is an update, then $\{u\}\varphi$ is also a DL formula. Note that this definition is recursive, such that φ in turn may have the form $\{u'\}\varphi'$, in which case the whole formula looks like $\{u\}\{u'\}\varphi'$. The strategies try to transform such subsequent updates into a single parallel update. As a special case, φ may not contain any modality (i.e., it is purely first-order). This situation occurs in the current proof in form of the sequent `==> {i:=3 || j:=7}p(i,j)` (close to the **OPEN GOAL**, after the rule application of **emptyModality** in the current proof). Now that the modality is gone, the update `{i:=3 || j:=7}` is applied in form of a *substitution*, to the formula following the update, `p(i,j)`. The reader can follow this step when scrolling down the proof. Altogether, this leads to a delayed turning of program assignments into substitutions in the logic, as compared to other variants of DL (or of Hoare logic). We will return to the generation, parallelization, and application of updates on page 524.

Employing Active Statements

We now focus on the connection between programs in modalities on the one hand, and taclets on the other hand. For that, we load `updates.key`. When moving the mouse around over the single formula of the **Current Goal**,

```
\<{ i=1;
    j=3;
    i=2;
  }\> i = 2
```

we realize that, whenever the mouse points anywhere between (and including) "`\<{`" and "`}\>`," the whole formula gets highlighted. However, the first statement is highlighted in a particular way, with a different color, regardless of which statement we point to. This indicates that the system considers the first statement `i=1;` as the *active statement* of this DL formula.

Active statements are a central concept of the DL calculus used in KeY. They control the application/applicability of taclets. Also, all rules which modify the program inside of modalities operate on the active statement, by rewriting or removing it. Intuitively, the active statement stands for the statement to be executed next. In the current example, this simply translates to the *first* statement.

We click anywhere within the modality, and *pre*select (only) the taclet **assignment**, just to view the actual taclet presented in the tooltip:

```
─── Tooltip ────────────────────────────────────────────────────────────
assignment {
  \find (
    \modality{#allmodal}{ ..
                             #loc=#se;
                         ... }\endmodality post
  )
  \replacewith (
    {#loc:=#se}
      \modality{#allmodal}{ ..   ... }\endmodality post
  )
}
──────────────────────────────────────────────────────────── Tooltip ───
```

The \find clause tells us how this taclet matches the formula at hand. First of all, the formula must contain a modality followed by a (not further constrained) formula post. Then, the first argument of \modality tells which kinds of modalities can be matched by this taclets, in this case all #allmodal, including ⟨.⟩. in particular. And finally, the second argument of \modality, .. #loc=#se; ... specifies the code which this taclet matches on. The convention is that everything between ".." and "..." matches the *active statement*. Here, the active statement must have the form #loc=#se;, i.e., a statement assigning a simple expression to a location, here i=1;. The "..." refers to the rest of the program (here j=3;i=2;), and the match of ".." is empty, in this particular example. Having understood the \find part, the \replacewith part tells us that the active statement moves out into an update.

After applying the taclet, we point to the active statement j=3;, and again preselect the **assignment**. The taclet in the tooltip is the same, but we note that it matches the highlighted *sub*formula, below the leading update. We suggest to finish the proof by pressing the play button.

The reader might wonder why we talk about *active* rather than *first* statements. The reason is that our calculus is designed in a way such that *block statements* are not normally *active*. By *block* we mean both unlabeled and labeled Java blocks, as well as try-catch blocks. If the first statement inside the modality is a block, then the active statement is the first statement *inside* that block, if that is not a block again, and so on. This concept prevents our logic from being bloated with control information. Instead, the calculus works inside the blocks, until the whole block can be *resolved*, because it is either empty, or an abrupt termination statement is active, like break,

continue, throw, or return. The interested reader is invited to examine this by
loading the file activeStmt.key.

Afterwards, one can see that, as a first step in the proof, one can pull out the
assignment i=0;, even if that is nested within a labeled block and a try-catch block.
We suggest to perform this first step interactively, and prove the resulting goal
automatically, for inspecting the proof afterwards.

Now we are able to round up the explanation of the ".." and "..." notation
used in DL taclets. The ".." matches the opening of leading blocks, up to the first
nonblock (i.e., active) statement, whereas "..." matches the statements following
the active statement, plus the corresponding closings of the opened blocks.[12]

Executing Programs Symbolically

So far, all DL examples we have been trying the prover on in this chapter had in
common that they worked with concrete values. This is very untypical, but served the
purpose of focusing on certain aspects of the logic and calculus. However, it is time
to apply the prover on problems where (some of) the values are either completely
unknown, or only constrained by formulas typically having many solutions. After
all, it is the ability of handling symbolic values which makes theorem proving more
powerful than testing. It allows us to verify a program with respect to *all* legitimate
input values!

First, we load the problem symbolicExecution.key:

—— KeY Problem File ——————————————————————————————————

```
\predicates { p(int,int); }
\functions { int c; }
\programVariables { int i, j; }
\problem {
        {i:=c}
          \<{ j=(i=i+1)+3;
             }\> p(i,j)
}
```

————————————————————————————————————— KeY Problem File ——

This problem is a variation of executeByProving.key (see above), the difference
being that the initial value of i is *symbolic*. The c is a logical *constant* (i.e., a function
without arguments), and thereby represents an unknown, but fixed value in the range
of int. The update {i:=c} is necessary because it would be illegal to have an
assignment i=c; inside the modality, as c is not an element of the Java language, not
even a program variable. This is another important purpose of updates in our logic:
to serve as an interface between logical terms and program variables.

The problem is of course as unprovable as executeByProving.key. All we
want this time is to let the prover compute the symbolic values of i and j, with

---

[12] ".." and "..." correspond to π and ω, respectively, in the rules in Chapter 3.

respect to c. We get those by clicking on the play button and therefore running KeY's
proof search strategy on this problem which results in ==> p(1+c,4+c) being the
remaining **OPEN GOAL**. This tells us that 1+c and 4+c are the final values of i and j,
respectively. By further inspecting the proof, we can see how the strategy performed
symbolic computation (in a way which is typically very different from interactive
proof construction). That intertwined with the 'execution by proving' (see 15.2.3)
method discussed above forms the principle of *symbolic execution*, which lies at the
heart of the KeY prover.

   Another example for this style of formulas is the \problem which we load from
postIncrement.key:

—— KeY Problem File ————————————————————————————————

```
\functions { int c; }
\programVariables { int i; }
\problem {
        {i:=c}
            \<{ i=i*(i++);
               }\> c * c = i
}
```

———————————————————————————————————— KeY Problem File ——

The validity of this formula is not completely obvious. But indeed, the obscure
assignment i=i*(i++); computes the square of the original value of i. The point
is the exact evaluation order within the assignment at hand. It is of course crucial
that the calculus emulates the evaluation order exactly as it is specified in the Java
language description by symbolic execution, and that the calculus does not allow any
other evaluation order. We prove this formula automatically here.

Quantifying over Values of Program Variables

A DL formula of the form $\langle p \rangle \varphi$, possibly preceded by updates, like $\{u\}\langle p \rangle \varphi$, can
well be a subformula of a more complex DL formula. For instance in $\psi \rightarrow \langle p \rangle \varphi$, the
diamond formula is below an implication (see also formula (15.1)). A DL subformula
can actually appear below arbitrary logical connectives, including quantifiers. The
following problem formula from quantifyProgVals.key is an example for that.

—— KeY Problem File ————————————————————————————————

```
\programVariables { int i; }
\problem {
        \forall int x;
          {i := x}
            \<{ i = i*(i++);
               }\> x * x = i
}
```

———————————————————————————————————— KeY Problem File ——

Please observe that it would be illegal to have an assignment i=x; inside the modality, as x is not an element of the Java language, but rather a logical variable.

This formula literally says that, \forall initial values i, it holds that after the assignment i contains the square of that value. Intuitively, this seems to be no different from stating the same for an *arbitrary but fixed* initial value c, as we did in postIncrement.key above. And indeed, if we load quantifyProgVals.key, and as a first step apply the taclet **allRight**, then the **Current Goal** looks like this:

—— KeY Output ——————————————————————————————————————
```
==>
 {i:=x_0}
   \<{ i=i*(i++);
      }\> x_0 * x_0 = i
```
—— KeY Output ——

Note that x_0 cannot be a logical variable (as was x in the previous sequent), because it is not bound by a quantifier. Instead, x_0 is a *Skolem constant*.

We see here that, after only one proof step, the sequent is essentially not different from the initial sequent of postIncrement.key. This seems to indicate that quantification over values of program variables is not necessary. That might be true here, but is not the case in general. The important proof principle of *induction* applies to quantified formulas only.

Proving DL Problems with Program Variables

So far, most DL \problem formulas *explicitly* talked about *values*, either concrete ones (like 2) or symbolic ones (like the logical constant a and the logical variable x). It is however also common to have DL formulas which do not talk about any (concrete or symbolic) values explicitly, but instead only talk about *program variables* (and thereby *implicitly* about their values). As an example, we use yet another variation of the post increment problem, contained in postIncrNoUpdate.key:

—— KeY Problem File ——————————————————————————————————
```
\programVariables { int i, j; }
\problem {
        \<{ j=i;
            i=i*(i++);
           }\> j * j = i
}
```
—— KeY Problem File ——

Here, instead of initially updating i with some symbolic value, we store the value of i into some other program variable. The equation after the modality is a claim about the relation between (the implicit values of) the program variables, in a state after program execution. When proving this formula automatically with KeY, we see that the proof has no real surprise as compared to the other variants of post increment. Please observe, however, that the entire proof does not make use of any symbolic value, and only talks about program variables, some of which are introduced within the proof.

Demonstrating the Update Mechanism

In typical applications of the KeY prover, the user is not concerned with the update mechanism. Still, this issue is so fundamental for the KeY approach that we want to put the reader in the position to understand its basic principles. We do this by running an example in a much more interactive fashion than one would ever do for other purposes. (For a theoretical treatment, please refer to Section 3.4).

Let us reconsider the formula

$$x < y \rightarrow \langle t = x; \ x = y; \ y = t; \rangle \, y < x$$

and (re)load the corresponding problem file, exchange.key (see above 15.2.3) into the system. Also, we make sure that the "One Step Simplifier" button in the toolbar is unselected such that we can illustrate the update mechanism fully transparent.

The initial **Current Goal** looks like this:

```
—— KeY Output ——————————————————————————————————————————
==>
      x < y
  -> \<{ t=x;
          x=y;
          y=t;
        }\> y < x
————————————————————————————————————————— KeY Output ——
```

We prove this sequent interactively, just to get a better understanding of the basic steps usually performed by automated strategies.

We first apply the **impRight** rule on the single formula of the sequent. Next, the first assignment, t=x;, is simple enough to be moved out from the modality, into an update. We can perform this step by pointing on that assignment, and applying the **assignment** rule. In the resulting sequent, that assignment got removed and the update {t:=x}[13] appeared in front of the modality. We perform the same step on the leading assignment x=y;. Afterwards, the sequent has the two subsequent updates {t:=x}{x:=y} leading the formula.

This is the time to illustrate a very essential step in KeY-style symbolic execution, which is *update parallelization*. A formula $\{u_1\}\{u_2\}\varphi$ says that φ is true after the *sequential* execution of u_1 and u_2. Update parallelization transforms the sequential steps (u_1 and u_2) into a *single*, parallel step $u_1 \,\|\, u_2'$, leading to the formula $\{u_1 \,\|\, u_2'\}\varphi$,

---

[13] Strictly speaking, the curly brackets are not part of the update, but rather surround it. It is however handy to ignore this syntactic subtlety when discussing examples.

where u_2' is the result simplifying $\{u_1\}\, u_2$, i.e., applying u_1 to the u_2. This will get clearer by continuing our proof in slow motion.

With the mouse over the curly bracket of the leading update, we select the rule **sequentialToParallel2**. (Its tooltip tells the same story as the previous sentences.) The resulting, parallel update is `{t:=x || {t:=x}x:=y}`. As t does not appear on the right side of `x:=y`, the parallel update can be simplified to `{t:=x || x:=y}`. (Parallelization is trivial for independent updates.) In the system, we select `{t:=x}x:=y`, and apply **simplifyUpdate3**. Then, by using the **assignment** rule a third time, we arrive at the nested updates `{t:=x || x:=y}{y:=t}` (followed by the empty modality). Parallelizing them (application of the rule **sequentialToParallel2**) results in the single parallel update `{t:=x || x:=y || {t:=x || x:=y}y:=t}`. Applying the rule **simplifyUpdate3** simplifies the rightmost of the three updates, `{t:=x || x:=y}y:=t` and removes `x:=y`, as it has no effect on `y:=t`.

Only now, when processing the resulting update `{t:=x}y:=t` further, we are at the heart of the update parallelization, the moment where updates turn from *delayed* substitutions to real substitutions. The reader can see that by applying the rule **applyOnElementary** on `{t:=x}y:=t`, and then **applyOnPV** (apply on Program Variable) on `{t:=x}t`. With that, our parallel update looks like `{t:=x || x:=y || y:=x}`. Its first element is not important anymore, as t does not appear in the postcondition `x < y`. It can therefore be dropped (**simplifyUpdate2** on the leading curly bracket). The reader may take a moment to consider the result of symbolic execution of the original Java program, the final update `{x:=y || y:=x}`. It captures the effect of the Java code `t=x;x=y;y=t;` (in so far as it is relevant for remainder for the proof) in a *single, parallel* step. The right-hand sides of the updates `x:=y` and `y:=x` are evaluated in the *same* state, and assigned to the left-hand sides at once.

With the empty modality highlighted in the **OPEN GOAL**, we can apply the rule **emptyModality**. It deletes that modality, and results in the sequent `x < y ==> {x:=y || y:=x}(y < x)`. When viewing the (parallel) update as a substitution on the succeeding formula, it is clear that this sequent should be true. The reader is invited to show this interactively, by using the rules **applyOnRigidFormula**, **simplifyUpdate1** and **applyOnPV** a few times, followed by **close**.

Let us stress again that the above demonstration serves the single purpose of gaining insight into the update mechanism. Never ever would we apply the aforementioned rules interactively otherwise. The reader can replay the proof automatically, with the One Step Simplifier switched on or off, respectively. In either case, the proof is quite a bit longer than ours, due to many normalization steps which help the automation, but compromise the readability.

Using Classes and Objects

Even though the DL problem formulas discussed so far all contained real Java code, we did not see either of the following central Java features: classes, objects, or method calls. The following small example features all of them. We consider the file `methodCall.key`:

—— KeY Problem File (15.1) ————————————————————

```
\javaSource "methodExample/"; // location of class definitions
\programVariables { Person p; }
\problem {
        \forall int x;
          {p.age:=x} // assign initial value to "age"
            (   x >= 0
              -> \<{ p.birthday();
                    }\> p.age > x)
}
```

———————————————————————————————— KeY Problem File ——

The \javaSource declaration tells the prover where to look up the sources of classes
and interfaces used in the file. In particular, the Java source file Person.java is
contained in the directory methodExample/. The \problem formula states that a
Person is getting older at its birthday(). As a side note, this is an example where
an update does not immediately precede a modality, but a more general DL formula.

Before loading this problem file, we look at the source file Person.java in
methodExample/:

—— Java ——————————————————————————————————————

```
public class Person {
    private int age = 0;
    public void setAge(int newAge) { this.age = newAge; }
    public void birthday() { if (age >= 0) age++; }
}
```

—— Java ——

When loading the file into the KeY system, the reader may recognize a difference
between the proof obligation given in the problem file and the initial proof obligation
in the KeY system:

—— KeY Output (15.2) ————————————————————————————

```
==>
 \forall int x;
   {heap:=heap[p.age := x]}
     (   x >= 0
      -> \<{ p.birthday();
            }\> p.age >  x)
```

———————————————————————————————————— KeY Output ——

Note that, in the display of the prover, the update {p.age:=x} from the problem
file is now written as {heap:=heap[p.age := x]}. Both updates are no different;
the first is an abbreviation of the second, using a syntax which is more familiar
to programmers. The expanded version, however, reveals the fact that this update,
whether abbreviated or not, changes the value of a variable named heap. We explain
this in the following, thereby introducing the representation of object states in KeY.

In the context of object-oriented programming, the set of all objects—including their internal state—is often referred to as the *heap*. This is an implicit data structure, in so far as it cannot be directly accessed by the programmer. Instead, it is implicitly given via the creation and manipulation of individual objects. However, in KeY's dynamic logic, the heap is an explicit data structure, and is stored in a variable called heap (or a variant of that name).[14] For the sake of clarity, we first discuss the abstract data type of heaps in a classical algebraic notation, before turning to KeY's concrete syntax shortly. Let us assume two functions *store* and *select* with the following type signature:

$$store : Heap \times Object \times Field \times Any \rightarrow Heap$$

$$select : Heap \times Object \times Field \rightarrow Any$$

store models the writing of a value (of *Any* type) to a given field of a given object, in a given heap. The result is a new heap. The function *select* looks up the value of a given field of a given object, in a given heap. The following axioms describe the interplay of *store* and *select*.

$$select(store(h,o,f,x),o,f) \doteq x$$

$$f \neq f' \vee o \neq o' \quad \rightarrow \quad select(store(h,o,f,x),o',f') \doteq select(h,o',f')$$

Please observe that we deliberately simplified these axioms for presentation. The real formalization has to distinguish select functions for different field types, has to check type conformance of *x*, and take special care of object creation. Please refer to Section 2.4.3 for a full account on this.

However, in the user interface of the KeY system, the above notation would give unreadable output for real examples. In particular, we would get deeply nested *store* terms during symbolic execution of a program (with one *store* per assignment to a field). Therefore, KeY uses the following, shorter syntax. Instead of *store(h,o,f,x)*, we write h[o.f:=x], denoting a heap which is identical to h everywhere but at o.f, whose value is x. With that, a nested store like *store(store(h,o1,f1,x1),o2,f2,x2)* becomes h[o1.f1:=x1][o2.f2:=x2], presenting the heap operations in their natural order. The *select* operation is also abbreviated. Instead of *select(h,o,f)*, we write o.f@h, denoting the access to o.f in heap h. With that, the above axioms become

$$o.f@h[o.f:=x] = x \tag{15.2}$$

$$f \neq f' \vee o \neq o' \quad \rightarrow \quad o'.f'@h[o.f:=x] = o'.f'@h \tag{15.3}$$

Please note that the symbol := in h[o.f:=x] does not denote an update. Instead, it is part of the mix-fix presentation ⊔[⊔.⊔:=⊔] of *store*. In particular, h[o.f:=x] does not, in itself, change h. Instead, it constructs a new heap that is (in most cases) different from h. An actual change to h has to be done extra, in an update like

---

[14] The object representation described here is implemented in KeY 2.0 onward, and significantly differs from the earlier object representation which was described in the first book about KeY [Beckert et al., 2007].

h := h[o.f:=x]. Only after that, h has a new value, given by applying *store* to the old value of h.

In proofs, during symbolic execution, KeY uses largely a specific heap variable called exactly heap, which is constantly modified in updates (resulting from assignments). There are some exceptions, however, where a proof node talks about more than one heap, for instance to distinguish the heap before and after execution of a method call. But as the one variable called heap dominates the picture, special shorthand notations are offered for this case. The select expression o.f@heap can be abbreviated by o.f, and the update heap := heap[o.f:=x] can be abbreviated by o.f:=x. Note that these abbreviations only apply to the single variable called exactly heap, not otherwise.

After this excursion on heap manipulation and presentation, let us look back to the KeY problem file methodCall.key, and KeY's presentation after loading the problem, see (15.2 from above). We now know that, in methodCall.key, the update p.age:=x abbreviates heap := heap[p.age:=x], and that the postcondition p.age > x abbreviates p.age@heap > x. The first abbreviation was immediately expanded by KeY when loading the file, whereas the second one will be expanded later-on during the proof.

Calling Methods in Proofs

We now want to have a closer look at the way KeY handles method calls. We make sure that methodCall.key is (still) loaded and set the option **Arithmetic treatment** in the **Proof Search Strategy** tab to **Basic** and the option **Method treatment** to **Contract** or **Expand**. The reader is encouraged to reflect on the validity of the problem formula a little, before reading on.—Ready?—Luckily, we have a prover at hand to be certain, so we press the play button.

The strategy stops with the a number of **OPEN GOAL**s, one of them being p = null, x_0 >= 0 ==> [15]. There are different ways to read this goal, which however are logically equivalent. One way of proving any sequent is to show that its left-hand side is false. Here, it would be sufficient to show that p = null is false. An alternative viewpoint is the following: in a sequent calculus, we always get a logically equivalent sequent by throwing any formula to the respective other side, but negated. Therefore, we can as well read the **OPEN GOAL** as if it was x_0 >= 0 ==> p != null. Then, it would be sufficient to show that p != null is true.

Whichever reading we choose, we cannot prove the sequent, because we have no knowledge whatsoever about p being null or not. When looking back to our problem formula, we see that indeed the formula is not valid, because the case where p is null was forgotten. The postcondition p.age > x depends on the method body of birthday() being executed, which it cannot in case p is null. Interpreting the **Proof** pane leads to the same reading. The first split, triggered by the taclet **methodCall**,

---

[15] Note that the particular index of the name x_0 can differ.

leads to two unclosed proof branches. The shorter one, marked as **Null Reference (p = null)**, leads immediately to an **OPEN GOAL** where the strategy gets stuck.

The file `methodCall2.key` contains the patch of the problem formula. The problem formula from above is preceded by `p != null ->`. We load that problem, and let KeY prove it automatically without problems.

We now look at the first split in the proof (and click on the node before the split). Like in the previous proof, the first split was triggered by the taclet **methodCall**. Then, in the branch marked as **Normal Execution (p != null)**, the first inner node looks like this:

—— KeY Output (15.3) ————————————————————————————————

```
x_0 >= 0
==>
p = null,
{heap:=heap[p.age:=x_0]}
  \<{ p.birthday()@Person;
    }\> p.age >= 1 + x_0
```
—— KeY Output ——

We should not let confuse ourselves by `p = null` being present here. Recall that the comma on the right-hand side of a sequent essentially is a logical *or*. Also, as stated above, we can always imagine a formula being thrown to the other side of the sequent, but negated. Therefore, we essentially have `p != null` as an *assumption* here. Another thing to comment on is the `@Person` notation in the method call. It represents that the calculus has decided which *implementation* of `birthday` is to be chosen (which, in the presence of inheritance and hiding, can be less trivial than here, see Section 3.7.1).

At this point, the strategy was ready to apply **methodBodyExpand**.[16] After that, the code inside the modality looks like this:

```
method-frame(source=birthday()@Person,this=p): {
  if (this.age >= 0) {
    this.age++;
  }
}
```

This `method-frame` is the only really substantial extension over Java which our logic allows inside modalities. It models the execution stack, and can appear nested in case of nested method calls. Apart from the class and the `this` reference, it can also specify a return variable, in case of nonvoid methods. However, the user is rarely concerned with this construction, and if so, only passively. We will not discuss this construct further here, but refer to Section 3.6.5 instead. One interesting thing to note here, however, is that method frames are considered as *block statements* in the sense of our earlier discussion of active statements, meaning that *method frames are never active*. For our sequent at hand, this means that the active statement is

---

[16] This is the case even if **Method treatment** was chosen to be **Contract** instead of **Expand**. If no contract is available, the **Contract** strategy will still expand the method body.

if (this.age>=0) {this.age++;}. The rule **methodBodyExpand** has also introduced the update heapBefore_birthday:=heap. This is necessary because, in
general, the formula succeeding the modality may refer to values that were stored in
the heap at the beginning of the method call. (An example for that is presented in
Section 15.3.) However, in the current proof, this update is simplified away in the
next step, because in the formula following the modality, there is no reference to
values in the heap from before calling the method.

Controlling Strategy Settings

The expansion of methods is among the more problematic steps in program verification (together with the handling of loops). In place of recursion, an automated proof
strategy working with method expansion might not even terminate. Another issue is
that method expansion goes against the principle of *modular* verification, without
which even midsize examples become infeasible to verify. These are good reasons
for giving the user more control over this crucial proof step.

KeY therefore allows the user to configure the automated strategies such that
they *refrain* from expanding methods automatically.[17] We try this out by loading
methodCall2.key again, and selecting **None** as the **Method treatment** option in the
Proof Search Strategy tab. Then we start the strategy, which now stops exactly at
the sequent which we discussed earlier (Figure 15.3). We can highlight the active
statement, apply first the taclet **methodCall**. After this step we *could* call **method-
BodyExpand** interactively. KeY would then *only* apply this very taclet, and stop
again.

Controlling Taclet Options

We draw out attention back to the proof of methodCall2.key. This proof has a
branch for the null case (**Null Reference (p=null)**), but that was closed after a few
steps, as p = null is already present, explicitly, on the right side of the sequent
(**close**). It is, however, untypical that absence of null references can be derived so
easily. Often, the "null branches" complicate proofs substantially.

In the KeY system the handling of null references and other runtime exceptions
can be adjusted by setting *taclet options* We open the taclet option dialogue, via the
main menu **Options** → **Taclet options**. Among the option categories, we select the
runtimeExceptions, observe that **ban** is chosen as default, and change that by selecting
allow instead. Even if the effect of this change on our very example is modest, we
try it out, to see what happens in principle.[18]. We then load methodCall.key and
push the play button. The proof search strategy stops with two open goals in the **Null
Reference (p = null)** branch. Allowing runtime exceptions in the KeY system results

---

[17] For a discussion of loop treatment, please refer to Chapter 3 and Section 16.3.

[18] Please note that changing back to default settings of KeY can be enforced by deleting the .key
directory in the user's home directory and restarting KeY.

in the treatment of these exceptions as specified in the Java language specification, i.e., that exceptions are thrown if necessary and have to be considered. KeY is able to not only consider explicit exceptions, such as throwing exceptions "by-hand," it is also able to map the behavior of the JVM, i.e., to treat implicit exceptions. The proof tree branches at the point where the strategy reaches the method call **p.birthday** in the modality. The branching of the proof tree results from the taclet **methodCall**. One branch deals with the case, that the object on which the method is called is nonnull and the other branch deals with the case that the object is null. Depending on the setting of the taclet option **runtimeException** the *null branch* representing the exceptional case in the proof looks different. At the moment we have set the option for runtime exceptions to allow. Therefore, in the *null branch* the method call in the modality is replaced by `throw new java.lang.NullPointerException ()`. So an exception is instantiated and thrown which allows the verified code to catch it and to continue execution in the exceptional case. In this case the exception has to be symbolically executed and it has to be proven that the postcondition also holds after the exception had occurred in the program.

Loading the same file with setting the option **runtimeException** to **ban** results in a proof stopping in the *null-branch* as well. If the user bans runtime exceptions in the KeY system, KeY treats any occurrence of a runtime exception as an irrecoverable program failure. The reader can reproduce this by comparing the node before the branching of the proof—into **Null Reference (p=null)** and **Normal Execution (p!=null)**— and the nodes after the split. In the node after the split the modality and the formula succeeding the modality (postcondition) in the succedent is fully replaced by false. This means that the program fails and therefore the postcondition will be false. If the succedent has more formulas than the modality and the postcondition, it is still possible to close the proof with the remaining parts of the sequent (in our case the context). The formula is replaced by false for two reasons. The first reason is that we do not want to take the runtime exceptions into account, therefore we replace the modality as well as the postcondition by false. Now the prover can not consider the case of an exception in a modality like it is the case in the option set to allow. Secondly, it makes the verification easier because the user and the prover do not have to deal with the symbolic execution of the implicit exception. For the remaining examples we switch the option **runtimeException** to **ban**.

We briefly mention another very important taclet option, the **intRules**. Here, the user can choose between different semantics of the primitive Java integer types `byte`, `short`, `int`, `long`, and `char`. The options are: the mathematical integers (easy to use, but not fully sound), mathematical integers with overflow check (sound, reasonably easy to use, but unable to verify programs which depend on Java's modulo semantics), and the true modulo semantics of Java integers (sound, complete, but difficult to use). This book contains a separate section on Java integers (Section 5.4), discussing the different variants in the semantics and the calculus. Please note that KeY 2.6 comes with the mathematical integer semantics chosen as default option, to optimize usability for beginners. However, for a sound treatment of integers, the user should switch to either of the other semantics.

15.3 Understanding Proof Situations

We have so far used simple toy examples to introduce the KeY system to the reader. However, the application area of the KeY system is verification of real-world Java programs, which are specified using the Java Modeling Language (JML). Proving the correctness of larger programs with respect to their specification can be a nontrivial task. s In spite of a high degree of automation, performing the remaining interactive steps can become quite complex for the user.

In this section we give some hints for where to search for the necessary information, and how to proceed the verification process.

We will introduce these hints on an example which will be described in more detail in Chapter 16.

There are several potential reasons why the automated strategy stops in a state where the proof is still open.

We first start with a simple case: the number of proof steps (adjustable in the slider in the **Proof Search Strategy** pane) is reached. In this case, one may simply restart the automated strategy by pressing the play button in the toolbar again and let the prover continue with the proof search. Or alternatively, first increase the number of maximal rule applications in the slider and then restart the strategy to try to continue with the automated proof search. This can already lead to a closed proof.

However, if incrementing the number of proof steps does not lead to a successful proof, one of the following reasons may be responsible for the automated strategy to stop:

- there is a bug in the specification, e.g., an insufficient precondition,
- there is a bug in the program
- the automated proof search fails to find a proof and

  - (some) rule applications have to be done manually,
  - or automated strategies have to be adjusted,
  - or both.

In the first two cases there is a mismatch between the source code and the specification, and the automated proof search strategy is not able to find a proof because there is none. Here the user has to review the source code and the specification in order to fix the bug.

In the third case we are limited by the proof complexity of dynamic logic. Here the user has to guide the prover by providing the right information, e.g., instantiations of quantifiers, such that the prover can carry on.

We cannot give a nostrum that would allow the user to decide which of the three cases is responsible for the prover to stop. (In fact, this case distinction is undecidable.) We rather reach a point in the interactive proof process where the user may have to understand aspects of the open goal in order to provide the right information or to identify mistakes in the program or in the specification. In the following, we give some hints for the comprehension of open goals.

The first step in understanding what happened during the proof process is to have a look at the proof tree. The user should start at the original proof obligation and follow the proof tree to the open goal(s). The *labels* at the nodes in the proof tree already give good hints what happened. The user may first draw the attention to the labels which are highlighted light-blue. These indicate the nodes where taclets have been applied that perform symbolic execution. Here the user gets an impression which point in the control flow of the program is presented in the open goal. Moreover, looking at *branching points* in the proof tree can give very useful insights. Looking closer into the node before the proof branches may give good hints about what is (supposed to be) proven in either of the branches.

Recall the example dealing with a method call (methodCall.key, KeY Problem File (15.1), page 526), where the proof splits into two branches: the case where the object on which the method is called is assumed to be not null (**p!=null** on the left side of the sequent, or, equivalently, **p=null** on the right side of the sequent) and the case where the object is assumed to be null (**p = null** on the left side of the sequent). The labels as well as the taclet applied to the node directly before the proof split give the information what has to be proven (i.e., in the mentioned example that the postcondition holds in both cases, p being null and p being not null).

The next step in understanding the proof situation is to take a closer look at the sequent of an open goal. First of all the sequent consists of a number of formulas. Depending on the progress of the symbolic execution of the program during proof construction and the original formula, there will also be a formula containing a modal operator and Java statements.

A good strategy is to first finish the symbolic execution of the program by letting the prover continue with the proof search on the branch with the open goal, such that the modality is removed from the sequent. This strategy is also implemented in the KeY system as so called macro proof step, which basically is a collection of proof steps and strategies and accessible by right-clicking onto the sequent arrow and selecting the context menu entry **Auto Pilot → Finish Symbolic Execution**.

If this task is successful, we are often left with a formula in pure first-order logic of which the validity has to be shown. However, this strategy does not always succeed. If the user is left with a sequent still containing a modal operator, the reader should be aware that the sequent remains in the prestate. This means that all formulas in the sequent refer to the state before executing the program. (But please observe that *sub*formulas, following updates or modalities, are evaluated in different states.)

When directly looking at the sequent of an open goal the user should also keep in mind the intuitive meaning of sequents: the left-hand side of the sequent is assumed and one of the right-hand side formulas has to be proven. As a special case, a sequent is valid if the left-hand side is contradictory, which may have to be exhibited by further proof steps.

The user should also keep in mind that $\Gamma \Rightarrow o = null, \Delta$ is equivalent to $\Gamma, o \neq null \Rightarrow \Delta$. This means that, instead of intuitively trying to prove $o = null$ or Δ, we can think of proving Δ under the assumption $o \neq null$, which is effectively the same. The reader may again recall an example from methodCall.key, where this was discussed earlier.

When the user is left with a pure first-order logic formula, it may be the case that parts of the invariants or the postcondition can not be proven. To identify those parts, there is a strategy which in many cases helps to get further insights. This strategy is also implemented as proof macro **Full Auto Pilot** and it is accessible by right-clicking onto the sequent arrow and selecting the context menu entry **Auto Pilot** → **Full Auto Pilot**. We will first describe how this method basically works and apply this method to an example afterwards.

After exhausting the automated strategy, the reader should split the proof interactively doing case distinctions of each conjunct of the postcondition using for example the taclet **andRight** or the cut rule. (This can also be achieved by using the proof macro **Propositional** → **Propositional Expansions w splits**.) After this case distinction each branch contains only one conjunct of the postcondition. Now the user should try to close each branch separately by either using the automated proof search strategy on each open goal or by applying the proof macro **Close provable goals below** to the node before the splits (right-clicking onto the node in the **Proof** pane in the proof tree and selecting the proof macro) The branches which do not close may not be provable and give hints on which part of the postcondition might be problematic.

For this we load the file `PostIncMod.java`, which is a slightly modified version of the first example in Chapter 16. For demonstration purposes we have incorporated a little mistake in the code or its specifications. For a detailed description of the example we point the reader to Chapter 16.

—— Java + JML ————————————————————————————————

```
public class PostIncMod{
  public PostIncMod rec;
  public int x,y;

  /*@ public invariant rec.x >= 0 && rec.y>= 0; @*/

  /*@ public normal_behavior
    @ requires true;
    @ ensures rec.x == \old(rec.y)+1 && rec.y == \old(rec.y)+1;
    @*/
  public void postInc(){
    rec.x = rec.y++;
  }
}
```

————————————————————————————————— Java + JML ——

The special Java comments `/*@ ... @*/` mark JML annotations in the Java code. The keyword `normal_behavior` states that the method `postInc()` terminates without throwing an exception. The method contract consists of a pre- and a postcondition. The meaning of the contract is that if the caller of the method fulfills the precondition, the callee guarantees the postcondition to hold after termination. In this example the precondition is **true** and the postcondition says that after the successful termination of the method the field `rec.x` is equal to the value of the field `rec.y` before the method call (indicated by the keyword `\old`) increased by one. Similarly, the field `rec.y` is equal to the value of the field `rec.y` before the method call increased by 1. For a more detailed description of JML we point the reader to Chapter 7. The reader is encouraged to determine what the method `postInc()` performs.

When loading this file, the **Proof Management** dialogue will open. In its **Contract Targets** pane, we make sure that the folder **PostIncMod** (*not* **PostInc**) is expanded, and therein select the method **postInc()** we want to verify. We are asked to select a contract (in this case, there is only one), and press the **Start Proof** button. The reader may make sure that the One Step Simplifier is turned on, and start the automated proof search strategy. The prover will stop with one open goal where the modality is already removed.

The reader may now search for the node where the empty modality is about to be removed from the sequent (the last node on the open branch which is highlighted in light blue and labeled with { }) and select that node. In the case at hand, the automated strategy searched a little too far, so we undo some automated rule applications in order to understand the case that could not be proved. For that we left-click on the *next* node in the proof tree (where the empty modality is removed), and select the context menu item **Prune Proof**. The open goal should now look similar to the following:

```
——— KeY Output —————————————————————————————————
wellFormed(heap),
self.<created> = TRUE,
PostIncMod::exactInstance(self) = TRUE,
measuredByEmpty,
self.rec.x >= 0,
self.rec.y >= 0
==>
self.rec = null,
self = null,
{heapAtPre:=heap || exc:=null ||
 heap:=
     heap[self.rec.y:= 1 + self.rec.y][self.rec.x:=self.rec.y]}
   (self.rec.y = self.rec.x
   & self.rec.y@heapAtPre = -1 + self.rec.y
   & self.<inv>
   & exc = null)
————————————————————————————————————— KeY Output ———
```

This is the point in the proof process where the prover has processed the entire Java method `postInc()`. The effects of the method execution are accumulated in the (parallel) update, which precedes the properties that must hold after `postInc()` (the formulas connected with &). To determine which of the parts of the postcondition does not hold (if any), we highlight the last formula of the sequent (by focusing the leading { of the update), and apply the rule **andRight**, which splits one of the conjuncts. We repeat this step for as long as the is more than one conjuncts left.[19] Now we have a closer look at the different sequents.

We start with the node whose last formula is:

—— KeY Output ——————————————————————————————————
```
{heapAtPre:=heap || exc:=null ||
 heap:=heap[self.rec.y:=1+self.rec.y][self.rec.x:=self.rec.y]}
  (self.rec.y@heapAtPre = -1 + self.rec.y)
```
—————————————————————————————————— KeY Output ——

Focusing on (the leading { of) this formula, we apply the rule **One step Simplification**. This will basically apply, and thereby resolve, the parallel update as a *substitution* on the equation `self.rec.y@heapAtPre` =`-1 + self.rec.y`(`@heap`). (Recall that the field access `self.rec.y`, without @, abbreviates `self.rec.y@heap`). Therefore, the last formula of the new sequent is

—— KeY Output ——————————————————————————————————
```
self.rec.y = -1 + self.rec.y@heap[self.rec.y:=1+self.rec.y]
                             [self.rec.x:=self.rec.y]
```
—————————————————————————————————— KeY Output ——

This formula states that the value of `self.rec.y`(@heap) is equal to −1 plus the value `self.rec.y` on a heap that is constructed from `heap` through the two given *store* operations. It can be instructive for the reader to try to understand whether, and why, this formula is true. One way to do that is to, *mentally*, apply the axiom (15.3) (page 527), which removes the [`self.rec.x:=self.rec.y`]. Then apply the axiom (15.2), which turns `self.rec.y@heap[self.rec.y:=1+self.rec.y]` into `1+self.rec.y`. To prove this branch the reader may now left-click on the sequent arrow and select the context menu entry **Apply rules automatically here**.

We now switch to the open goal with the following last formula:

—— KeY Output ——————————————————————————————————
```
{heapAtPre:=heap || exc:=null ||
 heap:=heap[self.rec.y:=1+self.rec.y][self.rec.x:=self.rec.y]}
  (self.rec.y = self.rec.x)
```
—————————————————————————————————— KeY Output ——

We again apply the rule **One step Simplification** onto the shown formula. The new last formula is

—— KeY Output ——————————————————————————————————
```
self.rec.y@heap[self.rec.y:=1+self.rec.y]
                [self.rec.x:=self.rec.y]
  =
```

---

[19] For postconditions with a lot of conjunctions this task can be tedious. Therefore, the KeY system offers a proof macro called **Propositional Expansions w/ splits** which the user may apply instead.

```
self.rec.x@heap[self.rec.y:=1+self.rec.y]
                [self.rec.x:=self.rec.y]
```
── KeY Output ──

This formula says that, in a heap constructed from heap with the two given *stores*, the values of `self.rec.y` and `self.rec.x` are the same. This is not true, however. The user can see that by, again *mentally*, applying the axioms (15.3) and (15.2) to the left side of the equation, resulting in `1 + self.rec.y`, and axiom (15.2) to the right side of the equation, resulting in `self.rec.y`.

With this technique we have encountered a mistake in our postcondition. We should have stated `rec.x==\old(rec.y)` instead of `rec.x==\old(rec.y)+1` in the JML specification. The reason is that the postincrement expression (in the Java implementation) returns the old value. A corrected version of the problem is included in file `PostIncCorrected.java`. The reader is encouraged to load this file and use the automated strategy to prove the problem. For further examples on using the KeY system we point the reader to the tutorial chapter (Chapter 16).

15.4 Further Features

Besides the introduced features and mechanisms in this chapter, the KeY systems employs a variety of different features. In the following we will give a glimpse into some other useful features of KeY.

Employing External Decision Procedures

Apart from strategies, which apply taclets automatically, KeY also employs external decision procedure tools for increasing the automation of proofs. If formulas contain a lot of equations and inequations over terms that represent structures from different theories it can be a good idea to use SMT solvers instead of a full theorem prover. SMT solvers implement highly-efficient algorithms for deciding the satisfiability of formulas over specific theories, in contrast to full theorem provers, which are designed to work on many different domains. We refer to [Bradley and Manna, 2007] and [Kroening and Strichman, 2008] for a more detailed introduction and description of decision procedures and their applications.

The field of decision procedures is very dynamic, and so is the way in which KeY makes use of them. The user can choose among the available decision procedure tools by selecting the main menu item **Options → SMT Solvers**. We first load `generalProjection.key` and then choose **SMT solvers Options** via the main menu item **Options**. This opens the **Settings for Decision Procedure** dialogue. The user can now adjust general SMT options as well as settings for individual solvers.

In the **General SMT Options** pane, we can choose for instance the timeout for the SMT solvers. Timeouts are important when working with SMT solvers, as the search process can last very long, without necessarily leading anywhere. Here we suggest using as a first step the default timeout settings. However, for more complex problems, it can be useful to increase the timeout, to give the solver a better chance to find a proof. For now we select the external decision procedure tool Z3[20] in the menu on the left-hand side in the dialogue. Now we are able to adjust some settings for the solver if needed, but for this example we leave the default settings and click **Okay**. In the tool bar the **Run Z3** button now appears and we can press it. This opens a dialogue which shows the application of Z3 and whether it was successful. In this case the dialogue says valid and the reader is now able to press the button **Apply**. This closes the proof in one step(!), as the **Proof** tab is telling us. Decision procedures can be very efficient on certain problems. On the down side, we sacrificed proof transparency here.

In a more realistic setting, we use decision procedures towards the end of a proof (branch), to close first-order goals which emerged from proving problems that originally go beyond the scope of decision procedures.

Counterexample Generator

A feature that comes in handy when deciding whether a proof obligation is invalid is the counter example generator in KeY. This feature is accessible by pressing the toolbar button ❷ when a proof state is loaded. The mechanism translates the negation of the given proof obligation to an SMT specification and uses an SMT solver to decide the validity of this formula. To use this feature, the SMT solver Z3_CE has to be configured in the SMT solver options dialogue.

Model Search

If a sequent contains a lot of (in)equations, the KeY system offers the possibility to adjust the proof search strategy to systematically look for a model. This strategy is accessible via the **Proof Search Strategy** tab. It is a support for nonlinear inequations and model search. In addition, this strategy performs multiplication of inequations with each other and systematic case distinctions (cuts).

The method is guaranteed to find counterexamples for invalid goals that only contain polynomial (in)equations. Such counterexamples turn up as trivially unprovable goals. It is also able to prove many more valid goals involving (in)equations, but will in general not terminate on such goals.

---

[20] To use an external SMT solver it has to be installed beforehand and the path to the executable of the solver has to be set in the **Settings for Decision Procedure** dialogue.

Test Case Generation

Another feature of KeY is the automated generation of test cases, achieving high code coverage criteria by construction. This feature is called KeYTestGen. It constructs and analyses a (partial) proof tree for a method under test, extracts path conditions, generates test data, and synthesizes test code. This includes the generation of test oracles, or alternatively the usage of the OpenJML runtime checker. Test case generation is accessible by pressing the button ♺ right after starting a proof for the method under test. The usage and underlying principles of test generation with KeY are described in detail in Chapter 12. In particular, the 'Quick Tutorial' (Section 12.2) offers a quick introduction into the usage of KeYTestGen to a new user.

15.5 What Next?

In this chapter, we introduced the usage of the KeY prover, in parallel to explaining the basic artifacts used by KeY, the logic, the calculus, the reasoning principles, and so on. As we did not assume the reader to be familiar with any of these concepts prior to reading this text, we hope we have achieved a self contained exposition. Naturally, this imposed limits on how far we could go. The examples were rather basic, and discussed in depth. Demonstrating the usage of KeY in more realistic scenarios is not within the scope of this chapter. However, this book contains the tutorial 'Formal Verification with KeY' (Chapter 16), which lifts the usage of KeY to the next level. It discusses more realistic examples, more involved usage of the tool, and solutions to archetypal problems of verification. We therefore encourage the reader to not stop here, but continue to learn more about how KeY can be used for program verification.

Chapter 16
Formal Verification with KeY: A Tutorial

Bernhard Beckert, Reiner Hähnle, Martin Hentschel, Peter H. Schmitt

16.1 Introduction

This chapter gives a systematic tutorial introduction on how to perform formal program verification with the KeY system. It illustrates a number of complications and pitfalls, notably programs with loops, and shows how to deal with them. After working through this tutorial, you should be able to formally verify with KeY the correctness of simple Java programs, such as standard sorting algorithms, gcd, etc. This chapter is intended to be read with a computer at hand on which the KeY system is up and running, so that every example can be tried out immediately. The KeY system, specifically its version 2.6 used in this book, is available for download from www.key-project.org. The example input files can be found on the web page for this book, www.key-project.org/thebook2, as well as in the `examples` directory of your KeY system's installation.

In principle, this chapter can be read on its own, but one should be familiar with basic usage of the KeY system and with some fundamental concepts of KeY's program logic. Working through Chapter 15 gives sufficient background. The difference between Chapter 15 and the present chapter is that the former focuses on usage and on interaction with the KeY system by systematically explaining the input and output formats, as well as the possibilities for interaction with the system. It also uses exclusively the KeY GUI (see Figure 1.1) and is concerned with problems formulated in first-order logic or dynamic logic. Figure 15.1 on page 496 displays an overview of the entire verification process.

In the present chapter we mainly look at JML annotated Java programs as inputs and we target the verification process as a whole, as illustrated in Figure 16.1. It shows the whole work flow, including specification annotations written in the Java Modeling Language (JML), the selection of verification tasks, symbolic execution, proving of first-order proof obligations, followed by a possible analysis of a failed proof attempt. In addition, there is a section on how to perform verification using the Eclipse integration of the KeY system.

© Springer International Publishing AG 2016
W. Ahrendt et al. (Eds.): Deductive Software Verification, LNCS 10001, pp. 541–570, 2016
DOI: 10.1007/978-3-319-49812-6_16

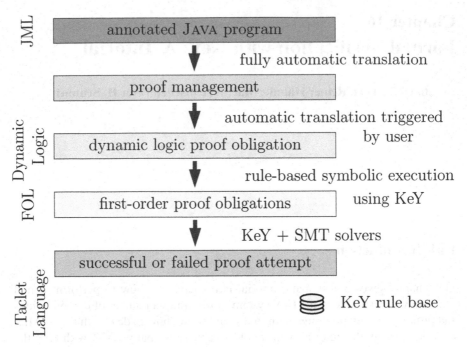

Figure 16.1 The KeY verification workflow

When the input to the KeY system is a `.java` rather than a `.key` file, then it is assumed that the Java code has annotations in JML in the form of structured comments of the source code. Chapter 7 provides a thorough introduction to JML. We give sufficient explanations to understand the examples in this chapter to make it self-contained (after all, JML is marketed as being easily understandable to Java programmers), but we avoid or gloss over the finer points and dark corners of that language.

The organization of the material in this chapter is as follows: In Section 16.2 we illustrate the basic principles of program verification with KeY by way of a simple, loop-free program: JML annotations, loading of problems, selection of proof tasks, configuration of the prover, interactive verification, representation of the symbolic heap. This is followed by Section 16.3 which gives a hands-on introduction into the craft of designing adequate loop invariants and how they are used in KeY. Sections 16.4 and 16.5 walk you through a more complex example (selection sort on arrays). We demonstrate advanced aspects of finding a proof: understanding intermediate states and open subgoals, specifying complex functional properties, working with method contracts, working with model elements in specifications, using strategy macros, guiding the prover when it cannot find a proof itself. Finally, Section 16.6 describes how the Eclipse integration of KeY can be used to automatically manage proofs so that user interaction is only required if a proof is not automatically closable.

16.2 A Program without Loops

```
1  public class PostInc{
2      public PostInc rec;
3      public int x,y;
4
5      /*@  public invariant
6      @        rec.x>=0 && rec.y>=0;
7      @*/
8
9      /*@ public normal_behavior
10     @ requires true;
11     @ ensures rec.x == \old(rec.y) &&
12     @         rec.y == \old(rec.y)+1;
13     @*/
14     public void postinc() {
15             rec.x = rec.y++;
16     }
17 }
```

Listing 16.1 First example: Postincrement

We start with a first simple Java program shown in Listing 16.1. The class PostInc has two integer fields x and y declared in line 3. The only method in the class, postinc(), declared in lines 14–15, sets x to y and increments y. To make things a little more interesting these operations are not performed on the this object, but on the object given by the field rec in line 2. The rest of the shown code are JML comments. In lines 5–6 an invariant is declared. An invariant, as the name is supposed to suggest, is—roughly—true in all states. The states during which the variables contained in the invariant are manipulated have, e.g., to be excepted from this requirement. The details of when invariants precisely are required to hold are surprisingly thorny. Detailed explanations are contained in Section 7.4. For now it suffices to understand that invariants may be assumed to hold at every method call and have to be established after every method termination.

Lines 9–13 are filled with a JML method contract. A contract typically consists of two clauses (we will later see more than two): a precondition signaled by the keyword **requires** and a postcondition following the keyword **ensures**. As with real-life contracts, there are two parties involved in a method contract. The user of a method has to make sure that the precondition is true when the method is called and may depend on the fact that the postcondition is true after termination of the method. The second party, the method provider, has the liability to guarantee that after termination of the method the postcondition is true, provided the precondition was met in the calling state. In the example there is no precondition, more precisely the precondition is the Boolean constant *true* that is true in any state. The postcondition in this case is just the specification of the postincrement operator _++. We trust that the reader has figured out that an JML expression of the form \old(exp) refers to the value of

exp before the execution of the method. The postcondition in itself does not make
any claims on the termination of the method. It is a partial correctness assertion: if
the method terminates, then the postcondition will be true. In the specific example,
termination is asserted by the declaration of the specification case in line 9 as a
`normal_behavior`. When a normal behavior method is called in a state satisfying
its precondition, it will terminate and not throw an exception.

To see what KeY does with the annotated program from Figure 16.1, start the
KeY system as explained in the beginning of Section 15.2. The file `PostInc.java`
is loaded by **File → Load** (or selecting ▦ in the tool bar) and navigating through the
opened file browser. This is the same as loading `.key` files as described in Chapter 15;
the result however is different. The **Proof Management** window will pop up. You will
notice that not only the file you selected has been loaded but also all other `.java`
files in the same directory. So, you could just as well have selected the directory
itself. You may now select in the **Proof Management** window a `.java` file, a method
and a contract. For this experiment we choose the contract `JML normal_behavior`
`operation contract 0` for method `postinc()` in file `PostInc.java` and press
the **Start Proof** button. The verification task formalized in Dynamic Logic will now
show up in the **Current Goal** pane. Since we try to discharge it automatically we do
not pay attention to it. We rather look at the **Proof Search Strategy** tab in the lower
left-hand pane and press the **Defaults** button in its top right corner. You may slide the
maximal rule application selector down to 200 if you wish. All that needs to be done
is to press the **Start** button (to the left of the **Defaults** button or in the tool bar). A
pop-up window will inform you that the proof has been closed and give statistics on
the number and nature of rule applications. In the **Proof** tab of the original window
the proof can be inspected.

The fact that the invariant `rec.x>=0 && rec.y>=0` can be assumed to be true
when the method `postinc()` is called did not contribute to establish the postcondition. But, the automatic proof did include a proof that after termination the invariant
is again true. You can convince yourself of this by investigating the proof tree. To do
this move the cursor in the **Proof** tab of the lower left-hand pane on the first node, or
any other node for that matter, of the proof tree and press the right mouse button. A
pop-up menu will appear. Select the **Search** entry. A search pane at the very bottom
of the **Proof** tab will show up. Enter `inv` in it. Press the ➡ button to the left of the text
field. The first hit, shown in the **Goal** pane, will be `self.<inv>` that corresponds to
the assumption of the invariant at the beginning. Another push on the ➡ button yields
the next hit of the form `h[self.<inv>]`. Here, `h` is a lengthy expression denoting
the heap after termination of the method. This is the formalization of the claim that
the invariant is true in the poststate. The green folder symbol shows that this claim
could be proved successfully. You can now save the proof by selecting **File → Save**.
Let us agree that we accept the suggested file name `PostInc.proof`. We remark,
that you can also save a partial proof and later load it again to complete it.

There is one more topic that we want to discuss with the `PostInc` example at
hand: pretty printing. We start by loading the file `PostInc.proof` that contains the
finished proof for the verification task we have just gone through. After loading
finishes the tree of the closed proof can be inspected in the **Proof** tab. Click on proof

node 13:exc=null;. The **Inner Node** pane now shows the sequent at this proof node. We first focus on the second line self.<created> = TRUE. In the **View** menu the option **Use pretty syntax** is checked in the standard setting. Uncheck it and let us investigate what happened. Line 2 now reads

boolean::select(heap,self,java.lang.Object::<created>) = TRUE.

Here, boolean::select is the ASCII rendering of the function $select_{boolean}$. In general A::select renders the functions $select_A$ introduced in Figures 2.4 and 2.11. In the same formula, <created> is expanded to java.lang.Object::<created>. We thus first observe that pretty printing omits the typing of functions, predicates and fields which in most cases is either fixed in the vocabulary or can be inferred from the context. If nothing helps, you may have to resort to switching pretty printing off. But, the important part is that pretty printing hides the dependence of evaluations on the current heap which is modeled by the attribute heap. This parallels the habit that most programmers omit most of the time to explicitly name the this object. For a field f of type B in class A and a term t of static type A, the following abbreviation will be used for pretty printing:

$$PP(B::select(heap,t,A::\$f)) = PP(t).f$$

Note, that in the next line PostInc::exactInstance(self) = TRUE remains unchanged by pretty printing since the functions $exactInstance_A$ do not depend on the heap.

When running a Java program all evaluations are done with respect to the current heap. But, in verifying properties of programs we need to talk about evaluations in different heaps. It is frequently the case that we want to compare the value of a field before the program is run with its value in the terminating state. What does pretty printing do in case evaluation is not with respect to the current heap? To see an example we look at the line that contains the end \> of the ASCII version of the diamond operator:

self.rec.y@heapAtPre = self.rec.x

Without pretty printing it looks

—— KeY Output ———————————————————————————

```
int::select(heapAtPre,
            PostInc::select(heapAtPre,
                            self,
                            PostInc::$rec),
            PostInc::$y)
 =
int::select(heap,
            PostInc::select(heap,self,PostInc::$rec),
            PostInc::$x)
```

————————————————————————————————— KeY Output ——

The general rule may be stated as

$$PP(B::select(H,t,A::f)) = PP(t).f@H .$$

Applying this literally to the term at the right (upper) side of the above equation we would obtain:

```
(self.rec@heapAtPre).y@heapAtPre
```

There is a second rule that allows the pretty printer to abbreviate `(t0.t1@H).t2@H` by `t0.t1.t2@H`.

Another pretty printing feature, which does not occur in the current example but will pop up in the next section, concerns array access. The pretty printed expression `a[pos2]@H` stands for the full version `int::select(H,a,arr(pos2))`.

The heap independent function $arr : Int \rightarrow Field$ (see Figures 2.4 and 2.11) associates with every integer i a field that stands for the access to the i-th entry in an array. Note, that JFOL is again more liberal than Java. We may write `A::select(h,a,arr(i))` even for i greater than the array length, for negative i, or even when a is not of array type.

The general pretty printing rule is

```
PP(A::select(H,e,arr(a))) = PP(e)[PP(a)]@H
```

if the declared type of `e` is `A[]`. Furthermore, `@H` will be omitted if `H` equals `heap`.

16.3 A Brief Primer on Loop Invariants

16.3.1 Introduction

Finding suitable loop invariants is considered to be one of the most difficult tasks in formal program verification and it is arguably the one that is least amenable to automation. For the uninitiated user the ability to come up with loop invariants that permit successful verification of nontrivial programs is bordering on black magic. We show that, on the contrary, the development of loop invariants is a craft that can be learned and applied in a systematic manner.

We highlight the main difficulties during development of loop invariants, such as strengthening, generalization, weakening, introducing special cases, and we discuss heuristics on how these issues can be attacked. Systematic development of loop invariants also involves close interaction with a formal verification tool, because it is otherwise too easy to overlook errors. To this end, we demonstrate a number of typical interaction patterns with the KeY system.

This section has necessarily some amount of overlap with Section 3.7.2, but it is written in a less formal manner and it concentrates on the pragmatics of loop invariant rules rather than on their formal definition. It is assumed that you have acquired a basic understanding of how the KeY prover works, for example, by reading Chapter 15. Even though proving problems involving recursive methods share some problems with proofs about loops, we concentrate here on the latter, because KeY uses somewhat different technical means to deal with recursion. Some information on proving recursive programs is found in Chapter 9.

16.3.2 Why Are Loop Invariants Needed?

Students who start in Computer Science are often puzzled by the question why such a complex and hard to grasp concept as loop invariants is required in the first place. In the context of formal verification, however, their need is easily motivated. In Chapter 3 it is explained how the calculus of JavaDL realizes a symbolic execution engine for Java programs. When, during symbolic execution, a loop[1] is encountered, symbolic execution attempts to unwind the loop, using the rule from Section 3.6.4:

$$\text{loopUnwind} \quad \frac{\implies \langle \pi \ \text{if} \ (e) \ \{ \ p \ \text{while} \ (e) \ p \ \} \ \omega\rangle\phi}{\implies \langle \pi \ \text{while} \ (e) \ p \ \omega\rangle\phi}$$

If the loop guard is evaluated to true in the current symbolic state, then the loop body p is symbolically executed once and afterwards the program pointer is at the beginning of the loop once again. Otherwise, symbolic execution continues with the code ω following the loop.

Obviously, this works only well, when the number of iterations of the loop is bounded by a small constant. This is not the case in general, however. A loop guard might, for example, look like i < a.length, where a is an arbitrary array of unknown length.

To reason about unbounded loops or even about loops whose body is executed very often (for example, 0 <= i && i < Integer.MAX_VALUE), some kind of induction principle is necessary that permits to prove properties of unbounded structures in a finite manner.

16.3.3 What Is A Loop Invariant?

First of all, a loop invariant always relates to some loop that occurs at a specific location in a given program. In the following we assume it is clear which loop is meant when we speak of "the loop."

In the context of KeY, a loop invariant is a formula $inv \in \text{DLFml}$ that holds in the program state at the beginning of the loop and in the state immediately after each execution of the loop body. If the loop terminates, this means that the invariant holds also in the state where continuation of the given program after the loop commences. As a consequence, if we manage to prove that a formula inv is a loop invariant, then

---

[1] To avoid obscuring the essential points with technical complexities, we concentrate in this section on while loops. Moreover, we assume that the loop body does not throw any exceptions and does not contain break, continue, or return statements.

it can be used during symbolic execution of the continuation after the loop. In this way, loop invariants indeed allow us to reason about programs containing unbounded loops.

The considerations in the previous paragraph can be formalized in a first attempt at a loop invariant rule for JavaDL. To simplify things a little, we assume that the program in the loop guard and loop body do not access the heap.

$$\frac{\begin{array}{ll} \Gamma \implies \{u\}inv, \Delta & \text{(initially valid)} \\ inv, g \doteq TRUE \implies [p]inv & \text{(preserved by body)} \\ inv, g \doteq FALSE \implies [\pi\ \omega]\varphi & \text{(use case)} \end{array}}{\Gamma \implies \{u\}[\pi\ \texttt{while}(g)\,p;\ \omega]\varphi, \Delta}\ \text{loopInvariant1}$$

The first premiss states that *inv* holds in the program state at beginning of the loop, the second premiss states that if *inv* holds in any state that evaluates the loop guard to true—i.e., the loop is entered—then it also holds in the final state after symbolic execution of the loop body, provided that it terminates. Finally, the third premiss permits to use the invariant plus the negated loop guard to prove correctness of the continuation (use case).

Soundness of the loop invariant rule rests on an inductive argument that runs as follows:

Induction Hypothesis: For any $n \geq 1$ the invariant *inv* holds in the state at the beginning of the n-th execution of the loop body.

Induction Base: The invariant *inv* holds in the state at the beginning of the first execution of the loop body, i.e., in the state where symbolic execution of the loop commences. This is exactly what the first premiss says.

Induction Step: If *inv* holds in the state at the beginning of the n-th execution of the loop body, and if the loop is entered at least one more time, then *inv* holds again after execution of the loop body, i.e., in the state at the beginning of the $n+1$-st execution of the loop body.

The problem is that we do not know in which state we are at the beginning of the n-th execution. This problem can be addressed by proving a somewhat more general induction step which does not require that knowledge:

"For *any* program state, if *inv* holds in it at the beginning of the n-th execution of the loop body, and if the loop is entered at least one more time, then *inv* holds again in the state after execution of the loop body."

The latter clearly implies the *Induction Step* above and it is exactly what is expressed in the second premiss of the invariant rule. Observe that the contexts Γ, Δ, and $\{u\}$ were removed from the sequent to ensure that the induction step is indeed valid in any program state.

Similarly, we don't know in which state we are when the loop terminates, so the context information is erased from the third premiss as well. This means that any information from the context that might be needed in the proof of the continuation must be part of the loop invariant. Obviously, this is not very practical and we will come back to this issue. But now let us look at our first concrete loop invariant.

16.3.4 Goal-Oriented Derivation of Loop Invariants

We start by the observation that *any* loop has the trivially valid invariant true. Indeed, a glance at the invariant rule above shows that its first two premisses are straightforward to prove whenever $inv \equiv$ true. But this trivial invariant is, of course, normally useless to prove correctness of the continuation (i.e., the third premiss). In general, we need to find a nontrivial formula to serve as loop invariant, but which?

Often, it is a good idea to think about what we would like to prove, i.e., to work in a goal-oriented manner. Consider the following formula in .key file input syntax:[2]

```
——— KeY ———
n >= 0 & wellFormed(heap) ==>
{i := 0} \[{
  while (i < n) {
    i = i + 1;
  }
}\] (i = n)
                                                              ——— KeY ———
```

Look at the postcondition i = n to be proven. What, in addition to the negated guard i >= n, is needed to show it? Obviously, the formula i <= n is sufficient. Therefore, let us take this formula as a candidate for our loop invariant. To establish that $inv \equiv i \leq n$ is an invariant we must instantiate the loop invariant rule with inv as above, $\Gamma \equiv n \geq 0, u \equiv i := 0, g \equiv i < n, p \equiv i = i + 1$; and empty Δ, π, ω. The instantiated (initially valid) premiss becomes

$$n \geq 0 \Longrightarrow \{i := 0\}(i \leq n)$$

After update application the sequent's succedent becomes $0 \leq n$, making the sequent obviously provable. Instantiation of the second premiss (preserved by body) and simplification of the guard expression yields:

$$i \leq n, i < n \Longrightarrow [i = i + 1;](i \leq n)$$

The sequent's succedent becomes after symbolic execution of the assignment and update application $i + 1 \leq n$, which is clearly provable from the antecedent. Therefore, $inv \equiv i \leq n$ is indeed a loop invariant that suffices to prove the postcondition at hand.

It is not always the case that a loop is the final statement before the postcondition. In this case, it is necessary to infer the difference between the state after the loop and the final state before the postcondition. For this reason, in the presence of multiple loops it is a good idea

---

[2] Even for programs that do not access the heap it is necessary to have the well-formedness assumption in order to render the problem provable. This is to exclude initial states that cannot be obtained in the Java runtime environment. We include the well-formedness constraint, because we want to give actually provable examples, but we leave it out from the subsequent reasoning steps for readability. The declaration of program variables, for example "int i, n;," is omitted in the following.

- to develop the invariant of the loop that is closest to the end of the program first, and
- to develop the invariant of the outermost loop first, in the case of nested loops.

16.3.5 Generalization

Let us look at a slightly more complex example, where x and y are program variables of type integer and x_0, y_0 are first-order constants of the same type.

—— KeY ——————————————————————————————————————
```
x = x0 & y = y0 & y0 >= 0 & wellFormed(heap) ==>
\[{
  while (y > 0) {
    x = x + 1;
    y = y - 1;
  }
}\] (x = x0 + y0)
```
——— KeY ——

Starting again from the postcondition, we see that the postcondition bears no obvious relation to the guard. Hence, our first attempt at finding a loop invariant is simply to use the postcondition itself: $inv \equiv x \doteq x_0 + y_0$. This formula, however, is clearly not valid at the beginning of the loop, and neither is it preserved by the loop body.

A closer look at what happens in the loop body reveals that both x and y are modified, but only the former is mentioned in the invariant. It is obvious that the invariant must say something about the relation of x and y to be preserved by the loop body. What could that be? The key observation is that in the loop body first x is increased by one and then y is decreased by one. Therefore, the *sum* of x and y stays invariant. Together with the observation that x initially has the value x_0 and y the value y_0, we arrive at the invariant candidate $inv \equiv x + y \doteq x_0 + y_0$, which is indeed initially valid as well as preserved by the loop body.

Is this a good invariant? Not quite: the postcondition is not provable from $x + y \doteq x_0 + y_0 \land y \leq 0$. It would be sufficient, if we knew that $y \geq 0$. And indeed, we have not made use of the precondition $y_0 \geq 0$ which states that the initial value of y is nonnegative. The loop guard ensures that y is positive when we enter the loop and in the loop body it is decreased only by one, therefore, $y \geq 0$ is a loop invariant as well. Using the combined invariant $inv \equiv x + y \doteq x_0 + y_0 \land y \geq 0$ it is easy to prove the example. In summary, for this example we made use of some important heuristics:

1. Generalize the postcondition into a relation about the variables modified in the loop body that is preserved.
2. Look for unused information in the proof context that can be used to derive additional invariants.

3. Loop invariants are closed under conjunction: if inv_1 and inv_2 are loop invariants of the same loop, then so is $inv_1 \wedge inv_2$.

16.3.6 Recovering the Context

Recall from Section 16.3.3 that our rule loopInvariant1 throws away the proof context from the second and third premiss to ensure soundness. Let us look at an example that illustrates the problem with this approach. Assume we want to prove something about the following program, where a has type int[]:

```
—— Java + JML ———————————————————————————
int i = 0;
while(i < a.length) {
  a[i] = 1;
  i++;
}
————————————————————————————— Java + JML ——
```

Whatever property we are going to prove about the loop, we will need the precondition a $\neq$ null $\in \Gamma$ to make sure that the array access does not throw a null pointer exception. As we throw away the context, it will be necessary to add a $\neq$ null to any loop invariant. This may seem not so bad, but now assume that Γ contains a complex class invariant that is needed during the proof of the continuation after the loop. Again, this has to be added to the invariant. Loop invariants tend to become impractically bulky when they are required to include relevant parts of the proof context.

A closer look at the loop body of the program above shows that while the content of the array a is updated, the object reference a itself is untouched and, therefore, a precondition such as a $\neq$ null $\in \Gamma$ is an implicit invariant of the loop body. What we would like to have is a mechanism that automatically includes all those parts of the context into the invariant whose value is unmodified by the loop body.

As it is undecidable whether the value of a given program location is modified in a loop body, this information must in general be supplied by the user. On the level of JML annotations this is done with the directive "assignable $l_1, \ldots, l_n$;", where the l_i are program locations or more general expressions of type \locset. These may contain a wildcard "*" where an index or a field is expected to express that all fields/entries of an object might get updated. For the loop above a correct specification of its assignable locations would be "assignable i, a[*];." KeY accepts that assignable clause, but actually ignores the local variable i. Instead its loop invariant rule checks the loop body and guard for any assignments to local variables and adds these implicitly to the assignable clause. Hence, only heap locations need to be specified as part of the assignable clause.

The intended effect of an assignable clause is that any knowledge in the proof context that depends on the value of a location mentioned in that assignable clause

is erased in the second and third premiss of the invariant rule. How is this realized
at the level of JavaDL? The main idea is to work with suitable updates. For value
types, such as i in the example above, it is sufficient to add an update of the form
$\{i := c\}$, where c is a fresh constant of the same type as i. Such an update assigning
fresh values to locations is called *anonymizing update*; details about their structure
are explained in Section 9.4.1. A context preserving invariant rule, based on the rule
LOOPINVARIANT1 above, therefore, looks as follows:

$$\frac{\begin{array}{ll} \Gamma \implies \{u\}inv, \Delta & \text{(initially valid)} \\ \Gamma \implies \{u\}\{v\}(inv \wedge g \doteq TRUE \to [p]inv), \Delta & \text{(preserved by body)} \\ \Gamma \implies \{u\}\{v\}(inv \wedge g \doteq FALSE \to [\pi\,\omega]\varphi), \Delta & \text{(use case)} \end{array}}{\Gamma \implies \{u\}[\pi\,\texttt{while}(g)\,p;\,\omega]\varphi, \Delta}$$

where $\{v\}$ is the anonymizing update for the assignable clause
`assignable` $l_1, \ldots, l_n;$.

Observe that the proof context Γ, Δ, $\{u\}$ has been reinstated into the second and
third premiss. For object types (e.g., a[*]) more complex conditions about the heap
must be generated. KeY does this automatically for assignable clauses specified in
JML and we omit the gory details. The interested reader is referred to Section 8.2.5.

Assignable clauses should be as "tight" as possible, i.e., they should not contain
any location that cannot be modified by the loop they refer to. On the other hand,
assignable clauses must be sound: they must list all locations that possibly can be
modified. In Java care must be taken, because it is possible to modify locations even
in the guard expression. An unsound assignable clause renders the invariant rule
where it is used unsound as well. For this reason, KeY generates proof obligations
for all assignable clauses that ensure their soundness.[3] The exception are local
variables where it is possible to compute a sound assignable clause by a simple
static analysis and KeY does that automatically, even when no assignable clause is
explicitly stated. Otherwise, the default declaration, when no assignable clause is
stated, is "`assignable \everything;`." This should be avoided.

We close this subsection by stating the example from above with JML annotations
that are sufficient for KeY to prove it fully automatic:

—— Java + JML ——————————————————————————

```
public int[] a;
/*@ public normal_behavior
  @   ensures (\forall int x; 0<=x && x<a.length; a[x]==1);
  @   diverges true; // termination not proven
  @*/
public void m() {
  int i = 0;
  /*@ loop_invariant
```

---

[3] This proof obligation is part of the (preserved by body) branch. For ease of presentation it is not
included in the rule above.

```
@   0 <= i && i <= a.length &&
@   (\forall int x; 0<=x && x<i; a[x]==1);
@   assignable a[*];
@*/
while(i < a.length) {
  a[i] = 1;
  i++;
}
}
```
———————————————————————————————— Java + JML ——

Observe that the local variable i is not listed in the assignable clause and that the JML default a ≠ null needs not to be stated in the invariant.

To maximize automation of KeY in the presence of loops, the setting **Invariant** should be chosen in the **Loop Treatment** option of the **Proof Search Strategy** settings (see Chapter 15). This causes the prover to look for `loop_invariant` and `assignable` declarations in the input file and applies the loop invariant rules without user interaction. In addition, it can be useful to set option **Quantifier Treatment** to **No Splits with Progs** (which avoids splitting during symbolic execution) and, if the program contains arithmetic operators * or /, to set option **Arithmetic Treatment** to **DefOps**.

16.3.7 Proving Termination

Programs with loops may not terminate, but so far we have only looked at partial correctness and at terminating programs. Consider, for example, the sequent:

$$\Longrightarrow [\texttt{i = 17; while (true) \{\}}]\, \texttt{i} \doteq 42$$

Is it provable? It turns out that our formalism so far can correctly handle this example: with the trivial invariant `true` and the declaration `assignable \nothing`; this is proven automatically. Indeed, for the trivial invariant, the (initially valid) and (preserved by body) branches are always closable. The negated guard gives `false` and from that anything is provable, including the stated postcondition. The initialization in front of the loop is completely irrelevant and could have been left out.

On the other hand, to prove *termination* of a loop we need additional machinery. In KeY we use well-founded orders, i.e. partial orders without infinite descending chains. In this chapter we use only the natural numbers in their standard ordering $0 < 1 < 2 < \cdots$. The idea is to define an arithmetic expression d over program variables that is proven to become strictly smaller, but not negative, in each loop iteration. This is called *decreasing term* or *variant*. Since any natural number has only a finite number of predecessors, it follows that a loop with a decreasing term must terminate after a finite number of iterations.

The principle is illustrated in Figure 16.2. Assume that, when we execute the loop body the first time, the decreasing term d is evaluated to $N \geq 0$. In the next iteration it must be evaluated to a value smaller than N, and so on. After a finite number of rounds 0 is reached. As d must be nonnegative, the loop must terminate then.

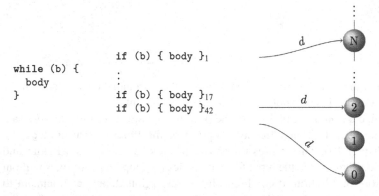

Figure 16.2 Mapping loop execution into a well-founded order

The loop invariant rule for total correctness can now be derived from the version for partial correctness in a straightforward manner, by simply adding the decreasing term with the according proof obligations:

1. We must strengthen the invariant *inv* by stating that the decreasing term d stays nonnegative, resulting in $inv \wedge d \geq 0$.
2. The postcondition of the (preserved by body) branch must state that the value of d is strictly less than it was at the beginning of the execution of the loop body.

The result is the following *invariant rule with context preservation for termination*:

$$\Gamma \implies \{u\}inv, \Delta$$
$$\Gamma \implies \{u\}\{v\}(inv \wedge g \doteq TRUE \wedge d \geq 0 \wedge d' \doteq d \to \langle p \rangle (inv \wedge d \geq 0 \wedge d > d')), \Delta$$
$$\frac{\Gamma \implies \{u\}\{v\}(inv \wedge g \doteq FALSE \to \langle \pi\, \omega \rangle \varphi), \Delta}{\Gamma \implies \{u\}\langle \pi\, \text{while}(g)\, p;\, \omega \rangle \varphi, \Delta}$$

where $\{v\}$ is the anonymizing update for the assignable clause **assignable** $l_1, \ldots, l_n;$. Moreover, d' is a fresh integer constant.

At the level of JML, total correctness is achieved by

1. removing the partial correctness directive **diverges true;** from the surrounding contract and
2. adding a directive "**decreasing** $d;$," where d is a decreasing term.

This causes KeY to create suitable proof obligations with total correctness modalities and to choose the terminating version of the invariant rule.

To prove that the loop in the example from the previous subsection terminates, it is sufficient to remove the **diverges true;** directive and to add the directive "**decreasing a.length - i;**" to the loop specification.

Sometimes a termination witnessing decreasing term of type integer is very difficult or even impossible to find. JML and KeY support more general **decreases** clauses working, e.g., with pairs or sequences. Details can be found in Section 9.1.4 on the verification of terminating recursive methods.

16.3.8 A More Complex Example

We use a slightly more complex example to illustrate a few more heuristics that can be useful when developing loop invariants. Below is the JML specification and Java implementation of method gcdHelp that computes the greatest common divisor (gcd) of two integers _big and _small under the normalizing assumption that _big is at least as large as _small which in turn is not negative. It can be used to implement a method gcd for arbitrary numbers (not shown here).

```
—— Java + JML ————————————————————————————————————————
public class Gcd {
  /*@ public normal_behavior
    @ requires _small >= 0 && _big >= _small;
    @ ensures _big != 0 ==>
    @   (_big % \result == 0 && _small % \result == 0 &&
    @     (\forall int x;
    @             x > 0 && _big % x == 0 && _small % x == 0;
    @             \result % x == 0));
    @ assignable \nothing;
    @*/
  private static int gcdHelp(int _big, int _small) {
    int big = _big; int small = _small;
    while (small != 0) {
      final int t = big % small;
      big = small;
      small = t;
    }
    return big;
  }
}
——————————————————————————————————————————— Java + JML ——
```

A result is only defined for the nontrivial case when _big is positive. In this case, the returned value must be a common divisor of both _big and _small which is ensured by "_big % \result == 0 && _small % \result == 0." In addition, the returned value must be the *greatest* common divisor. This is expressed by the quantified formula which states that any positive x that is a common divisor of _big and _small must also be a divisor of the result and hence not greater.

The code above does not yet specify a loop invariant. We must supply a specification of the loop that allows us to prove the given contract. Obviously, the loop doesn't modify any location that is visible outside, therefore, we use **assignable** \nothing;. The decreases term is also straightforward: small is initially nonnegative and certainly it decreases whenever the loop is entered, therefore, we use "**decreasing** small;."

To develop the loop invariant we look first at the requires clause to see what could be preserved. A quick check tells us that the properties of _big and _small also hold for the variables big and small that are used in the loop (we introduced these fresh names, because this results in a more readable invariant). Therefore, the first part of our invariant is:

$$small >= 0 \; \&\& \; big >= small$$

What else can we say about the boundaries of big and small? For example, can big become zero? Certainly not in the loop body, because it is assigned the old value of small which is ensured by the loop guard to be nonzero. However, it is admissible to call the method with _big being zero, so big > 0 might not initially be valid. Only when _big is non zero, we can assume big > 0 to be an invariant. Hence, we add the *relative* invariant

$$\_big \; != \; 0 \; ==> \; big \; != \; 0 \; . \tag{16.1}$$

But what is the *functional* property that the loop preserves? In the end we need to state something about all common divisors x of _big and _small. Which partial result might have been achieved during execution of the loop? A natural conjecture is to say something about the common divisors of big and small: in fact these should be *exactly* the common divisors of _big and _small. Because, if not, we could run in danger to "loose" one of the divisors during execution of the loop body. This property is stated as

```
(\forall int x; x > 0; (_big % x == 0 && _small % x == 0)
                  <==> (big % x == 0 && small % x == 0));
```

We summarize the complete loop specification below. With it, KeY can prove total correctness of gcdHelp fully automatically in a few seconds.

—— Java + JML ——

```
int big = _big; int small = _small;
/*@ loop_invariant small >= 0 && big >= small &&
  @ (big == 0 ==> _big == 0) &&
  @ (\forall int x; x > 0; (_big % x == 0 && _small % x == 0)
  @                  <==> (big % x == 0 && small % x == 0));
```

```
  @ decreases small;
  @ assignable \nothing;
  @*/
while (small != 0) {
  final int t = big % small;
  big = small;
  small = t;
}
return big; // will be assigned to \result
```
—— Java + JML ——

Perhaps the reader wonders why the loop invariant is actually sufficient to achieve the postcondition of the contract, specifically, why is it the case that the returned value, i.e., the final value of big after the loop terminates, is a divisor of both _big and _small? Now, this needs only to be shown when big is positive, because of (16.1). In that case, the third part of the invariant can be instantiated with x/big. Using that small == 0 (the negated loop guard) then completes the argument. This kind of reasoning is easily within the first-order inference capabilities of KeY.

16.3.9 Invariants: Concluding Remarks

The discussion in this section hopefully demonstrated that loop invariants must be systematically developed: they don't come out of thin air or appear magically after staring at a program for long enough. The process of loop invariant discovery is comparable to bug finding: it is a cycle consisting of analysis of the target program, generation of an informed conjecture and then confirmation or refutation of the conjecture. If the latter happens, the reasons for failure must be analyzed and they form the basis of the next attempt.

Good starting points for invariant candidates are the postcondition (what, in addition to the negated loop guard is needed to achieve it?) and the precondition of the problem's contract. Another source is the result of symbolic execution of one loop guard and body. But one such execution yields usually no invariant: it is necessary to relate the state before and after symbolic execution of the loop body to each other in the invariant. A good question to ask is: how can I express the partial result computed by one execution of the loop body? Often, symbolic execution of a few loop iterations can give good hints.

If a loop invariant that suffices to prove the problem at hand seems elusive, don't forget that your program or your specification of it might be buggy. Ask yourself questions such as: does the postcondition really hold in each case? Are assumptions missing from the precondition? Another possibility is that you attempt to use a stronger loop invariant than is required. The *Model Search* feature of the KeY prover (see Section 15.4) can be very useful to generate counter examples that give a hint, in case some proof goal stays open.

For complex loops, it is often the case that several rounds of strengthening and weakening of the invariant candidate is required, before a suitable one is found. In this case, it is a good idea to develop invariants incrementally. This is possible, because invariants are closed under conjunction. Start with simple value bounds and well-formedness assumptions. These may exhibit flaws in the target program or specification already. It is also a good idea to work with *relativized* invariants that can be tested separately. For example, it can be simpler to test $cnd \rightarrow inv$ and $\neg cnd \rightarrow inv$ separately than to work with inv directly.

Remember that there is no single loop invariant that is suitable to prove the problem at hand, but there are typically many reformulations that do the trick. There could be simpler formulations than the first one that comes to mind. In particular, try to avoid quantified formulas as much as possible in invariants, because they are detrimental to a high degree of automation in proof search.

It is recommended to use the KeY prover to confirm or to refute conjectures about invariants, as symbolic execution by hand is slow and error-prone. If a loop occurs within a complex context (for example, nested with/followed by other loops) it can be useful to formulate the invariant as a separate contract and look at just that proof obligation in isolation.

In this section we tried to give some practical hints on systematic development of loop invariants. There is much more to say about this topic. For example, so as not obscure the basic principles we left out the complications arising from heap access or from abrupt termination of loop bodies. More information on how JavaDL handles these issues can be found in Chapter 3. More complex examples of loop invariants can be found in the subsequent section and in Part V of this book.

16.4 A Program with Loops

Listing 16.2 shows the code of a Java class `Sort` implementing the selection sort algorithm. This is a simple, not very effective sorting algorithm, see e.g. [Knuth, 1998, Pages 138—141 of Section 5.2.3]. The integer array to be sorted is stored in the field `int[]` `a` of the class `Sort`. At every stage of the algorithm the initial segment `a[0]` `...a[pos-1]` is sorted in decreasing order. The tail `a[pos]` `...a[a.length-1]` is still unsorted but every entry `a[i]` in the tail is not greater than `a[pos-1]`. At the beginning `pos=0`. On termination `pos=a.length-1`, which means that `a[0]` `...a[a.length-2]` is sorted in decreasing order and `a[a.length-1]` is not greater than `a[a.length-2]`. Thus the whole array is indeed sorted.

To proceed from one stage in the algorithm to the next, as long as `pos` is still strictly less than `a.length-1`, an index `idx` is computed such that `a[idx]` is maximal among `a[pos]` `...a[a.length-1]`, the entries `a[idx]` and `a[pos]` are swapped and `pos` is increased by one.

The main part of this algorithm is implemented in the method `sort()` in lines 26 to 46 of Listing 16.2. The index of a maximal entry in the tail `a[pos]`

```
1  public class Sort {
2    public int[] a;
3
4    /*@ public normal_behavior
5      @ requires a.length > 0 && 0<= start && start < a.length;
6      @ ensures (\forall int i; start<=i && i<a.length;a[\result] >= a[i]);
7      @ ensures start <= \result && \result < a.length;
8      @*/
9    int /*@ strictly_pure @*/ max(int start) {
10     int counter = start;
11     int idx = start;
12     /*@ loop_invariant  start<=counter && counter<=a.length &&
13       @     start<=idx && idx<a.length  && start<a.length &&
14       @     (\forall int x; x>=start && x<counter; a[idx]>=a[x]);
15       @ assignable \strictly_nothing;
16       @ decreases a.length - counter;
17       @*/
18     while (counter < a.length) {
19       if (a[counter] > a[idx])
20         idx = counter;
21       counter = counter+1;
22     }
23     return idx;
24   }
25
26   /*@ public normal_behavior
27     @ requires a.length > 0;
28     @ ensures (\forall int i; 0 <= i && i<a.length-1; a[i] >= a[i+1]);
29     @*/
30   void sort() {
31     int pos = 0;
32     int idx = 0;
33     /*@ loop_invariant 0<=pos && pos<=a.length && 0<=idx && idx<a.length
34       @   && (\forall int x; x>=0 && x<pos-1; a[x]>=a[x+1]) &&
35       @   (pos>0 ==>(\forall int y; y>=pos && y<a.length; a[pos-1]>=a[y]));
36       @ assignable a[*];
37       @ decreases a.length - pos;
38       @*/
39     while (pos < a.length-1) {
40       idx = max(pos);
41       int tmp = a[idx];
42       a[idx] = a[pos];
43       a[pos] = tmp;
44       pos = pos+1;
45     }
46   }
47 }
```

Listing 16.2 Second example: Sorting an array

...a[a.length-1] of the array is returned by the method call max(pos). Method max(int start) is given in lines 9–24 in Listing 16.2.

The specification of sort() says that this method terminates without an uncaught exception (line 26) and upon termination array a is sorted in decreasing order (line 28). The only precondition, a.length>0, required of method sort() is stated in line 27. Inspection shows that the code would also handle the case a.length=0 correctly. But, the loop invariant would have to be rephrased. As it stands 0<=idx && idx<a.length would not be true at the beginning of the loop. There is no need to also require that a is not the null object since JML tacitly takes this as the default.

The loop invariant starts in line 33 with the statement that the local variables pos and idx stay within their bounds. The remaining two lines formalize the informal description of the algorithm given a above: The formula in line 34 says that the initial segment a[0] ...a[pos-1] is sorted in decreasing order while line 35 contains the formalization of the description that every entry a[i] for pos <= i < a.length+ is not greater than a[pos-1]. This is not true for pos=0, so the condition pos>0 ==> has to be prefixed. Line 31 specifies the locations that may at most be changed by the loop body. See Section 16.3.6 for a general introduction of the use of **assignable** clauses. Also pos and idx may be changed in the loop body, but the KeY system can figure this out by itself. Only possible changes to heap locations need to be declared.

To allow the system to prove termination of the loop an integer expression is needed that is never negative and strictly decreases in each loop iteration. The term a.length-pos given in the **decreases** clause in line 37 serves this purpose. See the previous Section 16.3.7 for a gentle introduction to termination proofs.

Let us now turn to the contract for method max. This method is declared to be **strictly_pure** in line 9, which means that is does not change any field of any existing object and also does not create new objects. The precondition, line 5, requires the parameter start to be within the bounds of array a. The conjunctive part a.length>0 is here for the same reason as in the precondition of sort. The postcondition ensures that the returned index, denoted by the JML keyword result, is taken from the tail segment start, ...a.length-1, line 7, and that a[result] is indeed maximal among a[start], ...a[a.length-1], line 6.

The loop invariant begins in lines 12 – 13 with a declaration that the method parameter start and the local variables counter and idx stay within their intended ranges. In Section 16.3.9 it was proposed as a guideline for finding invariants to look at the postcondition and the loop guard. This advice works very well in the case at hand. In the end, i.e., when counter=a.length, we want a[idx] to be maximal among a[start],..., a[a.length-1]. This suggests as an invariant that a[idx] be maximal among a[start],..., a[counter-1]. This is formalized in the formula in line 14. The frame condition in the **assignable** clause in line 15, and the **decreases** clause in line 16 are self explanatory.

The KeY system verifies the contracts for both methods automatically with the settings **Java verif. std.** Make sure that **Max. Rule Applications** is at least 6000. Let us inspect the finished proof. For this open the **Proof** tab in the lower left-hand pane, place the cursor over any node, activate the menu by a right mouse click and select the **Hide Intermediate Proofsteps** entry. After opening some of the green folder symbols

Figure 16.3 Condensed finished proof tree

the proof tree looks as in Figure 16.3 on the left. The proof goals Use Axiom at the top and Show Axiom Satisfiability at the bottom of the first column refer to the type or class invariant. This JML concepts was already alluded to in Section 15.3. A type invariant is a formula that is stipulated to be true in any *visible* state. E.g., a type invariant is assumed to be true at every method call and must be verified to be true after method termination, or as is the case in the situation under study, the invariant axiom is assumed to be true at the beginning of a while loop and has to be established after its termination. For the class Sort the invariant a!=null is automatically generated from the JML default. In general, the user may specify any invariant he believes to be useful. To guard against the possibility that the chosen invariant is inconsistent, the proof goal Show Axiom Satisfiability is generated and has to be discharged, which is absolutely trivial in the present situation.

The three proof goals on the second vertical line in the screenshot 16.3 are generated when symbolic execution reaches the while loop. As explained in Section 16.3.2, the new goals are *Invariant Initially Valid*, *Body Preserves Invariant* and *Use Case*. The interesting branch is *Body Preserves Invariant* which has been unfolded three times. We skip the next three columns in screenshot 16.3 and turn to the three goals Post(max), Exceptional Post(max), and Pre(max). They are generated when symbolic execution reaches the method call max. According to the proof settings the method call to max is not symbolically executed, its contract is used instead. This involves verifying that its precondition, Pre(max), is satisfied and continuing in case max terminates exceptionally with the proof branch labeled *Exceptional Post(max)* and in case of normal termination, *Post(max)*, with the respective guarantees ensured by the contract in both cases.

There is one more issue that can be demonstrated already with the small example program under investigation. How precise should a postcondition be? There is the notion of a strongest postcondition, but this is not always expressible in first-order logic and may also be undesirably complicated. The postcondition of method max in line 6 of Listing 16.2, e.g., is not the strongest possible. One could add that \result is the least index of a maximal value among a[start] ... a[a.length-1]:

```
(\forall int i; start <= i && i < \result; a[i]<\result)
```

But, that would complicate verification without being necessary in the present context. Thus, how precise the postcondition should be may depend in what it is being used for.

16.5 Data Type Properties of Programs

Listing 16.3 contains the same Java code as Listing 16.2. Also the contract for method max is the same. The differences lie in the contract for method sort in lines 30–33 and in the declaration of *model fields* in lines 4–6. In the postcondition for method sort in line 28 in Listing 16.2 an important assurance is missing: that the array a after termination is a permutation of the array when the method was called. More precisely, we want to say that there is a permutation σ of the integers $0, \ldots, a.length - 1$ such that for all $0 \leq i < a.length$ we have $a_{new}[i] = a_{old}[\sigma(i)]$. To formalize this statement we introduce the abstract data type *Seq* of finite sequences. This data type is described in detail in Section 5.2. For this tutorial it will suffice to think of a finite sequence as mathematical function σ whose domain of definition is a finite initial segment of the positive integers. In general the range of values of σ is quite liberal. Here, we only encounter finite sequences of integers. A permutation is then defined as a finite sequence that is a surjective, and thus also injective, function from its domain onto its domain. The data type *Seq* contains a binary predicate $seqPerm(s_1, s_2)$ with the intended meaning, that sequence s_1 is a permutation of s_2. This is not to be confused with the unary predicate $seqNPerm(s)$ which says that s is a permutation, i.e., that s is a bijective function from $[0, seqLen(a))$ onto $[0, seqLen(a))$, where predictably $seqLen(s)$ is the length of sequence s.

This seems to be the right time to point out a troubling obstacle to our idea to use sequences and permutation to formulate the intended postcondition of method sort: sequences and permutations do not occur anywhere in the Java code and Java code is all JML allows us to talk about. As a solution JML offers the declaration of *model fields*. In line 4 of Listing 16.3 a model field of class SortPerm named seqa of type \seq is declared. Here, \seq simply is the JML name for the data type *Seq*. A model field is a field that is only used for modeling purposes. Written as a special comment, like all JML specifications, it is ignored by the Java compiler. Values to model fields are assigned by the JML represents clause. In line 5 of Listing 16.3 seqa is assigned the sequence that corresponds to the field a. The transformation from a state-dependent Java array to a state-independent object of data type *Seq* is effected by the built-in function *array2seq*. The data type *Seq* and also the function *array2seq* are not part of official JML. It belongs to our project specific extension of JML, that we hope will at some time also be adopted in the official version. In the meantime we will use the escape sequence \dl_ to signal to the JML parser that the following item is not JML syntax and is to be passed unchanged on to the translator from JML into our internal logic *JavaDL*. After these explanations we see that line 32 in Listing 16.3 formalizes the postcondition we want: the sequence corresponding to array a after method termination is a permutation of the sequence corresponding to array a at method invocation. Since again *seqPerm* is not part of official JML we have to use the escape \dl_seqPerm.

Now, that we understand the specification let us see how we can prove it. We start with the taclet base configuration. To this end load any file containing JML annotated Java code and select a contract target. This is necessary since the menu item we are looking for, **Taclet Options**, is not active when no proof is loaded. Clicking on menu

```
1  public class SortPerm {
2    public int[] a;
3
4    /*@ model \seq seqa;
5      @ represents seqa = \dl_array2seq(a);
6      @*/
7
8    /*@ public normal_behavior
9      @ requires a.length > 0 && 0<= start && start < a.length;
10     @ ensures (\forall int i;start<=i && i<a.length; a[\result] >= a[i]);
11     @ ensures start <= \result && \result < a.length;
12     @*/
13   int /*@ strictly_pure @*/ max(int start) {
14     int counter = start;
15     int idx = start;
16     /*@ loop_invariant  start<=counter && counter<=a.length &&
17       @    start<=idx && idx<a.length  && start<a.length &&
18       @    (\forall int x; x>=start && x<counter; a[idx]>=a[x]);
19       @ assignable \strictly_nothing;
20       @ decreases a.length - counter;
21       @*/
22     while (counter<a.length) {
23       if (a[counter] > a[idx])
24         idx=counter;
25       counter=counter+1;
26     }
27     return idx;
28   }
29
30   /*@ public normal_behavior
31     @ requires a.length > 0;
32     @ ensures  \dl_seqPerm(seqa,\old(seqa));
33     @*/
34   void sort() {
35     int pos = 0;
36     int idx = 0;
37     /*@ loop_invariant 0<=pos && pos<=a.length && 0<=idx && idx<a.length
38       @    && \dl_seqPerm(seqa,\old(seqa));
39       @ assignable a[*];
40       @ decreases a.length - pos;
41       @*/
42     while (pos < a.length-1) {
43       idx = max(pos);
44       int tmp = a[idx];
45       a[idx] = a[pos];
46       a[pos] = tmp;
47       pos = pos+1;
48     }
49   }
50 }
```

Listing 16.3 Third example: Permutations

item **Options, Taclet Options** after a proof is loaded opens the **Taclet Base Configuration** window. Somewhere in the middle of the list you see moreSeqRules. Clicking
on it shows the two options **moreSeqRules:off** and **moreSeqRules:on**. By default this
option is turned off, but we will need it to reason about permutations. After pushing
the **OK** button, the system will inform you that you have to instantiate a new proof for
the changes to take effect. Do this, now by loading the file SortPerm.java. Since
KeY loads all Java files in a directory we have to select in the **Proof Management**
window the file SortPerm and the method sort(). This proof will not close automatically. The prover will need a little help from us. We want to keep interactions to
a minimum but at the same time have control over what the prover tries to do. This is
where strategy macros come into play.

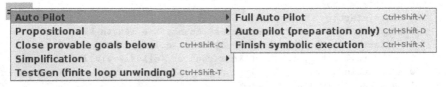

Figure 16.4 Strategy macros

Placing the cursor over the sequent separation arrow ==> a click on the right mouse
button will display the list of strategy macros shown in the screenshot 16.4 above.
Alternatively, you can press the left mouse button and select the **Strategy macros**
menu. For now, we select the **Full Auto Pilot** which does the following:

1. Finish symbolic execution   (another macro in itself)
2. Separate proof obligations
3. Expand invariant definitions
4. Close provable goals   (another macro in itself)

Alternatively one could click on the left mouse button to obtain a selection of possible
next steps. Among them is one named **Apply rules automatically here** which starts the
proof search strategy only for the current goal/formula. This differs from the macro
Close provable goals below in that it runs till the maximal number of proof steps is
exhausted and may thus stop in a proof situation that is hard to figure out. So, let us
apply the **Full Auto Pilot** macro with the maximal number of rule applications set to
5000. One goal remains. Inspection of the proof tree shows that the open goal claims
that the loop invariant is preserved by an execution of the loop body. Above the
sequent separator ==> we find the assumption seqPerm(s1,t1), where s1 denotes
the model field seqa at the beginning of an arbitrary loop iteration and t1 stands for
seqa at the beginning of the loop. Below the sequent separator ==> we find the claim
seqPerm(s2,t2). Here t2 is a different representation for the same sequence as t1,
in which the represents clause for seqa has not yet been applied. Also s2 denotes
the value of seqa at the end of the arbitrary loop execution. Thus s2 is obtained
from s1 by swapping two entries. So we need to prove: if s1 is a permutation of
t1 (=t2) and s2 is a swap of s1, then also s2 is a permutation of t1 (=t2). There
is fortunately a taclet that provides exactly this argument. Place the cursor over the

occurrence of `seqPerm` below the sequence separator, press the left mouse button and select from the presented suggestions the taclet seqPermFromSwap. Since the system cannot decide when it is useful to apply this taclet, i.e., when `s2` is a swap of `s1`, the heuristics of this taclet forbids automatic application. User interaction is thus needed here.

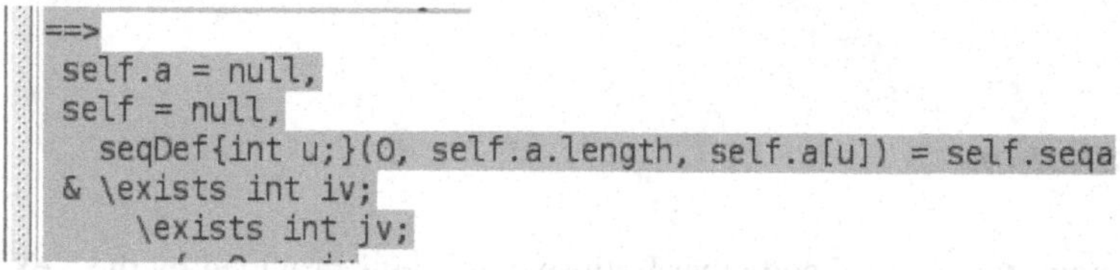

```
==>
  self.a = null,
  self = null,
    seqDef{int u;}(0, self.a.length, self.a[u]) = self.seqa
  & \exists int iv;
    \exists int jv;
```

Figure 16.5 After `seqPermFromSwap`

After rule application the lower (right) part of the sequent starts as shown in the Snapshot 16.5. Remember that the right side of a sequent is a comma separated disjunction. We may thus assume `self.a != null` and `self != null` and try to prove the remaining conjunction. Place the cursor over the conjunction symbol & and select the taclet andRight for the next step. This splits the previous conjunctive goal into two goals, one for each conjunct. Applying the macro **Close provable goals below** we see that KeY can prove both goals on its own. Make sure that **Max. Rule Applications** is at least 10 000.

16.6 KeY and Eclipse

As we have seen in the previous sections the KeY system is powerful enough to close a proof fully automatically in many situations. All that needs to be done is to load the source code, select a contract and start the proof search strategy. After a single contract has been proven successfully, the proof remains in the almost proven state until the correctness of all applied contracts is shown as well. Our goal for this section will be to achieve overall correctness, so we are interested in proving all available proof obligations.

To achieve overall correctness is an arduous path and very likely we will not be able to achieve it the first time. Some proofs might remain open caused by defective method implementations or by too weak or wrong specifications. In such cases we have to modify code or specifications. Previously unclosed proofs can then be retried on the new code version. But also already closed proofs have to be redone since the modification may have violated them.

Tool support for verification in such an ongoing software development process requires the ability to react on source file changes and to store proofs consistently with the sources. This can't be achieved by the KeY system alone simply by the fact that it operates on a specific version of source files. Modifications always have to be done in a different tool which is typically an integrated development environment (IDE) like Eclipse.

In the following subsections we describe the usage of KeY's Eclipse integration [Hentschel et al., 2014c]. The main contribution is an automatic proof management for all proof obligations in the whole project. After each change possibly outdated proofs are determined and automatically redone. User interaction is only required if a proof is not automatically closable.

16.6.1 Installation

The Eclipse integration of KeY and other Eclipse extensions provided by the KeY project can be added to an existing Eclipse installation via an update-site. The supported Eclipse versions and the concrete update-site URLs are available on the KeY website (www.key-project.org). When reading the following sections for the first time, we strongly recommend to have a running Eclipse installation with the verification features at hand, so that they can be tried out immediately. We assume that the reader is familiar with the Java perspective of the Eclipse IDE.

16.6.2 Proof Management with KeY Projects

Eclipse is a platform for different purposes including software development in different programming languages. Source files are organized in projects of different kinds associated with *Builders* that are automatically invoked when the project content changes. A *Java Project* is used to develop Java applications and the associated *Java Builder* automatically compiles the contained source code.

KeY's Eclipse integration provides a new project kind named *KeY Project* which is an extended Java project. The additional functionality is that the *KeY Builder* automatically performs relevant proofs whenever source or proof files are modified.

To start we create an example KeY project which is automatically filled with some content. All we have to do is to open the *New Example* wizard, select *KeY/KeY Project Example* and finish the wizard. An empty KeY project can be created with the help of the eponymous *New Project* wizard. Alternatively, it is possible to convert an existing Java project into a KeY project via its context menu.

Performed proofs are automatically maintained in folder *proofs* as shown in Figure 16.6. For each proof obligation a *.proof* file named after it exists.

The advantage of the maintained project structure is the compatibility with version control systems. Thus a KeY Project can be directly shared and source files with proofs are always committed and updated in a consistent way. Even a comparison between different versions is possible.

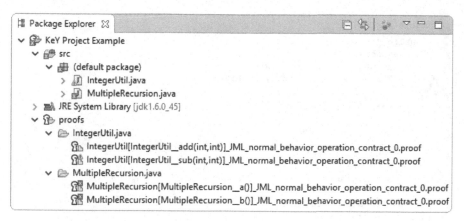

Figure 16.6 KeY project with example content

16.6.3 Proof Results via Marker

Each time the KeY Builder completed a proof, the user is immediately informed about the proof result. This is done directly in the source code as close as possible to the proven proof obligation via so called *Marker*. As Figure 16.7 demonstrates, markers are shown as icons next to the line number within the *Java Editor*. In this example the method add is successfully proven (ℹ information marker) whereas the proof of method sub is still open (⚠ warning marker).

The presence of warning and error markers can also be seen in view *Package Explorer*. Whenever a Java source file contains a warning (⚠) or error marker (⊗), an overlay image is added to the file icon. In case that a file contains both, warning and error markers, only the more urgent error icon is shown. In addition, the most urgent marker type is also delegated to parent folders and the project. This can be seen in Figure 16.6 where the default package has an error overlay image, because the error in class MultipleRecursion is more urgent than the warning in class IntegerUtil.

To find out why the proof of method sub was not closed by the proof search strategy all we have to do is to move the mouse over the marker icon. In general two reasons are possible: First, the strategy could be not powerful enough to close it or second, because the implementation or its specifications are defective.

Here, the implementation is obviously defective. We can easily fix it by replacing return x + y with return x - y. When we save the file now, the KeY Builder will be triggered. It performs the proofs again and updates the result marker. It is also possible to inspect and to interactively continue proofs using the *quick fix* functionality (i.e., left click on the marker icon). This opens the proof in the original user interface of KeY as earlier discussed in this chapter. Alternatively, a proof can be inspected using the Symbolic Execution Debugger (see Chapter 11). When an interactively completed proof is saved back to its original location, the KeY Builder will be triggered and in turn update the result marker.

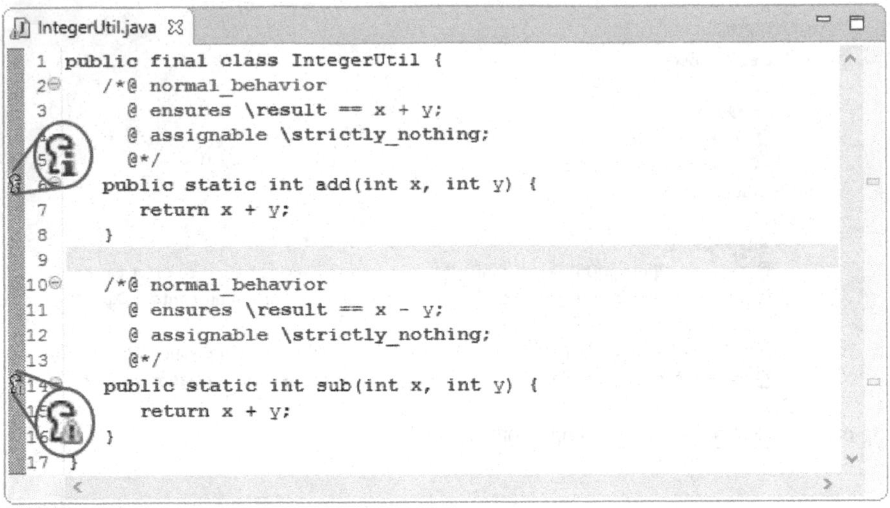

Figure 16.7 Closed and open proof marker

The *Use Operation Contract* rule requires to introduce another marker kind. Whereas in general the applicability of rules depends only on the current sequent, the application of method contracts requires a global correctness management to avoid cyclic contract applications of all proofs shown in the same proof management dialog. Such cycles are problematic because it allows one to prove everything, even false. To avoid cyclic contract applications in the KeY system, the rule which would cause a cycle is not applicable. The drawback is that other proofs and the order in which they are done can influence the current proof result.

This approach does not work for a KeY Project, because we can finish a single proof interactively without caring about other proofs. Consequently, the global correctness check is performed as last step during a built. If a cycle is detected, participating proofs are highlighted with an error marker (🔒). An example is shown in Figure 16.8 where methods a and b successfully prove **false**. Both proofs apply the contract of the called method which forms a cycle indicated by the error marker. The tooltip of such marker lists all participating proofs and it is our task to modify at least one of them to break the cycle.

16.6.4 The Overall Verification Status

The view *Verification Status* is the best opportunity to inspect the overall verification status. Figure 16.7 shows the status of the example project before fixing the defect in method sub. The two progress bars at the top indicate how many proofs are already successfully proven and how many methods are specified. Absolute numbers are shown in the tooltips of the progress bars.

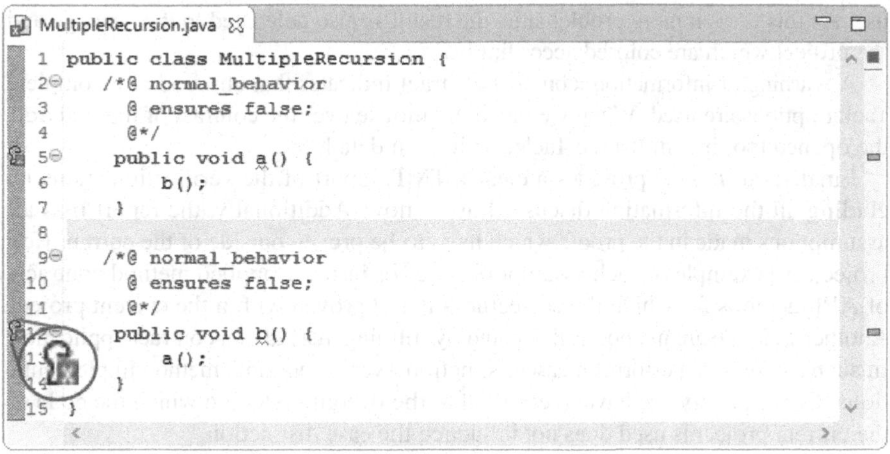

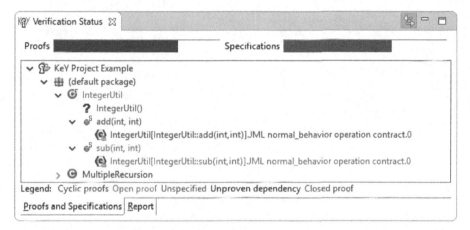

Figure 16.8 Recursive specification marker

Figure 16.9 The overall verification status

The tree in the middle reflects the code and the specification structure. The color of each item shows its verification result as specified by the legend below the tree. The *most problematic* result is always delegated to ancestors. It is defined as the minimal element in the following ordered list (worst to best): (i) *cyclic proofs* (the usage of specifications forms a cycle; colored red), (ii) *open proof* (colored orange), (iii) *unspecified* (no proof obligation available; colored gray), (iv) *unproven dependency* (proof is closed, but an applied specification is not verified yet; colored blue) and (v) *closed proof* (colored green). Here the only contract of method add is successfully proven whereas the one of sub is still open. The default constructor of class IntegerUtil is unspecified. The most problematic result below class IntegerUtil is the open proof and consequently, it is colored with this result. Finally, class MultipleRecursion contains proofs forming a cyclic specification use. As this is even more problematic, the result is also delegated to the package and the project which are colored accordingly.

A warning or information icon on a contract indicates that unsound or incomplete Taclet options are used. When we move the mouse over the contract of method add, the opened tooltip will list the Taclet options in detail.

Finally, tab *Report* provides a clear HTML report of the verification status including all the information discussed up to now. Additionally, the report lists all assumptions made in the proofs which have to be proven outside of the current KeY project. An example of such assumptions are for instance applied method contracts of API methods for which the correctness is not proven within the current project. Another example are method calls treated by inlining instead of a contract application. In such a case KeY performs a case distinction over all possible method implementations. Consequently, we have to ensure that the overall system in which the code of the current project is used does not influence the case distinction.

Chapter 17
KeY-Hoare

Richard Bubel and Reiner Hähnle

17.1 Introduction

In contrast to the other book chapters that focus on verification of real-world Java program, here we introduce a program logic and a tool based on KeY that has been designed solely for teaching purposes (see the discussion in Section 1.3.3). It is targeted towards B.Sc. students who get in contact with formal program verification for the first time. Hence, we focus on program verification itself, while treating first-order reasoning as a black box. We aimed to keep this chapter self-contained so that it can be given to students as reading material without requiring them to read other chapters in this book. Even though most of the concepts discussed here are identical to or simplified versions of those used by the KeY system for Java, there are subtle differences such as the representation of arrays, which we point out when appropriate.

Experience gained from teaching program verification using Hoare logic [Hoare, 1969] (or its sibling the weakest precondition (wp) calculus [Dijkstra, 1976]) as part of introductory courses exposed certain short-comings when relying solely on text books with pen-and-paper exercises:

- Using the original Hoare calculus requires to "guess" certain formulas, while using the more algorithmic wp-calculus requires to reason backwards through the target program, which is experienced as nonnatural by the students.
- Doing program verification proofs by hand is tedious and error-prone even for experienced teachers. The reason is that trivial and often implicit assumptions like bounds or definedness of values are easily forgotten. Hence, pen-and-paper proofs often contain undiscovered minor bugs due to too weak or incomplete specifications.
- First-order logic reasoning is typically not a part of an introduction to program verification. But this is difficult to avoid in standard formulations of program verification where the reduction of programs to first-order proof obligations and first-order reasoning is interleaved.

© Springer International Publishing AG 2016
W. Ahrendt et al. (Eds.): Deductive Software Verification, LNCS 10001, pp. 571–589, 2016
DOI: 10.1007/978-3-319-49812-6_17

KeY-Hoare mitigates the identified short-comings as follows: The first issue is addressed by reusing the idea of symbolic state updates from JavaDL (see Chapter 3). We designed a calculus to realize a symbolic execution style of reasoning in the same spirit as the JavaDL calculus, but we stay close to the formalism used in a Hoare-style calculus that extends standard Hoare triples to Hoare quadruples including symbolic state updates. This is only a small change, which does not impede the students from using standard text books (for example, [Tennent, 2002, Huth and Ryan, 2004]). Our target programming language is a simple imperative while programming language with scalar arrays. The remaining two issues have been solved by providing an easy-to-use tool which implements our modified Hoare calculus on top of the powerful first-order reasoning engine of KeY. Specifically, the discharge of first-order proof obligations can be treated as a black box.

This chapter is an extended version of the paper [Hähnle and Bubel, 2008] adding support for arrays, *total* correctness and worst-case execution time analysis.

17.2 The Programming Language

For KeY Hoare we focus on a simple imperative programming language whose syntax is defined by the following grammar:

$\langle Program \rangle ::= (\langle Statement \rangle)?$

$\langle Statement \rangle ::= \langle EmptyStatement \rangle \mid \langle AssignmentStatement \rangle \mid$
$\qquad\qquad\quad \langle CompoundStatement \rangle \mid \langle ConditionalStatement \rangle \mid$
$\qquad\qquad\quad \langle LoopStatement \rangle$

$\langle EmptyStatement \rangle ::= \text{';'}$

$\langle AssignmentStatement \rangle ::= \langle Location \rangle = \langle Expression \rangle \text{';'}$

$\langle CompoundStatement \rangle ::= \langle Statement \rangle \langle Statement \rangle$

$\langle ConditionalStatement \rangle ::= \texttt{if } \text{'('} \langle BoolExp \rangle \text{')'}$
$\qquad\qquad\qquad\qquad\quad \text{'\{'} \langle Statement \rangle \text{'\}'} \texttt{ else } \text{'\{'} \langle Statement \rangle \text{'\}'}$

$\langle LoopStatement \rangle ::= \texttt{while} \text{'('} \langle BoolExp \rangle \text{')'} \text{ '\{'} \langle Statement \rangle \text{'\}'}$

$\langle Expression \rangle ::= \langle BoolExp \rangle \mid \langle IntExp \rangle$

$\langle BoolExp \rangle ::= \langle IntExp \rangle \langle CompOp \rangle \langle IntExp \rangle \mid \langle IntExp \rangle == \langle IntExp \rangle \mid$
$\qquad\qquad\quad \langle BoolExp \rangle \langle BoolOp \rangle \langle BoolExp \rangle \mid \,! \langle BoolExp \rangle \mid$
$\qquad\qquad\quad \langle Location \rangle \mid \texttt{true} \mid \texttt{false}$

$\langle IntExp \rangle ::= \langle IntExp \rangle \langle IntOp \rangle \langle IntExp \rangle \mid \mathbb{Z} \mid \langle Location \rangle$

$\langle CompOp \rangle ::= < \mid <= \mid >= \mid > \qquad\qquad\qquad \langle BoolOp \rangle ::= \& \mid | \mid ==$

$\langle IntOp \rangle ::= * \mid / \mid \% \mid + \mid - \qquad \langle Location \rangle ::= \texttt{IDENT} \mid \texttt{IDENT}[\langle IntExp \rangle]$

The grammar used in the implementation is slightly more complex as it incorporates the usual precedence rules for operators and allows one to use parenthesized expressions. We point out some important design decisions:

1. The programming language has only two incomparable types called **boolean** and **int**, in particular, no array types exist. To simplify the semantics of arith-

metic operations, the type `int` represents the mathematical integers $\mathbb{Z}$ and not a finite integer type with overflow.

2. Program variables and arrays (referred to as ⟨*Locations*⟩ by the grammar) are declared globally outside of the program, i.e., there are no local program variables and arrays can only be manipulated, but not created at runtime. Arrays are unbounded and their elements are uniquely indexed by any integer. This avoids the need for checking boundaries when accessing array elements and to define exceptional behavior in case an array access is out of bounds.

3. *Locations* are program variables or array access expressions, e.g., `a[i]` (with `i` being an integer expression such as a program variable or number literal). Arrays themselves are scalar arrays, referenced by name. They are neither locations nor expressions. Let `a` and `b` denote two arrays of element type `int` then `a == b` is not a valid comparison expression and `a = b;` is not a valid assignment statement. On the other hand, `a[7] == b[8]` or `a[i] = b[j];` are syntactically valid. In addition, as `a` and `b` are different names, they denote different arrays. This avoids the aliasing problem for arrays (that is present in Java), e.g., `a[i]` and `b[i]` are never aliases in our language.

17.3 Background

17.3.1 First-Order Logic

Specifying a program means to express what a program is supposed to do in contrast to how to do it. To be able to machine-check whether a given implementation (which describes *how* to compute a function) adheres to its specification, we need to define a formal language in which to write the specification as we needed one (the programming language) to write the implementation.

The language of our choice is typed first-order logic as a small but well studied formal language suitable to express state-based properties about the behavior of programs. Terms and formulas are inductively defined as usual, but we also allow expressions of the programming language as terms. This does not cause any problems, as all expressions of our programming language are side effect free.

As usual the atomic formulas of our logic are either formulas of the form $P(t_1, \ldots, t_n)$ with a (user-defined) predicate symbol P of arity n and terms $t_1, \ldots, t_n$ of appropriate type or $s \doteq t$ with the reserved *equality* symbol $\doteq$ taking arbitrary terms as arguments.

Program variables are *not* modeled as first-order variables but as constants (0-ary functions). Therefore, it is not possible to quantify over program variables. This modeling is identical to the one used by JavaDL (see Chapter 3). Program variables are special constant symbols in the sense that they are *nonrigid* symbols. In contrast to *rigid* symbols which are evaluated by a classical interpretation function and variable assignment, *nonrigid* symbols (and hence program variables) are evaluated with respect to a (program) state. As a consequence the value of rigid symbols is fixed and cannot be changed by a program, while nonrigid program variables can be evaluated differently depending on the current execution state. A common usage of rigid function symbols is to "store" the initial value of a program variable so that one can refer to that value in a later execution state. In addition, built-in symbols with a fixed semantics, such as equality $\doteq$ and arithmetic operators of the programming language, are rigid symbols.

In JavaDL the only nonrigid symbols are program variables, but for KeY-Hoare it is useful to implement as well nonrigid unary function symbols f that map `int` values to values of type `int` or `boolean`. They are used to model arrays. We permit the notation $f[i]$ instead of $f(i)$ to resemble more closely the array syntax used in programs.

Many program logics, including the original logic by Hoare [1969], model program variables with first-order (rigid) variables. The disadvantage is that this requires to introduce so called *primed* variables as in [Boute, 2006]. Each state change during symbolic execution then causes the introduction of fresh primed variables. The increase in the number of symbols required to specify and to prove a problem compromises the readability of proofs considerably. Readability, however, is a central issue where interactive usability is concerned—not only for students at the beginner level. A further point in favor of nonrigid symbols is to avoid confusion for students who may just have gotten used to the static viewpoint of first-order logic.

Some useful *conventions*: program variables are typeset in *typewriter* font, logical variables in *italic*. When we specify a program π we assume that all program variables of π are contained in the first-order signature with their correct type. The *semantics* of first-order formulas is interpreted over fixed domain models. Specifically, all Boolean terms are interpreted over {`true`, `false`} and all integer terms over $\mathbb{Z}$. There are built-in function symbols for arithmetic including +, -, *, / and % and integer comparison operators <=, <, > and >= with their standard meaning. For the concrete formula syntax see Section 17.7.2. Apart from that, all semantic notions such as satisfiability, model, validity, etc., are completely standard and as defined in Chapter 2.

17.3.2 Hoare Calculus

Before we define our own version, we present a standard version of the Hoare [1969] calculus (without arrays) to introduce some basic notions and to identify some problematic design decisions that we avoid in our approach. As usual, the behavior of programs is specified with *Hoare triples*:

$$\{P\}\,\pi\,\{Q\} \tag{17.1}$$

Here, P and Q are closed first-order formulas and π is a program over locations $L = \{l_1, \ldots, l_m\}$. The meaning of a Hoare triple is as follows: *for each first-order* model $\mathcal{M} = (D, I)$ and program state s of P, if π is started with initial values $i_k = val_{\mathcal{M}, s, \beta}(l_k)$ $(1 \leq k \leq m)$ and if π terminates with final values f_k, then $\mathcal{M}, s_{l_1, \dots, l_m}^{f_1, \dots, f_m}, \beta$ is a model of Q.

We can paraphrase this in a slightly more informal, but more intuitive, manner: for a given program π over locations $\{l_1, \dots, l_m\}$, let us call an assignment of values $l_k = v_k$ $(1 \leq k \leq m)$ a *state* s of π. What the Hoare triple then says is that if we start π in any state satisfying the *precondition* P, if π terminates, then we end up in a final state that satisfies *postcondition* Q.

The standard Hoare rules are displayed in Figure 17.1. We use the following conventions for schematic variables occurring in the rules: e is an expression, b is a Boolean expression, x is a program variable, s, s1, s2 are statements. P, Q, R, I are closed first-order formulas. Here $P\{x/e\}$ is the formula arising from P by replacing every occurrence of the constant x by the expression e.

$$\text{assignment } \frac{}{\{P\{x/e\}\}\, x\texttt{=e};\, \{P\}}$$

$$\text{composition } \frac{\{P\}\,\texttt{s1}\,\{R\} \qquad \{R\}\,\texttt{s2}\,\{Q\}}{\{P\}\,\texttt{s1 s2}\,\{Q\}} \qquad\qquad \text{skip } \frac{}{\{P\}\,;\,\{P\}}$$

$$\text{conditional } \frac{\{P \wedge \texttt{b} \doteq \texttt{true}\}\,\texttt{s1}\,\{Q\} \qquad \{P \wedge \texttt{b} \doteq \texttt{false}\}\,\texttt{s2}\,\{Q\}}{\{P\}\,\texttt{if(b)\{s1\}else\{s2\}}\,\{Q\}}$$

$$\text{loop } \frac{\{I \wedge \texttt{b} \doteq \texttt{true}\}\,\texttt{s}\,\{I\}}{\{I\}\,\texttt{while(b)\{s\}}\,\{I \wedge \texttt{b} \doteq \texttt{false}\}}$$

$$\text{weakeningLeft } \frac{P \rightarrow Q \qquad \{Q\}\,\texttt{s}\,\{R\}}{\{P\}\,\texttt{s}\,\{R\}} \qquad \text{weakeningRight } \frac{\{P\}\,\texttt{s}\,\{Q\} \qquad Q \rightarrow R}{\{P\}\,\texttt{s}\,\{R\}}$$

$$\text{oracle } \frac{}{P} \quad (P \text{ any valid first-order formula})$$

Figure 17.1 Rules of standard Hoare calculus.

17.4 Hoare Logic with Updates

The standard formulation of Hoare logic in Figure 17.1 has a number of *drawbacks* in usability that are particularly problematic when used for teaching purposes:

- The assignment rule computes directly the weakest preconditions from a given postcondition. Therefore the calculus requires to reason backwards through the program. This is obviously unnatural as it requires the user to understand a reached program state by "executing" the program in opposite direction to its control flow.
- The compositional rule splits the proof into two subgoals and requires to provide a formula describing the intermediate state reached in between both statements. The standard formalization of the Hoare calculus requires this formula to be guessed instead of being algorithmically inferred.

- The rules for the conditional statement and loops require to apply an additional weakening rule as preparatory step. As weakening is a purely first-order reasoning rule, it would be preferable to defer this step until the program is completely eliminated and to hide it as part of the first-order reasoning process.

We overcome these issues by introducing an explicit notation that describes finite parts of symbolic program states. This allows us to recast Hoare logic as forward symbolic execution.

17.4.1 State Updates

State updates in our logic are almost identical to those introduced in Chapter 3. But since we use scalar arrays and an implicit heap, the updates in this chapter are closer to the original variant used in previous versions of the KeY system [Beckert et al., 2007, Rümmer, 2006].

A (state) *update* is an expression of the form $\langle Location \rangle := \langle FOLTerm \rangle$. Actually, this is only the most simple form of an update, called *elementary update*. Complex updates are defined inductively: if $\mathcal{U}$ and $\mathcal{V}$ are updates, then so are $\mathcal{U}, \mathcal{V}$ (*sequential update*), and $\mathcal{U} \parallel \mathcal{V}$ (*parallel update*) and $\mathcal{U}(\mathcal{V})$ (*update application*). Sequential updates as an explicit construct are available only in KeY-Hoare, but not in JavaDL.

The most important kind of update is the parallel update. Consider a parallel update of the form $\mathcal{U} = l_1 := t_1 \parallel \cdots \parallel l_m := t_m$. Let (D, I) be a first-order model with domain D, interpretation I and let β denote a variable assignment. Assume a given program state s. Then the update takes us into a state $s_{\mathcal{U}}$ such that:

$$s_{\mathcal{U}}(x) = \begin{cases} t_k & \text{if } x = l_k \text{ and } l \notin \{l_{k+1}, \ldots, l_m\} \\ s(x) & \text{if } x \notin \{l_1, \ldots, l_m\} \end{cases} \tag{17.2}$$

$$s_{\mathcal{U}}(a)(i) = \begin{cases} t_k & \text{if } k = \max\{j \in \{1 \ldots m\} | a[t'] = l_j \wedge val_{D,I,s,\beta}(t') = i\} \text{ exists} \\ s(a)(i) & \text{otherwise} \end{cases}$$
$$\tag{17.3}$$

In words: the value of the locations occurring in $\mathcal{U}$ are overwritten with the corresponding right-hand side. Equation (17.2) defines the case for program variables and (17.3) for arrays. The condition $l \notin \{l_{k+1}, \ldots, l_m\}$ in (17.2) ensures that the rightmost update in $\mathcal{U}$ "wins" if the same location occurs more than once on the left-hand side in $\mathcal{U}$. Similarly, the max operator in the array case. Apart from that, all updates are executed in parallel.

Updates are similar to a preamble or fixture as used in unit testing [Myers, 2004]: a piece of code that gets you into a certain state. There is, however, a difference between updates and code: the right-hand side of an update may contain a symbolic first-order term, not merely a program expression. This feature is often used to initialize a program with "arbitrary, but fixed" values.

The significance of parallel updates lies in the following property, formally stated in Lemma 17.1 below. Let us call two updates $\mathcal{U}$ and $\mathcal{V}$ *equivalent* if $s_\mathcal{U} = s_\mathcal{V}$ for any state s. Then for each update $\mathcal{U}$ there exists an equivalent *parallel* update $\mathcal{V}$ of the form $l_1 := t_1 \parallel \cdots \parallel l_m := t_m$.

17.4.2 Hoare Triples with Update

We extend the classical Hoare triple to a Hoare quadruple by placing an update $\mathcal{U}$ in front of any program like this: $[\mathcal{U}]\pi$. If we are in state s the meaning is that the program is started in state $s_\mathcal{U}$. Within Hoare logic we use updates as follows (identical to JavaDL):

$$\{P\}[\mathcal{U}]\pi\{Q\} \tag{17.4}$$

where, P, Q, and π are as above, and $\mathcal{U}$ is an update over the signature of P and π. We enclose updates in square brackets to increase readability. Either one of $\mathcal{U}$ and π can be empty. The meaning of this *Hoare triple with update* is as follows: if s is any state satisfying the *precondition P* and we start π in $s_\mathcal{U}$, then, if π terminates, we end up in a final state that satisfies *postcondition Q*. The Hoare triple with updates is equivalent to the dynamic logic formula:

$$P \rightarrow \{\mathcal{U}\}[\pi]Q$$

17.4.3 Hoare Style Calculus with Updates

In Figure 17.2 we state the rules of a Hoare calculus with updates that has some new features when compared to the Hoare calculus of Figure 17.1:

- Composition is turned into left-to-right symbolic execution. Thereby the intermediate formula R is computed by rule application and needs not to be guessed. While this is sufficient for completeness, it does not subsume the composition rule as a whole as it lacks its implicit weakening.
- Weakening is delayed until after all program rules have been applied and becomes part of first-order verification condition checking.
- We use updates for computing the result of assignments.

One advantage of weakest precondition calculation [Dijkstra, 1976] as well as backward-execution style Hoare calculus is that an assignment can be computed by simple substitution and no renaming of old variables is necessary. The price to be paid for that is the not very intuitive backward-execution of programs. The KeY program logic uses updates to achieve weakest precondition computation with *forward* symbolic execution. In our eyes, this is a major pedagogical advantage: not only follows program rule application the natural execution flow in imperative programs, but the whole proof process is compatible with established paradigms such as symbolic debugging (see Chapter 11).

$$\text{assignment}_{pv} \ \frac{\{P\}\,[\mathcal{U},\mathtt{x}:=\mathtt{e}]\,\mathtt{s}\,\{Q\}}{\{P\}\,[\mathcal{U}]\,\mathtt{x=e;s}\,\{Q\}} \qquad \text{assignment}_{arr} \ \frac{\{P\}\,[\mathcal{U},\mathtt{a[i]}:=\mathtt{e}]\,\mathtt{s}\,\{Q\}}{\{P\}\,[\mathcal{U}]\,\mathtt{a[i]=e;s}\,\{Q\}}$$

$$\text{exit} \ \frac{\vdash P \to \mathcal{U}\,(Q)}{\{P\}\,[\mathcal{U}]\,\{Q\}} \qquad\qquad \text{skip} \ \frac{\{P\}\,[\mathcal{U}]\,\mathtt{s}\,\{Q\}}{\{P\}\,[\mathcal{U}]\,\mathtt{;s}\,\{Q\}}$$

$$\text{conditional} \ \frac{\{P \wedge \mathcal{U}\,(\mathtt{b} \doteq \mathtt{true})\}\,[\mathcal{U}]\,\mathtt{s1;s}\,\{Q\} \qquad \{P \wedge \mathcal{U}\,(\mathtt{b} \doteq \mathtt{false})\}\,[\mathcal{U}]\,\mathtt{s2;s}\,\{Q\}}{\{P\}\,[\mathcal{U}]\,\mathtt{if(b)\{s1\}else\{s2\}s}\,\{Q\}}$$

$$\text{loop} \ \frac{\vdash P \to \mathcal{U}\,(I) \qquad \{I \wedge \mathtt{b} \doteq \mathtt{true}\}\,[]\,\mathtt{s1}\,\{I\} \qquad \{I \wedge \mathtt{b} \doteq \mathtt{false}\}\,[]\,\mathtt{s}\,\{Q\}}{\{P\}\,[\mathcal{U}]\,\mathtt{while(b)\{s1\}s}\,\{Q\}}$$

Figure 17.2 Rules of Hoare calculus with updates.

In the KeY logic as well as in the presented version of Hoare logic the rules have a "local" flavor in the sense that each judgment (i.e., node) in the proof tree relates to an elementary symbolic state transition during program execution.

We use the same conventions for schematic variables as above, but in addition, let $\mathcal{U}$ be an update and $\mathtt{s}$ is either a statement or the empty string. The rules are depicted in Figure 17.2. Let us briefly discuss each of them.

The *assignment* rules become easy as assignments are directly turned into updates. We can turn the whole assignment into an update in a single step, because in our simple language expressions have no side effects. Hence, we do not need to introduce temporary variables to capture expression evaluation as in JavaDL. The same holds for guards. Because we moved composition of substitutions into updates, we can now evaluate programs left-to-right. The weakest precondition calculation is moved into the update rules (see Figure 17.3 below).

There is one new rule called exit that is applied when a program is fully symbolically executed. At this point, the update is applied which computes the weakest precondition of the symbolic program state $\mathcal{U}$ with respect to the postcondition Q. Then it is checked whether the given precondition implies the weakest precondition. The premise of the exit rule (as well as the left-most premise of the loop rule) are purely first-order verification conditions. This is indicated by a turnstile in order to make clear that we left the language of Hoare triples.

The conditional rule simply adds the guard expression as a branch condition to the precondition. Of course, we must evaluate the guard in the current state $\mathcal{U}$. As mentioned above, this requires expressions to have no side effects. It has the advantage that path conditions can easily be read off each proof node.

The loop rule is a standard invariant rule. We exploit again that expressions have no side effects, but also that we have no reference types. The chosen formulation stresses the analogies to the conditional rule. The first premise says that the precondition must be strong enough to ensure that the invariant holds after reaching the state at the beginning of the loop. In the second premise we are not allowed to use P, because P might have been affected by executing $\mathcal{U}$. In addition, we must reset the update to the empty one. In other words, started in *any* state where the loop invariant and condition hold the invariant must hold again after execution of the loop body. In practice, one uses as a starting point for the invariant those parts of P that are unaffected by $\mathcal{U}$. In those parts that *are* modified, one typically generalizes a suitable term and adds that to the invariant. More advice on how to choose a loop invariant can be found in Section 16.3.

17.4.4 Rules for Updates

We still need rules that handle our explicit state updates. Specifically, we need to (i) turn sequential into parallel updates (Section 17.4.1) and (ii) apply updates to terms, formulas, and to other updates. For the first task we use a Lemma from [Rümmer, 2006] (in specialized form):

Lemma 17.1. *For any updates* $\mathcal{U}$*,* $x := t$ *and* $a\,[t_{idx}] := t$ *the updates*

- $\mathcal{U}$*,* $x := t$ *and* $\mathcal{U} \parallel x := \mathcal{U}(t)$ *are equivalent;*
- $\mathcal{U}$*,* $a\,[t_{idx}] := t$ *and* $\mathcal{U} \parallel a\,[\mathcal{U}(t_{idx})] := \mathcal{U}(t)$ *are equivalent.*

The resulting rule is depicted together with the other update application rules in Figure 17.3. These are rewrite rules that can be applied whenever they match. We use the same schematic variables as before and, in addition, t, t_{idx} are first-order terms, $\mathcal{P}$ is a parallel update of the form $l_1 := t_1 \parallel \cdots \parallel l_m := t_m$, y is a first-order variable, F is a rigid n-ary function or predicate symbol, $\Box$ is a propositional connective, and λ is a quantifier.

$$\mathcal{U}, x := t \rightsquigarrow \mathcal{U} \parallel x := \mathcal{U}(t) \qquad\qquad \mathcal{U}, a[t_{idx}] := t \rightsquigarrow \mathcal{U} \parallel a[\mathcal{U}(t_{idx})] := \mathcal{U}(t)$$

$$\mathcal{P}(x) \rightsquigarrow \begin{cases} t_k & \text{if } x = l_k \text{ and } l \notin \{l_{k+1}, \ldots, l_m\} \\ x & \text{if } x \notin \{l_1, \ldots, l_m\} \end{cases} \qquad \mathcal{U}(y) \rightsquigarrow y$$

$$\mathcal{P}(a[t_{idx}]) \rightsquigarrow \text{if } \mathcal{P}(t_{idx}) \doteq t_{idx_{i_k}} \text{ then } t_{i_k} \text{ else } \ldots \text{ else if } \mathcal{P}(t_{idx}) \doteq t_{idx_{i_1}} \text{ then } t_1 \text{ else } a[\mathcal{P}(t_{idx})]$$
$$\text{for } \mathcal{P} \downarrow_a = (i_1, \ldots, i_k)$$

$$\mathcal{U}(F(t_1, \ldots, t_n)) \rightsquigarrow F(\mathcal{U}(t_1), \ldots, \mathcal{U}(t_n)) \qquad \mathcal{U}(P \Box Q) \rightsquigarrow \mathcal{U}(P) \Box \mathcal{U}(Q)$$
$$\mathcal{U}(\lambda y. P) \rightsquigarrow \lambda y. \mathcal{U}(P), \ y \notin fv(\mathcal{U})$$

Figure 17.3 Rewrite rules for update computation.

The top row in Figure 17.3 contains the rules that turn sequential updates into parallel updates. The second row contains rules for applying updates to program and to first-order variables. There is a strong similarity between the first rule and the semantics definition of an update (17.2) on p. 576, while first-order variables are rigid and can never be changed by an update.

The third row shows the rule for applying a parallel update to an array access term. This rewrite rule is more complex as we cannot syntactically decide whether two array access expressions refer to the same location and we need in addition to compare the indices for equality. This comparison manifests itself in a cascade of conditional terms that check which (if any) elementary update of the parallel update is applicable. The comparisons must be performed backwards, because of the last-one-wins semantics of updates (corresponding to the max operator in the semantics definition of updates (17.3) on p. 576). In the rule we denote with $\mathscr{P} \downarrow_a$ the tuple $(i_1, \ldots, i_k)$ such that $i_z \in \mathscr{P} \downarrow_a \Leftrightarrow l_{i_z} = a[t_{idx_{i_z}}]$ for some term $t_{idx_{i_z}}$ and such that from $z_1 < z_2$ it follows that $i_{z_1} < i_{z_2}$ (with $0 < z_1, z_2 \leq k$). Intuitively, $\mathscr{P} \downarrow_a$ enumerates (order-preserving) all updates to array a by the parallel update $\mathscr{P}$.

Example 17.2. We demonstrate briefly how an application of a parallel update to an array access term is rewritten. Given the parallel update

$$\mathscr{V} := a[i] := 3 \parallel m := 5 \parallel a[j] := 4 \parallel b[m] := 10$$

The term $\mathscr{V}(a[m])$ becomes

$$\text{if } \mathscr{V}(m) \doteq j \text{ then } 4 \text{ else if } \mathscr{V}(m) \doteq i \text{ then } 3 \text{ else } a[\mathscr{V}(m)]$$

with $\mathscr{V} \downarrow_a = (1,3), l_1 = a[i]$ $(t_{idx_1} = i)$ and $l_3 = a[j]$ $(t_{idx_3} = j)$. Further applications of the update rewrite rules results in

$$\text{if } 5 \doteq j \text{ then } 4 \text{ else if } 5 \doteq i \text{ then } 3 \text{ else } a[5]$$

It can be easily seen that the resulting conditional term evaluates to 4, if for instance $i \doteq j \doteq \mathscr{V}(m)(= 5)$ holds which is according to the last one-wins semantics.

The fourth and fifth row contain rules for complex terms and for formulas. These are merely homomorphism rules propagating the update to the subterms/-formulas. In quantified formulas, again, first-order variables cannot be affected, but as they may occur in updates one has to ensure that no name clashes occur ($fv(\mathscr{U})$ returns the set of first-order variables not bound in $\mathscr{U}$). Update application can be seen as substitution of program variables with their new values with additional aliasing checks in case of arrays.

There is no rule to apply updates to programs. Updates accumulate during the reasoning process until symbolic execution of the target program terminates. Applying the update to the postcondition Q then computes its weakest precondition with respect to the taken path condition.

17.5 Using KeY-Hoare

We illustrate how to prove correctness of a program using the KeY-Hoare tool along a small example. Consider the program searchMax

```
max = a[0];
i = 1;
while (i < len) {
        if (max < a[i]) {
                max = a[i];
        } else {}
```

```
        i = i + 1;
}
```

which retrieves the value of a maximal element of the first `len` elements of an array a.
The determined maximal value is stored in program variable `max`. We observe that
the intended functionality assumes implicitly that the value of program variable `len`
is at least one as otherwise no maximal element exists. Formalizing this natural
language specification yields the following initial Hoare triple with updates (where
the initial update is empty):

$$\{\texttt{len} >= 1\} \, [] \, \texttt{searchMax} \, \{\backslash\text{forall int } j \, (j >= 0 \wedge j < \texttt{len} \rightarrow \texttt{max} >= \texttt{a}[j]); \, \}$$

Such an initial Hoare triple can be easily specified in a text-based format (described
in Section 17.7.3) and loaded into the KeY-Hoare system as a proof obligation.

Moving the mouse pointer over the displayed Hoare triple allows the user to
apply the calculus rules described in Section 17.4.3 using a simple point-to-click
interface. After clicking on the highlighted program (incl. the preceding updates
for some rules) a popup menu with all applicable rules is shown (see screenshot
below). There is exactly one applicable rule for each program construct and the
system offers exactly this rule:[1] by applying the program rules the user symbolically executes the program step by step. The only nontrivial interaction is to provide the loop invariant for the loop rule. In the example entering the invariant
$\backslash$forall int j $(j >= 0 \wedge j < \texttt{i} \rightarrow \texttt{max} >= \texttt{a}[j]);$ suffices to close the proof.

Whenever first-order verification conditions are reached, the system offers a rule
Update Simplification that applies the update rules from Figure 17.3 automatically.
At this point, the user can opt to push the green Go button ▶. Then the built-in first-
order theorem prover tries to establish validity automatically. For simple problems
discussed in the introductory courses, such as `searchMax`, this works quite well and
the reason that a proof could not be found is rarely rooted in insufficient reasoning
power of the underlying theorem prover. In the majority of cases an unclosable
proof points to a problem in the code or specification. It is worth to mention that the
problem is at least as often a too weak or wrong specification as it is a bug in the
code.

Inspecting open proof goals usually gives a good hint where to find the bug or
which (implicit) assumption is missing. The system allows the student to follow
the symbolic execution of the program and to concentrate on getting invariants and
specification right without needing to deal with first-order reasoning which is done
in the background by the system. It is possible to inspect and undo previous proof
steps as well as to save and load proofs.

---

[1] The other rules displayed are propositional rules that can be applied anytime and they can be
ignored.

17.6 Variants of the Hoare Logic with Updates

17.6.1 Total Correctness

The previous sections focused on partial correctness of programs, i.e., termination was ignored and nonterminating programs satisfied their specification trivially. In this section we explain the necessary changes to our calculus such that for the Hoare triple

$$\{P\}\,[\mathscr{U}]\,\pi\,\{Q\}$$

to be valid, the program π must not only adhere to its functional specification but also terminate when started in an initial state $s_{\mathscr{U}}$ such that s satisfies P. In other words, to establish the validity of a total correctness Hoare triple, we have to prove *total correctness* of the program π. Total correctness is supported by our tool KeY-Hoare.

The calculus rules for total correctness are identical to those presented in Section 17.4 except for the loop invariant rule. The new version of the loop invariant rule is given in Figure 17.4. To ensure that a while loop terminates one has to provide a term *dec* which decreases strictly monotonic after each execution of the loop body, but stays nonnegative. The first branch of the while rule now ensures additionally that the given term is initially greater or equal to zero. The second branch checks also that after each loop iteration *dec* is strictly smaller than before, but still nonnegative. To be able to access the old value of *dec*, the rule introduces a fresh (not yet used) rigid function *oldDec* to capture the value of *dec* at the beginning of the loop iteration.

$$\text{loop}_\text{T}\ \frac{\begin{array}{l} \vdash\ P \to \mathscr{U}\,(I \land dec \mathrel{>}= 0) \\ \{I \land \mathtt{b} \doteq \mathtt{true} \land oldDec \doteq dec\}\,[]\,\mathtt{s1}\,\{I \land dec \mathrel{>}= 0 \land dec < \text{oldDec}\} \\ \{I \land \mathtt{b} \doteq \mathtt{false}\}\,[]\,\mathtt{s}\,\{Q\} \end{array}}{\{P\}\,[\mathscr{U}]\,\mathtt{while(b)\{s1\}s}\,\{Q\}}$$

where *oldDec* is a new function symbol of arity $size(fv(dec))$ ($fv(dec)$ denotes the set of free first-order variables in *dec*)

Figure 17.4 Loop invariant rule for total correctness.

The total correctness proof for the maximum search example of Section 17.5 is almost identical for total correctness, except that when applying the loop invariant rule the decreasing term *dec* has to be provided in addition to the loop invariant. For the example, it suffices to instantiate *dec* with the expression `len-i`.

17.6.2 Worst-Case Execution Time

The most advanced variant of our Hoare logic with updates is concerned with reasoning about simple properties about the worst-case execution time (WCET) of a program [Harmon and Klefstad, 2007]. The calculus to reason about WCET is presented in Figure 17.5.

$$\text{assignment}_{\mathsf{ET}} \ \frac{\{P\}\,[\,\mathscr{U}, \mathtt{x} := \mathtt{e}, eT := eT + 1]\,\mathtt{s}\,\{Q\}}{\{P\}\,[\,\mathscr{U}\,]\,\mathtt{x=e}\,;\,\mathtt{s}\,\{Q\}}$$

$$\text{skip}_{\mathsf{ET}} \ \frac{\{P\}\,[\,\mathscr{U}, eT := eT + 1]\,\mathtt{s}\,\{Q\}}{\{P\}\,[\,\mathscr{U}\,]\,;\,\mathtt{s}\,\{Q\}} \qquad\qquad \text{exit}_{\mathsf{ET}} \ \frac{\vdash P \to \mathscr{U}(Q)}{\{P\}\,[\,\mathscr{U}\,]\,\{Q\}}$$

$$\text{conditional}_{\mathsf{ET}} \ \frac{\begin{array}{l}\{P \wedge \mathscr{U}(\mathtt{b} \doteq \mathtt{true})\}\,[\,\mathscr{U}, eT := eT + 1]\,\mathtt{s1}\,;\,\mathtt{s}\,\{Q\}\\[2pt] \{P \wedge \mathscr{U}(\mathtt{b} \doteq \mathtt{false})\}\,[\,\mathscr{U}, eT := eT + 1]\,\mathtt{s2}\,;\,\mathtt{s}\,\{Q\}\end{array}}{\{P\}\,[\,\mathscr{U}\,]\,\mathtt{if(b)\{s1\}else\{s2\}}\,\mathtt{s}\,\{Q\}}$$

$$\text{loop}_{\mathsf{ET}} \ \frac{\begin{array}{l}\vdash P \to \mathscr{U}(I \wedge dec >= 0)\\[2pt] \{I \wedge \mathtt{b} \doteq \mathtt{true} \wedge \text{oldDec} \doteq dec\}\\[2pt] \qquad\qquad [eT := eT + 1]\,\{\mathtt{s1}\}\,\{I \wedge dec >= 0 \wedge dec < \text{oldDec}\}\\[2pt] \{I \wedge \mathtt{b} \doteq \mathtt{false}\}\,[eT := eT + 1]\,\mathtt{s}\,\{Q\}\end{array}}{\{P\}\,[\,\mathscr{U}\,]\,\mathtt{while(b)\{s1\}}\,\mathtt{s}\,\{Q\}}$$

where

- oldDec is a new function symbol of arity $size(\mathit{fv}(dec))$ as above
- eT stands for the reserved program variable executionTime which does not occur elsewhere

Figure 17.5 Loop invariant rule for execution time reasoning

The basic idea for the WCET-calculus is taken from [Hunt et al., 2006]. To keep track of the number of executed instructions, an implicitly declared global program variable executionTime is introduced. This program variable cannot be directly accessed or modified by a program, but is increased implicitly as a side effect when symbolically executing a statement. Standard statements like assignment cause the counter to be increased by one, while in case of a branching statement like a conditional or a loop the guard evaluation costs an additional unit.

Assume a program countdown which decreases the counter variable timer to zero. A Hoare triple containing a WCET specification to be proven is shown in Figure 17.6.

```
{ startVal >= 0 & executionTime = 0}

[timer := startVal]

while (timer>0) {
  timer = timer -1;
}

{ timer = 0 & executionTime = 2*startVal + 1}
```

Figure 17.6 Worst-case execution time specification

The functional part of the specification states that if the program is started in an initial state with program variable timer set to a nonnegative value then in its final state the program variable timer has the value zero. We use a rigid constant

symbol startVal to capture the initial value of timer so that we can refer to it in
the postcondition.

The WCET part of the specification is added to the pre- and postcondition as a
simple conjunction. The precondition states additional knowledge about the initial
value of the execution time counter. In most cases one requires that the initial value
of the executionTime counter is either equal to a fixed nonnegative but unknown
value, or as in this example, zero.

The postcondition can be used to specify either the exact number of execution
steps performed by the algorithm (as done here) or it can simply state an upper bound
for the expected execution time. The countdown algorithm is expected to require
$2 * \text{startVal} + 1$ time units until completion. The justification for this number is
as follows: the timer is decreased by one in each loop iteration, hence, there are
startVal loop iterations where each iteration costs 2 time units (evaluation of the
loop guard plus decreasing the timer variable) plus one additional cost unit for the
final evaluation of the loop guard which terminates the loop.

Again the only nontrivial interaction is the application of the loop invariant rule.
Providing

        timer>=0 & executionTime = 2*(startVal-timer)

as loop invariant and timer as decreasing term allows us to close the proof.

17.7 A Brief Reference Manual for KeY-Hoare

We conclude this chapter with a brief reference manual for KeY-Hoare to describe
the installation, input format and usage of the tool in detail.

17.7.1 Installation

The tool KeY-Hoare is available at www.key-project.org/download/hoare in three
versions: (i) a source code version, (ii) a bytecode version and as (iii) *Java Web start*
version which allows the user to install and start KeY-Hoare with a single click. We
describe here only the Web Start installation, detailed installation instructions for the
other options can be found on the website.

Java Web Start is included in all recent JDK and JRE distributions of Java. It
provides a simple way to run and install Java applications. If Java is installed, almost
all web browsers know how to handle Java Web Start URLs out-of-the-box; if not,
the file type jnlp needs to be associated with the application javaws. Otherwise a
click on the Web Start link on the mentioned website loads and starts KeY-Hoare.
We use a self-signed certificate, which is not trusted by a standard Java installation.
You need to accept our certificate as an exception in the dialog box that pops up.

Instead of using a browser Java Web Start can also be used from the command
line:

```
javaws http://www.key-project.org/download/hoare/download/webstart/KeY-Hoare.jnlp
```

After the first start no internet connection is required and KeY-Hoare can be started in offline mode by executing `javaws -viewer` and selecting the KeY-Hoare entry in the list of available applications.

17.7.2 Formula Syntax

The predicate symbols and function symbols >, >=, <, <= and = as well as +, -, *, / and % are reserved symbols for which the usual infix notation and precedence rules are in place.

These arithmetic relations and operations are supported with their canonical signature and meaning. The modulo operation is defined as $x\%y := x - (x/y) * y$. Consequently, the values of the terms $0\%y$ and $x\%0$ are undefined. As in JavaDL, undefinedness is modeled by underspecification. This means that an integer value specified as $x/0$ is a valid term/expression whose value is not specified a priori and may be assigned a different integer value by different first-order interpretations.

The concrete syntax of propositional connectives is !, &, |, ->, <-> with their obvious meaning. First-order quantified formulas are written as follows:

⟨*QuantifiedFormula*⟩ ::= ⟨*Quantifier*⟩ ⟨*Type*⟩ ⟨*LogicalVariable*⟩ ; ⟨*FOLFormula*⟩
⟨*Quantifier*⟩ ::= **\forall** | **\exists**

Example 17.3. The following formula expresses that any common divisor x of the integers a and b is as well a divisor of the integer r.

```
\forall int x; ((x > 0 & a % x = 0 & b % x = 0) -> r % x = 0))
```

17.7.3 Input File Format

Input files for KeY-Hoare must have .key or .proof as file extension. By convention .key files contain only the problem specification, i.e., the Hoare triple to be proven together with the necessary program variable, array and user-defined rigid function declarations. In contrast, .proof files include in addition (partial) proofs for the specified problem and are created when saving a proof.

The input file grammar is given in Figure 17.8. As an example the input file for the example `searchMax` is shown in Figure 17.7. An input file consists of four sections:

1. The section starting with keyword \functions declares all required rigid function symbols used, for example, to assign input program variables to an arbitrary but fixed value as described in Section 17.4.1. In Figure 17.7 this section is empty.

```
\functions {}

\arrays {
        int[] a;
}

\programVariables {
        int i;
        int len;
        int max;
}

\hoare {

        { len >=1 }

        \[{
                max = a[0];
                i = 1;
                while (i<len) {
                        if (max < a[i]) {
                                max = a[i];
                        } else {}
                        i = i + 1;
                }
        }\]

        { \forall int j; (j>=0 & j<len -> max >=a[j]) }

}
```

Figure 17.7 Input file for the searchMax example.

2. The next section starting with keyword \arrays declares the arrays that may be used by the program or specification. In Figure 17.7 this section declares one integer typed array a. In addition to integer typed arrays, Boolean typed arrays are available.
3. The section starting with keyword \programVariables declares *all* program variables used in the program. Local variable declarations within the program are not allowed. Multiple declarations are permitted.
4. The section starting with keyword \hoare contains the Hoare triple with updates to be proven valid, i.e., the program and its specification. If total correctness or worst-case execution time of a program should be proven, the keyword \hoare is replaced by the keyword \hoareTotal, respectively, \hoareET.

⟨*InputFile*⟩ ::= ⟨*Functions*⟩? ⟨*ProgramVariables*⟩? ⟨*HoareTriple*⟩?

⟨*Functions*⟩ ::= \functions '{'⟨*FunctionDeclaration*⟩*'}'
⟨*FunctionDeclaration*⟩ ::= ⟨*Type*⟩ ⟨*Name*⟩ ('('⟨*Type*⟩(','⟨*Type*⟩)*')')?';'

⟨*Arrays*⟩ ::= \arrays '{'⟨*ArrayDeclaration*⟩*'}'
⟨*ArrayDeclaration*⟩ ::= ⟨*Type*⟩[] ⟨*Name*⟩(',' ⟨*Name*⟩)*';'

⟨*ProgramVariables*⟩ ::=\programVariables '{'⟨*ProgramVariableDeclaration*⟩*'}'
⟨*ProgramVariableDeclaration*⟩ ::= ⟨*Type*⟩ ⟨*Name*⟩(',' ⟨*Name*⟩)*';'

⟨*HoareTriple*⟩ ::= (\hoare | \hoareTotal | \hoareET) '{'
            ⟨*PreCondition*⟩ ⟨*Update*⟩ ⟨*Program*⟩ ⟨*PostCondition*⟩
            '}'

⟨*PreCondition*⟩ ::= ⟨*FOLFormula*⟩

⟨*Update*⟩ ::= '[' (⟨*AssignmentPair*⟩ (\|⟨*AssignmentPair*⟩)*)? ']'
⟨*AssignmentPair*⟩ ::= ⟨*Name*⟩ ':=' ⟨*FOLTerm*⟩

⟨*Program*⟩ ::= '\[{' ⟨*WhileProgram*⟩ '}\]'
⟨*PostCondition*⟩ ::= ⟨*FOLFormula*⟩

⟨*Type*⟩ ::= int | boolean
⟨*Name*⟩ ::= character sequence not starting with a number

Figure 17.8 Input file grammar

17.7.4 Loading and Saving Problems and Proofs

After starting KeY-Hoare (see Section 17.7.1) the prover window becomes visible
(the screenshot on p. 580 is displayed in enlarged form in Figure 17.9). The prover
window consists of a menu- and toolbar, a status line and a central part split into a
left and a right pane. The upper left pane displays a list of all loaded problems. The
lower left pane offers different tabs for proof navigation or strategy settings. The
right pane displays the currently selected subgoal or an inner proof node.

Before we explain the various subpanes in more detail, the first task is to load
a problem file. This can be done either by selecting Load in the File menu or by
clicking on the icon 📁 in the toolbar (📁 reloads the most recently loaded problem).
In the file dialogue window that pops up the users can choose one of the examples
provided (e.g., searchMax.key) or their own files.

After the file has been loaded the right pane of the prover window displays the
Hoare triple as specified in the input file. The proof tab in the left pane should display
the proof tree consisting of a single node. The first time during a KeY-Hoare session
when a problem file is loaded the system loads a number of libraries which takes a
few seconds.

(Partial) proofs can be saved at any time by selecting the menu item Save in the File menu and entering a file name ending with the file extension .proof.

17.7.5 Proving

First a few words on the various parts of the prover window. The upper part of the left pane displays all loaded problems. The lower part provides some useful tabs:

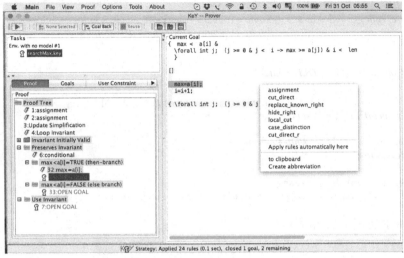

Figure 17.9 Screen shot of KeY-Hoare system

The Proof tab   shows the constructed proof tree. A left click on a node updates the right pane with the node's content (a Hoare triple with updates). Using a right click offers a number of actions like pruning, searching, etc.

The Goals tab   lists all open goals, i.e., the leaves of the proof tree that remain to be justified.

The Proof Search Strategy tab   allows one to tune automated proof search. In case of KeY-Hoare only the maximal number of rule applications before an interactive step is required, and (de-)activation of the autoresume mode can be adjusted.

All other tabs   are not of importance for KeY-Hoare.

The right pane displays the content of a proof node in two different modes depending on whether the node is (a) an inner node or a leaf justified by an axiom or (b) it represents an open proof goal.

(a) Inner Node View   is used for inner nodes of the proof tree. It highlights the formula which had been in focus at time of rule application as well as possible necessary side formulas. The applied rule is listed on the bottom of the view.

(b) Goal View   is used when an open goal is selected. This view shows the Hoare triple to be proven and allows the user to apply rules. Moving the mouse cursor

over the expressions within the node highlights the smallest enclosing term or formula at the current position. A left click creates a popup window showing all applicable rules for the currently highlighted formula or term.

17.7.6 Automation

A few remarks on automation: in our examples, the necessary interactive proof steps consisted of manual application of program rules and invocations of the strategies to simplify/prove first-order problems. To avoid having to start the automatic strategies manually one can activate the `autoresume` mode. This will invoke the strategies on all open goals after each manual rule application and simplify them as far as possible. In standard mode they will not apply program rules.

For pedagogic reasons the application of the program rules which execute a program symbolically are not performed automatically, but need to be applied interactively. Except for the loop invariant rule which requires the user to provide a loop invariant (and, if termination plays a role, a decreasing term) all other rules could be applied automatically, because they are deterministic and require no input. To enable automatic application of program rules (except loop) one can set the environment variable `TEACHER_MODE` to an arbitrary value. With both options (autoresume and teacher mode) activated the only required interaction in the examples above is the application of the loop invariant.

Part V
Case Studies

Chapter 18
Functional Verification and Information Flow Analysis of an Electronic Voting System

Daniel Grahl and Christoph Scheben

Electronic voting (e-voting) systems which are used in public elections need to fulfill a broad range of strong requirements concerning both safety and security. Among those requirements are reliability, robustness, privacy of votes, coercion resistance and universal verifiability. Bugs in or manipulations of an e-voting system can have considerable influence on society. Therefore, e-voting systems are an obvious target for software verification. In addition, it makes an excellent target for a formal analysis of secure information flow. While the individual ballots must remain confidential, the public election result depends on these secrets. We will employ the precise analysis technique introduced in Chapter 13, that readily includes support for this kind of declassification.

We report on an implementation of an electronic voting system in Java. It is based on the sElect system by Küsters et al. [2011], but reduced to its essential functionality. Even though the actual components are clearly modularized, the challenge lies in the fact that we need to prove a highly nonlocal property: After all voters have cast their ballots, the server calculates the correct votes for each candidate w.r.t. the original ballots. This case study proves the preservation of privacy of votes. Altogether the considered code comprises 8 classes and 13 methods in about 150 lines of code of a rich fragment of Java. The presentation in this chapter follows the works by Scheben [2014] and Grahl [2015].

18.1 Electronic Voting

Elections form a part of everyday life that has not (yet) been fully conquered by computerized systems. This is partly due to the relatively high effort—elections do not occur often—and partly due to little public trust in e-voting security. The public discussion of this issue—in Germany at least—has revealed a high demand for secure systems and in turn a projection of high costs to construct them that lead to the introduction of electronic voting being suspended. Systems for electronic casting and tallying of votes that are in the field in other countries (e.g., the Netherlands, the

© Springer International Publishing AG 2016
W. Ahrendt et al. (Eds.): Deductive Software Verification, LNCS 10001, pp. 593–607, 2016
DOI: 10.1007/978-3-319-49812-6_18

USA) are known to expose severe vulnerabilities. Apart from vote casting, computers are actually used in other activities related to elections such as voter registration or seat allocation.

A general goal is that electronic voting is at least as secure as voting with paper ballots. This includes *confidentiality* of individual votes. In particular they must not be attributable to a particular voter. But there is also an *integrity* issue: the final election result must reproduce the original voter intention; no vote must be lost, none must be manipulated. In paper-based elections, this mostly depends on trust in the election authorities and observers. In electronic voting, the idea is to issue a receipt to the voter, a so-called *audit trail*, for casting their ballot. After the votes have been tallied, the voters can then check on a public bulletin board whether their vote has actually been counted. This is called *verifiability* of the vote. To achieve verifiability and confidentiality of individual ballots/votes at the same time appears to be contradictory. The proposed solution is cryptography—that allows trails to be readable only to the voter. Some electronic voting systems also try to rule out voter *coercion* (by threatening or bribing). The idea is that trails and bulletin boards are of a form such that an attacker cannot distinguish the votes even if a coerced voter is trying to reveal his or her vote. This way, electronic voting may be even more secure than voting using paper ballots.[1] As it requires highest security guarantees, electronic voting has been frequently designated as a natural target for verification, e.g., by Clarkson, Chong, and Myers [2008].

18.2 Overview

We consider the sElect system implemented by Küsters et al., to be reduced to its essential functionality. In this system, a remote voter can cast one single vote for some candidate. This vote is sent through a secure channel to a tallying server. The secure channel is used to guarantee that voter clients are properly identified and cannot cast their vote twice. The server only publishes a result—the sum of all votes for each candidate—once all voters have cast their vote. The main modification compared to the original implementation by Küsters et al. is that messages are transmitted synchronously instead of asynchronously.

As described by Beckert et al. [2012], the goal is to show that no confidential information (i.e., votes) are leaked to the public. Obviously, the election result—a public information—does depend on confidential information. This is a desired situation. In order to allow this, the strong information flow property needs to be weakened, or parts of the confidential information need to be *declassified*. Section 13.5 shows how such a property can be formalized using Java Dynamic Logic and proven in the KeY verification system.

---

[1] An important practical aspect of elections is *fairness*. As argued by Bruns [2008], fairness requires a profound understanding of verifiability and confidentiality not only to security experts, but to any eligible voter. This issue is usually not considered with the present, complex systems.

Secure declassification—in the sense that parts of the secret information is purposely released (which is different from other uses of the term 'declassification' denoting the release of *any* information under certain constraints)—depends to a certain extent on functional correctness. In an election, the public result is the sum of the votes that result from secret ballots. In general, this cannot be dealt with using lightweight static analyses, such as type systems or program dependency graphs, which are still predominant in the information flow analysis world. Instead, the problem demands for semantically precise information flow analyses as provided by the direct formalization of noninterference in dynamic logic (Section 13.5).

18.2.1 Verification of Cryptographic Software

The sElect system uses cryptography and other security mechanisms. From a functional point of view, cryptography is extremely complex and it seems largely infeasible to reason about it formally. In particular, the usual assumption in cryptography that an attacker's deductive power is polynomially bounded—this is called a Dolev/Yao attacker [Dolev and Yao, 1983]—cannot be reasonably formalized. As a matter of fact, even encrypted transmission does leak information and therefore *strong secrecy* of votes—which can be expressed as noninterference—is not fulfilled: the messages sent over the network depend on the votes and could theoretically be decrypted by an adversary with unbounded computational power. As a consequence, information flow analysis techniques—like the ones presented in Section 13.5—would classify the sElect system insecure, although it is secure from a cryptographic point of view.

Küsters et al. [2011] proposed a solution to this problem: the authors showed that the real encryption of the system can be replaced by an implementation of *ideal encryption*. Ideal encryption completely decouples the sent message from the secret. Even an adversary with unbounded computational power cannot decrypt the message. The receiver can decrypt the message through some extra information sent over a secret channel which is not observable by adversaries. Küsters et al. showed that if—in the system with ideal encryption—votes do not interfere with the output to the public channel, then the system with real encryption guarantees privacy of votes. Therefore, it is sufficient to analyze the system with ideal encryption.

18.2.2 Verification Approach

Our approach combines functional verification and information flow verification, both performed with KeY. The properties are specified using the Java Modeling Language (see Chapter 7), including the extensions introduced in Section 13.4. All involved components are completely verified for their functional behavior. Additionally, the proof of confidentiality is based on a dynamic logic formalization of noninterference and theorem proving as laid out by Scheben [2014, Chapter 9]. The functional verification lays a foundation for the confidentiality proofs as they use functional method contracts.

In order to obtain an implementation of the system that is practically verifiable, we have implemented a simplified system ourselves. In fact, we have implemented several prototypes one after another, verified each of them, and refined it (and its specification) to produce the next one. This chapter describes the final implementation of this series, see [Grahl, 2015, Chap. 9] for the complete scene.

An alternative to the above approach is outlined in Section 18.4.1. It combines functional correctness proofs in KeY with lightweight static information flow analysis as proposed by Küsters et al. [2015]. The target program is transformed in such a way that there is no declassification of information. We then prove in the KeY system that this transformation preserves the original functional behavior. This allows the static analyzer JOANA [Hammer, 2009, Graf et al., 2013]—which is sound, but incomplete—to report the absence of information flow.

18.2.3 System Description

Figure 18.1 shows a UML class diagram of the considered e-voting system. The implementation comprises, besides the clients (class Voter) and the server, an interface to the environment and a setup. The main method of the setup models the e-voting process itself. This is necessary because the security property—that privacy of votes is preserved up to the result of the election—can only be formulated with respect to a complete e-voting process rather than only the implementation of the client and the server alone. This means that we do not have a composition of distributed components, but a simulation of their interaction in a sequential program.

The basic protocol works as follows: First, voters register their respective client to the server, obtaining a unique identifier. Then, they can send their vote along with their identifier (once). Meanwhile, the server waits for a call to either receive one message (containing a voter identifier and a vote) or to close the election and post the result. In the former case, it fetches a message from the network. If the identifier is invalid (i.e., it does not belong to a registered voter) or the (uniquely identified) voter has already voted, it silently aborts the call. In any other case, the vote is counted for the respective candidate. In the latter case, the server first checks whether a sufficient condition to close the election holds,[2] and only then a result (i.e., the number of votes per candidate) is presented. This is illustrated in the sequence diagram in Figure 18.2.

This simplified representation hides many aspects essential to real systems. We assume both a working identification and that identities cannot be forged. We assume that the network does not leak any information about the ballot (i.e., voter identifier and vote). This is meant to be assured through means of cryptography. The network may leak—and probably will in practice—other information such as networking

---

[2] In the present implementation, this is when all voters have voted.

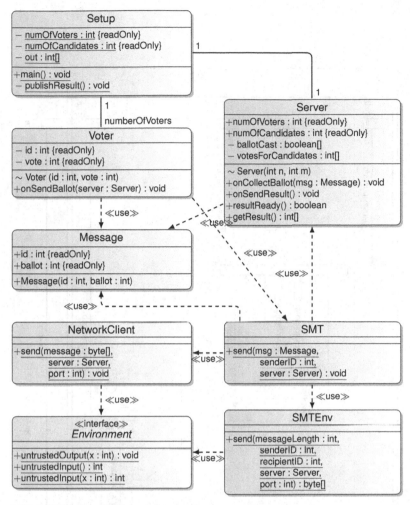

Figure 18.1 UML class diagram of the e-voting system

credentials. We do not need to assume that the network communication is loss-less or must not produce spurious messages.

Listing 18.1 shows the implementation of `Setup#main()`. Essentially, the adversary decides in the loop which client should send its vote next, until the server signals that the result of the election is ready. More precisely, the adversary is modeled through a call to the method `Environment.untrustedInput()`, that decides which client should send its vote. When subsequently the method `onSendBallot()` is called on the corresponding `Voter` object, the client sends its secret vote (stored in the attribute `vote`) to the server (synchronously), with the help of ideal encryption. In its `onCollectBallot()` method, the server immediately counts the vote—provided that the voter did not vote before. Finally, the server is asked by a call to the method

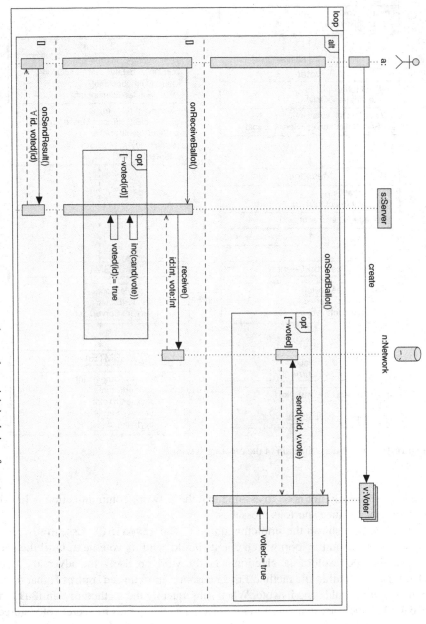

Figure 18.2 The overall protocol of the e-voting system. Here, the actor represent the nondeterministic choice of events.

```
 1  /*@ normal_behavior
 2   @ requires (\forall int j; 0 <= j && j < numberOfVoters;
 3   @                          !server.ballotCast[j]);
 4   @ requires (\forall int i; 0 <= i && i < numberOfCandidates;
 5   @                          server.votesForCandidates[i]==0);
 6   @ ensures (\forall int i; 0 <= i && i < numberOfCandidates;
 7   @               server.votesForCandidates[i] ==
 8   @                   (\num_of int j; 0 <= j && j < numberOfVoters;
 9   @                                   voters[j].vote == i));
10   @ diverges true;
11   @*/
12  public void main () {
13      while ( !server.resultReady() ) { // possibly infinite loop
14          // let adversary decide send order
15          final int k = Environment.untrustedInput(voters.length);
16          final Voter v = voters[k];
17          v.onSendBallot(server);
18      }
19      publishResult();
20  }
```

Listing 18.1 Implementation and functional contract for the Setup#main() method

resultReady() whether the result of the election is ready. If so, the loop terminates
and the result is published by a call to the method publishResult().

18.3 Specification and Verification

The overall functional property to prove is that—after all votes have been cast (and
collected by the server)—the server posts the correct number of votes per candidate.
More precisely, the 'correct number' corresponds to the sum of votes for each
candidate as on the ballots filled in by the voters. The information flow property to
prove is that no information other than the election result is released.

18.3.1 Specification

The functional contract for the main method is shown in Listing 18.1. In the preconditions, we assume that no voter has cast their vote yet (or more precisely, the
server has not yet marked the vote as cast) and all candidates have zero votes (in
the server). The postcondition states that the number of votes for each candidate
is exactly the number of voters who voted for them. This is expressed using the
generalized quantifier \num_of (see Section 7.2.2) in Line 8. The explicit **diverges**
clause allows this method to not terminate.

The functional specification is augmented with an information flow contract in Listing 18.2. The contract states that—under the condition that the server is initialized correctly—

1. the state of the environment, abstracted by `Environment.envState`, depends at most on its initial value as well as on the number of voters (Line 6);
2. The array `out` itself as well as each of its entries (containing the final result of the election, Lines 8f.) depend at most on

   - the number of candidates,
   - the number of voters, and
   - for each candidate—the correct sum of all votes for them (Lines 10ff.);

3. at most locations of the server, the environment and the result array are changed; and
4. the election might not terminate (because the adversary might block votes of voters forever, Line 16).

The `\declassifies` keyword is syntactic sugar (see Section 13.4), but stresses that the array `out` only depends on a well-considered part of the secret—the correct result of the election.

```
1  /*@ normal_behavior
2  @ requires     (\forall int j; 0 <= j && j < numberOfVoters;
3  @                !server.ballotCast[j]);
4  @ requires     (\forall int i; 0 <= i && i < numberOfCandidates;
5  @                server.votesForCandidates[i]==0);
6  @ determines  Environment.envState
7  @                \by Environment.envState, numberOfVoters;
8  @ determines  out, (\seq_def int i; 0; out.length; out[i])
9  @                \by numberOfCandidates, numberOfVoters
10 @     \declassifies (\seq_def int i; 0; numberOfCandidates;
11 @                (\num_of int j;
12 @                   0 <= j && j < numberOfVoters;
13 @                         voters[j].vote == i));
14 @ assignable  Environment.rep, out,
15 @                server.ballotCast[*], server.votesForCandidates[*];
16 @ diverges true;
17 @*/
18 public void main () { ... }
```

Listing 18.2 Information flow contract for the `main()` method

In order to show that `main()` fulfills its contract, we need a loop invariant (Listing 18.3). In the loop invariant, we talk about a bounded sum (indicated by the keyword `\num_of` in Line 4) that is defined through a nontrivial induction scheme: the elements are not added linearly, but only under stuttering and permutation. This makes it—at least the current machinery—impossible to prove the invariant automatically. The information flow part of the loop invariant in Lines 12ff. states that

1. the knowledge of the environment (`Environment.envState`),

```
1  /*@ maintaining \invariant_for(this);
2   @ maintaining (\forall int i; 0 <= i && i < numberOfCandidates;
3   @                    server.votesForCandidates[i] ==
4   @                        (\num_of int j; 0 <= j && j < numberOfVoters;
5   @                            server.ballotCast[j]
6   @                            && voters[j].vote == i));
7   @ maintaining    resultReady
8   @               == (\forall int j; 0 <= j && j < numberOfVoters;
9   @                        server.ballotCast[j]);
10  @ assignable Environment.rep,
11  @           server.ballotCast[*], server.votesForCandidates[*];
12  @ determines Environment.envState, resultReady, numberOfVoters,
13  @               (\seq_def int i; 0; numberOfVoters;
14  @                   server.ballotCast[i])
15  @           \by \itself;
16  @*/
```

Listing 18.3 Loop invariant for the loop in `Setup#main()`

2. the fact whether the result of the election is ready,
3. the number of voters, and
4. the information which voter has already voted (stored in the cells of the array `Server#ballotCast`)

depend at most on

(a) the initial knowledge of the environment,
(b) whether the result of the election initially was ready,
(c) the initial number of voters, and
(d) the initial information which voter has already voted.

As the field `Setup.out` is not modified by the loop, it does not need to be mentioned explicitly in the loop invariant. The fact that the array `Setup.out` itself as well as each of its entries depend at most on

- the number of candidates,
- the number of voters, and
- for each candidate the correct sum of all respective votes for them

can be derived from the contract of `publishResult()` (Listing 18.4) in combination with the assurance of the loop invariant that the server calculates the result correctly. Note that the functional knowledge that the server calculates the result correctly is necessary for proving the declassification. Here, the tight integration of functional and information flow-verification in our approach pays off.

The preservation of the loop invariant is proved with the help of contracts for the methods `untrustedInput()`, `onSendBallot()` and `resultReady()`. The method `untrustedInput()` is declared in the interface `Environment` (Listing 18.5). This interface provides the connection to the environment which is controlled by the attacker. It models all global sources and sinks. The state of the environment is encapsulated in a (ghost) field of type sequence. As any computable

```
/*@ normal_behavior
  @ requires (\forall int i; 0 <= i && i < numberOfCandidates;
  @                   server.votesForCandidates[i] ==
  @                      (\num_of int j; 0 <= j && j < numberOfVoters;
  @                          voters[j].vote == i));
  @ assignable out;
  @ determines  out, (\seq_def int i; 0; out.length; out[i])
  @         \by  numberOfCandidates, numberOfVoters,
  @              server.votesForCandidates
  @         \declassifies (\seq_def int i; 0; numberOfCandidates;
  @                          (\num_of int j;
  @                              0 <= j && j < numberOfVoters;
  @                              voters[j].vote == i));
  @*/
private void publishResult () { ... }
```

Listing 18.4 Information flow contract of `publishResult`.

information can be encoded into a sequence of integers, this is a valid abstraction. Each method of the `Environment` has a contract which, in essence, guarantees that the environment cannot access any other part of the e-voting system. More precisely, each method is required to meet the following restrictions: 1. The final state of the environment depends at most on its initial state and the parameters of the method. 2. If the method has a result value, then also this result value depends at most on the initial state of the environment and the parameters of the method. 3. At most the state of the environment (represented by field `envState`) is modified. The untrusted input from the environment needs to be sanitized, but still the main loop may not terminate as voters are requested to cast their votes for an arbitrary number of times.

The specification of `Environment` in Listing 18.5 establishes evidence that the information flow specification and verification approach presented in Chapter 13 can be used for the specification and verification of interfaces and consequently also for the specification and verification of open and interactive systems.

The method `Voter#onSendBallot()` generates a new message containing the vote of the voter and sends it over the network as shown in Listing 18.6. The network component is modeled by the classes `NetworkClient` and `SMT` (for 'secure message transfer'). In the implementation, they mainly encapsulate a single message. `Setup#onSendBallot()` has two contracts. Both require that the invariant of the server holds, and they ensure that the final state of the environment depends at most on its initial value. They differ in the functional part: the first contract additionally requires that the voter has not voted yet. In this case, the contract ensures that the server counted the vote correctly by incrementing the value of `Server#votesForCandidates[vote]`. The second contract requires that the voter did already vote and guarantees in this case that the server does not count the vote again.

The complete specification (for both functional correctness and information flow security) of the system consists of approximately 270 lines of JML.

```
public interface Environment {
    //@ public static ghost \seq envState;

    //@ public static model \locset rep;
    //@ public static represents rep = \locset(envState);
    //@ accessible rep : \locset(envState);

    /*@ normal_behavior
      @ ensures     true;
      @ assignable  rep;
      @ determines  Environment.envState, \result
      @             \by Environment.envState;
      @*/
    //@ helper
    public static int untrustedInput();

    /*@ normal_behavior
      @ ensures     true;
      @ assignable  rep;
      @ determines  Environment.envState
      @             \by Environment.envState, x;
      @*/
    //@ helper
    public static void untrustedOutput(int x);

    /*@ normal_behavior
      @ ensures     0 <= \result && \result < x;
      @ assignable  rep;
      @ determines  Environment.envState, \result
      @             \by Environment.envState, x;
      @*/
    //@ helper
    public static int untrustedInput(int x);

}
```

Listing 18.5 Declaration of the interface `Environment`.

18.3.2 Verification

For the functional verification of this implementation, there are 13 methods to be considered, with a total of 150 lines of (executable) code and approximately 140 lines of specification. The specification includes class invariants, method contracts, and loop invariants. Given our overall experience in formal specification, a 1:1 ratio of code against specification seems reasonable. Most method contracts can be proven without much effort. For instance, the proof of the `Voter#onSendBallot()` method

```
/*@ normal_behavior
  @ requires     ! server.ballotCast[id];
  @ requires     \invariant_for(server);
  @ ensures          server.votesForCandidates[vote]
  @                  == \old(server.votesForCandidates[vote])+1;
  @ ensures      server.ballotCast[id];
  @ assignable   server.votesForCandidates[vote],
  @              server.ballotCast[id], Environment.rep;
  @ determines   Environment.envState \by \itself;
  @ also normal_behavior
  @ requires     server.ballotCast[id];
  @ requires     \invariant_for(server);
  @ ensures          \old(server.votesForCandidates[vote])
  @                  == server.votesForCandidates[vote];
  @ ensures      \old(server.ballotCast[id])
  @                  == server.ballotCast[id];
  @ assignable   Environment.rep;
  @ determines   Environment.envState \by \itself;
  @*/
public void onSendBallot(Server server) {
    Message message = new Message(id, vote);
    //@ set message.source = this;
    SMT.send(message, id, server);
}
```

Listing 18.6 Contract of `Voter#onSendBallot()`

consists of 2,400 proof steps and takes 6 s, performed by the KeY prover without further interaction.[3]

Mostly due to its unconventional loop condition, the `main()` method could not be verified automatically. To prove equality of sums, we had to apply the split_sum rule several times interactively. This rule rewrites a sum comprehension into two comprehensions over split ranges. In addition, we have added some rules representing lemmas dealing with bounded sums to the rule base of KeY; and we have proven their soundness. The proof for `main()` finally took about 63,000 proof steps, only ten of which were applied by hand. The computation time for the automated parts of the proofs was 580 s.[4]

---

[3] Time measurements have been taken on standard desktop computer (1 processor core, 1.5 GHz, 4 GiB RAM, Debian/Linux).

[4] Please note that it is difficult to give figures for manual proofs. Firstly, the human interaction is necessary and therefore cannot be compared against computation time. Secondly, the time for the remaining automated rule application is not reliable as it may include time for rules applied automatically, but reverted by the user.

Information Flow Analysis

The subsequent verification of the information flow properties of the system took about four days. The final information flow proof consists of 23 subproofs with about 7,800 proof steps including some user interactions. The optimizations described in Section 13.5.1 have proven to be indispensable for the scalability of the self-composition approach.

18.4 Discussion

In the course of this chapter, we presented an approach to verify a Java implementation of an electronic voting system. Analyses of such systems mostly target the design or the system level. Even a system like the one presented here—which can be considered small if measured in lines of code—poses a major challenge to formal verification at code level. Therefore, it is not surprising that the proofs were laborious.

Actually, far more effort than in conducting the interactive proofs needed to be put into understanding the system and developing an appropriate specification. Apart from representing the high-level design, an appropriate specification needs to be correct w.r.t. the program. This in turn requires early proof attempts with prototype implementations. Our approach to first verify a very basic version and to refine it later on turned out to be helpful in this regard. It provided clear, reachable milestones.

An interesting point is that the main complexity resides in the synthetic setup that is used to model a deployed system and not in the components that are actually used. It is well-known that tools intended for code verification do not perform well at system level verification. As already noted by Woodcock et al. [2008], verifying software that was not originally produced for the purpose of verification almost always constitutes an ill-fated endeavor. While not of the size of system described by Woodcock et al., we experienced this phenomenon in the (original) sElect system by Küsters et al. The starting point of our verification was a final piece of software. In particular, specifications had to be conceived by ourselves, using only the present source code and informal descriptions of the components' behavior. Although there are no guidelines to produce well-verifiable programs, we believe that adherence to common software engineering guidelines would render formal specification and verification more feasible.

18.4.1 A Hybrid Approach to Information Flow Analysis

In order to perform an information flow analysis on a 'more realistic' implementation of the sElect system, Küsters et al. [2015] describe a hybrid approach that combines functional verification in KeY with a lightweight information flow analysis based on *program dependency graphs* [Hammer, 2009]. In order to get the JOANA tool [Graf et al., 2013] to accept declassification, the original program is transformed such that it does not have any illegal information flow by construction.

This technique is based on a simulation of noninterference in the Java code. The secret here is only a single bit (stored in the static field Setup.secret). In the setup, two arrays of voter objects are created according to the environment to simulate two possible high inputs. The program aborts in case they yield nonequivalent results. At this point in the program execution, both high inputs are incomparable modulo the declassified property (i.e., the result of the election). Then one array is chosen, depending on the secret, to be used in the main loop.

Since the functional property and the actual implementation did not change in comparison to Section 18.3.2, there are only new verification targets, namely 1. the Setup() constructor, that establishes the above described setup and 2. the so-called 'conservative extension' method, that is called after the election has terminated. The extension effectively eliminates the declassification through overwriting the result, as computed by the actual implementation, with a precomputed correct result. The central goal was to prove that this extension is really ineffective (which is an even stronger property than conservatism).

Both require significant interaction in proving, while having the automated prover apply several thousands of rules in between each interactive step. Interestingly, this is mainly due to the sheer size of the code under investigation, but not to any particularly pattern that is hard to prove. After all, the proof for main() consists of over 200,000 proof steps, of which some 100 were applied by hand. The labor invested in verifying it approximately amounts to three weeks full time.

18.4.2 Related Work

To the best of our knowledge, this is the first time that preservation of privacy of votes could be shown *on the code level* for a (simple) e-voting system. Systems like Bingo Voting [Bohli et al., 2009] Civitas [Clarkson et al., 2008], Helios [Adida, 2008], or Scantegrity [Chaum et al., 2009]—which are much more elaborate—provide guarantees on the design level, but it is not clear whether their implementations preserve these guarantees. Clarkson et al. [2008] mention that their Civitas system has been checked for information flows with JIF [Myers, 1999], but it is not stated clearly which properties have been checked.

Bär [2008] specified functional properties of a Java implementation of the Bingo Voting system with the Java Modeling Language. These specifications have been partially checked with the (unsound and incomplete) ESC/Java2 tool by Beck [2010]. Kiniry et al. [2006] report on the Dutch KOA remote voting system, that has been used in the European Parliament election in 2004 for a small group of voters. In order to specify the (offline) vote counting module with JML and subsequently analyze it with ESC/Java2, they reimplemented the KOA system in Java.

While using ideal cryptographic functionality in code verification can be seen as state of the art, there are other approaches that include formal reasoning about cryptographic guarantees [Stern, 2003]. Barthe, Grégoire, and Béguelin [2009] present a framework in which adversaries can be modeled as probabilistic polynomially bounded `while` programs. A probabilistic relational Hoare logic—extending Benton's logic [2004]—allows one to formally reason about these adversaries, that is implemented in the EasyCrypt system [Barthe et al., 2013b].

18.4.3 Conclusion

This case study clarified the boundaries to which verification scales with the KeY prover. Going even further, we performed first experiments with replacing synchronous by asynchronous message transfer. Again, the client and server components can be verified with reasonable effort, but the setup is largely intractable.

Nevertheless, this case study serves as a benchmark and has pushed forward several performance improvements in the KeY system. This includes both improvements in the strategy (i.e., moving to a more tractable complexity class) and practical implementation changes.

The e-voting case study shows that precise information flow verification techniques as the ones presented in Chapter 13 are essential for the verification of complex information flow properties, in particular for the verification of semantic declassification. It also shows that the optimizations introduced in Section 13.5.1 are indispensable for the feasibility of the self-composition approach.

Chapter 19
Verification of Counting Sort and Radix Sort

Stijn de Gouw, Frank S. de Boer, Jurriaan Rot

Sorting is an important algorithmic task used in many applications. Two main aspects of sorting algorithms which have been studied extensively are complexity and correctness. [Foley and Hoare, 1971] published the first formal correctness proof of a sorting algorithm (Quicksort). While this is a handwritten proof, the development and application of (semi)-automated theorem provers has since taken a huge flight. The major sorting algorithms Insertion sort, Heapsort and Quicksort were proven correct by Filliâtre and Magaud [1999] using the proof assistant Coq. Recently, Sternagel [2013] formalized a proof of Mergesort within the interactive theorem prover Isabelle/HOL.

In this chapter we discuss the formalization of the correctness of *Counting sort* and *Radix sort* in KeY, based on the paper [de Gouw et al., 2014]. Counting sort is a sorting algorithm based on arithmetic rather than comparisons. Radix sort is tailored to sorting arrays of large numbers. It uses an auxiliary sorting algorithm, such as Counting sort, to sort the digits of the large numbers one-by-one. The correctness of Radix sort requires the *stability* of the auxiliary sorting algorithm. Stability here means that the order between different occurrences of the same number is preserved. To the best of our knowledge, stability has only been formalized in higher-order logic [Sternagel, 2013].

We provide the first mechanized correctness proof of Counting sort and Radix sort. Several industrial case studies have already been carried out in KeY [Ahrendt et al., 2012, Mostowski, 2005, 2007]. In contrast to most industrial code, which is large but relatively straightforward, Counting sort and Radix sort are two relatively small but ingenious and nonstandard algorithms with inherently complex correctness proofs.

19.1 Counting Sort and Radix Sort Implementation

Counting sort is a sorting algorithm based on addition and subtraction rather than comparisons. Here we consider a version of Counting sort that takes as input an array

© Springer International Publishing AG 2016
W. Ahrendt et al. (Eds.): Deductive Software Verification, LNCS 10001, pp. 609–618, 2016
DOI: 10.1007/978-3-319-49812-6_19

a of *large numbers* in base-*k* and a column index *m*. Each large number is represented by an array of digits with the least significant digit first, thus *a* is a two dimensional array of nonnegative integers (i.e., $a[1][0]$ is the least significant digit of the second large number in *a*). It then sorts the large numbers in *a* based solely on the value of their $m+1$-th digit. Listing 19.1 shows the Java implementation. The worst-case time complexity is in $\mathcal{O}(n+k)$, where *n* is the number of elements in a^1.

```java
public static int[][] countSort(int[][] a, int k, int m) {
  int[] c = new int[k]; //initializes to zero
  int[][] res = new int[a.length][];

  for(int j=0; j<a.length; j++) {
    c[a[j][m]]=c[a[j][m]]+1;
  }
  for(int j=1; j<k; j++) {
    c[j]=c[j]+c[j-1];
  }
  for(int j=a.length-1; j>=0; j--) {
    c[a[j][m]]=c[a[j][m]]-1;
    res[c[a[j][m]]]=a[j];
  }
  return res;
}
```

Listing 19.1 Counting sort

Intuitively, the algorithm works as follows. After the first loop, for an arbitrary value $i \in [0 : k-1]$, $c[i]$ contains the number of times that *i* occurs in column *m* of *a*. During the second loop, the partial sums of *c* are computed (i.e., $c[i] = c[0] + \ldots + c[i]$), so that $c[i]$ contains the number of elements in (column *m* of) *a* that are less than or equal to *i*. At this moment, for every value *i* occurring in *a*, $c[i]$ can thus be interpreted as being the index in the sorted array before which the large number with value *i* in column *m* should occur — if there are multiple such large numbers, then these should be placed to the left. Indeed in the final loop, *c* is used to place the elements of *a* in the resulting sorted array *res* by, for each element $a[i]$, first decreasing $c[a[i][m]]$ by one and then placing $a[i]$ at position $c[a[i][m]]$. Notice that equal elements are thus inserted from right to left — so by starting at the last element of *a* and counting down, the algorithm becomes *stable*. Thus, the order on the previous digits is preserved.

Figure 19.1 shows an example execution of the last loop of a call to method countSort(a, 3, 2), where the input array *a* contains respectively the arrays 1 0 2, 2 1 1 and 0 2 1 (representing the numbers 201, 112 and 120), with digits in base $k = 3$; sorting is done based on column $m = 2$, which has the digits 2, 1 and 1 respectively. The far left shows the contents of *res* and *C* just before the first iteration of the last loop. In the first iteration, the number 120 (the last number of the input

---

[1] Note that this does not conflict with the well-known lower bound of $n\lg(n)$, since that holds for sorting algorithms based on comparing array elements.

Content of the array *res*:

```
null       null       2 1 1       2 1 1
null ⟹ 0 2 1 ⟹ 0 2 1 ⟹ 0 2 1
null       null       null        1 0 2
```

Content of the array *C*:

```
0 2 3 ⟹ 0 1 3 ⟹ 0 0 3 ⟹ 0 0 2
```

Figure 19.1 Iterations of the last loop in Counting sort with input arrays 1 0 2, 2 1 1 and 0 2 1.

```
1 0 2       0 2 1       1 0 2       2 1 1
0 2 1 ⟹ 1 0 2 ⟹ 2 1 1 ⟹ 0 2 1
2 1 1       2 1 1       0 2 1       1 0 2
```

Figure 19.2 Successive iterations of the Radix sort loop, highlighting the column processed by `stableSort`.

array) is placed at its sorted position in row 2, as indicated by the highlighted value 2 of that step in the *C* array.

Radix sort sorts an array of large numbers digit-by-digit, using an auxiliary stable sorting algorithm `stableSort` to sort on each individual digit. This is reminiscent of the typical way one sorts a list of words: letter by letter. A suitable candidate for `stableSort` is the implementation of Counting sort given in Listing 19.1. An implementation of Radix sort is given in Listing 19.2. We assume that all large numbers in *a* have the same length (in particular, all of them have *a*[0].*length* digits).

```
1  public static int[][] radixSort(int[][] a, int k) {
2    for(int i=0; i<a[0].length; i++) {
3      a = stableSort(a,k,i);
4    }
5    return a;
6  }
```

Listing 19.2 Radix sort

The call to `stableSort(a, k, i)` sorts *a* by the *i*-th column. The array *a* is sorted column by column, starting from the least significant digit at index 0 up to the most significant digit at index $a[0].length - 1$. Notice that it is essential for Radix sort that this auxiliary algorithm is stable, so that the order induced by the earlier iterations is preserved on equal elements in the *i*-th column.

Figure 19.2 illustrates an example run of the algorithm, showing the contents of the array *a* after each loop iteration. The input array, representing the large numbers 201, 120 and 112 with digits in base $k = 3$, is shown on the far left and the sorted output is shown on the far right.

19.2 High-Level Correctness Proof

As we have seen in the previous section, the correctness of Radix sort depends on the *stability* of the auxiliary sorting algorithm. In this section, we formalize the property of being "stable" and give a high-level proof of the correctness and the stability of Counting sort. Subsequently we prove the correctness of Radix sort. All contracts and invariants are formalized in JML.

To avoid getting side-tracked by technicalities, and to simplify the presentation, we assume in the high-level proof that all arrays have positive length, and there are no "Array Index Out of Bounds Exceptions." We drop these assumptions in the mechanized proofs and show in Section 19.3 how this affects the specifications and corresponding correctness proofs.

The following JML contract specifies a generic sorting algorithm that sorts a two-dimensional array based solely on the numbers occurring in a given column m:

```
/*@ public normal_behavior
  @    requires
  @        k > 0 && 0 <= m && m < a[0].length
  @     && (\forall int row; 0 <= row && row < a.length;
  @            a[row].length == a[0].length)
  @     && (\forall int row; 0 <= row && row < a.length;
  @            0 <= a[row][m] && a[row][m] < k);
  @    ensures
  @        \dl_seqPerm(\dl_array2seq(\old(a)),
  @                    \dl_array2seq(\result))
  @     && (\forall int row;
  @            0 <= row && row < \result.length-1;
  @               \result[row][m] <= \result[row+1][m]);
  @*/
public static int[][] countSort(int[][] a, int k, int m);
```

Listing 19.3 Generic sorting contract

As explained in Section 8.1.2.9, the `\dl_` prefix is an escape sequence that allows referencing functions defined in JavaDL in JML specifications. The JavaDL function *array2seq* converts an array into a sequence and the JavaDL predicate *seqPerm* is true if the two sequences passed as parameters are permutations of each other. Chapter 5 has a precise definition of the predicate *seqPerm* .

The precondition, specified by the JML **requires** clause, states that all large numbers have the same length $a[0].length$, and furthermore that all digits in the m-th column are bounded by k. In the postcondition (**ensures**), the formula $seqPerm(array2seq(old(a)), array2seq(\result))$ guarantees that the returned array $\result$ is a permutation of the input array a. The second conjunct of the postcondition states that $\result$ is sorted with respect to column m.

The above contract specifies correctness, but not stability. The contract below formalizes stability, by ensuring that if two different large numbers have the same value for the $m+1$-th digit, then their original relative order from the input array is preserved:

```
/*@ public normal_behavior
  @    requires
  @          0 <= m && m < a[0].length
  @       && (\forall int row; 0 <= row && row < a.length;
  @                a[row].length == a[0].length);
  @    ensures
  @       (\forall int row; 0 <= row && row < \result.length-1;
  @                \result[row][m] == \result[row+1][m]
  @          ==> (\exists int i,j;
  @                 0 <= i && i < j && j < a.length;
  @                       \result[row]==\old(a[i])
  @                    && \result[row+1]==\old(a[j])));
  @*/
public static int[][] countSort(int[][] a, int k, int m);
```

Listing 19.4 Contract specifying stability

19.2.1 General Auxiliary Functions

For a human readable proof of Counting sort, and for both the specification and proof of Radix sort, it is absolutely crucial to introduce suitable abstractions. We therefore define the following auxiliary functions:

Name	Meaning
$val(b,r,d,a)$	$\sum_{i=0}^{d}(a[r][i] * b^i)$
$cntEq(x,r,a,c)$	$\|\{i \mid 0 \le i \le r \wedge a[i][c] = x\}\|$
$cntLt(x,a,c)$	$\|\{i \mid 0 \le i < a.length \wedge a[i][c] < x\}\|$
$pos(x,r,a,c)$	$cntEq(x,r,a,c) + cntLt(x,a,c)$

Intuitively, $val(b,r,d,a)$ is the large number represented in base b which is stored in row r of the array of large numbers a (and d is the index of the last digit). The function $cntEq$ counts the number of elements in the array segment $a[0 \ldots r][c]$ equal to x in some fixed column c. The function $cntLt$ counts the number of elements in the array segment $a[0 \ldots a.length - 1][c]$ smaller than x in the column c. As a consequence of these definitions, $pos(a[i][c],i,a,c) - 1$ is the position of $a[i]$ in the sorted version of a.

The function val can easily be implemented in JML using the built-in constructs sum and product. The value of $cntEq(x,r,a,c)$ (and similarly $cntLt(x,a,c)$) can be represented in JML by:

```
\sum int i; 0<=i && i<=r; (x==a[i][c]) ? 1 : 0
```

19.2.2 Counting Sort Proof

With the above definitions in place, we are ready to prove that the implementation of Counting sort satisfies the contract in Listing 19.4. To this end, we devise the loop invariants of Counting sort. The first loop (Listing 19.1, lines 4–5) sets $c[i]$ to the number of occurrences of the value i in $a[0 \ldots j-1][m]$. Thus we use the invariant:

—— Java + JML ——————————————————————————————

```
    0 <= j && j <= a.length
&& \forall int i; c[i] == cntEq(i, j-1, a, m);
```

———————————————————————————————— Java + JML ——

The second loop replaces each $c[i]$ with its partial sum. We formalize this by the following invariant:

—— Java + JML ——————————————————————————————

```
    1 <= j && j <= k
&& (\forall int i; 0 <= i && i <= j-1;
        c[i] == cntEq(i, a.length-1, a, m) + cntLt(i, a, m))
&& (\forall int i; j <= i && i < k;
        c[i] == cntEq(i, a.length-1, a, m));
```

———————————————————————————————— Java + JML ——

The second conjunct ranges over the elements in c which have already been replaced by their partial sum. The third conjunct ranges over the elements which have not been processed yet (and hence, obey the postcondition of the first loop).

The invariant of the last loop is as follows:

—— Java + JML ——————————————————————————————

```
   -1 <= j && j < a.length
&& (\forall int i; 0 <= i && i < a.length;
        c[a[i][m]] == pos(a[i][m], j, a, m))
&& (\forall int i; j+1 <= i && i < a.length;
        res[pos(a[i][m], i, a, m)-1] == a[i]);
```

———————————————————————————————— Java + JML ——

Recall that $pos(a[i][m], i, a, m) - 1$ is the position of $a[i]$ in the sorted version of a. Thus the second conjunct intuitively means that $c[a[i][m]] - 1$ points to the position in which $a[i]$ should be stored in the sorted array. The assertion about res in the third conjunct expresses that res is the sorted version of a. This invariant gives rise to several proof obligations. We discuss the most interesting ones. For readability we abbreviate the invariant by I. Furthermore, whenever it is clear from the context we denote $pos(x, i, a, m)$ by $pos(x, i)$ and $pos(a[i][m], i)$ by $pos(i)$. Thus for example, $pos(i) - 1$ is the index of $a[i]$ in the sorted version of a.

Our first proof obligation states that pos obeys a weak form of injectivity.

$$\forall i \in [j : a.length - 1] : pos(i) = pos(j) \rightarrow a[j] = a[i]$$

This follows from the definitions of *pos*, *cntEq* and *cntLt*. The next verification condition characterizes the behavior of *pos*.

$$\forall i \in [0:a.length-1] : a[i][m] = a[j][m] \rightarrow pos(a[j][m],j) - 1 = pos(a[i][m],j-1)$$
$$\wedge \ a[i][m] \neq a[j][m] \rightarrow pos(a[i][m],j) = pos(a[i][m],j-1)$$

The truth of the first conjunct follows from the fact that $cntEq(a[j][m],j,a,m) - 1 = cntEq(a[j][m],j-1,a,m)$. The second conjunct holds since $cntEq(x,j,a,m) = cntEq(x,j-1,a,m)$ whenever $x \neq a[j][m]$. The next verification condition states that after the execution of the loop (i.e., when $j = -1$), *res* must be sorted:

$$\forall i \in [0:a.length-2] : I \wedge j = -1 \rightarrow res[i][m] \leq res[i+1][m]$$

This is true since the invariant implies $res[pos(i)-1] = a[i]$ for $i \in [0:a.length-1]$. But as remarked above, $pos(i) - 1$ is the position of $a[i]$ in the sorted version of a, hence *res* is sorted.

The final proof obligation concerns the proof of stability:

$$\forall r \in [0:a.length-2] : I \wedge j = -1 \wedge res[r][m] = res[r+1][m]$$
$$\rightarrow \exists i,j(0 \leq i < j < a.length) : res[r] = a[i] \wedge res[r+1] = a[j]$$

Fix some arbitrary $r \in [0:a.length-2]$. We must show that $I \wedge j = -1 \wedge res[r][m] = res[r+1][m]$ implies $\exists i,j(0 \leq i < j < a.length) : res[r] = a[i] \wedge res[r+1] = a[j]$. Since the function $i \mapsto pos(i)$ is a bijection on $[1:a.length]$ we must have $r = pos(i) - 1$ and $r + 1 = pos(j) - 1$ for some $i,j \in [0:a.length-1]$. Hence, only $i < j$ remains to show. This follows from the fact that $pos(i) < pos(j)$, together with the monotonicity property $pos(x,n) \leq pos(x,n+1)$ for all n (which follows from the earlier characterization of the behavior of *pos*). This proves the stability of our Counting sort implementation.

19.2.3 Radix Sort Proof

The correctness of Radix sort relies on the correctness of the stable sorting algorithm used in Radix sort. In the proof below, we assume only the contract of the generic stable sorting algorithm, instead of a particular implementation. This has the advantage that instead of being tied to Counting sort, *any* stable algorithm can be used within Radix sort, as long as it satisfies the contract of `stableSort`. Given the definitions of the auxiliary functions, the specification of Radix sort is as follows:

—— Java + JML ——————————————————————————————

```
/*@ public normal_behavior
  @   requires
  @       k > 0
  @    && (\forall int j; 0 <= j && j < a.length;
  @              a[j].length == a[0].length)
```

```
@       && (\forall int j,m;   0 <= j && j < a.length
@                           && 0 <= m && m < a[j].length;
@             0 <= a[j][m] && a[j][m] < k);
@    ensures
@       \dl_seqPerm(\dl_array2seq(\old(a)),
@                       \dl_array2seq(\result))
@       && (\forall int row; 0 <= row && row < a.length-1;
@               val(k,row,\old(a[0].length)-1,\result)
@             <= val(k,row+1,\old(a[0].length)-1,\result));
@*/
public static int[][] radixSort(int[][] a, int k);
```
———————————————————————————————— Java + JML ——

The last conjunct in the precondition informally means that all digits that appear in a are nonnegative and bounded by k. The formula `\forall int row` (...) in the postcondition expresses that the large number in each row of the returned array is smaller or equal to the number in the next row, when interpreted in base k.

The correctness proof of Radix sort is based on the following loop invariant I:

—— JML ————————————————————————————————————

```
  0 <= i && i <= a[0].length && a != null
&& \dl_seqPerm(\dl_array2seq(a), \dl_array2seq(\old(a)))
&& (\forall int row; 0 <= row && row < a.length;
      \val(k,row,i-1,a) <= \val(k,row+1,i-1,a));
```
—— JML ——

Intuitively, the formula `\forall int row` (...) states that a is sorted with respect to the first i digits. When proving that the body of the loop preserves I, the main verification condition that arises states that the invariant follows from the postcondition of the procedure call, provided that the invariant was true initially. We refer to the contents of a before the call by introducing a logical variable A in the contract of `stableSort` as follows: we add $A = a$ to the precondition and substitute A for $old(a)$ in the postcondition. Let $post'$ be the resulting postcondition. Formally the main verification condition is then as follows:

$$I[a := A] \land post'[\result := a] \rightarrow$$
$$\forall row \in [0 : a.length - 1] : val(k, row, i, a) \leq val(k, row + 1, i, a)$$

To see why this formula is valid, consider an arbitrary row $r \in [0 : a.length - 2]$. Given the assumption $I[a := A] \land post'[\result := a]$, we must prove $val(k, r, i, a) \leq val(k, r+1, i, a)$. From $post'[\result := a]$ we infer $a[r][i] \leq a[r+1][i]$. We distinguish two cases.

- $a[r][i] < a[r+1][i]$. Then also $a[r][i] * k^i < a[r+1][i] * k^i$. Clearly $val(k, r, i - 1, a) < k^i$, since $val(k, r, i - 1, a)$ is a number with i digits in base k, while k^i has $i + 1$ digits in base k. But $val(k, r, i, a) = val(k, r, i - 1, a) + a[r][i] * k^i$, hence $val(k, r, i, a) \leq val(k, r + 1, i, a)$.

- $a[r][i] = a[r+1][i]$. Then it suffices to prove $val(k,r,i-1,a) \leq val(k,r+1,i-1,a)$. But $post'[\backslash result := a]$ implies that $a[r] = A[m]$ and $a[r+1] = A[n]$ for some m, n (with $0 \leq m < n < a.length$), so it suffices to prove $val(k,m,i-1,A) \leq val(k,n,i-1,A)$. But the invariant implies $val(k,r_1,i-1,A) \leq val(k,r_2,i-1,A)$ if $r_1 < r_2$. Instantiating r_1 with m and r_2 with n gives the desired result.

This concludes the proof of Radix sort.

19.3 Experience Report

In this section we discuss our practical experience with KeY. The following table summarizes some statistics of the proofs in KeY:

	Counting Sort	Radix Sort
Rule applications	96.260	114.309
User interactions	743 (0.8%)	762 (0.7%)

"Rule applications" serves as a measure for the length of the proofs: this row contains the total number of proof rule applications used in the proofs, whereas "User interactions" indicates the number of proof rule applications that were applied manually by the authors (i.e., required creativity). The statistics show that the degree of automation of KeY for both algorithms was over 99%.

The mechanized proofs are significantly larger than the high-level proofs, for several reasons. First, we used the automatic proof strategies of KeY as much as possible, but the strategies do not always find the shortest proofs. Second, in the actual mechanized proofs we also showed termination. Fortunately this did not require much creativity: the ranking functions (loop variants) are trivial to find and prove since all loops that occur are for-loops. After appropriate ranking functions were given, the proof of termination was automatic. A third reason for the large proofs is that Java has several features that were ignored in the high-level proofs but complicate the mechanized KeY proofs.

One such Java feature is the fact that arrays are bounded. For example, to ensure that the assignment res[c[a[j]]] = a[j]; does not lead to index out-of-bounds exceptions, KeY generates *four* proof obligations: j must be within the bounds of the array a (this condition must be proven twice, since $a[j]$ occurs twice), and $a[j]$ and $c[a[j]]$ must be within the array bounds of respectively C and *res*. This duplication of proofs, caused by multiple references to the same array element, could be avoided by changing the Java source to int tmp = a[j]; res[c[tmp]] = tmp;. KeY was able to automatically prove that the array references to c in the first two loops did not violate the array bounds, and similarly for a in the third loop. The references to *res* and c in the third loop required some user interactions. In particular, it required proving that $1 \leq pos(i) \leq a.length$. Still, overall, less than 5% of the rule applications concerned array bounds.

The part of the proof by far responsible for the most rule applications (over 60%!) surprisingly is unrelated to deriving validity of the verification conditions discussed in the previous section. Instead it concerns proving that the value of our auxiliary functions *cntEq*, *cntLt*, *pos* and *val* is the same in different heaps that arise during execution (despite using the tightest possible assignable clauses in all loops and contracts). Note first that these functions indeed depend on the contents of the heap, since their value depends on the contents of an array (the array object a passed as a parameter), and arrays are allocated on the heap. Since the heap is represented explicitly by a term in KeY, the actual KeY formalization of the definitions of these functions contain an additional parameter *Heap*. In fact, since a is the only parameter of the auxiliary functions which has a class type, the value of the auxiliary functions depends *only* on the part of the heap containing a; other parts of the heap are simply not visible. However, the program never changes the contents of a: only parts of the heap irrelevant to the value of the auxiliary functions are changed. Unfortunately, currently KeY cannot detect this, nor can the user specify it, without unrolling the definition of the auxiliary functions. After unrolling, KeY could prove in most (but not all) cases automatically that the heap was only changed in ways irrelevant to the value of the auxiliary functions, though at the expense of a huge number of rule applications due to the size of the involved heap terms. One partial workaround for this is to surround any reference to the auxiliary functions by old in the loop invariants. This seemingly small change, which causes all occurrences of auxiliary functions to be evaluated in the same (old) heap, resulted in a reduction of the Radix sort proof from 169.030 rule applications to a little over the current 114.309! This change also reduced the number of manual user interactions by about 30%. A further potential improvement would be to use model methods that return the value of the auxiliary functions (instead of using the auxiliary functions directly), as the user can specify an `accessible` clause for model methods (see Section 7.9.1).

One final discussion point concerns the permutation predicate *seqPerm*. The detailed JavaDL formalization of this predicate and the sequence data type can be found in Chapter 5. The sequence data type and corresponding permutation predicates have been newly added to KeY 2.x but so far, little was known about the implications regarding automation. The present case study provides some empirical results: about 20% of the total manual interactions concerned reasoning about sequences.

Part VI
Appendices

Appendix A
Java Modeling Language Reference

Daniel Grahl

This appendix serves as a comprehensive reference for the syntax and semantics the dialect of the Java Modeling Language (JML) that is used in the KeY system, version 2.6. The extensions for information flow introduced in Section 13.4 are also included. Section A.1 presents the full syntax of JML as it is supported by the KeY system. In Section A.2, the semantics of JML expressions is given through a translation to JavaDL. Refer to Chapters 7ff. for in depth explanations and a discussion on these items. Contract semantics are not covered here; they are treated extensively in Section 8.2. We cover the issue of well-definedness in Section A.3.

A.1 JML Syntax

The syntax of JML is heavily intertwined with the syntax of the Java language. The JML reference manual [Leavens et al., 2013] presents a complete grammar for Java enriched with (standard) JML specifications. This includes every grammatical feature—from lexical tokens to compilation units. Here, in this appendix, we take on another approach in not reiterating the entire Java syntax, but indicating where the given definitions would be injected into it. This section only describes syntax; we assume that it is clear from the context how to produce expressions that are well-typed; in doubt, refer to the JML reference manual [Leavens et al., 2013].

Since JML has been designed for other analysis approaches, not all constructs that are introduced in the JML reference manual [Leavens et al., 2013]do make sense for the KeY approach. We present only that part of the syntax for which we can give a formal semantics. Please note that the targeted subset of Java does not include all Java 5–8 features, such as autoboxing, generics, etc. We also omit the JML delimiters //@ (end of line style) and /*@ @*/ (block style). We structure this section after the different locations where JML specifications may appear.

The grammar is given in a Backus Naur style using the postfix operators $^?$ (optional occurrence), * (any number of occurrences), and $^+$ (at least one occurrence).

Table A.1 Additional class members in JML

—— JML Syntax ————————————————————————————————

⟨*ClassElem*⟩ ::= ⟨*ClassSpec*⟩ | ⟨*MMthd*⟩
⟨*ClassSpec*⟩ ::= ⟨*Visibility*⟩$^?$ (⟨*ClassInv*⟩ | ⟨*FieldDecl*⟩ | ⟨*Represents*⟩ | ⟨*MAccess*⟩) ;
⟨*ClassInv*⟩ ::= ⟨*StaticOrInstance*⟩$^?$ ⟨*ClassInvKw*⟩ ⟨*BoolExpr*⟩
⟨*StaticOrInstance*⟩ ::= `static` | `instance`
⟨*ClassInvKw*⟩ ::= `invariant` | `constraint` | `initially` | `axiom`
⟨*FieldDecl*⟩ ::= (`ghost` | `model`) ⟨*Type*⟩ ⟨*Id*⟩$^+$
⟨*Represents*⟩ ::= `represents` ⟨*Id*⟩ = ⟨*Expr*⟩ | `represents` ⟨*Id*⟩ `\such_that` ⟨*BoolExpr*⟩
⟨*MAccess*⟩ ::= `accessible` ⟨*Id*⟩ : ⟨*LocSetExpr*⟩ ⟨*Mby*⟩$^?$
⟨*MMthd*⟩ ::= ⟨*Contract*⟩ (`no_state` | `two_state`)$^?$ `model` ⟨*Type*⟩ ⟨*Id*⟩ (⟨*Params*⟩)
                            { `return` ⟨*Expr*⟩; }
⟨*Params*⟩ ::= (⟨*Type*⟩ ⟨*Id*⟩ (, ⟨*Type*⟩ ⟨*Id*⟩)*)$^?$

——————————————————————————————————————— JML Syntax ——

In Table A.1, the rule ⟨*ClassElem*⟩ refers to elements which may additionally
appear as a Java class member (see [Gosling et al., 2013, Sect. 8.2]). Rule ⟨*Id*⟩ refers
to valid identifiers in Java (see ibid., Sect. 6) for types (i.e., classes or interfaces),
variables, fields, and methods.

Table A.2 Contract grammar in JML

—— JML Syntax ————————————————————————————————

⟨*Contract*⟩ ::= `also`$^?$ ⟨*SpecCase*⟩ (`also` ⟨*SpecCase*⟩)*
⟨*SpecCase*⟩ ::= ⟨*Visibility*⟩$^?$ ⟨*Behavior*⟩$^?$ ⟨*Clause*⟩*
⟨*Visibility*⟩ ::= `public` | `protected` | `private`
⟨*Behavior*⟩ ::= `normal_behavior` | `normal_behaviour` |
                    `exceptional_behavior` | `exceptional_behaviour`
⟨*Clause*⟩ ::= (⟨*Requires*⟩ | ⟨*Ensures*⟩ | ⟨*Signals*⟩ | ⟨*SignalsOnly*⟩ | ⟨*Diverges*⟩ |
                ⟨*Determs*⟩ | ⟨*Assign*⟩ | ⟨*Acc*⟩ | ⟨*Mby*⟩) ; | {| ⟨*Clause*⟩* |}
⟨*Requires*⟩ ::= (`requires` | `pre`) ⟨*BoolExpr*⟩
⟨*Ensures*⟩ ::= (`ensures` | `post`) ⟨*BoolExpr*⟩
⟨*Signals*⟩ ::= (`signals` | `ensures`) (⟨*Type*⟩ ⟨*Id*⟩$^?$) ⟨*BoolExpr*⟩
⟨*SignalsOnly*⟩ ::= ⟨*Type*⟩ (, ⟨*Type*⟩)* | `\nothing` | `\everything`
⟨*Diverges*⟩ ::= `diverges` ⟨*BoolExpr*⟩
⟨*Determs*⟩ ::= `determines` (⟨*Exprs*⟩ | `\nothing`) `\by` (⟨*Exprs*⟩ | `\itself` | `\nothing`)
        (`\declassifies` ⟨*Exprs*⟩ | `erases` ⟨*Exprs*⟩)$^?$ (`\new_objects` ⟨*Exprs*⟩)$^?$
⟨*Assign*⟩ ::= ⟨*AssignKw*⟩ (⟨*LocSetExpr*⟩ (, ⟨*LocSetExpr*⟩)*) |
                    `\nothing` | `\strictly_nothing` | `\everything`)
⟨*AssignKw*⟩ ::= `assignable` | `modifiable` | `modifies`
⟨*Acc*⟩ ::= `accessible` (⟨*LocSetExpr*⟩ (, ⟨*LocSetExpr*⟩)* | `\nothing` | `\everything`)
⟨*Mby*⟩ ::= `measured_by` ⟨*Exprs*⟩

——————————————————————————————————————— JML Syntax ——

Table A.2 shows the grammar used for method contracts. Contracts can appear
immediately before method declarations (modulo whitespace; see ibid., Sect. 8.4).

The standard JML clauses interpreted by KeY are limited to **requires, ensures, signals, signals_only, diverges, assignable, accessible, measured_by**. For all of these, their synonyms are defined, too (not all are shown here). Other clauses can still be parsed in KeY, but will be ignored. Additionally, the **determines** clause (see Section 13.4) extends standard JML.

Table A.3 shows modifiers in addition to Java's modifiers (see ibid., Sects. 8.1.1, 8.3.1, 8.4.3, 9.1.1). Note that, technically, the **nullable** and **non_null** are also modifiers, but for more readable semantics we treat them as type information.

Table A.3 Modifiers in JML

──── JML Syntax ───

⟨*Mod*⟩ ::= **pure** | **strictly_pure** | **helper** | **model** | **nullable_by_default**

── JML Syntax ────

Table A.4 shows annotations that may appear inside method bodies, such as loop invariants, block contracts [Wacker, 2012], or ghost assignment statements. Set statements may appear whenever the Java language expects a statement [Gosling et al., 2013, Sect. 14.5], block contracts may appear immediately before a statement block, and loop invariants must appear immediately before a loop statement (**while**, (enhanced) **for**, or **do** loops; see ibid., Sects. 14.12ff.). As a technical restriction of the implementation of KeY, any annotation statement must not be the last statement in a statement block.

Table A.4 JML annotation grammar

──── JML Syntax ───

⟨*Annot*⟩ ::= ⟨*LoopInv*⟩ | ⟨*BlockCntr*⟩ | ⟨*SetStm*⟩ | ⟨*Assert*⟩ | **unreachable;**
⟨*LoopInv*⟩ ::= (⟨*LoopInvClause*⟩ ;)⁺ (⟨*VariantClause*⟩ ;)? (⟨*Assign*⟩ ;)? (⟨*Determs*⟩ ;)?
⟨*LoopInvClause*⟩ ::= (**maintaining** | **loop_invariant**) ⟨*BoolExpr*⟩
⟨*VariantClause*⟩ ::= (**decreasing** | **decreases**) ⟨*Exprs*⟩
⟨*BlockCntr*⟩ ::= **also**? ⟨*BSpecCase*⟩ (**also** ⟨*BSpecCase*⟩)*
⟨*BSpecCase*⟩ ::= ⟨*BBehavior*⟩? ⟨*BClause*⟩*
⟨*BBehavior*⟩ ::= **behavior** | **normal_behavior** | **exceptional_behavior** |
                   break_behavior | **continue_behavior** | **return_behavior**
⟨*BClause*⟩ ::= ⟨*Breaks*⟩; | ⟨*Returns*⟩;| ⟨*Clause*⟩
⟨*Breaks*⟩ ::= (**breaks** | **continues**) ⟨*Id*⟩? ⟨*BoolExpr*⟩
⟨*Returns*⟩ ::= **returns** ⟨*BoolExpr*⟩
⟨*SetStm*⟩ ::= **set** ⟨*Loc*⟩ **=** ⟨*Expr*⟩;
⟨*Assert*⟩ ::= **assert** ⟨*BoolExpr*⟩;

── JML Syntax ────

Table A.5 shows the grammar for expressions in JML. This treatment is complete; all other Java expressions are not valid in JML and thus are rejected by KeY's parser. Rule ⟨*Literal*⟩ refers to (integer) literals of any type or numeral system (see ibid., Sect. 15.8.1).

Table A.5 JML expression grammar

—— JML Syntax ——————————————————————————

$\langle Exprs \rangle$ ::= $(\langle Expr \rangle,)^*$ $\langle Expr \rangle$
$\langle Expr \rangle$ ::= $\langle BoolExpr \rangle$ | $\langle IntExpr \rangle$ | $\langle LocSetExpr \rangle$ | $\langle SeqExpr \rangle$ | `this` | `null`
$\langle BoolExpr \rangle$ ::= `!`$\langle BoolExpr \rangle$ | $\langle BoolExpr \rangle \langle BinaryBoolOp \rangle \langle BoolExpr \rangle$ |
      $\langle Expr \rangle \langle EqOp \rangle \langle Expr \rangle$ | $\langle IntExpr \rangle \langle CompareOp \rangle \langle IntExpr \rangle$ |
      $(\langle Quant \rangle\ \langle Type \rangle\ \langle Id \rangle^+;\ (\langle BoolExpr \rangle;)^?\ \langle BoolExpr \rangle)$ |
      `\invariant_for(`$\langle Expr \rangle$`)` | `\static_invariant_for(`$\langle Type \rangle$`)` |
      `\fresh(`$\langle Expr \rangle$`)` | `\nonnullelements(`$\langle Expr \rangle$`)` |
      `\is_initialized(\type(`$\langle Type \rangle$`)` |
      `\reach(`$\langle Id \rangle$`, `$\langle Expr \rangle$`, `$\langle Expr \rangle(,\ \langle IntExpr \rangle)^?$`)` | $\langle Expr \rangle$ `instanceof` $\langle Type \rangle$ |
      `\typeof(`$\langle Expr \rangle$`)` $\langle TypeOp \rangle$ `\type(`$\langle Type \rangle$`)` | `\subset(`$\langle SeqExpr \rangle$`, `$\langle SeqExpr \rangle$`)` |
      `\disjoint(`$\langle SeqExpr \rangle\ (,\ \langle SeqExpr \rangle)^+$`)` | `\new_elems_fresh(`$\langle LocSetExpr \rangle$`)` |
      `true` | `false` | $\langle GenExpr \rangle$
$\langle BinaryBoolOp \rangle$ ::= `&&` | `&` | `||` | `|` | `==>` | `<==` | `<==>` | `<=!=>` | `^`
$\langle EqOp \rangle$ ::= `==` | `!=`
$\langle CompareOp \rangle$ ::= `<` | `<=` | `>` | `>=`
$\langle TypeOp \rangle$ ::= `==` | `<:`
$\langle Quant \rangle$ ::= `\forall` | `\exists`
$\langle IntExpr \rangle$ ::= `-`$\langle IntExpr \rangle$ | `~`$\langle IntExpr \rangle$ | $\langle IntExpr \rangle \langle BinaryIntOp \rangle \langle IntExpr \rangle$ |
      $\langle IntExpr \rangle \langle BinaryIntOpBitw \rangle \langle IntExpr \rangle$ | $\langle Comprehension \rangle$ | `\index` |
      $\langle Expr \rangle$`.length` | $\langle Literal \rangle$ | $\langle GenExpr \rangle$
$\langle BinaryIntOp \rangle$ ::= `+` | `-` | `*` | `/` | `%`
$\langle BinaryIntOpBitw \rangle$ ::= `<<` | `>>` | `>>>` | `&` | `|` | `^`
$\langle Comprehension \rangle$ ::= $(\langle ComprOp \rangle\ \langle Type \rangle\ \langle Id \rangle^+;\ (\langle BoolExpr \rangle;)^?\ \langle IntExpr \rangle)$ |
      $(`\num_of`\ \langle Type \rangle\ \langle Id \rangle^+;\ (\langle BoolExpr \rangle;)^?\ \langle IntExpr \rangle)$
$\langle ComprOp \rangle$ ::= `\sum` | `\product` | `\max` | `\min`
$\langle GenExpr \rangle$ ::= $\langle BoolExpr \rangle$`?` $\langle Expr \rangle$`:` $\langle Expr \rangle$ | `\result` | `\old(`$\langle Expr \rangle$`)` |
      `\pre(`$\langle Expr \rangle$`)` | `(\lblneg` $\langle Id \rangle\ \langle Expr \rangle$`)` | `(\lblpos` $\langle Id \rangle\ \langle Expr \rangle$`)` |
      `\dl_`$\langle Id \rangle$`(`$\langle Exprs \rangle^?$`)` | `\exception` |
      $(\langle Type \rangle)\ \langle Expr \rangle$ | $\langle Loc \rangle$ | $(\langle Expr \rangle`.`)^? \langle Id \rangle(\langle Exprs \rangle^?)$ |
      $(\langle Type \rangle)\ \langle SeqExpr \rangle[\langle IntExpr \rangle]$ | `(*` $\langle JavaDLTerm \rangle$ `*)`

$\langle Loc \rangle$ ::= $(\langle Expr \rangle`.`)^? \langle Id \rangle$ | $\langle Type \rangle`.`\langle Id \rangle$ | $\langle Expr \rangle[\langle IntExpr \rangle]$
$\langle LocSetExpr \rangle$ ::= $\langle Expr \rangle`.`\langle Id \rangle$ | $\langle Expr \rangle[\langle IntExpr \rangle]$ | $\langle Expr \rangle[\langle IntExpr \rangle`..`\langle IntExpr \rangle]$ |
      $\langle Expr \rangle[*]$ | $\langle Expr \rangle`.*`$ | `\empty` | `\everything` |
      $\langle LocSetOp \rangle(\langle LocSetExpr \rangle, \langle LocSetExpr \rangle)$ |
      `\infinite_union(`$\langle Type \rangle\ \langle Id \rangle;\ (\langle BoolExpr \rangle;\ )^?\langle LocSetExpr \rangle$`)` |
      `\reachLocs(`$\langle Id \rangle$`, `$\langle Expr \rangle(,\ \langle IntExpr \rangle)^?$`)` | $\langle GenExpr \rangle$
$\langle LocSetOp \rangle$ ::= `\intersect` | `\set_union` | `\set_minus`
$\langle SeqExpr \rangle$ ::= `\seq_empty` | `\seq_singleton(`$\langle Expr \rangle$`)` | `\values` |
      `\seq_concat(`$\langle SeqExpr \rangle$`, `$\langle SeqExpr \rangle$`)` |
      $\langle SeqExpr \rangle[\langle IntExpr \rangle`..`\langle IntExpr \rangle]$ | $\langle GenExpr \rangle$
      $(`\seq_def`\ \langle Type \rangle\ \langle Id \rangle;\langle IntExpr \rangle;\ \langle IntExpr \rangle;\ \langle Expr \rangle)$
$\langle Type \rangle$ ::= `boolean` | `byte` | `char` | `short` | `int` | `long` | `\bigint` | `\seq` |
      `\locset` | $\langle NullMod \rangle^?\ \langle Id \rangle([])^*$
$\langle NullMod \rangle$ ::= `nullable` | `non_null`

——————————————————————————————— JML Syntax ——

A.2 JML Expression Semantics

This section contains semantics for JML expressions, given as translations into JavaDL. Tables A.6–A.8 contain translations for Boolean expressions (yielding formulas). For some of the logical operators two or more alternatives with the same semantics exist.[1] All other tables contain translations to terms. See Section 8.1 for details.

Table A.6 Translation of Boolean JML operators

$e \in$ JExp (alternatives)			**JavaDL** $\lfloor e \rfloor \in$ DLFml
`!A`			$\neg \lfloor A \rfloor$
`A && B`	`A & B`		$\lfloor A \rfloor \wedge \lfloor B \rfloor$
`A || B`	`A | B`		$\lfloor A \rfloor \vee \lfloor B \rfloor$
`A ==> B`	`B <== A`		$\lfloor A \rfloor \rightarrow \lfloor B \rfloor$
`A <==> B`	`A == B`		$\lfloor A \rfloor \leftrightarrow \lfloor B \rfloor$
`A <=!=> B`	`A^B`	`A != B`	$\neg(\lfloor A \rfloor \leftrightarrow \lfloor B \rfloor)$
`(\forall T x1, ... xn; A; B)`			$\forall \lfloor T \rfloor x_1; \dots \forall \lfloor T \rfloor x_n; (\bigwedge_{i=1}^{n} \text{inRange}_T(x_i) \wedge \lfloor A \rfloor \rightarrow \lfloor B \rfloor)$
`(\exists T x1, ... xn; A; B)`			$\exists \lfloor T \rfloor x_1; \dots \exists \lfloor T \rfloor x_n; (\bigwedge_{i=1}^{n} \text{inRange}_T(x_i) \wedge \lfloor A \rfloor \wedge \lfloor B \rfloor)$

Table A.7 Translation of special Boolean JML operators

JML expression e	**JavaDL** $\lfloor e \rfloor \in$ DLFml
`\invariant_for(o)`	$Object{::}inv(\text{heap}, \lfloor o \rfloor)$
`\static_invariant_for(T)`	$\lfloor T \rfloor{::}\$inv(\text{heap})$
`\fresh(o)`	$select_{boolean}(\text{heap}^{pre}, \lfloor o \rfloor, created) \doteq FALSE \wedge \lfloor o \rfloor \neq \text{null}$
`\nonnullelements(a)`	$\lfloor a \rfloor \neq \text{null} \wedge \forall i.(0 \leq i < \lfloor a \rfloor.length$
	$\rightarrow select_{Object}(\text{heap}, \lfloor a \rfloor, arr(i)) \neq \text{null})$
`\is_initialized(\type(T))`	$\lfloor T \rfloor.{<}classInitialised{>} \doteq TRUE$
`\reach(f, o1, o2, n)`	$reach(\text{heap}, allObjects(\text{f}), \lfloor o_1 \rfloor, \lfloor o_2 \rfloor, \lfloor n \rfloor)$
`\reach(f, o1, o2)`	$\exists\ int\ n;\ reach(\text{heap}, allObjects(\text{f}), \lfloor o_1 \rfloor, \lfloor o_2 \rfloor, n)$
`\typeof(x) == \type(T)`	$exactInstance_{\lfloor T \rfloor}(\lfloor x \rfloor)$
`x instanceof T`	$instance_{\lfloor T \rfloor}(\lfloor x \rfloor)$

Table A.8 Predicates on location sets

JML expression e	**JavaDL** $\lfloor e \rfloor \in$ DLFml
`\subset(s,t)`	$subset(\lfloor s \rfloor, \lfloor t \rfloor)$
`\disjoint(s1, ..., sn)`	$\bigwedge_{1 \leq i < j \leq n} disjoint(\lfloor s_i \rfloor, \lfloor s_j \rfloor)$
`\fresh(s)`	$subset(\lfloor s \rfloor, unusedLocs(\text{heap}^{pre}))$
`\new_elems_fresh(s)`	$subset(\lfloor s \rfloor, union(\{\text{heap} := \text{heap}^{pre}\}\lfloor s \rfloor, unusedLocs(\text{heap}^{pre})))$

Table A.9 Translation of Java integer expressions. Depending on the type of subexpressions, there are different translations: The right-most column applies if at least one operand is of type \bigint, else if at least one operand is of type long, the center column applies, and else the left column applies. Note that there is no cast to \bigint. Refer to Section 5.4 for a detailed explanation on these functions.

$e \in$ JExp	$\lfloor e \rfloor \in \mathrm{Trm}_{int}$, $type_{ML}(e) = $ int	$\lfloor e \rfloor \in \mathrm{Trm}_{int}$, $type_{ML}(e) = $ long	$\lfloor e \rfloor \in \mathrm{Trm}_{int}$, $type_{ML}(e) = $ \bigint
$- n$	$javaUnaryMinusInt(\lfloor n \rfloor)$	$javaUnaryMinusLong(\lfloor n \rfloor)$	$-\lfloor n \rfloor$
$n + m$	$javaAddInt(\lfloor n \rfloor, \lfloor m \rfloor)$	$javaAddLong(\lfloor n \rfloor, \lfloor m \rfloor)$	$\lfloor n \rfloor + \lfloor m \rfloor$
$n - m$	$javaSubInt(\lfloor n \rfloor, \lfloor m \rfloor)$	$javaSubLong(\lfloor n \rfloor, \lfloor m \rfloor)$	$\lfloor n \rfloor - \lfloor m \rfloor$
$n * m$	$javaMulInt(\lfloor n \rfloor, \lfloor m \rfloor)$	$javaMulLong(\lfloor n \rfloor, \lfloor m \rfloor)$	$\lfloor n \rfloor * \lfloor m \rfloor$
n / m	$javaDivInt(\lfloor n \rfloor, \lfloor m \rfloor)$	$javaDivLong(\lfloor n \rfloor, \lfloor m \rfloor)$	$jdiv(\lfloor n \rfloor, \lfloor m \rfloor)$
$n \% m$	$javaModInt(\lfloor n \rfloor, \lfloor m \rfloor)$	$javaModLong(\lfloor n \rfloor, \lfloor m \rfloor)$	$jmod(\lfloor n \rfloor, \lfloor m \rfloor)$
$(T) n$	$castToByte(\lfloor n \rfloor)$, $castToShort(\lfloor n \rfloor)$, $castToInt(\lfloor n \rfloor)$, $castToLong(\lfloor n \rfloor)$, or $castToChar(\lfloor n \rfloor)$		
$\sim n$	$javaBitwiseNegation(\lfloor n \rfloor)$		
$n << m$	$javaShiftLeftInt(\lfloor n \rfloor, \lfloor m \rfloor)$	$javaShiftLeftLong(\lfloor n \rfloor, \lfloor m \rfloor)$	—
$n >> m$	$javaShiftRightInt(\lfloor n \rfloor, \lfloor m \rfloor)$	$javaShiftRightLong(\lfloor n \rfloor, \lfloor m \rfloor)$	—
$n >>> m$	$javaUnsignedShiftRightInt(\lfloor n \rfloor, \lfloor m \rfloor)$	$javaUnsignedShiftRightLong(\lfloor n \rfloor, \lfloor m \rfloor)$	—
$n \& m$	$javaBitwiseAndInt(\lfloor n \rfloor, \lfloor m \rfloor)$	$javaBitwiseAndLong(\lfloor n \rfloor, \lfloor m \rfloor)$	—
$n \mid m$	$javaBitwiseOrInt(\lfloor n \rfloor, \lfloor m \rfloor)$	$javaBitwiseOrLong(\lfloor n \rfloor, \lfloor m \rfloor)$	—
$n \hat{\ } m$	$javaBitwiseXOrInt(\lfloor n \rfloor, \lfloor m \rfloor)$	$javaBitwiseXOrLong(\lfloor n \rfloor, \lfloor m \rfloor)$	—

Table A.10 Translation of comprehension expressions (generalized quantifiers)

JML expression e	JavaDL $\lfloor e \rfloor \in \mathrm{Trm}_{int}$	
(\sum T x; n <= x && x < m; t)	$(T')bsum\{int\ x\}(\lfloor n \rfloor, \lfloor m \rfloor, \lfloor t \rfloor)$	$[T] = int$, t of type T'
(\sum T x1, ... xn; A; t)	$(T')sum\{T\ x_1\}(\ldots, sum\{T\ x_n\}(\bigwedge_{i=1}^{n} \mathrm{inRange}_T(x_i) \wedge \lfloor A \rfloor, \lfloor t \rfloor)\ldots)$	t of type T'
(\num_of T x; n <= x && x < m; B)	$(T')bsum\{int\ x\}(\lfloor n \rfloor, \lfloor m \rfloor, \mathrm{if}\ (\lfloor B \rfloor)\ \mathrm{then}\ (1)\ \mathrm{else}\ (0))$	$[T] = int$, t of type T'
(\num_of T x1, ... xn; A; B)	$(T')sum\{T\ x_1\}(\ldots, sum\{T\ x_n\}(\bigwedge_{x=1}^{n} \mathrm{inRange}_T(x_i) \wedge \lfloor A \rfloor, \mathrm{if}\ (\lfloor B \rfloor)\ \mathrm{then}\ (1)\ \mathrm{else}\ (0))\ldots)$	t of type T'
(\product T x; n <= x && x < m; t)	$(T')bprod\{int\ x\}(\lfloor n \rfloor, \lfloor m \rfloor, \lfloor t \rfloor)$	$[T] = int$, t of type T'
(\product T x1, ... xn; A; t)	$(T')prod\{T\ x_1\}(\ldots, prod\{T\ x_n\}(\bigwedge_{i=1}^{n} \mathrm{inRange}_T(x_i) \wedge \lfloor A \rfloor, \lfloor t \rfloor)\ldots)$	t of type T'
(\max T x1, ... xn; A; t)	$max\{T\ x_1\}(\ldots, max\{T\ x_n\}(\bigwedge_{i=1}^{n} \mathrm{inRange}_T(x_i) \wedge \lfloor A \rfloor, \lfloor t \rfloor)\ldots)$	t of type T'
(\min T x1, ... xn; A; t)	$min\{T\ x_1\}(\ldots, min\{T\ x_n\}(\bigwedge_{i=1}^{n} \mathrm{inRange}_T(x_i) \wedge \lfloor A \rfloor, \lfloor t \rfloor)\ldots)$	t of type T'

Table A.11 Restrictions on JavaDL types to match JML types

JML Type T'	JavaDL type $\lfloor T' \rfloor$	Restriction formula $\mathrm{inRange}_{T'}(x)$
boolean	$boolean$	$true$
byte	int	$inByte(x)$
char	int	$inChar(x)$
short	int	$inShort(x)$
int	int	$inInt(x)$
long	int	$inLong(x)$
\bigint	int	$true$
nullable T	$T \sqsubseteq Object$	$select_{boolean}(\mathrm{heap}, x, created) \doteq TRUE \vee x \doteq null$
nonnull T	$T \sqsubseteq Object$	$select_{boolean}(\mathrm{heap}, x, created) \doteq TRUE \wedge x \neq null$
nonnull $T[]^n$	$T[]^n$	$select_{boolean}(\mathrm{heap}, x, created) \doteq TRUE \wedge nonNull(\mathrm{heap}, x, n)$
\locset	$LocSet$	$disjoint(x, unusedLocs(\mathrm{heap}))$
\seq	Seq	$true$

Table A.12 Translation of special JML operators of arbitrary type

JML expression e	**JavaDL** $\lfloor e \rfloor \in \mathrm{Trm}_{Any}$
$A?\ B:\ C$	if $(\lfloor A \rfloor)$ then $(\lfloor B \rfloor)$ else $(\lfloor C \rfloor)$
\result	res
\old$(A)$	$\{\mathtt{heap} := \mathtt{heap}^{pre} \| \mathtt{p}_1 := \mathtt{p}_1^{pre} \| \ldots \| \mathtt{p}_n := \mathtt{p}_n^{pre}\} \lfloor A \rfloor$ (in loop invs.)
\old$(A)$	$\{\mathtt{heap} := \mathtt{heap}^{pre}\} \lfloor A \rfloor$ (in method contracts)
\pre$(A)$	$\{\mathtt{heap} := \mathtt{heap}^{pre}\} \lfloor A \rfloor$
(\lblneg $x\ A$)	$\lfloor A \rfloor$
(\lblpos $x\ A$)	$\lfloor A \rfloor$
\dl_func$(p1,\ \ldots,\ pn)$	$func(\mathtt{heap}, \lfloor p1 \rfloor, \ldots \lfloor pn \rfloor)$
(* $term$ *)	$term$
\index	$index$

Table A.13 Reference expressions

	$e \in$ JExp	$\lfloor e \rfloor \in \mathrm{Trm}_{Any}$
self reference	this	self
local variable	v	v
field access	o.f	$select_{T'}(\mathtt{heap}, \lfloor o \rfloor, C\text{::}\mathtt{f})$
static field access	C.f	$select_{T'}(\mathtt{heap}, \mathtt{null}, C\text{::}\$\mathtt{f})$
array access	$a[i]$	$select_{T'}(\mathtt{heap}, \lfloor a \rfloor, arr(\lfloor i \rfloor))$
array length	a.length	$length(\lfloor a \rfloor)$
pure method	o.pm$(p1,\ldots,pn)$	$C\text{::}pm(\mathtt{heap}, \lfloor o \rfloor, \lfloor p1 \rfloor, \ldots, \lfloor pn \rfloor)$
static pure method	C.pm$(p1,\ldots,pn)$	$C\text{::}pm(\mathtt{heap}, \mathtt{null}, \lfloor p1 \rfloor, \ldots, \lfloor pn \rfloor)$
model field	o.mf	$C\text{::}mf(\mathtt{heap}, \lfloor o \rfloor)$
static model field	C.mf	$C\text{::}mf(\mathtt{heap}, \mathtt{null})$

A.3 JML Expression Well-Definedness

As explained in Section 8.1.4, in JML, validity depends on the absence of undefinedness. According to the JML reference manual [Leavens et al., 2013], a Boolean
expression is satisfied in a state if has the truth value true and "does not cause an
exception to be raised." Our translation from JML to JavaDL above ignores this.

KeY can generate well-definedness proof obligations as shown in Section 8.3.3.
Table A.16 below gives the full definition of the well-definition operator ω, which
provides a formula $\omega(e)$ to every JML expression e, such that e is well-behaving in a
state s if and only if $s \vDash \omega(e)$.

---

[1] These operators may differ in the way well-definedness of expressions is evaluated, see Section A.3
below.

Table A.14 JML location set expressions

JML expression e	**JavaDL** $\lfloor e \rfloor \in \mathrm{Trm}_{LocSet}$
$o.\mathtt{f}$	$\{(\lfloor o \rfloor, \mathtt{f})\}$
$\mathtt{\backslash singleton}(o.\mathtt{f})$	$\{(\lfloor o \rfloor, \mathtt{f})\}$
$a[i]$	$\{(\lfloor a \rfloor, arr(\lfloor i \rfloor))\}$
$a[i..j]$	$arrayRange(\lfloor a \rfloor, \lfloor i \rfloor, \lfloor j \rfloor)$
$a[*]$	$allFields(\lfloor a \rfloor)$
$o.*$	$allFields(\lfloor o \rfloor)$
$\mathtt{\backslash empty}$	$empty$
$\mathtt{\backslash nothing}$	$empty$
$\mathtt{\backslash everything}$	$setMinus(allLocs, unusedLocs(\mathtt{heap}))$
$\mathtt{\backslash intersect}(s,t)$	$intersect(\lfloor s \rfloor, \lfloor t \rfloor)$
$\mathtt{\backslash set\_union}(s,t)$	$union(\lfloor s \rfloor, \lfloor t \rfloor)$
$\mathtt{\backslash set\_minus}(s,t)$	$setMinus(\lfloor s \rfloor, \lfloor t \rfloor)$
$\mathtt{\backslash infinite\_union}(T\ x;\ b;\ t)$	$\text{infiniteUnion}\{\lfloor T \rfloor\, x\}(\ \text{if } (inRange_T(x) \wedge \lfloor b \rfloor) \text{ then } (\lfloor t \rfloor) \text{ else } (empty)\ )$
$\mathtt{\backslash reachLocs}(\mathtt{f, o, n})$	$\text{infiniteUnion}\{Object\, o'\}(\ \text{if } (reach(\mathtt{heap}, allObjects(f), \lfloor o \rfloor, o', \lfloor n \rfloor))\ \text{then } (allFields(o')) \text{ else } (empty)\ )$
$\mathtt{\backslash reachLocs}(\mathtt{f, o})$	$\text{infiniteUnion}\{Object\, o'\}(\ \text{if } (\exists\, int\ n;\ reach(\mathtt{heap}, allObjects(f), \lfloor o \rfloor, o', n))\ \text{then } (allFields(o')) \text{ else } (empty)\ )$

Table A.15 JML sequence expressions

JML expression e	**JavaDL** $\lfloor e \rfloor \in \mathrm{Trm}_{Any}$
$\mathtt{\backslash seq\_concat}(s1,\ s2)$	$seqConcat(\lfloor s1 \rfloor, \lfloor s2 \rfloor)$
$\mathtt{\backslash seq\_empty}$	$seqEmpty$
$(T)s[i]$	$seqGet_T(\lfloor s \rfloor, \lfloor i \rfloor)$
$s.\mathtt{length}$	$seqLen(\lfloor s \rfloor)$
$\mathtt{\backslash seq\_singleton}(e)$	$seqSingleton(\lfloor e \rfloor)$
$s[i..j]$	$seqSub(\lfloor s \rfloor, \lfloor i \rfloor, \lfloor j \rfloor)$
$(\mathtt{\backslash seq\_def\ \backslash bigint}\ x;\ i;\ j;\ t)$	$seqDef\{int\, x\}(\lfloor i \rfloor, \lfloor j \rfloor, \lfloor t \rfloor)$
$\mathtt{\backslash values}$	$values$

Table A.16 Definition of the well-definedness operator ω

JML expression $e \in$ JExp	JavaDL formula $\omega(e) \in$ DLFml	
x, this, super, null, \result	*true*	for x a literal or local variable
$\circ A$	$\omega(A)$	$\circ \in \{\,!\,, -, \sim\}$
$A \circ B$	$\omega(A) \wedge \omega(B)$	$\circ \in \{==, !=, <=, >=, <, >, +,$ $-, *, \&, \|, <==>, \hat{}\,, >>, <<, >>>\}$
$\backslash f(A)$	$\omega(A)$	$f \in \{\texttt{fresh}, \texttt{new\_elems\_fresh}\}$
$\backslash f(A,\ B)$	$\omega(A) \wedge \omega(B)$	$f \in \{\texttt{set\_union}, \texttt{intersect},$ $\texttt{set\_minus}, \texttt{subset}, \texttt{disjoint}\}$
A / B, $\ A \% B$	$\omega(A) \wedge \omega(B) \wedge B \neq 0$	
$A \,\&\&\, B$	$\omega(A) \wedge (\lfloor A \rfloor \to \omega(B))$	
$A ==> B$	$\omega(A) \wedge (\lfloor A \rfloor \to \omega(B))$	
$A \,\|\,\| \, B$	$\omega(A) \wedge (\neg\lfloor A \rfloor \to \omega(B))$	
$A <== B$	$\omega(A) \wedge (\neg\lfloor A \rfloor \to \omega(B))$	
$A ? B : C$	$\omega(A) \wedge (\lfloor A \rfloor \to \omega(B))$ $\wedge (\neg\lfloor A \rfloor \to \omega(C))$	
$o.\texttt{f}$	$\omega(o) \wedge o \neq \texttt{null}$	for an instance field f, also if used as location
$\texttt{C.f}$	*true*	for a static field C.f, also if used as location
$o.\texttt{m}(a_1, \ldots, a_n)$	$\omega(o) \wedge o \neq \texttt{null} \wedge$ $\bigwedge_{i=1}^{n} \omega(a_i) \wedge$ $pre[a_i/\texttt{p}_i, o/\texttt{self}]$	
$\texttt{new C}(a_1, \ldots, a_n)$	$\bigwedge_{i=1}^{n} \omega(a_i) \wedge$ $pre[a_i/\texttt{p}_i, o/\texttt{self}]$	
$a[i]$	$\omega(a) \wedge a \neq \texttt{null} \wedge \omega(i) \wedge$ $0 \le i \wedge i < length(a)$	array access, sequence access also if used as location.
$a[i..j]$	$\omega(a) \wedge a \neq \texttt{null} \wedge$ $\omega(i) \wedge \omega(j) \wedge$ $0 \le i \wedge i \le j \wedge j < length(a)$	array range (location set)
$o[*], o.*$	$\omega(o) \wedge o \neq \texttt{null}$	
$o.\texttt{length}$	$\omega(o) \wedge o \neq \texttt{null}$	for an array o
$(\backslash Q \ T \ v; A; B)$	$\forall \lfloor T \rfloor \, v; \ \big(\omega(A) \wedge (\lfloor A \rfloor \to \omega(B))\big)$	$Q \in \{\texttt{forall}, \texttt{exists}, \texttt{min}, \texttt{max}$ $\texttt{infinte\_union}, \texttt{sum}, \texttt{product}\}$
$(\backslash\texttt{seq\_def}\ T \ v; A; B; C)$	$\forall\texttt{int}\ v; (\lfloor A \rfloor \le v < \lfloor B \rfloor \to \omega(C))$ $\wedge\ \omega(A) \wedge \omega(B)$	$T \in \{\texttt{int}, \backslash\texttt{bigint}\}$
$(T)t$	$\omega(t) \wedge instance_{\lfloor T \rfloor}(\lfloor t \rfloor) \doteq TRUE$	
t instanceof T	$\omega(t)$	
$\backslash\texttt{old}(A)$	$\{\texttt{heap} := \texttt{heap}^{pre}\}\omega(A)$	
$\backslash\texttt{invariant\_for}(A)$	$\omega(A) \wedge A \neq \texttt{null}$	

Appendix B
KeY File Reference

Wojciech Mostowski and Richard Bubel

B.1 Predefined Operators in JavaDL

This appendix lists syntax and semantics of all predefined function and predicate symbols of JavaDL.

B.1.1 Arithmetic Function Symbols

function symbol	typing and informal semantics
+	$int \times int \to int$ addition
−	$int \times int \to int$ subtraction
*	$int \times int \to int$ multiplication
/	$int \times int \to int$ Euclidian division
%	$int \times int \to int$ remainder for /
−	$int \to int$ unary minus
jdiv	$int \times int \to int$ division rounding towards 0
jmod	$int \times int \to int$ remainder for *jdiv*
shiftright	$int \times int \to int$ shift right for unbounded bitvectors
shiftleft	$int \times int \to int$ shift left for unbounded bitvectors

function symbol	typing and informal semantics
unsignedshift	$int \times int \times int \to int$
	unsigned shift for bitvectors of the size specified as third argument
binaryAnd	$int \times int \to int$
	binary 'and' for unbounded bitvectors
binaryOr	$int \times int \to int$
	binary 'or' for unbounded bitvectors
binaryXOr	$int \times int \to int$
	binary 'xor' for unbounded bitvectors
$\ldots, -1, 0, 1, 2, \ldots$	*int*
	integer numbers
FALSE	boolean
	constant for truth value false
TRUE	boolean
	constant for truth value true
null	Null
	constant for null element
(A) (for any $A \in$ TSym)	$Any \to A$
	cast to type A
max_byte	*int*
max_short	*int*
max_int	*int*
max_long	*int*
max_char	*int*
	maximum number of respective Java type
min_byte	*int*
min_short	*int*
min_int	*int*
min_long	*int*
min_char	*int*
	minimum number of respective Java type

B.1.2 Arithmetic Function Symbols with Modulo Semantics

These arithmetic functions realize Java's modulo semantics faithfully. The bitvector operations are defined for the bit sizes of their respective type (*int* 32-bit, *long* 64-bit).

function symbol	typing and informal semantics
unaryMinusJint	*int*
unaryMinusJlong	*int*
	unary minus

function symbol	typing and informal semantics
addJint	$int \times int \rightarrow int$
addJlong	$int \times int \rightarrow int$
	addition
subJint	$int \times int \rightarrow int$
subJlong	$int \times int \rightarrow int$
	subtraction
mulJint	$int \times int \rightarrow int$
mulJlong	$int \times int \rightarrow int$
	multiplication
divJint	$int \times int \rightarrow int$
divJlong	$int \times int \rightarrow int$
	division
modJint	$int \times int \rightarrow int$
modJlong	$int \times int \rightarrow int$
	modulo
shiftrightJint	$int \times int \rightarrow int$
shiftrightJlong	$int \times int \rightarrow int$
	binary shift-right
unsignedshiftrightJint	$int \times int \rightarrow int$
unsignedshiftrightJlong	$int \times int \rightarrow int$
	unsigned binary shift-right
shiftleftJint	$int \times int \rightarrow int$
shiftleftJlong	$int \times int \rightarrow int$
	binary shift-left
orJint	$int \times int \rightarrow int$
orJlong	$int \times int \rightarrow int$
	binary or
xorJint	$int \times int \rightarrow int$
xorJlong	$int \times int \rightarrow int$
	binary xor
andJint	$int \times int \rightarrow int$
andJlong	$int \times int \rightarrow int$
	binary and
negJint	int
negJlong	int
	binary negation
moduloByte	int
moduloShort	int
moduloInt	int
moduloLong	int
moduloChar	int
	computation of overflow

B.1.3 Predicate Symbols for Arithmetics and Equality

predicate symbol	typing and informal semantics
$<$	$int \times int$ less than
$<=$	$int \times int$ less than or equal
$>$	$int \times int$ greater than
$>=$	$int \times int$ greater than or equal
$\doteq$	$Any \times Any$ equality
$\neq$	$Any \times Any$ inequality
arrayStoreValid	$Any \times Any$ holds iff an array store operation is valid for the given arguments

B.1.4 Arithmetic Function Symbols whose Meaning Depends on the Chosen Integer Semantics

These arithmetic functions depend on the chosen integer semantics (see Section 5.4). They are usually introduced by the translation of JML or when symbolically executing arithmetic expressions (and moving them into the sequent).

function symbol	typing and informal semantics
javaUnaryMinusInt	$int \rightarrow int$
javaUnaryMinusLong	$int \rightarrow int$ translation of Java's unary minus operator for the promoted type *int/long*
javaBitwiseNegationInt	$int \rightarrow int$
javaBitwiseNegationLong	$int \rightarrow int$ translation of Java's unary bitwise negation operator for the promoted type *int/long*
javaAddInt	$int \times int \rightarrow int$
javaAddLong	$int \times int \rightarrow int$ translation of Java's addition operator for the promoted type *int/long*
javaSubInt	$int \times int \rightarrow int$
javaSubLong	$int \times int \rightarrow int$

function symbol	typing and informal semantics
	translation of Java's substraction operator for the promoted type *int/long*
javaMulInt	$int \times int \rightarrow int$
javaMulLong	$int \times int \rightarrow int$
	translation of Java's multiplication operator for the promoted type *int/long*
javaMod	$int \times int \rightarrow int$
	translation of Java's remainder operator for both promoted types *int* and *long*
javaDivInt	$int \times int \rightarrow int$
javaDivLong	$int \times int \rightarrow int$
	translation of Java's division operator for the promoted type *int/long*
javaShiftRightInt	$int \times int \rightarrow int$
javaShiftRightLong	$int \times int \rightarrow int$
	translation of Java's shift right operator for the promoted type *int/long*
javaShiftLeftInt	$int \times int \rightarrow int$
javaShiftLeftLong	$int \times int \rightarrow int$
	translation of Java's shift left operator for the promoted types*int/long*
javaUnsignedShiftRightInt	$int \times int \rightarrow int$
javaUnsignedShiftRightLong	$int \times int \rightarrow int$
	translation of Java's unsigned shift right operator for the promoted type *int/long*
javaBitwiseOrInt	$int \times int \rightarrow int$
javaBitwiseOrLong	$int \times int \rightarrow int$
	translation of Java's bitwise-or operator for the promoted type *int/long*
javaBitwiseAndInt	$int \times int \rightarrow int$
javaBitwiseAndLong	$int \times int \rightarrow int$
	translation of Java's bitwise-and operator for the promoted type *int/long*
javaBitwiseXOrInt	$int \times int \rightarrow int$
javaBitwiseXOrLong	$int \times int \rightarrow int$
	translation of Java's bitwise-xor operator for the promoted type *int/long*
javaCastByte	$int \rightarrow int$
javaCastShort	$int \rightarrow int$
javaCastInt	$int \rightarrow int$
javaCastLong	$int \rightarrow int$
javaCastChar	$int \rightarrow int$
	translation of Java's cast operator to the corresponding type

B.1.5 Predicate Symbols Depending on the Chosen Integer Semantics

predicate symbol	typing and informal semantics
inByte	*int*
inShort	*int*
inInt	*int*
inLong	*int*
inChar	*int*
	holds iff argument in range of respective Java Card type

B.1.6 Heap Related Function and Predicate Symbols

function symbol	typing and informal semantics
create	*Heap × Object → Heap* returns a new heap coinciding with the old one where the specified object is created
A :: select	*Heap × Object × Field → A* looks up the value at the given heap for the program location specified by the 2nd and 3rd argument and casts it to sort *A*
store	*Heap × Object × Field × any → Heap* returns the heap resulting from updating the given heap at program location specified by the second and third argument to value specified as fourth argument
anon	*Heap × LocSet × Heap → Heap* constructs a new heap from both given heaps; the returned heap coincides with the first heap on i) the set of created objects; ii) on all program locations of created objects that are *not* in the set of locations given as second argument. In all other cases the heap coincides with the second heap.
memset	*Heap × LocSet × any → Heap* returns a new heap coinciding with the given heap except for the program locations in the given set of locations, which are set to the value given as third argument
length	*Object → int* assigns each object an integer
null	*→ Null* the `null` constant

predicate symbol	typing and informal semantics
wellFormed	*Heap*
	characterizes valid Java heaps

B.1.7 Location Sets Related Function and Predicate Symbols

function symbol	typing and informal semantics
empty	$\rightarrow LocSet$
	\unique symbol for the empty set
allLocs	$\rightarrow LocSet$
	\unique symbol for the set of all locations
singleton	$Object \times Field \rightarrow LocSet$
	returns a location set containing only the location given as argument
union	$LocSet \times LocSet \rightarrow LocSet$
	returns the union of the location sets
intersect	$LocSet \times LocSet \rightarrow LocSet$
	returns the intersection of the location sets
setMinus	$LocSet \times LocSet \rightarrow LocSet$
	returns the set difference of the location sets
infiniteUnion{true}	$LocSet \rightarrow LocSet$
	variable binding function in the first argument; returns the infinite union $\bigcup_x L(x)$ of the location sets $L(x)$
allFields	$Object \rightarrow LocSet$
	returns the smallest location set of all locations whose object component is the object given as argument
allObjects	$Field \rightarrow LocSet$
	returns the smallest location set of all locations whose field component is the field given as argument
arrayRange	$Object \times int \times int \rightarrow LocSet$
	returns the location set of all array elements between the index given as second argument (incl.) and the index given as third argument (incl.) of the array given as first argument
freshLocs	$Heap \rightarrow LocSet$
	all locations of objects that are not created in the given heap

predicate symbol	typing and informal semantics
elementOf	*Object × Field × LocSet* holds iff the location specified by the first two arguments is an element of the location set given as third argument
subset	*LocSet × LocSet* holds iff the first location set is a subset of (or equal to) the second location set
disjoint	*LocSet × LocSet* holds iff both location sets are disjoint
createdInHeap	*LocSet × Heap* holds if the locations in the set are either static fields or belong to objects that are created in the heap given as second argument

B.1.8 Finite Sequence Related Function and Predicate Symbols

function symbol	typing and informal semantics
seqEmpty	*→ Seq* the empty sequence
seqSingleton	*any → Seq* singleton sequence with exactly the element given as argument
seqConcat	*Seq × Seq → Seq* concatenates two sequences to a single one
seqSub	*Seq × int × int → Seq* returns the subsequence of the first sequence ranging from the first argument (incl.) to the second argument (excl.); if the second argument is less or equal than the first one the empty sequence is returned
seqReverse	*Seq → Seq* reverses the sequence
seqDef{int x}(false, false, true)	*int × int × any → Seq* the defining constructor for sequences (see Section 5.2)
seqSwap	*Seq × int × int → Seq* swaps the two elements at the specified indexes

function symbol	typing and informal semantics
seqRemove	$Seq \times int \to Seq$ removes the element at the specified index
seqNPermInv	$Seq \to Seq$
array2seq	$Heap \times Object \to Seq$ converts the array into a sequence
A :: seqGet	$Seq \times int \to A$ retrieves the element at the specified index and casts it to type *A*; if out of bounds the element *seqGetOutside* is returned
seqLen	$Seq \to int$ returns the length of the sequence
seqIndexOf	$Seq \times any \to int$ returns the first index of the element (second argument) in the given sequence; otherwise unspecified
seqGetOutside	$\to any$ unspecified element returned when trying to access an element outside a sequence's bounds

predicate symbol	typing and informal semantics
seqPerm	$Seq \times Seq$ holds iff the first sequences is a permutation of the other
seqNPerm	Seq holds if the sequence *s* is a permutation of the integers $0, \ldots, seqLen(s) - 1$

B.1.9 Map Related Function and Predicate Symbols

function symbol	typing and informal semantics
mapForeach{*false,false,true*}	$boolean\,any \to Map$ the defining constructor for maps
mapEmpty	$\to Map$ the empty map

function symbol	typing and informal semantics
mapSingleton	*any* × *any* → *Map* map with one entry where the key is given as the first argument and the value as second argument
mapUpdate	*Map* × *any* → *Map* concatenates two sequences to a single one
mapRemove	*Map* × *any* → *Map* removes the entry whose key equals the key given as second argument from the map
mapGet	*Map* × *any* → *any* retrieves the value associated with the key given as second argument; returns the unspecified element *mapUndef*, if no such value is found
mapUndef	→ *any* unspecified unique element

predicate symbol	typing and informal semantics
inDomain	*Map* × *any* holds iff the map contains the key given as second argument

B.2 The KeY Syntax

The KeY system accepts different kinds of inputs related to JavaDL. From the user point of view these inputs can be divided into the following categories:

- system rule files,
- user defined rule files,
- user problem files/proofs with optional user defined rules,
- JavaDL terms and formulas required by the interaction component of the KeY system.

From the system's perspective the division is similar, but on top of this, the distinction between schematic mode and term (normal) mode is very important:

- in schematic mode schema variables can be defined and used (usually in definition of rules/taclets) and concrete terms or formulas are forbidden,

- in normal mode schema variables and all other schematic constructs are forbidden, while concrete terms and formulas are allowed.

Additionally, most of terms and formulas constructs can appear in both schematic and normal mode, but take slightly different form depending on the mode.

In either case, all inputs the KeY system accepts follow the same syntax—the KeY syntax (or, as sometimes it is sometimes referred to, .key file syntax).

On the implementation level, the parsing of the KeY input is done on two levels. One parser (called term, taclet, or problem parser) is used to parse all the input up to modalities, and a second parser (schematic Java parser) is used to parse all Java program blocks inside the modalities. Thus, on occasion, slightly different conventions may apply when input material inside the modality is considered as compared to input outside of the modality.

Finally, note that the syntax described here reflects the syntax of the KeY system snapshot available before the book was printed. The KeY syntax undergoes minor changes during system development, thus the publicly available KeY system may differ slightly in its input syntax.

B.2.1 Notation, Keywords, Identifiers, Numbers, Strings

Expressions in the `type-writer` font are KeY syntax tokens or identifiers. Keywords are annotated with **`bold type-writer`** font. In the KeY system the convention is to use an escape character, backslash \, to mark (almost) all keywords, and some KeY specific operators, like modalities. This is necessary to avoid collisions between KeY system keywords/operators and possible Java identifiers/operators.

An identifier in the KeY system can be one of the following:

—— KeY Syntax ——————————————————————————————

`lettersdigits_#`	starts with a letter, can contain letters, digits, underscore, and hash characters
`identifier`	like the first one, an identifier can start with a single dollar character
`<letters>`	identifier enclosed in <>, used to annotate implicit attributes, only letters allowed
`\letters_`	If not a reserved keyword, a sequence of letters and underscores starting with a backslash is also an identifier
`singledigit`	In special cases, when used as a function symbol, e.g., 1(...), a single digit is also an identifier

——————————————————————————————————— KeY Syntax ——

A keyword is a reserved identifier that starts with a backslash \ and contains only letters and underscores. An exception from this rule are keywords **`true`**, **`false`**, and modality symbols. Some examples of identifiers and the list of all keywords:

—— KeY Syntax ——

Identifiers:
```
varName #varName operation@pre
<transient> \non_keyword_ident
```

Keywords and keyword-escaped symbols:
```
\include \includeLDTs \javaSource \withOptions
\optionsDecl \settings

\sorts \generic \proxy \extends \oneof \abstract
\locset \seq \bigint

\schemaVariables \schemaVar \modalOperator
\program \formula \term \update \variables \variable
\skolemTerm \skolemFormula \termlabel

\forall \exists \sub \subst \ifEx \if \then \else

\rules \find \add \assumes \replacewith \addrules \addprogvars
\heuristics \noninteractive \trigger \avoid
\sameUpdateLevel \inSequentState \closegoal
\antecedentPolarity \succedentPolarity
\displayname \helptext \lemma

\varcond \typeof \elemTypeOf \new \newLabel \not \same
\subsub \strict \staticMethodReference \notFreeIn
\static \final \isReferenceArray \isReference \dependingOn
\instantiateGeneric \inType \hasSort \isConstant \isEnumType
\isArray \isArrayLength \isStaticField \isLocalVariable
\isAbstractOrInterface \isInductVar \isObserver
\containsAssignment \containerType \applyUpdateOnRigid
\disjointModuloNull \simplifyIfThenElseUpdate
\dropEffectlessElementaries \dropEffectlessStores
\enumConstant \freeLabelIn \fieldType

\heuristicsDecl \programVariables \predicates \functions
\unique

\problem \proof \contracts \modifies \proofScript \invariants

\< \> \[ \] \[[ \]] \diamond \box \throughout
\diamond_transaction \box_transaction \throughout_transaction
\modality \endmodality
true false $lmtd
```
—— KeY Syntax ——

An integer number in KeY can be given in a decimal or hexadecimal form with infinite precision. An integer constant can have a negation sign:

—— KeY Syntax ———————————————————————————————

Decimal integers:
```
1 2 -3 10 -20 1234567890123456789012345678
```

Hexadecimal integers:
```
0x01 -0xA 0xFFAABBCC0090ffaa
```

——————————————————————————————— KeY Syntax ——

The KeY system can also recognize strings and character constants in its input. Strings and characters in KeY are practically the same as strings and characters in Java, with the same special characters and character quoting rules:

—— KeY Syntax ———————————————————————————————

```
"A␣string␣with␣a␣line␣break␣at␣the␣end.\n"
'A' '0' '\t' '\r' '0x0020'
```

——————————————————————————————— KeY Syntax ——

Finally, in the following expressions in ⟨*italics*⟩ represent parsing rules in regular expression form with operators ::= (definition), | (alternative), ? (zero or one occurrence), * (zero or more occurrences), + (one or more occurrences), and () grouping. Whenever necessary, explanations are given to explain intuitive meaning of the rules. Identifiers are denoted with ⟨*identifier*⟩, numbers with ⟨*number*⟩, strings and characters with ⟨*string*⟩ and ⟨*character*⟩ respectively.

B.2.2 Terms and Formulas

We start with describing KeY's syntax rules to construct a valid JavaDL term or formula. On the syntax level, terms are hardly distinguishable from formulas, that is, from the parser point of view, a formula is a term with a special top-level sort (a "formula" sort). In general, many of the following syntax rules are only applicable if the involved expressions have the right sort. On the implementation level, semantic checks are performed next to syntax checks when expressions are parsed.

B.2.2.1 Logic Operators

The logic operators for building terms or formulas are the following:

—— KeY Syntax ———————————————————————————————

⟨*formula*⟩ ::= ⟨*term*⟩
⟨*term*⟩   ::= ⟨*term₁*⟩ (<-> ⟨*term₁*⟩)*
⟨*term₁*⟩ ::= ⟨*term₂*⟩ (-> ⟨*term₁*⟩)?
⟨*term₂*⟩ ::= ⟨*term₃*⟩ (| ⟨*term₃*⟩)*

⟨*term₃*⟩ ::= ⟨*term₄*⟩ (& ⟨*term₄*⟩)*
⟨*term₄*⟩ ::=   ! ⟨*term₄*⟩
          | ⟨*modalityTerm*⟩
          | ⟨*quantifierTerm*⟩
          | ⟨*equalityTerm*⟩

——— KeY Syntax ——

Intuitively, negation ! is the strongest operator and it is right associative, then comes left associative conjunction &, then left associative disjunction |, then *right* associative implication ->, and finally, left associative equivalence <->.

   Possible modalities are the following:

—— KeY Syntax ———————————————————————————————————————

⟨*modalityTerm*⟩ ::= ⟨*modalityBlock*⟩ ⟨*term₄*⟩

⟨*modalityBlock*⟩ ::=
       \< ⟨*javaBlock*⟩ \> | \[⟨*javaBlock*⟩ \] | \[[⟨*javaBlock*⟩ \]]
     | \diamond ⟨*javaBlock*⟩ \endmodality
     | \box ⟨*javaBlock*⟩ \endmodality
     | \throughout ⟨*javaBlock*⟩ \endmodality
     | \diamond_transaction ⟨*javaBlock*⟩ \endmodality
     | \box_transaction ⟨*javaBlock*⟩ \endmodality
     | \throughout_transaction ⟨*javaBlock*⟩ \endmodality
     | \modality{⟨*modalityName*⟩} ⟨*javaBlock*⟩ \endmodality

⟨*modalityName*⟩ ::= ⟨*identifier*⟩

——— KeY Syntax ——

In the last alternative, ⟨*modalityName*⟩ can be either a concrete modality (diamond, box, diamond_trc, etc.), or a schema variable representing a set of modalities if the expression is parsed in the schematic mode.

   As mentioned earlier, Java blocks inside modalities are parsed separately, we describe the corresponding syntax in Section B.2.5.

   Next, a quantifier takes the following form:

—— KeY Syntax ———————————————————————————————————————

⟨*quantifierTerm*⟩ ::=
     \forall ⟨*variableBinding*⟩ ⟨*term₄*⟩
   | \exists ⟨*variableBinding*⟩ ⟨*term₄*⟩

——— KeY Syntax ——

A variable binding takes the following form:

—— KeY Syntax ———————————————————————————————————————

⟨*variableBinding*⟩ ::= ⟨*singleVariableBinding*⟩ | ⟨*multipleVariableBinding*⟩

——— KeY Syntax ——

Then, depending on the parsing mode, variable binding can take the following forms, in normal mode:

—— KeY Syntax ——————————————————————————

⟨*singleVariableBinding*⟩ ::= ⟨*sortExp*⟩ ⟨*varName*⟩ ;

⟨*multipleVariableBinding*⟩ ::=
  (⟨*sortExp*⟩ ⟨*varName*⟩ (; ⟨*sortExp*⟩ ⟨*varName*⟩)+)

⟨*varName*⟩ ::= ⟨*identifier*⟩

———————————————————————————— KeY Syntax ——

And in the schematic mode:

—— KeY Syntax ——————————————————————————

⟨*singleVariableBinding*⟩ ::= ⟨*schemaVarName*⟩ ;

⟨*multipleVariableBinding*⟩ ::= (⟨*schemaVarName*⟩ (; ⟨*schemaVarName*⟩)+)

⟨*schemaVarName*⟩ ::= ⟨*identifier*⟩

———————————————————————————— KeY Syntax ——

In the former, ⟨*varName*⟩ is any valid KeY identifier and ⟨*sortExp*⟩ is a valid sort name as explained shortly, in the latter ⟨*schemaVarName*⟩ is also any valid KeY identifier associated with a proper schema variable. A sort expression takes the following form:

—— KeY Syntax ——————————————————————————

⟨*sortExp*⟩ ::= ⟨*sortName*⟩ ([])∗

———————————————————————————— KeY Syntax ——

A sort name ⟨*sortName*⟩ is any valid KeY sort, including fully qualified sorts that reflect Java types.

—— KeY Syntax ——————————————————————————

```
\forall (int i; int j) true
\exists java.lang.Object o_set; true
```

———————————————————————————— KeY Syntax ——

In the remainder of this appendix ⟨*variableBinding*⟩ and ⟨*sortExp*⟩ are going to be referenced often.

Finally, an ⟨*equalityTerm*⟩ expresses (in-)equality between two atomic terms:

—— KeY Syntax ——————————————————————————

⟨*equalityTerm*⟩ ::=
    ⟨*atomicTerm₁*⟩ (= ⟨*atomicTerm₁*⟩)?
  | ⟨*atomicTerm₁*⟩ (!= ⟨*atomicTerm₁*⟩)?

———————————————————————————— KeY Syntax ——

The inequality operator != is simply a syntactic sugar: a != b is the same as !a = b (note that = binds stronger than !).

B.2.2.2 Atomic Terms

Atomic terms are build in the following way. The top-level atomic term is:

—— KeY Syntax ————————————————————————————————————

$\langle atomicTerm_1 \rangle$ ::=
    $\langle atomicTerm_2 \rangle$ ($\langle intRelation \rangle$ $\langle atomicTerm_2 \rangle$)? $\langle termLabel \rangle$?

$\langle intRelation \rangle$ ::= < | <= | > | >=

$\langle termLabel \rangle$ ::= << $\langle label \rangle$ (, $\langle label \rangle$)* >>)?

$\langle label \rangle$ ::= $\langle identifier \rangle$ (($\langle string \rangle$ (, $\langle string \rangle$)*))?

—— KeY Syntax ——

The rule $\langle intRelation \rangle$ represents a possible integer comparison relation in the infix form. Of course, such relation can be only used if the sort of $\langle atomicTerm_2 \rangle$ permits this. The infix relation expressions (as well as infix integer binary operators, like +, -, *, etc., see below) are only a short hand notation for corresponding function symbols, like lt, geq, add, or mul. Term labels can be attached to atomic terms. It is not yet possible to declare supported term labels in input files; this must be done on the Java level. Further definitions for atomic terms are the following:

—— KeY Syntax ————————————————————————————————————

$\langle atomicTerm_2 \rangle$ ::=
    $\langle atomicTerm_3 \rangle$ ($\langle arithOp_1 \rangle$ $\langle atomicTerm_3 \rangle$)*

$\langle atomicTerm_3 \rangle$ ::=
    $\langle atomicTerm_4 \rangle$ ($\langle arithOp_2 \rangle$ $\langle atomicTerm_4 \rangle$)*

$\langle atomicTerm_4 \rangle$ ::=
        - $\langle atomicTerm_4 \rangle$
    | ($\langle sortExp \rangle$) $\langle atomicTerm_4 \rangle$
    | $\langle atomicTerm_5 \rangle$

$\langle arithOp_1 \rangle$ ::= + | -

$\langle arithOp_2 \rangle$ ::= * | / | %

—— KeY Syntax ——

Intuitively, all binary arithmetic operators are left associative, and *, /, % bind stronger than + and -. Unary minus and sort casts (definition of $\langle atomicTerm_4 \rangle$) are strongest and right associative. Next, the definition for $\langle atomicTerm_5 \rangle$ is the following:

—— KeY Syntax ———————————————————————————————

$\langle atomicTerm_5 \rangle$ ::=
    $\langle accessTerm \rangle$
  | $\langle locsetTerm \rangle$
  | $\langle substitutionTerm \rangle$
  | $\langle updateTerm \rangle$

———————————————————————————————— KeY Syntax ——

Access terms are defined in the following way:

—— KeY Syntax ———————————————————————————————

$\langle accessTerm \rangle$ ::=
    $\langle primitiveTerm \rangle$ $\langle arrayAttributeQueryAccess \rangle*$

$\langle primitiveTerm \rangle$ ::=
    $\langle staticQuery \rangle$
  | $\langle staticAttribute \rangle$
  | $\langle functionPredicateTerm \rangle$
  | $\langle variable \rangle$
  | $\langle conditionalTerm \rangle$
  | $\langle specialTerm \rangle$
  | $\langle abbrTerm \rangle$
  | ($\langle term \rangle$)
  | **true**
  | **false**
  | $\langle number \rangle$
  | $\langle character \rangle$
  | $\langle string \rangle$

$\langle arrayAttributeQueryAccess \rangle$ ::=
    $\langle arrayOrSequenceAccess \rangle$ | $\langle attributeAccess \rangle$ | $\langle queryAccess \rangle$

$\langle arrayOrSequenceAccess \rangle$ ::= [$\langle atomicTerm_1 \rangle$]

$\langle attributeAccess \rangle$ ::= . $\langle attributeExp \rangle$

$\langle queryAccess \rangle$ ::= . $\langle queryExp \rangle$

$\langle staticAttribute \rangle$ ::= $\langle typeReference \rangle$. $\langle attributeExp \rangle$

$\langle staticQuery \rangle$ ::= $\langle typeReference \rangle$. $\langle queryExp \rangle$

$\langle attributeExp \rangle$ ::= $\langle attributeName \rangle$ $\langle classLocator \rangle$?

$\langle queryExp \rangle$ ::= $\langle queryName \rangle$ $\langle classLocator \rangle$? ($\langle argumentList \rangle$?)

⟨*classLocator*⟩ ::= @(⟨*typeReference*⟩)

⟨*argumentList*⟩ ::= (⟨*term*⟩ (, ⟨*term*⟩)*)

⟨*attributeName*⟩ ::= ⟨*identifier*⟩

⟨*queryName*⟩ ::= ⟨*identifier*⟩

—— KeY Syntax ——

Class locator expressions are used to resolve possible collisions between attribute names when Java name shadowing occurs. Class locator expressions are obligatory when such a collision takes place, otherwise they are optional. Class locators can only occur in normal term parsing mode, not in the schematic mode. A ⟨*typeReference*⟩ is a fully qualified Java type expression, for example:

—— KeY Syntax ——
```
java.lang.Object
int[]
```
—— KeY Syntax ——

The package qualifier can be skipped, if there are no ambiguities. An ⟨*attributeName*⟩ is either a concrete attribute name, or a schema variable representing one, again depending on the parsing mode. ⟨*queryName*⟩ is similar to ⟨*attributeName*⟩, however in the current version of the KeY system, query expressions can only appear in normal parsing mode, thus ⟨*queryName*⟩ always represents a concrete method/query name. The decision whether an access is an array access or a sequent access ($A :: seqGet$) is resolved by semantic checks on the type of the accessed entity.

Before we describe what are the lowest level building blocks for terms, we first go back to the definition of ⟨*substitutionTerm*⟩ and ⟨*updateTerm*⟩:

—— KeY Syntax ——
⟨*substitutionTerm*⟩ ::=
    { \subst ⟨*singleVariableBinding*⟩ ⟨*atomicTerm₁*⟩ } ⟨*term₄*⟩

⟨*locsetTerm*⟩ ::=
    { (⟨*atomicTerm₁*⟩,⟨*atomicTerm₁*⟩)) (, (⟨*atomicTerm₁*⟩,⟨*atomicTerm₁*⟩)))* }

⟨*updateTerm*⟩ ::= { ⟨*parallelUpdate*⟩ } (⟨*term₄*⟩ | (⟨*parallelUpdate*⟩)))

⟨*parallelUpdate*⟩ ::= ⟨*singleUpdate*⟩ (|| ⟨*singleUpdate*⟩)*

⟨*singleUpdate*⟩ ::= ⟨*atomicTerm₁*⟩ := ⟨*atomicTerm₁*⟩
—— KeY Syntax ——

The above definitions mean that, in particular, the following terms are going to be parsed like this:

—— KeY Syntax ——————————————————————

`{\subst int i; 2} i = i`   is parsed as `({\subst int i; 2} i) = i`

`{i := 1} i = i`   is parsed as `({i := 1} i) = i`

`{ i := 1 || {i := 1} (j := i+1)} j = 2`

`{ i := 1 || {i := 1} (j := i+1 || z := 3)} j = 2`

Not parsable is the following
`{ {i := 1} j := i + 1 } j = 2`
because update on update applications must be parenthesized
——————————————————————————— KeY Syntax ——

Function and predicate expressions are constructed in the following way:

—— KeY Syntax ——————————————————————

⟨*functionPredicateTerm*⟩ ::=
  ⟨*funcPredName*⟩ (({ ⟨*singleVariableBinding*⟩ })? (⟨*argumentList*⟩))?

⟨*funcPredName*⟩ ::= ⟨*identifier*⟩
——————————————————————————— KeY Syntax ——

Simple variables, conditional terms, and abbreviations are defined as follows:

—— KeY Syntax ——————————————————————

⟨*variable*⟩ ::= ⟨*identifier*⟩

⟨*abbrTerm*⟩ ::= @ ⟨*identifier*⟩

⟨*conditionalTerm*⟩ ::=
  (\if | \ifEx ⟨*variableBinding*⟩) (⟨*formula*⟩)
    \then (⟨*term*⟩) \else (⟨*term*⟩)
——————————————————————————— KeY Syntax ——

A variable can be a logic or a program variable (normal parsing mode), or a schema variable (schematic mode). An abbreviation expression refers to an identifier that contains a term abbreviation. A special term is built in the following way:

—— KeY Syntax ——————————————————————

⟨*specialTerm*⟩ ::=
    ⟨*metaTerm*⟩
  | \inType (-? ⟨*schemaVariable*⟩
          | ⟨*schemaVariable*⟩ ⟨*arithOp*⟩ ⟨*schemaVariable*⟩)

⟨*metaTerm*⟩ ::= ⟨*metaOperator*⟩ ((⟨*argumentList*⟩))?

$\langle arithOp \rangle ::= + \mid - \mid * \mid / \mid \%$

$\langle schemaVariable \rangle ::= \langle identifier \rangle$

$\langle metaOperator \rangle ::= \langle identifier \rangle$

——————————————————————————— KeY Syntax ——

Special terms can only occur in the schematic mode. Meta-terms are used to construct
taclet meta-operator expressions. Currently, valid meta-operator identifiers are the
following:

—— KeY Syntax ———————————————————————————

```
#add #sub #mul #div #mod #pow #less #greater #leq #geq #eq
#ShiftLeft #ShiftRight #BinaryAnd #BinaryOr #BinaryXOr
#arrayBaseInstanceOf #constantvalue #enumconstantvalue
#divideMonomials #divideLCRMonomials
#introAtPreDefs #memberPVToField #addCast #ExpandQueries
```

——————————————————————————— KeY Syntax ——

Note that different meta-constructs are used inside modalities for schematic Java
code blocks.

Finally, the remaining term building blocks are number $\langle number \rangle$ constants, string
$\langle string \rangle$ and character $\langle character \rangle$ constants, grouping with parenthesis (), and logic
constants **true** and **false**.

Here are some examples of properly built terms and formulas. In normal mode:

—— KeY Syntax ———————————————————————————

```
false -> true
\forall int i; (i + i = 2 * i & i - i = 0)
\forall int i; (add(i, i) = mul(2, i) & sub(i, i) = 0)
\exists java.lang.Object[] o; o != null
java.lang.Object::instance(o) = TRUE
\< {i = 1;} \> i = 1
sum{int x;}(low, upper, x*x)
```

——————————————————————————— KeY Syntax ——

And in schematic mode:

—— KeY Syntax ———————————————————————————

```
\forall #v; (#v + #v = 2 * #v & #v - #v = 0)
\exists #v; #v != null
any::instance(#v) = TRUE
#o.#a != #se0 + #se1
#add(#se0, #se1) = 0
```

——————————————————————————— KeY Syntax ——

B.2.3 Rule Files

All rule files (system and user defined) are parsed only in schematic mode. On the top level, a rule file has the following form:

—— KeY Syntax ————————————————————————

⟨*ruleFile*⟩ ::= ⟨*libraryIncludeStatement*⟩∗ ⟨*ruleFileDeclarations*⟩∗ ⟨*ruleBlock*⟩∗

————————————————————————————— KeY Syntax ——

B.2.3.1 Library and File Inclusion

The KeY system supports file inclusion on two levels: (low) file level, and (high) library level. File inclusion statements can appear *anywhere* in the KeY input, and take the following form:

—— KeY Syntax ————————————————————————

⟨*fileInclusion*⟩ ::= **\includeFile** " ⟨*fileName*⟩ ";

————————————————————————————— KeY Syntax ——

The effect of **\includeFile** is that KeY unconditionally redirects its input to the indicated file ⟨*fileName*⟩. When the indicated file is read in, the parsing in the current file continues. File inclusion nesting is allowed and its depth is not limited by the KeY system itself.

Library file inclusion can be done with the following statements:

—— KeY Syntax ————————————————————————

⟨*libraryIncludeStatement*⟩ ::= (**\include** | **\includeLDTs**)
    ⟨*libraryFileName*⟩ (, ⟨*libraryFileName*⟩)∗ ;

————————————————————————————— KeY Syntax ——

The major feature of the library inclusion statements is that each library file is going to be read in once, even if the same library is requested multiple times (for example, because of circular dependencies). On the implementation level, when the library files are read in **\includeLDTs** performs slightly different operations than **\include**.

B.2.3.2 Rule File Declarations

Each rule file can have the following declarations:

—— KeY Syntax ————————————————————————

⟨*ruleFileDeclarations*⟩ ::=
    ⟨*ruleSetsDecl*⟩
  | ⟨*optionsDecl*⟩
  | ⟨*sortsDecls*⟩

```
|   ⟨schemaVariablesDecl⟩
|   ⟨functionsDecl⟩
|   ⟨predicatesDecl⟩
```
——————————————————————————————————— KeY Syntax ——

Rule sets and options are declared in the following way:

—— KeY Syntax ———————————————————————————————————

⟨ruleSetsDecl⟩ ::= **\heuristicsDecl** { (⟨ruleSetName⟩ ;)* }

⟨optionsDecl⟩ ::= **\optionsDecl** { (⟨oneOptionDecl⟩ ;)* }

⟨oneOptionDecl⟩ ::= ⟨optionName⟩ : { ⟨optionValue⟩ (, ⟨optionValue⟩)* }

⟨ruleSetName⟩ ::= ⟨identifier⟩   ⟨optionName⟩ ::= ⟨identifier⟩
                          ⟨optionValue⟩ ::= ⟨identifier⟩
——————————————————————————————————— KeY Syntax ——

Examples of valid rule set and option declarations are:

—— KeY Syntax ———————————————————————————————————
```
\heuristicsDecl {
    simplify_int;
    simplify_prog;
}

\optionsDecl {
  programRules:{Java, None};
  runtimeExceptions:{ban, allow, ignore};
}
```
——————————————————————————————————— KeY Syntax ——

Sorts are declared in the following way:

—— KeY Syntax ———————————————————————————————————

⟨sortsDecl⟩ ::= **\sorts** { (⟨oneSortDecl⟩ ;)* }

⟨oneSortDecl⟩ ::=
        \object ⟨sortNameList⟩
    | **\generic** ⟨sortNameList⟩
            (**\extends** ⟨sortNameList⟩)? (**\oneof** { ⟨sortNameList⟩ })?
    | **\proxy** ⟨sortNameList⟩
    | ⟨sortName⟩ **\extends** ⟨sortNameList⟩
    | ⟨sortNameList⟩

⟨sortNameList⟩ ::= ⟨sortName⟩ (, ⟨sortName⟩)*
——————————————————————————————————— KeY Syntax ——

The definition of ⟨*sortName*⟩ has been given earlier. Note, that here ⟨*sortName*⟩ may be (only in some places) required to be a simple ⟨*identifier*⟩, and cannot be a fully qualified sort name. Schema variables are declared in the following way:

—— KeY Syntax ————————————————————————————

⟨*schemaVariablesDecl*⟩ ::=
  \schemaVariables {
    (⟨*schemaVarDecl*⟩ ;)∗
  }

⟨*schemaVarDecl*⟩ ::=
    \modalOperator { ⟨*operatorList*⟩ **}** ⟨*variableList*⟩
  | **\formula** ⟨*schemaModifiers*⟩? ⟨*variableList*⟩
  | **\function** ⟨*schemaModifiers*⟩? ⟨*variableList*⟩
  | **\program** ⟨*schemaModifiers*⟩? ⟨*programSchemaVarSort*⟩ ⟨*variableList*⟩
  | **\term** ⟨*schemaModifiers*⟩? ⟨*sortName*⟩ ⟨*variableList*⟩
  | **\termlabel** ⟨*schemaModifiers*⟩? ⟨*variableList*⟩
  | **\update** ⟨*schemaModifiers*⟩? ⟨*variableList*⟩
  | (**\variables** | **\variable**) ⟨*sortName*⟩ ⟨*variableList*⟩
  | **\skolemTerm** ⟨*sortName*⟩ ⟨*variableList*⟩
  | **\skolemFormula** ⟨*variableList*⟩

⟨*programSchemaVarSort*⟩ ::= ⟨*identifier*⟩

⟨*schemaModifiers*⟩ ::= [⟨*identifier*⟩ (, ⟨*identifier*⟩)∗]

⟨*variableList*⟩ ::= ⟨*identifier*⟩ (, ⟨*identifier*⟩)∗

⟨*operatorList*⟩ ::= ⟨*identifier*⟩ (, ⟨*identifier*⟩)∗
————————————————————————————————— KeY Syntax ——

Schema variable modifiers can be list, rigid, or strict. The list of currently defined program schema variable sorts is the following:

—— KeY Syntax ————————————————————————————

```
LeftHandSide Variable StaticVariable LocalVariable
Expression SimpleExpression NonSimpleExpression
NonSimpleExpressionNoClassReference
ConstantPrimitiveTypeVariable
ConstantStringVariable StringLiteral NonStringLiteral

SimpleJavaBooleanExpression SimpleStringExpression
SimpleNonStringObjectExpression
AnyJavaTypeExpression JavaBooleanExpression JavaByteExpression
JavaCharExpression JavaShortExpression JavaIntExpression
JavaLongExpression JavaByteShortExpression
```

JavaByteShortIntExpression JavaShortIntLongExpression
JavaIntLongExpression JavaCharByteShortIntExpression
JavaBigintExpression AnyNumberTypeExpression

SimpleInstanceCreation NonSimpleInstanceCreation
InstanceCreation ArrayCreation ArrayInitializer
SpecialConstructorReference

Statement Switch
MultipleVariableDeclaration VariableInitializer
ArrayPostDeclaration ArrayLength
MethodBody NonModelMethodBody ProgramMethod ExecutionContext
NonSimpleMethodReference ForUpdates LoopInit Guard

Catch Label MethodName Type NonPrimitiveType ClassReference
———————————————————————————————————— KeY Syntax ——

Some examples of properly declared schema variables:

—— KeY Syntax ——————————————————————————————————————
```
\schemaVariables {
  \modalOperator {diamond, box, throughout} #puremodal;
  \formula post, inv, post1;
  \program Type #t, #t2 ;
  \program[list] Catch #cs ;
  \term[rigid,strict] H h;
  \variables G x;
```
————————————————————————————————————— KeY Syntax ——

Function and predicate declarations are very similar to each other, the only difference
is that there is no result type specified for predicates:

—— KeY Syntax ——————————————————————————————————————

⟨*functionsDecl*⟩ ::=
   \functions ⟨*optionSpecs*⟩? {
       (⟨*oneFunctionDecl*⟩ ;)*
   }

⟨*predicatesDecl*⟩ ::=
   \predicates ⟨*optionSpecs*⟩? {
       (⟨*onePredicateDecl*⟩ ;)*
   }

⟨*oneFunctionDecl*⟩ ::=
   (\unique)? ⟨*sortExp*⟩ ⟨*funcPredName*⟩ ⟨*binder*⟩? ⟨*argumentSorts*⟩?

⟨*binder*⟩ ::=
  { (`true` | `false`) (, (`true` | `false`))∗

⟨*onePredicateDecl*⟩ ::=
  ⟨*funcPredName*⟩ ⟨*binder*⟩? (⟨*argumentSorts*⟩?

⟨*argumentSorts*⟩ ::= (⟨*sortExp*⟩ (, ⟨*sortExp*⟩)∗)

⟨*optionSpecs*⟩ ::= (⟨*optionSpecList*⟩)

⟨*optionSpecList*⟩ ::=
  ⟨*oneOptionSpec*⟩ (, ⟨*oneOptionSpec*⟩)∗

⟨*oneOptionSpec*⟩ ::= ⟨*optionName*⟩ : ⟨*optionValue*⟩

———————————————————————————————— KeY Syntax ——

In the above the option specification tells the system that the declared functions or predicates should only be visible when the specified option is active. Some function and predicate declaration examples:

—— KeY Syntax ————————————————————————————

```
\functions(intRules:javaSemantics) {
  int unaryMinusJint(int);
  \unique Field <created>;
  int sum{false, false, true}(int, int, int);
}

\predicates {
  Acc(java.lang.Object, any);
}
```

———————————————————————————————— KeY Syntax ——

The sum declaration states that sum binds a variable in the third argument, but not in the two other arguments.

B.2.3.3 Rules

Rules (taclets) are defined in **\rules** blocks this way:

—— KeY Syntax ——————————————————————————————
⟨*ruleBlock*⟩ ::= **\rules** ⟨*optionSpecs*⟩? { (⟨*taclet*⟩ ;)∗ }
——————————————————————————————— KeY Syntax ——

The option specification has the same meaning as for the function and predicate declarations. Each taclet can have additional (per taclet) option specifications and local schema variable declarations. The syntax for a taclet is:

—— KeY Syntax ——————————————————————————————
⟨*taclet*⟩ ::= **\axioms** { (⟨*taclet*⟩ | ⟨*axiom*⟩)∗ } |
  ⟨*identifier*⟩ ⟨*optionSpecs*⟩? {
    (**\schemaVar** ⟨*schemaVarDecl*⟩ ;)∗
    ⟨*contextAssumptions*⟩? ⟨*findPattern*⟩?
    ⟨*applicationRestriction*⟩? ⟨*variableConditions*⟩?
    (⟨*goalTemplateList*⟩ | **\closegoal**)
    ⟨*tacletModifiers*⟩∗ ⟨*trigger*⟩∗
  }

⟨*axiom*⟩ ::= ⟨*identifier*⟩ { ⟨*formula*⟩ }

⟨*contextAssumptions*⟩ ::= **\assumes** (⟨*schematicSequent*⟩)
⟨*findPattern*⟩ ::= **\find** (⟨*termOrSequent*⟩)

⟨*applicationRestriction*⟩ ::= **\inSequentState** | **\sameUpdateLevel**
  | **\antecedentPolarity** | **\succedentPolarity**

⟨*variableConditions*⟩ ::= **\varcond** (⟨*variableConditionList*⟩)
⟨*variableConditionList*⟩ ::= ⟨*variableCondition*⟩ (, ⟨*variableCondition*⟩)∗

⟨*goalTemplateList*⟩ ::= ⟨*goalTemplate*⟩ (; ⟨*goalTemplate*⟩)∗

⟨*schematicSequent*⟩ ::= ⟨*termList*⟩? ==> ⟨*termList*⟩?
⟨*termList*⟩ ::= ⟨*term*⟩ (, ⟨*term*⟩)∗
⟨*termOrSequent*⟩ ::= ⟨*term*⟩ | ⟨*schematicSequent*⟩

⟨*tacletModifiers*⟩ ::= **\heuristics** (⟨*identifierList*⟩)
  | **\noninteractive** | **\displayname** ⟨*string*⟩ | **\helptext** ⟨*string*⟩

⟨*trigger*⟩ ::= **\trigger** { ⟨*variable*⟩ } ⟨*term*⟩ (**\avoid** ⟨*termList*⟩)∗

⟨*identifierList*⟩ ::= ⟨*identifier*⟩ (, ⟨*identifier*⟩)∗
——————————————————————————————— KeY Syntax ——

A variable condition can be one of the following:

```
── KeY Syntax ───────────────────────────────────────────
⟨variableCondition⟩ ::=
    \new ( ⟨variable⟩ , ⟨typeCondExp⟩
        | \dependingOn ( ⟨variable⟩ )
        | \dependingOnMod ( ⟨variable⟩ )
        )
  | \newLabel ( ⟨variable⟩ )
  | \applyUpdateOnRigid ( ⟨variable⟩ , ⟨variable⟩ , ⟨variable⟩ )
  | \dropEffectlessElementaries (
            ⟨variable⟩, ⟨variable⟩, ⟨variable⟩ )
  | \dropEffectlessStores (
            ⟨variable⟩ , ⟨variable⟩ , ⟨variable⟩, ⟨variable⟩ , ⟨variable⟩ )
  | \simplifyIfThenElseUpdate (
            ⟨variable⟩, ⟨variable⟩ , ⟨variable⟩ , ⟨variable⟩, ⟨variable⟩ )
  | \differentFields ( ⟨variable⟩ , ⟨variable⟩ )
  | \fieldType ( ⟨variable⟩ , ⟨sortExp⟩ )
  | \containsAssignment ( ⟨variable⟩ )
  | \isEnumType ( ⟨typeCondExp⟩ )
  | ( \different | \metaDisjoint ) ( ⟨variable⟩ , ⟨variable⟩ )
  | \equalUnique ( ⟨variable⟩ , ⟨variable⟩, ⟨variable⟩ )
  | \notFreeIn ( ⟨variable⟩ ( , ⟨variable⟩ )+ )
  | \hasSort
                ( ⟨variable⟩ , ( ⟨sortExp⟩ | \elemSort ( ⟨sortExp⟩ ) ) )
  | \isReference ( [non_null] )? ( ⟨typeCondExp⟩ )
  | \isObserver ( ⟨variable⟩ )    |    \enumConstant ( ⟨variable⟩ )
  | \hasSubFormulas ( ⟨variable⟩ )
  | \hasLabel ( ⟨variable⟩ , ⟨identifier⟩ )
  | \not? \freeLabelIn ( ⟨variable⟩, ⟨variable⟩ )
  | \not? \staticMethodReference (
            ⟨variable⟩ , ⟨variable⟩ , ⟨variable⟩ )
  | \not? ( \isThisReference | \isReferenceArray ) ( ⟨variable⟩ )
  | \not? ( \isArray | \isArrayLength ) ( ⟨variable⟩ )
  | \not? ( \isConstant | \final | \static ) ( ⟨variable⟩ )
  | \not? ( \isLocalVariable | \isStaticField ) ( ⟨variable⟩ )
  | \not? \isAbstractOrInterface ( ⟨typeCondExp⟩ )
  | \not? ⟨typeComparison⟩ ( ⟨typeCondExp⟩ , ⟨typeCondExp⟩ )

⟨typeCondExp⟩ ::= (\typeof | \containerType) ( ⟨variable⟩ ) | ⟨sortExp⟩

⟨typeComparison⟩ ::= \same | \disjointModuloNull | \strict? \sub
─────────────────────────────────────────── KeY Syntax ──
```

The goal specification is defined as follows:

—— KeY Syntax ————————————————————————————————

⟨*goalTemplate*⟩ ::=
    ⟨*optionSpecs*⟩ { ⟨*oneGoalTemplate*⟩ }
  | ⟨*oneGoalTemplate*⟩

⟨*oneGoalTemplate*⟩ ::=
  ⟨*branchName*⟩?
    ⟨*replaceGoal*⟩ ⟨*addGoal*⟩? ⟨*addRules*⟩? ⟨*addProgramVars*⟩?
    | ⟨*addGoal*⟩ ⟨*addRules*⟩?
    | ⟨*addRules*⟩

⟨*branchName*⟩ ::= ⟨*string*⟩ :

⟨*replaceGoal*⟩ ::= \replacewith (⟨*termOrSequent*⟩)

⟨*addGoal*⟩ ::= \add (⟨*schematicSequent*⟩)

⟨*addRules*⟩ ::= \addrules (⟨*taclet*⟩ (, ⟨*taclet*⟩)∗)

⟨*addProgramVars*⟩ ::= \addprogvars (⟨*variable*⟩ (, ⟨*variable*⟩)∗)
——————————————————————————————————— KeY Syntax ——

Some examples of properly formed taclets:

—— KeY Syntax ————————————————————————————————
```
eliminateVariableDeclaration {
    \find (\<{.. #t #v0; ...}\> post)
    \replacewith (\<{..   ...}\> post)
    \addprogvars(#v0)
    \heuristics(simplify_prog, simplify_prog_subset)
    \displayname "eliminateVariableDeclaration"
};

makeInsertEq {
    \find (sr = tr ==>)
    \addrules ( insertEq { \find (sr) \replacewith (tr) } )
    \heuristics (simplify)
};

cut {
    "cut:␣#b␣TRUE":  \add (#b ==>);
    "cut:␣#b␣FALSE": \add (==> #b)
};
```
——————————————————————————————————— KeY Syntax ——

B.2.4 User Problem and Proof Files

User problem and proof files are almost the same, the only difference is that the problem file does not contain a \proof section. User problem and proof files have some additional elements as compared to rules files, and all the elements of the rule files can be present in a problem/proof file:

—— KeY Syntax ————————————————————————————

⟨userProblemProofFile⟩ ::=
    ⟨proverSettings⟩?
    ⟨javaSource⟩?
    ⟨libraryIncludeStatement⟩*
    ⟨tacletOptionActivation⟩?
    ⟨programVariablesDecl⟩?
    ⟨ruleFileDeclarations⟩*
    ⟨contracts⟩*
    ⟨ruleBlock⟩*
    (⟨problem⟩ | ⟨proofobligation⟩) ⟨proof⟩? | ⟨chooseContract⟩

———————————————————————————————————— KeY Syntax ——

The following simple definitions cover most of the problem/proof file syntax:

—— KeY Syntax ————————————————————————————

⟨proverSettings⟩ ::= \settings { ⟨string⟩ }

⟨javaSource⟩ ::= \javaSource " ⟨fileName⟩ ";

⟨tacletOptionActivation⟩ ::= \withOptions ⟨optionSpecList⟩ ;

⟨programVariablesDecl⟩ ::= \programVariables { (⟨progVarDecl⟩ ;)* }

⟨progVarDecl⟩ ::= ⟨typeReference⟩ ⟨variableList⟩

⟨problem⟩ ::= \problem { ⟨formula⟩ }

⟨proofobligation⟩ ::= \proofObligation { ⟨string⟩ }

⟨proof⟩ ::= \proof { ⟨proofTree⟩ }

———————————————————————————————————— KeY Syntax ——

The \programVariables section defines program variables local to the problem, for example:

—— KeY Syntax ————————————————————————————

```
\programVariables { java.lang.Object o; }

\problem {
  \< {o = new Object();} \> o != null
}
```

—————————————————————————————— KeY Syntax ——

The parameter to \settings is a string containing the description of prover settings in a category/property list form, similar to this:

—— KeY Syntax ————————————————————————————

```
\settings {
"#Proof-Settings-Config-File
#Wed␣Aug␣18␣17:49:41␣CEST␣2016
[StrategyProperty]VBT_PHASE=VBT_SYM_EX
[SMTSettings]useUninterpretedMultiplication=true
[StrategyProperty]METHOD_OPTIONS_KEY=METHOD_CONTRACT
[StrategyProperty]USER_TACLETS_OPTIONS_KEY1=USER_TACLETS_OFF
[StrategyProperty]USER_TACLETS_OPTIONS_KEY2=USER_TACLETS_OFF
...
}
```

—————————————————————————————— KeY Syntax ——

The \proof contains a proof tree in the form of Lisp-like nested lists. Since proof trees are in principle not supposed to be edited by the user manually, we skip the detailed description of the proof tree syntax. An example of a proof tree is the following:

—— KeY Syntax ————————————————————————————

```
\proof {
(keyLog "0" (keyUser "woj" ) (keyVersion "0.2184"))

(branch "dummy␣ID"
  (rule "concrete_and_1" (formula "1") (term "0")
    (userinteraction "n"))
  (rule "concrete_and_2" (formula "1") (term "1")
    (userinteraction "n"))
  (rule "concrete_eq_4" (formula "1") (userinteraction "n"))
  (rule "concrete_not_2" (formula "1") (userinteraction "n"))
  (rule "close_by_true" (formula "1") (userinteraction "n"))
)
}
```

—————————————————————————————— KeY Syntax ——

The \proofObligation contains the name of the proof-obligations to be proven:

—— KeY Syntax ————————————————————————————————
```
\proofObligation "#Proof Obligation Settings
#Wed Aug 22 15:59:39 CEST 2012
name=Matrix22[Matrix22\\:\\:strassen(Matrix22,Matrix22)].
                    JML normal_behavior operation contract.0
contract=Matrix22[Matrix22\\:\\:strassen(Matrix22,Matrix22)].
                    JML normal_behavior operation contract.0
class=de.uka.ilkd.key.proof.init.FunctionalOperationContractPO
";
```
————————————————————————————————————— KeY Syntax ——

B.2.4.1 Method Contracts

Method contracts can be expressed directly in JavaDL and are specified in the \contracts section of an input file using the following KeY syntax:

—— KeY Syntax ————————————————————————————————
⟨contracts⟩ ::=
  \contracts {
     (⟨oneContract⟩ ;)*
  }

⟨oneContract⟩ ::=
  ⟨identifier⟩ {
     ⟨programVariablesDecl⟩?
     ⟨prePostFormula⟩
     \modifies ⟨term⟩
     (\heuristics (⟨identifierList⟩))?
     (\displayname ⟨string⟩)?
  }

⟨prePostFormula⟩ ::=
  ⟨formula⟩ -> ⟨modalityBlock⟩ ⟨formula⟩
————————————————————————————————————— KeY Syntax ——

Here program variables are declared locally for a contract. The contract formula ⟨prePostFormula⟩ has to be in special form (Hoare Triple)—the program blocks appearing inside the modality are limited to single method body reference expression and special exception catching constructs. The term provided after the \modifies keyword has to be of type \locset.

We conclude this subsection with an example of a contract written in JavaDL:

—— KeY Syntax ————————————————————————————
```
\contracts {
  Demoney_setUndefined {
    \programVariables {
      byte b;
      fr.trustedlogic.demo.demoney.Demoney demoney;
    }
    demoney.definedParamFlags != null ->
    \<{
      demoney.setUndefined(b)
         @fr.trustedlogic.demo.demoney.Demoney;
    }\> demoney.definedParamFlags != null
    \modifies allFields(demoney.definedParamFlags)
    \displayname "setUndefined"
  };
}
```
——————————————————————————————— KeY Syntax ——

B.2.5 Schematic Java Syntax

In principle, inside a JavaDL modality any valid Java code block can be placed, that
is, any Java code block that would be allowed in a Java method implementation. On
top of that, the KeY system allows extensions to the regular Java syntax. We are
not going to discuss the Java syntax, we assume that in this context it is common
knowledge. Similarly to terms, different rules for the code inside a modality apply
when the schematic mode is used for parsing the rule files, as explained below. Java
blocks that appear inside a modality have to be surrounded with a pair of braces {}.
In the following, Java keywords that appear in Java blocks are marked with **bold**.

B.2.5.1 Method Calls, Method Bodies, Method Frames

In normal parsing mode the following construct can be used to refer to method's
body/implementation:

—— KeY Syntax ————————————————————————————
$\langle methodBody \rangle ::=$
  $(\ \langle resultLoc \rangle\ =\ )?$
    $\langle staticClassOrObjectRef \rangle\ .\ \langle methodName \rangle$
      $\langle methodArguments \rangle\ @\ \langle classReference \rangle\ ;$
——————————————————————————————— KeY Syntax ——

The following are properly constructed method body references:

—— KeY Syntax ——————————————————————————————
```
o.method()@MyClass;
result = pack.StaticClass.method(o, 2)@pack.StaticClass;
```
———————————————————————————————— KeY Syntax ——

On the top level, any Java block can also be enclosed in a method frame to provide the method execution context. A method frame expression takes the following form:

—— KeY Syntax ——————————————————————————————
⟨*methodFrame*⟩ ::=
 method-frame(result -> ⟨*resultLoc*⟩ ,
         source = ⟨*methodName*⟩ ⟨*methodArguments*⟩@⟨*classReference*⟩
         (, this = ⟨*variable*⟩)?) : {
   ⟨*javaBlock*⟩
 }
———————————————————————————————— KeY Syntax ——

For example:

—— KeY Syntax ——————————————————————————————
```
\<{ method-frame(result->j, source=m()@MyClass, this=c) : {
        this.a=10;
        return this.a;
     }
}\> ...
```
———————————————————————————————— KeY Syntax ——

B.2.5.2 Exception Catching in Contracts

When a JavaDL method contract is constructed a method body reference inside the modality can be enclosed in an exception catching construct to allow exceptional specification of a method. The syntax is the following:

—— KeY Syntax ——————————————————————————————
⟨*contractExceptionCatch*⟩ ::=
    #catchAll(⟨*classReference*⟩ ⟨*variable*⟩) { ⟨*methodBody*⟩ }
———————————————————————————————— KeY Syntax ——

For example:

—— KeY Syntax ——————————————————————————————
```
#catchAll(Exception e) {
  o.method()@MyClass;
}
```
———————————————————————————————— KeY Syntax ——

B.2.5.3 Inactive Java Block Prefix and Suffix

In the schematic mode several extensions to the Java syntax are available. First, the
inactive prefix and suffix of the Java block can be given with `..` and `...`, following
this syntax:

—— KeY Syntax ————————————————————————————————

⟨*inactivePrefixSuffix*⟩ ::= `..` ⟨*javaBlock*⟩ `...`

—————————————————————————————————————— KeY Syntax ——

The inactive prefix and suffix constructs can be seen as special cases of program
schema variables.

B.2.5.4 Program Schema Variables

Any program part inside the modality can be replaced with a corresponding schema
variable, provided a schema variable of a proper kind is provided to match the given
element in Java code. Additionally some elements of the inactive prefix can also be
matched with a schema variable to refer to the execution context data. For example,
the following are valid schematic Java blocks:

—— KeY Syntax ————————————————————————————————

```
.. #loc = #se; ...              Assignment
.#ex.. #lb: throw #se; ...      Execution Context & Label
.. #t #v = #exp; ...            Variable declaration
.. #se.#mn(#selist);            Method call
```

—————————————————————————————————————— KeY Syntax ——

B.2.5.5 Meta-Constructs

When in schematic mode, the KeY system offers a variety of meta-constructs to
perform local program transformations and new code introduction related to the
corresponding symbolic execution rules of Java code. Such meta-constructs can only
be used in the modalities that are part of the **\replacewith** or **\add** taclet goal
specifiers. For example the following meta-construct can be used to introduce proper
method body reference into the analyzed Java code:

—— KeY Syntax ————————————————————————————————

```
.. #method-call(#se.#mn(#selist)); ...
```

—————————————————————————————————————— KeY Syntax ——

The full list of schematic Java meta-constructs is the following:

—— KeY Syntax ——————————————————————————————

```
#unwind-loop #enhancedfor-elim #for-to-while #unpack
#switch-to-if #do-break #evaluate-arguments
#resolve-multiple-var-decl #typeof #length-reference

#method-call #expand-method-body
#constructor-call #special-constructor-call

#create-object #post-work
#array-post-declaration #init-array-creation

#static-initialization #isstatic #static-evaluate
```
—————————————————————————————— KeY Syntax ——

B.2.5.6 Passive Access in Static Initialization

Finally, the static initialization rules extend Java syntax with the passive (or raw) access operator:

—— KeY Syntax ——————————————————————————————

⟨*passiveAccessExp*⟩ ::= @(⟨*attributeVariableAccess*⟩)

—————————————————————————————— KeY Syntax ——

The passive access operator @ can be used both in normal (only when appropriate) and schematic mode.

References

Jean-Raymond Abrial. *The B Book: Assigning Programs to Meanings*. Cambridge University Press, August 1996. (Cited on page 240.)

Ben Adida. Helios: Web-based open-audit voting. In Paul C. van Oorschot, editor, *Proceedings of the 17th USENIX Security Symposium, 2008, San Jose, CA, USA*, pages 335–348. USENIX Association, 2008. (Cited on page 606.)

Wolfgang Ahrendt, Thomas Baar, Bernhard Beckert, Martin Giese, Elmar Habermalz, Reiner Hähnle, Wolfram Menzel, and Peter H. Schmitt. The KeY approach: Integrating object oriented design and formal verification. In Manuel Ojeda-Aciego, Inma P. de Guzmán, Gerhard Brewka, and Luís Moniz Pereira, editors, *Proceedings of the 8th European Workshop on Logics in Artificial Intelligence (JELIA)*, volume 1919 of *LNCS*, pages 21–36. Springer, October 2000. (Cited on page 13.)

Wolfgang Ahrendt, Andreas Roth, and Ralf Sasse. Automatic validation of transformation rules for Java verification against a rewriting semantics. In Geoff Sutcliff and Andrei Voronkov, editors, *Proceedings, 12th International Conference on Logic for Programming, Artificial Intelligence and Reasoning, Montego Bay, Jamaica*, volume 3835 of *LNCS*, pages 412–426. Springer, December 2005. (Cited on pages 12 and 64.)

Wolfgang Ahrendt, Richard Bubel, and Reiner Hähnle. Integrated and tool-supported teaching of testing, debugging, and verification. In Jeremy Gibbons and José Nuno Oliveira, editors, *Second International Conference on Teaching Formal Methods, Proceedings*, volume 5846 of *LNCS*, pages 125–143. Springer, 2009a. (Cited on page 7.)

Wolfgang Ahrendt, Frank S. de Boer, and Immo Grabe. Abstract object creation in dynamic logic. In Ana Cavalcanti and Dennis Dams, editors, *FM 2009: Formal Methods, Second World Congress, Eindhoven, The Netherlands. Proceedings*, volume 5850 of *LNCS*, pages 612–627, 2009b. (Cited on page 56.)

Wolfgang Ahrendt, Wojciech Mostowski, and Gabriele Paganelli. Real-time Java API specifications for high coverage test generation. In *Proceedings of the 10th International Workshop on Java Technologies for Real-time and Embedded Systems*, JTRES '12, pages 145–154, New York, NY, USA, 2012. ACM. (Cited on pages 6 and 609.)

Wolfgang Ahrendt, Jesús Mauricio Chimento, Gordon J. Pace, and Gerardo Schneider. A specification language for static and runtime verification of data and control properties. In Nikolaj Bjørner and Frank de Boer, editors, *Formal Methods - 20th International Symposium, Oslo, Norway, Proceedings*, volume 9109 of *LNCS*, pages 108–125. Springer, 2015. (Cited on page 519.)

Elvira Albert, Miguel Gómez-Zamalloa, and Germán Puebla. Test data generation of bytecode by CLP partial evaluation. In Michael Hanus, editor, *Logic-Based Program Synthesis and Transformation, 18th International Symposium, LOPSTR, Valencia, Spain, Revised Selected Papers*, volume 5438 of *LNCS*, pages 4–23. Springer, 2009. (Cited on page 4.)

Elvira Albert, Richard Bubel, Samir Genaim, Reiner Hähnle, and Guillermo Román-Díez. Verified resource guarantees for heap manipulating programs. In Juan de Lara and Andrea Zisman, editors, *Fundamental Approaches to Software Engineering - 15th International Conference, FASE 2012, Held as Part of the European Joint Conferences on Theory and Practice of Software, ETAPS 2012, Tallinn, Estonia. Proceedings*, volume 7212 of *LNCS*. Springer, 2012. (Cited on page 4.)

Eyad Alkassar, Mark A. Hillebrand, Wolfgang J. Paul, and Elena Petrova. Automated verification of a small hypervisor. In Gary T. Leavens, Peter W. O'Hearn, and Sriram K. Rajamani, editors, *Verified Software: Theories, Tools, Experiments, Third International Conference, VSTTE, Edinburgh, UK*, volume 6217 of *LNCS*, pages 40–54. Springer, 2010. (Cited on page 9.)

Afshin Amighi, Stefan Blom, Marieke Huisman, and Marina Zaharieva-Stojanovski. The VerCors project: Setting up basecamp. In Koen Claessen and Nikhil Swamy, editors, *Proceedings of the sixth workshop on Programming Languages meets Program Verification, PLPV 2012, Philadelphia, PA, USA*, pages 71–82. ACM, 2012. (Cited on pages 3, 240, 241 and 377.)

Afshin Amighi, Stefan Blom, Saeed Darabi, Marieke Huisman, Wojciech Mostowski, and Marina Zaharieva-Stojanovski. Verification of concurrent systems with VerCors. In Marco Bernardo, Ferruccio Damiani, Reiner Hähnle, Einar Broch Johnsen, and Ina Schaefer, editors, *Formal Methods for Executable Software Models - 14th International School on Formal Methods for the Design of Computer, Communication, and Software Systems, SFM 2014, Bertinoro, Italy, Advanced Lectures*, volume 8483 of *LNCS*, pages 172–216. Springer, 2014a. (Cited on page 350.)

Afshin Amighi, Stefan Blom, Marieke Huisman, Wojciech Mostowski, and Marina Zaharieva-Stojanovski. Formal specifications for Java's synchronisation classes. In Alberto Lluch Lafuente and Emilio Tuosto, editors, *22nd Euromicro International Conference on Parallel, Distributed, and Network-Based Processing, PDP 2014, Torino, Italy*, pages 725–733. IEEE Computer Society, 2014b. (Cited on pages 3 and 378.)

Paul Ammann and Jeff Offutt. *Introduction to Software Testing*. Cambridge University Press, New York, NY, USA, 2008. (Cited on pages 421 and 448.)

Torben Amtoft, Sruthi Bandhakavi, and Anindya Banerjee. A logic for information flow in object-oriented programs. In J. Gregory Morrisett and Simon L. Peyton Jones, editors, *Proceedings of the 33rd ACM SIGPLAN-SIGACT Symposium on Principles of Programming Languages, POPL 2006, Charleston, South Carolina, USA*, pages 91–102. ACM, 2006. (Cited on page 454.)

Saswat Anand, Edmund K. Burke, Tsong Yueh Chen, John Clark, Myra B. Cohen, Wolfgang Grieskamp, Mark Harman, Mary Jean Harrold, Phil McMinn, Antonia Bertolino, J. Jenny Li, and Hong Zhu. An orchestrated survey of methodologies for automated software test case generation. *Journal of Systems and Software*, 86(8):1978–2001, 2013. (Cited on page 448.)

Sven Apel, Wolfgang Scholz, Christian Lengauer, and Christian Kästner. Detecting dependences and interactions in feature-oriented design. In *IEEE 21st International Symposium on Software Reliability Engineering, ISSRE 2010, San Jose, CA, USA*, pages 161–170. IEEE Computer Society, 2010. (Cited on page 17.)

Thanassis Avgerinos, Alexandre Rebert, Sang Kil Cha, and David Brumley. Enhancing symbolic execution with veritesting. In Pankaj Jalote, Lionel C. Briand, and André van der Hoek, editors, *36th International Conference on Software Engineering, ICSE '14, Hyderabad, India, 2014*, pages 1083–1094. ACM, 2014. (Cited on page 450.)

Nathaniel Ayewah, David Hovemeyer, J. David Morgenthaler, John Penix, and William Pugh. Using static analysis to find bugs. *IEEE Software*, 25(5):22–29, 2008. (Cited on page 412.)

Thomas Baar. Metamodels without metacircularities. *L'Objet*, 9(4):95–114, 2003. (Cited on page 2.)

Thomas Baar, Bernhard Beckert, and Peter H. Schmitt. An extension of dynamic logic for modelling OCL's @pre operator. In Dines Bjørner, Manfred Broy, and Alexandre V. Zamulin, editors, *Perspectives of System Informatics, 4th International Andrei Ershov Memorial Conference, PSI 2001, Akademgorodok, Novosibirsk, Russia, Revised Papers*, volume 2244 of *LNCS*, pages 47–54. Springer, 2001. (Cited on page 249.)

Michael Balser, Wolfgang Reif, Gerhard Schellhorn, Kurt Stenzel, and Andreas Thums. Formal system development with KIV. In Thomas S. E. Maibaum, editor, *Fundamental Approaches to*

Software Engineering, Third Internationsl Conference, FASE 2000, Held as Part of the European Joint Conferences on the Theory and Practice of Software, ETAPS 2000, Berlin, Germany. Proceedings, volume 1783 of *LNCS*, pages 363–366. Springer, 2000. (Cited on pages 10, 239 and 353.)

Anindya Banerjee, Michael Barnett, and David A. Naumann. Boogie meets regions: A verification experience report. In Natarajan Shankar and Jim Woodcock, editors, *Verified Software: Theories, Tools, Experiments, Second International Conference, VSTTE 2008, Toronto, Canada. Proceedings*, volume 5295 of *LNCS*, pages 177–191, New York, NY, 2008a. Springer. (Cited on page 350.)

Anindya Banerjee, David A. Naumann, and Stan Rosenberg. Regional logic for local reasoning about global invariants. In Jan Vitek, editor, *ECOOP 2008 - Object-Oriented Programming, 22nd European Conference, Paphos, Cyprus, Proceedings*, volume 5142 of *LNCS*, pages 387–411, New York, NY, 2008b. Springer. (Cited on page 350.)

Michael Bär. Analyse und Vergleich verifizierbarer Wahlverfahren. Diplomarbeit, Fakultät für Informatik, KIT, 2008. (Cited on page 606.)

Michael Barnett, Robert DeLine, Manuel Fähndrich, K. Rustin M. Leino, and Wolfgang Schulte. Verification of object-oriented programs with invariants. *Journal of Object Technology*, 3(6): 27–56, 2004. (Cited on pages 210, 215 and 348.)

Michael Barnett, Bor-Yuh Evan Chang, Robert DeLine, Bart Jacobs, and K. Rustan M. Leino. Boogie: A modular reusable verifier for object-oriented programs. In Frank S. de Boer, Marcello M. Bonsangue, Susanne Graf, and Willem P. de Roever, editors, *Formal Methods for Components and Objects, 4th International Symposium, FMCO 2005, Amsterdam, The Netherlands, 2005, Revised Lectures*, volume 4111 of *LNCS*, pages 364–387. Springer, 2006. (Cited on pages 10 and 216.)

Mike Barnett, K. Rustan M. Leino, and Wolfram Schulte. The Spec# programming system: an overview. In Gilles Barthe, Lilian Burdy, Marieke Huisman, Jean-Louis Lanet, and Traian Muntean, editors, *Construction and Analysis of Safe, Secure and Interoperable Smart devices (CASSIS), International Workshop, Marseille, France, Revised Selected Papers*, volume 3362 of *LNCS*, pages 49–69. Springer, 2005a. (Cited on pages 241 and 348.)

Mike Barnett, David A. Naumann, Wolfram Schulte, and Qi Sun. 99.44% pure: Useful abstractions in specification. In *ECOOP Workshop FTfJP'2004 Formal Techniques for Java-like Programs*, pages 51–60, January 2005b. (Cited on page 210.)

Mike Barnett, Manuel Fähndrich, K. Rustan M. Leino, Peter Müller, Wolfram Schulte, and Herman Venter. Specification and verification: the Spec# experience. *Communications ACM*, 54(6): 81–91, 2011. (Cited on page 349.)

Clark Barrett, Aaron Stump, and Cesare Tinelli. The SMT-LIB standard: Version 2.0. In A. Gupta and D. Kroening, editors, *Proceedings of the 8th International Workshop on Satisfiability Modulo Theories (Edinburgh, UK)*, 2010. (Cited on pages 12 and 18.)

Gilles Barthe, Pedro R. D'Argenio, and Tamara Rezk. Secure information flow by self-composition. In *17th IEEE Computer Security Foundations Workshop, (CSFW-17), Pacific Grove, CA, USA*, pages 100–114, Washington, USA, 2004. IEEE CS. (Cited on page 454.)

Gilles Barthe, Mariela Pavlova, and Gerardo Schneider. Precise analysis of memory consumption using program logics. In Bernhard K. Aichernig and Bernhard Beckert, editors, *Third IEEE International Conference on Software Engineering and Formal Methods (SEFM 2005), Koblenz, Germany*, pages 86–95. IEEE Computer Society, 2005. (Cited on page 230.)

Gilles Barthe, Lilian Burdy, Julien Charles, Benjamin Grégoire, Marieke Huisman, Jean-Louis Lanet, Mariela Pavlova, and Antoine Requet. JACK: A tool for validation of security and behaviour of Java applications. In Frank S. de Boer, Marcello M. Bonsangue, Susanne Graf, and Willem P. de Roever, editors, *Formal Methods for Components and Objects, 5th International Symposium, FMCO 2006, Amsterdam, The Netherlands, Revised Lectures*, volume 4709 of *LNCS*, pages 152–174, Berlin, 2007. Springer. (Cited on page 240.)

Gilles Barthe, Benjamin Grégoire, and Santiago Zanella Béguelin. Formal certification of code-based cryptographic proofs. In Zhong Shao and Benjamin C. Pierce, editors, *Proceedings of the*

36th ACM SIGPLAN-SIGACT Symposium on Principles of Programming Languages, POPL 2009, Savannah, GA, USA, pages 90–101. ACM, January 2009. (Cited on page 607.)

Gilles Barthe, Juan Manuel Crespo, and César Kunz. Relational verification using product programs. In Michael Butler and Wolfram Schulte, editors, *FM 2011: Formal Methods - 17th International Symposium on Formal Methods, Limerick, Ireland. Proceedings*, volume 6664 of *LNCS*, pages 200–214. Springer, 2011. (Cited on page 483.)

Gilles Barthe, Juan Manuel Crespo, Sumit Gulwani, César Kunz, and Mark Marron. From relational verification to SIMD loop synthesis. In Alex Nicolau, Xiaowei Shen, Saman P. Amarasinghe, and Richard W. Vuduc, editors, *ACM SIGPLAN Symposium on Principles and Practice of Parallel Programming, PPoPP '13, Shenzhen, China, 2013*, pages 123–134. ACM, 2013a. (Cited on page 5.)

Gilles Barthe, Boris Köpf, Federico Olmedo, and Santiago Zanella Béguelin. Probabilistic relational reasoning for differential privacy. *ACM Transactions on Programming Languages and Systems*, 35(3):9, 2013b. (Cited on page 607.)

Patrick Baudin, Pascal Cuoq, Jean-Christophe Filliâtre, Claude Marché, Benjamin Monate, Yannick Moy, and Virgile Prevosto. *ACSL: ANSI/ISO C Specification Language*. CEA LIST and INRIA, 2010. Version 1.5. (Cited on page 241.)

Christoph Baumann, Bernhard Beckert, Holger Blasum, and Thorsten Bormer. Lessons learned from microkernel verification – specification is the new bottleneck. In Franck Cassez, Ralf Huuck, Gerwin Klein, and Bastian Schlich, editors, *Proceedings Seventh Conference on Systems Software Verification, SSV 2012, Sydney, Australia*, volume 102 of *EPTCS*, pages 18–32, 2012. (Cited on page 2.)

Kent Beck. *JUnit Pocket Guide: quick lookup and advice*. O'Reilly, 2004. (Cited on pages 416 and 421.)

Tobias Beck. Verifizierbar korrekte Implementierung von Bingo Voting. Studienarbeit, Fakultät für Informatik, KIT, March 2010. (Cited on page 606.)

Bernhard Beckert and Daniel Bruns. Formal semantics of model fields in annotation-based specifications. In Birte Glimm and Antonio Krüger, editors, *KI 2012: Advances in Artificial Intelligence - 35th Annual German Conference on AI, Saarbrücken, Germany. Proceedings*, number 7526 in LNCS, pages 13–24. Springer, 2012. (Cited on page 310.)

Bernhard Beckert and Christoph Gladisch. White-box testing by combining deduction-based specification extraction and black-box testing. In Yuri Gurevich and Bertrand Meyer, editors, *Tests and Proofs, First International Conference, TAP 2007, Zurich, Switzerland. Revised Papers*, volume 4454 of *LNCS*, pages 207–216. Springer, 2007. (Cited on page 416.)

Bernhard Beckert and Sarah Grebing. Evaluating the usability of interactive verification systems. In Vladimir Klebanov, Bernhard Beckert, Armin Biere, and Geoff Sutcliffe, editors, *Proceedings of the 1st International Workshop on Comparative Empirical Evaluation of Reasoning Systems, Manchester, United Kingdom, 2012*, volume 873 of *CEUR Workshop Proceedings*, pages 3–17. CEUR-WS.org, 2012. (Cited on page 8.)

Bernhard Beckert and Reiner Hähnle. Reasoning and verification. *IEEE Intelligent Systems*, 29(1): 20–29, Jan.–Feb. 2014. (Cited on pages 2, 3 and 18.)

Bernhard Beckert and Vladimir Klebanov. Must program verification systems and calculi be verified? In *Proceedings, 3rd International Verification Workshop (VERIFY), Workshop at Federated Logic Conferences (FLoC), Seattle, USA*, pages 34–41, 2006. (Cited on page 64.)

Bernhard Beckert and Wojciech Mostowski. A program logic for handling Java Card's transaction mechanism. In Mauro Pezzè, editor, *Proceedings, Fundamental Approaches to Software Engineering (FASE), Warsaw, Poland*, volume 2621 of *LNCS*, pages 246–260. Springer, 2003. (Cited on pages 354 and 376.)

Bernhard Beckert and André Platzer. Dynamic logic with non-rigid functions: A basis for object-oriented program verification. In U. Furbach and N. Shankar, editors, *Proceedings, International Joint Conference on Automated Reasoning, Seattle, USA*, volume 4130 of *LNCS*, pages 266–280. Springer, 2006. (Cited on page 65.)

Bernhard Beckert and Steffen Schlager. Software verification with integrated data type refinement for integer arithmetic. In Eerke A. Boiten, John Derrick, and Graeme Smith, editors, *Integrated*

Formal Methods, 4th International Conference, IFM 2004, Canterbury, UK. Proceedings, volume 2999 of *LNCS*, pages 207–226. Springer, 2004. (Cited on page 51.)

Bernhard Beckert and Steffen Schlager. Refinement and retrenchment for programming language data types. *Formal Aspects of Computing*, 17(4):423–442, 2005. (Cited on page 51.)

Bernhard Beckert, Martin Giese, Elmar Habermalz, Reiner Hähnle, Andreas Roth, Philipp Rümmer, and Steffen Schlager. Taclets: a new paradigm for constructing interactive theorem provers. *Revista de la Real Academia de Ciencias Exactas, Físicas y Naturales, Serie A: Matemáticas*, 98(1):17–53, 2004. Special Issue on Symbolic Computation in Logic and Artificial Intelligence. (Cited on page 11.)

Bernhard Beckert, Reiner Hähnle, and Peter H. Schmitt, editors. *Verification of Object-Oriented Software: The KeY Approach*. Number 4334 in LNCS. Springer, 2007. (Cited on pages IX, 16, 230, 240, 272, 306, 376, 384, 527 and 576.)

Bernhard Beckert, Daniel Bruns, Ralf Küsters, Christoph Scheben, Peter H. Schmitt, and Tomasz Truderung. The KeY approach for the cryptographic verification of Java programs: A case study. Technical Report 2012-8, Department of Informatics, Karlsruhe Institute of Technology, 2012. (Cited on page 594.)

Bernhard Beckert, Thorsten Bormer, and Markus Wagner. A metric for testing program verification systems. In Margus Veanes and Luca Viganò, editors, *Tests and Proofs. Seventh International Conference, TAP 2013, Budapest, Hungary*, volume 7942 of *LNCS*, pages 56–75. Springer, 2013. (Cited on page 65.)

Bernhard Beckert, Daniel Bruns, Vladimir Klebanov, Christoph Scheben, Peter H. Schmitt, and Mattias Ulbrich. Information flow in object-oriented software. In Gopal Gupta and Ricardo Peña, editors, *Logic-Based Program Synthesis and Transformation, 23rd International Symposium, LOPSTR 2013, Madrid, Spain, Revised Selected Papers*, number 8901 in LNCS, pages 19–37. Springer, 2014. (Cited on page 460.)

Bernhard Beckert, Vladimir Klebanov, and Mattias Ulbrich. Regression verification for Java using a secure information flow calculus. In Rosemary Monahan, editor, *Proceedings of the 17th Workshop on Formal Techniques for Java-like Programs, FTfJP 2015, Prague, Czech Republic*, pages 6:1–6:6. ACM, 2015. (Cited on page 428.)

Jesper Bengtson, Jonas Braband Jensen, Filip Sieczkowski, and Lars Birkedal. Verifying object-oriented programs with higher-order separation logic in coq. In Marko van Eekelen, Herman Geuvers, Julien Schmaltz, and Freek Wiedijk, editors, *Interactive Theorem Proving: Second International Conference, ITP 2011, Berg en Dal, The Netherlands. Proceedings*, pages 22–38. Springer, 2011. (Cited on page 316.)

Nick Benton. Simple relational correctness proofs for static analyses and program transformations. In Neil D. Jones and Xavier Leroy, editors, *Proceedings of the 31st ACM SIGPLAN-SIGACT Symposium on Principles of Programming Languages, POPL 2004, Venice, Italy*, pages 14–25. ACM, 2004. (Cited on pages 5, 483 and 607.)

Dirk Beyer. Software verification and verifiable witnesses — (report on SV-COMP 2015). In Christel Baier and Cesare Tinelli, editors, *Tools and Algorithms for the Construction and Analysis of Systems - 21st International Conference, TACAS 2015, Held as Part of the European Joint Conferences on Theory and Practice of Software, ETAPS 2015, London, UK. Proceedings*, volume 9035 of *LNCS*, pages 401–416. Springer, 2015. (Cited on pages 4 and 18.)

Joshua Bloch. *Effective Java: Programming Language Guide*. The Java Series. Addison-Wesley, 2nd edition, 2008. (Cited on page 261.)

Arjan Blom, Gerhard de Koning Gans, Erik Poll, Joeri de Ruiter, and Roel Verdult. Designed to fail: A USB-connected reader for online banking. In Audun Jøsang and Bengt Carlsson, editors, *Secure IT Systems - 17th Nordic Conference, NordSec 2012, Karlskrona, Sweden. Proceedings*, volume 7617 of *LNCS*, pages 1–16. Springer, 2012. (Cited on page 353.)

Stefan Blom and Marieke Huisman. The VerCors Tool for verification of concurrent programs. In Cliff B. Jones, Pekka Pihlajasaari, and Jun Sun, editors, *FM 2014: Formal Methods - 19th International Symposium, Singapore. Proceedings*, volume 8442 of *LNCS*, pages 127–131. Springer, 2014. (Cited on page 378.)

Jens-Matthias Bohli, Christian Henrich, Carmen Kempka, Jörn Müller-Quade, and Stefan Röhrich. Enhancing electronic voting machines on the example of Bingo voting. *IEEE Transactions on Information Forensics and Security*, 4(4):745–750, 2009. (Cited on page 606.)

Greg Bollella and James Gosling. The real-time specification for Java. *IEEE Computer*, pages 47–54, June 2000. (Cited on page 5.)

Alex Borgida, John Mylopoulos, and Raymond Reiter. "... And nothing else changes": On the frame problem in procedure specifications. *IEEE Transactions on Software Engineering*, 21(10): 785–798, 1995. (Cited on pages 233 and 321.)

Bernard Botella, Mickaël Delahaye, Stéphane Hong Tuan Ha, Nikolai Kosmatov, Patricia Mouy, Muriel Roger, and Nicky Williams. Automating structural testing of C programs: Experience with PathCrawler. In Dimitris Dranidis, Stephen P. Masticola, and Paul A. Strooper, editors, *Proceedings of the 4th International Workshop on Automation of Software Test, AST 2009, Vancouver, BC, Canada*, pages 70–78. IEEE Computer Society, May 2009. (Cited on page 449.)

Raymond T. Boute. Calculational semantics: Deriving programming theories from equations by functional predicate calculus. *ACM Transactions on Programming Languages and Systems*, 28 (4):747–793, 2006. (Cited on page 574.)

Robert S. Boyer, Bernard Elspas, and Karl N. Levitt. SELECT—A formal system for testing and debugging programs by symbolic execution. *ACM SIGPLAN Notices*, 10(6):234–245, June 1975. (Cited on page 383.)

John Boyland. Checking interference with fractional permissions. In Radhia Cousot, editor, *Static Analysis, 10th International Symposium, SAS 2003, San Diego, CA, USA. Proceedings*, volume 2694 of *LNCS*, pages 55–72. Springer, 2003. (Cited on pages 378 and 379.)

Aaron R. Bradley and Zohar Manna. *The Calculus of Computation: Decision Procedures with Applications to Verification*. Springer, 2007. (Cited on page 537.)

Cees-Bart Breunesse and Erik Poll. Verifying JML specifications with model fields. In *ECOOP workshop on Formal Techniques for Java-like Programs (FTfJP'03), Darmstadt*, number 408 in Technical Report, ETH Zürich, pages 51–60, July 2003. (Cited on page 350.)

Cees-Bart Breunesse, Néstor Cataño, Marieke Huisman, and Bart Jacobs. Formal methods for smart cards: an experience report. *Science of Computer Programming*, 55:53–80, 2005. (Cited on page 226.)

Daniel Bruns. Elektronische Wahlen: Theoretisch möglich, praktisch undemokratisch. *FIfF-Kommunikation*, 25(3):33–35, September 2008. (Cited on page 594.)

Daniel Bruns. Formal semantics for the Java Modeling Language. Diploma thesis, Universität Karlsruhe, 2009. (Cited on pages 195, 215, 243, 245 and 350.)

Daniel Bruns. Specification of red-black trees: Showcasing dynamic frames, model fields and sequences. In Wolfgang Ahrendt and Richard Bubel, editors, *10th KeY Symposium, Nijmegen, the Netherlands*, 2011. Extended Abstract. (Cited on page 296.)

Richard Bubel. *Formal Verification of Recursive Predicates*. PhD thesis, Universität Karlsruhe, 2007. (Cited on page 306.)

Richard Bubel, Andreas Roth, and Philipp Rümmer. Ensuring the correctness of lightweight tactics for Java Card dynamic logic. *Electronic Notes in Theoretical Computer Science*, 199:107–128, 2008. (Cited on pages 138 and 144.)

Richard Bubel, Reiner Hähnle, and Benjamin Weiß. Abstract interpretation of symbolic execution with explicit state updates. In Frank S. de Boer, Marcello M. Bonsangue, and Eric Madeleine, editors, *Formal Methods for Components and Objects, 7th International Symposium, FMCO 2008, Sophia Antipolis, France, Revised Lectures*, volume 5751 of *LNCS*, pages 247–277. Springer, 2009. (Cited on pages IX, 171, 454, 471 and 474.)

Richard Bubel, Reiner Hähnle, and Ulrich Geilmann. A formalisation of Java strings for program specification and verification. In Gilles Barthe and Gerardo Schneider, editors, *Software Engineering and Formal Methods - 9th International Conference, SEFM 2011, Montevideo, Uruguay. Proceedings*, volume 7041 of *LNCS*, pages 90–105. Springer, 2011. (Cited on page IX.)

Richard Bubel, Antonio Flores Montoya, and Reiner Hähnle. Analysis of executable software models. In Marco Bernardo, Ferruccio Damiani, Reiner Hähnle, Einar B. Johnsen, and Ina Schaefer, editors, *Executable Software Models: 14th International School on Formal Methods for the Design of Computer, Communication, and Software Systems, Bertinoro, Italy*, volume 8483 of *LNCS*, pages 1–27. Springer, June 2014a. (Cited on page 16.)

Richard Bubel, Reiner Hähnle, and Maria Pelevina. Fully abstract operation contracts. In Tiziana Margaria and Bernhard Steffen, editors, *Leveraging Applications of Formal Methods, Verification and Validation, 6th International Symposium, ISoLA 2014, Corfu, Greece*, volume 8803 of *LNCS*, pages 120–134. Springer, October 2014b. (Cited on page 9.)

Lilian Burdy, Yoonsik Cheon, David Cok, Michael Ernst, Joe Kiniry, Gary T. Leavens, K. Rustan M. Leino, and Erik Poll. An overview of JML tools and applications. In Thomas Arts and Wan Fokkink, editors, *Eighth International Workshop on Formal Methods for Industrial Critical Systems (FMICS 03), Proceedings*, volume 80 of *Electronic Notes in Theoretical Computer Science*, pages 73–89. Elsevier, 2003a. (Cited on page 239.)

Lilian Burdy, Antoine Requet, and Jean-Louis Lanet. Java applet correctness: A developer-oriented approach. In Keijiro Araki, Stefania Gnesi, and Dino Mandrioli, editors, *FME 2003: Formal Methods, International Symposium of Formal Methods Europe, Pisa, Italy. Proceedings*, volume 2805 of *LNCS*, pages 422–439. Springer, 2003b. (Cited on page 353.)

Jacob Burnim and Koushik Sen. Heuristics for scalable dynamic test generation. In *23rd IEEE/ACM International Conference on Automated Software Engineering (ASE 2008), L'Aquila, Italy*, pages 443–446. IEEE Computer Society, 2008. (Cited on page 450.)

Rod M. Burstall. Program proving as hand simulation with a little induction. In *IFIP Congress '74, Stockholm*, pages 308–312. Elsevier/North-Holland, 1974. (Cited on pages 12 and 383.)

Cristian Cadar, Daniel Dunbar, and Dawson R Engler. KLEE: Unassisted and automatic generation of high-coverage tests for complex systems programs. In Richard Draves and Robbert van Renesse, editors, *8th USENIX Symposium on Operating Systems Design and Implementation, OSDI 2008, San Diego, CA, USA, Proceedings*, pages 209–224. USENIX Association, 2008a. (Cited on page 450.)

Cristian Cadar, Vijay Ganesh, Peter M. Pawlowski, David L. Dill, and Dawson R. Engler. EXE: automatically generating inputs of death. *ACM Transactions on Information and System Security (TISSEC)*, 12(2), 2008b. (Cited on page 450.)

Cristian Cadar, Patrice Godefroid, Sarfraz Khurshid, Corina S. Pasareanu, Koushik Sen, Nikolai Tillmann, and Willem Visser. Symbolic execution for software testing in practice: preliminary assessment. In Richard N. Taylor, Harald Gall, and Nenad Medvidovic, editors, *Proceedings of the 33rd International Conference on Software Engineering, ICSE 2011, Waikiki, Honolulu , HI, USA*, pages 1066–1071. ACM, 2011. (Cited on page 449.)

Néstor Cataño, Tim Wahls, Camilo Rueda, Víctor Rivera, and Danni Yu. Translating B machines to JML specifications. In Sascha Ossowski and Paola Lecca, editors, *Proceedings of the ACM Symposium on Applied Computing, SAC 2012, Riva, Trento, Italy*, pages 1271–1277, New York, NY, USA, 2012. ACM. (Cited on page 240.)

Néstor Cataño and Marieke Huisman. CHASE: A static checker for JML's assignable clause. In Lenore D. Zuck, Paul C. Attie, Agostino Cortesi, and Supratik Mukhopadhyay, editors, *Verification, Model Checking, and Abstract Interpretation, 4th International Conference, VMCAI 2003, New York, NY, USA. Proceedings*, volume 2575 of *LNCS*, pages 26–40. Springer, 2003. (Cited on page 240.)

Patrice Chalin. Improving JML: For a safer and more effective language. In Keijiro Araki, Stefania Gnesi, and Dino Mandrioli, editors, *FME 2003: Formal Methods, International Symposium of Formal Methods Europe, Pisa, Italy. Proceedings*, volume 2805 of *LNCS*, pages 440–461. Springer, 2003. (Cited on page 231.)

Patrice Chalin. JML support for primitive arbitrary precision numeric types: Definition and semantics. *Journal of Object Technology*, 3(6):57–79, June 2004. Special issue: ECOOP 2003 Workshop on FTfJP. (Cited on page 232.)

Patrice Chalin. A sound assertion semantics for the dependable systems evolution verifying compiler. In *29th International Conference on Software Engineering (ICSE 2007), Minneapolis, MN, USA*, pages 23–33. IEEE Computer Society, 2007. (Cited on page 286.)

Patrice Chalin and Frédéric Rioux. Non-null references by default in the Java modeling language. *SIGSOFT Software Engineering Notes*, 31(2), September 2005. (Cited on page 246.)

Patrice Chalin and Frédéric Rioux. JML runtime assertion checking: Improved error reporting and efficiency using strong validity. In Jorge Cuellar, Tom Maibaum, and Kaisa Sere, editors, *FM 2008: Formal Methods, 15th International Symposium on Formal Methods, Turku, Finland. Proceedings*, volume 5014 of *LNCS*, pages 246–261. Springer, 2008. (Cited on page 286.)

Patrice Chalin, Perry R. James, and Frédéric Rioux. Reducing the use of nullable types through non-null by default and monotonic non-null. *Software, IET*, 2(6):515–531, 2008. (Cited on page 246.)

Patrice Chalin, Robby, Perry R. James, Jooyong Lee, and George Karabotsos. Towards an industrial grade IVE for Java and next generation research platform for JML. *STTT*, 12(6):429–446, 2010. (Cited on page 239.)

Crystal Chang Din, Richard Bubel, and Reiner Hähnle. KeY-ABS: A deductive verification tool for the concurrent modelling language ABS. In Amy P. Felty and Aart Middeldorp, editors, *Automated Deduction - CADE-25 - 25th International Conference on Automated Deduction, Berlin, Germany. Proceedings*, volume 9195 of *LNCS*, pages 517–526. Springer, 2015. (Cited on page 6.)

David Chaum, Richard T. Carback, Jeremy Clark, Aleksander Essex, Stefan Popoveniuc, Ronald L. Rivest, Peter Y. A. Ryan, Emily (Emily Huei-Yi) Shen, Alan T. Sherman, and Poorvi L. Vora. Scantegrity II: End-to-end verifiability by voters of optical scan elections through confirmation codes. *IEEE Transactions on Information Forensics and Security*, October 2009. (Cited on page 606.)

Zhiqun Chen. *Java Card Technology for Smart Cards: Architecture and Programmer's Guide.* Addison-Wesley, June 2000. (Cited on pages 353 and 354.)

Yoonsik Cheon. *A Runtime Assertion Checker for the Java Modeling Language.* PhD thesis, Department of Computer Science, Iowa State University, Ames, 2003. Technical Report 03-09. (Cited on page 239.)

Yoonsik Cheon. Automated random testing to detect specification-code inconsistencies. In Dimitris A. Karras, Daming Wei, and Jaroslav Zendulka, editors, *International Conference on Software Engineering Theory and Practice, SETP-07, Orlando, Florida, USA*, pages 112–119. ISRST, 2007. (Cited on page 239.)

Yoonsik Cheon and Gary T. Leavens. A quick overview of Larch/C++. *Journal of Object-oriented Programing*, 7(6):39–49, 1994. (Cited on page 240.)

Dave Clarke, John Potter, and James Noble. Ownership types for flexible alias protection. In Bjørn N. Freeman-Benson and Craig Chambers, editors, *Proceedings of the 1998 ACM SIGPLAN Conference on Object-Oriented Programming Systems, Languages & Applications (OOPSLA '98), Vancouver, British Columbia, Canada*, pages 48–64, Vancouver, Canada, October 1998. ACM. (Cited on pages 13 and 348.)

Edmund M. Clarke, Orna Grumberg, and Doron A. Peled. *Model Checking.* The MIT Press, 1999. (Cited on page 6.)

Michael R. Clarkson, Stephen Chong, and Andrew C. Myers. Civitas: Toward a secure voting system. In *2008 IEEE Symposium on Security and Privacy (S&P 2008), Oakland, California, USA*, pages 354–368. IEEE Computer Society, 2008. (Cited on pages 594 and 606.)

Ellis S. Cohen. Information transmission in computational systems. In Saul Rosen and Peter J. Denning, editors, *Proceedings of the Sixth Symposium on Operating System Principles, SOSP 1977, Purdue University, West Lafayette, Indiana, USA*, pages 133–139. ACM, 1977. (Cited on page 454.)

Ernie Cohen, Markus Dahlweid, Mark Hillebrand, Dirk Leinenbach, Michał Moskal, Thomas Santen, Wolfram Schulte, and Stephan Tobies. VCC: A practical system for verifying concurrent C. In Stefan Berghofer, Tobias Nipkow, Christian Urban, and Makarius Wenzel, editors, *Theorem Proving in Higher Order Logics, 22nd International Conference, TPHOLs 2009*, volume 5674 of *LNCS*, pages 23–42, Berlin, August 2009. Springer. (Cited on pages 241 and 349.)

David R. Cok. Reasoning with specifications containing method calls and model fields. *Journal of Object Technology*, 4(8):77–103, 2005. (Cited on page 350.)

David R. Cok. Adapting JML to generic types and Java 1.6. In *Seventh International Workshop on Specification and Verification of Component-Based Systems (SAVCBS 2008)*, number CS-TR-08-07 in Technical Report, pages 27–35, 2008. (Cited on pages 195 and 237.)

David R. Cok. OpenJML: JML for Java 7 by extending OpenJDK. In Mihaela Bobaru, Klaus Havelund, Gerard Holzmann, and Rajeev Joshi, editors, *NASA Formal Methods - Third International Symposium, NFM 2011, Pasadena, CA, USA. Proceedings*, volume 6617 of *LNCS*, pages 472–479. Springer, Berlin, 2011. (Cited on pages 239 and 426.)

David R. Cok and Joseph Kiniry. ESC/Java2: Uniting ESC/Java and JML. In Gilles Barthe, Lilian Burdy, Marieke Huisman, Jean-Louis Lanet, and Traian Muntean, editors, *Post Conference Proceedings of CASSIS: Construction and Analysis of Safe, Secure and Interoperable Smart devices, Marseille*, volume 3362 of *LNCS*, pages 108–128. Springer, 2005. (Cited on pages 195 and 240.)

David R. Cok and Gary T. Leavens. Extensions of the theory of observational purity and a practical design for JML. In *Seventh International Workshop on Specification and Verification of Component-Based Systems (SAVCBS 2008)*, number CS-TR-08-07 in Technical Report, pages 43–50, 4000 Central Florida Blvd., Orlando, Florida, 32816-2362, 2008. School of EECS, UCF. (Cited on page 210.)

Stephen A. Cook. Soundness and completeness of an axiom system for program verification. *SIAM Journal of Computing*, 7(1):70–90, 1978. (Cited on page 65.)

Patrick Cousot and Radhia Cousot. Abstract interpretation: A unified lattice model for static analysis of programs by construction or approximation of fixpoints. In *Proceedings of the 4th ACM SIGACT-SIGPLAN Symposium on Principles of Programming Languages*, POPL '77, pages 238–252, New York, NY, USA, 1977. ACM. (Cited on pages 167 and 168.)

Lajos Cseppento and Zoltán Micskei. Evaluating symbolic execution-based test tools. In *2015 IEEE 8th International Conference on Software Testing, Verification and Validation (ICST)*, pages 1–10. IEEE Computer Society, April 2015. (Cited on page 449.)

Marcello D'Agostino, Dov Gabbay, Reiner Hähnle, and Joachim Posegga, editors. *Handbook of Tableau Methods*. Kluwer, Dordrecht, 1999. (Cited on page 11.)

Ádám Darvas and Rustin Leino. Practical reasoning about invocations and implementations of pure methods. In Matthew B. Dwyer and Antónia Lopes, editors, *Fundamental Approaches to Software Engineering, 10th International Conference, FASE 2007, Held as Part of the Joint European Conferences, on Theory and Practice of Software, ETAPS 2007, Braga, Portugal. Proceedings*, volume 4422 of *LNCS*, pages 336–351. Springer, 2007. (Cited on page 210.)

Ádám Darvas and Peter Müller. Reasoning about method calls in interface specifications. *Journal of Object Technology*, 5(5):59–85, 2006. (Cited on page 210.)

Ádám Darvas and Peter Müller. Formal encoding of JML Level 0 specifications in JIVE. Technical Report 559, ETH Zurich, 2007. (Cited on pages 195 and 243.)

Ádám Darvas, Reiner Hähnle, and Dave Sands. A theorem proving approach to analysis of secure information flow. In Roberto Gorrieri, editor, *Workshop on Issues in the Theory of Security, WITS*. IFIP WG 1.7, ACM SIGPLAN and GI FoMSESS, 2003. (Cited on pages 5 and 278.)

Ádám Darvas, Reiner Hähnle, and David Sands. A theorem proving approach to analysis of secure information flow. In Dieter Hutter and Markus Ullmann, editors, *Security in Pervasive Computing, Second International Conference, SPC 2005, Boppard, Germany. Proceedings*, volume 3450 of *LNCS*, pages 193–209. Springer, 2005. (Cited on pages IX, 5, 278 and 454.)

Ádám Darvas, Farhad Mehta, and Arsenii Rudich. Efficient well-definedness checking. In Alessandro Armando, Peter Baumgartner, and Gilles Dowek, editors, *Automated Reasoning, 4th International Joint Conference, IJCAR 2008, Sydney, Australia. Proceedings*, LNCS, pages 100–115, Berlin, Heidelberg, 2008. Springer. (Cited on page 286.)

Stijn de Gouw, Frank S. de Boer, and Jurriaan Rot. Proof pearl: The key to correct and stable sorting. *J. Automated Reasoning*, 53(2):129–139, 2014. (Cited on page 609.)

Stijn De Gouw, Jurriaan Rot, Frank S. De Boer, Richard Bubel, and Reiner Hähnle. OpenJDK's java.utils.collection.sort() is broken: The good, the bad and the worst case. In Daniel Kroening and Corina Pasareanu, editors, *Computer Aided Verification - 27th International Conference,*

CAV 2015, San Francisco, CA, USA. Proceedings, Part I, volume 9206 of *LNCS*, pages 273–289. Springer, July 2015. (Cited on page 9.)

Dorothy E. Denning. A lattice model of secure information flow. *Communications of the ACM*, 19 (5):236–243, 1976. (Cited on page 454.)

Krishna Kishore Dhara and Gary T. Leavens. Weak behavioral subtyping for types with mutable objects. *Electronic Notes in Theoretical Computer Science*, 1:91–113, 1995. This issue contains revised papers presented at the Eleventh Annual Conference on Mathematical Foundations of Programming Semantics, (MFPS XI), Tulane University, New Orleans, 1995. Managing editors: Michael Mislove and Maurice Nivat and Christos Papadimitriou. (Cited on page 219.)

Edsger W. Dijkstra. *A Discipline of Programming*. Prentice-Hall, 1976. (Cited on pages 571 and 577.)

Crystal Chang Din. *Verification Of Asynchronously Communicating Objects*. PhD thesis, Faculty of Mathematics and Natural Sciences, University of Oslo, March 2014. (Cited on page 6.)

Dino Distefano and Matthew J. Parkinson. jStar: towards practical verification for Java. In Gail E. Harris, editor, *Object-Oriented Programming, Systems, Languages, and Applications (OOPSLA)*, pages 213–226, New York, NY, 2008. ACM. (Cited on page 316.)

Huy Q. Do, Richard Bubel, and Reiner Hähnle. Exploit generation for information flow leaks in object-oriented programs. In Hannes Federath and Dieter Gollmann, editors, *ICT Systems Security and Privacy Protection - 30th IFIP TC 11 International Conference, SEC 2015, Hamburg, Germany. Proceedings*, volume 455 of *LNCS*, pages 401–415. Springer, 2015. (Cited on page 17.)

Quoc Huy Do, Eduard Kamburjan, and Nathan Wasser. Towards fully automatic logic-based information flow analysis: An electronic-voting case study. In Frank Piessens and Luca Viganò, editors, *Principles of Security and Trust, 5th Intl. Conf., POST, Eindhoven, The Netherlands*, volume 9635 of *LNCS*, pages 97–115. Springer, 2016. (Cited on pages IX, 5 and 189.)

Danny Dolev and Andrew C. Yao. On the security of public key protocols. *IEEE Transactions on Information Theory*, 29(2):198–208, 1983. (Cited on page 595.)

Felix Dörre and Vladimir Klebanov. Pseudo-random number generator verification: A case study. In Arie Gurfinkel and Sanjit A. Seshia, editors, *Proceedings, Verified Software: Theories, Tools, and Experiments (VSTTE)*, volume 9593 of *LNCS*. Springer, 2015. (Cited on page 455.)

Gilles Dowek, Amy Felty, Hugo Herbelin, Gérard Huet, Chet Murthy, Catherine Parent, Christine Paulin-Mohring, and Benjamin Werner. The Coq proof assistant user's guide. Rapport Techniques 154, INRIA, Rocquencourt, France, 1993. Version 5.8. (Cited on pages 2 and 108.)

Christian Engel. A translation from JML to JavaDL. Studienarbeit, Fakultät für Informatik, Universität Karlsruhe, February 2005. (Cited on pages 195 and 243.)

Christian Engel and Reiner Hähnle. Generating unit tests from formal proofs. In Bertrand Meyer and Yuri Gurevich, editors, *Tests and Proofs, First International Conference, TAP 2007, Zurich, Switzerland. Revised Papers*, volume 4454 of *LNCS*. Springer, 2007. (Cited on pages IX, 4 and 416.)

Michael D. Ernst, Jeff H. Perkins, Philip J. Guo, Stephen McCamant, Carlos Pacheco, Matthew S. Tschantz, and Chen Xiao. The Daikon system for dynamic detection of likely invariants. *Science of Computer Programming*, 69(1–3):35–45, December 2007. (Cited on page 240.)

Michael E. Fagan. Design and code inspections to reduce errors in program development. *IBM Systems Journal*, 15(3):182–211, 1976. (Cited on pages 18 and 413.)

Azadeh Farzan, Feng Chen, José Meseguer, and Grigore Roşu. Formal analysis of Java programs in JavaFAN. In Rajeev Alur and Doron A. Peled, editors, *Proceedings, 16th International Conference on Computer Aided Verification (CAV)*, volume 3114 of *LNCS*, pages 501–505. Springer, 2004. (Cited on page 64.)

Dennis Felsing, Sarah Grebing, Vladimir Klebanov, Philipp Rümmer, and Mattias Ulbrich. Automating regression verification. In *29th IEEE/ACM International Conference on Automated Software Engineering (ASE 2014)*, ASE '14, pages 349–360. ACM, 2014. (Cited on pages 17 and 483.)

Jean-Christophe Filliâtre and Nicolas Magaud. Certification of sorting algorithms in the system Coq. In *Theorem Proving in Higher Order Logics: Emerging Trends*, Nice, France, 1999. (Cited on page 609.)

Jean-Christophe Filliâtre, Léon Gondelman, and Andrei Paskevich. The spririt of ghost code. In Armin Biere, Swen Jacobs, and Roderick Bloem, editors, *Computer Aided Verification - 26th International Conference, CAV 2014, Held as Part of the Vienna Summer of Logic, VSL 2014, Vienna, Austria. Proceedings*, volume 8559 of *LNCS*, pages 1–16. Springer, 2014. (Cited on page 269.)

John S. Fitzgerald, Peter Gorm Larsen, and Marcel Verhoef. Vienna development method. In Benjamin W. Wah, editor, *Wiley Encyclopedia of Computer Science and Engineering*. John Wiley & Sons, Inc., 2008. (Cited on page 240.)

Cormac Flanagan and K.Rustan M. Leino. Houdini, an annotation assistant for ESC/Java. Technical Report 2000-003, DEC-SRC, December 2000. (Cited on page 240.)

Robert W. Floyd. Assigning meanings to programs. In J. T. Schwartz, editor, *Mathematical Aspects of Computer Science*, volume 19 of *Proceedings of Symposia in Applied Mathematics*, pages 19–32, Providence, Rhode Island, 1967. American Mathematical Society. (Cited on pages 194 and 234.)

M. Foley and C. A. R. Hoare. Proof of a recursive program: Quicksort. *Computer Journal*, 14(4): 391–395, 1971. (Cited on page 609.)

Nathan Fulton, Stefan Mitsch, Jan-David Quesel, Marcus Völp, and André Platzer. Keymaera X: an axiomatic tactical theorem prover for hybrid systems. In Amy P. Felty and Aart Middeldorp, editors, *Automated Deduction - CADE-25 - 25th International Conference on Automated Deduction, Berlin, Germany. Proceedings*, volume 9195 of *LNCS*, pages 527–538. Springer, 2015. (Cited on page 6.)

Stefan J. Galler and Bernhard K. Aichernig. Survey on test data generation tools. *International Journal on Software Tools for Technology Transfer*, 16(6):727–751, 2014. (Cited on page 448.)

Jean H. Gallier. *Logic for Computer Science: Foundations of Automatic Theorem Proving*. Wiley, 1987. (Cited on pages 27 and 35.)

Flavio D. Garcia, Gerhard Koning Gans, Ruben Muijrers, Peter Rossum, Roel Verdult, Ronny Wichers Schreur, and Bart Jacobs. Dismantling MIFARE classic. In Sushil Jajodia and Javier Lopez, editors, *Proceedings of the 13th European Symposium on Research in Computer Security*, volume 5283 of *LNCS*, pages 97–114. Springer, 2008. (Cited on page 353.)

Tobias Gedell and Reiner Hähnle. Automating verification of loops by parallelization. In Miki Herrmann, editor, *Logic for Programming, Artificial Intelligence, and Reasoning, 13th International Conference, LPAR 2006, Phnom Penh, Cambodia. Proceedings*, LNCS, pages 332–346. Springer, October 2006. (Cited on page 68.)

Ullrich Geilmann. Formal verification using Java's String class. Studienarbeit, Chalmers University of Technology and Universität Karlsruhe, November 2009. (Cited on page 161.)

Robert Geisler, Marcus Klar, and Felix Cornelius. InterACT: An interactive theorem prover for algebraic specifications. In Martin Wirsing and Maurice Nivat, editors, *Algebraic Methodology and Software Technology, 5th International Conference, AMAST '96, Munich, Germany. Proceedings*, volume 1101 of *LNCS*, pages 563–566. Springer, 1996. (Cited on page 108.)

Steven M. German and Ben Wegbreit. A synthesizer of inductive assertions. *IEEE Transactions on Software Engineering*, SE-1(1):68–75, March 1975. (Cited on page 234.)

Martin Giese. Taclets and the KeY prover. In David Aspinall and Christoph Lüth, editors, *Proc. User Interfaces for Theorem Provers Workshop, UITP, Rome, 2003*, volume 103 of *Electronic Notes in Theoretical Computer Science*, pages 67–79. Elsevier, 2004. (Cited on page 108.)

Martin Giese. A calculus for type predicates and type coercion. In Bernhard Beckert, editor, *Automated Reasoning with Analytic Tableaux and Related Methods, International Conference, TABLEAUX 2005, Koblenz, Germany. Proceedings*, volume 3702 of *LNCS*, pages 123–137. Springer, 2005. (Cited on page 35.)

Christoph Gladisch. Verification-based test case generation for full feasible branch coverage. In Antonio Cerone and Stefan Gruner, editors, *Proceedings, Sixth IEEE International Conference on Software Engineering and Formal Methods, SEFM 2008, Cape Town, South Africa*, pages 159–168. IEEE Computer Society, 2008. (Cited on pages IX, 434 and 436.)

Christoph Gladisch and Shmuel Tyszberowicz. Specifying a linked data structure in JML for formal verification and runtime checking. In Leonardo de Moura and Juliano Iyoda, editors, *Formal Methods: Foundations and Applications - 16th Brazilian Symposium, SBMF 2013, Brasilia, Brazil. Proceedings*, volume 8195 of *LNCS*, pages 99–114. Springer, 2013. (Cited on pages 296 and 300.)

Christoph David Gladisch. *Verification-based software-fault detection*. PhD thesis, Karlsruhe Institute of Technology, 2011. (Cited on pages 416 and 436.)

Patrice Godefroid, Michael Y. Levin, and David Molnar. SAGE: Whitebox fuzzing for security testing. *Queue*, 10(1):20, 2012. (Cited on page 450.)

Kurt Gödel. Über formal unentscheidbare Sätze der Principia Mathematica und verwandter Systeme I. *Monatshefte für Mathematik und Physik*, 38:173–198, 1931. (Cited on page 65.)

Joseph A. Goguen and José Meseguer. Security policies and security models. In *IEEE Symposium on Security and Privacy*, pages 11–20, 1982. (Cited on page 454.)

Michael J. C. Gordon, Robin Milner, and Christopher P. Wadsworth. *Edinburgh LCF*, volume 78 of *LNCS*. Springer, 1979. (Cited on page 10.)

James Gosling, Bill Joy, Guy Steele, Gilad Bracha, and Alex Buckley. *The Java Language Specification, Java SE 7 Edition*. The Java Series. Addison-Wesley, Boston, Mass., 2013. (Cited on pages 52, 53, 54, 55, 60, 91, 156, 197, 237, 247, 622 and 623.)

Jürgen Graf, Martin Hecker, and Martin Mohr. Using JOANA for information flow control in Java programs – A practical guide. In Stefan Wagner and Horst Lichter, editors, *Software Engineering (Workshops)*, volume 215 of *Lecture Notes in Informatics*, pages 123–138. Gesellschaft für Informatik, 2013. (Cited on pages 596 and 605.)

Daniel Grahl. *Deductive Verification of Concurrent Programs and its Application to Secure Information Flow for Java*. PhD thesis, Karlsruhe Institute of Technology, 29 October 2015. (Cited on pages IX, 351, 593 and 596.)

Jim Gray. Why Do Computers Stop and What Can Be Done About It? Technical Report 85.7, PN87614, Tandem Computers, June 1985. (Cited on page 384.)

Wolfgang Grieskamp, Nikolai Tillmann, and Wolfram Schulte. XRT — exploring runtime for .NET architecture and applications. *Electronic Notes in Theoretical Computer Science*, 144(3):3–26, 2006. Proceedings of the Workshop on Software Model Checking (SoftMC 2005), Software Model Checking, Edinburgh, UK, 2005. (Cited on page 384.)

John V. Guttag and James J. Horning. *Larch: Languages and Tools for Formal Specification*. Springer, 1993. (Cited on page 194.)

Elmar Habermalz. Interactive theorem proving with schematic theory specific rules. Technical Report 19/00, Fakultät für Informatik, Universität Karlsruhe, 2000a. (Cited on page 108.)

Elmar Habermalz. *Ein dynamisches automatisierbares interaktives Kalkül für schematische theoriespezifische Regeln*. PhD thesis, Universität Karlsruhe, 2000b. (Cited on page 108.)

Reiner Hähnle. Many-valued logic, partiality, and abstraction in formal specification languages. *Logic Journal of the IPGL*, 13(4):415–433, July 2005. (Cited on page 280.)

Reiner Hähnle and Richard Bubel. A Hoare-style calculus with explicit state updates. In Zoltán Instenes, editor, *Proc. Formal Methods in Computer Science Education (FORMED)*, Electronic Notes in Theoretical Computer Science, pages 49–60. Elsevier, 2008. (Cited on pages X, 7, 15 and 572.)

Reiner Hähnle, Wolfram Menzel, and Peter Schmitt. Integrierter deduktiver Software-Entwurf. *Künstliche Intelligenz*, pages 40–41, December 1998. (Cited on page 1.)

Reiner Hähnle, Markus Baum, Richard Bubel, and Marcel Rothe. A visual interactive debugger based on symbolic execution. In Jamie Andrews and Elisabetta Di Nitto, editors, *Proc. 25th IEEE/ACM International Conference on Automated Software Engineering, Antwerp, Belgium*, pages 143–146. ACM Press, 2010. (Cited on pages 8, 384 and 412.)

Reiner Hähnle, Nathan Wasser, and Richard Bubel. Array abstraction with symbolic pivots. In Erika Ábrahám, Marcello Bonsangue, and Broch Einar Johnsen, editors, *Theory and Practice of Formal Methods: Essays Dedicated to Frank de Boer on the Occasion of His 60th Birthday*, pages 104–121. Springer, 2016. (Cited on pages 184 and 187.)

Christian Hammer. *Information Flow Control for Java – A Comprehensive Approach based on Path Conditions in Dependence Graphs*. PhD thesis, Universität Karlsruhe (TH), July 2009. (Cited on pages 596 and 605.)

Christian Hammer, Jens Krinke, and Gregor Snelting. Information flow control for Java based on path conditions in dependence graphs. In *IEEE International Symposium on Secure Software Engineering (ISSSE 2006)*, pages 87–96. IEEE, March 2006. (Cited on page 454.)

David Harel. *First-Order Dynamic Logic*. Springer, 1979. (Cited on page 65.)

David Harel. Dynamic logic. In D. Gabbay and F. Guenthner, editors, *Handbook of Philosophical Logic*, volume II: Extensions of Classical Logic, chapter 10, pages 497–604. Reidel, Dordrecht, 1984. (Cited on page 49.)

David Harel, Dexter Kozen, and Jerzy Tiuryn. *Dynamic Logic*. MIT Press, 2000. (Cited on pages 12, 49 and 330.)

Trevor Harmon and Raymond Klefstad. A survey of worst-case execution time analysis for real-time Java. In *21th International Parallel and Distributed Processing Symposium (IPDPS 2007), Proceedings, Long Beach, California, USA*, pages 1–8. IEEE Press, 2007. (Cited on page 582.)

Maritta Heisel, Wolfgang Reif, and Werner Stephan. Program verification by symbolic execution and induction. In Katharina Morik, editor, *GWAI-87, 11th German Workshop on Artificial Intelligence, Geseke, 1987, Proceedings*, volume 152 of *Informatik Fachberichte*, pages 201–210. Springer, 1987. (Cited on page 12.)

Martin Hentschel, Richard Bubel, and Reiner Hähnle. Symbolic execution debugger (SED). In Borzoo Bonakdarpour and Scott A. Smolka, editors, *Runtime Verification, 14th International Conference, RV, Toronto, Canada*, volume 8734 of *LNCS*, pages 255–262. Springer, 2014a. (Cited on pages X, 8 and 384.)

Martin Hentschel, Reiner Hähnle, and Richard Bubel. Visualizing unbounded symbolic execution. In Martina Seidl and Nikolai Tillmann, editors, *Proceedings of Testing and Proofs (TAP) 2014*, LNCS, pages 82–98. Springer, July 2014b. (Cited on pages IX and 386.)

Martin Hentschel, Stefan Käsdorf, Reiner Hähnle, and Richard Bubel. An interactive verification tool meets an IDE. In Emil Sekerinski Elvira Albert and Gianluigi Zavattaro, editors, *Proceedings of the 11th International Conference on Integrated Formal Methods*, volume 8739 of *LNCS*, pages 55–70. Springer, 2014c. (Cited on pages X and 566.)

Martin Hentschel, Reiner Hähnle, and Richard Bubel. Can formal methods improve the efficiency of code reviews? In Erika Ábrahám and Marieke Huisman, editors, *Integrated Formal Methods, 12th International Conference, IFM, Reykjavik, Iceland*, volume 9681 of *LNCS*, pages 3–19. Springer, 2016. (Cited on pages 8 and 18.)

Mihai Herda. Generating bounded counterexamples for KeY proof obligations. Master thesis, Karlsruhe Institute of Technology, January 2014. (Cited on page 439.)

C. A. R. Hoare. An axiomatic basis for computer programming. *Communications of the ACM*, 12 (10):576–580, 583, October 1969. (Cited on pages 7, 208, 234, 349, 571 and 574.)

C. A. R. Hoare. Procedures and parameters: An axiomatic approach. In Erwin Engeler, editor, *Symposium on Semantics of Algorithmic Languages*, volume 188 of *Lecture Notes in Mathematics*, pages 102–116. Springer, Berlin, Heidelberg, 1971. (Cited on page 299.)

C. A. R. Hoare. Proof of correctness of data representations. *Acta Informatica*, 1:271–281, 1972. (Cited on page 302.)

C.A.R. Hoare and Jayadev Misra. Verified software: Theories, tools, experiments vision of a grand challenge project. In Bertrand Meyer and Jim Woodcock, editors, *Verified Software: Theories, Tools, Experiments, First IFIP TC 2/WG 2.3 Conference, VSTTE 2005, Zurich, Switzerland, Revised Selected Papers and Discussions*, volume 4171 of *LNCS*, pages 1–18. Springer, 2005. (Cited on page 289.)

Gerard J. Holzmann. *The SPIN Model Checker*. Pearson Education, 2003. (Cited on pages 6 and 7.)

Falk Howar, Dimitra Giannakopoulou, and Zvonimir Rakamaric. Hybrid learning: interface generation through static, dynamic, and symbolic analysis. In Mauro Pezzè and Mark Harman, editors,

International Symposium on Software Testing and Analysis, ISSTA, Lugano, Switzerland, pages 268–279. ACM, 2013. (Cited on page 18.)

Engelbert Hubbers and Erik Poll. Reasoning about card tears and transactions in Java Card. In Michel Wermelinger and Tiziana Margaria, editors, *Proc. Fundamental Approaches to Software Engineering (FASE), Barcelona, Spain*, volume 2984 of *LNCS*, pages 114–128. Springer, 2004. (Cited on page 377.)

Engelbert Hubbers, Wojciech Mostowski, and Erik Poll. Tearing Java Cards. In *Proceedings, e-Smart 2006, Sophia-Antipolis, France*, 2006. (Cited on page 374.)

Marieke Huisman and Wojciech Mostowski. A symbolic approach to permission accounting for concurrent reasoning. In *14th International Symposium on Parallel and Distributed Computing (ISPDC 2015)*, pages 165–174. IEEE Computer Society, 2015. (Cited on pages 378 and 380.)

Marieke Huisman, Wolfgang Ahrendt, Daniel Bruns, and Martin Hentschel. Formal specification with JML. Technical Report 2014-10, Department of Informatics, Karlsruhe Institute of Technology, 2014. (Cited on page 193.)

Marieke Huisman, Vladimir Klebanov, and Rosemary Monahan. VerifyThis 2012. *International Journal on Software Tools for Technology Transfer*, 17(6):647–657, 2015. (Cited on page 289.)

James J. Hunt, Fridtjof B. Siebert, Peter H. Schmitt, and Isabel Tonin. Provably correct loops bounds for realtime Java programs. In *JTRES '06: Proceedings of the 4th international workshop on Java technologies for real-time and embedded systems*, pages 162–169, New York, NY, USA, 2006. ACM. (Cited on page 583.)

Michael Huth and Mark Dermot Ryan. *Logic in computer science - modelling and reasoning about systems (2. ed.)*. Cambridge University Press, 2004. (Cited on page 572.)

Malte Isberner, Falk Howar, and Bernhard Steffen. Learning register automata: from languages to program structures. *Machine Learning*, 96(1–2):65–98, 2014. (Cited on page 18.)

ISO. ISO 26262, road vehicles – functional safety. published by the International Organization for Standardization, 2011. (Cited on page 424.)

Daniel Jackson. Alloy: A lightweight object modelling notation. *ACM Transactions Software Engineering and Methodology*, 11(2):256–290, April 2002. (Cited on page 438.)

Daniel Jackson. Alloy: A logical modelling language. In Didier Bert, Jonathan P. Bowen, Steve King, and Marina A. Waldén, editors, *ZB 2003: Formal Specification and Development in Z and B, Third International Conference of B and Z Users, Turku, Finland. Proceedings*, volume 2651 of *LNCS*, page 1. Springer, 2003. (Cited on page 240.)

Bart Jacobs and Frank Piessens. The VeriFast program verifier. Technical Report CW-520, Department of Computer Science, Katholieke Universiteit Leuven, August 2008. (Cited on pages 2 and 384.)

Bart Jacobs and Frank Piessens. Expressive modular fine-grained concurrency specification. In Thomas Ball and Mooly Sagiv, editors, *Proceedings of the 38th ACM SIGPLAN-SIGACT Symposium on Principles of Programming Languages, POPL 2011, Austin, TX, USA*, pages 271–282. ACM, 2011. (Cited on page 241.)

Bart Jacobs and Erik Poll. A logic for the Java Modeling Language. In Heinrich Hußmann, editor, *Proc. Fundamental Approaches to Software Engineering, 4th International Conference (FASE), Genova, Italy*, volume 2029 of *LNCS*, pages 284–299. Springer, 2001. (Cited on pages 195 and 243.)

Bart Jacobs and Jan Rutten. A tutorial on (co)algebras and (co)induction. *Bulletin of the European Association for Theoretical Computer Science*, 62:222–259, 1997. (Cited on page 252.)

Bart Jacobs, Hans Meijer, and Erik Poll. VerifiCard: A European project for smart card verification. *Newsletter 5 of the Dutch Association for Theoretical Computer Science (NVTI)*, 2001. (Cited on page 353.)

Bart Jacobs, Joseph Kiniry, and Martijn Warnier. Java program verification challenges. In Frank S. de Boer, Marcello M. Bonsangue, Susanne Graf, and Willem-Paul de Roever, editors, *Formal Methods for Components and Objects*, volume 2852 of *LNCS*, pages 202–219. Springer, 2003. (Cited on page 88.)

Bart Jacobs, Jan Smans, Pieter Philippaerts, and Frank Piessens. The VeriFast program verifier – a tutorial for Java Card developers. Technical report, Department of Computer Science, Katholieke Universiteit Leuven, Belgium, September 2011a. (Cited on page 377.)

Bart Jacobs, Jan Smans, Pieter Philippaerts, Frédéric Vogels, Willem Penninckx, and Frank Piessens. VeriFast: A powerful, sound, predictable, fast verifier for C and Java. In Mihaela Gheorghiu Bobaru, Klaus Havelund, Gerard J. Holzmann, and Rajeev Joshi, editors, *NASA Formal Methods - Third International Symposium, NFM 2011, Pasadena, CA, USA. Proceedings*, volume 6617 of *LNCS*, pages 41–55. Springer, 2011b. (Cited on pages 377 and 378.)

Bart Jacobs, Jan Smans, and Frank Piessens. Verification of unloadable modules. In Michael Butler and Wolfram Schulte, editors, *17th International Symposium on Formal Methods (FM 2011)*, pages 402–416. Springer, June 2011c. (Cited on page 350.)

JavaCardRTE. *Java Card 3 Platform Runtime Environment Specification, Classic Edition, Version 3.0.4*, Oracle, September 2012. (Cited on pages 5, 353 and 354.)

JavaCardVM. *Java Card 3 Platform Virtual Machine Specification, Classic Edition, Version 3.0.4*, Oracle, September 2012. (Cited on page 354.)

Trevor Jennings. SPARK: the libre language and toolset for high-assurance software engineering. In Greg Gicca and Jeff Boleng, editors, *Proceedigngs, Annual ACM SIGAda International Conference on Ada, Saint Petersburg, Florida, USA*, pages 9–10. ACM, 2009. (Cited on page 5.)

Ran Ji. *Sound programm transformation based on symbolic execution and deduction*. PhD thesis, Darmstadt University of Technology, Department of Computer Science, 2014. (Cited on pages IX, 482, 491 and 492.)

Ran Ji and Reiner Hähnle. Information flow analysis based on program simplification. Technical Report TUD-CS-2014-0877, Department of Computer Science, 2014. (Cited on page 492.)

Ran Ji, Reiner Hähnle, and Richard Bubel. Program transformation based on symbolic execution and deduction. In Robert M. Hierons, Mercedes G. Merayo, and Mario Bravetti, editors, *Software Engineering and Formal Methods: 11th International Conference, SEFM 2013, Madrid, Spain*, volume 8137 of *LNCS*, pages 289–304. Springer, 2013. (Cited on pages IX and 5.)

Einar Broch Johnsen, Reiner Hähnle, Jan Schäfer, Rudolf Schlatte, and Martin Steffen. ABS: A core language for abstract behavioral specification. In Bernhard Aichernig, Frank S. de Boer, and Marcello M. Bonsangue, editors, *Proceedigns, 9th International Symposium on Formal Methods for Components and Objects (FMCO 2010)*, volume 6957 of *LNCS*, pages 142–164. Springer, 2011. (Cited on page 6.)

Cliff B. Jones. Tentative steps toward a development method for interfering programs. *ACM Transactions on Programming Languages and Systems*, 5(4):596–619, 1983. (Cited on page 351.)

Neil D. Jones, Carsten K. Gomard, and Peter Sestoft. *Partial evaluation and automatic program generation*. Prentice-Hall, 1993. (Cited on page 475.)

Kari Kähkönen, Tuomas Launiainen, Olli Saarikivi, Janne Kauttio, Keijo Heljanko, and Ilkka Niemelä. LCT: An open source concolic testing tool for Java programs. In Pierre Ganty and Mark Marron, editors, *Proceedings of the 6th Workshop on Bytecode Semantics, Verification, Analysis and Transformation (BYTECODE'2011)*, pages 75–80, 2011. (Cited on page 450.)

Michael Karr. Affine relationships among variables of a program. *Acta Informatica*, 6(2):133–151, 1976. (Cited on page 234.)

Ioannis T. Kassios. Dynamic frames: Support for framing, dependencies and sharing without restrictions. In Jayadev Misra, Tobias Nipkow, and Emil Sekerinski, editors, *FM 2006: Formal Methods, 14th International Symposium on Formal Methods, Hamilton, Canada. Proceedings*, volume 4085 of *LNCS*, pages 268–283, Berlin, 2006. Springer. (Cited on pages 13, 320 and 322.)

Ioannis T. Kassios. The dynamic frames theory. *Formal Aspects Computing*, 23(3):267–288, 2011. (Cited on pages IX, 241, 290, 320 and 322.)

Shmuel Katz and Zohar Manna. Towards automatic debugging of programs. *ACM SIGPLAN Notices*, 10(6):143–155, 1975. Proceedings of the International Conference on Reliable software, Los Angeles. 1975. (Cited on page 383.)

Moritz Kiefer, Vladimir Klebanov, and Mattias Ulbrich. Relational program reasoning using compiler IR. In *8th Working Conference on Verified Software: Theories, Tools, and Experiments (VSTTE)*, 2016. To appear. (Cited on page 483.)

James C. King. Symbolic execution and program testing. *Communications of the ACM*, 19(7): 385–394, July 1976. (Cited on pages 4, 67 and 383.)

Joseph R. Kiniry, Alan E. Morkan, Dermot Cochran, Fintan Fairmichael, Patrice Chalin, Martijn Oostdijk, and Engelbert Hubbers. The KOA remote voting system: A summary of work to date. In Ugo Montanari, Donald Sannella, and Roberto Bruni, editors, *Proceedings of Trustworthy Global Computing (TGC)*, volume 4661 of *LNCS*, pages 244–262. Springer, 2006. (Cited on page 606.)

Laurie Kirby and Jeff Paris. Accessible independence results for Peano Arithmetic. *Bulletin of the London Mathematical Society*, 14(4), 1982. (Cited on page 40.)

Michael Kirsten. Proving well-definedness of JML specifications with KeY. Studienarbeit, KIT, 2013. (Cited on pages 254 and 287.)

Vladimir Klebanov. Precise quantitative information flow analysis – a symbolic approach. *Theoretical Computer Science*, 538:124–139, 2014. (Cited on page 470.)

Vladimir Klebanov, Peter Müller, Natarajan Shankar, Gary T. Leavens, Valentin Wüstholz, Eyad Alkassar, Rob Arthan, Derek Bronish, Rod Chapman, Ernie Cohen, Mark Hillebrand, Bart Jacobs, K. Rustan M. Leino, Rosemary Monahan, Frank Piessens, Nadia Polikarpova, Tom Ridge, Jan Smans, Stephan Tobies, Thomas Tuerk, Mattias Ulbrich, and Benjamin Weiß. The 1st Verified Software Competition: Experience report. In Michael Butler and Wolfram Schulte, editors, *FM 2011: Formal Methods - 17th International Symposium on Formal Methods, Limerick, Ireland. Proceedings*, volume 6664 of *LNCS*, pages 154–168. Springer, 2011. (Cited on pages 18 and 289.)

Gerwin Klein, June Andronick, Kevin Elphinstone, Gernot Heiser, David Cock, Philip Derrin, Dhammika Elkaduwe, Kai Engelhardt, Rafal Kolanski, Michael Norrish, Thomas Sewell, Harvey Tuch, and Simon Winwood. seL4: Formal verification of an operating system kernel. *Communications of the ACM*, 53(6):107–115, June 2010. (Cited on page 9.)

Donald E. Knuth. *The Art of Computer Programming, Volume 3: Sorting and Searching*. Addison–Wesley, third edition, 1998. (Cited on page 558.)

Dexter Kozen and Jerzy Tiuryn. Logics of programs. In Jan van Leeuwen, editor, *Handbook of Theoretical Computer Science*, volume B: Formal Models and Semantics, chapter 14, pages 789–840. The MIT Press, 1990. (Cited on page 49.)

Daniel Kroening and Ofer Strichman. *Decision Procedures: An Algorithmic Point of View*. Springer, 1 edition, 2008. (Cited on page 537.)

Daniel Kroening and Michael Tautschnig. CBMC - C bounded model checker - (competition contribution). In Erika Ábrahám and Klaus Havelund, editors, *Proceedings, 20th International Conference on Tools and Algorithms for the Construction and Analysis of Systems (TACAS)*, volume 8413 of *LNCS*, pages 389–391. Springer, 2014. (Cited on page 97.)

Ralf Küsters, Tomasz Truderung, and Andreas Vogt. Verifiability, Privacy, and Coercion-Resistance: New Insights from a Case Study. In *32nd IEEE Symposium on Security and Privacy, S&P 2011, Berkeley, California, USA*, pages 538–553, Oakland, California, USA, 2011. IEEE Computer Society. (Cited on pages 593, 594, 595 and 605.)

Ralf Küsters, Tomasz Truderung, Bernhard Beckert, Daniel Bruns, Michael Kirsten, and Martin Mohr. A hybrid approach for proving noninterference of Java programs. In Cédric Fournet and Michael Hicks, editors, *28th IEEE Computer Security Foundations Symposium*, pages 305–319. IEEE Computer Society, 2015. (Cited on pages 596 and 605.)

Leslie Lamport. What good is temporal logic? In R. E. A. Mason, editor, *Proceedings of the IFIP Congress on Information Processing*, pages 657–667, Amsterdam, 1983. North-Holland. (Cited on page 291.)

Butler W. Lampson. A note on the confinement problem. *Commun. ACM*, 16(10):613–615, 1973. (Cited on page 454.)

Daniel Larsson and Reiner Hähnle. Symbolic fault injection. In Bernhard Beckert, editor, *Proc. 4th International Verification Workshop (Verify) in connection with CADE-21 Bremen, Germany*, volume 259, pages 85–103. CEUR Workshop Proceedings, July 2007. (Cited on page 17.)

Gary T. Leavens. *Verifying Object-Oriented Programs that use Subtypes*. PhD thesis, Massachusetts Institute of Technology, December 1988. (Cited on pages 219, 260, 292 and 293.)

Gary T. Leavens and Yoonsik Cheon. Preliminary design of Larch/C++. In Ursula Martin and Jeannette M. Wing, editors, *Proceedings of the First International Workshop on Larch, 1992*, Workshops in Computing, pages 159–184, New York, NY, 1993. Springer. (Cited on page 194.)

Gary T. Leavens and Krishna Kishore Dhara. Concepts of behavioral subtyping and a sketch of their extension to component-based systems. In Gary T. Leavens and Murali Sitaraman, editors, *Foundations of Component-Based Systems*, pages 113–135. Cambridge University Press, 2000. (Cited on pages 219 and 293.)

Gary T. Leavens and David A. Naumann. Behavioral subtyping is equivalent to modular reasoning for object-oriented programs. Technical Report 06-36, Department of Computer Science, Iowa State University, Ames, Iowa, 50011, December 2006. (Cited on pages 219 and 293.)

Gary T. Leavens and William E. Weihl. Specification and verification of object-oriented programs using supertype abstraction. *Acta Informatica*, 32(8):705–778, 1995. (Cited on page 293.)

Gary T. Leavens and Jeanette M. Wing. Protective interface specifications. *Formal Aspects of Computing*, 10(1):59–75, 1998. (Cited on page 281.)

Gary T. Leavens, Jean-Raymond Abrial, Don Batory, Michael Butler, Alessandro Coglio, Kathi Fisler, Eric Hehner, Cliff Jones, Dale Miller, Simon Peyton-Jones, Murali Sitaraman, Douglas R. Smith, and Aaron Stump. Roadmap for enhanced languages and methods to aid verification. In Stan Jarzabek, Douglas C. Schmidt, and Todd L. Veldhuizen, editors, *Generative Programming and Component Engineering, 5th International Conference, GPCE 2006, Portland, Oregon, USA. Proceedings*, pages 221–236, New York, NY, USA, 2006a. ACM. (Cited on page 289.)

Gary T. Leavens, Albert L. Baker, and Clyde Ruby. Preliminary design of JML: a behavioral interface specification language for Java. *ACM SIGSOFT Software Engineering Notes*, 31(3): 1–38, 2006b. (Cited on pages 193 and 253.)

Gary T. Leavens, K. Rustan M. Leino, and Peter Müller. Specification and verification challenges for sequential object-oriented programs. *Formal Aspects of Computing*, 19(2):159–189, 2007. (Cited on page 289.)

Gary T. Leavens, Erik Poll, Curtis Clifton, Yoonsik Cheon, Clyde Ruby, David Cok, Peter Müller, Joseph Kiniry, Patrice Chalin, Daniel M. Zimmerman, and Werner Dietl. *JML Reference Manual*, May 31, 2013. Draft Revision 2344. (Cited on pages IX, 2, 13, 193, 208, 233, 243, 244, 245, 247, 248, 253, 261, 262, 280, 322, 328, 621 and 628.)

Dirk Leinenbach. *Compiler Verification in the Context of Pervasive System Verification*. PhD thesis, Saarland University, Saarbrücken, 2008. (Cited on page 473.)

K. Rustan M. Leino. *Towards Reliable Modular Programs*. PhD thesis, California Institute of Technology, 1995. Available as Technical Report Caltech-CS-TR-95-03. (Cited on page 289.)

K. Rustan M. Leino. Data groups: Specifying the modification of extended state. In Bjørn N. Freeman-Benson and Craig Chambers, editors, *Proceedings of the 1998 ACM SIGPLAN Conference on Object-Oriented Programming Systems, Languages & Applications (OOPSLA '98), Vancouver, British Columbia, Canada*, volume 33, pages 144–153. ACM, October 1998. (Cited on pages 320 and 347.)

K. Rustan M. Leino. Efficient weakest preconditions. *Information Processing Letters*, 93(6): 281–288, 2005. (Cited on page 76.)

K. Rustan M. Leino. Dafny: An automatic program verifier for functional correctness. In Edmund M. Clarke and Andrei Voronkov, editors, *Logic for Programming, Artificial Intelligence, and Reasoning - 16th International Conference, LPAR-16, Dakar, Senegal, 2010, Revised Selected Papers*, volume 6355 of *LNCS*, pages 348–370. Springer, 2010. (Cited on pages 2, 7, 10, 241 and 348.)

K. Rustan M. Leino and Michał Moskal. VACID-0: Verification of ample correctness of invariants of data-structures, Edition 0. In Gary T. Leavens, Peter W. O'Hearn, and Sriram Rajamani, editors, *Verified Software: Theories, Tools, Experiments, Third International Conference, VSTTE, Edinburgh, UK*, Edinburgh, UK, 2010. (Cited on page 296.)

K. Rustan M. Leino and Peter Müller. Object invariants in dynamic contexts. In Martin Odersky, editor, *European Conference on Object-Oriented Programming*, volume 3086 of *LNCS*, pages 491–516. Springer, 2004. (Cited on page 215.)

K. Rustan M. Leino and Peter Müller. A verification methodology for model fields. In Peter Sestoft, editor, *European Symposium on Programming (ESOP)*, volume 3924 of *LNCS*, pages 115–130, New York, NY, March 2006. Springer. (Cited on page 350.)

K. Rustan M. Leino and Greg Nelson. An extended static checker for Modula-3. In Kai Koskimies, editor, *Compiler Construction, 7th International Conference, CC'98, Held as Part of the European Joint Conferences on the Theory and Practice of Software, ETAPS'98, Lisbon, Portugal. Proceedings*, volume 1383 of *LNCS*, pages 302–305. Springer, 1998. (Cited on page 240.)

K. Rustan M. Leino and Greg Nelson. Data abstraction and information hiding. *ACM Transactions on Programming Languages and Systems*, 24(5):491–553, September 2002. (Cited on pages 302 and 322.)

K. Rustan M. Leino, Greg Nelson, and J.B. Saxe. ESC/Java user's manual. Technical Report SRC 2000-002, Compaq System Research Center, 2000. (Cited on pages 195 and 240.)

K. Rustan M. Leino, Arnd Poetzsch-Heffter, and Yunhong Zhou. Using data groups to specify and check side effects. In *Proceedings of the ACM SIGPLAN 2002 Conference on Programming Language Design and Implementation (PLDI'02)*, volume 37(5), pages 246–257, New York, NY, June 2002. ACM. (Cited on page 348.)

K. Rustan M. Leino, Peter Müller, and Jan Smans. Verification of concurrent programs with Chalice. In Alessandro Aldini, Gilles Barthe, and Roberto Gorrieri, editors, *Foundations of Security Analysis and Design*, volume 5705 of *LNCS*, pages 195–222. Springer, 2009. (Cited on pages 350 and 378.)

Xavier Leroy. Formal certification of a compiler back-end or: programming a compiler with a proof assistant. In J. Gregory Morrisett and Simon L. Peyton Jones, editors, *Proceedings of the 33rd ACM SIGPLAN-SIGACT Symposium on Principles of Programming Languages, POPL 2006, Charleston, South Carolina, USA*, pages 42–54. ACM, 2006. (Cited on page 473.)

Xavier Leroy. A formally verified compiler back-end. *J. Automated Reasoning*, 43(4):363–446, 2009. (Cited on page 473.)

Barbara Liskov. Data abstraction and hierarchy. *SIGPLAN Notices*, pages 17–34, May 1988. (Cited on pages 218, 219 and 292.)

Barbara Liskov and Jeanette M. Wing. Specifications and their use in defining subtypes. In Andreas Paepcke, editor, *Proceedings of the 8th Annual Conference on Object-Oriented Programming Systems, Languages and Applications*, pages 16–28, Washington DC, USA, 1993. ACM Press. (Cited on pages 217 and 292.)

Barbara Liskov and Jeannette M. Wing. A behavioral notion of subtyping. *ACM Transactions on Programming Languages and Systems*, 16(6):1811–1841, November 1994. (Cited on pages 218 and 292.)

Sarah M. Loos, David W. Renshaw, and André Platzer. Formal verification of distributed aircraft controllers. In Calin Belta and Franjo Ivancic, editors, *Proc. 16th Intl. Conference on Hybrid Systems: Computation and Control, HSCC, Philadelphia, PA, USA*, pages 125–130. ACM, 2013. (Cited on page 6.)

Claude Marché and Nicolas Rousset. Verification of Java Card applets behavior with respect to transactions and card tears. In *Fourth IEEE International Conference on Software Engineering and Formal Methods (SEFM 2006), Pune, India*, pages 137–146. IEEE CS Press, 2006. (Cited on page 377.)

Claude Marché, Christine Paulin-Mohring, and Xavier Urbain. The Krakatoa tool for certification of Java/JavaCard programs annotated with JML annotations. *J. Logic and Algebraic Programming*, 58:89–106, 2004. (Cited on pages 195, 239 and 353.)

John McCarthy. Towards a mathematical science of computation. In Cicely M. Popplewell, editor, *Information Processing 1962, Proceedings of IFIP Congress 62, Munich, Germany*, pages 21–28. North-Holland, 1962. (Cited on page 41.)

John McCarthy and James Painter. Correctness of a compiler for arithmetic expressions. *Mathematical Aspects of Computer Science*, 19:33–41, 1967. Proceedings of Symposia in Applied Mathematics. 1967. (Cited on page 473.)

José Meseguer and Grigore Rosu. Rewriting logic semantics: From language specifications to formal analysis tools. In D. Basin and M. Rusinowitch, editors, *Automated Reasoning, Second*

International Joint Conference, IJCAR 2004, Cork, Ireland, Proceedings, volume 3097 of *LNCS*, pages 1–44. Springer, 2004. (Cited on page 64.)

Bertrand Meyer. From structured programming to object-oriented design: The road to Eiffel. *Structured Programming*, 1:19–39, 1989. (Cited on page 246.)

Bertrand Meyer. Applying "design by contract". *IEEE Computer*, 25(10):40–51, October 1992. (Cited on pages 13, 194, 289 and 291.)

Bertrand Meyer. *Object-Oriented Software Construction*. Prentice-Hall, 1997. (Cited on pages 194 and 291.)

Alysson Milanez, Dênnis Sousa, Tiago Massoni, and Rohit Gheyi. JMLOK2: A tool for detecting and categorizing nonconformances. In Uirá Kulesza and Valter Camargo, editors, *Congresso Brasileiro de Software: Teoria e Prática*, pages 69–76, 2014. (Cited on page 239.)

Robin Milner and Richard Weyhrauch. Proving compiler correctness in a mechanized logic. *Machine Intelligence*, 7:51–72, 1972. Proceedings of the 7th Annual Machine Intelligence Workshop, Edinburgh, 1972. (Cited on page 473.)

Andrzej Mostowski. On a generalization of quantifiers. *Fundamenta Mathematicæ*, 44(1):12–36, 1957. (Cited on page 248.)

Wojciech Mostowski. Formalisation and verification of Java Card security properties in dynamic logic. In Maura Cerioli, editor, *Fundamental Approaches to Software Engineering (FASE), Edinburgh, Proceedings*, volume 3442 of *LNCS*, pages 357–371. Springer, April 2005. (Cited on pages 354, 376 and 609.)

Wojciech Mostowski. Formal reasoning about non-atomic Java Card methods in Dynamic Logic. In Jayadev Misra, Tobias Nipkow, and Emil Sekerinski, editors, *Proceedings, Formal Methods (FM) 2006, Hamilton, Ontario, Canada*, volume 4085 of *LNCS*, pages 444–459. Springer, August 2006. (Cited on pages 354 and 376.)

Wojciech Mostowski. Fully verified Java Card API reference implementation. In Bernhard Beckert, editor, *Proceedings of 4th International Verification Workshop (VERIFY) in connection with CADE-21, Bremen, Germany, 2007*, 2007. (Cited on pages 3, 6, 354, 376 and 609.)

Wojciech Mostowski. Dynamic frames based verification method for concurrent Java programs. In Arie Gurfinkel and Sanjit A. Seshia, editors, *Verified Software: Theories, Tools, and Experiments: 7th International Conference, VSTTE, San Francisco, CA, USA, Revised Selected Papers*, volume 9593 of *LNCS*, pages 124–141. Springer, 2015. (Cited on pages 3, 378 and 380.)

Wojciech Mostowski and Erik Poll. Malicious code on Java Card smartcards: Attacks and countermeasures. In *Smart Card Research and Advanced Application Conference CARDIS 2008*, volume 5189 of *LNCS*, pages 1–16. Springer, September 2008. (Cited on pages 354 and 361.)

Wojciech Mostowski and Mattias Ulbrich. Dynamic dispatch for method contracts through abstract predicates. In *Proceedings of the 14th International Conference on Modularity, MODULARITY 2015, Fort Collins, CO, USA*, pages 109–116. ACM, 2015. (Cited on pages 311 and 316.)

Wojciech Mostowski and Mattias Ulbrich. Dynamic dispatch for method contracts through abstract predicates. *Transactions Modularity and Composition*, 1:238–267, 2016. (Cited on page 311.)

Peter Müller. *Modular Specification and Verification of Object-Oriented Programs*, volume 2262 of *LNCS*. Springer, Berlin, 2002. (Cited on pages 296, 348 and 350.)

Peter Müller, Arnd Poetzsch-Heffter, and Gary T. Leavens. Modular specification of frame properties in JML. *Concurrency and Computation: Practice and Experience*, 15(2):117–154, February 2003. (Cited on pages 233 and 348.)

Peter Müller, Arnd Poetzsch-Heffter, and Gary T. Leavens. Modular invariants for layered object structures. *Science of Computer Programming*, 62(3):253–286, October 2006. (Cited on page 215.)

Oleg Mürk, Daniel Larsson, and Reiner Hähnle. KeY-C: A tool for verification of C programs. In Frank Pfenning, editor, *Proc. 21st Conference on Automated Deduction (CADE), Bremen, Germany*, volume 4603 of *LNCS*, pages 385–390. Springer, 2007. (Cited on page 16.)

Andrew C. Myers. JFlow: practical mostly-static information flow control. In Andrew W. Appel and Alex Aiken, editors, *POPL '99, Proceedings of the 26th ACM SIGPLAN-SIGACT Symposium on Principles of Programming Languages, San Antonio, TX, USA*, pages 228–241, New York, NY, USA, 1999. ACM. (Cited on pages 454 and 606.)

Glenford J. Myers. *Art of Software Testing*. John Wiley & Sons, second edition, 2004. (Cited on page 576.)

Aleksandar Nanevski, Anindya Banerjee, and Deepak Garg. Verification of information flow and access control policies with dependent types. In *32nd IEEE Symposium on Security and Privacy, S&P 2011, Berkeley, California, USA*, pages 165–179, may 2011. (Cited on page 455.)

David A. Naumann. Observational purity and encapsulation. *Theoretical Computer Science*, 376 (3):205–224, 2007. (Cited on page 210.)

Tobias Nipkow, Lawrence C. Paulson, and Markus Wenzel. *Isabelle/HOL — A Proof Assistant for Higher-Order Logic*, volume 2283 of *LNCS*. Springer, 2002. (Cited on pages 2, 10 and 108.)

Bashar Nuseibeh. Ariane 5: Who dunnit? *IEEE Software*, 14(3):15–16, May / June 1997. (Cited on page 230.)

Kirsten Nygaard and Ole-Johan Dahl. The development of the SIMULA languages. In Richard L. Wexelblat, editor, *History of Programming Languages*, ACM monograph series. Academic Press, 1981. (Cited on page 291.)

Peter W. O'Hearn, John C. Reynolds, and Hongseok Yang. Local reasoning about programs that alter data structures. In Laurent Fribourg, editor, *Computer Science Logic, 15th International Workshop, CSL 2001. 10th Annual Conference of the EACSL, Paris, France. Proceedings*, volume 2142 of *LNCS*, pages 1–19. Springer, 2001. (Cited on pages 241 and 349.)

Peter W. O'Hearn, Hongseok Yang, and John C. Reynolds. Separation and information hiding. In Neil D. Jones and Xavier Leroy, editors, *Proceedings of the 31st ACM SIGPLAN-SIGACT Symposium on Principles of Programming Languages, POPL 2004, Venice, Italy*, pages 268–280. ACM, January 2004. (Cited on page 241.)

Peter W. O'Hearn, Hongseok Yang, and John C. Reynolds. Separation and information hiding. *ACM Transactions on Programming Languages and Systems*, 31(3):11:1–11:50, April 2009. (Cited on page 349.)

Sam Owre, S. Rajan, John M. Rushby, Natarajan Shankar, and Mandayam K. Srivas. PVS: Combining specification, proof checking, and model checking. In Rajeev Alur and Thomas A. Henzinger, editors, *Computer Aided Verification, 8th International Conference, CAV '96, New Brunswick, NJ, USA, 1996, Proceedings*, volume 1102 of *LNCS*, pages 411–414. Springer, 1996. (Cited on page 108.)

Pierre Le Pallec, Ahmad Saif, Olivier Briot, Michael Bensimon, Jérome Devisme, and Marilyne Eznack. NFC cardlet development guidelines v2.2. Technical report, Association Française du Sans Contact Mobile, 2012. (Cited on pages 354, 355 and 360.)

Matthew Parkinson. Class invariants: The end of the road? In *International Workshop on Aliasing, Confinement and Ownership (IWACO)*, volume 23. ACM, 2007. position paper. (Cited on page 349.)

Matthew Parkinson and Gavin Bierman. Separation logic and abstraction. *SIGPLAN Notices*, 40(1): 247–258, January 2005. (Cited on pages 349 and 350.)

Corina S. Păsăreanu, Willem Visser, David Bushnell, Jaco Geldenhuys, Peter Mehlitz, and Neha Rungta. Symbolic PathFinder: integrating symbolic execution with model checking for Java bytecode analysis. *Automated Software Engineering*, 20(3):391–425, 2013. (Cited on page 449.)

Christine Paulin-Mohring. Introduction to the Coq proof-assistant for practical software verification. In Bertrand Meyer and Martin Nordio, editors, *Tools for Practical Software Verification*, volume 7682 of *LNCS*, pages 45–95. Springer, 2012. (Cited on page 10.)

Guillaume Petiot, Nikolai Kosmatov, Alain Giorgetti, and Jacques Julliand. How test generation helps software specification and deductive verification in Frama-C. In Martina Seidl and Nikolai Tillmann, editors, *Tests and Proofs - 8th International Conference, TAP 2014, Held as Part of STAF 2014, York, UK. Proceedings*, LNCS, pages 204–211. Springer, 2014. (Cited on page 449.)

André Platzer. An object-oriented dynamic logic with updates. Master's thesis, Universität Karlsruhe, Fakultät für Informatik, September 2004. (Cited on page 65.)

André Platzer. *Logical Analysis of Hybrid Systems: Proving Theorems for Complex Dynamics*. Springer, 2010. (Cited on page X.)

André Platzer and Jan-David Quesel. KeYmaera: A hybrid theorem prover for hybrid systems. In Alessandro Armando, Peter Baumgartner, and Gilles Dowek, editors, *Automated Reasoning,*

4th International Joint Conference, IJCAR, Sydney, Australia, volume 5195 of *LNCS*, pages 171–178. Springer, 2008. (Cited on pages 6 and 16.)

Arndt Poetzsch-Heffter. *Specification and Verification of Object-Oriented Programs*. PhD thesis, Technical University of Munich, 1997. Habilitation thesis. (Cited on page 215.)

Nadia Polikarpova, Julian Tschannen, Carlo A. Furia, and Bertrand Meyer. Flexible invariants through semantic collaboration. In Cliff B. Jones, Pekka Pihlajasaari, and Jun Sun, editors, *FM 2014: Formal Methods – 19th International Symposium, Singapore. Proceedings*, volume 8442 of *LNCS*, pages 514–530. Springer, 2014. (Cited on page 349.)

Nadia Polikarpova, Julian Tschannen, and Carlo A. Furia. A fully verified container library. In Nikolaj Bjørner and Frank D. de Boer, editors, *FM 2015: Formal Methods - 20th Intl. Symp., Oslo, Norway*, volume 9109 of *LNCS*, pages 414–434. Springer, 2015. (Cited on page 3.)

Guillaume Pothier, Éric Tanter, and José Piquer. Scalable omniscient debugging. In Richard P. Gabriel, David F. Bacon, Cristina Videira Lopes, and Guy L. Steele Jr., editors, *Proceedings of the 22nd Annual ACM SIGPLAN Conference on Object-Oriented Programming, Systems, Languages, and Applications, OOPSLA 2007, Montreal, Quebec, Canada*, pages 535–552. ACM, 2007. (Cited on page 383.)

Vaughan R. Pratt. Semantical considerations on Floyd-Hoare logic. In *17th Annual IEEE Symposium on Foundation of Computer Science, Houston, TX, USA. Proceedings*, pages 109–121. IEEE Computer Society, 1977. (Cited on pages 12 and 49.)

Arun D. Raghavan and Gary T. Leavens. Desugaring JML method specifications. Technical Report TR #00-03e, Department of Computer Science, Iowa State University, 2000. Current revision from May 2005. (Cited on pages 206 and 255.)

Henrique Rebêlo, Gary T. Leavens, Mehdi Bagherzadeh, Hridesh Rajan, Ricardo Lima, Daniel M. Zimmerman, Márcio Cornélio, and Thomas Thüm. Modularizing crosscutting contracts with AspectJML. In Walter Binder, Erik Ernst, Achille Peternier, and Robert Hirschfeld, editors, *13th International Conference on Modularity, MODULARITY '14, Lugano, Switzerland. Proceedings*, pages 21–24, New York, NY, USA, 2014. ACM. (Cited on page 239.)

John C. Reynolds. User-defined types and procedural data structures as complementary approaches to data abstraction. In Carl A. Gunter and John C. Mitchell, editors, *Theoretical Aspects of Object-Oriented Programming: Types, Semantics, and Language Design*, Foundations of Computing, pages 13–24. The MIT Press, 1994. Reprint of the original 1975 paper. (Cited on page 252.)

John C. Reynolds. Separation logic: A logic for shared mutable data structures. In *Proc. 17th IEEE Symposium on Logic in Computer Science*, pages 55–74, Washington, DC, USA, 2002. IEEE Computer Society. (Cited on pages 349 and 378.)

Robby, Edwin Rodríguez, Matthew B. Dwyer, and John Hatcliff. Checking JML specifications using an extensible software model checking framework. *International Journal on Software Tools for Technology Transfer, STTT*, 8(3):280–299, 2006. (Cited on page 239.)

Stan Rosenberg, Anindya Banerjee, and David A. Naumann. Decision procedures for region logic. In Viktor Kuncak and Andrey Rybalchenko, editors, *Verification, Model Checking, and Abstract Interpretation - 13th International Conference, VMCAI 2012, Philadelphia, PA, USA. Proceedings*, volume 7148 of *LNCS*, pages 379–395, Berlin Heidelberg, 2012. Springer. (Cited on page 350.)

Andreas Roth. *Specification and Verification of Object-oriented Software Components*. PhD thesis, Universität Karlsruhe, 2006. (Cited on page 296.)

RTCA. DO-178C, Software considerations in airborne systems and equipment certification. published as RTCA SC-205 and EUROCAE WG-12, 2012. (Cited on page 424.)

James Rumbaugh, Ivar Jacobson, and Grady Booch. *The Unified Modeling Language Reference Manual*. Object Technology Series. Addison-Wesley, Reading/MA, 2nd edition, 2010. (Cited on page 240.)

Philipp Rümmer. Proving and disproving in dynamic logic for Java. Licentiate Thesis 2006-26L, Department of Computer Science and Engineering, Chalmers University of Technology, Göteborg, Sweden, 2006. (Cited on pages 576 and 579.)

Christoph Scheben. *Program-level Specification and Deductive Verification of Security Properties.* PhD thesis, Karlsruhe Institute of Technology, 2014. Karlsruhe, KIT, Diss., 2014. (Cited on pages 454, 455, 456, 457, 458, 460, 463, 467, 593 and 595.)

Christoph Scheben and Peter H. Schmitt. Verification of information flow properties of Java programs without approximations. In Bernhard Beckert, Ferruccio Damiani, and Dilian Gurov, editors, *Formal Verification of Object-Oriented Software International Conference, Turin, FoVeOOS 2011, Revised Selected Papers*, volume 7421 of *LNCS*, pages 232–249. Springer, 2012. (Cited on pages 455 and 458.)

Christoph Scheben and Peter H. Schmitt. Efficient self-composition for weakest precondition calculi. In Cliff B. Jones, Pekka Pihlajasaari, and Jun Sun, editors, *FM 2014: Formal Methods - 19th International Symposium, Singapore. Proceedings*, volume 8442 of *LNCS*, pages 579–594. Springer, 2014. (Cited on pages 455 and 462.)

Steffen Schlager. Handling of integer arithmetic in the verification of Java programs. Diplomarbeit, University of Karlsruhe, July 10 2002. (Cited on pages 230 and 245.)

Peter H. Schmitt. A computer-assisted proof of the Bellman-Ford lemma. Technical Report 2011,15, Karlsruhe Institute of Technology, Fakultät für Informatik, 2011. (Cited on page 280.)

Peter H. Schmitt and Mattias Ulbrich. Axiomatization of typed first-order logic. In Nikolaj Bjørner and Frank de Boer, editors, *FM 2015: Formal Methods - 20th International Symposium, Oslo, Norway. Proceedings*, volume 9109 of *LNCS*, pages 470–486. Springer, 2015. (Cited on page 47.)

Peter H. Schmitt, Mattias Ulbrich, and Benjamin Weiß. Dynamic frames in Java dynamic logic. In Bernhard Beckert and Claude Marché, editors, *Formal Verification of Object-Oriented Software - International Conference, FoVeOOS 2010, Paris, France. Revised Selected Papers*, volume 6528 of *LNCS*, pages 138–152. Springer, 2010. (Cited on page IX.)

Ulrik P. Schultz, Julia L. Lawall, and Charles Consel. Automatic program specialization for Java. *ACM Transactions on Programming Languages and Systems*, 25:452–499, 2003. (Cited on page 491.)

Jan Smans, Bart Jacobs, Frank Piessens, and Wolfram Schulte. An automatic verifier for Java-like programs based on dynamic frames. In José Luiz Fiadeiro and Paola Inverardi, editors, *Fundamental Approaches to Software Engineering, 11th International Conference, FASE 2008, Held as Part of the Joint European Conferences on Theory and Practice of Software, ETAPS 2008, Budapest, Hungary. Proceedings*, volume 4961 of *LNCS*, pages 261–275, Berlin, April 2008. Springer. (Cited on page 348.)

Jan Smans, Bart Jacobs, and Frank Piessens. Implicit dynamic frames. *ACM Trans. Program. Lang. Syst*, 34(1):2, 2012. (Cited on pages 350 and 378.)

Ian Sommerville. *Software Engineering*. Pearson, 10th edition, 2015. (Cited on pages 2 and 18.)

J. Michael Spivey. *Z Notation - a reference manual (2. ed.)*. Prentice Hall International Series in Computer Science. Prentice Hall, 1992. (Cited on page 240.)

Kurt Stenzel. *Verification of Java Card Programs*. PhD thesis, Institut für Informatik, Universität Augsburg, Germany, July 2005. (Cited on page 239.)

Jacques Stern. Why provable security matters? In Eli Biham, editor, *Advances in Cryptology - EUROCRYPT 2003, International Conference on the Theory and Applications of Cryptographic Techniques, Warsaw, Poland. Proceedings*, volume 2656 of *LNCS*, pages 449–461. Springer, 2003. (Cited on page 607.)

Christian Sternagel. Proof pearl — A mechanized proof of GHC's mergesort. *Journal of Automated Reasoning*, pages 357–370, 2013. (Cited on page 609.)

Alexander J. Summers, Sophia Drossopoulou, and Peter Müller. The need for flexible object invariants. In *International Workshop on Aliasing, Confinement and Ownership in Object-Oriented Programming, (IWACO) at ECOOP 2008, Paphos, Cyprus*, pages 1–9. ACM, 2009. (Cited on page 350.)

Robert D. Tennent. *Specifying Software: a Hands-On Introduction*. Cambridge University Press, 2002. (Cited on page 572.)

Nikolai Tillmann and Jonathan de Halleux. Pex–white box test generation for .net. In Bernhard Beckert and Reiner Hähnle, editors, *Tests and Proofs*, volume 4966 of *LNCS*, pages 134–153. Springer, 2008. (Cited on page 450.)

Nikolai Tillmann and Wolfram Schulte. Parameterized unit tests. In Michel Wermelinger and Harald Gall, editors, *Proc. 10th European Software Engineering Conference/13th ACM SIGSOFT Intl. Symp. on Foundations of Software Engineering, 2005, Lisbon, Portugal*, pages 253–262. ACM Press, 2005. (Cited on page 4.)

Kerry Trentelman. Proving correctness of Java Card DL taclets using Bali. In Bernhard Aichernig and Bernhard Beckert, editors, *Third IEEE International Conference on Software Engineering and Formal Methods (SEFM 2005), Koblenz, Germany*, pages 160–169, 2005. (Cited on page 64.)

Thomas Tuerk. A formalisation of smallfoot in HOL. In Stefan Berghofer, Tobias Nipkow, Christian Urban, and Makarius Wenzel, editors, *Theorem Proving in Higher Order Logics, 22nd International Conference, TPHOLs 2009, Munich, Germany. Proceedings*, volume 5674 of *LNCS*, pages 469–484. Springer, 2009. (Cited on page 241.)

Mattias Ulbrich. A dynamic logic for unstructured programs with embedded assertions. In Bernhard Beckert and Claude Marché, editors, *Formal Verification of Object-Oriented Software - International Conference, FoVeOOS 2010, Paris, France. Revised Selected Papers*, volume 6528 of *LNCS*, pages 168–182. Springer, 2011. (Cited on page 473.)

Mattias Ulbrich. *Dynamic Logic for an Intermediate Language. Verification, Interaction and Refinement*. PhD thesis, Karlsruhe Institut für Technologie, KIT, 2013. (Cited on pages 36 and 473.)

Bart van Delft and Richard Bubel. Dependency-based information flow analysis with declassification in a program logic. *Computing Research Repository (CoRR)*, 2015. (Cited on page 471.)

Joachim van den Berg and Bart Jacobs. The LOOP compiler for Java and JML. In Tiziana Margaria and Wang Yi, editors, *Proc. 7th International Conference on Tools and Algorithms for the Construction and Analysis of Systems (TACAS), Genova, Italy*, volume 2031 of *LNCS*, pages 299–312, 2001. (Cited on page 195.)

Sergiy A. Vilkomir and Jonathan P. Bowen. Formalization of software testing criteria using the Z notation. In *25th International Computer Software and Applications Conference (COMPSAC 2001), Invigorating Software Development, Chicago, IL, USA*, pages 351–356. IEEE Computer Society, 2001. (Cited on pages 424 and 425.)

David von Oheimb. *Analyzing Java in Isabelle/HOL: Formalization, Type Safety and Hoare Logic*. PhD thesis, Technische Universität München, 2001. (Cited on page 64.)

Simon Wacker. Blockverträge. Studienarbeit, Karlsruhe Institute of Technology, 2012. (Cited on pages 238, 466 and 623.)

Jos Warmer and Anneke Kleppe. *The Object Constraint Language: Precise Modelling with UML*. Object Technology Series. Addison-Wesley, Reading/MA, 1999. (Cited on pages 1, 13 and 240.)

Nathan Wasser. Generating specifications for recursive methods by abstracting program states. In Xuandong Li, Zhiming Liu, and Wang Yi, editors, *Dependable Software Engineering: Theories, Tools, and Applications - First International Symposium, SETTA 2015, Nanjing, China. Proceedings*, pages 243–257. Springer, 2015. (Cited on page 189.)

Benjamin Weiß. Predicate abstraction in a program logic calculus. In Michael Leuschel and Heike Wehrheim, editors, *Integrated Formal Methods, 7th International Conference, IFM 2009, Düsseldorf, Germany. Proceedings*, volume 5423 of *LNCS*, pages 136–150. Springer, 2009. (Cited on page 474.)

Benjamin Weiß. *Deductive Verification of Object-Oriented Software — Dynamic Frames, Dynamic Logic and Predicate Abstraction*. PhD thesis, Karlsruhe Institute of Technology, Karlsruhe, January 2011. (Cited on pages IX, 241, 243, 251, 290, 306, 307, 319, 322, 335, 336, 338 and 341.)

Florian Widmann. Crossverification of while loop semantics. Diplomarbeit, Fakultät für Informatik, KIT, 2006. (Cited on page 101.)

Niklaus Wirth. Modula: a language for modular multiprogramming. *Software Practice and Experience*, 7:3–35, 1977. (Cited on page 291.)

Peter Y. H. Wong, Elvira Albert, Radu Muschevici, José Proença, Jan Schäfer, and Rudolf Schlatte. The ABS tool suite: modelling, executing and analysing distributed adaptable object-oriented systems. *International Journal on Software Tools for Technology Transfer, STTT*, 14(5):567–588, 2012. (Cited on page 6.)

Jim Woodcock, Susan Stepney, David Cooper, John A. Clark, and Jeremy Jacob. The certification of the mondex electronic purse to ITSEC level E6. *Formal Aspects of Computing*, 20(1):5–19, 2008. (Cited on page 605.)

Jooyong Yi, Robby, Xianghua Deng, and Abhik Roychoudhury. Past expression: encapsulating pre-states at post-conditions by means of AOP. In *Proceedings of the 12th annual international conference on Aspect-oriented software development, (AOSD), Fukuoka, Japan*, pages 133–144. ACM, 2013. (Cited on page 249.)

Lei Yu. A formal model of IEEE floating point arithmetic. *Archive of Formal Proofs*, 2013, 2013. (Cited on page 3.)

Marina Zaharieva-Stojanovski and Marieke Huisman. Verifying class invariants in concurrent programs. In Stefania Gnesi and Arend Rensink, editors, *Fundamental Approaches to Software Engineering - 17th International Conference, FASE 2014, Held as Part of the European Joint Conferences on Theory and Practice of Software, ETAPS 2014, Grenoble, France. Proceedings*, volume 8411 of *LNCS*, pages 230–245. Springer, 2014. (Cited on page 216.)

Karen Zee, Viktor Kuncak, and Martin C. Rinard. Full functional verification of linked data structures. In Rajiv Gupta and Saman P. Amarasinghe, editors, *Programming Language Design and Implementation (PLDI)*, pages 349–361, New York, NY, 2008. ACM. (Cited on page 296.)

Andreas Zeller. *Why programs fail—A guide to systematic debugging*. Elsevier, 2nd edition, 2006. (Cited on page 412.)

Hong Zhu, Patrick A. V. Hall, and John H. R. May. Software unit test coverage and adequacy. *ACM Computing Surveys*, 29(4):366–427, 1997. (Cited on page 423.)

Daniel M. Zimmerman and Rinkesh Nagmoti. JMLUnit: The Next Generation. In B. Beckert and C. Marché, editors, *Formal Verification of Object-Oriented Software - International Conference, FoVeOOS 2010, Paris, France. Revised Selected Papers*, volume 6528 of *LNCS*. Springer, 2010. (Cited on page 239.)

Index